The Drug Development Process

DRUGS AND THE PHARMACEUTICAL SCIENCES

DRUGS AND THE PHARMACEUTICAL SCIENCES

A Series of Textbooks and Monographs

edited by

James Swarbrick
AAI, Inc.
Wilmington, North Carolina

1. Pharmacokinetics, *Milo Gibaldi and Donald Perrier*
2. Good Manufacturing Practices for Pharmaceuticals: A Plan for Total Quality Control, *Sidney H. Willig, Murray M. Tuckerman, and William S. Hitchings IV*
3. Microencapsulation, *edited by J. R. Nixon*
4. Drug Metabolism: Chemical and Biochemical Aspects, *Bernard Testa and Peter Jenner*
5. New Drugs: Discovery and Development, *edited by Alan A. Rubin*
6. Sustained and Controlled Release Drug Delivery Systems, *edited by Joseph R. Robinson*
7. Modern Pharmaceutics, *edited by Gilbert S. Banker and Christopher T. Rhodes*
8. Prescription Drugs in Short Supply: Case Histories, *Michael A. Schwartz*
9. Activated Charcoal: Antidotal and Other Medical Uses, *David O. Cooney*
10. Concepts in Drug Metabolism (in two parts), *edited by Peter Jenner and Bernard Testa*
11. Pharmaceutical Analysis: Modern Methods (in two parts), *edited by James W. Munson*
12. Techniques of Solubilization of Drugs, *edited by Samuel H. Yalkowsky*
13. Orphan Drugs, *edited by Fred E. Karch*
14. Novel Drug Delivery Systems: Fundamentals, Developmental Concepts, Biomedical Assessments, *Yie W. Chien*
15. Pharmacokinetics: Second Edition, Revised and Expanded, *Milo Gibaldi and Donald Perrier*
16. Good Manufacturing Practices for Pharmaceuticals: A Plan for Total Quality Control, Second Edition, Revised and Expanded, *Sidney H. Willig, Murray M. Tuckerman, and William S. Hitchings IV*
17. Formulation of Veterinary Dosage Forms, *edited by Jack Blodinger*

18. Dermatological Formulations: Percutaneous Absorption, *Brian W. Barry*
19. The Clinical Research Process in the Pharmaceutical Industry, *edited by Gary M. Matoren*
20. Microencapsulation and Related Drug Processes, *Patrick B. Deasy*
21. Drugs and Nutrients: The Interactive Effects, *edited by Daphne A. Roe and T. Colin Campbell*
22. Biotechnology of Industrial Antibiotics, *Erick J. Vandamme*
23. Pharmaceutical Process Validation, *edited by Bernard T. Loftus and Robert A. Nash*
24. Anticancer and Interferon Agents: Synthesis and Properties, *edited by Raphael M. Ottenbrite and George B. Butler*
25. Pharmaceutical Statistics: Practical and Clinical Applications, *Sanford Bolton*
26. Drug Dynamics for Analytical, Clinical, and Biological Chemists, *Benjamin J. Gudzinowicz, Burrows T. Younkin, Jr., and Michael J. Gudzinowicz*
27. Modern Analysis of Antibiotics, *edited by Adjoran Aszalos*
28. Solubility and Related Properties, *Kenneth C. James*
29. Controlled Drug Delivery: Fundamentals and Applications, Second Edition, Revised and Expanded, *edited by Joseph R. Robinson and Vincent H. Lee*
30. New Drug Approval Process: Clinical and Regulatory Management, *edited by Richard A. Guarino*
31. Transdermal Controlled Systemic Medications, *edited by Yie W. Chien*
32. Drug Delivery Devices: Fundamentals and Applications, *edited by Praveen Tyle*
33. Pharmacokinetics: Regulatory • Industrial • Academic Perspectives, *edited by Peter G. Welling and Francis L. S. Tse*
34. Clinical Drug Trials and Tribulations, *edited by Allen E. Cato*
35. Transdermal Drug Delivery: Developmental Issues and Research Initiatives, *edited by Jonathan Hadgraft and Richard H. Guy*
36. Aqueous Polymeric Coatings for Pharmaceutical Dosage Forms, *edited by James W. McGinity*
37. Pharmaceutical Pelletization Technology, *edited by Isaac Ghebre-Sellassie*
38. Good Laboratory Practice Regulations, *edited by Allen F. Hirsch*
39. Nasal Systemic Drug Delivery, *Yie W. Chien, Kenneth S. E. Su, and Shyi-Feu Chang*
40. Modern Pharmaceutics: Second Edition, Revised and Expanded, *edited by Gilbert S. Banker and Christopher T. Rhodes*
41. Specialized Drug Delivery Systems: Manufacturing and Production Technology, *edited by Praveen Tyle*
42. Topical Drug Delivery Formulations, *edited by David W. Osborne and Anton H. Amann*
43. Drug Stability: Principles and Practices, *Jens T. Carstensen*

44. Pharmaceutical Statistics: Practical and Clinical Applications, Second Edition, Revised and Expanded, *Sanford Bolton*
45. Biodegradable Polymers as Drug Delivery Systems, *edited by Mark Chasin and Robert Langer*
46. Preclinical Drug Disposition: A Laboratory Handbook, *Francis L. S. Tse and James J. Jaffe*
47. HPLC in the Pharmaceutical Industry, *edited by Godwin W. Fong and Stanley K. Lam*
48. Pharmaceutical Bioequivalence, *edited by Peter G. Welling, Francis L. S. Tse, and Shrikant V. Dinghe*
49. Pharmaceutical Dissolution Testing, *Umesh V. Banakar*
50. Novel Drug Delivery Systems: Second Edition, Revised and Expanded, *Yie W. Chien*
51. Managing the Clinical Drug Development Process, *David M. Cocchetto and Ronald V. Nardi*
52. Good Manufacturing Practices for Pharmaceuticals: A Plan for Total Quality Control, Third Edition, *edited by Sidney H. Willig and James R. Stoker*
53. Prodrugs: Topical and Ocular Drug Delivery, *edited by Kenneth B. Sloan*
54. Pharmaceutical Inhalation Aerosol Technology, *edited by Anthony J. Hickey*
55. Radiopharmaceuticals: Chemistry and Pharmacology, *edited by Adrian D. Nunn*
56. New Drug Approval Process: Second Edition, Revised and Expanded, *edited by Richard A. Guarino*
57. Pharmaceutical Process Validation: Second Edition, Revised and Expanded, *edited by Ira R. Berry and Robert A. Nash*
58. Ophthalmic Drug Delivery Systems, *edited by Ashim K. Mitra*
59. Pharmaceutical Skin Penetration Enhancement, *edited by Kenneth A. Walters and Jonathan Hadgraft*
60. Colonic Drug Absorption and Metabolism, *edited by Peter R. Bieck*
61. Pharmaceutical Particulate Carriers: Therapeutic Applications, *edited by Alain Rolland*
62. Drug Permeation Enhancement: Theory and Applications, *edited by Dean S. Hsieh*
63. Glycopeptide Antibiotics, *edited by Ramakrishnan Nagarajan*
64. Achieving Sterility in Medical and Pharmaceutical Products, *Nigel A. Halls*
65. Multiparticulate Oral Drug Delivery, *edited by Isaac Ghebre-Sellassie*
66. Colloidal Drug Delivery Systems, *edited by Jörg Kreuter*
67. Pharmacokinetics: Regulatory • Industrial • Academic Perspectives, Second Edition, *edited by Peter G. Welling and Francis L. S. Tse*
68. Drug Stability: Principles and Practices, Second Edition, Revised and Expanded, *Jens T. Carstensen*

69. Good Laboratory Practice Regulations: Second Edition, Revised and Expanded, *edited by Sandy Weinberg*
70. Physical Characterization of Pharmaceutical Solids, *edited by Harry G. Brittain*
71. Pharmaceutical Powder Compaction Technology, *edited by Göran Alderborn and Christer Nyström*
72. Modern Pharmaceutics: Third Edition, Revised and Expanded, *edited by Gilbert S. Banker and Christopher T. Rhodes*
73. Microencapsulation: Methods and Industrial Applications, *edited by Simon Benita*
74. Oral Mucosal Drug Delivery, *edited by Michael J. Rathbone*
75. Clinical Research in Pharmaceutical Development, *edited by Barry Bleidt and Michael Montagne*
76. The Drug Development Process: Increasing Efficiency and Cost-Effectiveness, *edited by Peter G. Welling, Louis Lasagna, and Umesh V. Banakar*
77. Microparticulate Systems for the Delivery of Proteins and Vaccines, *edited by Smadar Cohen and Howard Bernstein*
78. Good Manufacturing Practices for Pharmaceuticals: A Plan for Total Quality Control, Fourth Edition, Revised and Expanded, *Sidney H. Willig and James R. Stoker*

ADDITIONAL VOLUMES IN PREPARATION

Pharmaceutical Statistics: Practical and Clinical Applications, Third Edition, *Sanford Bolton*

Aqueous Polymeric Coatings for Pharmaceutical Dosage Forms: Second Edition, *edited by James W. McGinity*

The Drug Development Process

edited by
Peter G. Welling
Parke-Davis Pharmaceutical Research
Ann Arbor, Michigan

Louis Lasagna
Tufts Center for the Study
of Drug Development
Boston, Massachusetts

Umesh V. Banakar
St. Louis College of Pharmacy
St. Louis, Missouri

Marcel Dekker, Inc. New York • Basel • Hong Kong

Library of Congress Cataloging-in-Publication Data

The drug development process : increasing efficiency and cost-effectiveness / edited by Peter G. Welling, Louis Lasagna, Umesh V. Banakar.
p. cm. — (Drugs and the pharmaceutical sciences ; v. 76)
Includes bibliographical references and index.
ISBN 0-8247-9727-2 (hardcover : alk. paper)
1. Drugs—Research. 2. Pharmaceutical industry. I. Welling, Peter G. II. Lasagna, Louis. III. Banakar, Umesh V. IV. Series.
[DNLM: 1. Drug Evaluation. 2. Drug Screening. 3. Drug Industry—organization & administration. 4. Drug Design. W1 DR893B v.76 1996 / QV 771 D7939 1996]
RM301.25.D77 1996
615'.19—dc20
DNLM/DLC
for Library of Congress 96-24681
CIP

The publisher offers discounts on this book when ordered in bulk quantities. For more information, write to Special Sales/Professional Marketing at the address below.

This book is printed on acid-free paper.

Marcel Dekker, Inc.
270 Madison Avenue, New York, New York 10016

Current printing (last digit):
10 9 8 7 6 5 4 3 2 1

PRINTED IN THE UNITED STATES OF AMERICA

Foreword

In 1976, Comroe and Dripps published the results of their study analyzing the essential information needed to produce the top 10 clinical advances in cardiovascular and pulmonary medicine in the previous 30 years [1]. Some of their findings are relevant to the subject of this book. First, it is striking how long the lag time can be from a scientific discovery to an advance in clinical practice based on that discovery. Second, Comroe and Dripps differentiated basic from nonbasic research according to whether the scientists attempted to determine the mechanisms for the effects observed. Thus, studies in sick people could be basic if they probed mechanisms, whereas studies in cells or of enzymes could be nonbasic if they described events but did not probe for mechanisms.

The relevance of these findings to the future health of the public, as the consequences of cost containment in health care impact on the pharmaceutical industry, cannot be overemphasized. The drug discovery process is often perceived as a straight line proceeding from the discovery of a screening technique for a desired pharmacological effect to the synthesis of compounds for screening, to the preclinical development of leading candidates for introduction into humans, to the introduction into humans in Phase I, to the clinical trials in Phases II and III, to the filing of the New Drug Application (or other registration documents), to regulatory approval, to commercial launch and marketing. In reality, the process is more varied and complicated than such a direct progression. As pointed out by Comroe and Dripps, it actually starts much earlier, with all sorts of discoveries, often not oriented to any goal other than the understanding of some biological process. These discoveries, frequently paid for by government or foundation funds, are what produce the conceptual basis that culminates in the drug discovery screen. The lag time from discovery to development of the screen can be years or decades, and it is the drug discovery and development process that enables these earlier discoveries to be translated into improvements in health care. Factors that impede this process block the earlier discoveries from achieving their potential for improving the health of the public.

Another oversimplification is the idea that work progresses directly from preclinical research to clinical development. There is a clinical research phase between preclinical research and clinical development as a drug moves along the path to becoming a medicine. This clinical research phase provides information that is essential for the rational development of the drug. Clinical research can also substantially impact on preclinical research and candidate drug selection. Innovative compounds that may never be useful medicines can be used to test novel drug concepts that are of critical relevance to a major drug discovery program. In fact, when done imaginatively and well, some of this clinical research meets the Comroe and Dripps definition of basic research: it searches for mechanisms of observed effects. When done by rote and poorly, it adds nothing to the drug discovery process and leaves to chance aspects of the pivotal Phase III trials that will spell the success or failure of a new potential breakthrough drug.

During the new era of cost containment, when prices are being discounted and time means money to the innovative pharmaceutical company, the drug development process must be carried out with maximum efficiency and cost-effectiveness. Making such platitudinous statements and implementing them are very different things. The unpredictability of some human responses to drugs makes managing drug development more challenging and difficult than managing an industrial process that obeys the laws of physics and chemistry. Maintaining a corporate culture that supports a scientific point of view during the studies in humans while maintaining an appropriate focus on product without dulling the imagination of the scientist doing the discovery part of drug development is a major management challenge as money gets tighter, formularies become more restrictive, and liability seems to grow. Yet this is precisely what is needed to continue to develop innovative products that society needs, and for which society has invested in the basic research—and continues to invest for the future.

The contributors to this book have thought and written about a variety of subjects that need to be considered in "re-engineering" the drug development process to meet the challenges of the future. This book gives the reader the opportunity to think with these experts as they address specific problems faced by those trying to increase the efficiency and effectiveness of the drug development process.

Marcus M. Reidenberg, M.D.
Cornell University Medical College
New York, New York

REFERENCE

1. Comroe, J. H., and Dripps, R. D., Scientific basis for the support of biomedical science, *Science 192*: 105 (1976).

Preface

Drug development in the pharmaceutical industry has historically been a slow and expensive process. This has been exacerbated during the last decade by spiraling costs and ever-increasing demands by regulatory agencies worldwide on the content and quality of submission packages to support the marketing of new drugs. Recent estimates have placed the overall cost of successfully developing a single drug entity, from discovery to marketplace, at over $300 million. The potential for this cost to increase even further, considered against the backdrop of cost containment in the health care industry in general—and in pharmaceuticals in particular—has provided incentive to reexamine the drug development process and has provoked discussions as to how it can be made more efficient and cost-effective.

This text has been prepared with these goals in mind. Experts were invited to contribute chapters expressly to challenge current approaches to drug development used by industry and required by regulatory agencies and to present alternatives that may generate a better overall approach. Authors were asked to be provocative and to "throw out ideas," however speculative, that might help improve what must be considered an extremely inefficient process.

Contributions were sought from a variety of areas. Experts with many years of experience in the business were invited to provide comment on the drug development process, where it is going, and where it should be going. Contributions were also sought from representatives from the many disciplines involved in drug development, including pharmacology, chemistry, biotechnology, pharmacokinetics, metabolism, regulatory affairs, pharmaceutics, marketing, and, of course, management, again with the charge of challenging the present system and suggesting alternatives. Our intention has been to describe different potential approaches for those engaged in the difficult and regulation-bound drug development process. If we have sown some seeds and increased the reader's awareness of the challenges to be met and opportunities to be grasped, then we have succeeded in our task.

We wish to thank the contributing authors, who willingly took time away from busy schedules to contribute in their areas of specialization. We thank also our administrative colleagues who were responsible for preparing manuscripts. Particular thanks are due to Ms. Theresa Davis, who administratively kept the whole thing together and thereby made our tasks much easier.

Peter G. Welling
Louis Lasagna
Umesh V. Banakar

Introduction: Whither Drug Development?

This is a crucial time for drug development. The tremendous advances achieved in the past half-century have merely whetted the public's appetite for solutions to the many therapeutic needs currently unmet by the progress made to date. Most cancers, once they have spread beyond the reach of the surgeon's scalpel, are incurable. Alzheimer's disease—whose sufferers were once fittingly compared by Nobelist Elie Wiesel to a book whose pages are falling out one by one, leaving nothing at the end but dusty covers—increases yearly in prevalence and is only slightly treatable by current medications. AIDS, the modern plague, is associated with a host of opportunistic infections and neoplasms, some of which are treatable, but the fundamental infection can be halted only temporarily by current therapy, and a vaccine is nowhere in sight. Vaccines to prevent many other infections are needed. Neurological and muscular diseases are typically unresponsive to drugs. Cystic fibrosis patients now can live into their 30s (and occasionally longer), but a normal life span eludes most victims of this genetic abnormality.

Why have we not solved these problems? It is certainly not because of the FDA, although this regulatory agency at times slows the access to market of some good drugs. The fault lies in the failure of science to come up with solutions. The future, like the past, is likely to depend on the following factors to develop new remedies: resources, brains, hard work, and luck. The process of drug development is cumbersome, lengthy, and fearfully expensive. The time from discovery to marketing has doubled in the last 30 years, owing to excessive regulatory requirements, the changing state of the art, and human error and inefficiency.

The traditional pharmaceutical companies have been profitable but, in an environment of high risk, they have plowed back into research a higher percentage of their profits than any other industry. Today, there is a tendency to retreat somewhat on this philosophy, and the threats of Congress to cut NIH funds and funding for grants pose the possibility of grievous harm to the unmatched nonindustrial U.S. research establishment, which has in the past contributed important scientific building blocks to the drug development process.

The drug industry is under attack worldwide as being excessively profitable, and cost containment efforts in country after country are often directed at pharmaceutical expenditures, even though drugs are generally considered the most cost-effective form of therapy, and drug costs constitute a small percentage of any country's total health care budget.

How profitable should the drug industry be? I have no magic number to propose, but it seems obvious that a company must be profitable enough to justify investment in a risky, lengthy, and expensive process. Turning the drug industry into a public utility would likely lower the cost of those drugs already available, but would represent a cruel blow to the hopes and prayers of all those suffering from diseases now essentially untreatable.

The new biotechnology industry—perhaps 1300 companies in the United States—faces special problems. Few of these companies are currently profitable, and many will disappear from the scene because their venture capital will all be spent before any product makes it to market. Absorption by traditional pharmaceutical companies will at least temporarily salvage some biotech firms, but many others seem doomed, despite the enormously exciting promise of the field.

Health care reform is in the wind, and great changes are being made, even in the absence of Washington-imposed schemes. Managed care, capitation-based reimbursement, and the need to contain health care costs would seem to lead inevitably to certain changes. Needless drug prescribing, like unnecessary lab tests, x-rays, or surgery, is a rational target. But the "fat" in health care is finite, and the ability of science to come up with new drugs, new devices, new vaccines, new tests, new organ transplants, and new orthopedic joint replacements seems limitless. Some of these advances will save money, but many will not, even though they prolong life or improve its quality. If an arbitrary percent of gross national product is set as a cap on health care expenditures, rationing would seem inevitable. Indeed, we already see it in the Oregon Medicaid program, where it was deemed more appropriate (given a fixed budget) to spend money on pediatric vaccines than on a liver transplant for a chronic alcoholic.

This kind of rationing is different from the sort seen in times of earthquake, flood, or war, where triage sacrifices a few to save many others. This new type is a painful pill for many to swallow. (There has, of course, always been inequity of access to health care in most countries, since geography, education, and personal wealth can determine whether one gets care. An Eskimo on the shores of Hudson Bay will not receive the same care as a resident of Toronto, and, if one is wealthy enough, waiting lines for cataract or hip or coronary bypass surgery can be avoided simply by traveling to another city or another country.)

Whatever happens, it is clear that in the future a new drug will need persuasive evidence that it is better, safer, cheaper, or more convenient to take—i.e., possesses some comparative advantage over older competitors—if it is to be dispensed by HMOs and paid for by third parties. Pharmacoeconomic studies are the order of the day, even though we are only beginning to appreciate how to do them well and convincingly. Whether the FDA should be engaged in approving the use of such data is now being debated, but the obligation to do the studies is more evident with each passing day.

These are troubled times in many ways, but they are also challenging times. We all have a stake in first-class drug development, and it is hoped that this book will in some way contribute constructively to the process.

Louis Lasagna, M.D., D.Sc.
Tufts Center for the Study of Drug Development
Boston, Massachusetts

Contents

Contributors

Rebecca J. Anderson, Ph.D. R & D Budgets and Planning, Boehringer Ingelheim Pharmaceuticals, Inc., Ridgefield, Connecticut

Umesh V. Banakar, Ph.D. Professor of Pharmaceutics and Director of Research, St. Louis College of Pharmacy, St. Louis, Missouri

Bret Berner, Ph.D. Executive Director of Development, Cygnus, Inc., Redwood City, California

Alan Bye, Ph.D. International Director, Glaxo-Wellcome Inc., Research Triangle Park, North Carolina

D. Bruce Campbell, Ph.D. Director of International Scientific Affairs, Servier Research and Development Ltd., Fulmer, Slough, England

Jim Cassidy, M.D., Ph.D. Professor of Oncology, University of Aberdeen, Aberdeen, Scotland

W. J. C. Currie, M.D. Executive Director, Clinical and Regulatory Development, Merck & Co., Inc., Rahway, New Jersey

Dai Davies, Ph.D. Clinical Pathology Laboratory, Zeneca Pharmaceuticals, Cheshire, England

Jan Gugliotti, M.B.A. CSC Index, Cambridge, Massachusetts

James E. Higgins, Ph.D. Executive Vice President and Director of Biometrics, Health Decisions, Inc., Chapel Hill, North Carolina

Karolyn Jackson, Ph.D. Clinical Pathology Laboratory, Zeneca Pharmaceuticals, Cheshire, England

Agis Kydonieus, Ph.D. Vice President, R & D, ConvaTec, A Bristol-Myers Squibb Company, Princeton, New Jersey

Gary D. Lightfoot Senior Vice President of Market Development, Pharmaco International Inc., Austin, Texas

Michael C. Makoid, Ph.D. Associate Professor of Pharmaceutical Sciences, School of Pharmacy & Allied Health Professions, Creighton University, Omaha, Nebraska

Vaila M. Marshall Senior Director of Regulatory Affairs and Clinical Quality Assurance, Pfizer Central Research, Kent, England

J. Robert Powell, Pharm.D. International Director, Clinical Pharmacology, Glaxo-Wellcome Inc., Research Triangle Park, North Carolina

Paul D. Rubin, Ph.D. Vice-President, Glaxo-Wellcome Inc., Research Triangle Park, North Carolina

Martha M. Rumore, Pharm.D. Associate Professor, Pharmacy Administration, Arnold & Marie Schwartz College of Pharmacy, Long Island University, Brooklyn, New York

Albert J. Siemens, Ph.D. Executive Vice President, ClinTrials Research Inc., Research Triangle Park, North Carolina

John C. Somberg, M.D. Professor of Medicine and Pharmacology, and Chief of the Division of Clinical Pharmacology and Cardiology, Finch University of Health Sciences/The Chicago Medical School, North Chicago, Illinois

Terry R. Stouch, Ph.D. Bristol-Myers Squibb Pharmaceutical Research Institute, Princeton, New Jersey

John Thompson, M.A. Senior Advisor, CSC Index, Cambridge, Massachusetts

John R. Vogel, Ph.D. Drug Development Consultant, John R. Vogel Associates, Inc., Oldwick, New Jersey

Peter G. Welling, Ph.D. Vice President, Pharmacokinetics and Drug Metabolism, Parke-Davis Pharmaceutical Research, Warner-Lambert Company, Ann Arbor, Michigan

1

The Evolving Drug Discovery and Development Process

John C. Somberg

Finch University of Health Sciences/The Chicago Medical School
North Chicago, Illinois

I. INTRODUCTION

Change is part of the human condition, but often we fail to notice the pace of change. When change is rapid, even being part of the system does not obscure the results of the rapid change taking place. The drug development process is undergoing considerable change; one can even discern a major revolutionary process that is ongoing. Over the last 100 years, we have evolved through several stages of drug development, but perhaps all that has passed will pale in comparison to the dramatic information age before us that will markedly alter the environment in which we work and the drug development process.

To deny the forces of change is to make a fundamental error that will swamp even the most powerful and wealthiest of companies engaged in drug discovery and development. The evolution of the computer age gave IBM the opportunity to expand and alter its business from analog systems and adding machines to punch cards and then to complex computer systems. As the computer age developed, IBM led with the innovative personal computer although actually this innovation was copied from others. Recently, the lead has been lost by IBM because the language of the machine and the "software" has become the core of the information age, along with the chips that permit the exponential growth in machine computing performance. Thus, Microsoft, just a concept 20 years ago, is more dominant in today's information age than IBM. Remaining a leader in technology advances, IBM leads in new fundamental patents and has a strong marketing and sales force to market a robust product line. It kept up in technology, but its management failed to perceive the salient change in the information age from large computers to small, and then the importance of the operation language that controls information processing, analysis, and communication.

Drug development is in an analogous situation. We have seen an evolution from the age of botanicals to the age of chemical synthetic discovery and now to the age of biotechnology and gene manipulation, which is dawning before us. Each area still can develop, but the shift in direction is fundamental to our scientific development. Even taking these major changes into account, drug discovery and development will be fundamentally altered by the information age. The concept of the information age first conceived by Alvin and Heidi Toffler has been correctly perceived by them to be revolutionary in its effects on society, just as the first two waves were in their era. The agricultural revolution and the industrial revolution were fundamental changes in society, as will be the information age. The Tofflers describe an era in their book entitled *Future Shock* [1], when the pace of change in modern life is so great as to disenfranchise individuals from the process that society is undergoing. While this is a real problem for society and a problem with political dimensions, failure of our institutions and our corporate structures to adjust will bring considerable societal and economic disruption. For these reasons, an understanding of the evolution of drug discovery and development and how this evolution will be affected by the information age is essential for those working in drug discovery and development.

II. THE AGE OF BOTANICALS

Anthropologists tell us that from the early hunter–gatherer groups, man made use of herbals. Whether they were foods, items of religious significance, or used as medication cannot be clearly discerned. As civilization progressed, remedies from plants developed further. The earliest folklore relates stories of plant medicinals. The Bible contains passages eluding to medicinal herbs and plants. In fact, all the major religions discuss plant remedies as part of their sacred works. There are many stories in pharmacology relating to the use of medicinal plants and the work of herbalists in the early discovery of drugs. I recall from my yearly lecture in pharmacology on inotropic agents, the story of William Withering, the physician from Birmingham, England, who on his charity rounds in Shropshire saw that an herbal potion was used successfully to treat a woman with dropsy (CHF). Withering's botanical training in Edenbrough permitted him to identify the probable active ingredient, the leaf of the foxglove plant. After ten years of clinical experimentation, he developed a series of case studies deliminating the dose range from minimal effective dose to toxicity. He categorized the adverse side-effect profile of the digitalis leaf and its potentially life-threatening toxicities. He noted the adverse outcomes and carefully chronicled the conditions that the drug was most useful in treating. While he found the agent to increase urine volume and, thus, to have diuretic properties, he commented in his thesis that the drug had a powerful action on the motion of the heart and thus recognized its cardiotonic action years before it was actually proven. Withering was a masterful botanist (he chronicled the plants of Great Britain later in his life). He was an exemplary clinical pharmacologist and demonstrated the best in botanical drug discovery and testing, given the skills of his day. But Withering's observations may not be unique. The effect of the foxglove on disease is known to be part of European plant folklore. The use of the glycoside yielding plants and the use of the skin of the toad for medicinal purposes goes back to ancient Egypt, as well as being mentioned in Chinese herbal writings. Confucius talks of glycoside plants for edematous states and cardiac glycosides are a significant component of Chinese herbal medications. While Withering's observations were a defining moment for modern medicine, botanicals of similar action were used over 2000 years ago. Clearly botanicals have been important to therapeutic advances. Whether we are discussing digitalis or atropine or any number of other drugs, plants have contributed much to drug discovery. The use of quinidine in atrial fibrillation and quinine to treat malaria are other examples of the important role botanicals have played in therapeutics. In fact, in the 1700s and 1800s botanicals were the only source of drugs for development. Anti-infective agents have depended on extracts from molds and fungus for a very long time. Recent therapies are derived from nature with some chemical modifications to improve activity. We often think of the age of botanicals as one that has gone by, but even though the use of botanicals was the first step in drug discovery and development, it continues to this day to play a major role. While reserpine was used for 1000 years in India and parts of China, it was only in the 1950s that it was purified and used as an effective antihypertensive agent. The recent use of taxol in oncology is an example of a botanical that was in very short supply. Until a synthetic pathway for commercial production was developed, the bark of the Yew tree became a very valuable commodity and caused the Yew tree to be endangered. In fact, some companies like Schaman Pharmaceuticals have made it their corporate purpose to discover and develop pharmaceuticals from botanical sources. We read of Merck and Company and Pfizer, to name two of the corporate giants, who have formed special alliances with botanical gardens, countries in South America or Africa, or both, to find new drug products. Is this a denial of the evolution of drug discovery, a last chance for the botanical pioneers, or a shrewd business decision? I would venture to say a bit of each. The biodiversity of the planet, the potential to find new antibacterials and other potentially useful pharmaceuticals is great. However, the need to assay so many compounds for a host of disease states and the imperfect capacity of our assays makes the odds of success much less than one might first estimate. Another critical aspect to the drug development process from botanicals is the fallacy of uniqueness. By this I mean the assumption that nature will provide a unique agent that can be purified and have a salutary action on a disease state with little to no organ toxicity. These assumptions are naive and may not be sustainable. However the biodiversity may provide chemical structures that can be modified or redesigned and can be useful starting points for the drug discovery process. However, we must be smart enough to use the information that we collect. Techniques are going to be needed for the categorization and analysis of what the botanic explorers find.

Another question is once we find a useful agent, can we utilize today's technology to amplify its utility and ensure its availability in industrial quantities? These considerations are most important to industry. Supplies of plant pharmaceuticals can be very limited. We need to employ the technologies of recombinant DNA biotechnology to provide commercial quantities once these botanicals are discovered. It may be that the chemical synthetic process is cheaper and this also must be considered as an alternative supply route once the novelty of the compound and its utility in clinical practice has been established. There are indeed potential drugs that can be obtained through botanical sources. However, a systematic program is going to be needed to develop and explore possible leads and then to provide for adequate quantities of the substance.

The evolutionary process has created a great biodiversity. This does offer great potential, but we must realize that there is a limited window of opportunity. Man has unfortunately negatively impacted on our environment—and perhaps this adverse impact of the industrialization of the world is unavoidable—but as a result the biodiversity is diminished and the potential for development is also diminished. To be able to utilize the remaining diversity is a challenge and one that has been assumed by a number of recently devised projects. To successfully deal with the challenge requires the application of the most modern techniques. The most important might well be those related to the handling of the vast information that can be collected. Clearly computer applications for exploration and categorization of the plant world with automated processes for analysis and chemical categorization with innovative storage, organization, and retrieval, will be required to make the drug discovery process effective. The systematic computerization of knowledge in ethnobotany and pharmacognosy with emphasis on plant categorization across primitive societies will be helpful to sustain the discovery process. Using sophisticated computer techniques to look for similarities in medicinal plant use among primitive peoples to ascertain potentially useful observations can greatly aid the ethnobotanist. The goal is that these computerized techniques will replace the hundreds, if not thousands, of years needed for serendipitous observations such as that made by William Withering 200 years ago that led to the introduction of the digitalis glycosides in clinical medicine.

III. CHEMICAL SYNTHETIC DISCOVERY

Over the last 75 years, the majority of new molecules have come from synthetic chemistry. In cardiology, beta blockers and calcium channel blockers have revolutionized cardiovascular therapeutics. Beta agonists in respiratory therapy and H_2 antagonists in gastrointestinal ulcer disease therapy are two other examples of the work of synthetic chemists that has greatly changed our treatment of patients. These advances represent creations of synthetic chemistry, but also the well-proven model of finding a useful transmitter in a physiologic system, finding a receptor on which the transmitter acts, and then modifying the agonist's structure to find a specific antagonist. This has worked well with major advances in a number of fields. As new receptors and new physiologic systems are revealed, the synthetic chemist will surely continue to make considerable contributions to the field of drug discovery. For instance, as the role of the endothelium is understood better, its impact on pharmaceutical research has greatly expanded. What was once called EDRF (Endotheliol Derived Relaxing Factory) has been characterized as a locally released gas, nitric oxide. Studies on endothelial function have found endogenous substances involved in the modulation of vasodilation and vasoconstriction at the local endothelial level. There are endogenous substances opposing the vasodilating properties of nitric oxide. Endothelin is one of these transmitters and the development of specific endothelin antagonists is an exciting new field. Whether these endothelin antagonists will be effective therapies in angina, hypertension, or congestive heart failure remains to be determined, but the process shows that the synthetic discovery of drugs, combined with physiologic transmitter research, is still spawning drugs of great potential. Even here, with well-established approaches, we see the influence of the information age. Employing computers to determine receptor structure and thus possible receptive blockers has become a useful tool in the drug discovery process. Computer-assisted drug synthesis has great potential. In fact, there is at least one company that has this technology central to its commercial activities. The revolution in this aspect of synthetic chemistry is analogous to the computer revolution in the animation industry. Where dozens of artists once toiled, there are now computers creating "life-like" animations that were not feasible previously. The same revolution that the company Silicone Graphics created for animation will be occurring for the chemical synthetic industry. Besides design, the categorization of synthetic pathways can readily be computerized. The application of computer sciences to chemistry will also lead to considerable advances in this field. The application of computers to the steps beyond modeling systems, such as identifying chemical structures and automatically developing synthetic approaches, will be of considerable impact. Synthetic antagonists with optimum potency can be developed from a host of chemical possibilities.

With a heightened receptor selectivity and potency, the increased yield of these procedures will be noticeable.

However, the information age applications to synthetic modeling will be inherently limited unless we can improve our screening techniques. For many years, I have given considerable thought to the link between drug synthesis, discovery, and development. Almost 15 years ago, I had the good fortune to visit Janssen Pharmaceuticals and discuss the drug discovery process with Paul Janssen, a genius in the field. I was most impressed with his grasp of chemistry, his diverse interests, and his unparalleled success in the discovery of novel entities. Janssen was a chemist looking for novel compounds that could then be assessed to find biologic activity. A promising new compound would be processed through hundreds of models, looking for possible pharmacologic activity. The question arose about the ability to screen for biologic activity, a critical linkage point in the discovery and development process, and one to which the efficiencies and great possibilities of the information age can be effectively applied.

The Janssen approach fascinated me, but to this day has created deep abiding concerns. Since I have been interested in the field of antiarrhythmic drug development for many years and have participated in all stages of drug development from chemical synthesis to the clinical arena of programmed electrical stimulation studies, I was particularly interested in Janssen's approach as applied to antiarrhythmic pharmacology. I had been working on Lorcainide, a drug Janssen developed at Bersa, and wondered how this compound came out of discovery and how it compared to other agents screened. Janssen employed a costly dog model of PVC suppression post-coronary artery ligation. Lorcainide, being a Ic Vaughan Williams' agent, was most effective in this model as a sodium channel blocker with slow "on and off" kinetics to the sodium channel would be predicted to act in this type of model. But PVC suppression and the Ic agents have not shown prolongation of life in post-MI studies. The type-III agents appear to be most effective clinically, although not definitively shown to prolong life in randomized controlled trials. However, a meta-analysis of drugs of the type-III variety and, specifically, amiodarone, have suggested them to be far more effective with much less proarrhythmia than the sodium channel blockers. One might wonder what would be the effect of the clinically valuable agent amiodarone in the screening model that Janssen was using to pick out his antiarrhythmic to go into development. In fact, the records at Bersa were so accurate that the scientists in that department could look up the results in a few minutes and describe the actions of other known antiarrhythmic agents in the drug model. The answer they gave me was that amiodarone was much less effective and, in fact, hardly effective at all in the model in which Lorcainide was so very effective. It is no wonder that the pharmaceutical industry in the 80s found a host of Ic agents (flecainide, encainaide, lorcainide, propafenone, indecainide, ethmozine, etc.), since that is what their assays were best at picking up as active agents. Thus the model is so very important in the drug discovery process and will often determine development. We could synthesize thousands of compounds and select for development a few that fit the characteristics being sought by the model employed in the screening process, but these may not be optimum for therapy. This is a major problem and one not given enough consideration. We can only think of the possibility that there may be hundreds, if not thousands, of compounds buried in analytical hoppers such as Janssen's Bersa research establishment that could have been extremely useful, but were discarded because they were not identified as biologically active in an inherently flawed screening model.

In addition to the problem of the model used in drug screening there is also a fundamental difference in discovery between mass screening and receptor-targeted research. The latter has proved more successful in the last decade, but some major advances have come out of pure chemistry and follow-up screening to determine biologic activity. Can the revolution of the information age and computer sciences be applied to synthesis and screening? This is a cogent question that will challenge us in the coming years. I believe a revolution will occur here too. Synthesis on a grand scale will be tied to automated focused biological-activity screening that will permit the evaluation of tens of thousands of molecules on a daily basis. Clearly, how we screen will determine the validity of this approach.

While we are in transition from the age of synthetic chemistry to biotechnology and gene manipulation, synthetic discovery still will play a major role in advancing the therapeutic armormentarium.

IV. BIOTECHNOLOGY AND GENE MANIPULATION

The area of biotechnology and gene manipulation is in its early stages, but has already made considerable impact. The largest pharmaceutical companies are busy positioning themselves by acquiring or "joint venturing" with the biotechnology companies, usually small start-up enterprises. They are undertaking these acquisitions to be prepared to benefit from the coming revolution in biotechnology and gene manipulation products and procedures. Biotechnology has not advanced as rapidly as some have predicted. The science has made tremendous strides, but a number of factors have limited the advances and commercialization. The scale-up and commercialization of biotechnology processes is limited by expense and the difficulties that are technologically imposed. The first generation of compounds have been effective at times, as growth hormone and rTPA demonstrate. However, there have been major failures such as the antibodies to counteract the effects of septic shock. While the science permits the creation of drugs to evaluate, the compounds themselves may not be effective. This dichotomy stems from our imperfect knowledge of the pathophysiology of disease states, such as in the case with gram negative sepsis and shock. Another is the problem of a constantly changing target such as the case with the AIDS virus. Genentech and Amgen have been successful in bringing drugs to the marketplace, but even these companies have struggled to remain viable and maintain adequate cash flow to undertake research and development for the next generation of products. The hundreds, if not thousands, of smaller companies may not fare as well and it is safe to predict that only a small fraction will indeed find a successful product. Besides the discrepancy between the ability to make a compound and its clinical efficacy, there are the problems of corporate capitalization and effective drug development. The mergers of biotech concerns and the established pharmaceutical industry will go beyond improved capitalization and will bring more expertise in drug development and the regulatory approval process to this fledgling industry. But there are further impediments to success. Many of the products of biotechnology synthesis are proteins that are not orally active. A major area of research is going to be to convert the intravenously active compounds to ones with a facilitated means of delivery. Novel drug delivery systems to overcome the problems of lack of oral activity will be crucial. Carrier molecules, topical transport enhancers, and nasal absorption enhancers are but a few of the possible solutions to the drug delivery problem that considerably hampers the biotechnology field. Another approach has been the development of chemical molecules that have similar key structural elements that may permit the chemical compound to act like the protein molecule. If this is possible, we may find ourselves using the tools of biotechnology to enhance the drug discovery process through chemical synthesis. Despite the problems and the inherent limitations, the field of biotechnology will greatly increase the possibilities of compounds available for drug development and, in fact, development in many novel areas that have been very much lacking in therapies. With the initial cost being so great, the pressures for successful development are further heightened and thus the critical elements of the development process will need to be clear if we are not to repeat the mistakes of yesterday. For example, demonstrating the blood-clot lysing capabilities of recombinant tissue plasminogen activator (rTPA) and reversal of an acute MI in development was not enough for commercial viability of the product. Genentech persisted and undertook to perform a comparative study of rTPA with streptokinase to demonstrate the superiority of the rTPA product. The superiority of the rTPA combined with an aggressive marketing strategy permitted Genentech to dominate the thrombolytic market. In the development process of biotechnology products, their value and place in the therapeutic armamentarium may be as important as the demonstration of efficacy in a pivotal trial. The pharmacoeconomic impact of new therapies—the very great expense of the biotechnology-derived drugs, the benefits of the drug, its place in therapy, and especially its cost-benefit ratio—will become critical in the product's success.

V. GENE THERAPY

Gene manipulation strategies may lie at the core of disease treatment. It seems that not a day goes by without a new gene being "discovered" that is the cause of a well-known disease. That there would be a single gene responsible for a metabolic disease like gout or homocystinuria, for example, seems reasonable. That a single gene mutation could cause a condition like Eulers Danos syndrome also seems reasonable. But breast cancer, lupus erythematosus, or coronary artery disease caused by a single abnormal gene is a surprise to say the least. A building body of evidence supports many of these claims. This is exciting and may represent a new age of possible effective therapies for some of the most important conditions affecting man. But the identification of the gene itself, though an important first step, is only the initial part of a very long process to cure the disease. The techniques for gene modification are rudimentary and certainly need further study. An area of cardiology where gene therapy should be most promising is restenosis following acute angioplasty. Angioplasty entails placing a catheter in the coronary vessel, inflating a balloon at the tip of the catheter, pushing aside the atherosclerotic lesion. This is rather a successful technique; however, a major problem limiting the success of angioplasty is reocclusion. At the time of the initial angioplasty, there are stimuli that are initiated that cause cell proliferation of the media leading to restenosis. The medial cells that proliferate are very homogeneous, and this process seems to occur quite rapidly and in 20–60% of individuals having a single-vessel angioplasty. But even this simple model for gene therapy has proven a difficult target. There has been some very interesting work done with antisense therapy with promise shown in the area of restenosis. Clinical trials are currently in progress using antisense material. However so much of the methodology is new, and this impedes the clinical development. The use of viral vector to insert the material in the medial cells turning off protein synthesis is one limitation. A major question arises, can the virus replicate? Will the gene be correctly inserted or will additional genetic material of the virus be inserted? Thus, the validation and safety aspects are formidable and can markedly slow the development process. As experience increases with product development and manufacture and guidance for developing clinical trials improves, the overall time for developing gene manipulation strategies will be improved. We are only at the frontiers of gene manipulation; the possibilities are phenomenal. Will the promise be realized? This question cannot be answered at this time, but the prospect of preventing diseases of such great magnitude or even treating such serious diseases as cancer in advanced stages is so exciting that the concept is scientifically irresistible.

VI. THE DEVELOPERS

Along with the evolution in the process of discovery and the tremendous influence of the revolution in information handling, changes in the participants in the development process will also have considerable impact. There is also an evolution occurring in the parties to the development process. Observing the trends makes one think of the theories of the origins of the universe with oscillations in mass: accumulations, explosions, and reaccumulations, forming large aggregates and small break-off components. Perhaps the process started with the entrepreneurs who led the field successfully and developed the large corporate giants of today. Merck and Hoffman-LaRoche are examples of the one-man enterprises that expanded into major companies. In fact, the major companies dominate the pharmaceutical industry to an unparalleled extent. Perhaps 10 to 20 companies represent over 90% of new drugs emanating from the corporate phalanx. In fact, over the last 20 years, mergers have continued and indeed the last few years have seen even further consolidation of the pharmaceutical industry. One analyst reported in the *Wall Street Journal* that for a company to survive it must be able to compete with the major players in the pharmaceutical field. This is not just because of funding requirements for drug development programs, but because of the development impediments established by these very large competitors. These impediments can be simple, such as the number of patients exposed to a new entity, or more complex, such as a survival study or the use of experimental ancillary technologies that are prohibitively expensive and would not be automatically required for the development of a compound. These impediments can create an impression, both to the FDA and other companies, that they are requisite, which makes development of a second or third agent in the field much more difficult, time consuming, and expensive. The time factor is especially important since the longer it takes to develop a compound, the more dominance in the market the first drug has gained. Time is the same as money and the loss of product lead can all but destroy the market potential for an agent.

VII. SMALL DEVELOPMENT COMPANIES

Considering all these obstacles to development and the considerable regulatory maze, the trend to conglomeratization with bigger and bigger companies is not surprising. What is indeed surprising is the simultaneous opposing trend of the development of the very small niche start-up companies proliferating along with the ever-increasing size of the major players in pharmaceutical development. In fact, it is not just how small these companies are that is surprising, it is that they only encompass one aspect of the drug discovery and development process. Some companies are focusing on discovery, others specialize in clinical development. Some companies plan that once the NDA is granted, the company will license the product to a larger firm for marketing. Then there are other companies that neither discover or develop drugs but place their energies in the marketing of developed pharmaceuticals. One may argue that the niche enterprises are doomed to failure. But a number of factors combine to make this approach viable. The total overhead of the very large companies limits development to compounds expected to have sales of at least $100 million. At times a drug may have a smaller market and a large company will develop the product for public relations, to bolster sales of existing products in their product line, or out of sheer miscalculation of market potential. However, the small companies look to a potential market of $5 to $50 million a year as a bonanza. Their costs are far lower permitting adequate profit margins after development, marketing, discovery costs, and expenses for sales. Small companies cannot carry out clinical trials at the same level expected of a Pfizer or a Merck. Thus, the studies are fewer, smaller, and aimed at proving the efficacy and safety as directly as possible. Clearly, though, the niche company will play a major role in drug development. They will service areas not considered appropriate in terms of market size by the larger companies. They will represent the dynamic growth of academic entrepreneurs who look to the commercialization of their ideas especially in biotechnology and gene manipulation.

VIII. ACADEMICIANS AND ENTREPRENEURS

Many of these companies are investor driven and thus have intense dedication to development and success. But can a company with one or two products compete? It appears it can. There are a number of such examples. For instance, Medco Research developed a rather novel therapy for SVT, adenosine, and has become quite successful for a very small pharmaceutical company. While Medco is involved in the traditional pharmaceutical development approach of synthetic chemistry, they in fact developed an existing product not unique to the Medco research. However, most small companies are in the biotechnology field. The biotechnology industry seems most appropriate for the small-company approach. If the companies besides Genentech and Amgen can climb out of the start-up phase remains to be seen. Centicor, Genzyme, and US Bioscience have all made attempts, some more successful than others, but it is difficult to develop a viable product and then to sustain the research and development necessary for continued growth. But the trend is clearly established. Academicians with a novel idea no longer publish their results and go onto the next project. Rather, patents are obtained and a company is started. I marvel at the recent reports of a new technique in cardiothorasic surgery being performed using the laparoscopic approach. Instead of reading about the advances in JAMA, the discussion centers in the *Wall Street Journal* and the possible IPO that will be forthcoming. Entrepreneurs and academicians are forming alliances that may speed a procedure or chemical entity into a viable product for development. While the free exchange of ideas may be limited and scientific discourse suffer a bit, the possibility of widespread clinical use facilitated by commercial development is enhanced. The pros and cons of this approach are not for us to debate, but rather to accept as a trend that is ongoing and growing considerably. I do think that the nimbleness of these small dynamic companies, coupled with their lower overhead cost, offers considerable benefit to pharmaceutical discovery and development. Drugs are being developed that the larger concerns would not have considered. The advancement in niche areas like orphan drugs are for the most part being pursued by smaller companies. I believe this is a healthy trend and one that will force all of the industry to streamline. Combined with the trend of small niche companies in drug development has come the parallel corporate trend of downsizing and the hesitancy to expand divisions to take on temporary projects. More and more of the large companies are contracting for critical aspects of drug discovery and development. Compounds can be manufactured under contract. Consultants can put together manufacturing specifications and preclinical testing, and stability work can be done under contract. Clinical studies are performed by CROs with the data handled by contract statistical analysis. A consulting team can put together a NDA under the supervision of a small core group at corporate headquarters. This can be done for the small company or the very largest of the pharmaceutical giants. Parts of a projects can be subcontracted. Indeed it is not uncommon for intermediate-to-small projects at the largest companies to be entirely subcontracted. For these reasons, the CROs and other contract service companies (CSAs) have been most successful. A bonanza of new business has created exponential growth for these types of companies. The companies are competitive and the work relentless, but results are what makes the industry thrive and drug development has been speeded up considerably in some instances using this "piecework" approach.

There are dangers with the fragmented approach. Outside companies can be less dependable; projects can fall apart when the capitalization of the company is inadequate and they go under; and less than favorable schedules can sometimes develop since the project is not necessarily the highest priority of the contracting company. The fragmented approach can create situations wherein the contracting company is less able to alert the primary company to important clinical findings that should alter the development program or to serious toxicities that need to be taken into account. If studies are performed outside the United States, as they often are, the quality of the data and the important aspects of clinical-study acumen by the site investigators is often lacking. Important information about the drug may not be passed along and this can seriously impede the development process. In addition, corporate rapport with the site investigators may be lost and the important "seeding" of the market with experienced investigators with a product may not occur when contract organizations are involved and non-United States data is employed. However, there may be significant cost savings and increased patient accession with the CRO and foreign-study data approaches that may make their utilization advisable. Clearly a balanced program giving careful considerations to the limitations of CROs running the studies, providing statistical analysis, and complete monitoring services as well as CROs coordinating non-United States performed studies need to be carefully evaluated and balanced against the more traditional approaches to drug development.

IX. THE GOVERNMENT AND DRUG DEVELOPMENT

The influences of the federal government are pervasive in our society, from our tax structure to the actions of regulatory agencies. All aspects of industry, and especially the pharmaceutical industry, are greatly influenced. Some very manipulative politicians target the pharmaceutical industry as they target the "rich" in their rhetoric to pander to voters. But for the most part, there is a finely balanced tension between the Democrats representing more government and the Republicans representing less government and deregulation. This is, of course, a simplification, but one with historic justification. Clearly there is a trend against government as the provider of solutions. How the trend will develop in the short term is difficult to predict. Even with the progression away from government and regulation, the impact this trend may have on the pharmaceutical industry will remain substantial. The loosening of OSHA regulations and environmental impact statements are more likely than changes at the FDA. This is despite a lot of discussions by the new Republican congressional leadership regarding FDA. However, the specter of an unprotected public is a difficult political cry to oppose and one I believe not one readily taken on except for the most ardent of Republican zealots. The industry itself, especially the larger pharmaceutical companies, appears to support FDA rather vigorously. They operate successfully within its framework and, in a way, the FDA has become part of the process to limit competition and diminish the effectiveness of the smaller companies not able to compete against the more formidable pharmaceutical giants. Additionally, the FDA, especially at the scientific level, well serves industry, ensuring efficacy and safety and instilling a very high degree of confidence on the part of the public in pharmaceutical products. Thus, significant change from the status quo is unlikely in the immediate future.

X. GOVERNMENT RESEARCH

The importance of the defense and space-related technology on drug development has been minimal and will probably continue to be disappointing. A more effective utilization of research funding coming from space research and the military defense research consortium could be obtained by a granting system based along the NIH and NSF lines with more decentralization. While the NSF and NIH are most imperfect systems, they are far better at supporting the advancement of knowledge than the military's or space administration's approach. Whether the government turns in this direction cannot be predicted and, in fact, may be unlikely. However, the trend to very big scientific projects has slowed and a more reasonable, decentralized approach is taking shape under the new congressional leadership. I think this is especially encouraging since by supporting new programs, small programs, and diverse projects, we are more likely to see important advances as opposed to the results seen when the established industrial scientific complex and its bureaucracy is the only receiver of support.

Still, there is a paucity of government support for pharmaceutical-related research, clinical pharmacology research, and research related to drug development. This is truly unfortunate since there is tremendous public health benefit to be obtained in this area. I am not suggesting government to compete with industry, but in areas where industry is not working, or in more fundamental areas that lead to the discovery and development process or are ancillary to drug discovery and development, government could and should play an important role. However, a major component of the nation's public health research remains solely funded by for-profit pharmaceutical enterprises. The federal government's genome project appears much more promising for the biotechnology gene manipulation sector of drug discovery and development. This information is fundamental and will form the information base of so many discoveries in this area for the future. It is counter-productive for the government to patent its findings and not facilitate the dissemination and utilization of this information in research and practical product development, and it is very good indeed that this approach has stopped and the government is once again returning to its role as a facilitator, not a competitor. That the direction of the genome project is recoiling from the concept of patenting in competition with the private sector is a sign that the federal bureaucracy can be modified and be responsive to the needs of society.

XI. THE FDA REGULATORS

The drug development process occurs within the structure defined by the Food and Drug Administration. From initial clinical testing in Phase I to later Phase II and III clinical trials, the FDA has considerable influence and control while at the same time exercises a minimal degree of interference that is often surprising. Unlike European agencies, for example, the scientific levels of the Food and Drug Administration are most accessible at all stages of development from pre-IND, pre-Phase II or pre-NDA meetings, and the FDA can provide meaningful guidance in a drug development program. Yes, they will be the judges of the data presented and the "keepers of the regulations," but I believe their assistance comes more from experience in the drug development process. The scientific division chiefs and other senior individuals at FDA see a tremendous number of clinical trials, have often encountered clinical development problems, and can, without the disclosure of confidential information, provide considerable assistance to those involved in drug development. While an individual in a company may be involved in four or five compounds over a career in terms of major development programs, the FDA senior people may see that in a week and from many different perspectives. Clearly, the FDA is the nexus of pharmaceutical development information and training that unfortunately has not been tapped into as effectively as it should be.

To consult the FDA while involved in drug development is a most advisable approach. The FDA and industry working together on a product will often evolve a development program that is more effective and more efficient in time and resources. Too many may take FDA's advice as dictum. There is what could be termed "the shadow FDA." Those regulatory advisors in industry telling us what the FDA requires and wants, all too often offer distorted advice and impede effective drug development. The FDA should be looked upon as an important resource, with whom those pivotally involved in drug development in industry should communicate directly. Regulatory advisors, consultants, past regulators, facilitators, and legal advisors all have their place but should not be interposed between those individuals at companies who are critical links in drug development. No advice should be binding, but needs to be discussed and reasonable approaches taken. The individuals at the FDA are not omniscient. A development plan may not work out and may need substantial modification. Failure to realize this and blindly going forth after an FDA conference can lead to failure. Coming back to the FDA and saying, "But this is what we were instructed to do," is foolish and in a sense undercuts the free and open exchange of ideas between the regulators and the developers. Advice is what is given, and reproach later because of changing circumstances, developments in the field, or just lack of efficacy of a compound, cannot be blamed on the regulatory advisors. In fact, reproach later will deter the critical assistance from the FDA that can be so very helpful to a drug development team.

These impressions, of course, need to be modified in the context of the divisions and the individuals involved. There are differences among and between divisions, individuals, and those at FDA giving advice, and this needs to be factored into the equation. But clearly the most successful in development have created a working relationship with the FDA and made use of the extensive scientific experience these individuals have with drug development. Having been the organizer of a course on Cardiovascular Drug Development, Protocol Design, and Methodology for 15 years, I can attest to the unselfish assistance of so many senior individuals at the FDA. Their knowledge of the drug development field and their interest in successful drug development and in finding scientific truth is clear cut. While the course involves many leading academics and industry physicians who have considerable knowledge, each year the Symposium demonstrates that the FDA participants who are senior at the agency consistently demonstrate a broad knowledge of the field of drug development.

Clearly, the FDA can facilitate drug development further than what is currently being done. There are times that the delays are needless and the debate is not helpful, but the "drug lag" behind Europe, which so severely crippled therapeutics in the 50s, 60s, and the 70s, no longer exists as a problem. However, excessive drug regulation is not the goal. Rather more expeditious, less costly development in the information age is a goal that needs to be set by the FDA. A case-by-case review is no longer needed. To have each data point separately chronicled and meticulously reviewed for efficacy and toxicity by a junior reviewer is an immense waste of time. Having the primary reviewer recreate the NDA piece by piece and then producing their own summary is a laborious process that obviously can take a year or more. The NDA is put together by hundreds of individuals highly trained in the pharmaceutical industry and having one or two people go through this on a line-by-line basis and check every data point and reanalyze the presentations is going to be a most arduous time-consuming process. Quality assurance techniques are in place to ensure accuracy and integrity of a NDA data base. The FDA could make use of these techniques and clearly the FDA will need to strengthen procedures by the century's end and apply sophisticated computer techniques to make the analyses as expeditious as possible. To keep up with the information age, the FDA will be one of the links in the drug development process that is most stressed by forthcoming change. User fees and more FDA revenues are not the answer, and placing the cost of submission beyond the capacity of small start-up companies is ill advised. Using these funds for more and more reviewers to expand the laborious almost hand approach to data review is fallacious. Many of these programs are not objected to by the giants of industry and are in fact encouraged because they once again appease those who want to speed up the process and at the same time create impediments for the more formative, dynamic, small companies: creating anticompetitive practices in which the FDA is an unwitting ally.

I have often heard the statement that the FDA needs to "take its time" to "plow through each data point" to protect the public. By never approving a drug, the FDA would be the most protective, since no adversity would ensue from approved drugs. However, the adverse effects of no therapeutic advances would be intolerable. Thus, a compromise in the tension between the regulators charged to protect the public and the public's need for new effective therapies needs to be struck. The use of the information revolution to facilitate drug development needs to be explored. We are at the beginning of this exciting period and the government will evolve slower perhaps than other centers in the development process, but it will indeed evolve.

A number of approaches are possible. The use of quality assurance techniques for partial-to-comprehensive data verification on a random basis certainly needs to be validated and then applied. Perhaps data analysis performed by certified groups that are paid for by the company, but at the same time are licensed by the FDA, would eliminate the need for data re-entry and reapplication of analytical techniques. The focusing in on quick review techniques for the critical pivotal studies and ascertaining their veracity needs to be placed at the top of the review list. With the acceptance of efficacy, rapid computerized analysis of toxicity of a product and comparison of the results to those obtained with other agents could permit an estimation of the agent's potential benefits and toxicity. This could facilitate early presentation of the NDA material to an advisory committee that would be able to understand its place in the therapeutic armamentarium and decide whether a more prolonged thorough evaluation is needed or an early release could be considered. Of course an early release might be combined with a more prolonged preliminary period where information is collected on adverse experiences and efficacy and these items then used for continued drug evaluation.

The process of approving a drug, getting very little additional information after the approval, and once approved, having it remain on the market forever is really as wrong as a very slow and time-consuming initial development process. The fact that it is so difficult to get a drug off the market and that we have so little postmarketing information validates the regulators' approach of making the initial approval stringent indeed. It would be far better to look to a system such as that in Great Britain where there may be a more provisional stage of approval, where there is a very detailed program of postmarketing surveillance that makes it quite simple for practitionists to participate. We must understand that drugs can be marketed and then knowledge and information developed that changes our initial impression. A drug could be severely limited in its labeling, have warnings issued to physicians who will be using it, or possibly even taken off the market when our knowledge base on the product changes. I do not think a drug withdrawal should be looked at as a criticism of the FDA, but a realization that our knowledge continues to evolve. Unfortunately, I have read the transcripts of congressional committees led by inquisitors who severely criticize regulators when adversity is later discovered from an agent that was approved on quite a meritorious application. If we can get the ground rules straight and understand that our knowledge base evolves and that we might have to take a different regulatory decision-making course as this knowledge advances, then we can accept the earlier approval without faulting our regulatory colleagues. This approach is needed if we are to fundamentally change for the better the drug development process. This is a difficult change since so much of the process is developed by lawyers who look upon the process as a litigation, with guilt or innocence to be determined, instead of by scientists who are continuously learning as more information is collected.

XII. ISSUES AND CONCEPTS IN DRUG DEVELOPMENT

The field of drug development is vast and often specific to a given compound and the indications sought for its use. No chapter can provide an ABC guide to development. What is often a surprise is that development is applied in a general manner without a clear understanding of the market needs, without careful preclinical testing of the drug's effectiveness and especially its comparative effects to other available agents. In the remaining portions of this chapter, I am going to direct my thoughts to cardiovascular drug development; I believe that the discussion could be generalized to other areas of drug development as well.

When one is considering developing an antiarrhythmic, there is a need to go beyond the antiarrhythmic label. Are we discussing a drug aimed at the treatment of supraventricular arrhythmias or are we discussing a drug that will be used for the treatment of ventricular arrhythmias? Are we talking about arrhythmia prevention, acute conversion, or a long-term prophylaxis? What is the drug's mechanism of action? What is available for therapy alternatives? A sodium channel blocker needs to have a specific attribute: perhaps less toxicity; perhaps less proarrhythmia. One has to ask if animal studies unambiguously show the advantages of the drug, warranting the program to go forward. Some of these issues appear obvious, but some of the considerations are often not addressed in the preliminary stages of drug development. When the class I sodium channel blockers were made suspect after the CAST study, the rush was on to find and develop type-III amiodarone-like agents. However, there was no evidence that a pure type-III drug was superior to a mixed function agent like amiodarone that had beta blocking and some sodium channel blocking properties as well. Why industry went off on almost a quest for pure, specific potassium channel blockers is an interesting example of herd psychology. This is an area where animal models could have been developed to test the hypothesis of which drugs should be sought for development and which would be optimum for clinical testing. I believe this was not done. This is not an indictment of the pharmaceutical industry, but one of the entire academic community. The development of preclinical in vivo models is under emphasized. Could we not develop a CAST arrhythmia model in rats to look at post-MI mortality? Could not proarrhythmia be assessed in an atrial fibrillation animal model: It seems that counting bodies in rats, mice, or guinea pigs, for that matter, or other species is far less expensive and far less disturbing than assessing the impact of these agents on mortality and clinical trials. Clearly, the model needs to be validated, but this is certainly possible when the clinical outcome has been assessed in at least one large-scale clinical study. Another example is the ACE inhibitors and their use with post-MI and CHF patients. Indeed some of pioneering work was done by investigators accomplished in the animal laboratory. Besides clinical studies, an animal model does exist. But when the A-II receptor antagonists come to the fore for development, they are not evaluated in terms of mortality in the existing animal model. It would be useful to evaluate the A-II antagonists in this model since there are differences between the ACE inhibitors and the A-II antagonists. One difference is that the ACE inhibitor increases bradykinin while the A-II receptor blocker antagonizes the effects of angiotensin without changing the amounts of bradykinin in the system. This difference may be immaterial or bradykinin can even be deleterious and the A-II antagonists could show greater beneficial effect. Testing in an animal model though would go a long way toward testing this hypothesis and helping us design perhaps clinical studies to evaluate the A-II effects. Undoubtedly, animal studies employing models need to be validated, but they also need to be employed frequently to aid in determining an optimum development strategy. In models varying dose, varying the combination of drugs is feasible. In a definitive clinical mortality trial one dose of the therapy is probably all that is possible.

Another area in which modeling could be so very useful is the use of surrogate endpoints. Whether it be blood-pressure reduction, lipid lowering, VPC suppression, or thrombus dissolution, the endpoint often used clinically and the one that is so readily obtainable clinically is a surrogate endpoint. Surrogate endpoints are an important basis for drug development, but one that is quite precarious. Targeting PVCs for developing an antiarrhythmic in the 90s post-CAST is of no value and, in fact, would be the subject of ridicule. All surrogates are suspect and need to be validated. The possibility of validation, even if only partial, with animal studies is an area needing further evaluation.

XIII. PHARMACEUTICAL STRUCTURE

The structure of the group working on drug development is most important. Individuals that have familiarity with their field are requisite. Pharmacologists, pharmacokineticists, those with expertise in trial design, and individuals with strong preclinical study knowledge all are necessary components. Occasionally one or two individuals have the expertise, but often a team is needed to pursue the objective. At least an advisory group with broad expertise should be interposed in the development process to take a number of areas into consideration early in the planning stages. With an adequate structure, the resources must also be available. One cannot be ahead of the preclinical development program and make rational decisions. One needs the appropriate technology, but one also needs to coordinate resources in manufacturing (including placebos and positive controls) with packaging and regulatory considerations. Marketing needs to be involved. Developing a drug for supraventricular arrhythmias when the treatment of all arrhythmias is the goal of the company can be a disaster. While for medical reasons some groups will be excluded in SVT development, excluding groups with very severe LV dysfunction and ventricular arrhythmias from a general antiarrhythmic development program would not be acceptable. The capabilities of the compound must be assessed by the development group and fitted in with the corporate goals for that drug development of that compound. Then a rational drug development plan can be devised.

XIV. DOSE AND SERUM CONCENTRATION MEASUREMENTS

Perhaps the most fundamental issue in drug development is establishing the dose for a study. This is indeed a difficult area and one that is inadequately handled in many instances. It would be safe to say that perhaps 75% to 95% of all drugs are being employed at doses that are not optimum. Dose ranging is difficult, expensive, and time consuming, but so very important. Finding a minimally effective dose can help in reducing adverse side effects of agents and can be an important step in an effective drug development program. For years, the dose of the thiazide diuretics were perhaps 50 times the needed dose for antihypertensive therapy. This is both bad for drug development and bad for the patient taking the medication. We can do better than this, and more and more studies, due to FDA insistence, more often than not, are rather elegantly determining the effective dose range. It is also important to state that an effective dose range for one individual may not be an effective dose for another individual. Differences may not just be on an individual basis, but may vary within special populations. In fact, it is rather important to try to look at a more homogeneous population early on, and exclude the special populations, to come up with a reasonable dose range. The other population can be studied at a later date. In fact, later studies to establish dose in special populations are very important. The FDA has mandated the inclusion of women in studies because they have been woefully underrepresented previously. A drug's effect in the black population or oriental population is also very important to discern and clearly there are racial differences in drug handling that can significantly affect the appropriate dose for a given population. As important, is the consideration of the disease state in the different racial groups. While hypertension is very prevalent in the black population, they usually manifest low renin hypertension and ACE inhibitors do not seem to be very useful in treating hypertension in blacks. This is not a major problem for the effective treatment of hypertension since alternative agents can be used in the black population. However, the problem is certainly an important consideration in terms of heart failure therapy. Heart failure is common in the black population, often as an end result of hypertensive cardiovascular disease. Whether ACE inhibitors have the same salutary effects, reducing mortality in the black population as it does in the general heart-failure group, has still not been clearly determined. Establishing dose and also utility of an agent in special populations is a matter that needs more attention.

What we are usually faced with early on is the need for a dose to initiate clinical studies. Even the most rudimentary of Phase I and II studies need a starting dose. For first-time studies in man, perhaps exploring the lower estimated dose range from preclinical studies is optimum. Further dose escalation following a logarhythmic approach may then be appropriate. All exposures in man should be based on milligram-per-kilogram exposures in prior animal models with some previous experience in that model's correspondence to the human condition. Incremental dose escalation is helpful to give some guidance, but time/action relationships and accumulation of drug combine to limit this technique. Establishing a dose in fixed combination is especially important and the FDA does require a synergistic effect to be established for the combined compound A and B as contrasted to either A or B alone at the peak of their dose response curve.

Dose escalation studies to toxicity are to be avoided. The IRBs and clinical common sense are not going to tolerate dangerous dose escalations. Careful exploration, even to what appears to be astronomical doses, is appropriate in controlled situations when the lower doses have been explored. A log exploration is to be recommended as the most appropriate choice when possible exploration of 0.1, 1, and 10 is better than the more usual 1-, 5-, and 10-dose titration approach. If no toxicity is observed in man or if it is mild and none observed in animals at higher doses, the effects of higher doses should then be explored in man. If 10 is tolerated, then perhaps 50 and 100 should be explored to further determine the concentration-effect curve. As one creeps up to the higher doses, caution is certainly needed. I was involved in one study where we used doses of an oral nitrate preparation of 30, 60, 120, and then up to 240 mg. The 240 mg was looked upon in horror by most investigators and they were correct if that was the starting dose. Giving the 240 mg without previous titration would result in a lot of adverse side effects. However, the lower doses were explored first, then to get to that higher dose, there was a two or three step titration. This enhanced the safety while still exploring the full dose-response range of the agent.

Perhaps the most dependable approach is a parallel design with escalating dose in each group. Group comparisons are best and a dose can be established without having carryover effect from the previous dose and missing the peak action of the previous dose in the patient. But these are just guidelines to the selection process and by the very nature are simplifications. Each situation presents unique problems to consider and there is no one dose-finding technique for all circumstances.

Let us consider two situations that indeed impact on drug development. If we are developing an antiarrhythmic agent, what endpoint do we use to establish dose? At times PVCs have been employed although even for the Ia or Ic agents, the dose of PVC suppression may not correlate with the dose for VT suppression at programmed electrical stimulation (PES) and neither may correlate with a dose that reduces mortality over a six-month to one-year follow-up after electrophysiologic testing. The type-III agent is even more problematic since a dose at EP testing and the results at EP testing, for that matter, may or may not correlate with outcome. VPC suppression with a type-III agent would be even less likely to correlate with outcome. Using prolongation of the Action Potential Duration (APD) employing a monophasic action potential catheter (FRANZ catheter) may be the most promising technique with the type-III Vaughan Williams' agents since action potential prolongation is inherent in the pharmacodynamic action of the drug. Thus, dose should be tied to the critical marker of the electrophysiologic mechanism of action of the drug, which in this case is action potential duration prolongation.

Another approach that might improve results to obtain serum concentrations and correlating these to drug action. Serum concentration varies less and this is a potential advantage (at least this is the claim of Pk/Pd proponents). However, the correlation of serum concentration to drug action is not well established in most areas in cardiovascular therapeutics and, in fact, one can generalize to most areas of therapeutics. In cardiology, PK/PD relationships are virtually nonexistent. Serum concentrations of beta blockers do not correlate with drug action. Levels of antiarrhythmic agents do not really correlate with outcome. Myerburg and Associates once reported that if one obtains a minimal defined concentration with an antiarrhythmic agent (mostly type Is), patients had a better outcome than if a lower concentration was obtained (2).

But clearly defined target levels do not exist and studies have not reported any difference in blood levels in patients who were "protected" by Holter analysis or at programmed electrical stimulation testing compared to those who were not protected. In the field of CHF, dose is also a difficult and vexing question. Digitalis is employed at the most minimum of doses to avoid toxicity, whether high doses would be more beneficial is currently unknown since the spector of toxicity is what we try to avoid against clinically. The ACE inhibitors are a major contribution to the field and a number of studies have shown that they reduce mortality in patients with severe and also moderate congestive heart failure. But what dose is the most effective? What should be the dose that is targeted clinically? These are unanswered questions despite the body of evidence attesting to the efficacy of ACE inhibitors in congestive heart failure. The ACE inhibitors lower blood pressure and a dose of ACE that lowers BP, but does not cause prohibitive side effects, is one that is selected often for testing in clinical trials. We must ask ourselves: what is the correlation of the effect of the ACE inhibitor on blood pressure and the outcome in heart failure patients? The answer to this important question is clearly unknown. A substudy of the NIH program in heart failure (SOLVD) study reported that patients with a greater inhibition of converting enzyme did better than those showing a lower inhibition (3). Perhaps dose should be established on the basis of ACE inhibition. Clearly there is considerable confusion in the field and the confusion probably diminishes the use of ACE inhibitors because this degree of uncertainty to physicians decreases their likelihood of employing the ACE and encourages them to use such low doses of ACE as to be homeopathic.

Lipid therapy is another area where correlation of the dose has not been established for clinical effect. The surrogate of reduction in cholesterol is the target we have chosen for clinical therapy. However, in clinical studies a fixed dose was employed, cholesterol was reduced but was not necessarily pushed to a target cholesterol level. We see benefit in secondary prevention in some trials. This is very different than pushing to a target cholesterol and seeing what would happen in terms of outcome. However, the target cholesterol must be considered suspect since we really have no definitive evidence that it is the cholesterol lowering to a target level that is causing benefit. Do we know that the cholesterol target is optimum or should cholesterol be lowered even further? The Simvastatin Trial showing a marked secondary prevention gain may not relate to cholesterol lowering per se, but to changes caused in the vascular biology-altering plaque rupture proclivity and platelet aggregation (4). The gain in luminal diameter has only been modest as demonstrated by quantitative angiography studies and, thus the small improvement documented in luminal diameter is unlikely to be the mechanism of the mortality benefit. What dose should therefore be employed in the future lipid trials is another conundrum in drug development. We have certain doses that work. We have certain targets for cholesterol and perhaps studies are needed to validate the concept that lowering blood cholesterol to a target concentration will offer us the most benefit as compared to a fixed dose of a lipid-lowering agent.

XV. METHODOLOGIES AND DRUG DEVELOPMENT

There is considerable importance to sequential drug development. The coordination of Phase-I studies, dose finding, key pivotal studies, and then drug interaction trials with followup of special populations and further patient exposures, is a basic tenant of drug development. Further dose evaluations and studies looking at combination with other known concomitant drugs that would be used are important to drug development. The advantage of parallel studies as opposed to crossover design trials can be argued. Utility of placebo-controlled trials, as well as the place of positive control studies, are all important aspects of the decisions that need to be made in the development program. Especially important is how are drugs to be assessed and what indices ought to be employed. This is, in part, a discussion of surrogate endpoints, partly a discussion of medical approaches to a problem, and partly a discussion of philosophy. Recently I was discussing with FDA the development of an IV antiarrhythmic for the most life-threatening of ventricular arrhythmias, especially patients undergoing a cardiac arrest who are unresponsive to electroshock therapy. The discussion of the relevant endpoint is most critical. Is the relevant endpoint arrhythmia termination, survival at one hour, at 24 hours, or survival at 3, 6, or 12 months? There are no answers to these questions, but there are intervening factors that affect our decision of endpoint selection in drug development. These patients are critically ill. If nothing can be done for them, they will rapidly die. If they live for a few more minutes with the arrhythmia terminated, there is maybe enough time to utilize an assist device. If they live longer and stabilize, some will do well but most will be scheduled for a diagnostic procedure such as a cardiac catheterization with probable angioplasty to follow if a culprit coronary lesion is identified that can be technically approached. With all of the intervening therapies, the endpoints further out become a result of the initial intervention and the result also of the additional medical therapies provided. Thus the determination of outcome must be related to the intervention. In this case, the administration of the study antiarrhythmic agent—not a host of other procedures that will be performed—needs to be assessed. Looking at all endpoints might be most appropriate and useful, but the critical benefit that the antiarrhythmic can offer us is termination of an arrhythmia that previously could not be terminated.

The determination of dose and endpoints is critical. The appropriate statistical powering of the number of patients to enter and the type of study is very important. The subtleties of the selection of endpoint and dose is critical to the design and possible successful outcome to the study. As the clinical community becomes more sophisticated and more agents appear, more definitive outcomes are required. Thus in the field of cardiovascular drug development, mortality endpoints are often required to prove efficacy and safety. For an antiarrhythmic or a heart failure treatment agent, mortality has become critical. This is not at the exclusion of other concerns for mechanism and antiarrhythmic or anti-CHF effects, but still mortality is a powerful regulatory persuader. For an antiarrhythmic, the effect in the PES laboratory, the reduction in symptoms like syncope, and the reduction in death are to be hoped for and all correlate together to tell the story that the drug is antiarrhythmic. But still the effect on mortality outcome, and especially the effect on sudden death, is expected to be evaluated and to be associated with mortality reduction. When one moves along into the field of atrial fibrillation, the prevention of the arrhythmia is not felt to be sufficient, but rather remaining in sinus rhythm without adverse side effects, such as embolization or stroke, appears to be requisite. But are we testing an anticoagulant or an antiarrhythmic? Both could possibly prevent embolization and stroke, but by entirely different mechanisms. Thus, the antiarrhythmic effect must be demonstrated as well as a favorable outcome and each might require a different study to be demonstrated. The field of CHF drug development is a complex one. The ACE inhibitors demonstrate significant hemodynamic action and this is expected to correlate with a favorable mortality effect. However, establishing a dose on the hemodynamic actions may not be appropriate. Concomitant therapy with digitalis and diuretics may be beneficial or adverse. The beta blockers may have a significant role to play and maybe they have to be given concomitantly with the ACE inhibitor. Finally, when several studies have shown benefit, can approval for CHF therapy be based on hemodynamic surrogates and a class effect be granted in terms of mortality and ACE inhibition? Clearly further ACE-inhibition mortality studies are not possible and a positive control study would not prove comparability in terms of mortality since the number of patients to prove that would be prohibitive.

I believe that novel endpoints such as hemodynamic effects of a drug and the correlation with converting-enzyme inhibition can and will be employed. Valid animal models that show correlative results with the pivotal mortality studies in man with other agents of the class will lend credence to a class-effect claim. If, for an ACE inhibitor, one had an hemodynamic effect, one showed short-term improvement in exercise capacity in heart failure patients, one had similar effects on converting enzyme inhibition, and one also had data in an animal mortality study that showed there was benefit, all this would lead to the possibility of a mortality claim. However, potentially significant differences—and I emphasize the word potentially—may make one ACE inhibitor different enough from the others to question the class effect in terms of mortality. In this situation, animal models will be especially important in terms of mortality trials in man with new agents similar to the ACE inhibitors, the A-II antagonists.

XVI. INTEGRATING TECHNOLOGIES

Perhaps one of the most vexing questions in drug development relates to the often-observed problem of finding a field in evolution where the endpoints, diagnostic techniques, and methodologies are changing rapidly at times, making drug development part of the changing process. When I became interested in antiarrhythmic drug development, the technique of therapy selection employing programmed electrical stimulation was developing. The field was undergoing rapid change. Programmed electrical stimulation studies were not validated and, thus, using PES protection as an endpoint in drug development was a major leap of faith. Not to use the PES technique would have been remiss, but to solely utilize PES studies as an endpoint would have been a mistake for the development program. At that time, the appropriate role of PES was not defined clearly and different responses among the classes of drugs was also not known. Problems like this often appear in the preliminary stages of drug development. They can be even more problematic. While for antiarrhythmic drug development, PES studies still are utilized to demonstrate "drug effect" and in fact, not to expose a new antiarrhythmic to testing in the PES laboratory will raise serious regulatory questions. However, in the development of an antianginal agent, a similar evolution was occurring. Holter monitoring, identification of ischemia without chest pain, was being developed. A concept of silent ischemia was emerging. Using validating studies that employed techniques like the use of the nuclear vest was preceding, showing wall-motion abnormalities during silent ischemia, confirming that the EKG changes were not artifact or positional, but rather the ST depression without pain was true ischemia. In fact subsequent studies have found that when the episodes of silent ischemia are increased, the outcome to the patient is adverse and a reduction of silent-ischemic episodes correlates with an improved outcome. Other studies have not always found a correlation between overt anginal pain, its frequency, and silent ischemia. This is especially true in the diabetic population. The validation of the importance of silent ischemia endpoint was, and is, pretty good, especially in comparison to other endpoints often employed in drug development. However, utilizing silent-ischemia studies would not well serve the drug development program. The FDA does not recognize silent ischemia as an independent endpoint. The FDA grants no indication for the treatment of silent ischemia and maintains the singular primacy of the exercise anginal study for antianginal drug development. Indeed, there is no anti-ischemic drug development despite the widespread acceptance in the clinical cardiovascular specialists community of the importance of silent ischemia and the validity of the Holter methodology to assess silent ischemia. In this field a marked dichotomy has developed with trials designed to test a monotherapy in terms of exercise time to angina compared to a clinical cardiology approach of combined therapy with the assessment of reversible ischemia regardless of whether it is silent or overt anginal pain. In cardiology, the goal is to reduce the ischemic burden first procedurally, if possible, and then to provide medical therapy when ischemia is still present at rest or on exercise.

Knowledge of the nuances of the given field, the intricacies that the development drug process must abide by, is so very crucial. After organizing a course on Cardiovascular Drug Development for 15 years, I can appreciate the complexity of the process and the need for familiarity with the issues. Not to take part intimately in this evaluative process and to casually walk onto the scene, review other development plans, and discuss some issues with clinicians in the field will doom a plan to excessive expense and often whole aspects of a development plan will be in a direction that will not be productive or could lead to outright failure. No wonder the costs of development are so high and the results so poor.

XVII. DECISIONS IN DEVELOPMENT

With the development program underway, a number of branch points often develop that require critical decisions. Establishing dose, blinding studies, organizing centers, and dealing with IRBs are all part of development vagaries. Especially vexing is a need for studies clearly demonstrating effect and the IRBs pressures to optimize patient care and the administration of potentially beneficial established therapies. Tension develops between these cross purposes and the clinical demands are often pressing. Compromise is often needed, but the team guiding the development program needs to resist some of these substantial pressures. Compromises that limit one's knowledge about the drug are to be avoided. Developers must be encouraged to be relentless and not easily compromise study integrity. This is because all too often the perceived requirement for therapy is based on little evidence. I can remember a leader in the heart failure field blocking a comparative evaluation of an ACE inhibitor without digitalis even though so many doubt the effectiveness of the digitalis glycosides. Another situation was with a vociferous investigator who pushed very hard to prevent a study of digitalis acutely withdrawn in CHF patients receiving ACE inhibitors. It was "unethical" not to use digitalis. But this is despite the known incidence of up to 60% of patients with the diagnosis of CHF who are not being treated with ACE inhibitors. The question arises: is it unethical to withdraw digitalis and administer ACE inhibitors in patients?

The study prevailed and to this day is one of the best demonstrations of the utility of digitalis in patients with signs of pulmonary congestion (5).

There are many critical times in drug development that require a strong will and clear purpose to stay the course. The drug development program may come upon adversity in terms of adverse toxicity or lack of efficacy that may provoke serious questions about the continuation of the project. To fail to terminate a project appropriately may lead to needless expenditures and inappropriate liability. However, far too often programs are jettisoned prematurely when indeed the project needs further study. Premature cancellation of a study by a data-monitoring or safety board can be extremely adverse with the loss of further data collection that could show results quite different. If at all possible, a study should not be terminated based on a trend. The study should be pursued until statistical significance is found for the adverse endpoint. If additional precautions can be undertaken for patients' safety without study termination, this would be the recommended course to take.

An example of a trying period in development was the increased toxicity reported with the calcium channel blocker, bepridil. Since the drug prolonged the QT interval, it seemed appropriate not to administer the agent to patients with an already prolonged QT interval and with the most severe LV function. However this course would probably have limited the drug's prescribing and might have lead to the FDA placing a "black box labeling" with a statement that the drug might be unsafe for the population excluded or that it was possibly unsafe because the drug was not studied in this population. Because of these considerations, which were in opposition to the corporate plan for the drug, it was decided to expose the drug in the population that was previously excluded. With the change in the development strategy, the drug was exposed to patients with poor LV function and those with QT prolongation. With the randomization of the first patients, severe arrhythmias and death were experienced, whereas previously the safety record was pristine when the conservative entrance criteria were employed. Clearly, the suspicions of possible proarrhythmia were well founded in these high-risk patients. While development was continued and some of the studies were redirected, the change in strategy could well have lead to the termination of drug development.

A more limited indication can still lead to approval and appropriate drug availability while unselected drug exposure can lead to severe adversity and drug development termination. It is nice, in fact desirable, to develop a blockbuster product, but more often than not, reality needs to set in. An agent may continue in development for a more limited group and this may be appropriate given the pharmacodynamic and kinetic considerations for a given agent. A drug will eventually find its rightful place in the market in any event and thus initial self-deception wins nothing in the long run for the company.

XVIII. THE SCIENTIFIC ADVANCEMENT OF KNOWLEDGE

A major fault in the drug development process is that it is aimed solely at commercial success. Often this goal is compatible with scientific knowledge advancement. But this is not invariably the case. Forcing a development program to yield results can, and often does, backfire. A limited approval and a smaller initial market is better than a failed program. Appropriate studies helping physicians place the drug in the existing therapy context is requisite in many European countries, but, sadly, this is not the case in the United States. A drug can often receive approval showing efficacy in a condition such as hypertension. What we need are agents that work in people who do not respond to the first-line drugs, and agents that work in people that do not respond even to second-line agents. We need to know how the agent fits in these more difficult-to-treat populations. We unfortunately often do not know how the agents work in combination. Thus the approval process often does not provide the information the clinicians need or the marketers could use to further drug sales. These studies are often undertaken as part of a Phase-IV program since they are needed to assist marketing. The antihypertensive field is an example where a new agent needs to be positioned to make a significant impact. The A-II antagonists are an example of an exciting new category of treatment. The pharmaceutical industry does not want the A-II antagonists they are developing—that they are pouring funds into—to be limited to those patients who cannot tolerate the cough one sees with ACE inhibitors that occurs in between 8 and 15% of patients. The pharmaceutical industry would like a far larger market, but without further studies and only the ones necessary for gaining approval, physicians will not be helped to place these agents in the antihypertensive armormentarium. In fact, the economic forces at work in medicine of the 90s and beyond further inhibit a new agent's use by blocking entry into formularies and prescription plans, except for the most revolutionary of products.

The FDA has in fact brought up the subject of the importance of novelty of a drug in development and that the novel agents should be given expeditious consideration in development and regulatory review. We hear of the time wasted in the development of "me too" products. This pharmaceutical elitism fails to take into account the previous experience in pharmaceutical drug development. Often the first agent in a series is not the best and most prescribed drug. A drug developed later may have a kinetic advantage or a better side-effect profile. Second-generation H_2 blocker ranindine is favored over cimetidine by many because of fewer drug interactions or the more favorable side-effect profile reported with ranindine as compared to cimetidine. The first beta blocker, propranalol, has given way to the polar once-a-day beta blocker, atenelol, with what has been reported to be a lower CNS side-effect profile. The once-a-day ACE inhibitors appear to offer an advantage over the shorter acting agent in terms of patient compliance and effective antihypertensive therapy. In fact, the once-daily ACE inhibitors appear to be gaining in CHF therapy as well. Once again, the first agent of a class may not be the one with the greatest advantages or most frequent clinical use. A development program thus needs to define an agent so well that its attributes can be determined and used to gain approval and then permit the company to appropriately position the product to attract physician attention. Development plans need to go beyond the rudiments of the approval process.

A lack of information from the drug development process is a considerable liability. The selective publication of drug development information makes our knowledge very imperfect. The development program of a drug can be stopped and all we may know is the material from a single abstract. Recently, the development program of d-sotalol was stopped prematurely with the reporting of an adverse profile in the SWORD study. This has considerable impact in the antiarrhythmic drug development world because it suggests that pure type-III agents may not be nearly as safe as the mixed-function drugs such as sotalol, which has both type-III activity and beta-blocking activity. However, with so little information in the field for over a year now, the true ramifications cannot be discerned. This lack of early reporting limits the dissemination of information. So much information is lost due to the bias of both investigators and editors of journals against publishing negative or incomplete studies. However without the availability of this information, physicians may repeat the mistakes in development or other developers may retrace these same nonproductive paths in drug development because of a lack of effective information. This is why several years ago, I advocated the concept of a need for a repository of information on negative or adverse study outcomes that would provide sources from which those interested in drug development could learn of past mistakes and past failed ideas. Perhaps the "on-line journal of clinical trials" is well suited for this type of publication and would certainly enhance the rapidity of the information's availability. This information, I believe, would prove very valuable to those involved in drug development, those involved in designing clinical trials, and those involved in evaluating the efficacy of drugs in clinical testing. However, I am most unsure if we will ever be able to make use of the vast body of information that the pharmaceutical industry has accrued that will never see the light of day for publication. This sets back the field of clinical drug development and it sets back our understanding of pharmaceuticals. The process of publication, the disclosure of this information, would bring the drug development process and its literature closer to science than commercialism. This is a worthwhile goal to pursue.

XIX. FROM TRIAL RESULTS TO APPROVAL

The development process is unending and needs to be attended to throughout its course. Once the critical pivotal studies are ongoing, the next step needs to be planned. Adequate patient exposure needs to be ensured. Many of the patients need not be exposed to controlled randomized trials, but could be exposed through treatment studies or prolonged chronic exposure. However failure to maintain contemporaneous control groups can be quite devastating to a program. If liver enzyme elevations are noted just in a few patients, a program could be placed in severe jeopardy. However, if it is clear that both in the control group and in patients receiving the drug under development there is an elevation in liver enzymes, then the drug would appear exonerated and the development program would proceed unhindered. Controls are critical for the evaluation of adverse side effects as well as for the evaluation of drug efficacy.

Beside establishing safety through patient exposure, adequate drug interaction studies are needed. In cardiology, several drug-interaction studies are standard such as evaluating a possible interaction with digoxin. Others can be predicted by knowing the route of elimination of the new agent and if, for instance, the liver is involved, there is likely a need to study interactions with drugs that induce liver enzymes. If a drug is significantly protein bound, then agents that may displace it from its protein binding need to be evaluated. From the known pharmacodynamic and kinetic properties of the drug, potential interactions can be determined. Another aspect of the drug-interaction evaluation comes from the pharmacodynamic properties of a drug. For instance, if a drug is going to be used as an antianginal, it may be used in combination with a calcium channel blocker or beta blocker. Clearly, concomitant studies with the use of these combined agents are indicated to see if there is a dynamic interaction. These studies go a long way toward placing the drug in the proper context, aiding the physician in its use, and reassuring them in terms of safety.

Another critical aspect at this time is the exposure of special populations. Women need to be included in the drug development process at all stages, but especially in terms of drug efficacy and safety, adequate numbers of women are needed. While most antianginal, antihypertensive, and heart failure studies are performed on men, it turns out that as many, if not more, women are being treated with these medical therapies. It is appropriate to suspect that the pharmacodynamic response, as well as the kinetic handling of the drugs, may be different between genders and thus adequate exposure and careful comparison of the female group to the male group needs to be undertaken. In terms of kinetics the effect of drugs in other special populations, such as orientals and blacks, is most important. There is a well-known belief that the oriental population handles drugs in terms of elimination much more poorly and therefore much smaller doses are needed for effect and to essentially have the same degree of clearance from the body. While this is a general rule of thumb, it is something worth being looked at in the special population studies. There is also the aspect of pharmacodynamic action and this is so very important in the black population where some of the pathophysiology, such as in hypertension, may differ. For this reason, it seems appropriate to study ACE inhibitors, A-II blockers, and beta blockers in the black population as well as the white population. Often the exposure is there, but subset analysis has not been performed. This is, I believe, very important and it is especially incumbent upon the pharmaceutical industry to go back and review their data pool to see if the information that was so effective in the drug approval process can also aid physicians in knowing the utility of an agent in the subpopulations who might receive it. I think this is a responsibility of the pharmaceutical industry and one that should be vigorously upheld.

A drug development program must not be complacent while the NDA is being prepared and then reviewed. In some instances where a mortality study may be indicated, such as in heart failure, hemodynamic and exercise data may form the basis of the submission with the mortality study pending as the initial review process goes forward. As the study is completed, this type of information can be added to the NDA review or even after provisional drug approval is received. The concept of receiving approval of a drug pending the completion of a critical mortality trial has precedence in the field of heart failure and also lipid-lowering agents. Also, the planned post-marketing studies do not have to wait for approval, but can be initiated during the NDA preparation and review process.

The NDA preparation can be a target for streamlining and improvement. Clearly, the NDA needs to be structured in advance, the computer formats established, and as the data comes in, to be evaluated, refined, and then analyzed. The templates of summaries should already be in place, data fitted in, and obviously the information that is new and novel should be viewed and added to the data summaries. The NDA cannot take months to write after the data is collected, but needs to be put together in a short period of time to optimize the information-gathering techniques to shorten the submission process.

The FDA can go a long way in the facilitation of the review process. By utilizing disks provided by industry and by having systems compatible, the FDA reviewer can interact with the data and the company for a given section of the NDA. Queries can be immediately answered and facilitate the NDA application review. Clearly, as computer techniques become more sophisticated, we will be able to make use of the information-age advances by employing our computer systems to handle the vast data overload that is typical of an NDA application. It is also important that after the NDA is complete, most of its data is incorporated in papers that are rapidly put together. All too often industry waits for an investigator to come forward and publish a small excerpt of the database in which they were involved. This can give rise to a misleading impression of the data or the publication of data that does not have the power to stand statistical scrutiny. I have heard the FDA saying that the published data is unimportant and has no relation to the NDA they have just reviewed and, in fact, the published data is of little use. I find that abhorrent. It should be that the published data would be consonant with that in the NDA, and that the FDA, as physicians who are going to use the drug, could look at information in the public sector, evaluate it, and make a judgment. The scientific data in the public domain should be complete, accurate, and informative. That is not to say that the NDA would not be far more complex and thorough than a publication. That is to be expected, but the implication that the information is misleading or vastly incomplete is a considerable disservice to the scientific community and to the physicians who will use the drug clinically. This is especially important in terms of secondary claims or "off label" uses of a new drug that often will never undergo adequate study. Indeed, if the medical literature were more complete, the FDA could more readily rely on this information and permit its dissemination to physicians with the understanding that the information is not definitive and not the subject of FDA critical review.

While there have been a number of attempts to fully automate the NDA process with electronic data entry and electronic NDA submission, there have been limitations to most systems that have been undertaken. However, this has been tested only a very short period and certainly over the next few years electronic data entry, special data-handling techniques, automated quality assurance data handling, and NDA automated submissions will be the rule, not the exception.

The FDA reviewers will require considerable computer assistance. They will be able to rapidly cross-check the data bases to ensure data integrity, completeness, as well as establish a system that will permit checking parts of the data analysis and summaries for validity without going through a line-by-line analysis. Once this is done, the work of the FDA reviewer will be vastly simplified and he will be able to work with his superiors on-line through E-mail systems and through automated data-review algorithms that will permit a timely and much more thorough and complete evaluation of the database. Having the reviewers recreate the NDA piece by piece, make their own reviews and own analysis, and having the NDA broken up and reviewed individually in different sections of the FDA is a very laborious, time-consuming process that is at the heart of the slow-moving NDA review process. This could be expedited in the information age and this will be a great contribution to speeding up the process as well as ensuring the validity of the review.

At the completion of the submission of the NDA, one has to continue to consider a number of aspects in drug development. There will be ongoing studies; there will be studies spawned by some of the questions that have arisen during the development program in the NDA analysis. Phase-IV studies will be underway and should be planned. Many companies will embark upon seeding programs to enhance the experience of critical prescribers in the field with the product in question. Clearly these studies must be well controlled and well designed. They should also be monitored and they should be contrived in such a way as to produce useful exposure data. This both protects the drug, diminishing the chance for adversity during a critical period of regulatory review, and makes the expenditure of time and effort worthwhile by increasing patient exposure. When this is done in a controlled fashion, even a more serious blip on the curve will usually be ironed out with this being seen in a concomitantly treated population on a control or standard therapy. Uncontrolled exposure really places the drug in considerable jeopardy and every report that builds up on the reviewer's desk is another question, if you look at the data hard enough. The question will arise: was there a trend that has not been revealed so far? This will only slow the drug's evaluation.

Another area that needs attention is the development of the product insert. Clearly the entire development program has been aimed at determining the indications, the pharmacokinetics, the preclinical pharmacology, the adverse profile, and the appropriate doses. From the very beginning the product insert has been sketched out, but as the process has progressed, more information has been obtained and this should be a working document that has already been drafted and now is in its final stages. Also during this period, it is time to review the database and see if clues are given to other potential uses of the drug that could then be explored. If one is developing an antiarrhythmic agent and considerable benefit has been seen in the field of ventricular arrhythmias, possibly this is the time to start developing a program around a supraventricular arrhythmia indication. A drug that reduces sudden death mortality in the heart failure population such as what has been reported with vesnarinone, which has type-III antiarrhythmic properties, may need to be at this stage evaluated as an antiarrhythmic agent in other populations (6). Perhaps there are other niches that the drug could be fitted into and other uses explored. To many, this is something that the clinicians do, that is not worth the time and effort of industry. I think this is a very misguided approach. The benefits one can get, the additional information that can be disseminated, and the aid in prescribing guidelines can be helpful to all. If the drug turns out to be adverse in some situations, we then have guidelines and parameters to use to decide when not to use the drug. If it turns out that the drug is beneficial, that is even more reason for its use. There is a certain regulatory rapport that can be developed and confidence that can be built by exploring the scientific aspects of the drug that will help guide the medical community. These are very important considerations and ones that are often overlooked. In the field of antihypertensive therapy, a program that has defined hemodynamic action may naturally lead into the field of congestive heart failure. In the field of lipid-lowering therapy, one may have an agent that modulates vascular biology, that reduces second myocardial infarctions, and that might have a role in the prevention of death in ischemic heart disease. I think the time in the development process to plan out these further developmental strategies, which could lead to a far greater expansion of the market, would be after the NDA filing.

I have the impression there is a pervasive feeling that what one is looking for is the holy grail of approval and after that everything else will fall into place. Additional claims and additional indications are of dubious benefit. I think this is not correct. Experience has demonstrated that additional information in the medical literature leads to further indications for a drug. Having additional use of the drug may lead to further development and claims should be included in the product insert: physicians are more likely to use the product for the other indications when they have used it for the initial indication. In terms of costs, this is a far more economical means of promotion and a far more rational one. Depending upon "off-label" use rather than proceeding with additional studies is wrong, especially within our current regulatory framework that limits "off label" promotion. These types of studies are expensive, but I think industry could pursue a more collaborative approach with academia and government agencies. The need to monitor these studies as one would do for a pivotal trial, and for the same stipends to the investigators, is just not required. Still, the information may prove to be very useful and I think for collateral claims the FDA may depend more and more on published materials as long as they accurately contain the information necessary for review.

XX. CONCLUSION

Drug development and discovery is a most exciting field. It is creative, intellectually taxing, and organizationally demanding. Those involved are to be congratulated for undertaking efforts that are usually anonymous but that impact on clinical therapeutics to a considerable degree. The drug discovery process has gone through the botanical phase, the synthetic chemistry phase, and is now into a most exciting era of biotechnology and gene manipulation. There is an awful lot of hoopla in this arena, but we must remember, it is just one of the rings of a three-ring circus. There is a tremendous evolution in our understanding of medicine, disease processes, and our statistical evaluation of clinical trials and these are important evolving arenas that dynamically interact with the drug discovery process. A third arena, the drug development program itself, is being markedly affected by the Third Wave, the information age. We can only think back to when a chapter like this would be handwritten, typed on a typewriter with carbon paper, corrections made, and then a copy sent off to the publisher. Word processing has revolutionized this approach and will revolutionize it further in the next couple of years. This is the same revolution that totally changes the drug development process, facilitates it, and further facilitates the review of the database presented for review. All phases will undergo radical change and we will be better for it. This is a most exciting era and one that will be both fun and worthwhile to live through.

REFERENCES

1. A. Toffler, *Future Shock*. Random House, New York, 1970.
2. R. J. Myerburg, K. M. Kessler, I. Kiem, K. C. Pefkaros, C. A. Conde, D. Cooper, and A. Castellanos. Relationship Between Plasma Levels of Procainamide, Suppression of Premature Ventricular Complexes and Prevention of Recurrent Ventricular Tachycardia. *Circulation 64*: 280–289, 1981.
3. The SOLVD Investigators. Effect of Enalapril on Survival in Patients with Reduced Left Ventricular Ejection Fractions and Congestive Heart Failure. *New Engl. J. Med. 325*: 293–302, 1991.
4. Scandinavian Simvastatin Survival Study Group. Randomised Trial of Cholesterol Lowering in 4444 Patients with Coronary Heart Disease: the Scandinavian Simvastatin Survival Study (4S). *Lancet 344*: 1383–1389, 1994.
5. M. Packer, M. Gheorghiade, J. B. Young, P. J. Constantini, K. F. Adams, R. J. Cody, L. K. Smith, L. van Voorhees, L. A. Gourley, and M. K. Jolly for the RADIANCE Study. Withdrawal of Digoxin from Patients with Chronic Heart Failure Treated with Angiotensin-Converting-Enzyme Inhibitors. *New Engl. J. Med. 329*: 1–7, 1993.
6. A. M. Feldman, M. R. Bristow, W. W. Parmley, P. E. Carson, C. J. Pepine, E. M. Gilbert, J. E. Strobeck, G. H. Hendrix, E. R. Powers, R. P. Bain, and B. G. White for the Vesnarinone Study Group. Effects of Vesnarinone on Morbidity and Mortality in Patients with Heart Failure. *New Engl. J. Med. 329*: 149–155, 1993.

2

Redefining Competition in the Pharmaceutical Industry: A Time for Choice

John Thompson and Jan Gugliotti

CSC Index
Cambridge, Massachusetts

I. INTRODUCTION

As this chapter is written, the health care industry is in upheaval. Congress is considering a number of health care reform options, any one of which will drive out marginal players in the insurer and direct-care provider segments and significantly worsen the earnings squeeze in the drug sector. Every day, headlines announce new alliances, mergers, consolidations, and spinoffs within the pharmaceutical and other health care sectors as organizations try to shore themselves against rapid external change.

Potential congressional action is the latest but certainly not the only factor contributing to chaos in what had long been a stable, profitable industry, seemingly immune to the normal pressures of competition. Pharmaceuticals may simply be the last sector of the U.S. economy forced to acknowledge that its old model of competition—the search for and exploitation of blockbuster drugs—is no longer a viable market strategy for many if not the majority of firms. This chapter explores the urgent need for pharmaceutical executives to redefine their strategic and operating model in order to sustain their firms into the twenty-first century.

Look at the income statement of any one of the major drug firms. The vulnerability of this industry is obvious. The operating model that grew out of a continuous breakthrough strategy typically results in R & D expenses at 10% to 20% of sales and sales and marketing expenses at 30% to 40% of sales. You can argue (as some will) that these percentages are distorted by financial reporting practices. But in the end it simply will not be viable to continue spending this amount of money on R & D in a climate of fast follow-ons and generic substitutes or to finance armies of sale representatives calling on physicians with decreasing decision influence on prescription. The fundamental strategies and operating models of this industry must change radically.

II. EMBRACING AN UNKNOWN FUTURE

If our perception of the need for fundamental change is correct, or at least if it is shared by senior industry leaders, you might expect to hear more firms talking about fundamental change to the paradigm that says "we invent, then go to market." Everyone in this industry knows things are changing dramatically and quickly. A generation of blockbusters will come off patent in the next five years with little in the pipeline to replace them. Generic substitutes take markets overnight. Even patent-protected drugs face competition within two to three years after launch versus, historically, seven or more years of exclusive claims. As consolidated distribution networks decide which formulations will be sold and which will not, superior clinical performance will no longer be an overriding factor for market success. Government and other powerful third-party players who will not accept a $65 billion national drug bill will increasingly exert downward pressure on prices and margins. European-style price regulation is not unthinkable here.

But the biggest threat to the continued prosperity of drugs firms is not external change. It is the unwillingness to give up what created success in the past, the inability to define our new business, and the understandable reluctance to embrace an unknown future. Like GM, which grew too bloated and complacent to see the competition; like IBM, which misunderstood the effects of cloning its technology; like Sears, which miscalculated its ability to sustain premium prices under siege from discount houses—the more successful a firm has been in the past, the harder it is to embrace an unknown, less desirable future.

A. Coming to Terms with What You Can Be

We predict that one-third to one-half of the top international pharmaceutical companies will not be in the drug discovery and development business as a primary strategy within five years. We also fear that many competitors will not face this reality until their stock price takes a pounding—or worse. So what will a firm have to do right if it wants to avoid the slow, painful upheaval of a GM or an IBM?

We believe there are three key activities and decisions that need to occur almost simultaneously in order to reinvent any business:

1. Make a conscious, and realistic, decision about what value we choose to bring to our customers and come to terms with what we can be.

   As described in the recent *Harvard Business Review* article on the value disciplines, successful players across all industries stake out leading positions in one or, rarely, two of three basic value propositions:

   - Product Leadership—focused, disciplined programs that give us differentiating ability to understand unmet or emerging customer needs; skills, organization, and culture that let us outperform competitors in developing new products to meet those needs, and continuing investments aimed at maintaining leading-edge performance.
   - Operational Excellence—ruthless cost-cutting and quality-raising programs, enabling competition based on lowest price, hassle-free service, and guaranteed performance.
   - Customer Intimacy—bundling and customizing products and services to match intimately understood total customer needs.

   Winning organizations must be brutally realistic about where they have the best chance to compete. This means defining and being able to at least match best-in-the-industry performance for those things that are critical competitive factors in a given value arena. It also means hard truths about how we perform today. For example, drug firms that choose to continue to compete on product leadership will probably have to move new compounds from GLP animal studies to regulatory approval in five years or less to compete with firms like Glaxo and Merck that have demonstrated they can do so. The industry average cycle time is six years or more.

   An emerging adaptation of the value-disciplines model is the focused spin-off or reverse-synergy approach. A firm physically and organizationally separates into two or more stand-alone businesses. Each piece pursues a different value discipline and does so with unique, focused operating models. This allows firms that currently fall into the "black hole" of mediocrity because they are trying to integrate conflicting customer needs to salvage positions in multiple competitive arenas. In pharmaceuticals, it could mean establishing a separate organization to broadly serve the needs of a given therapeutic customer base. Or it could mean setting up a focused drug development organization free to sell its new products at Phase II or Phase III on the open market, to the highest bidder.

2. Design and implement a new operating model in support of the chosen value discipline.

   Use the chosen value discipline as the standard to question every activity, investment, organization structure, technology investment, performance measure, compensation scheme, and cultural norm that defines today's business model. Strong and courageous leadership must step forward at this stage to force hard choices about what we must stop doing as well as what we must start to do. Every aspect of operations, organization, and culture must be lined up with the need to excel in one dimension. Unsuccessful competitors fail to make clear choices and fail to successfully adapt.

   For most drug companies, even those that continue to compete in the product leadership arena, change will be wrenching. Discovery and development organizations will be under siege, forced to cut development portfolio from an average of 40+ compounds to 10 or fewer and dropping to one or two therapeutic areas. In order to make the right downsizing choices, Ph.D.s, MDs and MBAs will have to learn to listen to each other in a truly collaborative way when, traditionally, they neither understand nor particularly respect each other's viewpoints.

3. Scare the organization into making it happen.

   It would have been almost impossible for the pharmaceutical industry to have contemplated fundamental change like this in the late 1980s, even though a thoughtful analysis of the obvious forces in place then—DRGs, the rise of buying networks, the lessening influence of physicians in prescribing, a diminishing number of attractive candidates for licensing-in—would have raised serious doubts about the industry's ability to carry astronomical R & D and marketing costs on future revenue streams. Agreeing that there is a problem is particularly difficult when we are making tons of money and the future is not clearly known.

   Today the external threat is obvious. Now the issue for top leaders of pharmaceutical companies is to put the magnitude of the threat into sufficient perspective so that the organization agrees on the right problem to solve. We fear that the series of tactical initiatives most companies have begun to plug the earnings gap will not be a sufficient response, but will be sufficiently distracting until it is almost too late for effective change. Efforts aimed at improving work-flow design in one development function will not be successful when the real need is to redesign cross-functionally and structure for multidisciplinary collaboration. Budget squeezing and pricing reassessment will not be sufficient when what is really needed is fundamental restructuring to produce a product offering that brings new value to customers.

B. The Role of Leadership in Change

A key lesson that we can draw from these observations is how difficult discontinuous change will be for the drug industry. The cultural bedrock of a science-based organization that views itself as having been "put on this planet" to make medical breakthroughs will resist rational examination of alternative strategies.

Leadership plays three essential roles in pushing through changes that often feel like unnatural acts. One role is to continually articulate the need for change in terms of the organization's past performance and the ever-heightening competitive bar. Six year cycle times will not make the grade. Me-too therapeutic aims are not worth the investment.

The second role of leadership is to create a clear vision for the future of the company that is compelling, energizing, and attractive to individuals. Without a clear view of the future there is no context within which to make the decisions that have to be made today.

The third role, which most leaders do not recognize soon enough, is to anticipate and eliminate all of the inevitable organization responses that turn a clear strategic vision into conflict and confusions. Behaviors such as turf wars, task-force proliferation, analysis paralysis, values clash, and other types of informed resistance are inevitable and will stop any well-meaning change effort without a clear signal—such as a public hanging—that they will not be tolerated.

This is a time for choice: to choose whether to stay in the drug development business (where the conditions of survival include halving the drug development time) or to compete in the cost-effectiveness war with the distribution giants and the generics providers (where the cost of survival is quartering the sales force and changing the culture of the company). Those who make the wrong choice may fail, those who fail to make *any* choice and try to straddle the fence with a little drug development and a mediocre distribution system, will surely fail.

Most major companies accept that these are the choices to be made. But who will make them best? Those whose leadership is deeply entrenched in the way the business has been for the past 30 years or those imported from other industries to take over the mantle of recently fired CEOs? One knows too much about the past, the other knows too little about it.

Drug development will certainly continue, of that we can be sure. That it will be done faster by fewer companies, we may be certain. The present upheaval may even be a healthy wake-up call for the industry. What is dangerous, however, is the current interregnum of uncertainty with clinical testing cut back until companies get a better understanding of the reforms currently being considered by Congress. It is not the change that damages, it is the uncertainty and the absence of clear decisions. Those companies that fail to make these choices soon will surely fail.

3

The Impact of Liability and Cost Containment on the Drug Development Process

Martha M. Rumore

Long Island University
Brooklyn, New York

I. INTRODUCTION

The pharmaceutical industry of the 1990s is facing increasing challenges. The race to new drug approval is now further complicated by increased cost-containment pressures and liability concerns. The expectation for pharmaceutical companies to "economically" develop safe and efficacious drugs that provide added value to the health care marketplace has caused pharmaceutical companies to reevaluate their drug development process. Among the many trends and events that are shaping the future of new drug development, several are paramount. This chapter identifies and analyzes emerging cost-containment and product liability trends that have impacted on the drug development process. It concludes with a look at how these factors might affect future drug development and patient access to new pharmaceuticals.

II. PRODUCT LIABILITY ISSUES IN DRUG DEVELOPMENT

Product liability continues to be the creature of social policy and has changed as society's value system has changed. Just as a certain morbidity/mortality risk for surgery is accepted, we accept some benefit versus risk from any drug. For example, xerostomia may be an acceptable price to pay for the drug of choice, deafness may not be. A striking risk/benefit example is the risk of bone marrow suppression with cytotoxic drugs in treating neoplastic diseases. Although bone marrow suppression can be life threatening, the disease is lethal, so we take and accept the risk. Part of industry's problem is that there are no guidelines outlining the concept of risk/benefit. The best case is for a product to be so uniquely life saving or beneficial that no prudent person could argue that the benefit/risk balance is not acceptable [1].

Before 1970, relatively few product lawsuits were filed in the United States. Product liability litigation in the United States is rising, and in 1994, the pharmaceutical industry spent approximately 0.5% of total revenues just on legal fees [2]. That percentage is approximately double that spent by either the food or utilities industries [2]. Medical malpractice and product liability costs in the United States have increased from $900 million in 1974 to $9.2 billion in 1991 [3]. In 1992 there were 31,400 such cases, with roughly two out of five taking more than two years to resolve [4]. The increase is attributed to the belief that manufacturers should be strictly liable for all injuries associated with products, regardless of actual fault or consumer misuse. The courts have extended the liability of the manufacturer to include not only the actual consumer, but anyone who may be "foreseeably" affected by the product [5].

Certain drug categories have been characterized as "litogens," i.e., drugs causing lawsuits. The threat of enormous punitive damage awards has discouraged manufacturers from developing these "litogens." Product liability has also slowed other areas of research such as vaccines, Acquired Immune Deficiency Syndrome (AIDS), maternal drugs, and chemotherapy and has driven other products from the market (e.g., Bendectin). A February 1990 report by the National Research Council concluded that U.S. manufacturers might be unwilling to develop new contraceptive products for fear of product liability suits [6]. In fact, since 1970, the number of major U.S. pharmaceutical companies involved in contraceptive R & D has dropped from 20 to just two [7].

A. Basis of Liability in Drug Development

Pharmaceutical product liability lawsuits may be brought under a variety of theories including negligence in the design, testing, and manufacture of the product; strict liability for defective design or failure to warn; breach of express or implied warranty; fraud; and deceit and misrepresentation for a misbranded or deceptively advertised product. Defenses vary by jurisdiction but may include lack of appropriate proof of causation; assumption of the risk or contributory negligence; statute of limitations; and inability to identify a tortfeasor (e.g., multisource product). In some cases manufacturers have been relieved of liability by statute (e.g., Swine Flu Act) [8].

Strict liability in tort, as outlined by Restatement (Second) of Torts Section 402A, states that the seller of a defective and unreasonably dangerous product is liable for injury caused by the product [9]. The idea behind strict liability was to make the manufacturer carry the liability risk because the manufacturer was in the best position to allocate the risk more broadly—by increasing the price of the product and buying insurance [10]. A significant exception applying to pharmaceuticals is found in Comment K following Section 402A. Comment K exempts manufacturers of prescription drugs from strict liability for design defect, provided their products are properly prepared and contain appropriate directions and warnings of any known or knowable dangers that reasonably might be expected from their use. Comment K describes such products as "unavoidably unsafe" [11].

Manufacturers have affirmative duties to convey accurate information about their products. Fraud, deceit, misrepresentation of a material fact can occur via the product literature, sales personnel or other company representatives, advertisements and other product promotion. One of the major advantages of filing suit on the basis of intentional torts such as these is the possibility of obtaining an award of punitive damages.

In drug product liability litigation, the breach of warranty theory is generally asserted along with other theories. In warranty liability, no proof of negligence is necessary. The claimant does not have to prove that a manufacturer was aware of the product defect or should have discovered it. Liability for breach of warranty arises where persons are damaged because of a product's failure to live up to an express or implied representation of the manufacturer. It is distinguished from negligence liability in that it is not based on fault or failure of a manufacturer to exercise reasonable care.

Negligence is a failure to exercise that degree of care that a person of ordinary prudence would exercise under the same circumstances. Liability for negligence in pharmaceutical product cases is most likely to involve a failure to warn, or to warn adequately, of foreseeable harm. Since most theories of liability are based on the negligent failure of the manufacturer to test, discover, or warn, these are discussed in more detail here.

1. Product Design

The manufacturer has a duty to use reasonable care in the design of the product. According to the Restatement (Second) of Torts, a product is defective if it is in an "unreasonably dangerous" condition [9]. Proof that a safer alternative design exists or could have been utilized is an important factor [12]. In *Brouchu v. Ortho Pharmaceutical Corp.*, the court allowed the use of the design defect theory because a lower dose oral contraceptive was equally as effective in preventing contraception as the higher dose pill with less risk of stroke [13].

During the product development phase, a manufacturer is under a legal duty to anticipate both intended and unintended but foreseeable uses of a product. Expensive lawsuits follow when a new drug is removed from the market for adverse experiences (AEs) (e.g., temafloxacin). Building safety into a product is less costly than recalling a product that causes injuries and ensuing litigation [5].

2. Inadequate Materials

The manufacturer has a duty to ensure that the product is manufactured with reasonably safe materials and materials that are proper for its intended and foreseeable uses [5]. For example, plaintiffs have alleged they contracted polio because a killed virus polio vaccine was contaminated with live polio virus. Recently a settlement was reached in a class action suit brought by hemophiliacs infected with the AIDS virus in the early 1980s when they used anti-hemophiliac blood-clotting factors [14].

3. Failure to Test

The manufacturer has a duty to ensure sound laboratory, clinical trial, and manufacturing processes. Cases have been brought against manufacturers for failure to follow good laboratory practices (GLPs) or good manufacturing practices (GMPs). Appropriate tests and inspections are needed to ensure freedom from manufacturing defects. The manufacturer cannot escape liability by shifting responsibility for product inspection or testing to another (e.g., excipient manufacturer) [5]. Similarly, releasing a product for commercial distribution in the face of certain danger signs emanating from the test results could lead to product liability.

In addition to quality control testing, there is also a duty to test for safety during the preclinical and clinical product development phases. The manufacturer must test not only for apparent dangers of an investigational product but also for those dangers it should have discovered. In *Barson v. ER Squibb & Sons*, the company was liable for failure to conduct teratology tests that were not required by the Food and Drug Administration (FDA) at that time [15]. In *Tinnerholm v Parke-Davis & Co.*, the manufacturer was liable for negligent failure to test a drug under foreseeable market conditions [16]. Inadequate preclinical testing, failure to monitor AEs, failure to keep abreast of relevant scientific literature may all lead to a "failure to test" causation.

Satisfaction of the FDA requirements regarding testing will not protect the manufacturer from liability for failure to test [12]. Further, New Drug Application (NDA) test results are available to plaintiffs through discovery and the Freedom of Information Act (FOIA).

4. Inadequate Directions for Use, Labeling, and Advertisements

Most pharmaceutical product liability cases are based on a "failure to adequately warn" theory. Inadequate, outdated, or nonexistent product instructions or warnings may lead to liability. Under strict liability, even if a product is perfectly manufactured, it can be considered defective and unreasonably dangerous if not accompanied by adequate warnings. Some products are considered "unavoidably unsafe" and warning labels on these products eliminate or significantly reduce strict liability [5,9]. Manufacturers are exempt from "failure to warn" liability for unknown risks, as in those not yet detected for an investigational new drug (IND). However, in a number of court cases, product overpromotion (e.g., lack of fair balance) has been found to nullify the effect of adequate warnings.

B. Factors Shifting Liability to the Manufacturer

1. Adverse Experience Reporting Regulations

A number of factors are shifting product liability to the manufacturer. In general, failure of a pharmaceutical company to properly state the results of clinical trials constitutes fraud. Cases of mysterious vandalism of clinical investigator offices on the eve of FDA audits on the quality of data collected in support of NDAs have occurred [17]. Fraudulent data were recently associated with the National Surgical Adjuvant Breast and Bowel Cancer Project. Although safety testing fraud remains a problem, a company may inadvertently fail to link an investigational drug with an AE, as in the recent case of deaths caused by FIAU, an investigational drug for chronic hepatitis B. In 1994, a number of deaths were attributed to unknown side effects from newly approved drugs for epilepsy, migraine, and asthma. In response, the FDA recently revised regulations for AE reporting for investigational drugs and biologics [18]. The FDA has also amended the IND regulations to require a description of any adverse clinical or laboratory outcomes that investigators must immediately report to the sponsor [19]. Companies are required to estimate the expected incidence of deaths and serious AEs. Once the estimate is exceeded, the sponsor would have to notify all investigators and FDA within 15 days [20]. These regulations may increase the potential liability of manufacturers by establishing a presumption that the investigational drug was associated with the AE and injuries. These reports would be discoverable in any legal action and therefore would assist plaintiffs to prove causation [20].

2. New Demographic Requirements for Clinical Trials

Testing of investigational drugs in special patient populations (i.e., pregnant females, severe renal or hepatic impairment, pediatric, or geriatric) for which little safety data exists may increase industry liability. Only after a significant period of human exposure can there be firm data on which to base a conclusion that a drug poses an appreciable risk of harm to the human fetus or special patient populations.

In 1990, under National Institutes of Health (NIH) sponsorship, Abbott Laboratories, Inc. developed hyperimmune globulin for prevention of maternal AIDS transmission. Two years later, when the clinical trials were scheduled to begin, Abbott sought NIH indemnification for potential future liabilities. The NIH refused and Abbott decided not to release the drug for clinical trials using women of childbearing age [21]. In July 1993, the FDA issued the "Guideline for the Study and Evaluation of Gender Differences in the Clinical Evaluation of Drugs" [22]. This guideline allows for the participation of women of childbearing potential in early clinical trials and defines means of determining sufficient female inclusion. While only a guideline, the FDA has indicated in its "refusal to file" policy that it will refuse to accept NDAs for review without adequate demographic analysis by gender, age, or racial group [23].

The FDA also recently proposed an amendment to a 1979 regulation that required full clinical trials in the pediatric population as a basis for labeling for use in children. The rule would allow some pediatric labeling to be based on adult data when the disease treated is likely to be similar in adults and children [24]. However, the new rule requires manufacturers to examine existing information and submit an application for supplemental labeling by the end of 1996. Finally, it gives the FDA authority to request specific pediatric use data and ensure pediatric testing during new drug development for products that have potentially widespread use in children.

While manufacturers have not faced substantial litigation by clinical trial participants, inclusion of women or pediatric patients in early clinical trials may change that. There is a potential risk that any birth defect that occurs in the child of a woman who conceives while on an investigational drug could result in a lawsuit against the manufacturer by the offspring. Under current law, the offspring of women participating in clinical trials have the right to sue if health problems result. Additionally, approximately forty states allow suits on behalf of the fetus. This might be a problem in Phase I if healthy volunteers are involved or if reproductive/teratology animal studies have not been completed. Changes in federal law would be required to decrease any sponsor liability [25].

3. Miscellaneous Trends

In addition to regulatory actions, other trends that are shifting liability to pharmaceutical manufacturers include media sensationalization; extremely large settlements and judgements by juries; and contingency fees for plaintiffs' lawyers [1]. Companies are disrupted by the discovery process and the costs for defense are high.

The media coverage of AEs can lead to class action suits. In high media profile litigation, the costs to a company's reputation with the financial markets and the public may be astronomical. This has encouraged pharmaceutical product manufacturers to settle instead of defending their products. In the case of Bendectin, the company took the drug off the market in 1983 after 1800 lawsuits had been filed and the company faced increasingly burdensome product liability insurance costs. In *Havner v Merrell Dow Pharmaceuticals*, a jury ordered the manufacturer to pay $19.2 million to a couple who blamed the drug for their son's club feet [26]. In March 1994, the verdict was thrown out entirely by the Court of Appeals, which found there was no scientific evidence to support the jury's conclusions. The plaintiffs have appealed [27].

The widely prescribed sleeping pill, Halcion demonstrates the potential damage of media coverage. A recurring allegation accuses the company of relying on falsified clinical studies and bribing researchers to hide the truth about Halcion. The FDA was swept into a RICO (Racketeer Influenced and Corrupt Organization) suit, with plaintiffs contending the FDA improperly approved the drug [28]. The RICO Act describes punishable racketeering offenses. Questions were raised over the accuracy of an early Halcion clinical trial in the 1970s, known as protocol 321. The results of this trial were used in the product's NDA [29]. In 1992, an FDA panel found that Halcion was still safe and effective, but told the company to lower initial recommended dosages. Recently, a Federal Tort Claims Act action for $7.5 million was filed by a

Halcion user blaming the FDA for approving a dangerous drug [30]. As of January 1994, there were 49 suits pending nationwide. Of the 135 suits since 1983, 86 were dismissed or settled [31].

Finally, liability has been shifted to pharmaceutical manufacturers by the manufacturers themselves. In an effort to increase market share, several companies have offered indemnity for prescribers of their recently approved products (e.g., Norplant). In June 1994, about 1000 Norplant users joined a nationwide class action suit alleging that the manufacturer did not adequately warn them of the lengthy surgery and scarring that may occur when the implant is removed [32]. Other manufacturers "guarantee" their products in exchange for placement on managed care formularies.

C. Effects on the New Drug Development Process

What effects do the above issues have on new drug development? They increase the costs of research and development (R & D), require more studies to be done to show safety, channel R & D into areas with less risk, and force companies to move overseas.

Companies avoid pursuit of high risk products that may put them out of business. Product areas where manufacturers have been discouraged from investing in R & D because of enormous legal liability include contraceptive products, vaccines, and pediatric products. In other cases, venture capitalists are reluctant to invest in products when the risk of litigation is high. This liability climate tends to force some companies to move overseas. Liability is a substantial reason that companies are going overseas with their products. Other reasons include U.S. export restrictions and the U.S. regulatory system. There has been a visible shift of some preclinical R & D and manufacturing overseas to Europe or Japan [33–35]. United States companies have stringent data requirements for INDs. The data requirements are prompting more and more researchers to conduct clinical trials overseas. Europe has a much easier process for registering clinical trials [36]. Although the total number of commercial INDs filed with FDA has held at around 300–400 per year over the past decade, PhRMA data reveal that only about 20% of Phase I studies now are conducted in the United States, compared with about 50% 10 years ago [37]. A recent survey conducted by the Gallop Organization examined 58 U.S. medical electronics manufacturing companies. Forty percent said they had cut their workforce in the United States as a consequence of regulatory delays, and 22% said they had already moved U.S. jobs overseas [3]. For the first time, the American College of Cardiology has received more abstracts from outside the United States than from inside for its 1995 meeting [38]. The trend in the United States is toward allowing more and more foreign data and there have been instances where entire NDAs were based on foreign data. It is natural for companies to move overseas where liability is decreased. The U.S. liability climate raises the cost of product here so that when we export it, the potential for others to underprice increases.

In isolated cases, the government will indemnify a manufacturer for a needed product that is associated with liability. Lawsuits against vaccine manufacturers began to increase greatly during the 1970s [39]. It was partially out of concern that many pharmaceutical companies were getting out of the vaccine business that Congress in 1986 enacted the Childhood Vaccine Injury Act which established the Childhood Vaccine Compensation Program [40]. One of the purposes of this federally subsidized compensation program was to pay people with government funds outside the normal tort system in situations where inoculation is involuntary as in the case of childhood vaccines. This was an incentive for manufacturers to distribute these much-needed vaccines without fear of liability. Under this program, anyone claiming to have suffered injury from one of the listed childhood vaccines may file a petition with the U.S. Court for Federal Claims for compensation. More than 4800 claims were filed and because the awards were higher than predicted, Congress was forced to appropriate additional funds to deal with these extra cases. In 1976, under the Swine Flu Immunization Program, the government also agreed to indemnify vaccine manufacturers. Approximately 4179 claims were filed seeking a total of $3,211,072,540 of which the government paid out slightly less than $100 million [41]. These lawsuits continue with large awards to plaintiffs. In October 1994, a jury awarded $13.5 million to a patient who developed Guillain–Barre Syndrome resulting in paralysis [42].

These large judgements place increasing pressure on manufacturers to conduct pharmacoepidemiologic (PE) studies. The PE study can take place at any time during the drug development process and such studies have been used to refute unsubstantiated allegations about a product and avoid liability [1,43]. In the future, there will likely be a still greater demand for better pharmacoepidemiologic information to prevent drugs from becoming "litogens."

D. Product Liability Reform

There remains no uniform standard of product liability law in the United States and uncertainty prevails as the rules continue to vary from state to state. Insurance is often prohibitively expensive and some pharmaceutical companies self-insure. Others purchase only product-recall insurance to cover expenses incurred for recalls but not litigation.

Product liability legislation has been introduced in every Congress for the past 14 years. Each year the call for liability reform grows stronger from industry. Economic caps on awards and contingency fees redress only the symptoms of a disease that is deeply rooted in the liability system.

Several 1995 versions of proposed product liability reform legislation state that punitive damages shall not be awarded if a drug was approved by the FDA. Under this "government standards defense," the manufacturer could still be forced to pay actual damages—compensation for injuries or losses—to anyone harmed by the medication. Table 1 summarizes the key provisions in the legal reform bills passed by the House, those introduced by Sens. Jay Rockefeller (D–W.Va) and Slade Gorton (R–Wash.), and proposals made by Sen. Orin Hatch (R–Utah) [44,45].

Perhaps for products with great social benefit, liability risks should be adjusted accordingly with special liability protection. While there is optimism for passage of tort reform legislation in this Congress, various reforms have been proposed in the past to give manufacturers an absolute defense if the plaintiff was under the influence of alcohol or illegal drugs at the time of an accident; limited immunity from suit for certain needed products; provisions for out-of-court settlements; two-year statute of limitations to begin when the claimant discovers the harm or cause; and federal preemption and restriction of punitive damages [46].

Federal preemption has been interpreted for medical devices under the 1976 Medical Device Amendments. Courts have not allowed state suits [47].

Table 1 Proposed Tort Reform

Provision	House Bill	Rockefeller-Gorton Bill	Hatch Bill
Punitive damages	Immunity if FDA approved unless false information provided	No FDA defense	Includes FDA defense clause
Noneconomic damages	Limited to $250,000	No cap	Limited to $250,000
Statute of repose	Within 15 years	Twenty years	None
Statute of limitations	None	Two years	Two years
Joint and several liability	Abolishes joint liability for noneconomic damages, allows it for economic damages	Same	Same as House bill for noneconomic damages
Attorney	Imposes sanctions for frivolous filings	None	Same as House bill

There is also a series of recent court decisions that preclude individuals from maintaining lawsuits against device manufacturers on any grounds [47].

Medical malpractice or provider practice tort reform without product liability reform would shift the cost of litigation and liability solely to manufacturers and suppliers at the expense of health care innovation. Tort reform, including medical malpractice and product liability reform, could save more than $35 billion over a five-year period, according to a report by the National Medical Liability Reform Coalition [48]. Our current product liability and malpractice laws cause significant waste and add billions of dollars to the cost of drug development and health care. Tort reform could help to stop the siphoning of funds necessary for innovative drug development.

III. THE IMPACT OF COST CONTAINMENT ON DRUG DEVELOPMENT

Although pharmaceuticals represent only a small part of total health care costs, they have not escaped cost containment efforts for several reasons: (a) the industry has given the image of high profitability, (b) pharmaceuticals enjoy a protected and financially secure market (covered by public or private insurance), and (c) pharmaceuticals are easily identifiable in health care accounting, making intervention easy. Cost containment measures within and outside the industry have led not only to significant changes in new drug development but in a major restructuring of the pharmaceutical industry. New drug development plans aim to reduce redundancy and shorten timelines while capturing the socioeconomic data needed for rapid regulatory approval and effective product launch. Society is demanding more comparative information about pharmaceuticals. Pharmacoeconomic analysis and quality-of-life research has been used in setting price, gaining access to managed care providers, and demonstrating cost advantages. Insurers have focused on a two-pronged approach to cost-containment: utilization controls and containing prices.

The cost of drug development for a new chemical entity has risen to over $200 million, with an increase in average R & D investments from 11.3% of sales in 1975 to more than 16.7% in 1993 and 18.8% in 1994 (Figure 1) [49,50]. However, this also reflects the fact that sales fell even more than research budgets. Also, individual companies have stated that they will actually be decreasing their R & D budgets (Figure 2). The process of new drug development has become longer and more regulated (Figure 3). A recent study has shown that while priority drugs were approved in half the time as standard drugs, they spent 68% longer time in the development stage. The result is that the total time spent for developing, testing, reviewing, and approving priority drugs exceeded the time spent for standard drugs [51]. Aggregate R & D budgets

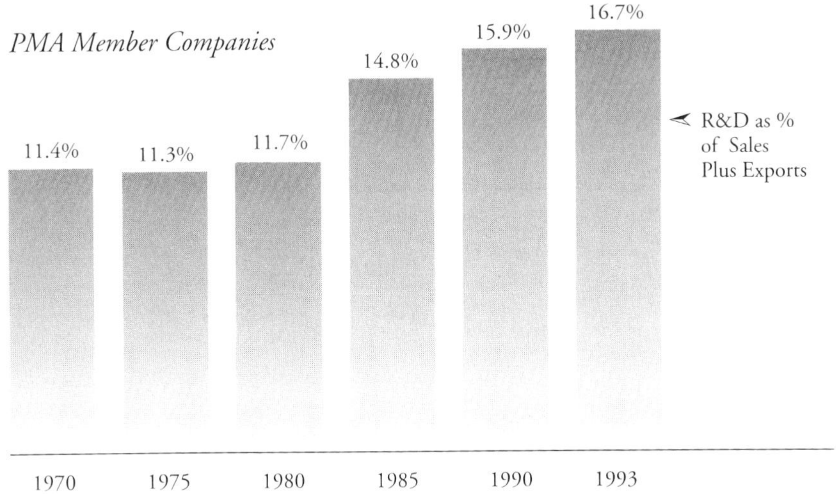

Year	R&D as % of Sales Plus Exports	Year	R&D as % of Sales Plus Exports	Year	R&D as % of Sales Plus Exports
1993	16.7%	1985	14.8%	1977	11.1%
1992	16.4	1984	14.3	1976	11.0
1991	16.2	1983	14.4	1975	11.3
1990	15.9	1982	13.8	1974	10.9
1989	16.5	1981	13.1	1973	11.2
1988	16.3	1980	11.7	1972	11.6
1987	15.8	1979	11.2	1971	11.2
1986	14.8	1978	10.9	1970	11.4

For 1994, R&D as % of Sales Plus Exports = 18.8%.

Fig. 1 Research and Development as a percent of sales. R & D Basis: Intramural and extramural company-financed domestic U.S. R & D expenditures for human-use and veterinary-use pharmaceuticals. Sales Basis: domestic U.S. sales plus U.S. exports (includes exports to other firms as well as intrafirm exports). Source: PhRMA, 1994.

are now between $500 and $1 billion per year per company and rising [52,53]. From a financial point of view, such an investment is only justified if it generates a return comparable to that which could be achieved by investing in other sectors of the economy. Over the past five years R & D expenditures have almost doubled, while the number of new drugs approved each year has remained relatively flat at approximately twenty-three [54]. Therefore, it costs more and more to bring a new drug to market and fewer and fewer failures

Dollars in millions

Company	Year of incorporation	Total assets 1992	Total sales 1987-1992	R&D 1987-1992
Abbott	1888	$6,499.1	$36,077.4	$3,358.4
Allergan	1948	829.4	4,011.5	363.5
American Home Products	1926	6,686.6	41,586.8	2,364.0
Baxter	1931	8,571.9	37,854.6	1,350.5
Bristol-Myers Squibb	1900	10,115.9	57,811.4	5,041.7
Carter-Wallace	1880	562.3	3,581.4	271.4
Eli-Lilly	1876	8,120.4	28,418.3	3,986.5
Glaxo[b]	1935	9,629.0	30,052.0	3,839.2
Johnson & Johnson	1887	11,127.1	65,124.9	5,013.9
Marion Merrell Dow	1950	2,980.3	10,099.8	1,439.5
Merck	1891	10,379.9	44,020.2	4,996.1
Novo Nordisk[b]	1940	2,615.1	7,563.7	980.0
Pfizer	1849	8,979.3	37,208.2	3,698.5
Rhone-Poulenc Rorer	1910	3,612.6	13,847.1	1,599.3
Schering-Plough	1908[a]	3,891.9	20,180.2	2,226.2
SmithKline Beecham[b]	1830	4,508.3	42,015.2	3,590.1
Syntex	1957	2,630.2	9,290.6	1,616.1
Upjohn	1886	4,311.6	18,099.1	2,652.8
Warner-Lambert	1920	3,817.7	27,320.8	2,096.5
Wellcome[b]	1880	3,349.3	15,267.4	2,121.6
Total		**$113,218.1**	**$549,430.2**	**$52,605.7**

Note: All amounts equal to 1990 dollars. Annual data were not available for some years.

[a]Schering-Plough was reorganized in 1970.

[b]Amounts calculated using average exchange rate for given year. All amounts, except Novo-Nordisk's R&D, taken from Compact Disclosure.

Source: Corporate annual reports and SEC 10K reports.

Fig. 2 Information on the top 20 pharmaceutical companies for years 1987 through 1992, assets as of 1992.

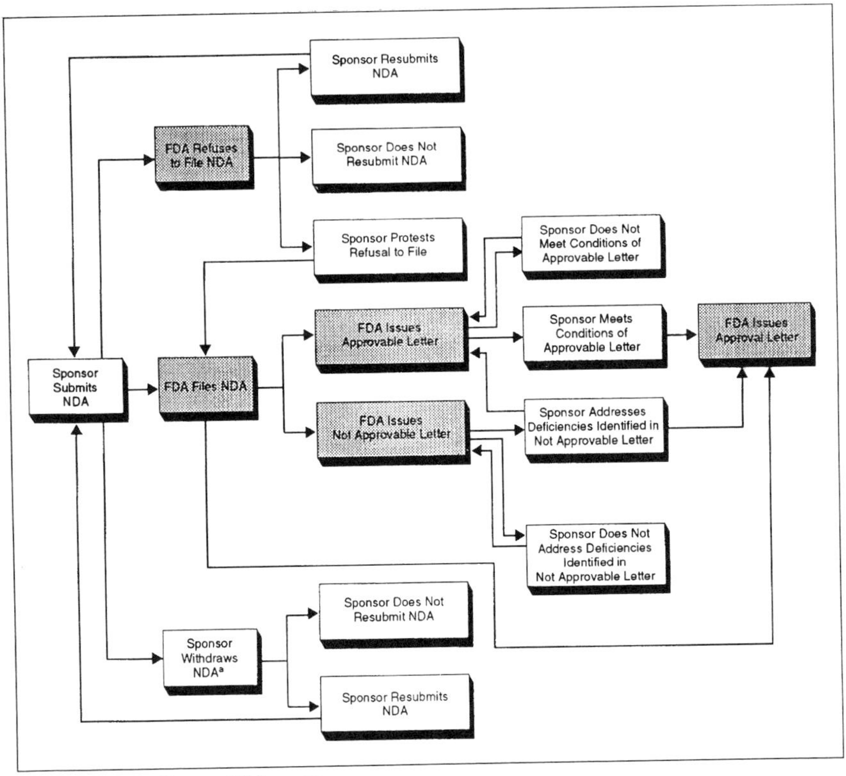

[a]Sponsor can withdraw NDA at any point in the process.

Fig. 3 The NDA review and approval process.

are affordable. The result is a focus on fewer projects per company and pressure to focus on truly important drugs, e.g., AIDS or cancer.

A. The Political and Regulatory Environment

In 1994, most pharmaceutical companies showed weak-to-modest results, reflecting intense price competition, discounts to managed care organizations, patent expiration for major drugs (e.g., Tagamet, Naprosyn), and a weak European market [55].

In addition to intensified competitive rivalry and profit pressures, pharmaceutical companies will continue to face further government scrutiny and intervention. There is a trend toward much more government involvement in research decisions. A number of health care and regulatory reforms threaten to control the prices of new pharmaceuticals and limit the funds available for R & D investment.

1. 1990 to the Present

Four federal laws enacted since 1990 have significantly impacted the new drug development process: OBRA '90, The Veteran Health Care Act of 1992, The Prescription Drug User Fee Act of 1992, the tax changes required by OBRA '93. The average annual cost to industry of these four new federal laws is $2.9 billion, which represents almost 20% of the pharmaceutical industry's total investment in R & D in 1995 [48,54].

Under the Prescription Drug User Fee Act of 1992, revenues raised from user fees paid by pharmaceutical manufacturers were to reduce NDA review times from 20 months to 12 months, ensuring that new drug advances reach the public as quickly as possible. The reduction in approval times is to be phased in over a five-year period. By the end of 1997, 90% of standard drugs are to be "acted on" (i.e., approval, approvable, or nonapprovable letter issued) within 12 months of submission, and 90% of priority drugs "acted on" within 6 months. In 1995, the FDA's new molecular entity (NME) average approval time was 19.2 months, a 30% decrease from the 1993 average approval time. For the 14 NMEs approved in 1995 that were assessed user fees, the average approval time was 15.6 months [56]. Although the average approval time has decreased, 1995 was not a record year for drug approvals: the number of NMEs approved went from 25 in 1993 to 28 in 1995. Acceleration of the time-to-market approval has a direct impact on both a company's stock price and the perceived value of the product. Based on a study of NME sales curves, accelerating approval by 12 months could translate to an average $4.5 million additional cash flow per product. If the product is a potential "blockbuster" the value could reach or exceed a million dollars per day [57]. This would have a profound effect on a company's new drug development.

The Medicaid rebate provision of the OBRA '90 Law will cost the pharmaceutical industry $10.2 billion from 1994 to 1998. The revenue-raising provisions of OBRA '93 included a higher corporate tax rate and changes to Section 936 of the tax code as well as an end to the ban on Medicaid formularies. The Veteran's Health Care Act of 1992 mandated discounts to the Department of Veterans Affairs and Department of Defense.

2. Health Care Reform

The Health Security Act proposed by President Clinton would have established an "Advisory Council on Breakthrough Drugs" to decide whether the prices on new drugs were reasonable. This was later replaced by an "Advisory

Council on Prescription Drug Prices," which would have examined and reported on the pricing of all prescription drugs both new and existing.

In a report by the Congressional Budget Office entitled "How Health Care Reform Affects Pharmaceutical R & D," it was estimated that under the President's proposed Health Security Act, profits from drug development would rise less than 3%. The report further predicted that the level of industry R & D might not change appreciably, but the placement of R & D investment might shift. As profits on drugs sold exclusively for the over-65 population would decrease, this would reduce the incentives to produce such drugs and shift it toward drugs aimed primarily at those under 65.

Although the Health Security Act is moot, Congress and the current administration are searching for cost containment and reductions in health care spending. Health reforms that have been proposed include unitary pricing provisions; user-fee exemptions for orphan products and small companies; any willing provider laws; drug-PAC (a consumer cost-effectiveness guide); repeal of the insurance industry's McCarren–Ferguson Act immunity that permits health plans to restrict providers; and coverage of investigational drugs.

The government is paying $18–19 billion annually for drugs, or nearly 35% of all prescription drugs purchased in the United States. They will continue to seek ways to pool all that leverage. Could a national formulary be created in the United States and what effect would this have on new drug development? It has been suggested that a professional/scientific body be created to supply comparative information on therapeutic and economic properties of pharmaceutical preparations and/or develop a therapeutic formulary for voluntary application [58]. A federal center for prescription drug cost-effectiveness assessments that would fund and coordinate research where there are no manufacturer incentives has also been suggested.

Biomedical research has been a Republican favorite. The 104th Congress, if true to its Republican history of deregulation of the pharmaceutical industry, may alter the Health Care Reform debate. This would stimulate private sector investment in R & D and possibly help reverse the increased FDA restrictions on marketing and economic claims. Pharmaceutical industry critics are no longer in command of subcommittees with investigative power. A Republican Congress may mean less government scrutiny and regulation, more R & D incentive legislation, and less oversight of vertical and horizontal integrations [59]. For example, complementing the FDA's proposed rule on pediatric labeling is a proposed pediatric study incentive. Six months of additional market exclusivity would be given to products for which pediatric studies have been conducted at the request of the Health and Human Services (HHS) secretary. The new Congress has already decided to study how the FDA is implementing the user-fee program and is expected to be receptive to industry complaints about drug approval delays.

3. Patent Reform and Technology Transfer

In 1980, Congress enacted the Bayh–Dole Act (P.L. 96-517) and in 1986, the Federal Technology Transfer Act, both intended to facilitate technology transfer from universities and other research-oriented institutions (e.g., NIH) to industry. Although it's a rare patent that emerges from this technology transfer that becomes a blockbuster commercial product, it has occurred (e.g., Retin-A).

Reasonable pricing clauses have impeded cooperative R & D agreements (CRADAs) between these institutions and industry. In 1994 legislation was proposed to increase NIH control over the prices of drugs that result from CRADAs. Although only applicable to NIH, it would have established a precedent for future expansion of the reasonable pricing principle to other government agencies. The NIH's CRADAs have dropped from 126 in 1992 to 26 in 1993 [36]. Many companies stated they would not enter into a CRADA with a reasonable pricing clause because there is no way to predict the effect on commercial development of a product. Recently the NIH and the Public Health Service Technology Transfer Board decided to terminate the "reasonable pricing" clause from existing and future CRADAs and non-CRADA licensing agreements thus maintaining industry's incentive to participate in them [60].

Under the Department of Justice's proposed "Antitrust Guidelines for the Licensing and Acquisition of Intellectual Property," a new methodology will be used for evaluating the impact of licensing and acquisition on R & D activities. In cases where the parties to the licensing process possess identifiable specialized assets necessary for certain types of R & D activity, the possible anticompetitive impact will be considered in innovation markets [61].

In 1992 Senator Pryor's Special Committee on Aging began exploring the feasibility of shortening patent terms as a detriment to pricing excesses. There have been subsequent proposed patent law changes. Perhaps the most significant changes to the U.S. patent laws is the recently enacted General Agreement on Tariffs and Trade (GATT) legislation [62]. Under the new law a patent will expire 20 years after the patent application is filed, instead of 17 years after the patent is granted. This means that regulatory delays in obtaining the patent will result in a shorter period of patent protection. Although the Patent and Trademark Office (PTO) claims the average pendency is 20–28 months, some biotech patents are still in the examination process 5–10 years after the initial application was filed. Many valuable years of potential return on R & D costs will be consumed before the product can be brought to market. These changes will effect the ability of start-up companies to attract venture capital [63]. For patents filed before June 8, 1995, the date from filing or issuance that provides the longer term (with a 14 year maximum) is the operative one.

The FDA has issued a policy that prevents Abbreviated New Drug Application (ANDA) approvals during the extended patent period. According to a new study, as a result of this decision for the next 17 years the American public will pay an estimated $6 billion in higher prices for 105 brand-name drugs because of GATT-induced delays in generic drug introductions [64]. Approximately 94 patents already extended under Waxman–Hatch will get new extensions. Capoten and Zantac will be protected until 1996 and 1997, respectively [65]. Clearly, this FDA decision represents a windfall to pioneer pharmaceutical companies.

Other intellectual property reforms have been suggested as cost-containment approaches. One suggestion is the use of a royalty system whereby drugs would be protected by copyright and licensed by a pharmaceutical company to other companies who wish to manufacture the same drug. This would require extensive changes to the copyright laws to enable pharmaceuticals to fall within the definition of copyrightable subject matter. While the effect this would have on U.S. R & D in unknown, a recent Government Accounting Office (GAO) report found that Canada's compulsory licensing program had a negative impact on Canadian R & D of pharmaceuticals [66].

Approximately 1346 independent pharmacies in the United States in 15 states have filed separate lawsuits against 27 drug manufacturers, wholesalers, and mail-order pharmacies, claiming the industry has priced drugs on a discriminatory basis that has damaged competition in the marketplace resulting in higher prices. These suits also allege manufacturers are using patent violations to block normal market forces. The pharmacies are also arguing in favor of mandatory licensing [67].

Conversely, in 1994 legislation was proposed that would have provided patent extensions and expedited approval to pharmaceutical manufacturers for products if they voluntarily submitted direct comparison studies. It was further suggested that the FDA "certify" these studies and disseminate them to health plans and practitioner groups via electronic bulletin boards and other means. Also, the Biotechnology Patent Protection Act, which has been winding its way through Congress in various versions since 1990, would prevent the importation of biotech products made outside the United States using a starting material patented in the United States. It would strengthen patent protection for biotechnology inventions and would have a beneficial effect on biotech new drug development.

4. *Orphan Drug Act Amendments*

The Orphan Drug Act of 1983 provided incentives to innovators conducting research on drugs with "limited commercial value." The FDA's Office of Orphan Product Development lists some 350 different orphan drugs under development as of December 31, 1994 [68]. Currently, orphan drug designations are allowed for drugs with a patient population below 200,000 or no reasonable expectation that development costs will be recovered. We have witnessed an unexpected paradox: the profitability of orphan drug development. The sales of several orphan products have far outstripped their original R & D costs.

In reaction, several amendments to the Orphan Drug Act have been proposed, none of which have been enacted into law, including a windfall profit tax on orphan drugs that become excessively profitable; removal of orphan status if the target populations exceeds 200,000; decreased exclusivity from seven to four years with an additional three years available for drugs with limited commercial potential [69]. Would changes to the Orphan Drug Act decrease orphan drug research incentives? Some believe that pharmaceutical companies will no longer be willing to drill all the dry holes needed to discover oil.

Other proposed changes to the Orphan Drug Act would encourage new drug development. One proposal is to amend the Orphan credit so that drugs developed to treat AIDS would be considered "orphan drugs." Another proposal extends or makes "permanent" the Orphan Drug Development tax credits that expire on June 30, 1995 [70].

5. Miscellaneous Reforms

Often uses of a product are discovered after FDA approval. Manufacturers do not follow up on such uses because approval of a supplemental NDA is required, and two full clinical trials must be carried out to obtain such approval. The cost becomes prohibitive. In addition to the cost involved, supplemental approval times are generally longer than the original applications for the same drugs and the product's patent may expire in the time it takes to do the clinical trials, allowing generic manufacturers to market the drug for the new and old indications, without the burden of research costs [53]. Although generic manufacturers cannot market their drugs for new indications for three years after the pioneer firm has obtained supplemental NDA approval, physicians can prescribe or pharmacists can dispense the generic for new indications. To resolve the problem of off-label uses, FDA has begun to encourage certain manufacturers to file supplemental NDAs that the FDA has suggested they will process more quickly than would normally be the case.

The Investigational New Drug (IND) approval process is fast becoming a significant impediment to R & D, prompting more and more researchers to conduct clinical trials overseas where regulatory requirements are less demanding. Only about 20% of Phase I studies are now conducted in the United States and while the actual number of clinical holds has not increased in recent years, there are more "informal holds" and "partial holds" imposed by the FDA [33]. Many believe more flexibility is needed in the approval of Phase I trials to prevent the bench-to-clinic bottleneck that is occurring. As a result, there is growing pressure to simplify and streamline the IND review process.

Finally, a Memorandum of Understanding was signed in 1994 that allows U.S. manufactured products to gain certification in Russia based on their market approval by the FDA. This should speed up product registration in Russia.

B. Market Forces Behind Health Economic Issues

There is a trend in healthcare toward total drug therapy management and integration of medical data on therapeutic outcomes. There is an increased demand for performance guarantees and an increased role for the pharmacist in disease management. Price regulators care very little whether the price set is sufficient either to provide a reasonable return on past company investment in R & D or to sustain an ongoing research program.

1. Managed Care

Last year was the first year that more than half of all prescriptions were paid by third-party payers, instead of out of pocket by patients. Managed care programs now influence about 80% of the market and therefore, play a critical role in addressing prescription cost containment.

Managed care plans negotiate price rebates from manufacturers in exchange for inclusion of their products on the formulary. The growth of managed care and its tendency toward therapeutic equivalence and therapeutic substitution have resulted in fewer new drugs reaching over $100 million in sales. Unfortunately, managed care and other drug insurance programs have sometimes adopted across-the-board controls on utilization where cost-containment stipulations do more to distort than support therapeutic considerations [14]. Patients are switched from one product to another simply because the Health Maintenance Organization (HMO) may obtain a better price from another company [71].

The risk that the "corporate negligence doctrine" will apply to managed care entities creates a duty on these entities to perform the proper investigation for data to support selection or exclusion of pharmaceuticals on their formularies. Under the theory of "liability for utilization management," or "Wickline liability" as it is commonly called, managed care organizations may face liability for injury resulting from adverse consequences of drugs on the formulary, even if they were carefully selected and monitored. The Wickline case highlights the issues that can arise when a third-party payor imposes utilization and monetary controls [72]. Denial of payment may constitute a denial of the use and medical benefit of a nonformulary drug [73].

Pharmacy benefit management companies (PBMs) have exerted intense scrutiny over the cost of a patient's pharmaceutical care and are becoming more involved with managing outcomes. One PBM executive recently described a scenario of risk sharing with manufacturer's warranting their products and if the product is not as efficacious as the manufacturer predicts, the manufacturer reimburses the PBM for the unsuccessful drug therapies [74]. We are now witnessing aggressive pricing strategies by brand-name companies on new products to compete with other brand-name products, backed by efficiency-based money back guarantees for the product (e.g., fluvastatin). The PBMs are benefiting from all of this and saving a great deal of money.

2. The Expanding Role of Formularies

Formularies are preferred lists of drugs developed for an institution by a committee of experts based on the needs of patients and the institution. They have been around for four decades and formularies are currently used by virtually all state Medicaid programs, 90% of the nation's hospitals, 93% of the HMOs, and 70% of nursing homes [75,76]. Unfortunately, they sometimes become merely cost-containment devices rather than techniques to improve the quality of patient care [77]. These formularies are moving to closed, restrictive categories.

Do sales losses resulting from the widespread use of formularies have a substantial adverse effect on the incentives to develop and market new drugs, particularly those that have small annual sales? Data examining availability on Medicaid formularies demonstrates that failure to gain reimbursement for two years after marketing, caused by delays in formulary approval, results in sharp limitation in sales [78]. One study found that only 20% of new drug introductions were accepted onto all six studied state Medicaid formularies. Interestingly, the group of drugs rated as significant therapeutic advances was the least available to Medicaid patients [79]. The study investigator concluded that losses of sales resulting from the widespread use of formularies have a substantial adverse effect on incentives to develop and market new drugs, particularly those that have low annual sales. There is no doubt that this affects new drug development but further research is needed to quantitate the magnitude of this effect.

3. Generic and "Me-Too" Drugs

Section 202 of the Drug Price Competition and Patent Term Restoration Act has led to stockpiling and flooding the market as soon as the patent expires. While this may provide quicker access to lower priced generics, innovator pharmaceutical companies face generic competition earlier and lost market share quicker.

The prescription share of generics has doubled since the mid-1980s and is expected to reach 50% in 1995 [49]. A large number of breakthrough drugs are coming off patent in the 1990s. Pushed by the generic embrace of managed-care providers, many consumers continued to seek out generic substitutes to branded products. However, pharmaceutical companies that once threatened to become major generic drug suppliers now appear to be backing off (e.g., Merck & Co.). Surprisingly, in 1994, the best-selling drugs appear to have held off the challenges of new generic and low-cost branded drugs. Some market inroads were made, but not the massive slippage predicted for all competing brands [80].

An even greater impact on the market life of a breakthrough product has come from the introduction of "me-too" drugs, which are chemically different from the breakthrough compound but are based on the same mechanism of action. They compete with the breakthrough drug before its patent expires. Me-too drugs have historically absorbed a large share of R & D budgets. From 1978 to 1991, 153 NMEs approved by FDA were classified as "little or no therapeutic gain," while only 42 were classified as "important therapeutic gain" [81]. Pharmaceutical manufacturers are finding it difficult to get me-too drugs added to managed care formularies, especially for crowded therapeutic areas (e.g., cephalosporins, beta blockers, Angiotensin-Converting Enzyme (ACE) inhibitors, nonsteroidal anti-inflammatory agents). Therefore it is even harder for companies to recoup their R & D investment in me-toos. In fact, seven out of ten marketed prescription drugs do not recoup the average cost of R & D [82]. For example, last year G.D. Searle stopped development of an antihypertensive because it was decided the drug was not sufficiently unique from the competition. Because health insurers efforts are making me-too drugs harder to market profitably, pharmaceutical manufacturers are now increasing their emphasis on potential breakthrough drugs.

4. *Price Controls*

Congress and consumer groups have accused the industry of outright greed. In 1993, seventeen companies representing two-thirds of the market publicly promised to voluntarily restrain price increases. As a result the increases in drug prices have dropped to below the inflation rate in the past year for the first time in decades (Table 2) [83,84]. Most new drugs still face competition from drugs in other classes and from other treatments such as surgery. Even new "breakthrough" drugs are being introduced at prices lower than those of existing market leaders [85]. This trend is likely to continue as managed care organizations require cost-effectiveness documentation and low prices to gain entrance to their formularies.

In almost every country, with the exception of the United States, there are strict price and budgetary controls on pharmaceuticals. There have been major pricing pressures in the past two years from health care reform in European countries and government-imposed price cuts in Japan. Pricing is a marginal option in the global market today. In certain countries this type of cost-containment measures have gone as far as they can. For example, how much further can pharmaceutical prices fall in countries such as Spain and Greece?

Table 2 Prescription Drug Price Increases

Year	Percentage
1990	9.9
1991	9.4
1992	5.7
1993	4.7

5. *Pharmacoeconomic and Outcomes Research*

The Boston Consulting Group has found that each year over 700 health economics studies are published, and each pharmaceutical company begins, on average, 23 new studies [86]. Pharmacoeconomic analysis, which assesses both costs and outcomes, has certainly gained importance in this era of cost containment. During the drug development process, pharmaceutical companies are looking more carefully at the price of other drugs in the same therapeutic class and the projected prescription volume. Quality of life studies are becoming pivotal in determining "cost effectiveness" or the value of a drug. The industry is incorporating quality of life data when making an economic case for their drugs. Government agencies are increasingly using pharmacoeconomic research in making formulary, pricing, and reimbursement decisions.

Federal regulations do not require that new therapies be superior to or less expensive than existing therapies, only that they be safe and effective. However, a greater number of NDA submissions now include pharmacoeconomic study data. The Division of Drug Marketing, Advertising, and Communications (DDMAC) in the Center for Drug Evaluation and Research at the FDA is "being drawn" into the cost-effectiveness research field as a result of its regulation of prescription drug advertising. They review economic drug claims as a basis of comparative advertising of cost effectiveness or claims that the drug cuts health care spending. There would be a tremendous increase in the number of pharmacoeconomic studies if the FDA would require them as a condition for NDA approval [87,88]. In preparation for more industry research on cost effectiveness and outcomes and in view of the numerous requests the FDA is receiving from companies for advice in an effort to get claims approved, the FDA has recently formed a task force to educate staff and intends to issue written guidance on the topic [89]. Economic research is also popular throughout the European Community and elsewhere. Australia and five providences in Canada, for example, now require pharmaceutical manufacturers to submit an economic analysis as a condition for approval and listing on the national or, in Canada, providencial formularies.

With some drug therapy that allows for earlier hospital or nursing home discharge, the cost savings is apparent. New antiulcer drugs costing about $900 per year have made ulcer surgery, which costs nearly $30,000, obsolete. Coronary bypass surgery costs over $40,000. Certain types of heart disease can be treated as effectively with medications costing approximately $300 per year. The annual cost for a new drug for schizophrenia costs about $4500 annually. This drug enables many schizophrenics to leave hospitals, where care can cost more than $70,000 per year. A recent three-year pharmacoeconomic study cofunded by the manufacturer and the National Institutes of Diabetes, Digestive, and Kidney Diseases, reported that captopril use in diabetic nephropathy could save Medicare approximately $2.6 billion over a 10-year period [89].

There is currently no best source for outcome research. The Agency for Health Care Policy and Research has conducted some research and will continue to fund studies on outcomes research and develop more clinical-practice guidelines. The FDA data are limited to direct comparisons of one agent against another. For example, the FDA may have studies comparing two calcium channel blockers but none that compared all of them to see which is the most effective for which subgroups of patients. Pharmaceutical companies have no incentive, for example, to show that older, less expensive drugs are more cost effective than a newer, more expensive one. Employers and managed care organizations would gain from such broad research but have not been willing to invest heavily in it. The recently conducted Blue Cross and Blue Shield Association Technology Evaluation (TEC) comparative trials on breast cancer are an exception.

In the future, pharmaceutical prices may be based on outcome, not cost, as FDA regulation of outcome research becomes more likely. Today, FDA approval carries diminished control over the market as utilization decisions are increasingly being made by health plans and government agencies. Approval by the FDA is now becoming only the first step in bringing a new product to market.

6. *Pharmaceutical Industry Structural Reform*

All of these economic factors call for changes in the traditional structure and operation of pharmaceutical companies. Growing numbers of reorganizations and downsizings are visible signs of the economic squeeze that industry is faced with. However, the paradigm of pharmaceutical company integrations can be viewed as a declaration of their commitment to research. What started in 1989 with SmithKline/Beecham and Bristol-Myers/Squibb continues with Roche/Syntex, American Home Products/Cyanamid and, most recently, Glaxo's bid for Burroughs Wellcome. Unlike the recent vertical integrations (e.g., Merck/Medco), horizontal integration is aimed at bolstering the company's drug discovery processes. Both Smith-Kline Beecham and Bristol-Myers Squibb were able to report strong growth in the years immediately following their mergers and introduced numerous new products ahead of key patent expiration [90].

Vertical integrations have resulted in pharmaceutical companies owning a large share of the Pharmaceutical Benefit Management market. Pharmaceutical companies are also purchasing wholesalers. Those manufacturers who have not vertically integrated may be shut out of the market.

It is economic constraints that cause pharmaceutical companies to favor a core package of clinical and nonclinical studies that may require only minor additions to be suitable for submission in different countries. It is becoming impossible to support development of a drug that will not be able to penetrate the three major markets of the United States, Europe, and Japan [91]. Globalization has been a reactive response to economic demands rather than a proactive initiative to meet world pharmaceutical needs. Due to the need to optimize a company's high cost and high-risk R & D investment, it became obvious that drug development could not continue on a fragmented country-by-country basis. Drug development has become the catalyst for globalization and is also the driving force for mergers, acquisitions, and joint ventures (Figure 4) [92].

Economics is also restructuring the biopharmaceutical industry. In 1992, figures from the U.S. Patent and Trademark Office (PTO) indicate that 69% of biotech health care patents were of U.S. origin. Although U.S. companies continue to maintain their worldwide lead in biotechnology research and more than 300 products are currently wending their way through the approval process, we are witnessing an increase in foreign biotechnology investment [93].

Pharmaceutical companies are forming webs of partnerships and corporate alliances with biotech companies and outplacing internally developed technology. More than 30 major agreements were made in just the first quarter of 1994 compared with 14 during the same period in 1993. In addition to strategic alliances, biotech companies are utilizing alternative financing options. These include PIPEs (private investments in public entities), double-edged SWORDS (stock warrant, off-balance-sheets, R & D financings), SIRRS (stock index reset rights) and others (Table 3) [94]. These new financing vehicles could constitute a major trend in the industry's method of raising capital. In fact, venture capital investments in biotech companies grew from $459 million in 1993 to $639 million in 1994 and an analysis of their financial statements indicates a 27% increase in R & D spending [95].

7. *Shifting R & D Costs*

Funds to support clinical trials are drying up. For example, in the area of cancer research, the National Cancer Institute at NIH now funds less than 15% of research proposals, mostly for laboratory research [96]. The pharmaceutical industry has, consequently, assumed a larger role in supporting cancer research.

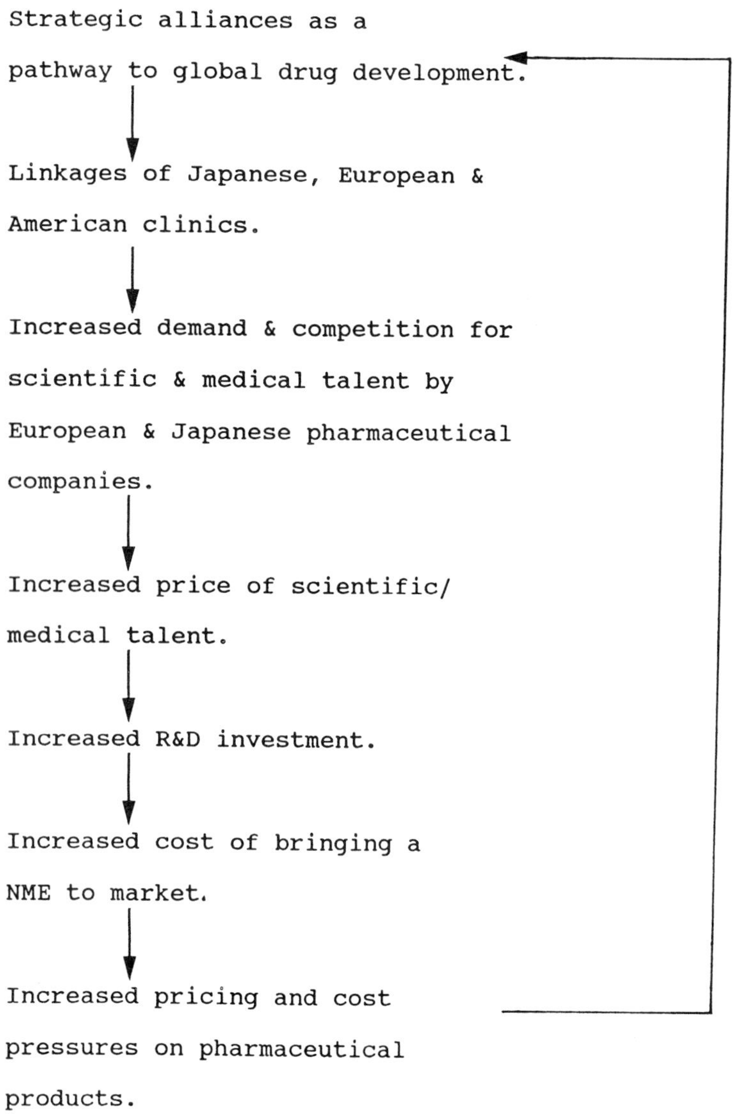

Fig. 4 Drug development as a catalyst for globalization.

Table 3 Biotech Creative Financing Mechanisms

SWORDS—stock warrant, off-balance-sheet, R & D financings. Allows companies to sell stock and warrants in a package that includes warrants from a large pharmaceutical company. If the biotech company fails, the investor retains the value of the warrants from the large company.
SIRRS—stock index reset rights. If the biotech stock does not reach a targeted price within a specified period, investors are issued additional shares to provide a cushion against losses.
PIPEs—private investments in public equities. Created in 1993 in an attempt to open the public equity market.
Regulation S filings—securities sold to foreign investors.
Novel partnering models—R & D focused spinout, royalty-based, joint venture, joint R & D, 60/40 without integration, selectively partnered.

Adapted from Refs. [94,95].

Further, major teaching hospitals that conduct clinical trials are facing severe revenue and budgetary cuts and insurance companies and Medicare are less willing to pay for the hospitalization and medical costs for patients treated with investigational drugs [50].

C. Effects on Innovation

Changes in the marketplace and cost containment strategies are affecting decisions made in drug development. Pharmaceutical companies are focusing on cost-cutting measures and streamlining research programs. Pharmaceutical companies will be less willing to have all their investigational efforts directed at compounds with higher failure rates than the norm, compounds that are more costly and/or that require the development and validation of clinical trial methodology. They will be more comfortable with a mix.

As a result of cost constraints there tends to be a "bottleneck" at the stage between promising laboratory data and clinical trials. Gaps have already been identified in funding "high-risk" research on diseases such as opportunistic infections. For example, the National Task Force on AIDS Drug Development intends to study industry barriers to AIDS drug discovery [97].

Market competition is resulting in pharmaceutical companies targeting cost-effective therapies and less on "me-too" drugs. Risks of a "no me-too policy" are that research will be aborted before companies know whether the drug will lead to incremental or major advances. Me-too drugs sometimes offer advantages in safety or efficacy over products that precede them. Companies will not develop specific products if they perceive themselves as trailing another company, only to see the front runner falter somewhere down the road [81].

There may be a shift from R & D on chronic disease drugs to acute therapies that typically have a shorter time line for new product development [85]. Passage of a Health Care Reform Act that would rachet down prices on therapies for Medicare patients could further divert R & D funds from chronic conditions that affect the elderly to those that are more predictable in terms of market success. At the same time few companies will invest in orphan drugs if projected costs are too high.

Phase IIIB studies are larger, or specialized, studies that concentrate on expanded populations and/or involve comparative studies with competitive products. These studies are conducted after NDA submission and are designed to provide supplemental information. We will continue to see pharmaceutical companies conducting more of these studies to obtain cost-effectiveness and product-comparison data as they vie for lean and restricted formularies. However, a trend is developing for inclusion of pharmacoeconomic and outcome analysis earlier than Phase III clinical trials or postmarketing. Today, some companies are conducting these studies prior to proceeding into expanded clinical trials. Because of the need to provide more information earlier to venture capital firms and investment companies, there is particular pressure to move these outcomes and cost-effectiveness studies earlier in the process for biotech development [88]. In the future, these trials will be undertaken in Phase II or even Phase I. However, this may actually inhibit new drug development, with the inherent risk of missing an opportunity. It is extremely difficult to evaluate the pharmacoeconomics of a drug in the artificial environment and economics of early clinical trials. The drug's pharmacoeconomic profile may be quite different after it has been used for some time in the market.

The proposed Health Security Act had a chilling effect on the pharmaceutical and venture capital dependent biotechnology industry. The Standard & Poor Drug Index of pharmaceutical stocks lost 22% of its value in 1992 and declined by an annual rate of 25% in 1993 [97]. Similarly, the American Biotech Index lost 32% of its value, initial public offerings decreased, and the actual number of companies declined. The result on new drug development was a decrease in the number of NMEs, biotech, and biologic drugs submitted to the FDA for approval [98]. In 1994, the number of significant biologics cleared by the Center for Biologics Evaluation and Research dropped to 15 from 23. In fact, the FDA has commissioned a study to examine the trend of declining biologics submissions [68]. Biotech R & D has been the first victim of health care reform.

Increased regulatory stringency for new drug approval has increased the cost of R & D per NME. This has reduced the expected rate of R & D return and, therefore, the level of investment. Decades of regulatory creep have increased research investments by about 13% per year per approved product while time lines have increased 5 years in two decades and the economic risks of failure have increased [98].

IV. CONCLUSION

The development of new prescription medications offers our greatest hope of controlling human suffering and the costs associated with diseases of aging. With nearly 17% of its revenue devoted to R & D, the U.S. pharmaceutical industry continues to maintain international leadership in finding solutions to health problems.

Cost-containment and product-liability considerations have become more controlling than innovation considerations in some aspects of new drug development. Although cost containment activities and product liability have no doubt been responsible for some portion of the decline in research productivity, the precise extent of their contribution to that decline is unknown [99]. Government-forced rebates and discounts, coercive pressures from the managed care industry, and the increasing preference for generics will foster intensified competition and squeeze revenues.

In the future, the therapies available to patients will be determined by decisions based on pharmacoeconomic and outcome-oriented research. The industry is already curbing prices through involvement with managed care programs and the increased competition from generics and "me-too" products. The specter of price regulation, government controls, and other market manipulations are expected to reduce industry profitability and consequently reduce investment in new drug research. Today's profits are an inaccurate measure of the continued viability of the pharmaceutical industry's innovative process. They merely show that the innovative process of the last decade was

Table 4 The Future: How to Nurture Drug Development

Accelerate drug development/approval
Reduce product liability disincentives
Continue harmonization of drug approval procedures between countries
Foster favorable environment for R & D collaboration and greater emphasis on interdisciplinary research
Eliminate trade barriers via multilateral trade negotiations
Reconsider patent laws
Co-marketing, merging, strategic alliances

Adapted from Ref. [100].

successful. The survivors in the future cost containment environment will be those with clearly defined corporate missions and R & D strategies.

The future depends on innovation, not imitation. New drug development can be encouraged in a number of ways (Table 4), and the rewards are great [100]. Who knows what dramatic drug discoveries remain to be found in a new synthetic compound, a fresh soil sample, or a plant obtained from some pristine forest? In any event, let us all hope that the cost containment and product liability approach that is governing drug development will be replaced by a more rational approach.

REFERENCES

1. M. M. Rumore and S. Strauss. Legal aspects of pharmacoepidemiology. *J. Pharmacoepidemiology 1*: 3, 1990.
2. 1994 Law Department Spending Survey. Price Waterhouse L.L.P., December 1994.
3. W. W. George. Medical technology and competitiveness in the world market. Reinventing the environment for innovation. Presented to the Food and Drug Law Institute 38th Annual Education Conference, Washington, D.C., December 1994.
4. Medical Malpractice and Product Liability Lawsuits—1992. U.S. Dept. of Justice, Washington, D.C., April 13, 1995.
5. D. Hoffmeister and J. Nygaard. What a product manager should know about products' liability in the 1990s. *Drug Info. J. 28*: 879, 1994.
6. National Research Council, Washington, D.C., February 1990.
7. PhRMA Advertisement. *Washington Post.* April 28, 1995.
8. 2 U.S.C. Sec. 247 (b)(j) (1983).
9. Restatement (Second) of Torts. Section 402A, comment g, (1965).
10. F. C. Woodside. Concepts and Relationships Underlying Injuries Involving Drug and Medical Devices. Drug Product Liability Reporter vol. 1, F. C. Woodside and M. Dixon, Eds., Matthew Bender, New York, 1989, p. 1–9.
11. Restatement (Second) of Torts. Section 402A, comment k, (1965).
12. L. D. Bauer and L. D. Stith. The Duty to Warn. Products Liability. Pharmaceutical Drug Cases, D. E. Vinson and A. H. Slaughter, Eds., Shephard's/McGraw Hill, New York, 1988, p. 129–130.
13. Brochu v Ortho Pharmaceutical Corp., 642 F2d 652 (1st Cir 1981).
14. Wadleigh v Rhone-Poulenc Rorer Inc, MDL-986.
15. Barson v E.R. Squibb & Sons, 682 P2d 832 (Utah 1984).
16. Tinnerholm v Parke-Davis & Co., 285 F Supp 432, 448 n 12 (SDNY 1968), modified, 411 F2d 48 (2d Cir 1969).
17. J. Braithwaite. Corporate Crime in the Pharmaceutical Industry. Routledge & Kegan Paul, London, 1984, p. 51.
18. 59 Fed. Reg. 54034 (Oct. 27, 1994).
19. 59 Fed. Reg. 54046 (Oct. 27, 1994).

20. J. N. Gibbs. FDA proposes new drug and biologic reporting requirements. *Regulatory Affairs Professionals Society Newsletter.* January 1995, p. 6.
21. Did liability block AIDS trial? *Science 257*: 316, 1992.
22. 59 Fed. Reg. 39406 (July 22, 1993).
23. U.S. FDA alters rules on women in clinical trials. *SCRIP* 1845: 15, August 10, 1993.
24. Specific Requirements on Content and Format of Labeling for Human Prescription Drugs; Revision of Pediatric Use Subsection in the Labeling, 21 CFR Part 201. Docket No. 92N-0165.
25. I. Green, M. M. Rumore, G. Torre, and L. Hyman. Drug clinical trials: Do women have equal access? *Regulatory Affairs 7*: 1, 1995.
26. Havner v Merrell Dow Pharmaceuticals Inc. 88-3915-F (Dist. Ct., Nueces Co., Texas), March 17, 1994.
27. $19.2 million verdict against Marion Merrell. *National Law J.* p. B2, July 4, 1994.
28. Racketeer Influenced and Corrupt Organization Act. P.L. 91-452, Sec. 1, 84 Stat. 22 (1970).
29. Upjohn v Oswald, 1992 —U-111 (High Ct.) England.
30. DHHS Federal Tort Claim 93-M-186.
31. A. Blum, Halcion[R] stirs litigation storm. *National Law J.* p. A1,A23, April 11, 1994.
32. Strain of Norplant's High Up-front Costs Has Subsided. U.S. General Accounting Office, HEHS-95-7, October 1994.
33. B. Bienz-Tadmor, Pheak Son Sea, and N. Bryant. Research and development, manufacturing, and marketing of biopharmaceuticals: an international comparison. *Drug Info. J. 29*: 523, 1995.
34. J. S. Benson and J. W. Boretos. Biomaterials and the future of medical devices. *Medical Device & Diagnostic Industry* p. 32–37, April 1995.
35. J. Wechsler. Getting to the heart of FDA's problems. *Pharm. Tech.* p. 14–20, May 1995.
36. J. Wechsler. Getting to first base. *Appl. Clin. Trials 3*: 12, 1994.
37. PhRMA Data. 1995.
38. W. W. George. Reinventing the environment for innovation. *Medical Device & Diagnostic Industry* p. 24–32, April 1995.
39. M. M. Rumore. Issues on vaccines. *Amer. Pharm. 32*: 7, 1992.
40. Childhood Vaccine Injury Act. P.L. 99-660 (1986).
41. R. P. Charron. An AIDS vaccine: It may take an Act of Congress. *J. NIH Research 6*: 84, 1994.
42. Farnes v E.R. Squibb & Sons, 92-10250-CA-01 (Cir. Ct., Monroe Co., FL.).
43. M. M. Rumore and S. Strauss. Pharmacoepidemiology: regulatory role of the pharmacist. *New York State J. Pharm. 11*: 42, 1991.
44. H. Berkman. Showdown in Senate on Tort Reform. *The National Law J.* p. A1, A26, May 1, 1995.
45. A. Blum. Tort Reform: Camel's Nose into State Law. *The National Law J.* p. A1, A22, March 20, 1995.
46. D. Barker. The effects of tort reform on medical malpractice insurance markets: an empirical analysis. *J. Health Politics, Policy and Law 17*: 143, 1992.
47. W. Griffen. Reforming medical device liability. *Medical Device & Diagnostic Industry*, p. 110, May 1994.

48. Drug makers address financial concerns of reform. *Pharm. Rep.* p. 3, Jan. 1994.
49. Pharmaceutical Manufacturers Association. Trends in U.S. Pharmaceutical Sales and R&D. 1990–1993 PMA Annual Survey Report, October 1993, p. 4, 7, 25.
50. J. Wechsler. Who will pay for R&D? *Appl. Clin. Trials 3*: 18, 1994.
51. K. I. Kaiten, M. Manocchia, M. Seibring, and L. Lasagna. The new drug approvals of 1990, 1991, and 1992: trends in drug development. *J. Clin. Pharmacol. 34*: 120, 1994.
52. J. Drews. The impact of globalization on pharmaceutical research and development. *Drug Info. J. 27*: 1059, 1993.
53. J. A. DiMasi. The cost of innovation in the pharmaceutical industry. *J. Health Econ. 10*: 107, 1991.
54. The Wilkerson Group. Integrated Health Care: Pharmaceutical Company Roles in a Seamless System. Wilkerson Pub., New York, March 1995, p. 46, 59.
55. E. Tanouye. Drug makers are expected to report modest results for the second quarter. *The Wall Street J.* p. A8, July 8, 1994.
56. FDA doing "good job" at meeting user fee review time goals. *FDC Reports—The Pink Sheet 58*: 11, January 22, 1996.
57. G. L. Barkdoll and K. A. McEvoy. Predicting the payoff from earlier approvals. *Pharm. Exec.* p. 46, November 1987.
58. T. Rucker. Public policy and drug costs: Legitimate and bastard options. *J. Research Pharm. Economics 4*: 3, 1992.
59. Wechsler. Politics and cost-effectiveness. *Appl. Clin. Trials 4*: 16, 1995.
60. PHS/NIH Terminate "Reasonable Pricing" Clause. *FDC Reports—The Pink Sheet*, p. 23, April 17, 1994.
61. T. Culbert and P. Saint-Antoine. Justice Department premieres its guidelines for the licensing and acquisition of intellectual property. *The National Law J.* p. B5, December 5, 1994.
62. 60 Fed. Reg. 20195 (April 25, 1995).
63. R. Rines and S. Kaltenheuser. Proposed patent laws would harm inventors. *The National Law J.* p. A23, November 24, 1994.
64. S. Schondelmeyer. Economic Impact of GATT Patent Extensions on Currently Marketed Drugs. PRIME Institute, March 1995.
65. FDA GATT Policy Prevents Generic Approvals During Extensions. *FDC Reports—The Pink Sheet*, p. 3, May 29, 1995.
66. United States General Accounting Office. Prescription Drugs. Companies Typically Charge More in the United States Than in Canada. GAO/T-HRD-93-5, February 22, 1993.
67. Drug Pricing Lawsuits. *Rx Ipsa Loquitur 22*: 3, 1995.
68. Data on File FDA's Office of Orphan Product Development, Bethesda, MD, December 1994.
69. Orphan Drugs with Sales Under Threshold Would Be Guaranteed Full Seven Years of Exclusivity Under Revision to Orphan Drug Amendments Proposed by HHS. *FDC Reports—The Pink Sheet 56*: 7, June 20, 1994.
70. AIDS Research Maximization Would be Aided by Permanent Restructured R&D and Orphan Drug Tax Credits. BIO Tells National Task Force on AIDS Subcommittee. *FDC Reports—The Pink Sheet 57*: 4–5, May 1, 1995.

71. Skyrocketing Prescription Drug Prices: Turning a Bad Deal into a Fair Deal. A Briefing Paper Prepared by the Majority Staff of the U.S. Senate Special Committee on Aging. David Pryor, Chairman, November 16, 1994.
72. Wickline v State of California. 288 Cal. Reptr. 661 (Cal. Ct. App. 1986).
73. D. Elden. Managed care liability relating to formularies and drug utilization management. *Managed Healthcare Pharmacy 1*: 15, 1992.
74. PBM evolution toward risk-sharing with manufacturers. *FDC Reports—The Pink Sheet 56*: T&G 3, June 20, 1994.
75. A. Farrar-Roff. Expanding role of formularies with eye on cost, compliance and care. *Pharmacy Today 1*: 25, 1995.
76. Marion Merrell Dow. Managed Care Digest—Long Term Care Edition, 1994.
77. E. Tanouye. Drug Marketers May Use Illegal Tactics to Sell. *The Wall Street J.*, August 23, 1994.
78. L. F. Soyka. Risks and benefits of global drug development: resource consideration. *Drug Info J. 27*: 1095, 1993.
79. D. S. Hilzenrath. Cutting back on "Me-too" drugs. *The Washington Post* p. C1, C2, April 26, 1994.
80. H. Grabowski. Medicaid Patients' access to new drugs. *Health Affairs 7*: 804, 1988.
81. E. Tanouye. Bestselling drugs held off low-cost challengers in '94. *The Wall Street J.* January 18, 1995.
82. P. R. Vagelos. Are prescription prices too high? *Science 252*: 1080, 1991.
83. *Historical Consumer Price Index for All Urban Consumers.* Bureau of Labor Statistics, 1993.
84. M. Kolassa. *Reductions in Pharmaceutical Price Growth.* Research Institute of Pharmaceutical Sciences, School of Pharmacy, University of Mississippi, February 1993.
85. J. Wechsler. Health reform threatens medical research. *Appl. Clin. Trials 2*: 12, 1993.
86. Boston Consulting Group. The Changing Environment for U.S. Pharmaceuticals. New York, NY, April 1993.
87. CBER will commission study to investigate declining submissions. *FDC Reports—The Pink Sheet 57*: 6, January 16, 1995.
88. J. Wechsler. Re-evaluating clinical trials: Devices, outcomes, and efficacy. *Appl. Clin. Trials 2*: 14, 1993.
89. FDA being "drawn into" cost effectiveness field through ad oversight, Kessler says, Agency is receiving cost studies with NDAs, "increasing role" predicted. *FDC Reports—The Pink Sheet 55*: 8, November 1, 1993.
90. E. Lewis. Captopril use in diabetic nephropathy. *New Engl. J. Med. 329*: 1619–22, 1993.
91. Glaxo bid for Wellcome follows SmithKline/Beecham, Bristol-Myers Squibb models. *FDC Reports—The Pink Sheet 57*: 7, January 30, 1995.
92. B. Tambi. Impact of global drug development on industry mergers, acquisitions and joint ventures. *Drug Info. J. 27*: 1089, 1993.
93. T.L. Copmann and C. R. Eaton. PMA Analysis. In Development Biotechnology Medicines. Pharmaceutical Manufacturers Association, Washington, D.C., 1993, p. 4.

94. G. S. Burill. Emerging trends: 1994 first quarter update. *BioPharm 7*: 22, June 1994.
95. G. S. Burill. Challenging conventional wisdom: projecting biotech's future. *BioPharm 7*: 48, November 1994.
96. M. M. Canan. Companies refocusing R&D as health debate begins. *Pharmaceutical Daily 1*: 1, September 24, 1993.
97. National Task Force on AIDS drug development to survey industry on drug discovery; Stumbling blocks include funding, staffing issues. *FDC Reports—The Pink Sheet 56*: 10, June 27, 1994.
98. W. Tucker. Health plans chilling effect on biotech. *The Washington Times*, July 11, 1994.
99. W. L. Thompson. Role of Portfolio Analysis in Corporate Strategic Decisions: New Economics of Health Care Worldwide. Portfolio Management '95. Barnett & Parexel, Aston, PA, 1995.
100. M. M. Rumore. The decline in new drug development. *Amer. Pharm. 32*: 73, 1992.

4

Managing the Overall Portfolio for Successful Discovery and Development

Rebecca J. Anderson

Boehringer Ingelheim Pharmaceuticals, Inc.
Ridgefield, Connecticut

I. INTRODUCTION: THE EXISTING SITUATION

For more than a decade now, pharmaceutical R & D expenditures in the United States have grown steadily at a rate of about 15% per year [1]. Over the same period the number of new drugs approved by the FDA has remained at approximately 23 per year [2]. Consequently, the investment in bringing a new chemical entity (NCE) to the pharmacist's shelf has risen steadily. Recent analysis now puts the development cost at $231 million [3], and there is every reason to believe the cost of drug development will continue to rise.

Interestingly, most pharmaceutical products are only marginally profitable. According to one study, the majority of pharmaceutical sales come from approximately the top 25% of pharmaceutical products [4]. About 55% of the profit from pharmaceuticals comes from 10% of drugs [5]. Only about 3 out of 10 drugs recover their development costs after taxes over the lifetime of the product [6]. For a sample of drugs introduced in the United States in the 1970s, it took 23 years after market launch to reach a positive net present value on the average R & D investment [7]. Changing market conditions now under way make it likely that newer products will have shorter effective lifetimes [8]. If this is true, the average NCE now being introduced would not pay back its development costs over its product lifetime. The conclusion from these analyses is that it is incumbent on a successful drug company to have an occasional blockbuster NCE to cover the cost of pharmaceutical R & D [7], since many drugs in the portfolio will not pay for their development.

Pharmaceutical R & D expenditures as a percent of sales climbed through the 1980s and reached a peak of 16.5% in 1989, as shown in Figure 1. There are a number of factors that have driven the cost of R & D upward, including inflation, the high cost of novel technologies, ever-increasing regulatory requirements, increased pressure to protect the environment, and more stringent worker safety requirements [9]. These factors have not diminished, nor are they expected to diminish in the future. Interestingly, over the past 5 years,

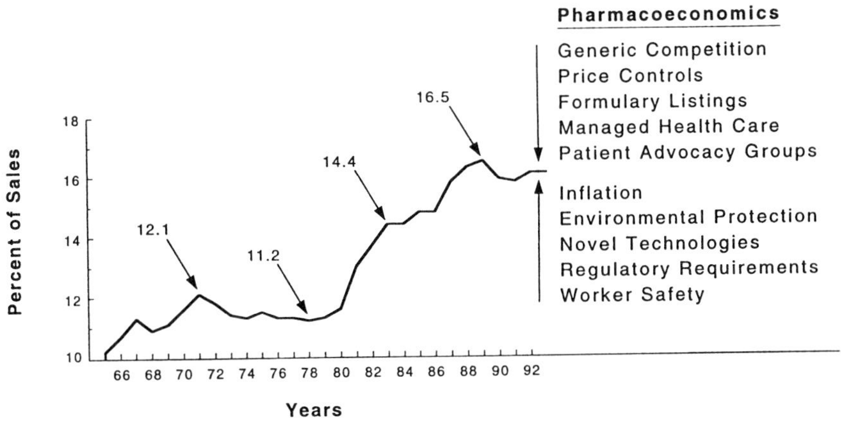

Fig. 1 Pharmaceutical R & D expenditures as a percent of sales. Some of the factors that have driven R & D costs upward and sales downward are shown to the right of the graph. (From Ref. [10].)

the fraction of income that companies are willing to invest in research has plateaued at about 16% [10], and there are reasons to believe the fraction will not go higher.

In the past, decisions about the choice of drug treatment were made by physicians, pharmacists, and opinion leaders who were primarily concerned about the properties of the drug, irrespective of cost. Now and in the future, other groups and factors are emerging that are forcing drug companies to adjust their marketing strategy [11]. These include the pressure of generic competition, the prospect of price controls and increased media coverage, the pressure from third party payment groups and managed health care organizations, and the influence of patient advocacy groups and consumer organizations. Since actions taken by companies to address these issues all tend to limit profitability, drug companies are re-examining expenditures. The successful companies of the future will find ways to produce high quality products more quickly and efficiently.

II. DIFFERENCES BETWEEN RESEARCH AND DEVELOPMENT

There are two quite different cultures that coexist within the R & D organization [12]. Some of the differences are listed in Table 1. Successful management of the R & D budget, as well as of R & D productivity, depends on under-

Table 1 Differences Between the Discovery and Development Environments

	Discovery	Development
Overall objective	Select a development candidate	Submit NDA or PLA
Corporate mandate	Broad, loosely defined	Narrow, focused
Compounds tested	Many and diverse	One
Types of studies used	Few	Many
Regulatory control	Little or none	Extensive
Timetable	Loose, flexible	Strict, constrained
Basis of recognition	Innovation	Speed
Culture	Chaotic	Structured
Workstyle	Entrepreneurial	Interdependent

standing these differences and creating an environment where both cultures can thrive and maximize their contribution to successful new products.

The goal of discovery scientists is to propose new substances for development. Typically they are given a great deal of latitude in how to go about this, as long as they stay within the company's general mission, which is usually defined in terms of targeted therapeutic areas or market segments. In fact, because innovative and breakthrough drugs are thought to have a significant market advantage, discovery scientists are encouraged to explore novel approaches in their attempts to discover a therapeutically beneficial substance, rather than follow a course already established by other drugs. One is more likely to see the entrepreneurial spirit in discovery laboratories, where individual scientists or small groups are free to explore their ideas without strict goal setting and accountability. This is because no timetable can be set for selecting a new development candidate until one of the hypotheses being tested shows promise and produces a chemical or biological lead substance as a starting point for further research. Even then, the timetable for optimizing a chemical series to select an acceptable development candidate cannot be predicted with certainty. Optimization may in fact not be possible. In the process of hypothesizing and testing, thousands of substances may be evaluated in a few, carefully chosen assay systems—a process that may be repeated many times until a sound hypothesis is validated by using a feasible assay system to produce a lead substance that fits the criteria for activity. All of this takes place in a culture that is at times chaotic and constantly changing direction, and for which the highest rewards and recognition go to those who produce a novel substance with commercial promise.

The scientists and physicians who support drug development work in a much different environment. For them, the drug substance, delivery system, and therapeutic indication have already been defined, at least conditionally. Consequently, their mandate from management is clear and direct: to move the product candidate through development so that a New Drug Application (NDA) or Product License Application (PLA) can be submitted as quickly as possible with the best chance of approval. A wide variety of studies must be carried out on this one drug, each designed to characterize its efficacy, safety, selectivity, or purity. Since much of the data generation is driven by strict and extensive regulatory guidelines, the development timetable is more predictable and lends itself to close management control. Furthermore, since many of the studies are interdependent, the development staff must work as an integrated, interactive team. All of this creates a culture that is highly structured and closely managed and in which speed and quality are the main criteria for reward and recognition.

III. MONITORING AND CONTROLLING R & D COSTS

In the future, a drug's success will depend not only on its safety and efficacy, but also on its economic benefit [13]. The pharmaceutical industry must adapt quickly to concerns about drug pricing. Clearly, a drug that is cheaper to develop and produce will command a significant market advantage over an identical drug that is priced higher. The first step in improving the return on investment under restricted pricing conditions is to contain investment costs through close monitoring and rational financial controlling.

A. Elements of the Budget

It is important to note that increased investment in R & D causes a disproportionate increase in the cost of developing each successful new product. In addition to the actual cash outlays, this investment carries an unusually high cost of capital because the expenditures are made early in a very long term development process [5]. In order to control R & D costs, one first needs to know where the costs come from. Table 2 shows the major elements of the R & D budget and their relative magnitude. The cost of drug discovery, especially for a company that emphasizes intramural research, is largely the cost of the scientific staff. Personnel-related costs may account for as much as 25–30% of the entire R & D budget. If intramural research is emphasized, materials and facilities needed by the scientific staff to support state-of-the-art research will also be high. Outside contracts usually supplement research, especially in areas in which intramural expertise does not exist or is not cost effective. In companies that do not emphasize intramural research, contracts will account for the majority of the discovery budget.

Table 2 Distribution of R & D Costs by Category

	Discovery	Development
Personnel	$$$	$$
Materials	$$	$
Facilities	$$	$
Contracts	$	$$
Support/Admin	$	$

In development, the intramural staff are also a valuable asset, especially for formulation and assay development, preparing novel delivery systems, and data handling when speed and control are essential. For these activities, skilled personnel and the facilities to support them are necessary components of the budget. However, a well-designed development program requires access to large numbers of suitable patients, and contract research organizations (CROs) contribute significantly to the development budget. Contract laboratories are also a viable and cost-effective option for nonclinical studies. This is especially true for development programs that require unconventional dosage forms, testing in nonstandard species, and dealing with situations in which intramural facilities or expertise are unavailable.

For both research and development, administrative overhead should be kept low. Current industry estimates [10] show that support services account for 20% of the R & D personnel and approximately 15% of the budget. Regulatory requirements for documentation encourage proliferation of administrative activities, but modern technologies are also available to automate and streamline these functions, which increases speed of information flow and decreases costs.

B. Considerations in Budget Control

A sufficient budget for research is much harder to predict than for development, because the milestones and accountability of discovery projects are harder to control. Serendipity often factors into the success of the research effort, as well as unanticipated breakthroughs in technologies that provide the tools for drug discovery. The time, cost, and chances for success are therefore much more variable in research than they are in development. As a result, budgeting drug discovery must be flexible: the company should provide as much funding as it can afford, avoid big swings in funding from year to year, and establish a balance between tolerance of high costs in projects that are moving slowly and the need to focus costs on high-priority, high-yield projects.

Preparing a sufficient budget to cover drug development is a more straightforward exercise. Much of the work, whether internal or external, is determined far in advance by the development plan and can be estimated by referring to similar experiences with previous projects. Historical information can also be helpful in estimating the cost of contingency plans, which would increase the budget, and the project failure rate, which would reduce it.

Accurate project cost accounting is important for effective budget control. Concerns over high-priced drug therapies are increasingly motivating companies to track the actual cost of product development. Monitoring costs from the earliest research effort through product registration will provide valuable data to justify the cost of the product development. Since companies must also cover the cost of good ideas that fail during development, development costs must be adjusted to account for these investments as well. Nevertheless, good project accounting provides a sound basis for these adjustments.

Since personnel can be such a significant component of the R & D budget, many companies have introduced monitoring systems to track the time employees spend on development projects as part of the project cost accounting procedure. The cost of materials purchased for specific projects, as well as contracts, can also be captured as project costs. However, lab supplies that are ordered in bulk and the facilities costs serve many projects and cannot be monitored on a project basis. In these cases an allocation procedure is used to spread unspecified costs to all projects, in proportion to the amount of work done on each one. Administrative support costs can be allocated to the projects on the same basis.

Increasingly, project managers are realizing that it makes good sense for the project to have its own budget and to be accountable for the expenses it incurs. By holding the team that is responsible for development of a compound also accountable for its expenses and for a competitive share of the budget, the team will be more cognizant and aggressive in seeking cost-effective options for conducting studies, assaying samples, and the like. Project budgeting is possible for development projects because the costs can be planned several years in advance. In discovery projects, this is more difficult.

IV. BALANCE BETWEEN RESEARCH AND DEVELOPMENT

With R & D budgets being more carefully scrutinized, one of the most difficult questions is how to divide the R & D budget between discovery and development activities. Discovery of a new development candidate is a very small cost relative to the cost of developing it. However, discovery efforts have a much higher failure rate, which significantly increases the cost of research needed to ensure one successful new product.

As an industry average, drug development is 60–70% of the total R & D budget, with the balance going to drug discovery [1]. However, no two drug companies are alike. There are small specialty drug companies seeking a niche market, large multinationals that cover all major therapeutic categories, and diversified health care product providers for which ethical pharmaceuticals are only one component of the product portfolio. The R & D budget for a small biotechnology company is almost totally devoted to research. At the other extreme, there are drug companies that focus almost exclusively on the development of products licensed or purchased from outside sources. The R & D budget for these firms is largely devoted to development.

In all these cases, the R & D budget is established to meet the needs of the company, not the other way around [14]. The question is not how the budget should be split between R & D, but rather, one should ask, What are the strategic objectives of the company? It is the company's strategic mission that defines the relative emphasis on discovery versus development. This defines the balance in the portfolio between the number of drug discovery approaches and the number of projects in development. Once a strategic mission is clearly stated, the budget to support the defined research objectives and development objectives is a straightforward exercise.

V. FACTORS THAT CONTRIBUTE TO R & D COSTS AND WAYS TO CONTROL THEM

The balance of costs between discovery and development is one thing; determining the appropriate cost of discovery and the cost of development is another. Research and development strategies should not be driven by the budget, but at the same time R & D should be sensitive to the ever-rising cost of doing work and find ways to control it. Table 3 lists five factors that are prerequisites for the success of R & D efforts [15]. These factors are usually considered as measures of scientific success. However, they can also be used as a means of assessing commercial success. Since productivity and success in R & D are increasingly being defined in financial terms, these factors provide the framework for identifying improvements in R & D operations in ways that improve cost-benefit.

A. Effectiveness

In order to do the right thing, the company must first decide what the right thing is. The company must identify what it does well (i.e., its core competencies) and what it wants to do well (i.e., its cutting-edge competencies) [14]. The

Table 3 Measures of Productivity and Success

Effectiveness:	Doing the right thing
Efficiency:	Doing the thing right
Quality:	Doing it best
Innovation:	Doing it smart
Integrity:	Telling it right and hearing it right

Source: Ref. [15].

amount of money a company spends on R & D should then be allocated to achieve success in these strategic areas, where the right people are working on the right projects.

Selecting the right people for the right job is critical; no amount of money can compensate for a poor quality scientific staff and skills that are inappropriately matched with projects [14]. When recruiting new personnel and reassigning existing staff, motivation and perseverance are the two most important characteristics to achieve success [16]. Perseverance is an inherent trait that should be used as a key selection criterion when recruiting new employees and should be a prime consideration when assigning resources to particularly difficult projects. Motivation is also an inherent trait. Although self-motivated individuals are more likely to be successful, motivation is strongly reinforced by success. In the absence of success, perseverance is the only force that will keep the company on course.

Identifying new product candidates comes from selecting the right research projects. To maximize the chances for success, though, research must be channeled in a balanced way along two lines: one that is consistent with the strategic goals of the company and one that encourages scientists to pursue intellectual challenges which emerge from their ongoing research. The first approach is pragmatic but guarantees a product portfolio with commercial value consistent with the corporate goals. The second approach stimulates scientific thinking to keep the portfolio from becoming trivial and shallow; these can sometimes provide solutions to problems unexpectedly [13,17]. Throwing money at research aimlessly does not shorten the discovery of new drugs or improve the likelihood of success. To receive management approval for either research approach, an attractive research idea should be presented as a proposal, which should include an hypothesis, rationale, a plan for testing the hypothesis, and a timetable for decision points. It is the responsibility of management to ensure that funds are available for both research approaches, but they must be based on sound proposals.

For the company to be effective, the choice of development candidates should also be based on the corporate mission: the drug must either fit one of the therapeutic areas of the company, round out a product line, or fill a portfolio gap in product introductions. Attractive candidates that do not fit strategically should not be pursued internally but may be good candidates for outlicensing. The decision to continue internal development of such a drug should be done only if it is so attractive that it justifies modifying the corporate strategy: this attractiveness may be based on entry into a new therapeutic area of future strategic importance, or it may enhance the company's image. Unlike discovery, drug development does depend to a large extent on the availability of resources, financial and otherwise. The size of the development budget is determined by the number of products in development and the timetable for project completions. Therefore, it is important to create a development portfolio that ensures that the development budget maximizes the chances for new product introductions. This requires ongoing steering by management throughout development, to keep the project in line with corporate goals.

B. Efficiency

Efficiency is squeezing the most out of what you have. Management must look critically at R & D and make the best use of its resources to maximize achievements with a minimum of cost and time.

Time is money. For pharmaceutical development, this is now true more than ever. For a $50 million product, there is an opportunity cost of $2 million for each month's delay in drug development [18]. For a major product, each day the NDA is delayed is a loss of $1 million in sales [19]. Each 400 days of additional effective patent life produces an additional $100 million in sales [5]. These statistics explain why decreasing drug development time is an important priority for pharmaceutical management. Reaching the market sooner provides an earlier return on the investment. Not only does the company's income increase from sales in earlier years, but also there is no extended drain on resources by prolonged development. In addition, the first product introduction in a therapeutic class holds a commanding lead in the marketplace that subsequent products cannot easily displace. Therefore, the financial benefit of a competitive advantage comes not only from providing sales in earlier years but also producing larger product sales than if the product were introduced as the third or fourth product in its class.

The financial winners of the future will be those who have as an objective the fastest development and approval for a main indication in all the major world markets [13]. Many approaches are used to decrease development time. One way is to smooth the major transitions between research and development and between development and commercialization [15,20]. Improved planning during preclinical development will ensure that enough bulk active ingredients are available to initiate key preclinical studies, as well as critical formulation work and the clinical program. Planning also ensures that adequate evaluation is done to understand the drug's metabolic fate in the species used for preclinical testing. These are often the most troublesome areas for delays in preclinical development.

In clinical development, steps should be taken to streamline the clinical program by carefully selecting the studies and the countries where studies are performed to ensure that the data are complementary and meet the regulatory requirements in the target countries [13]. The current industry trend is a strategy of coordinated, simultaneous development in all targeted countries [21]. A clinical program that is focused and appropriate in size has a competitive advantage [22].

The registration process is another target for improving efficiency. The chemical, preclinical and clinical requirements should all be addressed early in the planning process, and reassessed frequently during development to ensure that the plan and regulatory requirements stay in synchrony. Both the regulatory requirements and the development program change course many times during development, and reassessment is critical to maintain the shortest path. Efforts to harmonize regulatory requirements in major countries offer hope that future drug applications will be less troublesome. However, a variety of socio-economic concerns are likely to keep the requirements strict and numerous. For the foreseeable future, therefore, the most efficient registration package will likely be one that is constructed to meet the core requirements of key countries, such as the EEC, USA, and Japan, with modular sections that can be added or subtracted to meet country-specific requirements [17]. Such a package requires considerable advance planning, which should take place in conjunction with the development plan and which is actually constructed as each segment of the preclinical and clinical program is completed. Simultaneous, worldwide submissions are already a reality in some companies and, in the future, will be a necessity to stay competitive.

Finally, at all stages of the development process, the key to efficient development is a sound overall plan that includes contingency plans, rapid identification of bottlenecks, and vigorous resolution of each bottleneck when it appears [23]. Keeping the project on track is fundamentally a process of meeting target dates and milestones. It is up to management to set the objectives and target dates. This should be done after frank and open discussions with those who are charged with actually doing the work to ensure that the target dates are realistic [13]. Meeting the target dates then becomes a common goal to which both management and the team are committed. Constant diligence and attention to these fundamental activities will be the hallmark of successful companies in the future.

Table 4 Sources of Inefficiency in R & D

Lack of motivation
Inconsistency of funding
Lack of coordination
Unproductive research
Unfocused development
Slow project termination

Source: Ref. [15].

Effective time management of the development process is an admirable goal, but in order to shorten development time, one must first identify the root causes of inefficiency. Table 4 lists some common sources of inefficiency.

1. Motivation

Annual R & D costs are now approximately $175,000 per person, based on data from the PMA [10]. If the R & D staff is not motivated to operate at its peak potential, the company is paying for undelivered services, as illustrated in Figure 2. Once a high-quality staff is in place, the value of this R & D investment can be maximized by their efficient utilization. If properly guided, this simple adjustment can markedly increase the likelihood of success without any additions to the R & D budget. For research scientists and physicians, recognition from peers in the scientific community who acknowledge a significant medical contribution is a great motivator. For development scientists, recognition often comes from solving difficult technical problems during development and is usually a team effort. Nobody wants to work on a loser. So management can maximize productivity on commercially promising R & D projects by selectively recognizing and encouraging those who make significant contributions to projects that are strategically important to the company [24]. It is a simple and direct way for management to communicate clearly to the entire organization what it values, and it is an excellent opportunity to reinforce the company's strategic priorities by pointing out how a specific performance contributed to the company's success [20].

Rewarding performance in R & D has some special challenges. First, management is often hesitant to acknowledge good performance until it is clear that a drug is actually a proven winner in the marketplace. However, by the time a product reaches the market, many of the key contributors are gone and for those remaining the luster of their achievement has long since faded, in comparison to their current assignments.

Experience has shown that frequent rewards, even if they are small ones, are more important as motivators than a large one at the end. Rewards that

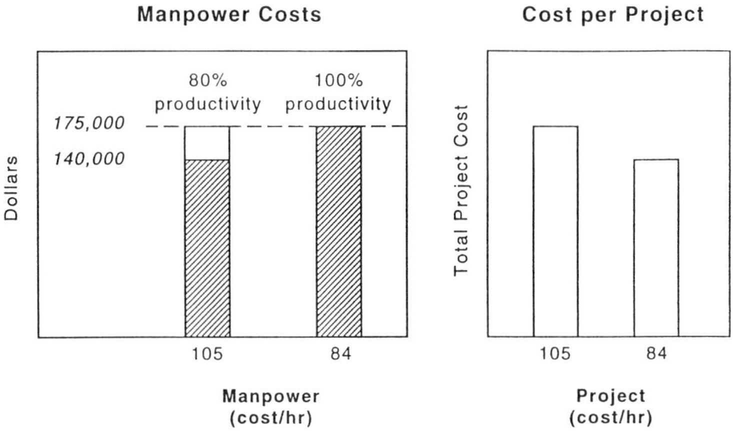

Fig. 2 Effect of productivity on project costs. The left panel shows that the average cost of work for R & D employees working at 100% efficiency is \$84 per hour, versus \$105 per hour when working at 80% efficiency. The right panel shows that the cost of development is significantly greater when the work costs \$105 per hour. Increasing worker productivity significantly reduces project costs without the need to reduce the R & D budget.

acknowledge the contribution quickly after the achievement are also more motivating than those that come after a long delay. In R & D, individual achievements should therefore be identified and rewarded as soon as possible after the contribution is made. For example, delivering a viable development candidate for preclinical testing is a significant achievement for a researcher, even if the drug never reaches clinical trials. Submitting a quality Investigational New Drug (IND) package is a significant achievement for a preclinical development team, even if the drug does not show clinical efficacy. From the point of view of motivation, the development process should be broken down into as many discrete contributory steps as possible, and management should be prepared to recognize and reward each of these contributions. Success is a great motivator for a scientist, but an achievement must be viewed by the recipient as a success. This can only happen if management recognizes and rewards it.

Second, R & D operations have a high failure rate, and management may resist rewarding failure, for fear of sending the wrong message about company priorities. However, a clear distinction should be made between drugs that fail and people who fail. The accomplishments of those who tried their best to achieve success should be recognized even though the project fails. A team should be rewarded for showing clear evidence that a product candidate has failed and recommending that it be dropped. Termination without producing a product under these conditions permits timely reallocation of the resources to more promising projects and is a good thing.

Finally, the reward must have value to the recipient, and there are wide individual differences in the perception of value. The 3M management discovered this when it allowed its teams to determine their own reward, with management approval [25]. Instead of a monetary reward, one team decided to send some of the key contributors to the official product launch ceremonies in the targeted market country. Another team asked for a dinner party for the team, as well as for 50 other contributors whose efforts they valued in the success of the project. There is a significant advantage in permitting the recipients to chose their own reward. One should be sensitive to these individual preferences and deliver an award that the recipient values.

2. Inconsistency

Inconsistency and frequent shifts in the level of financial support for individual projects is another significant source of inefficiency. Big swings in the R & D budget lead to uncertainty among the staff, discontinuity of the projects, and ultimately inefficient product development. Efficient R & D for one new product requires a sustained financial and management commitment for seven years or more. It is not uncommon for many internal and external competitive factors to change during this time, and the temptation to cut back support for a project is great. Research and development is not a profit-producing function of the company, and it is an easy target for budget cuts. If funding is allowed to fluctuate, the project cannot be optimally supported, and delays in development are inevitable. Worker morale and productivity also wax and wain when projects appear to be in favor one day and out of favor the next. Both of these situations increase the total project development cost. It requires a long term vision and an ongoing commitment by management to make adjustments that are financially responsible but also sustain high worker productivity and rapid development.

3. Lack of Coordination

Another factor affecting efficiency is the lack of coordination and continuity in product development from the test tube to the pharmacy shelf. Organizational structures often dictate separate divisions for discovery research, development, production, and marketing. Within each of these divisions there is usually good harmonization of goals and priorities. However, there is often discontinuity between divisions. A lack of common objectives and coordination across the organization can lead to costly development delays [13,14]. For example, the company may develop a scientifically attractive product for which there are no manufacturing facilities to produce it or for which the marketing department feels there is no market. For a company to operate efficiently, there must be a consensus and commitment to corporate goals, and the resources and facilities supporting the goals must be homogeneous across the organization to support both product development and commercialization [15, 26].

4. Research Productivity

The nature of research runs contrary to the usual notion of efficiency. The work is long term and unpredictable, since scientific discoveries do not follow a smooth, stepwise path. There are fits and starts as new insight is applied to a research problem, and often a quantum leap or the convergence of individually unimportant and seemingly unrelated facts leads to a breakthrough [13]. One cannot plan for this, but one does not have to be wasteful either. Drug discovery efforts can be focused to stay in line with the general corporate objectives while still maintaining an atmosphere that encourages creative intellectual pursuits. A useful management tool is a periodic assessment of research to review progress. Too frequent scrutiny is detrimental because it does not allow the freedom to take risks and explore potentially fruitful, if unorthodox, approaches. However, a formal review at reasonable intervals actually is beneficial because it forces scientists to review, organize, and rationalize their research direction, take stock of their progress, and solicit other scientific input. Research should move forward, not sideways, not backwards, and not stand still. If progress is not made, tough decisions need to be made to either focus the work, redirect it toward more profitable lines, or stop. Nothing drains the research budget more than projects that are stagnate and stale.

5. Development Productivity

Development projects are easier to run efficiently. At the beginning of the development project, there should be a detailed analysis, questioning all assumptions and background information leading to the decision to develop the substance [27]. The project risks, alternatives, and contingency plans should all be considered both from a technical and financial perspective. After the overall plan is formulated, there should be a detailed annual planning cycle to review and if necessary to revise the long term plan, in view of market changes, new competition, and changing regulatory requirements [27]. Formal review of development projects should be more frequent than research projects and should coincide with the availability of new project information [13]. The purpose of these reviews should be to check on the progress toward the current milestone and to mandate reasonable target dates for future milestones. The goal of development is to move the product through the pipeline as quickly as possible. Allocating additional financial and human resources can speed up development, but there is always the temptation to dilute the effort: attractive drug candidates tend to be embellished with burdensome additional indications or dosage forms; a drug in trouble tends to be salvaged by performing extra work to uncover redeeming marketable attributes no matter how remote [21]. Both courses are risky and can be very costly in terms of time and money. Drug development is a major financial investment, and it should be treated as such [27]. Efficient management of the investment, however, requires diligence and discipline, to maintain focus on the long-range corporate goals and avoid the many powerful temptations to pursue interesting but perhaps less lucrative alternative development paths.

6. Project Termination

Knowing when to quit is just as important as maintaining focus and is a significant mechanism for improving efficiency. Companies no longer can afford to fund open-ended research, on the slim chance that a novel drug mechanism might eventually be found using some yet-to-be-characterized research approach. Neither can they afford to explore every possible option to explain adverse findings, with the hope of salvaging a poor development candidate. It is hard to stop research that might lead to a profitable new product. It is hard to stop work on a development candidate that might hold some advantage therapeutically, despite problems in preclinical testing. It is hard on the scientific staff, who have invested a big part of their career in the effort and have strong ownership of their project. They may be unwilling or technically unable to retrain for a new R & D initiative. These are strong and compelling forces, but they are not financially sound. Research and development often is a black box, but it should not become a black hole.

Failure to terminate unproductive projects is one of the greatest financial drains both on the company as a whole and on resources that should be allocated to projects with a greater likelihood of success. The average R & D project consumes approximately $300,000 per month in internal resources. Allowing unproductive projects to continue has two financial disadvantages. First, there is the obvious wasteful expenditure on a project that will not yield a marketable product. In addition, there is a loss of productivity on other projects, because they are deprived of resources that are instead committed to the unproductive product, as illustrated in the example in Figure 3. The development of priority projects may be less than optimal if resources are limiting and not able to be assigned to it. Taking swift action to redirect valuable R & D resources toward more productive product candidates maximizes the chance for success, shortens development time, and minimizes waste.

Major research discoveries are often not planned or predicted in advance. Because of this, the decision to terminate a discovery project cannot be based solely on the failure to demonstrate constant, steady progress. Research projects should be set up with specific and realistic objectives in mind, with suffi-

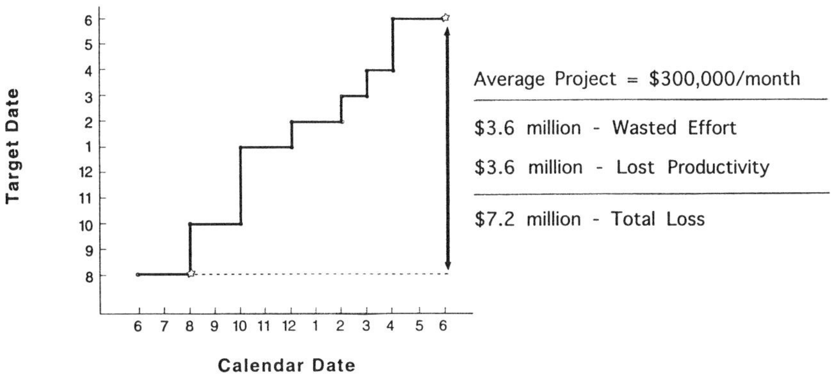

Fig. 3 Effect of delayed termination on R & D costs. The graph shows a series of adjustments by management over the course of one year, each time resetting and delaying the decision to terminate a project. For a project costing $300,000 per month in internal resources, the cost to R & D of the delayed decision is $3.6 million for unnecessary work done on the terminated project, plus $3.6 million in lost productivity on a higher priority project because resources from the unsuccessful project could not be assigned to it.

cient latitude for exploring unexpected findings. Approved projects should be measured periodically against their plan to assess progress. Projects that are not making adequate progress are easy to spot.

Development progress, on the other hand, can be more easily assessed. A development plan with milestone decisions is an integral part of drug development. A negative or unexpected observation should be taken very seriously as a harbinger of worse things to come [28]. This is because in development a drug moves progressively from more-controlled to less-controlled experimental conditions. If there are troublesome results early on, they will likely be compounded in larger, less-controlled studies. Problems do not magically go away. Many teams slip into salvage mode: trying to figure out why an unexpected result was seen; trying to bury it in statistics by increasing the number of observations through repeated retesting; or sidetracking the entire project by developing a whole new line of studies to overcome the problem. These are not wise approaches.

For both discovery and development projects, a back-up strategy that anticipates unexpected findings should be formulated as part of the original research or development plan. This strategy should include a clear understanding of the conditions under which the project should be terminated. When difficulties arise, as they invariably do, the back-up strategy should be consulted. As part of the project review, management should decide either to drop the original plan in favor of a new plan that plays to the strengths of the unexpected findings, or terminate the project outright. The important thing is that the project should not be allowed to stagnate or divert resources without a specific research or development objective in mind.

Communication is a key factor in termination of a project. A regular review cycle to assess progress against goals makes it obvious which projects are progressing and which are not. Termination of projects that have not met their objectives or have not overcome their problems should not come as a surprise to anyone. Management can ease the disruptions and disappointments caused by project terminations by pointing out to the R & D staff the need to maximize resource allocations on high-priority projects and reminding everyone of the benefits of staying focused on projects with the highest potential [13]. Scientists, like everyone else, want to be identified with a winner. If important strategic areas are clearly communicated to the company, workers will flock to them.

The financial realities of the future will dictate a much closer scrutiny of R & D expenditures than in the past, and smart management will become more pragmatic in the review of established projects, more selective in the approval of risky projects, and more willing to terminate those that repeatedly show no progress.

C. Quality

The purity, safety, and efficacy of drugs is taken for granted by the consuming public because of stringent regulatory requirements. In the past, drug companies viewed doctors and patients as their customers, for whom safety and efficacy were the only measures of product quality. In the future, the customers will include third party providers, formularies, and the government, and for them decisions of quality will be based on the quality of life and the cost of the product relative to its therapeutic benefit [29]. Successful companies in the future will be those that provide not only product quality but economic quality as well. Research and development resources must be concentrated on fewer projects, which are chosen to maximize the likelihood of producing truly important new drugs [17,21].

Drug companies also recognize regulatory agencies as a key customer. If they are not satisfied, the product will not reach the market at all. Therefore, increased emphasis on quality regulatory submissions promises to produce drug applications that can be reviewed more quickly and efficiently by the agency and probably stand a better chance of approval. Also, much of the pharmaceutical industry is adopting Total Quality Management (TQM) techniques to improve internal operations and customer service. In-process improvements for manufacturing drug product are the most readily addressed, but re-engineering in other areas is also taking place. For example, automated techniques for data processing and compiling computer assisted New Drug Applications (CANDAs) promise to take years off the development time and review process [30]. Similarly, improved systems for reporting adverse events not only will speed up reporting, but also will provide more complete information to the drug company and regulatory agencies. Successful companies of the future will be those that make quality a priority in all of their R & D operations, not just in the characteristics of their products.

D. Innovation

Innovativeness is one of the most important determinants of profitable pharmaceutical products. Breakthrough products provide a novel approach to treating disease, treat diseases that were previously untreatable, or better yet, expand the size of the market by providing treatment to patients who previously could not be treated or did not seek treatment; these products are almost always profitable.

Given the new climate for health care reform, successful pharmaceutical companies of the future will be more focused on innovation [8]. There are several reasons for this. First, the pay-off for successful novel drugs is bigger than for me-too drugs. Whereas me-too drugs will be faced with price constraints that match the price of other marketed drugs in the same class, novel drugs will probably be given more latitude for premium pricing because there are no alternative therapeutic agents [9]. Second, consumers are increasingly unwilling to pay a premium price for a product that provides a small incremental benefit [8]. The emergence of generic equivalents and the increasing freedom of consumers to receive generic equivalents, will severely limit the attractiveness of new drugs unless they can claim some advantage for the patient. Novel agents that offer a clear advantage in efficacy, adverse event profile, or drug delivery will enjoy more flexibility in pricing. Third, it is likely that in the future at least some regulatory agencies will permit only two or three drugs in a given class [29]. Companies that are fifth or sixth to the market may have a difficult time obtaining product approval. Finally, breakthrough drugs open up new markets by providing treatment options that previously did not exist. The early success of Tagamet came from large, unexpected sales to patients who were previously untreated because they were refractory to conventional medications and those who were previously undiagnosed and/or did not seek treatment [31]. Both consumers and the pharmaceutical company benefit from breakthrough products because the market is expanded to meet an unsatisfied medical need. For these reasons, pharmaceutical companies that are first to launch an innovative drug with clinical superiority are more likely to be successful [8].

Unfortunately, not every novel research idea will translate into a commercially attractive product with a demonstrable therapeutic advantage. Innovation cannot be mandated, but it can be encouraged. A critical mass of scientific talent, coupled with a good communication network, relevant technologies, and an adequate infrastructure provides an environment that fosters innovative research. Challenging scientists to discover drugs of a unique chemical class, which modify biological processes in a novel way to improve or reverse a pathological condition in the patient, is one way to create a breakthrough product. So is encouraging innovative formulations and novel delivery systems. Genetic engineering techniques also promise to open up whole new dimensions of drug treatment by reconfiguring biological substances into therapeutic agents.

A critical success factor for pharmaceutical companies in the future will be the ability to correctly identify these breakthrough products early in development. There is no proven method for predicting commercial success, but qualitative and quantitative analysis of the appropriate endpoints can be helpful. Quantitative analysis, such as determining the number of company patents that are cited as prior art by other patent applicants or clinical performance results, can be used to assess the value of the innovation [32]. Qualitative analysis, for example from an independent scientific advisory board who reviews reactions to papers presented at top scientific conferences or the value of publications, can be used to provide an unbiased assessment of the value of the company's research rationale and the technologies employed [33]. A plan for

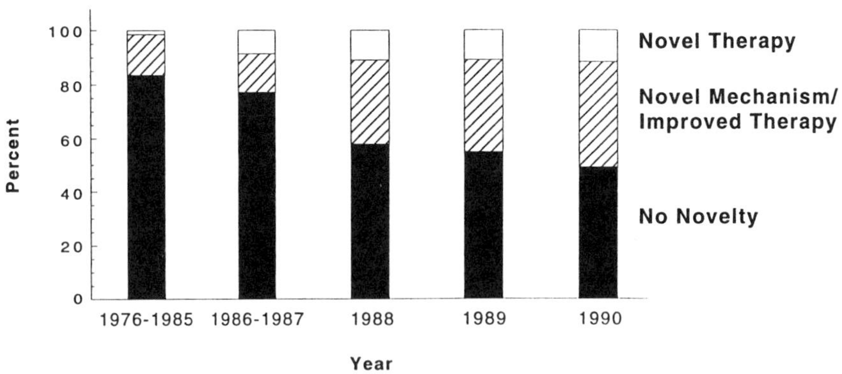

Fig. 4 Trend in innovative new project introductions. The graph shows a steady increase in the fraction of new drug introductions that claim a novel mechanism or therapeutic advance. (From Ref. [2].)

calculated risk, with clearly defined go/no go milestones, can provide a cost-effective strategy for determining the product potential. Consulting this plan early and frequently will help to focus the R & D effort on those projects that have the greatest commercial potential.

Market research, on the other hand, has not proven to be a reliable indicator of the commercial potential of novel products. While sales of me-too products can be estimated because there is an established market, there is no reasonable method for calculating sales of a novel product. Sales forecasts are usually underestimated because the market segment eventually served by the product is often not visible to the forecaster or is not appreciated as a future market.

Prior to 1985, less than 20% of the new drugs introduced in the United States claimed a novel therapeutic approach, a novel mechanism, or an improved therapeutic benefit [12]. Figure 4 shows that by 1990 the fraction of novel drugs had steadily increased to approximately 50%. Concurrent with this increased emphasis on novel products has been a trend toward greater profitability of new drugs. Figure 5 shows that drugs introduced in the early 1980s produced greater second year sales than those introduced in the 1970s. Similarly, drugs introduced in the late 1980s had greater second year sales than those introduced in the early 1980s. The profitability of new drugs is likely to be attenuated over the next decade, as drug sales become more price sensitive [5]. Novel drugs that offer enhanced therapeutic benefit to the patient will be

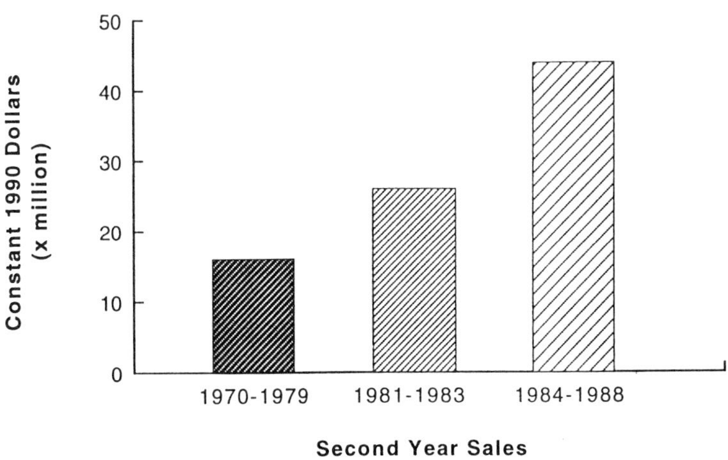

Fig. 5 Trend in sales of new product introductions. The graph shows a progressive increase in second-year sales of new drug introductions in the last two decades, measured in constant 1990 dollars. (From Ref. [5].)

one of the few factors that can counter the profit-limiting environment imposed by pharmacoeconomics.

The pharmaceutical industry has always been high risk for new product development. The increased emphasis on novel drugs will make the risk even higher, and many companies may languish [8]. There is an increasingly crowded field of competitors, all seeking a unique approach to therapy. Clearly, only a few of them will be able to move fast enough to launch a novel drug; others introducing their new products later in the same class suddenly become the me-too drugs. Finding novel approaches that are commercially viable therefore will become quite challenging and highly competitive.

E. Integrity

Personal and professional integrity in the pharmaceutical industry is high. It is driven not only by strict regulatory requirements that are designed to protect the consumer, but also by the ethics of science and medicine, which have never tolerated willful deception or distortion of scientific findings.

However, integrity may be compromised when the R & D environment constrains telling it right or hearing it right. The R & D staff must be open and honest with their management in order for projects to be evaluated fairly and acted upon appropriately. This will not happen if workers feel compelled to suppress bad news or delay actions while trying to find some redeeming value in the project [24]. This problem has been compounded by globalized drug development where cultural differences may impede communications and mislead management decision making. The reticence to admit failure and the desire to save face are very real forces that may not be fully appreciated but that can severely impact progress in development.

Hearing it right is equally important. Bright new ideas often struggle for lack of full management commitment. There is a tendency for the management of the industry leader to stick to an existing technology in which they lead and have invested heavily, rather than embrace an alternative cutting-edge technology that is needed to sustain their market position in the future [34]. While there may be a strategic objective of new product development and superficial commitment to it, management often does not put full support behind it. The R & D managers made their careers with the existing technologies, and in fact may have been promoted to their current position as a reward for those technical skills. Their preference will be to continue support work in this same area, both for the sake of their own reputation and because the alternatives are less familiar and they have less expertise with them. New ideas always take more convincing, but this is especially true when the decision makers come from an older school of thought. All the while, there is a risk of losing a competitive advantage as other companies capitalize on the same new ideas.

While there may be no willful or deliberate intention to deceive in these cases, the impact of not telling it right, not hearing it right, or both, can have a severe impact on new product progress. Some drugs may never be discovered because there is a lack of management confidence, support, or understanding. Promising product candidates may languish for lack of a full commitment, in favor of others with which management is more familiar or values more because of personal knowledge. Worst of all, the perception that R & D staff are not free to report bad news discourages risk-taking, stifles the most creative elements of the company, and cuts off the most important sources of future commercial successes. The successful companies of the future will be those that foster an atmosphere of mutual confidence and trust.

VI. THE R & D PORTFOLIO

A. Portfolio Considerations and Complications

Periodic evaluation of the R & D portfolio can have a major impact on improving R & D productivity. It can identify promising projects that are not being adequately resourced. It can identify projects that are not meeting the company's strategic objectives despite a major resource investment. It can identify projects that, although promising, do not fit the company's strategic plan. Taking appropriate actions, based on these findings, will focus R & D efforts along the most productive lines and divest those projects that do not fit. To be conducted properly, the portfolio analysis requires a considerable commitment from management and from many specialized functions. It is important therefore to approach this exercise with an appreciation of what things the portfolio analysis can and cannot accomplish and to be aware of the pitfalls that are commonly encountered while doing the analysis.

First, the accuracy of project assessment and the attractiveness of a product candidate change during the course of development, as more information is collected. All discovery projects are more risky than development candidates because very little is known about the product's characteristics. An early development candidate may be highly valued because it represents a novel mechanism of action that promises to treat refractory patients, whereas the same product in Phase III clinical trials may be rated very low because the novel mechanistic approach has not proven to be clinically beneficial. The market assessment will be much more realistic for a product nearing NDA submission than a product just entering clinical trials. These examples illustrate the importance of selecting standards and criteria for assessing projects that do not introduce biases due to the relative maturity of the project. All evaluation criteria should be normalized so that the product attractiveness is not distorted by unproven expectations.

Second, the goal of portfolio analysis is not to set a priority list. Priorities are important, but the outcome of a good portfolio analysis should be to establish a balanced portfolio that includes a variety of product types. Low-risk, high-reward projects are the most important product candidates and should be adequately supported. But some risky projects may be justified because they promise to be highly lucrative if successful. Likewise, some low-reward projects may be justified if there is confidence that the product promises a high likelihood of reaching its targeted market. Only those projects that carry a high risk and will deliver little or no return on investment if successful should be clear candidates for elimination. The rest should be chosen or rejected on the basis of their fit with the corporate strategies for short-term/long-term balance, high-reward/high-risk balance and low-risk/low-reward balance.

Third, the outcome of the portfolio analysis should be driven by the corporate mission, not the other way around. There is no formula for appropriate distribution of projects in the portfolio. Any portfolio may be appropriate, depending on how the strategic objectives of the company are defined. However, it is not prudent to allow the corporate vision to be defined by an unstructured project portfolio. Therefore, one important precursor to conducting a portfolio analysis is a clearly stated set of corporate goals to which the company is committed.

Fourth, portfolio analysis is a dynamic exercise consisting of a recurring cycle: analysis, review, evaluation, conclusions, decisions, and implementation. The frequency of this cycle should be dictated by the needs and requirements of the corporate goals. Since projects are constantly changing in value based on new information, there may be a temptation to adjust the portfolio too frequently. While major project milestones should be used as an opportunity to reassess the relative value of a project and its place in the portfolio, there is just as much harm in too frequent adjustments as there is in infrequent or irregular reviews. The review cycle should be timed to coincide with corporate strategic planning and long-range financial planning decisions.

Finally, it is not the results of the portfolio analysis that are important, rather it is the *process* of review that is valuable to the organization. It is easy to become overly analytical using fancy weighting scales and flashy graphics to quantitate and display the value of each project. However, the most effective portfolio analysis comes from thoughtful discussions by the company's decision makers, who evaluate the projects qualitatively with respect to business objectives now and in the future. Delegating the exercise to subordinates prevents involvement by key management decision makers. Those with the greatest knowledge of the projects and those making policy decisions for the company should be the ones directly involved in the analysis. The discussions, challenges, and explanations that are revealed in the process of comparing one project to the others, and defending this opinion to others who hold differing views, represent the most valuable aspect of the process. It is the only way informed decisions about the project's place in the portfolio can be made. The graphs and charts that follow this process are really of secondary importance; their only value is to communicate to the rest of the company the major conclusions coming from the portfolio discussions.

B. Dimensions and Criteria for Portfolio Analysis

Evaluation of the portfolio should take place in two stages. First, each project needs to be assessed for its individual strengths and weaknesses. Next, the projects need to be assessed as a group, either by therapeutic class, or the portfolio in its entirety. The group assessment gives an overview of the strengths and weaknesses of the aggregated portfolio.

All criteria used to assess projects can be classified in one of two dimensions. Risk is one dimension and measures the likelihood of success, based on feasibility factors. The other dimension is reward, which measures the financial return of the product, given that it is successful. The choice of evaluation criteria is critically important for a successful analysis, and the criteria must be quantitative. Unfortunately, criteria that are measurable are often irrelevant, and those that are relevant are usually unmeasurable [15]. The number of risk and reward factors does not have to be comprehensive, but the factors must be relevant and representative characteristics of the risk and reward value of the project, respectively. A well-defined corporate mission is helpful in selecting criteria that are in line with the strategic priorities of the company for reaching targeted markets and long-range sales objectives.

In order to compare one project with another, the evaluations must be quantitative [14]. It is important to keep the scaling simple and consistent with the precision of the projects being measured. Especially for projects in early development, there are probably far more characteristics that are unknown about the drug than those that are known; therefore, much of the assessment is educated guesswork, rather than soundly defensible fact. It is easy to fall into the traps of defining parameters with greater precision than what is known about the product and using statistical analysis schemes that are more complex than the conclusions that can be drawn from the available information. Both the rating scales and the calculations from them should be consistent with the relative uncertainty of the assessments themselves.

The portfolio analysis should be conducted separately for research projects and substances under development. The single event that distinguishes discovery projects from development projects is the identification of a development candidate. Discovery portfolios should focus on evaluation of the research approaches, since the value of a yet-to-be-named development candidate cannot be measured. Development portfolios, on the other hand, can evaluate and compare specific drugs with each other. Because of this, the evaluation criteria are different and should be chosen to assess the attractiveness of the research approach for discovery projects and the attractiveness of drugs as potential products for development projects.

C. Assessing the Discovery Portfolio

Assessing the discovery portfolio should be done in two ways. First, newly emerging research ideas should be evaluated as they arise, and a decision should be made whether to include them in the portfolio. Research is what keeps the pipeline stocked. Ideas that fit the strategic plan should be encouraged; those that do not should be redirected toward more suitable lines. Second, there should be a periodic review of ongoing research projects to determine whether the approach is making suitable progress and to assess whether each project still meets the original strategic expectations.

Some indices for assessing the risk and reward value of the projects in a research portfolio [35,36] are shown in Table 5. Risk can be divided into two categories: the risk associated with technical feasibility and that associated with therapeutic relevance. Either type of risk, if high, should stop the research effort. Technical feasibility assesses the wherewithal of the company to follow through on the research idea. Does the research staff have the right technical skills? Does the company have a critical mass of such manpower? Do these people have the proper facilities to test their ideas? Will the budget support this type of research effort, or is it too costly an approach? How much dependence is there on external resources to round out the technology base and are these resources complementary to the internal resources? How much time will it take to set up the appropriate technologies?

Therapeutic relevance assesses the relationship (or lack) of the drug's mechanism of action to its clinical efficacy. Does the pharmacologic mechanism of action target the etiology of the disease or symptomatology? How predictive are the laboratory model systems to clinical disease? Can the therapeutic target be influenced without disrupting other biological systems?

The relative reward potential can also be divided into two categories: the reward derived from the market value of the product and the rewards from having a favorable advantage over competitors. For research projects, there is no way to determine a market share because no drug has yet been identified. There is no way to predict with certainty which patients with the disease will respond to the drug, or whether adverse actions of the drug will limit prescribing to selected populations. Assessment of the market potential should therefore be limited to general questions. What is the size of the patient population for the target indication? If there are effective drugs already available to the patient, do they have limitations that this new product will overcome? Is this

Table 5 Criteria for Assessing Discovery Projects

	Factors	Examples of quantitative endpoints
Risk	Technical feasibility	People skills
		Research facilities
		Financially realistic goals
		Type of external support required
	Therapeutic relevance	Efficacy in vitro
		Efficacy in animal models
		Predictability of animal models
		In vivo selectivity of drug action
Reward	Market	Size of patient population
		Medical need
		Innovation
		Patent protection
	Competition	Value of core competencies

Sources: Refs. [35,36].

a novel approach to drug treatment? Does the company have secure patent protection for these discoveries?

For research projects, assessing the competition cannot be determined by market share. There is no way to determine how many competitors will launch similar products at the same time. However, one can gauge the competitive advantage by assessing the company's core competencies: how strong is the research approach compared to the competitors in terms of screening techniques, animal models, patent protection, and key collaborators?

In the future drug discovery will be driven by an environment that demands minimizing costs and maximizing the therapeutic benefit to the patient and other pharmaceutical customers. Innovation is the best means to achieve a major therapeutic advance and therefore produces the highest rewards. The dilemma is that truly novel research approaches, by definition, have no proven therapeutic relevance, are probably costly to implement, and usually require sophisticated technologies. There is no guarantee that these efforts will lead to identification of a new drug, there is no way to determine in advance how long it will take to identify a lead chemical structure using these approaches, and there are no guidelines on how long one should continue before giving up the search. Thus, while the most attractive research projects are those that yield high rewards at low risk, these projects are rare. Innovation is almost always associated with high risk. Innovative projects are certainly worth the risk, if the portfolio is balanced with other projects to offset the overall risk to the company. Furthermore, analysis using quantitative criteria not only assesses the value of the research activities but also provides an opportunity for periodic and rational adjustments in research direction in order to maintain focus.

D. Assessing the Development Portfolio

As with the discovery portfolio, the development portfolio should be assessed in two ways. First, each new drug candidate should be assessed when it is proposed for development to determine where it falls in the portfolio. Second, there should be a regular review of all the development projects to ensure that each project is making acceptable progress and that it still is fulfilling its original strategic expectations.

Since development candidates are known entities with specific properties, it is much easier to quantitate and rank the strengths and weaknesses of projects in the development portfolio. Some of the criteria that can be used to assess development projects [27,35,36] are shown in Table 6.

Technical feasibility assesses the wherewithal of the company to follow through with the development plan and generate a high-quality regulatory submission. Does the utilization of resources match the company's ability? Does the company have the right facilities to develop and manufacture the product? Is the clinical program designed to ensure patient recruitment, to

Table 6 Criteria for Assessing Development Projects

	Factors	Examples of quantitative endpoints
Risk	Technical feasibility	People skills
		Development facilities
		Clinical feasibility
		Type of external support required
	Therapeutic relevance	Clinical efficacy
		Clinical selectivity
		Clinical side effects
		Probability of regulatory approval
Reward	Market	Return on investment
		Profitability
		Long-term market trend
		Pharmacoeconomics
		Patent protection
	Competition	Advantage over existing therapies
		Value of core competencies
		Status of competitors

Sources: Refs. [27,35,36].

include measurable parameters, etc.? How much dependence is there on external resources, and do these resources complement the internal support?

Therapeutic relevance assesses the drug's potential for satisfying an unmet medical need. Does the drug have attractive properties in terms of efficacy, selectivity, and acceptable adverse effects? Do these features lead to a high probability of regulatory approval?

The market attractiveness should be quantitated in terms of return on the R & D investment, profitability, and pharmacoeconomics. Can the company afford to make the capital and market launch investments required by the drug? What is the likely profitability in terms of market segment, third-year profits, number of years until profitability and/or total product profits? Is the product entering a growing or aging market? Will the drug improve the quality of life at an acceptable price? Is there sufficient patent life after market launch?

In addition to core competencies, the competition should be quantitated in terms of advantages over existing therapies and the status of competing drugs under development. Does the company have the internal know-how to develop and market the drug successfully against competing drugs? Does the drug have a competitive advantage in efficacy, safety, convenience, compliance, or quality of life? What is the status of the competitors in terms of product quality, number of competing products, intensity of effort, and time to market?

E. Quantitative Assessment of the Portfolio and the Review Cycle

Quantitative scales should be attached to each criterion, ranging from low to high risk and low to high reward [35]. Ranking the relative risk and relative reward of each project in the portfolio then becomes a simple mathematical calculation, and the results can be plotted on a two dimensional graph of risk versus reward [37]. Figure 6 shows the value of the portfolio by plotting one endpoint of risk (clinical feasibility) against one endpoint of reward (third year profits). Figure 7 shows an example in which all the selected endpoints have been aggregated to show a composite grid of all risk and reward factors.

Two-dimensional grids can be constructed in this manner for the discovery portfolio and the development portfolio. The risk–reward grids are convenient, pictorial summaries of the status of the R & D projects. The risk–reward analysis should be formally updated at regular intervals to reflect new information, but not more frequently than once annually.

In addition to the risk–reward analysis of the portfolio, new R & D projects should be assessed ad hoc when they enter the research and development portfolios, respectively. This analysis should be identical to that used for projects

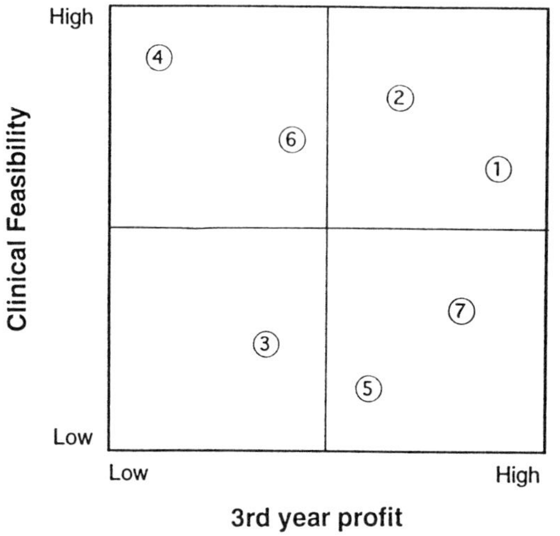

Fig. 6 Portfolio analysis of specific risk/reward factors. The graph plots individual development projects (in numbered circles) according to their value as measured by third-year profits (reward) and clinical feasibility (risk).

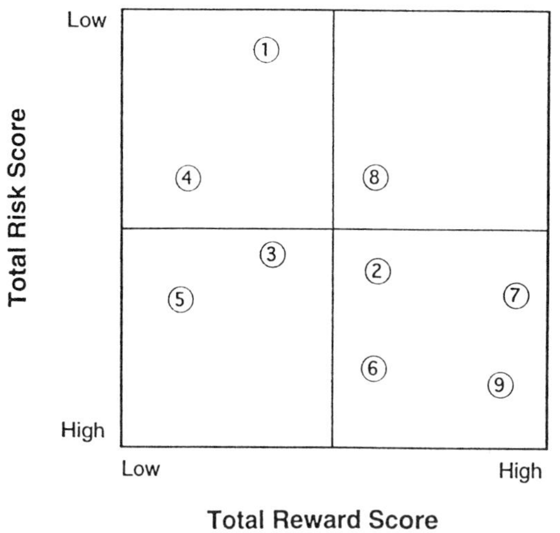

Fig. 7 Aggregated analysis of risk/reward factors. The graph plots individual projects (in numbered circles) according to the aggregated value of all risk and reward factors.

already in the portfolio, and the new project is added to the appropriate place in the grid based on its relative risk and reward characteristics.

The third type of project assessment is an evaluation of each project to assess its progress. For research projects, this can and should be done prior to the risk–reward assessment. The review of research projects is a valuable mechanism for scientists to organize their data in a way that demonstrates to themselves as well as to management what they have accomplished and what they propose to do. The research team should outline what yet needs to be done to identify a development candidate, how long it will take, and how much effort will be required, including known technical hurdles. With this information, the cost of research for completion of the planned research studies can be easily estimated.

Unlike the discovery portfolio, the development portfolio focuses on the strengths and weaknesses of specific drug substances. The internal criteria that characterize the drug's effects, the capabilities of the staff to develop it, and the external criteria that assess competing products and the marketplace should be assessed in financial terms whenever possible. As new information about the drug is generated in the development process, this information should be factored into an updated assessment of the candidate's value and place in the portfolio.

If development projects are reviewed with each new finding, estimates of the market value of the product will become more accurate. These financial and economic factors should be increasingly weighted in the latter stages of development in determining whether or not to proceed with development [27]. In the market of the future, the attractiveness of a product will depend not only on medical need but also on competitive pricing. Therefore, if the financial value of the product is no longer attractive, drug development should be terminated, no matter how far development has proceeded.

For research projects that are making good scientific progress, termination should be considered only if the costs are prohibitive or the time to reach a development candidate is excessively long. However, if progress has not been made in identifying a strategy that would lead to a development candidate, and it is not clear what steps should be taken to work toward a development candidate, the research should be terminated, no matter how scientifically intriguing.

F. Portfolio Review and Priority Setting

The objective of the portfolio is to maintain a collection of potential drug products that meet the strategic objectives of the company and are balanced between the high likelihood of reaching the market and a good return on their investment. Few drugs promise both a high likelihood of success and a high return. However, the portfolio as a whole should consist of promising product candidates that meet these requirements in the aggregate. Furthermore, adjustments should be made to reestablish the appropriate portfolio balance when projects either drop out or finish development.

A frequent failing of those who conduct a portfolio analysis is to rank the projects in a priority list, with the high-reward/low-risk projects at the top and the high-risk/low-reward projects at the bottom. The risk–reward grid is a graphic representation of the relative attractiveness of each project: high-reward, low-risk projects are most attractive, and low-reward, high-risk projects are least attractive. This is illustrated in Figure 8. But attractiveness should not be the only criterion for establishing a priority list.

Projects should be prioritized by comparing their relative attractiveness with their strategic value to the company [1]. An example of this quantitative analysis is shown in Figure 9. It is important to set strategic objectives that target specific markets, defined by therapeutic area and in some cases by specific market segment. In setting the long term direction of the pipeline, emphasis should not be on where the company is, but where it is going. The strategic goals must state clearly the position of the company 5–10 years from now, not restate the current situation. Some examples of endpoints that should be considered in assessing strategic value are listed in Table 7.

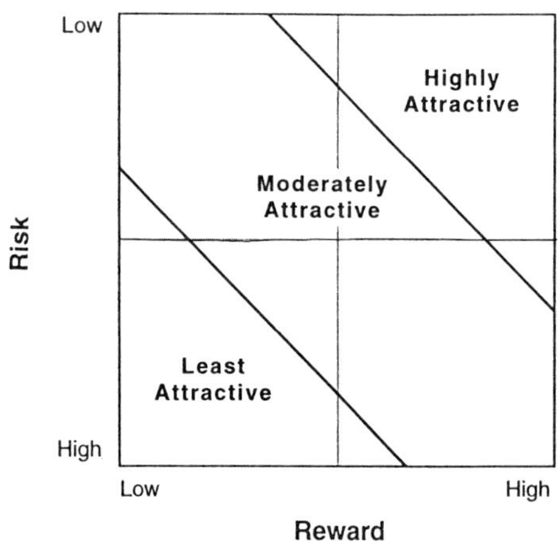

Fig. 8 Project attractiveness. The risk/reward grid is annotated to identify the most attractive (upper right), moderately attractive (diagonal center), and least attractive (lower left) projects in the portfolio.

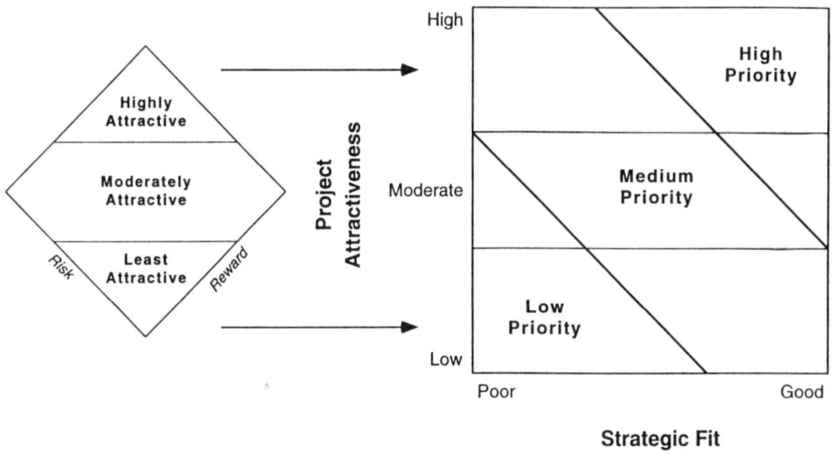

Fig. 9 Project attractiveness, adjusted for strategic fit. The grid showing project attractiveness (taken from Figure 8) is shown in the left panel, rotated so that the most attractive projects are at the top. In the right panel, the projects are plotted on a new grid that sorts them by attractiveness versus strategic fit. The annotation identifies projects with high (upper right), moderate (diagonal center), and low (lower left) priority.

Table 7 Factors for Determining the Strategic Value of Projects

Fits therapeutic areas or strategic markets targeted by the company
Long-range financial endpoints (target sales, profits)
Dominant presence in designated therapeutic areas
Superiority in selected technologies
Overall competitiveness
Fills a pipeline gap
Differentiation from competitors
Outpaces competitors
Entry in a new therapeutic area or strategic market for the company
Enhances company image
Humanitarian considerations
Needed to round out product line
Has long-term potential, despite short-term loss

Both the discovery and the development portfolios should be merged into one ranking that is based on their strategic fit. This gives a comprehensive priority ranking for all R & D projects in the portfolio, as shown in Figure 10. The results of this analysis may show, for example, that a highly attractive drug (high reward, low risk) does not fit with the therapeutic areas where the company has marketing strength. Such a product has great advantages as a licensing candidate. On the other hand, a drug that has a relatively low reward or high risk might be a good strategic fit because it is the only drug in the portfolio that can fill a pipeline gap. For each therapeutic target, one should seek a steady roll-out of market launches for drugs in the near-term (ready for regulatory submission), mid-term (entering clinical development), and long-term (ready for preclinical development). A gap in the product pipeline can be financially devastating. A drug that fills such a gap should receive a relatively high priority. If done properly, the product priorities should minimize biases that are dependent on the stage of development, emphasize those projects that are both highly attractive and fit well with strategic objectives, and equalize the value of discovery projects and development candidates.

G. Interpretation of the Portfolio Analysis and Action Steps

Having assessed the individual projects, rated the risk–reward value of the portfolios, and then prioritized them based on their strategic fit, the remaining step is to adjust resources to ensure that the projects receive resources that are consistent with their place in the portfolio [21]. The corporate strategy defines where the company is going. It is up to management to determine how to get there, by resourcing the projects in the portfolio consistent with strategic goals.

First, the portfolio should be examined as a whole. Are there the right number of projects in the portfolio, or is the company spread too thin? In order to answer this question, the company has to have some sense of how many projects can be adequately resourced. As greater emphasis is put on shortening development time, the number of development projects will need to be decreased [17,21]. The distribution of projects in the portfolio is also important. Of those that fit strategically, what is the level of risk of the portfolio? Adjustments should be made to ensure that projects represent a balance between profitability and feasibility.

Second, the projects at the top of the list should be considered. These are the projects that fit with the strategic plan, have a high reward potential and high likelihood of success. Are these projects moving at maximal speed? If not, what adjustments in manpower and budget will ensure the shortest development time? If nothing else is accomplished, resourcing these projects will quickly improve the product line. Is the value of the portfolio adequate? If the

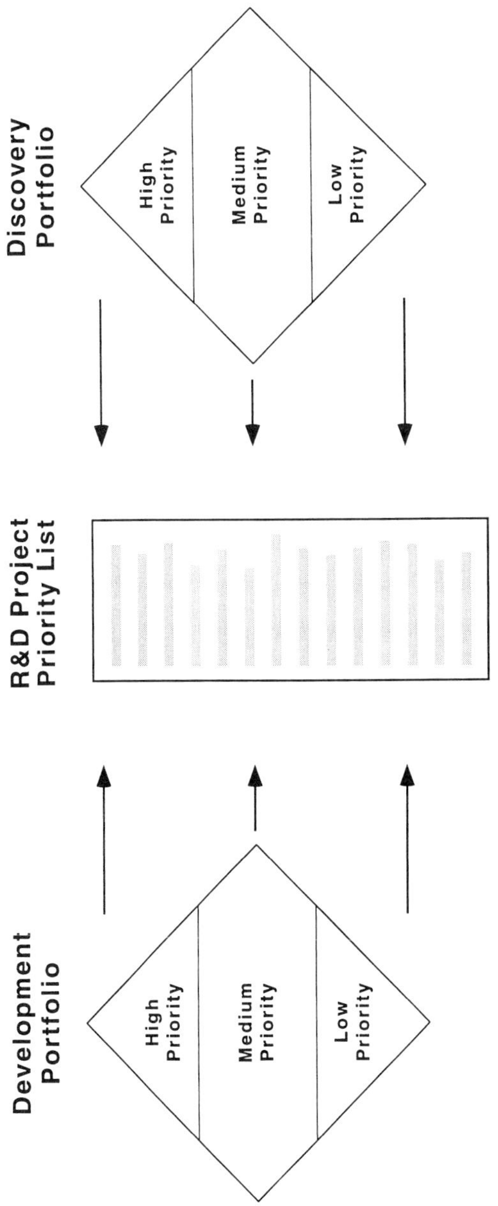

Fig. 10 Aggregated priority list. The discovery and development grids adjusted for strategic fit (taken from Figure 9) are shown in the left and right panels, annotated so that the highest priority projects are at the top. In the center panel, the projects from the discovery and development grids are placed in an aggregated priority list, which takes into account the risk, reward, and strategic fit of each project.

best projects are still a poor strategic fit, one of the major management actions should be to encourage the R & D staff to initiate work on new projects that are likely to increase the value of the portfolio. Finally, does the portfolio ensure a steady rollout of products, or are there pipeline gaps? If there are gaps, even a project with relatively low attractiveness may fill a critical, and strategic, place in the portfolio and should be elevated to a place among the high-priority projects.

Third, after addressing the concerns with high-priority projects, the projects at the bottom of the priority list should be carefully examined. Some may be highly attractive but simply do not fit the strategic plan. Intramural development should be redirected to ensure that these projects are groomed as attractive licensing candidates. Are there too many low-priority projects? If so, these should be culled selectively so that they are in balance with the high-priority projects. Projects that do not fit strategically should be promptly terminated, and the resources reallocated to higher priority projects.

Finally, the middle segment of the priority list should be examined. In view of the adjustments to resource the high-priority projects and reallocate resources from terminated projects, are there sufficient resources remaining to support the rest of the portfolio? If not, perhaps the company has defined too many strategic targets and this should be examined. Perhaps the company is just too successful in identifying promising product candidates. In this case, some product candidates can be selected for licensing but this should be done so that the remaining portfolio is optimized for the company's strategy and remains balanced in terms of pipeline, risk, and reward value. Projects in the middle deserve to be adequately resourced if the company is to remain competitive over time. If there are resource shortages, careful discussions need to take place in order to determine appropriate allocation of resources and whether prolonged development times due to resource shortages affect the competitive position of the products.

REFERENCES

1. F. M. Jacques, L. Linden and N. Selby. Turning the pipeline into a hit parade. *Pharmaceutical Executive 12*: 62, 1992.
2. PMA New Drug Approvals. Pharmaceutical Manufacturers Association, Washington, DC, 1992, p. 1.
3. J. A. DeMasi, R. W. Hansen, H. G. Grabowski, and L. Lasagna. Cost of innovation in the pharmaceutical industry. *J. Health Economics 10*: 107, 1991.
4. P. Joglekar and M. L. Paterson. A closer look at the returns and risks of pharmaceutical R&D. *J. Health Economics 5*: 153, 1986.
5. F. M. Scherer. *Pharmaceutical R&D: Costs, Risks and Rewards.* Office of Technology Assessment, OTA-H-522, US Government Printing Office, Washington, DC, 1993.

6. H. G. Grabowski. Blood money? Critics question high pharmaceutical profits. *Sci Am*: 115, August, 1993.
7. H. Grabowski and J. Vernon. A new look at the returns and risks to pharmaceutical R&D. *Management Science 36*: 804, 1990.
8. K. Wilson, K. Bryan, and R. Faulkner. The industry as patient: Bringing it back to health. *Pharmaceutical Executive 13*: 84, July, 1993.
9. P. Flanagan. Drug Prices: What's the Rationale? *Management Review*: 10, July, 1993.
10. PMA Annual Survey Report: Trends in US Pharmaceutical Sales and R&D. Pharmaceutical Manufacturers Association, Washington, DC, 1993.
11. W. vonWartburg. In The Management of Pharmaceutical R&D: The Keys to Success. D. Harnden and D. Macarthur, Eds. PJB Publications, Ltd., New York, 1990, p. 114.
12. J. Drews. Strategies for successfully managing pharmaceutical research and development in the 1990s. *Drug Information Journal 26*: 635, 1992.
13. D. Harnden and D. Macarthur. In The Management of Pharmaceutical R&D: The Keys to Success. PJB Publications, Ltd., New York, 1990.
14. I. Krause and J. Liu. Benchmarking R&D productivity. *Planning Review*: 16, January–February, 1993.
15. J. D. Coombes. In The Management of Pharmaceutical R&D: The Keys to Success. D. Harnden and D. Macarthur, Eds. PJB Publications, Ltd., New York, 1990, p. 120–124.
16. J. Drews. In The Management of Pharmaceutical R&D: The Keys to Success. D. Harnden and D. Macarthur, Eds. PJB Publications, Ltd., New York, 1990, p. 108.
17. J. Drews. The impact of globalization on pharmaceutical research and development. *Drug Information Journal 27*: 1059, 1993.
18. A. B. Chivvis, D. J. Mackie, and N. C. Selby. Playing to win the new game in pharmaceuticals. *Pharmaceutical Executive 7*: 50, 1987.
19. E. Broshy. A race to the finish in the development game. *Pharmaceutical Executive 11*: 70, 1991.
20. E. Rule. Squeeze time for speedier drug approvals. *Pharmaceutical Executive 13*: 72, 1993.
21. L. Soyka. Risks and benefits of global drug development: Resource consideration. *Drug Information Journal 27*: 1095, 1993.
22. E. Philipp and T. R. Weihrauch. Multinational drug development and clinical research: A bird's eye view of principles and practice. *Drug Information Journal 27*: 1121, 1993.
23. R. Sykes. In The Management of Pharmaceutical R&D: The Keys to Success. D. Harnden and D. Macarthur, Eds. PJB Publications, Ltd., New York, 1990, p. 112.
24. O. Harari. Working Smart: The New Strategic Imperative. *Management Review*: 30, May, 1994B.
25. M. K. Allio. 3M's sophisticated formula for teamwork. *Planning Review*: 19, November/December, 1993.
26. L. L. Miller. Risk/benefit assessment: The "greased pig" of drug development. *Drug Information Journal 27*: 1011, 1993.

27. B. Tiusanen. In The Management of Pharmaceutical R&D: The Keys to Success. D. Harnden and D. Macarthur, Eds. PJB Publications, Ltd., New York, 1990, p. 31–32.
28. D. Jack. In The Management of Pharmaceutical R&D: The Keys to Success. D. Harnden and D. Macarthur, Eds. PJB Publications, Ltd., New York, 1990, p. 106.
29. W. K. Brandt and M. Ingold. From Medicines to Markets. *Pharmaceutical Executive 14*: 48, 1994.
30. D. W. Johnson and A. A. Sinkula. Pharmaceuticals as Information. *Pharmaceutical Executive 14*: 52, 1994.
31. P. R. Nayak and J. M. Ketteringham. Breakthroughs! Rawson Associates, New York, 1986.
32. S. Osono. In The Management of Pharmaceutical R&D: The Keys to Success. D. Harnden and D. Macarthur, Eds. PJB Publications, Ltd., New York, 1990, p. 119.
33. Y. Kishida. In The Management of Pharmaceutical R&D: The Keys to Success. D. Harnden and D. Macarthur, Eds. PJB Publications, Ltd., New York, 1990, p. 119.
34. O. Harari. The Thomas Lawson Syndrome. *Management Review*: 58, Feb. 1994A.
35. C. Cronrath, R. Eckel, and U. Abshagen. Portfolio Analysis: A Valuable Tool for Focusing R&D. *Pharmaceutical Executive 13*: 84, 1993.
36. B. Spilker. *Multinational Pharmaceutical Companies: Principles and Practices*, 2nd ed. Raven Press, New York, 1994.
37. M. R. Monk and M. Smith. Product Portfolio Analysis: SmithKline to SmithKline Beecham. *J. Pharm. Marketing and Management 4*: 85, 1990.

5

Pharmaceutical Issues in Drug Development

Umesh V. Banakar

St. Louis College of Pharmacy
St. Louis, Missouri

Michael C. Makoid

Creighton University
Omaha, Nebraska

I. INTRODUCTION

> "Pills, until almost completely replaced by compressed tablets around the middle of this century, were the most widely used dosage form. By definition, they were small spherical or ovoid products incorporating a medicinal agent in a doughy matrix. The pill mass consisted of two parts: the active ingredient, and the excipient used to form the pill, giving it the proper consistency and acting as a diluent."

Great strides have been made in the management of disease through the intervention of drugs over the past decade. This has been effected with the concomitant recognition of various intricacies associated with the treatment of numerous diseases. Simultaneously, the area of the pharmaceutical technology has undergone a tremendous change in the last decade from the standpoint of maturation as well as implementation of innovative ideas in the process of drug development. This has been coupled with the various intriguing, if not fascinating, attempts to design and fabricate novel drug delivery systems. Yet, the primary concerns governing drug product development such as excipients in dosage forms, dissolution modeling in dosage form design, and the ever-bearing, *in vitro–in vivo* correlation have not been clearly understood. This chapter focuses on these three areas. First, it provides an insight into the importance of the role of excipients in pharmaceutical drug development. Second, it demonstrates the significance of simulation (modeling) of dissolution performance in the design of dosage forms through the use of the Makoid–Banakar function. Finally, it presents a new approach to correlate *in vitro–in vivo* data employing the System Response Correlation Concept.

II. ROLE OF EXCIPIENTS IN DRUG DEVELOPMENT

The choice of the proper excipient required, if not mandated, is dependent on the formulator's knowledge of chemistry, materia medica, and physics. The bulk of the final product in dosage forms such as tablet, capsule, etc., the speed of disintegration, rate of dissolution/release of drug, protection against moisture, and stability during storage, as well as compatibility, are determined by the excipient(s).

Excipients can be divided into three categories:

- adhesive,
- liquid, and
- dry or absorbent.

Adhesive excipients commonly used include such materials as syrup, honey, acacia, tragacanth mucilages, starch glycerides, glycerin, etc. Their purpose, by virtue of their nature, is to form a more viscous quasi-solid with the ingredients thus holding the mass in shape.

Liquid excipients are used where solvent action on the ingredients is warranted thus producing a mixture sufficiently adhesive to enable the formation of a mass.

Dry, also referred to as absorbent excipients, provide an increase in solidity when combined with the above two categories, enhancing the fluidity of the materials while forming them into their respective dosage forms. Dry excipients employed in the past, and even today, include magnesium carbonate/stearate, calcium phosphate, powdered acacia, kaolin, soap, cocoa butter, bread crumb, flour, powdered liquorice root, etc.

All dosage forms, conventional, nonconventional, past (cachets, pills), present (tablets, capsules), and future require inert materials as diluent excipients. Besides acting as bulking agents, i.e., fillers, the excipients in common use today often have ancillary functions such as binder action (sugar, pregelatinized starch), disintegration activity (microcrystalline cellulose, starch), or dissolution/release rate modifiers (polymers) particularly in the development and fabrication of pharmaceuticals/galenicals.

A. General Characteristics

The excipient must meet certain basic criteria for satisfactory performance in a final dosage form regardless of its physical and chemical functional characteristics. They MUST

- be unreactive with the drug substance(s);
- have no effect on the functions of other excipients;
- not interfere with the bioavailability of the active material nor influence the dissolution of the product;
- have no pharmaceutical and/or physiological activity;
- not promote nor contribute the physical properties, such as segregation of the granulation power blend, and should be able to be milled, if required, to match the particle size distribution of the active ingredient;
- have consistent and stable chemical and physical characteristics and properties from batch to batch and ideally between suppliers;
- be colorless or nearly so; and
- not support microbiological growth in the product nor contribute to microbiological load.

Chemically, modern solid dosage form excipients fall into two categories (Table 1):

- carbohydrates and modified carbohydrate excipients, and
- inorganic materials

While the excipients listed in Table 1 are more likely to be employed in conventional fast-release dosage forms, Table 2 lists categories of excipients (biopolymers) employed in nonconventional modified-release drug products. From their functional utility point of view, pharmaceutical excipients can be grouped as follows:

- fillers,
- disintegration promoters,
- glidants,
- lubricants,
- wetting agents,
- solubilizers,
- viscosity modifiers,
- surface-active modifiers,
- antioxidants,
- preservatives, and
- dissolution/release rate modifiers.

Excipients and active ingredients may be present in the dosage form in three different states of dispersion: homogeneous, heterogeneous, and in a specific structure. Likewise, their role and effect may also be different.

In the course of drug formulation, one must consider that the desired effect/functional performance of the drug may be altered by the quantity of an excipient present. The following possible relationships between the quantity

Table 1 Modern Solid-dosage Excipients

Carbohydrate and Modified Carbohydrate	Inorganic Materials
Celluloses (powdered and others)	Calcium phosphate
Sugars and sugar alcohols	Dicalcium phosphate
Lactose	Anhydrous dibasic calcium phosphate
Sucrose-based excipients	Tricalcium phosphate
Mannitol	Calcium sulfate dihydrate
Sorbital	Calcium carbonate
Dextrose-based excipients	Magnesium carbonate
Modified dextrose (dextrates)	Sodium chloride
Fructose	
Starches	
Starch	
Compressible starch (pregelatinized)	
Maltodextrins	

Table 2 Biopolymers in Modified Drug Delivery/Release

Nonbiodegradable	Biodegradable	Soluble	Hydrogels
Silicones	Polyactic/glycolic acid	Cellulose derivatives	p-HEMA
Polyethylene-vinyl acetate	Poly/acetones	Polyacrylic esters and polymethacrylic esters	PVA
Polyurethanes	Poly (D-(−)-3-hydroxy butyric acid)	Others	PEO
Others	Poly (ortho esters)	Carbopol resins	PVP
PVC	Polyanhydrides		Others
Polyamides			Dextrans

of the active ingredient necessary to achieve the desired effect and the amount of excipient present should be considered:

- the effect of the active ingredient is not influenced by the quantity of the excipient that is necessary for the preparation of the drug product;
- the effect of the active ingredient is increased in the presence of an increased amount of the excipient; a smaller quantity of the active ingredient is thus necessary to achieve the same effect;
- the effect of the active ingredient is decreased by increasing the quantity of the excipient; and
- the effect of the active ingredient is inhibited by the excipient only to a certain degree.

Table 3 lists the advantages and disadvantages offered by various excipients used in direct compression and wet granulation. Tables 4 and 5 document the characteristics of lactose diluents and the tableting properties of various cellulose excipients, respectively.

B. Performance Characteristics

During the past few years, tremendous interest has sprung up regarding the nature of excipient materials administered with an active drug. Excipients are typically chosen for inclusion in a formulation for specific formulation and are often classified by their intended mode of action. They can exert profound influences on the stability of the finished product, its bioavailability profile, and the ease with which the product can be manufactured. As a result, the performance characteristics of the excipients need to be assessed and established. They primarily pertain to

- functionality and
- reworkability

Table 3 Advantages and Disadvantages Offered by Various Excipients in Direct Compression and Wet Granulation

Excipient	Advantages	Disadvantages
Microcrystalline Cellulose	Directly compressible Binder activity High carrying capacity Hard tablets at low compression pressures Wicking action promotes fast tablet disintegration Protects granulation from overwetting while wet massing	Fair flowability Higher cost
Powdered Cellulose	Some degree of inherent lubricity, which minimizes ejection force Inexpensive	Poor flow Poor compressibility Poor binding properties, little interparticulate binding Low dilution potential
Sucrose	Good binder, produces strong granules and tablets Inexpensive Soluble	Needs high machine pressures, particularly with overwetted granulations Slight hygroscopic May produce gritty mouth feel Cariogenic Calorie contributor Not acceptable for diabetics
Compressible Sugar	Highly compressible Soluble Nonhygroscopic Free flowing Inexpensive Available commercially in colors	Not acceptable for diabetics Calorie contributor Cariogenic
Mannitol	White Nonhygroscopic Water soluble Compresses well when combined with other direct-compression excipients	Poor flow Needs high lubricant content

Table 3 Continued

Excipient	Advantages	Disadvantages
Mannitol (cont.)	Noncariogenic Low caloric value Good mouth feel, free of grittiness, sweet cooling taste	
Sorbitol	Highly compressible High solubility White Noncariogenic Good mouth feel, free of grittiness, sweet cooling taste	Very hygroscopic
Dextrose	Water soluble Some binding action Less hygroscopic than lactose Can be dried to low moisture content	Produces soft tablet On aging, disintegration time increases, hardness increases, friability decreases More browning of tablets in the presence of amines than with lactose
Dextrates	Water soluble Nonhygroscopic Free flowing Rapid dissolution Good mouth feel, free of grittiness, sweet cooling taste	Reactive with amines Contains 8–10% moisture Tablet hardness may increase after compression
Starch*	Inert Disintegrant activity Some lubricant action Good oil absorption properties	Contains up to 10% moisture Dried granulations can absorb moisture Produces a soft tablet
Pregelatinized Starch	Good binder Free flowing High dilution capacity Excellent carrier for incorporating dye systems in tablet granulations Self-lubricating Disintegrant activity	Needs high pressures to produce a hard tablet Binding properties reduced by lubricants; tends to soften when used with magnesium stearate For good flow, a glidant is required

*Wet granulation as capsule-filler material

Table 4 Characteristics of Lactose Diluents

Lactose, Monohydrate (Hydrous)
Not directly compressible and therefore used in wet granulation formulations
Produces a hard tablet
Tablet hardness tends to increase on storage
Disintegration time is not affected by tablet hardness
Soluble, but a disintegrant is needed
Drug release usually not affected by this material
Unreactive, except for discoloration when formulated with amines and alkaline materials
Contains approximately 5% moisture, and therefore is a potential source of instability with moisture-sensitive drugs
Poor flowability
Inexpensive
Lactose, Anhydrous
Directly compressible
Drug release from lactose-matrix tablets is not affected by this material
Not free flowing
Can pick up moisture at elevated humidities causing a change in tablet dimension
Unreactive, except for discoloration when formulated with amines and alkaline material
Inexpensive
Lactose, Spray-Dried
Directly compressible
Requires high compression pressures to produce hard tablets
Compressibility affected if allowed to dry below 3% moisture
Has high dilution capacity
Free flowing
Drug release from lactose-matrix tablets is not affected by this material
Disintegrant is needed
Requires a lubricant, but lubricants do not affect binding
May discolor in presence of amines, and excess moisture
Inexpensive

1. Functionality

Standardization of raw materials in drug products is necessary to manufacture any finished product with consistent quality, for their acceptance by regulatory authorities, and for a wide acceptance by pharmaceutical formulators. It has been pointed out that performance specification compendium need to be established. Unfortunately, such performance standards have not been included in pharmacopoeia primarily because their specifications have always been based

Table 5 Tableting Properties of Celluloses[a]

Material	Compressibility on tapping	Compactability, Hardness: Pressure ratio	Sensitivity to Lubricants	Tablet Weight Uniformity[b]	Disintegration[b] with disks	Disintegration[b] without disks
Avicel PH-1	++	+++	+++	++	+++	+++
Emcocel	++	+++	++	+++	+++	+++
Ex-Cel	na[c]	++	+++	na[c]	+++	+++
Medicel 101	+	+	+++	++	+	+
MCC type 101	+	++	++	+++	+++	na[c]
Senaq 101 L	++	++	+++	++	+++	++
Unimac MG-100	++	++	+	++	+++	+++
Avicel PH-102	++	+++	++	+++	+++	+++
Emcocel 90M	+++	+++	+	+++	+++	+++
Medicel 102	–	+	+++	+	++	++
MCC type 102	++	++	++	+++	+++	+++
Unimac MG-200	+++	++	–	+++	+++	+++

[a] Key: +++, excellent; ++, adequate; +, poor; –, inadequate
[b] Tablets lubricated with 0.5% magnesium stearate and prepared on rotary machines to a target crushing strength of 60 N (6.1 kg^f)
[c] Not available

on chemical parity and because it has not been possible to standardize performance criteria. With the exception of dissolution, the tests of purity and identity described in pharmacopoeia are generally very limited to their relevance to characterizing materials relative to their formulation functionality.

The literature is replete with examples demonstrating functional differences in excipients that depend on the particular material and circumstance. Control of functionality is as important as control of identity and purity. The following reasons can be cited:

1. Many excipients have multiple functions.
2. There is lack of awareness in some situations that the excipients behave differently, depending upon the vendor (or even from lot-to-lot), so much so that substitution from one source to that of another is not possible.

3. Scientists must establish a direct or indirect property to measure that enables establishing a specification and must standardize a test method by which to measure it.

Studies investigating the relationship of properties of excipients to their functionality are not new to the pharmaceutical literature. For example the basic properties of six commonly used direct-compression excipients have been studied. The properties include

- volumetric flow of the excipients,
- effect of particle size on binding,
- filler weight required to produce tablet of desired volume,
- dissolution and disintegration of drug of equal volume,
- dilution potential,
- lubricant sensitivity, and
- filler effect on tablet hardness and friability.

Bolhuis and Lerk (1973) studied 11 excipients including microcrystalline cellulose, powdered cellulose, lactose, dextrose, pregelatinized starch, dicalcium phosphate, and others as direct-compressible tablet excipients. The investigation compared the tableting characteristics of each excipient and studied the influence the various excipients had on each other in this regard. Direct-compression tablet formulations containing large amounts of noncompressible active ingredients were also tested. As with many such investigations, individual comparisons were clear; however, general rules were not apparent.

2. Reworkability

Information on the reworking potential of excipients, tablet diluents in particular, is sparse. Precompression, often referred to as slugging, is many times used for reworking tablet and capsule formulations. However, the mechanism by which precompression (slugging) facilitates bonding in the manufacture of these dosage forms is not fully understood. The "reworking potential" is defined as the ratio of the areas under the tensile strength–compression profiles for recompression and for initial compression (Fig. 1). Often the results show that recompression generally reduces tablet strength and that this reduction is more significant when the initial compaction is carried out at a higher pressure.

Armstrong and Lowndes (1984) evaluated the effect of reworking on formulations containing both microcrystalline cellulose and lactose. The compressed mixtures of the former and spray-dried lactose were characterized over a range of compaction pressures. Although the strength of the original compact was directly proportional to the content of microcrystalline cellulose, the quality of the tablets increased after reworking as spray-dried lactose was increased; however, tablet weight uniformity decreased. The higher the initial

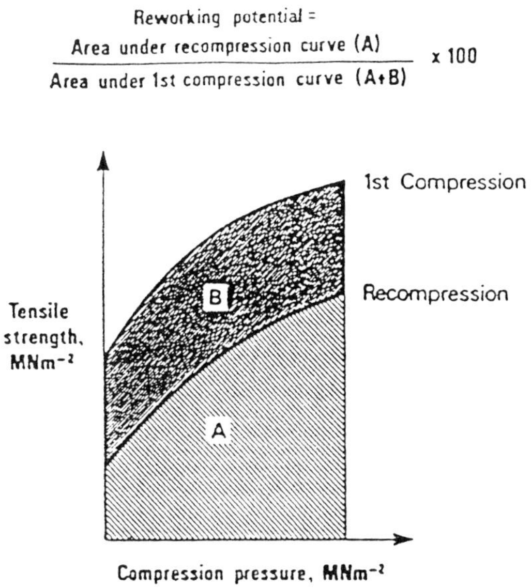

Fig. 1 Excipient reworkability.

tableting pressure, the lower the ability of the tablets to be reworked—an observation consistent with the concept of work-hardening during the initial compression.

3. Response to Force and Loading Rate

a. Modes of Deformation Aulton et al. (1974), suggested that "tableting materials which deform plastically, with little elastic recovery, should produce better quality tablets than more resilient materials." In their study, hardness determined by indentation under a fixed load and the elastic recovery from the indentation were measured over the faces of tablets prepared from direct-compression excipients. An elastic quotient was calculated, i.e., the fraction of the indentation that rebounds elastically on removal of the load of compression. The ratios indicate that the tablets prepared from direct-compression materials generally have a lower elastic recovery, and therefore must have undergone greater plastic deformation than the poorer tableting materials. Employing this concept as a single criterion in order of tableting performances, from good to less satisfactory, the excipients studied could be ranked as follows: compressible starch, dibasic calcium phosphate (dihydrate), sucrose, a dextrate (Celutab), anhydrous lactose, and microcrystalline cellulose. Microcrystalline cellulose, a notable exception to the correlation, exhibits a high elastic recovery but nevertheless binds well.

b. Effects on Compression Rate Armstrong and Blundell's study (1985) on rate-dependent deformation effects showed that the strength of tablets made from four directly compressible tablet excipients, Avicel, Emcompress, Fast Flow Lactose, and Starch 1500 (pregelatinized), were dependent on the speed of the rotary tablet press and hence on the rate of tablet compression. In virtually all cases, an increase in the tablet press-speed led to a reduction in tablet strength.

In general, tablets made from materials that consolidate by deformation such as Avicel, compressible starch, etc., are improved by increasing the time during which they are exposed to the compression force, i.e., the so-called dwell time. On the contrary, those materials such as lactose, dibasic calcium phosphate, etc., which consolidate by fragmentation, exhibit little dependence on press speed.

III. DOSAGE FORM DESIGN

A rational approach to dosage form design for any drug requires a complete understanding of its physicochemical and biopharmaceutical properties, which can have a tremendous impact on its bioavailability and thereby on its efficacy and toxicity profile. Thus, understanding these parameters is often tantamount to the selection and development of the optimum dosage form. Properties that dictate the selection and formulation of the dosage form include

- solubility and dissolution rate,
- partition coefficient (lipid-water),
- stability and/or degradation in the physiologic fluids,
- susceptibility to metabolic inactivation, and
- transport mechanism across biologic membranes.

Once the physicochemical and biopharmaceutical properties of the drug are determined and the desired plasma-concentration-time profile is defined, the pharmaceutical scientist can select and develop an efficacious dosage form by employing appropriate excipients.

A. Dissolution Testing

Dissolution testing of pharmaceutical solid dosage forms has emerged as the single most important test that, when carried out appropriately, will ensure the quality of the product. Interest in dissolution standards and their significance has been mounting steadily during the past decade. Knowledge of critical operating variables for a dissolution device is important to the pharmaceutical scientist interested in product development, quality control, and research applications. Since the recognition of the fact that the dissolution rate of a drug from its dosage form can often become the rate-limiting process in the physiologic availability of the drug, interest has been focused on the development of a reliable *in vitro* dissolution test method that can positively characterize the *in vivo* dissolution rate-controlled absorption of drugs.

The appreciation and understanding of the role of pharmaceutical ingredients and excipients in the dissolution assessment is of paramount importance to gauging product success. The performance of the pharmaceutical product, both *in vitro* and *in vivo*, is virtually a function of the appropriate selection of the drug ingredients and its complimentary excipient(s).

The primary objectives of all investigations of the dissolution rate are to correlate *in vitro* and *in vivo* test results and to establish that control specifications have been met in the commercial production batches entering the market. Factors of major importance that influence the dissolution rate are categorized as follows (Banakar, 1992a).

1. Physicochemical factors of the active ingredient
   a. Factors influencing dissolution
      - Polymorphism
      - Amorphous state and solvation
      - Chemical structure (acid, base, salt)
      - Complex formation, solid solution, eutectic mixture
      - Particle size
      - Presence of surface active agents
   b. The role of the surface
      - Particle size
      - Manufacturing variables
2. Composition and manufacturing methods for the drug product
   a. Tablets
      - Amount and type of excipients used
      - Applied tableting procedure
      - Size and size distribution of granules
      - Moisture content prior to tableting
      - Type and quantity of the disintegrating agent
      - Amount and type of surface active agent
      - Tableting pressure and rate
   b. Capsules
      - Amount and type of excipients
      - Granulating procedure
      - Size and size distribution of granules and powder particles

- Amount and type of surface active agents
- Properties of the capsule wall

3. Properties of the dosage form
    - Moisture content
    - Storage contents
    - Age of the drug product
4. Test Factors
    - Intensity, rate, and type of stirring
    - Fluid dynamics and geometrical factors
    - Concentration gradient between surface and bulk
    - Dissolution fluid composition
    - Temperature of the dissolution fluid

1. Pharmaceutical Ingredient (Active Principal)

Dissolution of the active ingredient is a prerequisite for absorption. In the case when the dissolution rate is the rate-determining step, i.e., the rate of dissolution is lower than the rate of diffusion to the site of absorption and/or the rate of absorption, then the particle size of the drug may play a very important role in the overall rate of absorption. However, decreasing the particle size in order to increase absorption may only be of importance with compounds of limited solubility (0.1 mg/mL or less). The role of particle size should be considered at solubilities of only 1 mg/mL or less.

A larger particle size may be employed if the dissolution rate is not as critical and the effect may be sustained over a longer period of time. Griseofulvin exhibits increased oral absorption following micronization thus making it possible to decrease the dose size. However, the decrease in particle size may be a "double-edged sword." As a consequence of increased concentration, chances of toxic effects may also increase.

One of the most frequently applied methods to enhance the dissolution rate is to make a salt of the acid or base form of the drug or to prepare coprecipitates. The salt form acts in aqueous solution as a buffer in the diffusion zone and changes its pH value. On precipitation, the prewetted particles of the precipitate are not ionized and, therefore, are more lipid-soluble thus increasing absorption. In the course of formulation, however, the stability of the different salts of the active ingredient in the digestive fluids must be compared. In the case of penicillin salts, the most soluble sodium salt yielded the least bioavailability since it was the most unstable form in the digestive fluid (Fig. 2). Sulfadimethoxine suspension is more bioavailable than its tablet formulation (Fig. 3)—another example.

The particle size and hence the exposed surface area of the suspended particles for intramuscular or subcutaneous administration is an important factor. The absorption rate of the drug generally increases with increasing surface

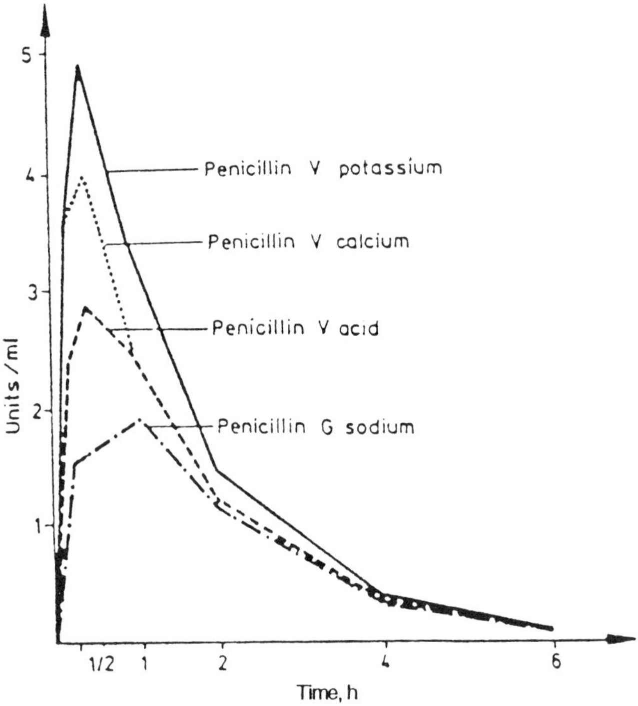

Fig. 2 Bioavailability profiles following oral administration of 400K units of different penicillin salts [*Antibiot. Med. Clin. Ther. 4*: 497, 1947].

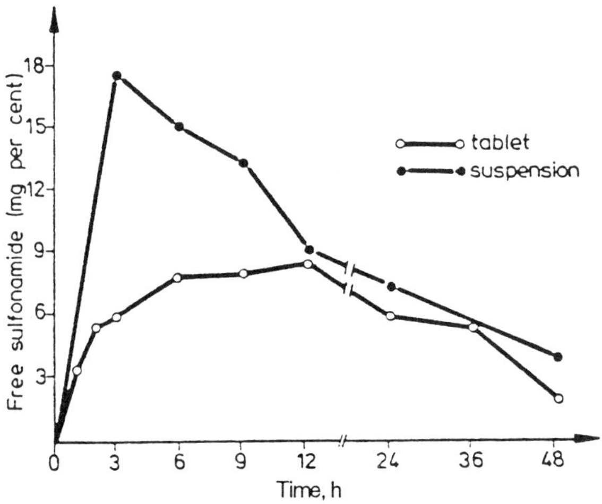

Fig. 3 Free sulfonamide blood levels in children following oral administration of sulfadimethoxine (1 mg/m^2) suspensions and tablets [*Am. J. Med. Sci. 239*: 142, 1960].

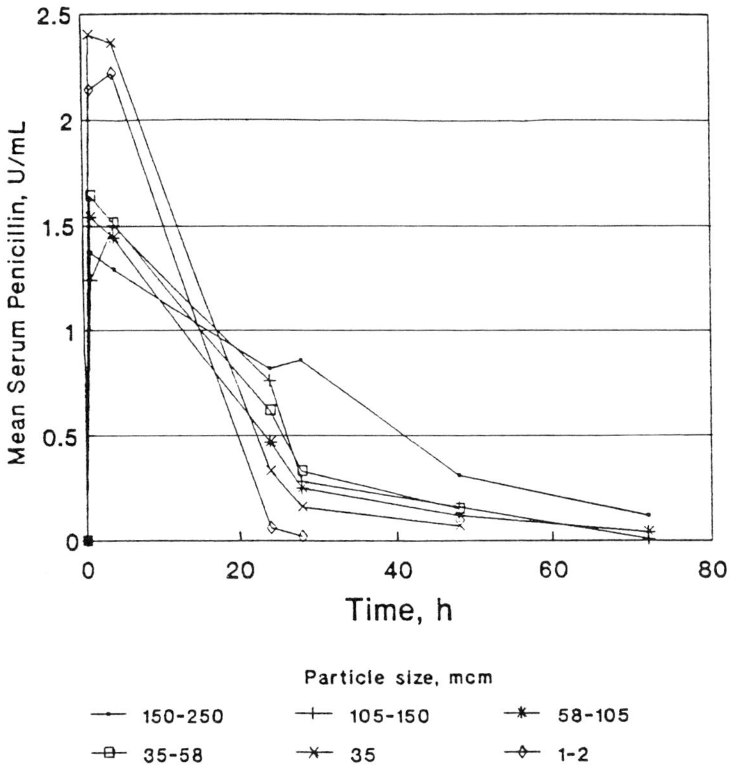

Fig. 4 Effect of particle size of penicillin G procaine administered in aqueous suspension (IM 300K U/mL) on the serum level in rabbits.

area; however, in some vehicles, there is a hydrophobic protecting layer, and the absorption may be retarded, if very small particles are present (Fig. 4).

In ointments and suppositories (semisolid heterogeneous systems) the particle size of the undissolved portion of the drug plays a significant role in achieving the desired effect. In these cases, by decreasing the particle size, an increase in the solubility and the quantity of the drug absorbed is observed. The optimal particle size should be determined in the course of drug formulation experimentation.

Based on observations of numerous experimental data, it may be inferred that the differences in the therapeutic effect of different drug products that contain the same active ingredient are most frequently the result of differences

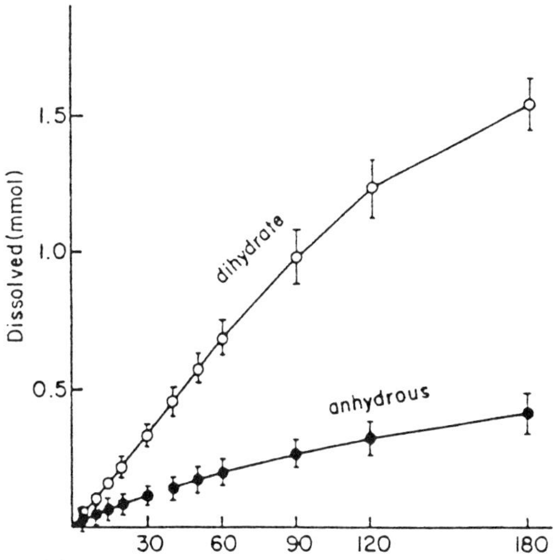

(a)

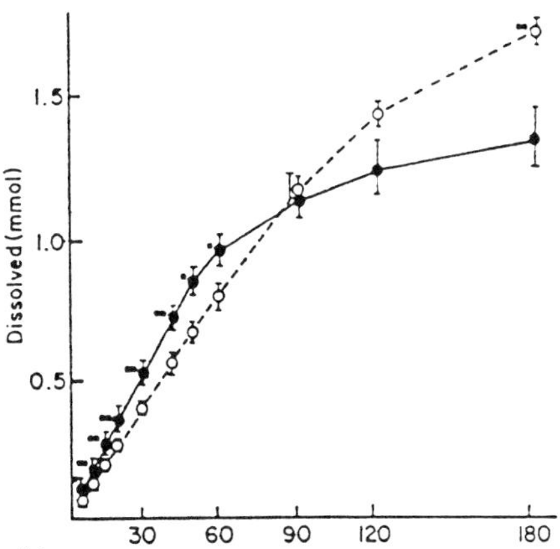

(b)

Fig. 5 (a) Dissolution behavior of carbamazepine anhydrate (filled circle) and dihydrate (open circle) in 0.1 N HCl; (b) Dissolution behavior of carbamazepine anhydrate (filled circles) and dihydrate (open circles) in 0.1 N HCl with 0.01% polysorbate 80 [*Int. J. Pharm. 14*: 103, 1983].

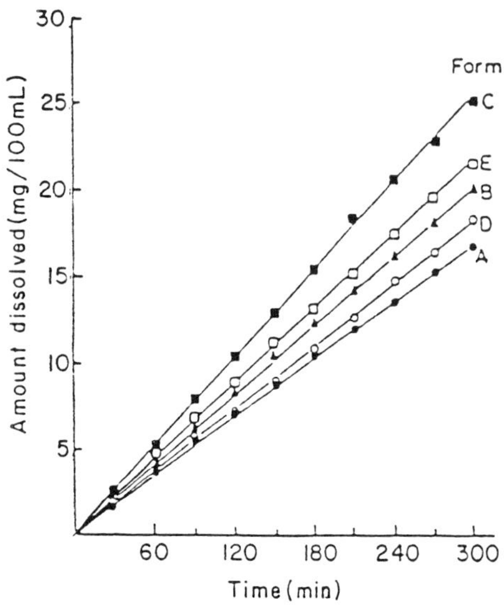

Fig. 6 Dissolution rates of phenylbutazone crystal forms (A–E) in 0.2 M phosphate buffer at pH 7.5 and 100 RPM [*J. Pharm. Pharmacol.* *35*: 208, 1983].

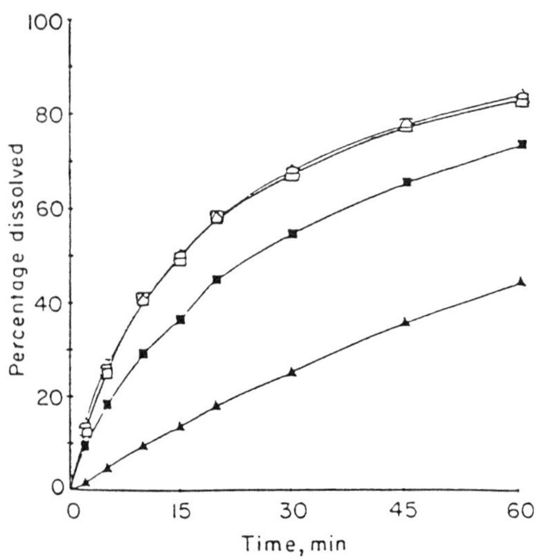

Fig. 7 Dissolution performance of diazepam determined with rotating basket at 100 RPM of formulations: P-2 (filled square), P-30 (filled triangle), S-2 (open square), and S-3- (open triangle) [*Int. J. Pharm.* *13*: 287, 1983].

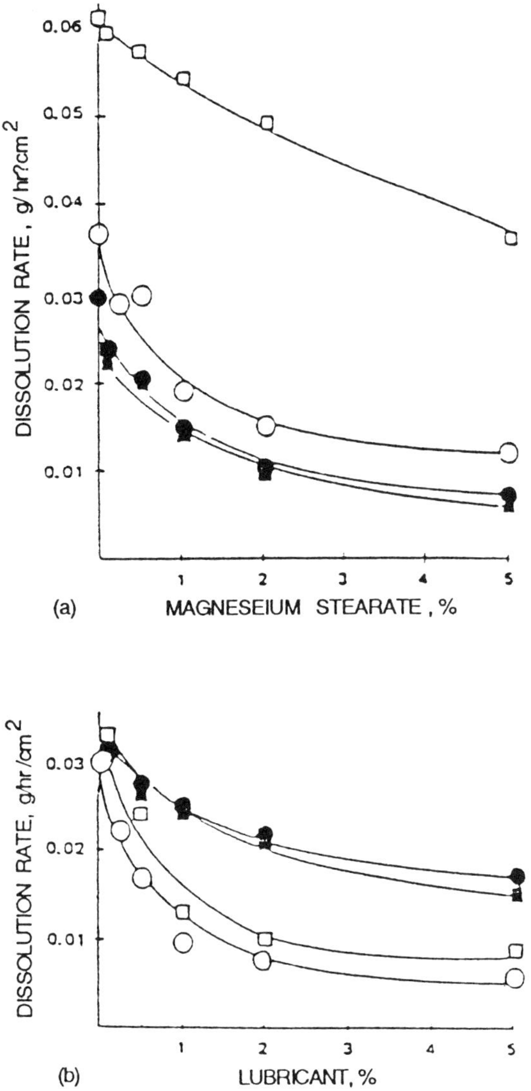

Fig. 8 (a) Effect of amount magnesium stearate on dissolution of 80/100 mesh materials compressed at 1135 kg. Formulations: SA (open circle), ASA (open square), SA with equimolar mixture of ASA and SA (filled circle), and ASA from equimolar mixture of ASA and SA (filled square). (b) Effect of amount calcium stearate and glyceryl monostearate on dissolution of 80/100 mesh equimolar mixture of ASA and SA compressed at 1135 kg. Formulations: SA with calcium stearate (open circle), ASA with calcium stearate (open square), SA with glyceryl monostearate (filled circle), and ASA with glyceryl monostearate (filled square) [*J. Pharm. Sci. 67*: 535, 1978].

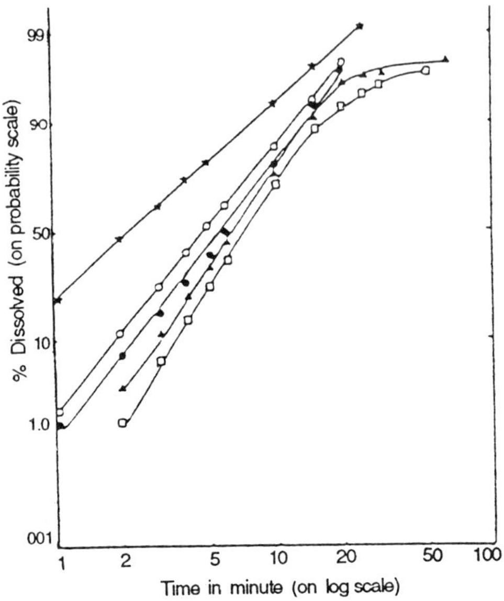

Fig. 9 Wagner plot on dissolution tests of tablets compressed at 20°C containing 0–10 × 10^{-5} M/g of light liquid paraffin: lactose 0 M/g (filled star), 0.5 × 10^{-5} M/g (filled circle), 1 × 10^{-5} M/g (open circle), 5 × 10^{-5} M/g (filled triangle), and 10 × 10^{-5} M/g (open square) [*Int. J. Pharm. 15*: 73, 1983].

in the rates at which the active ingredient(s) are liberated from the given dosage form.

Literature is replete with information about the characteristics of the active ingredient that can influence the dissolution and thereby the bioavailability performance of the drug and the drug product. Additionally, the use of excipients, virtually in all cases, in the fabrication of drug dosage form interferes with the dissolution performance of the drug and the drug product. Such intervention can be advantageous when the dissolution performance is enhanced for a poorly soluble drug, or the dissolution rate is controlled over a prolonged period for a drug appropriate for modified drug delivery. In several instances, however, the dissolution process, both rate and extent, is changed without notice (unpredictable). This is particularly true in case of fast-acting or rapid-release dosage forms. Figures 5–14 illustrate the effects of some of the critical variables that profoundly influence the dissolution performance of the drug

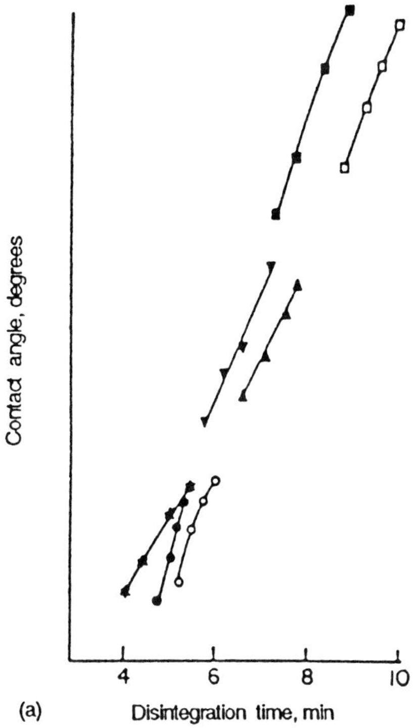

Fig. 10 (a) Correlation of contact angle of water on the powder compacts containing 0.5–10 × 10^{-5} M/g of paraffins and silicones with the disintegration time (min.) of the corresponding tablets compressed at 20°C: light liquid paraffin (filled circle), liquid paraffin (open circle), white soft paraffin (filled triangle), paraffin (open square), silicone dc 200/20 (filled star), silicone dc 200/50 (filled inverted triangle), and silicone dc 550 (filled square). (b) Correlation of contact angle of water on the powder compacts containing 0.5–10 × 10^{-5} M/g of paraffins with t_{90} and t_{100} of the corresponding tablets compressed at 20°C: light liquid paraffin –t_{90} (filled circle), t_{100} (open circle); liquid paraffin –t_{90} (filled inverted triangle), t_{100} (open inverted triangle); white soft paraffin –t_{90} (filled triangle), t_{100} (open triangle); paraffin wax –t_{90} (filled square), t_{100} (open square) [*Int. J. Pharm. 15*: 75, 1983].

and the drug product and that are germane to the characteristics of drug and excipients incorporated in the formulation.

2. Modeling Dissolution Behavior

The absorption of the active ingredient is regulated by physiochemical properties of the drug and the manner in which it is formulated. The primary prop-

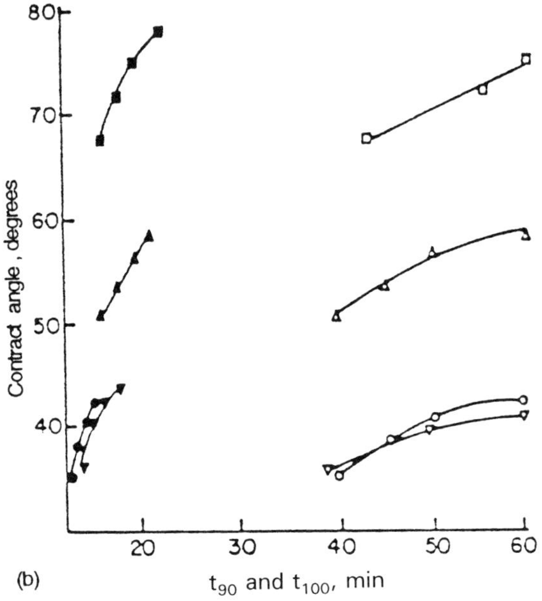

Fig. 10(b)

erties of the drug that influence absorption are solubility, distribution ratio (PC), pK, polarity, and the ability to form hydrogen bridges. Numerous *in vitro* methods can be used to estimate the absorption of the active ingredient. The following methods provide increasingly better approximations of *in vivo* conditions, but at the same time become increasingly more difficult and time-consuming to perform:

- Static distribution ratio of the compound between water and an organic phase (octanol, cyclohexane, heptane),
- Kinetic transport between two aqueous phases separated by a lipid model membrane,
- Model absorption through a segment of isolated intestine *in vitro*, and
- Model absorption through the oral membrane of a human subject

A drug product development program revolves around the recognition of the following factors:

1. The desired duration of activity,
2. The rate of release (delivery) over the desired duration of activity, and
3. The desired presence/absence of "burst effect" or immediate release of active ingredient.

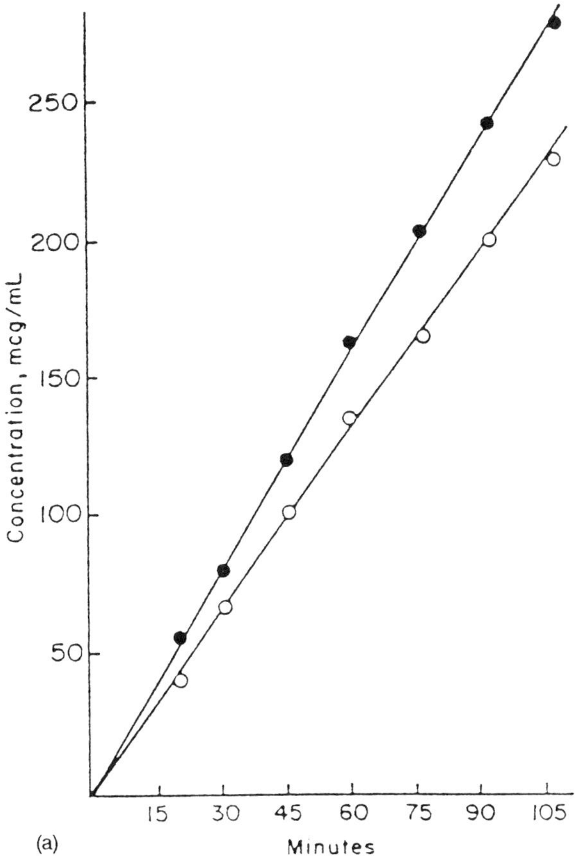

(a)

Fig. 11 Dissolution (a) and bioavailability (b) behavior of sulfathiazole compressed disks with dye; drug alone (filled circle), drug with FD&C Blue No. 1 (open circle) [*J. Pharm. Sci. 61*: 1857, 1970].

Virtually, the success of any drug delivery system, i.e., dosage form, is governed by the drug absorption performance, which is a function of drug release, assuming relatively rapid absorption following its dissolution. Hence, the above three considerations can be viewed in terms of the drug release/dissolution characteristics of the drug delivery system.

a. Makoid–Banakar Function (Makoid, Dufore, and Banakar, 1993) The process of the release of a drug from a solid dosage form can be graphed as a

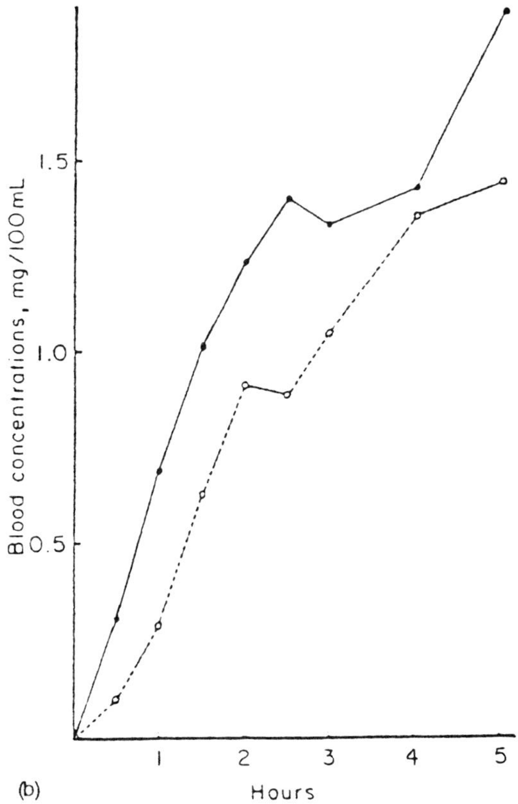

Fig. 11(b)

function of time. These time profiles asymptotically reach a plateau value and may or may not have a discernable lag-time and/or initial slow release phase (Fig. 15). The shape of the curve may vary depending on the relative importance of each of the factors, but in general, the cumulative amount released asymptotically reaches a value in the end.

There are several equations that can be used to mimic this process, each with its own set of parameters that carry with them almost the entire profile of information encoded within the framework of the system and the confines of the questions asked of (or by) the theory. To date, many models developed with the assistance of the computer have resulted in mathematical expressions

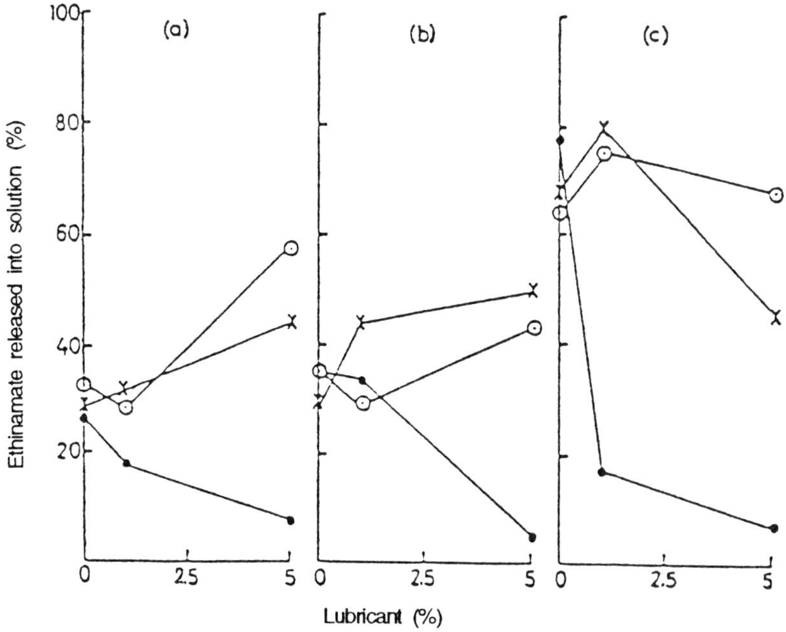

Fig. 12 Effect of lubricant amount on release of ethinamate from high fill-weight capsules after 40 min at 0 wetting agent (filled circle), low wetting agent (X), and high wetting agent (open circle) content for (a) 0 diluent, (b) low diluent, and (c) high diluent [*J. Pharm. Pharmacol. 22*: 163S, 1970].

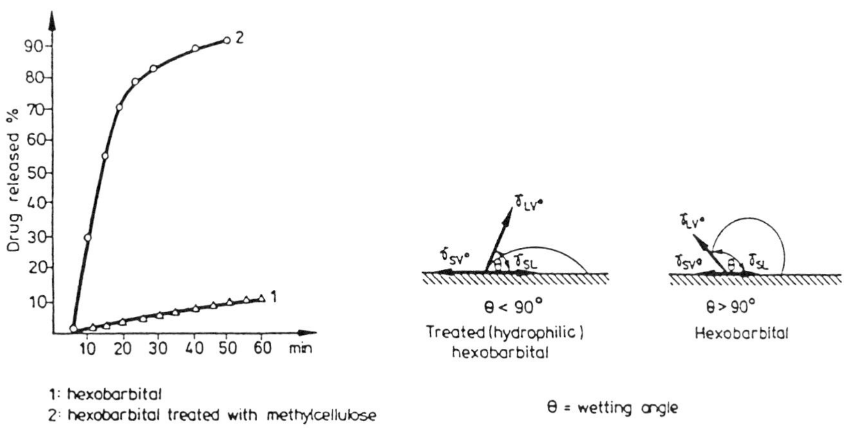

Fig. 13 Wettability of active ingredients in drug release [*Acta Pharm. Technol. 23*: 21, 1977].

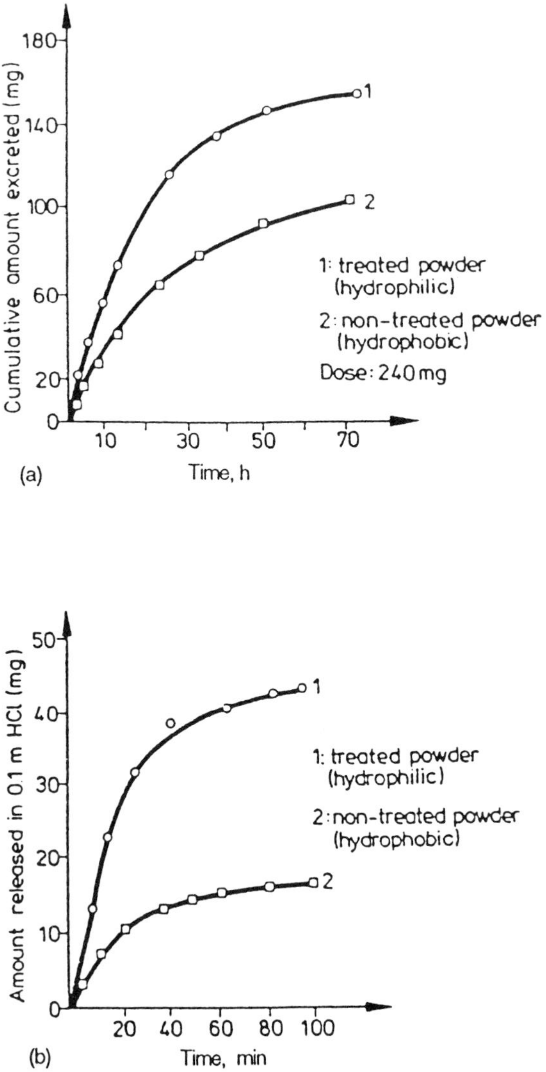

Fig. 14 (a) Dissolution rates of treated (hydrophilic) and nontreated (hydrophobic) griseofulvin in 0.1 N HCl from capsules. (b) Mean cumulative urinary excretion of griseofulvin after oral administration of 240 mg treated and nontreated powder [*J. Pharm. Pharmacol. 30*:479, 1978].

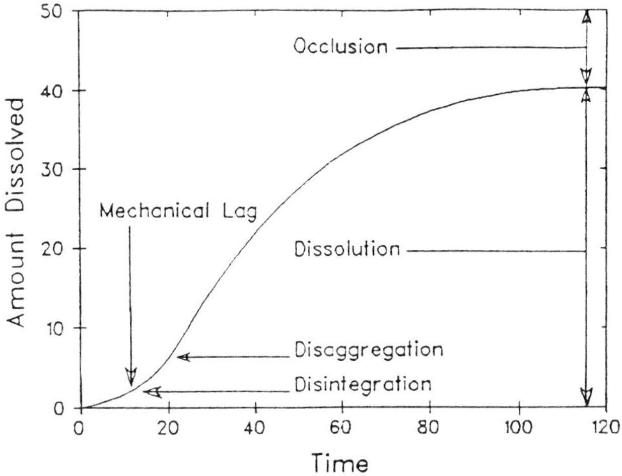

Fig. 15 Dissolution scheme [Carstensen, 2nd WI-Update Conf. 1982].

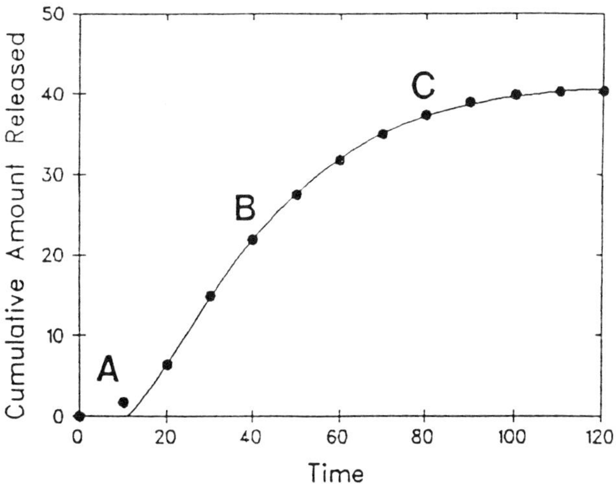

Fig. 16 Dissolution data according to Makoid–Banakar Function [data from *J. Pharm. Sci. 70*: 535, 1970].

that are often complicated, cumbersome, and difficult to "decode" in order to use them in either quality control or product development.

A more simplistic, yet comprehensive view of Fig. 15 is given by the Makoid–Banakar Function (Fig. 16). This function simply depicts a model in which there is a zero-order process (B segment of Fig. 16) being shut down by a first-order process.

A = Time shift; if A = +ve, the data has a time lag; if A = –ve, the data has a burst effect.
B = zero order release rate
C = first order shut down rate

Ind. Var.: TIME
Dep. Var.: F
Parameters: A B C
T: = (TIME–A)×UNIT (TIME–A)
FL: = UNIT (T–1/C)
FE: = B×T×EXP((–C)×T)
FM: = B/C×0.36788
F: = (1–F)×FE+FL×FM

where FL and FE are the amount (fraction) released during late and early phases, FM is the maximum amount (fraction) released, F is the cumulative amount (fraction) released.

Real time (TIME) is replaced by corrected time (T) to take into consideration the time shift parameter (A). By setting the first derivative of the function to zero, the time (T) to reach the peak is calculated and found to be:

$$T_{peak} = 1/C$$

By setting the time (T) equal to 1/C, the maximum amount released is found to be:

$$F_{max} = B/C \times EXP(-1) = B/C \times 0.36788$$

If the data exhibits a burst effect, the amount released immediately may be calculated by setting real time (TIME) = 0 in the function. Thus the burst amount would be equal to

$$F_{burst} = B \times A \times EXP(-C \times A)$$

b. Makoid–Banakar Function Modified for Gradual Early Release (Sigmoid Shape)

Ind. Var.: TIME
Dep. Var.: F
Parameters: A B C

TS = LN(B/A)/A
TL: = TS–1/A+1/B
TM: = 1/C + TL
T1: = TIME–TS
T2: = TIME–TL
T3: = TIME–TM
FE: = EXP(A×TIME)–1
FL: = B×T2×EXP((–C)×T1)
FM: = B/C×EXP(C/A–C/B–1)
FL1: = UNIT (–T1)
FL3: = UNIT (–T3)
F: = FL3×(FE×FL1+FL×(1–FL1)) + (1–FL3)×FM

Figure 17 depicts this model. The original equation has been modified to incorporate the initial gradual release phase. The switch between FE and FL is arbitrarily set to occur when the slopes of both functions (segments A and B) of Fig. 17 are equal to allow for a smooth transition.

c. Utility of Makoid–Banakar Functions in Product Development The use of these functions in drug product development is twofold.

1. The formulation scientist can decide a priori the value of T peak (duration of drug delivery) and A (+ve, –ve, or 0). In so doing, one can back calculate

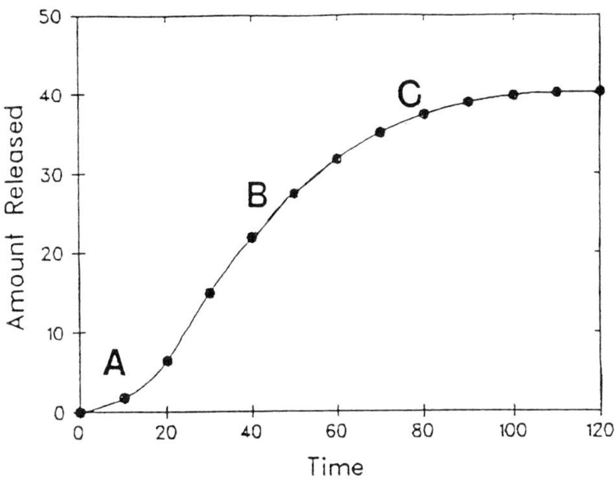

Fig. 17 Dissolution data fit to Makoid–Banakar function modified for gradual early release [data from *J. Pharm. Sci. 70*: 535, 1970].

parameters B and C. Thus, after the recognition of A, B, and C an "optimal dissolution profile" for that product can be generated. For a hypothetical drug, whose physicochemical properties warrant that T = 10 h and A = 0, the desired optimal dissolution profile is generated. The scientist can then work diligently with the available resources to achieve a formulation that performs accordingly. The data generated can be regressed with the "optimal profile" to determine the coefficient of correlation and determination and respective p value. Thus the effort will be more directed, less time consuming, and will save resources.

2. If formulation work for a drug is in progress wherein critical variables such as drug load, polymer:drug ratio, etc. are carefully being evaluated for their influence on dissolution performance, then these models can be employed for predicting the influence of the variables studied on the performance of the product. Let us assume the influence of drug:polymer ratio on dissolution performance of drug is being evaluated. A few series of drug:polymer ratios are processed to formulate the dosage form. The dissolution data respective to each formulation will yield T and A values and B and C values can be calculated/computed. The respective B and C values generated can be graphed as a function of drug:polymer ratio. The profile will provide valuable insight as to whether the intended objective—such as whether there is a proportional increase/decrease in duration of release with respect to various drug:polymer ratios—is being met. This can lead to valuable time-saving and resource-saving judgments.

d. Practical Experiences with the Makoid–Banakar Function While these equations might be useful in evaluation of dissolution and absorption profiles, the point regarding the utility of less complex equations may be made using one or two of the equations to evaluate data from the literature.

Comparison of Data Sets. Evaluation and reanalysis of data by Chau et al. (1980) fit to the Hill equation is shown in Fig. 18. Similar analyses can be done using any of the above equations. Some will fit better than others. However, all will fit the data to a relatively high degree. Using the Hill function, for example, the time lag, the time for 50% absorption, gamma-shape fixer, and the maximum percent of the drug absorbed can be obtained. These parameters can be easily compared between data sets just as the parameters of the Makoid–Banakar function will be compared subsequently.

We recently presented a paper in which the dissolution profiles of two sustained release theophylline products were evaluated. The products were from two different manufacturers (Key and Searle) and at three different strengths, under three different dissolution conditions. Using statistical analysis, it was determined if the fractions released at a given time, for a given product, strength, and condition pair were or were not significantly different. That, however, is

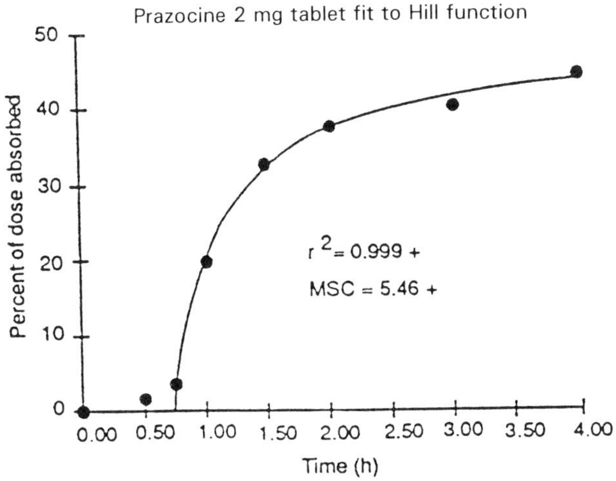

Fig. 18 Drug absorption data fit to the Hill Function.

not very useful information. Looking at Fig. 19, it should be apparent that there is a significant difference between the Theo-Dur product and the Theo-24 product. But just how is that difference quantified?

Using the Makoid–Banakar function, quantifiable differences become readily apparent. Looking at Table 6, which contains the parameters and results of statistical best fit analyses of the two release profiles, we see that

1. The Fraction Released Immediately (FRI) is 0 for Theo-24 and about 25% for the Theo-Dur,
2. The initial zero-order release rate constant (B) for Theo-Dur is about twice as fast as Theo-24,
3. The first-order shut-down rate constant (C) for Theo-Dur is about two to three times larger than Theo-24, yielding a peak-time (TMAX = 1/C) two to three times sooner, and
4. The fraction released at infinite time [FMAX = B/C×EXP(−1)] is also easily obtained.

In addition, other relationships become apparent when the data is subject to this type of analysis. It might even be possible to quantitate the effects of experimental conditions on the release profiles by this method. For example, a series of graphs of the release profiles of Theo-24 at various RPM showed what could be a difference in the profiles depending on the angular velocity.

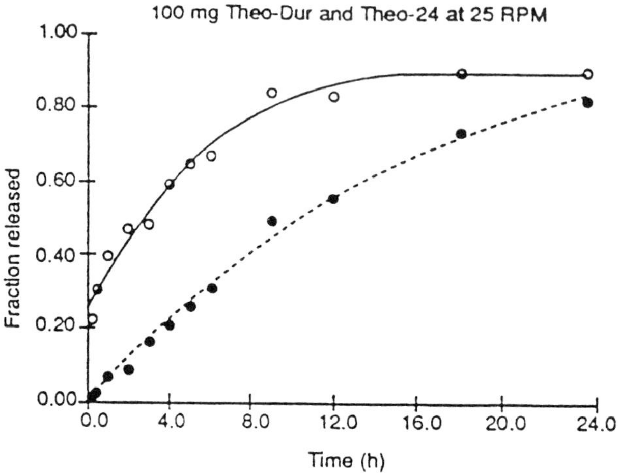

Fig. 19 Dissolution profile of Theo-Dur (open circles) and Theo-24 (closed circles).

A typical profile series is shown in Fig. 20. Three such profiles were generated, one for each strength.

When the release profiles for the three different strengths of Theo-24 are subjected to nonlinear regression analysis, and the initial zero-order release rate constant, B, is plotted versus the effect of agitation [Log (RPM)], the effect of agitation on release rate becomes apparent as shown in Fig. 21.

Formulation Development. If a release profile is changed by the addition of an excipient, either by changing the amount or some measurable, quantifiable characteristic such as molecular weight, hydrophile–lipophile balance (HLB), polymeric index, etc., in a homologous series, it is likely that the change in release profile is reflected in a change in one or more of the parameters in the

Table 6 Comparison of Parameters Obtained Using the Makoid–Banakar Function to Fit the Dissolution of Two Dosage Forms of Sustained Released Theophylline

	FRI	B	C	MSC	TMAX	FMAX
Theo-24	0	0.062	0.023	5.0	43.5	0.91
Theo-Dur	0.247	0.111	0.062	3.7	16.1	0.91

B and C are as previously described in the Makoid–Banakar function and FRI is the calculated fraction released immediately from the parameter A as described in the text.

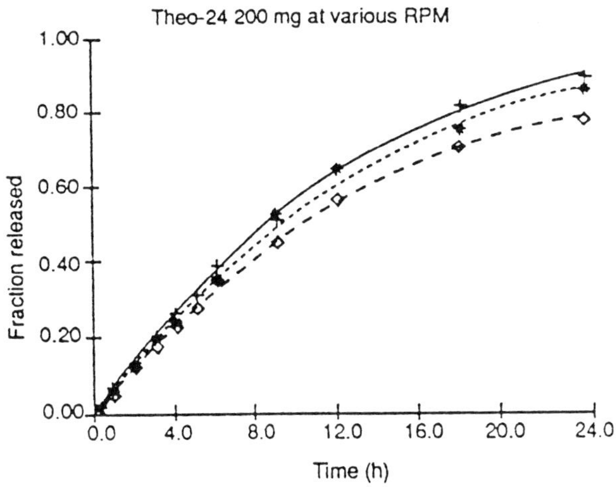

Fig. 20 Theo-24 release profiles at various RPM.

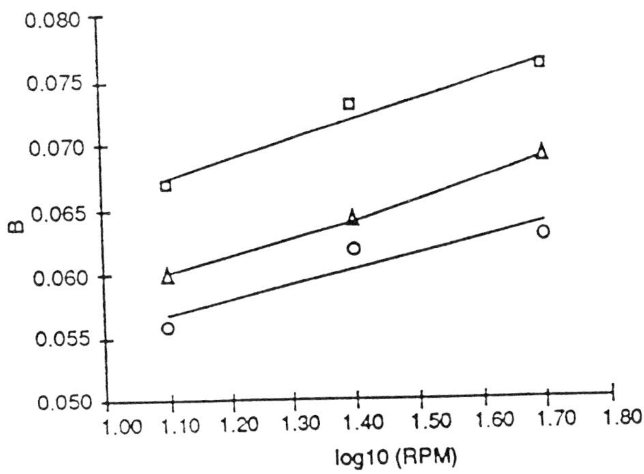

Fig. 21 The effect of agitation (RPM) on the initial zero-order rate constant (B) of three strengths of Theo-24 (100 mg: circle, 200 mg: triangle, 300 mg: square).

Makoid–Banakar function. A plot of the individual parameters versus the variable would yield insight into that variable's effect on the overall profile. If the preformulation decision has been made as to what the optimal release profile should look like, then these relationships would yield a working road map for experimental design. The model might quickly determine whether the presence of an excipient might yield a profile of the desired shape, without having to formulate and test all the permutations. While detailed information regarding the excipients is not readily available, the trend is to make such information more readily accessible, particularly in the area of polymers. Thus in the near future, the performance of formulations might be able to be predicted from a parameter (for example polymer index) of the polymer used.

Reviewing the recent literature yielded a couple of examples of release profiles as a function of an excipient that can be analyzed as we discussed. Gilbert and Whiteman (1991) presented a paper at the recent CRS meeting in which they presented the release profile of methylparahydroxybenzoate (MEPB) formulated in matrices of pluronics of various molecular weights. Graphs of B and C determined from the release profiles provided versus pluronic grade (molecular weight) (Figs. 22 and 23) show clear relationships that can be used to aid in formulation decision.

The parameters B and C are linked so that not all combinations of B and C are available using the pluronics and simply varying the molecular weight. If the optimal system parameters, as previously defined in the preformulation stages, fall on or close to the line in Fig. 24, then the molecular weight of

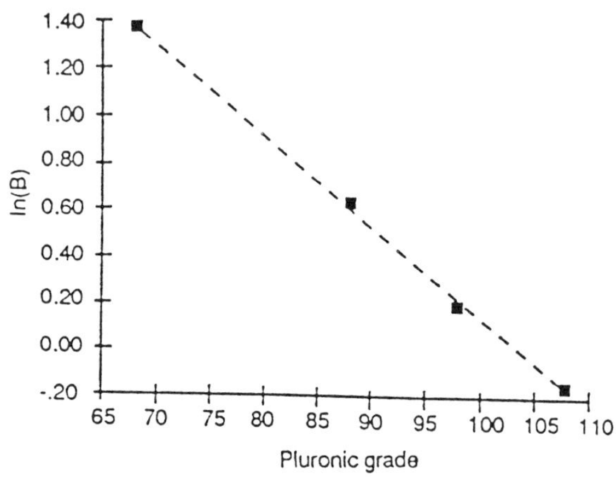

Fig. 22 Effect of molecular weight on the initial zero-order release constant in (B) of MEPB.

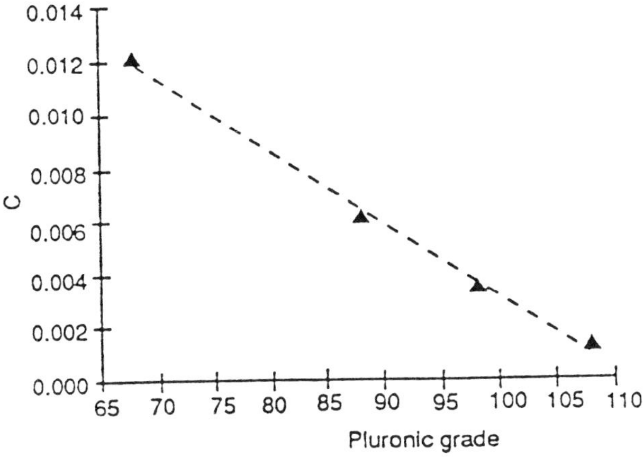

Fig. 23 Effect of molecular weight on the first order rate constant (C) of MEPB.

pluronic polymer is determined. If not, then the pluronics will not yield the optimal delivery system as designed unless some other variable could enter into the calculation (such as percent pluronic in the formulation). Given two variables (e.g. molecular weight and percent composition) a three-dimensional surface plot could be constructed that might yield the proper combination of

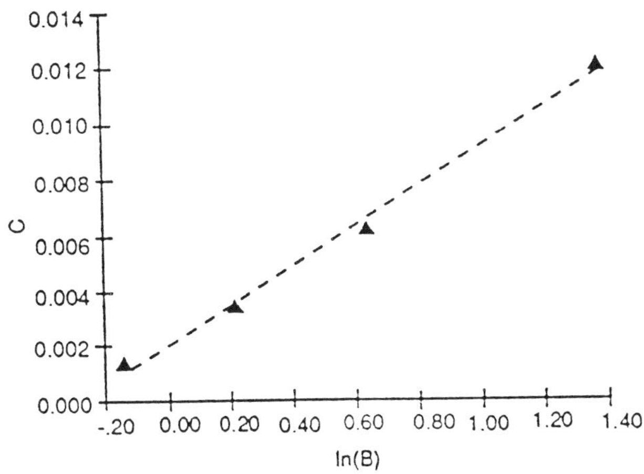

Fig. 24 Relationship between the parameters B and C for pluronics of varying molecular weight.

the variables to yield the sought after parameters, B and C. Or, conversely, a family of curves might be created for various polymer types and used as a ready reference for the formulation of sustained release products.

A second example comes from the same meeting where Lootens et al. (1991) presented a paper in which they evaluated the release of homidium bromide from a slow-release device. Parameters B and C determined from the release profiles provided versus percent of homidium bromide in the device (Figs. 25 and 26) show quantitatively the effect of the drug amount on the release profiles.

Clearly, these simple equations (Makoid–Banakar function and Modified Makoid–Banakar function) meet the requirements of the scientific process, even without a complex theory to give them credibility. These are practical equations that allow one to impose order on the chaos which surrounds us. They are useful only to the extent that they reduce the myriad of observations to manageable, understandable, and predictable parameters/variable sets. They are easy to utilize and thus have practical utility.

The relationships between the parameters themselves or the excipients need not be linear or log linear. They can be virtually any function (one hopes continuous or, at worst, reproducibly discontinuous). Asymptotic or parabolic functions between parameters and excipients might tell the concentration (or other independent variable) above which no change (or a deleterious change) is predicted to occur, which is exactly that happened when we consulted with a major drug company on the formulation of one of their sustained release products. The relationships between the parameters B and C themselves are linked

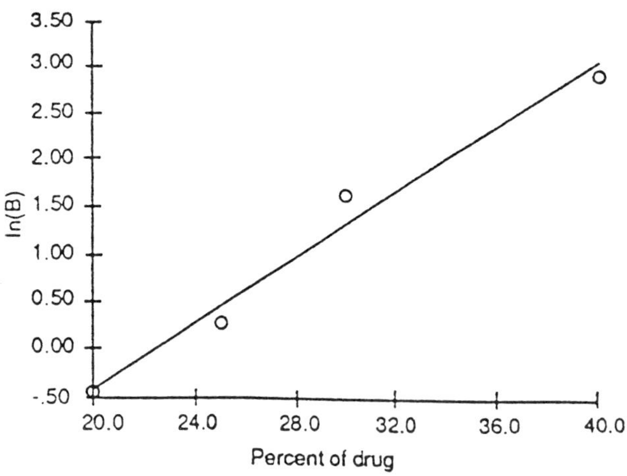

Fig. 25 Effect of drug load on parameter B.

to the excipient. Thus, as discussed in the Gilbert paper, the B, C relationship is fixed to the pluronic grade, as they would be with any independent variable. Consequently, not all combinations of B and C are available, as discussed, which in itself may save investigation time. All of the forgoing calculations resulted from a review of literature data, not data created to show relationships.

Let us now turn to the determination of the values of A, B, and C for a hypothetical optimal delivery system. Beauty is in the eyes of the beholder. Consequently, what comprises an "optimum" can be reasonably and logically argued. However, given that the decision to create a delivery system with a particular release profile has been made, what are the parameters necessary to create such a delivery system?

First question: How long should the product last (release drug)? You (or marketing, more likely) decide that the delivery system should release the drug for 10 h. If T_{peak} is 10 h, then 1/C is 10 h. Thus $C = 0.1\ h^{-1}$.

Second question: Do you want a time lag or burst effect?

—When A is zero, release begins at time zero.
—When A is positive, you get a time lag.
—When A is negative, you get a burst effect.

Third question: How much of the drug do you want to be released by T_{peak}? Assuming that you want it all gone by T_{peak} (FM = 1), B can be calculated from FM in the Makoid–Banakar function: $FM = B/C \times EXP(-1)$. Thus for our theoretical delivery system, $B = C/EXP(-1) = 0.1/0.368 = 0.272$.

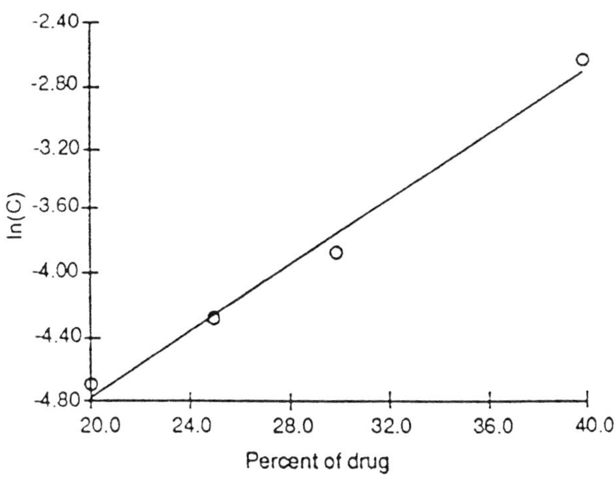

Fig. 26 Effect of drug load on parameter C.

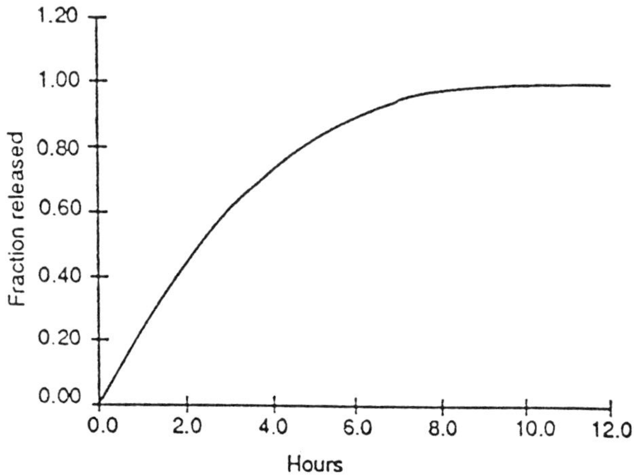

Fig. 27 Example of dissolution profile of an "optimal" delivery system.

Thus an "optimal" delivery system can be built (Fig. 27). The requirements are that A = 0, B = 0.272, and C = 0.1. We would then go back to the excipients that we use to develop the delivery system and, with a minimum of experimentation, find the ones that will give the proper values (or conversely, find the ones that we thought we could use will not, under any manipulation, give us the proper values). We used the Makoid–Banakar function to find our "optimal" delivery system's parameters in the above example. That is not the only function that could be used, nor is it necessarily the best one for all release profiles. It is simply one that fits the data that we observe.

The process is the important consideration:

1. Pick/create an equation that fits the data,
2. Make sure it has meaning/understanding for you,
3. Relate the parameters of the equation to the variables (excipients or processes),
4. Design your optimal system, and
5. Use a feed back loop—will your variables give you the optimal system? Yes, go with it; no, change variables.

IV. *IN VITRO–IN VIVO* CORRELATION

In vitro dissolution tests seem to be the most sensitive and reliable predictors of *in vivo* availability. Attempts to estimate physiologic availability, until recently, of a drug from a solid dosage form by *in vitro* methods have been confined to the measurement of the rates of disintegration and ultimate dissolution. Although official tests have great practical value, the fact that there is still a need for a test more directly related to bioavailability has been pointed out repeatedly. Since dissolution of a dosage form *in vivo* is often the rate-limiting factor determining the physiologic availability of a drug, the measurement of the *in vitro* dissolution rate or some related parameter is more likely to offer a meaningful indication of physiologic availability. If a correlation between the values of "good," "definite," "likely," or "poor" exists between this parameter and some parameter of bioavailability, then the relatively simple procedure of monitoring the dissolution profile should permit the prediction of *in vivo* availability.

The logic and interest behind correlating *in vitro* and *in vivo* dissolution parameters is twofold. First, *in vitro* values are used to evaluate different lots of a particular pharmaceutical product as a quality control check to ensure a desired physiologic performance. Second, *in vitro* values are used as a developmental tool for series of dosage forms to obtain a desired *in vivo* performance. These objectives can be best fulfilled when a relationship between the *in vitro* and *in vivo* parameters can be confirmed, but not when dissolution is merely defined under a random set of *in vitro* specifications.

A. Basics of *In Vivo–In Vitro* Correlations

Levy classified *in vivo–in vitro* correlations as follows:

1. Pharmacological correlations—based on clinical observations;
2. Semiquantitative correlations—based on blood levels or urinary excretion data; and
3. Quantitative correlations—resultant to absorption kinetics.

While most of the published correlations fall within the second class, the most valuable are those based on absorption kinetics.

Essentially, there are two basic types of correlations that are employed while comparing *in vivo–in vitro* data:

- Quantitative correlations
- Rank order correlations

All correlation techniques require linearity of the complete system under investigation. Erroneous interpretations are likely when absorption of undissolved particles occur or when absorption rate is changed significantly during gastrointestinal passage. Additionally, inter- and intraindividual variability in the bioavailability of the drug will seriously limit the meaningfulness of the correlation. Furthermore, inadequate *in vitro* test condition(s) without regard to physicochemical characteristics of the drug substance or the drug product could prevent a successful correlation. "Poor" *in vivo–in vitro* correlations according to F.I.P. guidelines are characterized by

- Differences in bioavailability data that are not observed in dissolution data,
- Order of rates reversed in the two sets,
- Significant differences in dissolution tests not observed in bioavailability data, and
- Dissolution being inconsistent (accelerated or decelerated) with bioavailability data.

The most important and most frequently employed techniques for correlating *in vivo* and *in vitro* data are

- Numerical deconvolution/convolution;
- Statistical moment analysis;
- Model dependent methods by
  —Loo–Riegelman, and
  —Wagner–Nelson; and
- Regression type correlation of distinct single *in vivo* and *in vitro* parameters

B. What Parameters Should Be Considered in *In Vivo–In Vitro* Correlations?

The answer to this question is not easy. The gastrointestinal tract presents a complex and continuously changing environment for pH, enzyme secretions, motility, presence of other substances, absorption surfaces, absorption routes, and others. The manner in which these various factors influence drug bioavailability depends on the drug, the dosage form, the dosage regimen, the dose level, and patient or subject characteristics.

In vivo absorption may, or may not, be dissolution-rate limited. The drug, the dosage form, or both may have variable stability in the presence of gastrointestinal secretions and other gastrointestinal components. To these factors must be added other complicating factors, such as drug–drug interactions, food effects, age effects, and special patient populations. These factors may have an unpredictable effect on the rate and extent of drug absorption. *In vivo* availability is thus influenced by many factors in an environment that is far more complex, variable, and unpredictable than an *in vitro* test environment.

Some of the subtle factors that profoundly affect drug absorption, and yet many times are overlooked, should be considered. They include blood flow and drug permeability, food and fluid volume, antacids, drug metabolism and intestinal mucosa, metabolic activity of the intestinal microflora, and dissolution rate. These have been discussed in an earlier publication (Banakar and Makoid, 1992).

1. Analogous and Nonanalogous Data Parameters

Numerous variables have been derived from *in vivo* and *in vitro* data that have been correspondingly correlated with *in vitro* and *in vivo* data, respectively, as illustrated in Table 7. Several investigators have argued over the relative importance of different *in vitro* dissolution parameters. However, it appears that the time for 50% of the drug to dissolve *in vitro* (T_{50}) is probably the best *in vitro* variable to correlate. Two factors that contribute to this observation are

1. By employing this value, one is not limiting or biasing the observation to any formal kinetic interpretation of data.
2. The T_{50} value indicates the central tendency of the *in vitro* dissolution performance.

It has been pointed out that instead of confining oneself to a specific observation point (value), it is more optimal to consider the entire dissolution profile from $T = 0$ to $T = \infty$ or some other parameter derived therefrom. This parameter often provides for a better and more meaningful indication of how the dosage form will perform *in vivo*.

The use of areas derived from plasma concentration time profiles involves the assumption that plasma clearance of drug is the same following different treatments. Additionally, the amount of drug absorbed per milliliter of the volume of distribution varies with the pharmacokinetic model applied for analysis. Use of this parameter involves assumptions such as assuming that the volume of distribution is the same following different treatments. Additionally, the estimation of the elimination rate constants after different treatments is not biased by measurement in a region where absorption is either incomplete or in progress. However, in such instances when elimination rate constant is estimated, absorption has ceased. Such differences and/or inconsistencies should be taken into consideration and thoroughly understood before any inferences are drawn.

The variables cited in Table 7 are meaningful in terms of the pharmacokinetic theory. It must be pointed out that estimation of relative bioavailability determined from parameters such as the amount excreted at a specific time, t, especially when t is less than ten biological-half-lives of the drug, cannot be employed for correlation. Also, area-under-the-plasma-concentration-time curve values of truncated blood-level-profiles when following concentration are measurable following one or multiple dosing and are inappropriate and should not be employed in correlating *in vitro–in vivo* data. The resultant correlations may not be valid in addition to the fact that they have less meaningful value.

Quantitative correlations of appropriate variables derived from *in vitro* dissolution data with appropriate variables derived from *in vivo* performance of the dosage form in human subjects must be established and demonstrated in

Table 7 *In Vitro* and *In Vivo* Parameters Commonly Used in Establishing Correlation

In Vivo Parameter[a]	In Vitro Parameter[a]	Formulation Type[b]	Drug/Active Moiety
$AUC_{(0-\infty)}$	$\%D_{15}$, D_{30}	Tablets	Promethazine
	k_d	Granules	Omeprazole
	$T_{50\%}$	Microcapsules	Bacampicillin hydrochloride
$AUC_{(0-\infty)}$	$\%D_{30}$	Tablets	Hydrocortisone
$AUC_{(0-24h)}$	$\%D_{30}$min	Capsules	Indomethacin
$AUC_{(0-6h)}$	$\%D_{30}$, $\%D_{60}$	Uncoated tablets, capsules (SR), tablets (SR)	Theophylline
$AUC_{(0-6h)}$	$\%D_{60}$, $1/T_{50\%}$	Tablets	Digoxin
AUC	$\log k_d$	Film-coated tablets and controlled-release tablets (insoluble matrix type)	Alproclate
	$\%D_{4h}$	Tablet (controlled release)	Quinidine gluconate
F% (rel. to soln.)	$\%D_{30}$	Tablets	Furosemide
F%	$T_{50\%}$	Tablets	Nalidixic acid
F%	$1/T_{50\%}$	Tablets	Digoxin
F% (6 h)	k_s	Uncoated tablets, capsules (SR), tablets (SR)	Theophylline
F% (1 h)	$\%D_{60\ mins}$	Uncoated tablets, capsules (SR), tablets (SR)	Theophylline
A_e (0–8 h)	$T_{50\%}$	Microcapsules	Bacampicillin hydrochloride
A_e (0–24 h) (steady state)	$\%D_{6h}$	Slow-release tablets	Terbutaline
A_e (0–48 h)	$\%D_{4h}$	Tablets (rapid and slow release)	Metformin
A_e (0–48 h)	$\%D_{60}$	Tablets and capsules	Triamterene-hydrochloro-thiazide
A_e (0–72 h) (single dose)	$\%D_{4h}$	Slow release	Terbutaline
A_e (0–72 h)	$\%D_{60}$	Tablets	Chlorothiazide
C_{max}	$\%D_{30}$	Suspensions	Trisulfapyrimidine
C_{max}	D_{60}		Nitrofurantoin

Table 7 *Continued*

In Vivo Parameter[a]	In Vitro Parameter[a]	Formulation Type[b]	Drug/Active Moiety
C_{max}	$T_{50\%}$	Microcapsules	Bacampicillin hydrochloride
C_{max}	$1/T_{50\%}$		Flufenamic acid
C_{max}	$\%D_{60\ min}$	Uncoated tablets, capsules (SR), tablets (SR)	Theophylline
C_{max}	k_d		Alproclate
In vivo release rate	In vitro release rate	OROS tablets	Oxprenolol
Time to invasion	Time for dissolution	Tablets	Molsidomine
$MDT_{in\ vivo}$	$MDT_{in\ vitro}$	Film-coated tablets	Alproclate
MT (invasion)	MDT (in vitro)	Tablets (extended release)	Theophylline

[a] $\%D_n$, percentage of dose dissolved in n minutes; $\%T_p$, time to dissolve p percent of the dose; F%, bioavailability percent (relative to solution or IV); AUC, area under the plasma concentration time curve; C_{max}, peak plasma concentration; A_e, amount of unchanged or total drug excreted in the urine; k_d, rate constant for dissolution; MDT, mean dissolution time.
[b] SR, Slow release.

order to arrive at pharmaceutically efficient dosage forms. Despite the huge number of such investigations undertaken and reports published, very few good correlations exist. The countless attempts to modify dissolution-rate testing equipment do not help in achieving a reasonably good and universal method that can be employed in designing a protocol for such *in vitro–in vivo* correlation experimentation. Such and many other factors have contributed to the development of varied and diversified theoretical as well as practical approaches in testing and correlating *in vitro* and *in vivo* data.

The selection of meaningful single parameters to characterize drug performance, both *in vitro* and *in vivo*, is of crucial importance. Empirical single *in vivo* parameters can be advantageous as their calculation may not require complex mathematical modeling, but they often exhibit enormous variability, e.g., C_{max}, T_{max}. Characterization of the entire concentration-time profile can be achieved by statistical moments by computation of parameters such as Mean Residence Time (MRT), Mean Dissolution Time (MDT), etc. (Yamaoka et al., 1978; Block and Banakar, 1988; Banakar and Block, 1984).

Sometimes dissolution and absorption profiles are better characterized by rate constants of their respective kinetic profiles. However, pharmacokinetic models have to be established, proven, and fitted to confirmed determinations in each single case.

Correlation parameters have to be selected according to their kinetic importance rather than empirically formed relation between any *in vivo* or *in vitro* data set. Quality, efficacy, and safety of a modified release preparation, for example, cannot possibly be anticipated by controlling the fraction absorbed in 1 h (Chung and Changkoo, 1987) (Fig. 28). The significance of such a correlation is very limited.

Another possibility is the occurrence of accidental linear correlation when nonanalogous data are compared, e.g., area under the curve (AUC) as a function of fraction of dose absorbed at a given time F(t), which do not represent any causal or functional relation. Such correlations are susceptible to malfunction and are extremely sensitive to slight variations in the testing procedure.

Misinterpretations can be avoided by correlating analogous *in vivo* and *in vitro* parameters. Analogous parameters (Banakar and Makoid, 1992b) are defined as analyzed data *in vitro* versus their respective calculated or predicted in vitro data and vice versa (Fig. 29). Some examples of analogous pairs are,

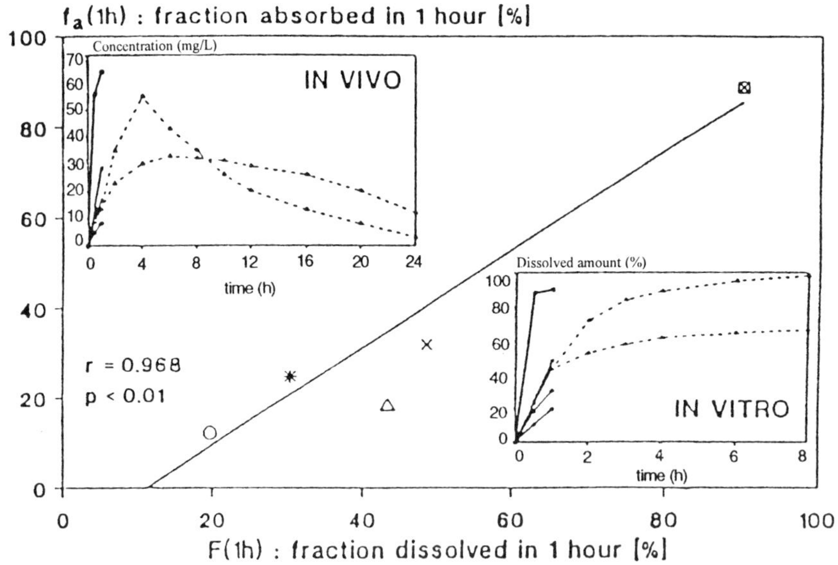

Fig. 28 *In vitro–in vivo* correlations for theophylline preparations [data from *J. Pharm. Sci. 76*: 784, 1987].

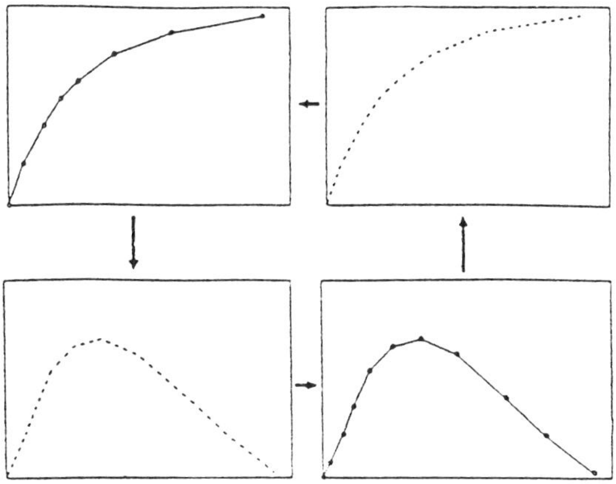

Fig. 29 Analogous data for *in vitro–in vivo* correlations. Measured data (-•-); calculated data (...) [from *Proc. Pharm. Tech. Conf.*, 1992, p. 162.]

MRT and MDT, $K_{diss.in\ vitro}$ and $K_{diss.\ in\ vivo}$ $F_{in\ vivo}$ and $F_{in\ vitro}$ (Table 8). The resultant correlations are more meaningful and dependable.

C. System Response Correlation Concept

The evolution of microcomputers and analytical software has resulted in the availability of phenomenal tools for the pharmaceutical researcher. When analysis was done mostly by hand, correlations were, per force, point, a single number derived from one graph compared to a single number derived from a second,

Table 8 Parameters Employed in *In Vitro–In Vivo* Correlation Determinations

In Vitro	In Vivo
AUC	AUC
K_r, K_d	K_a, K_d, K_r
T'_∞, T_{max}	C_{max}
F(t), T(F), $t_{63.2\%}$	$F_a(t)$, $T(F_a)$
MDT	MRT

e.g. peak time *in vivo* with *in vitro* dissolution, T50%. As would be expected, the first applications of computers to this kind of data were essentially not to change the end result but simply to get there faster. Recently, suggestions regarding *in vivo–in vitro* correlation have been made which depart from such classical analytical procedures. These suggestions begin to utilize the power of the computer for the very first time. The premise is that in order for data from one set to be comparable to data from another the two sets must be similar. The *in-vitro* dissolution profile of a tablet can be expressed in two forms as can the *in vivo* absorption data. Both may be expressed in cumulative-amount-versus-time or rate-versus-time terms. *In vitro* cumulative amount released and *in vivo* cumulative amount absorbed is a comparable pair as is *in-vitro* rate of release and *in vivo* rate of absorption while comparisons of rate with cumulative amount are not. Thus only similar parameters derived from comparable pairs would be allowed and the arbitrary combinations of parameters from dissimilar pairs would not. These are the current guidelines when submitting this type of data for regulatory approval.

It is well accepted that the movement of the individual drug molecules through the body compartment is governed by probability. The time course of drug concentrations in plasma can usually be regarded as a statistical distribution curve. The acceptance of a drug molecule in a biological fluid such as blood, i.e., absorption, can be conceived in terms of the biological system responding to the incoming drug molecule. Thus, the drug concentration-time profile can be viewed as system response-time profile. Similar argument can be presented in favor of *in vitro* dissolution test system and the drug dissolving (being accepted) in the dissolution medium. Thus both *in vitro* dissolution-time profile and blood/plasma-time profile as well as urinary excretion-time profile can be expressed as system response as a function of time (Fig. 30). Both *in vitro* and *in vivo* system response as a function of time are analogous and can be thus compared and correlated.

A logical extension of the concept of correlating analogous parameters is not to compare only similar parameters derived from similar data representations, but to compare those entire data sets directly. This would be done by

1. Fitting the data from similar pairs to equations through nonlinear regression analysis (MINSQ),
2. Using the ability of MINSQ to find intrinsic variables, to determine the times for the fractional system response, and
3. Plotting the correlated fractional system response times *in vivo* as a function of *in vitro*.

The plot of corresponding fractional system response times would yield a function that correlated the similar paired data sets. Stepping through this

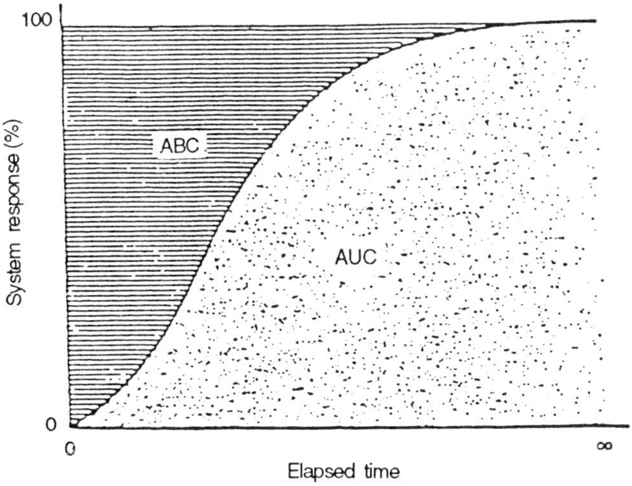

Fig. 30 Schematic illustration of system response as a function of elapsed time [from *Pharm. Tech.* 7: 103, 1984].

process with data from dissolution-time profiles (Fig. 31a) and plasma-concentration-time profiles (Fig. 31b) for six of seven commercially available phenobarbital tablet formulations demonstrates the utility of the process.

1. Treatment of Bioavailability Data

STEP 1: Curve-fit the plasma-concentration-time data to the equation in MINSQ format:

```
INDVARS: T
DEPVARS: CP
PARAMS: I KA K
CP = I×KA/(KA–K)×(EXP(–K×T)–EXP(–KA×T))
```
(1)

where I = FD/V and KA and K are the absorption rate constant and the elimination rate constant, respectively. This yields a standard plasma concentration versus time profile for each of the preparations.

STEP 2: Transform the plasma data.

Integration of the Cp versus T profile yields the cumulative AUC versus T profile. Using either the AUC from an intravenous dose (absolute bioavailability) or from the innovator oral product (comparative bioavailability), the fractional system response is calculated by:

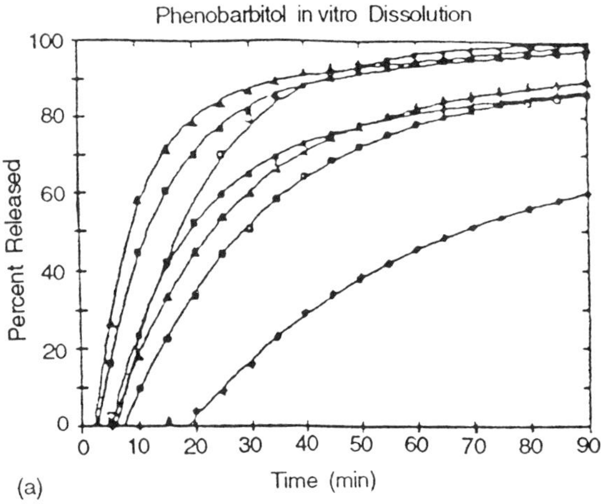

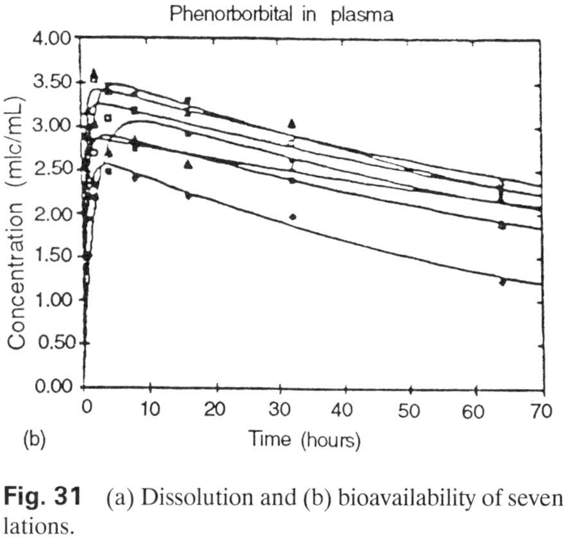

Fig. 31 (a) Dissolution and (b) bioavailability of seven phenobarbital tablet formulations.

INDVARS: T
DEPVARS: F
PARAMS: I KA K (2)
F = I×K×/AUC×KA/(KA–K)×((1–EXP(–K×T)/K)–
(1–EXP(–KA×T)/KA))

Placing parameters obtained from nonlinear regression analysis of the plasma profile (Eqn. 1) into the fractional system response profile (Eqn. 2) transforms the data into a data set similar to the fraction released from dissolution profile.

STEP 3: Compute the fractional response-time profile.

Simply making the independent variable the dependent variable and vice versa and adding limits to the now implicit variable T allows for the solution of T at various F, thus:

```
INDVARS: F
DEPVARS: T
PARAMS: I KA K                                              (3)
F = I×K×/AUC×KA/(KA–K)×((1–EXP(–K×T)/K)–
   (1–EXP(–KA×T)/KA))
O < T < TMAX
```

where TMAX is the maximum time of that profile.

By simulating the data set with the parameters obtained from Eqn. 1, Eqn. 2 will yield as many F versus T pairs for the profiles as needed. In general, 10 pairs are sufficient for most straight lines.

2. Treatment of Dissolution-Time Data

STEP 4: Curve-fit the dissolution-time data to the equation in MINSQ format

```
INDVARS: TIME
DEPVARS: F
PARAMS: A K                                                 (3)
T = (SQRT(TIME)–SQRT(A))×UNIT(SQRT(TIME)–SQRT(A))
F = (3×K×T–3×SQR(K×T)+(K×T)^3)
```

where A is the lag time and K is the Higuchi release-rate constant for single face planar release.

STEP 5: Compute the fractional response-time profile.

Again, making the independent variable the dependent variable and vice versa and adding limits to the now implicit variable TIME allows for the solution of TIME at various F, thus:

```
INDVARS: F
DEPVARS: TIME
PARAMS: A K                                                 (5)
T = (SQRT(TIME)–SQRT(A))×UNIT(SQRT(TIME)–SQRT(A))
F = (3×K×T–3×SQR(K×T)+(K×T)^3)
O < TIME < TIMEMAX
```

By simulating the data set with the parameters obtained from Eqn. 3, Eqn. 4 will yield as many F versus TIME pairs for the profiles as needed. In general, 10 pairs are sufficient for most straight lines.

3. In Vivo–In Vitro Correlation

STEP 6: Determine *in vivo–in vitro* correlation.

Plot the fractional system response time for dissolution (abscissa) versus the fractional system-response-time for AUC (ordinate) for the same fractional system response. Compute the coefficient of correlation, slope, and intercept (Fig. 32).

D. Discussion on System Response Correlation Concept

The computation and correlation of fractional system-response-time for dissolution and bioavailability provides a means for comparing analogous data sets in terms of how the product will perform both in the laboratory and in the biological (human) subject. This concept assumes that both the *in vitro* and *in*

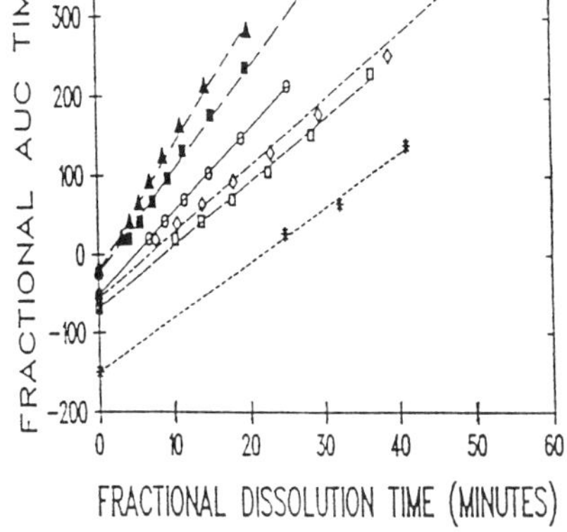

Fig. 32 *In vitro–in vivo* correlation for six phenobarbital tablet formulations based on system response correlation concept.

vivo systems behave linearly from a kinetic standpoint, both dissolution kinetics and pharmacokinetics. The intercept of such a correlation relates to the bioavailability while the slope relates to the dissolution rate. The correlation coefficients of such a comparison will be close to unity since the system response is computed as a back calculation from the observed fitting of data to a model. However the slope and the intercept of this correlation provide key information about the *in vitro* and *in vivo* performance of the formulation(s). Two products may be bioavailable but their rate and extent to which they dissolve both *in vitro* and *in vivo* may differ. In such cases, the intercept will be the same but the slope of such correlation will be different. In the six data sets shown in Fig. 32 two data sets clearly are superior, three sets are average, and one set is inferior. This pattern is reflected in the dissolution profiles, the plasma profiles, and the fractional system response profiles. Thus the correlation is successful in discriminating and separating out the formulations that are behaving differently in spite of their claims to be similar.

The utility of this approach is obvious in the development and assessment of bioequivalence, or the lack of, between products. Products having the same fractional response profile intercept would have the same bioavailability, whereas products having both slope and intercept the same would be bioequivalent. Simplistically, it means that the fractional system-response correlation profiles for the test formulation(s) and the reference formulation should be superimposable in order to unequivocally demonstrate bioequivalence. In practice, however, such superimposability may not be possible. In general, one might want to set guidelines for deeming a product as bioequivalent based on allowable deviation, at a prescribed confidence level, from the fractional system-response correlation profile obtained for the reference formulation. Such a permissible deviation at 95% confidence level is adequate and a test formulation falling within these limits can be deemed bioequivalent with the corresponding reference formulation.

REFERENCES

Armstrong, G. and Blundell, S. 1985. *J. Pharm. Pharmacol. 37*: 28P.
Armstrong G. and Lowndes, L. 1984. *Int. J. Pharm. 5*: 11.
Aulton, H. J., et al. 1974. *J. Pharm. Pharmacol. 26*: 59P.
Banakar, U. V. 1992a. Pharmaceutical Dissolution Testing. Marcel Dekker, New York.
Banakar, U. V. 1992b. Proc. Pharm. Tech. Conf. East Brunswick, NY, p. 149–181.
Banakar, U. V. and Makoid, M. C. 1992. *East. Pharm. XXXV (416)*: 17.
Block, L. H. and Banakar, U. V. 1988. *Drug Dev. Ind. 14*: 2143.
Bolhuis, F. and Lerk, C. F. 1973. *Pharm. Wkbld. 108*: 469.
Chau, H. M., et al. 1980. *Clin. Pharmacol. Ther. 28*: 6.

Chung, B. H. and Chang Koo, S., 1987. *J. Pharm. Sci. 76*: 784–788.
Gilbert, A. and Whiteman, S. 1991. *Proc. CRS Mtg. 18*: 256.
Lootens, D., et al. 1991. *Int. Sym CRS 18*.
Makoid, M. C., Dufore, A., and Banakar, U. V. 1993. *STP 3*: 49.
Yamaoka, K., et al. 1978. *J. Pharmacokinet. Biopharm. 6*: 547.

6

Novel Drug Delivery Systems

Bret Berner

Cygnus, Inc.
Redwood City, California

Agis Kydonieus

ConvaTec, A Bristol-Myers Squibb Company
Princeton, New Jersey

I. INTRODUCTION

As health care reform is debated in Congress, the fact remains that health care costs are 14% of GNP and 55 million Americans are uninsured or underinsured. Pharmaceuticals represent only 7% of the health care costs but still, as the Health Security Report on American People [1] indicates, prescription drugs constitute the largest cost of daily living for 45% of the people over 65.

It is unimaginable that price controls, price negotiation of new drugs, or other government restrictions will be imposed on pharmaceuticals. Such restrictions would stifle high risk research, which is necessary to discover the new pharmaceuticals to treat the diseases of our age: AIDS, Alzheimers, drug resistant infections, and others.

However, the attitude toward health care in the United States will never be the same. The passage of the Waxman-Hatch Act, allowing generic drugs to be marketed upon patent expiry and the emergence of large buying groups, HMOs and other organized buyers of health care services, shifted the price control from the pharmaceutical company to the person paying the bill. Mergers, acquisitions, strategic alliances, layoffs, and voluntary price controls were the result.

We believe that in the above mentioned environment of uncertainty and cost control, the development of novel drug delivery systems will flourish. Over 250 million dollars are required to bring a new drug to the market, but marketing approval of a novel drug delivery system can be secured for as little as ten million dollars. As the pharmaceutical companies adjust their strategies to one of disease management, novel drug delivery offers us the capability of developing a series of niche and line extensions to enhance the product line offered around the disease focus.

In addition to cost containment, novel drug delivery systems can impart important advantages such as extending the duration of drug activity, which allows greater patient compliance owing to elimination of multiple dosing schedules; reducing side effects due to optimization of the blood concentration-time profiles; addressing chronobiological issues by temporal optimization of dosing and by using feedback control self-regulatory polymers and other systems; and being the carriers of proteins and peptides and the vehicles for drug targeting.

A. Patient Compliance

The practical importance of compliance is obvious. If the patient does not comply, the therapeutic goal is not achieved and the cost of drugs prescribed but not taken becomes enormous. In the last few years, adherence to medication has been studied for hypertensives [2], antiasthmatics [3], allergics [4], diabetics [5], cancer [6], and ulcer patients [7], and the elderly [8]. In all cases where the effect of the dosage regimen was studied, the conclusion was that once per day medication gave the best compliance. Luscher, in his studies with hypertensives, indicated that 60–75% of the patients were well controlled, but one-third to one-fourth of the patients were noncompliant. He concluded that "with the advent of potent antihypertensive drugs, noncompliance has become the most important limiting factor in the management of hypertension." Vandereychen [9] in his article "Chronic Illness Behavior and Noncompliance with Treatment" concluded that improving adherence to treatment regimen may produce as great an impact upon disability and health as the development of new biomedical assessment and treatment techniques and may result in greater cost effectiveness of health care services.

Examples of novel systems that have made major impact in the patient compliance area include the Norplant birth control system and the Catapres TTS-Transdermal Therapeutic system. The Norplant birth control system is an implant containing the progestin levonogestrel and is effective for continuous reversible contraceptive protection for up to five years [10]. Norplant is composed of six dimethylsiloxane/methylvinylsiloxane copolymer capsules, 2.4 mm in diameter and 34 mm in length, each containing 36 mgs of levonogestrel. The capsules are implanted in a superficial plane beneath the skin of the upper arm and they should be removed by the end of the fifth year. The system releases 85 μg/day of drug initially, which declines to as low as 30 μg/day during its useful life. Blood plasma concentrations of 0.30 nanograms/mL over five years were observed in clinical trials [11]. The typical failure rate of the system in the first year is 0.2% compared to 3% with oral contraceptives, and second only to male sterilization in minimizing failure rate [12].

Catapres TTS for the treatment of hypertension is a transdermal system with each patch providing continuous systemic delivery of clonidine for seven days at an approximately constant rate. The drug clonidine is a potent antihypertensive agent that is delivered orally at 0.1 to 1.5 mg doses t.i.d. or b.i.d. Catapres TTS is a multilayered film 0.2 mm thick, with system areas of 3.5, 7.0, or 10.5 cm^2 with the amount of drug released being 0.1, 0.2, and 0.3 mg clonidine per day. Proceeding from the visible surface towards the surface that is attached to the skin are four layers: (a) a backing layer of pigmented polyester film; (b) a drug reservoir of clonidine, mineral oil, polyisobutylene, and colloidal silicone dioxide; (c) a microporous polypropylene membrane that controls the rate of delivery of clonidine from the system to the skin surface; and (d) an adhesive formulation of clonidine, mineral oil, polyisobutylene and colloidal silicone dioxide. Prior to use, a protective peel strip of polyester that covers layer d is removed [13].

In patients, one weekly application of the 0.1 mg/day system produces levels of clonidine in plasma that correspond to trough levels of an oral dose of 0.1 mg given twice daily, but the blood plasma levels for the Catapres TTS are more constant than those of oral medication [14]. In addition to seven day efficacy after each transdermal application versus 12 or 8 hour efficacy with use of tablets, Catapres TTS provides for a reduced side effect profile and controls hypertension with a lower daily dosage of clonidine. Drowsiness and dry mouth, the two important side effects of clonidine are reduced by transdermal therapy [15,16]. Catapres TTS sales have been increasing continuously since its introduction in 1985, with U.S. sales reaching $47 million in 1993 despite the fact that over 15% of the population using the patch develops skin sensitization.

B. Reduction of Side Effect Profile

As mentioned above, Catapres TTS was able to reduce side effects by lowering the daily dose of clonidine and by the elimination of peaking concentrations. Reduction of side effects can also be accomplished for drugs that are substantially metabolized during the first pass through the liver. Estradiol is a physiological hormone secreted by the ovaries and it is used therapeutically for systemic estrogen replacement for postmenopausal women and prevention of osteoporosis. A once-daily oral bolus of estradiol has been likened to "hitting the liver with a hammer" every 24 hours, so marked are the elevations in some hepatically derived proteins that result. These elevations have been postulated to cause certain serious side effects of exogenous estrogens, including hypertension, hyperlipidemia, and hypercoagulability [17]. Elimination of the rapid first-pass metabolism of estradiol to estrone and continuous control of the delivery of estradiol to the systemic circulation would minimize these problems. The Estraderm transdermal system addresses these issues. The system is comprised of four layers. Proceeding from the visible surface toward the surface attached to the skin, these layers are: (a) a transparent polyester film; (b) a drug reservoir of estradiol USP and alcohol USP gelled with hydroxypropyl cellulose; (c) an ethylene-vinyl acetate copolymer membrane; and (4) an adhesive formulation of light mineral oil and polyisobutylene. A protective liner (e) of siliconized polyethylene terephthalate film is attached to the adhesive surface and must be removed before the system can be used [18].

Since the skin does not significantly metabolize estradiol delivered from Estraderm, only 5% of the amount of drug used in oral dosing was required to achieve the same blood plasma levels. Clinical studies in postmenopausal women showed that Estraderm delivered therapeutically effective, physiologic levels of estradiol without the unusually high levels of estrone associated with hepatic metabolism of estradiol [19,20].

II. ROUTES OF ADMINISTRATION

As mentioned earlier, novel routes or forms of drug delivery may offer several advantages over conventional dosage forms. However, the desire to increase the speed of drug development can lead to immediate selection of conventional dosage forms. While the use of innovative approaches to drug delivery may have profound effects on the drug development process, the overall process and the probability of success may increase. A novel dosage form typically requires multiple Phase I or Phase IIa trials to research and optimize the dosage form, but Phase IIb and Phase III may be shorter, particularly if steady-state pharmacokinetics/pharmacodynamics in Phase IIa simplify the dose finding. This section serves as a guide to the novice in drug delivery to expand one's options and to understand its impact on development.

Any biological membrane in the human body is a potential portal for drug delivery. We elect to concentrate on the GI tract, transdermal, buccal, nasal, pulmonary, and parenteral delivery. Reviews including other routes such as vaginal, intrauterine, ocular, and rectal may be found elsewhere [21,22].

A. The GI Tract

Since oral delivery is the preferred route of drug delivery, problems in absorption, metabolism, or local tolerability define the rationale for other routes of delivery. Within the context of this review, 4 areas impinge on the drug development process: (a) the use of appropriate tools to screen absorption in the drug discovery process; (b) extended release dosage forms to lengthen the product life for short half-life drugs and the role of infusion studies in regions of the GI tract and scintigraphy in Phase I and IIa to define the dosage form; (c) niche therapies involving diseases of the local regions of the GI tract; and (d) oral peptide and protein delivery and whether this approach is realistic.

Transit through the GI tract may profoundly affect the performance of the dosage form. A median total transit time of 27.4 hours with a range of 5.1 to 38.3 hours was determined from the recovery of oral osmotic pumps [23]. Gastric emptying from the stomach with a pH of approximately 2 varies between 0.5 and 2 hours in the fasted state [24]. After feeding, larger dosage forms exit after the meal has emptied while small pellets empty with the meal [25,26]. Many factors may influence the gastric emptying time including caloric content, disease states, or various drugs. Transit through the small intestine is more reproducible and is typically 3–4 hours [27]. The values of pH in the duodenum and ileocecal junction are 5.8 ± 0.8 and 6.5 to 8.5, respectively [28], but the pH near the jejunal membrane may be 6.1 versus 7.2 in the bulk [29,30]. An increase in pH of 0.5–1.0 unit is typical of entry into the colon. Colonic transit is highly variable and is typically 10–20 hours [31].

Degradation of drugs may occur by hydrolysis in the stomach, by enzymatic digestion such as proteolysis in the small intestinal fluid, by metabolism in the gut wall, and by microorganisms in the colon. Extensive metabolism may also occur in the liver that is directly perfused by the portal blood supply leaving the intestine prior to entering the systemic circulation. Gut wall or hepatic first-pass metabolism may lead to highly variable or poor absorption of drug into the systemic circulation. Metabolized or intact drug may also be recirculated into the small intestine after biliary excretion.

In spite of these complications, prediction of drug absorption from the GI tract has had some success. Simple models correlate oil solubility or melting point with absorption through a lipid membrane [32,33] with water solubility added to account for dissolution in the fluid [34]. More complex hydrodynamic models of flow through tubes may also be useful [35,36,37]. The use of these physical parameters with the models in combination with measurements of absorption in cell culture, such as $CaCO_2$ [38], intestinal segments [39], or Ussing chambers can be invaluable screening tools when used as a guide to drug discovery to define structure/absorption/enzyme activity. The use of a physical model alone may particularly be in error for those ionized drugs that may be absorbed by active transport such as angiotensin-converting enzyme inhibitors and β-lactam antibiotics. While the models may not be definitive, the potential need for employing novel drug delivery or terminating projects may be highlighted early.

Oral controlled-release dosage forms may be designed to decrease the frequency of dosing by targeting a continuous delivery rate to the trough plasma levels resulting from steady-state dosing of the conventional dosage form. A variety of oral controlled-release dosage forms exist including microcapsules and coated pellets [40], ion exchange resins [41], hydrogels [42], and osmotic pumps [43]. Hydrogels may be reproducibly loaded with drug, designed to deliver over a wide range of delivery rates, and permit simple removal of monomers, initiators, stabilizers, and other species with unacceptable toxicological profiles. The cumulative release from a hydrogel is generally proportional to the square root of time, although there is extensive academic work on hydrogels that provide constant release. Such zero-order hydrogels release by such mechanisms as novel geometries [44], Case II diffusion [45], and dissolution-controlled systems [46]. When novel polymers are the basis of the controlled-release system, extensive toxicological studies are required and GMP scale-up and production issues are important. The uniqueness of the selection of these polymers should justify the time and cost.

Oral osmotic pumps (OROS) may be used to tailor the delivery rate to that of constant infusions. In practice, the limitations of drug solubilities and reasonable pressures are determined by the choice of membrane. Water diffuses down its activity gradient across a membrane impermeable to drug and exerts a constant pressure that forces the drug through a small hole. In the elementary osmotic pump, a semipermeable membrane, through which a delivery portal is drilled, surrounds a core of drug that may act as its own osmotic agent. In the case of Acutrim 16 hour steady-state control tablets (Ciba Consumer

Pharmaceuticals), an appetite suppressant, an elementary osmotic pump was designed to deliver 3.5 mg/h following a 20-mg bolus dose achieved by coating the semipermeable membrane with an immediate release fraction [47]. The plasma concentration of phenylpropanolamine remains at or above 60 ng/ml for 16 hours in contrast to the peaks associated with side effects from rapid-release dosage forms.

The push-pull OROS has a flexible impermeable partition spanning the interior of the semipermeable membrane and dividing the OROS into two compartments: (a) a drug compartment where the hole is present and (b) a compartment containing the osmotic agent. Procardia XL (marketed by Pfizer Inc.) delivers 20, 60, or 90 mg nifedipine, a calcium channel blocker, as a once-a-day dosage form [47]. It is an example of the use of a controlled-release dosage form to extend product life by using a patented dosage form to provide patent protection on a brand-name drug after the patent exclusivity on the chemical entity has expired (see below, Recent Successes).

The development of controlled-release oral dosage forms requires Phase I infusion studies in man in different regions of the GI tract, particularly duodenal and colonic infusions. Absorption or degradation from the colon may be a problem and needs to be examined. Inter- and intrasubject variation in absorption, particularly due to first-pass metabolism, may be characterized. Studies of transit recovering the osmotic pump [23], gamma scintigraphy [31], or Heidelberg capsules [28] can be helpful in understanding the performance of the dosage form. Differences in osmotic pressure in regions of the colon may necessitate compensation of the rate of drug delivery. However, it is likely that intersubject variation in GI transit may preclude designing release over too long a period. If diminished frequent side effects while maintaining efficacy is to be part of the labeling, pharmacokinetic/pharmacodynamic studies should be planned in Phase IIa. Minimal Phase III studies without Phase IIb would be a likely clinical program.

Extension of GI transit has been proposed for further decreasing the frequency of oral dosing. However, no such dosage forms are marketed, perhaps due to a lack of matching a therapeutic application of sufficient market potential to the technological possibilities. Dosage forms of various size or density have been investigated to delay gastric transit. Gastric transit has also been avoided by producing dosage forms that swell to become too large to pass through the pylorus. As the emptying time is typically within the range of emptying time for solids, these dosage forms have had limited success. A second approach is bioadhesion to soft mucosa or the mucus lining the GI tract [48,49]. Highly swollen hydrogels such as polyacrylic acid and carboxymethylcellulose may depend on entanglements and hydrogen bonding for this adhesion [50,51, 52]. Sialic acid with its negative charge may also be important for mucoadhesion. While polycarbophil has been shown to double the bioavailability of chlorthiazide in rats due to prolonged gastric retention, in humans and dogs the effects were smaller.

Many studies of the oral delivery of proteins may be found in the controlled-release literature. There has yet to be any convincing data of intact oral absorption of a protein *in vivo* at sufficiently high bioavailabilities to be commercially viable and with sufficiently low intra- and intersubject variability in bioavailability to be safe. Many results are based on pharmacodynamic rather than pharmacokinetic results and are subject to considerable error. The combination of proteolysis and the macromolecular and hydrophilic nature of proteins minimize absorption from the GI tract. The use of carrier systems such as micelles or lipid vehicles [53] or proteinoids [54] may follow the flux of chylomicrons into the lymphatic system, but absorption from the lymphatics is poorly characterized. While enhancers may increase passive absorption across many regions of the GI tract [55–58], such enhancement often depends on gross alterations of membrane properties that may also cause cellular lysis, inflammation, or at minimum, biochemical changes. When used in localized bursts, repair mechanisms may be able to handle such alterations.

Finally, proteins have been targeted to the colon, a region of lower proteolysis, to avoid proteolysis in the small intestine. However, the more thorough experiments still exhibit impractically low bioavailabilities. The colonic delivery systems use 3 basic approaches: (a) swelling upon sensing the pH change upon entering the colon, but this pH difference may be within the intersubject variation; (b) polymers that are subject to degradation by colonic bacteria; and (c) delayed release coatings or membranes that take advantage of the reproducibility of transit through the small intestine. The third approach has a faster development time in that conventional dosage forms may be modified without requiring new polymers with their extensive toxicological and processing requirements. A second more practical use of these colonic systems is for the niche of localized diagnosis and treatment of colonic diseases for which there are currently no convenient means of access.

B. Transdermal Delivery

A primary function of the skin is to protect the body from foreign insult and its three basic mechanisms of protection define the limitations of transdermal delivery: (a) the excellent barrier properties of the outermost layer, the stratum corneum, which is 10–20 μ thick and consists of keratinized epithelial cells joined by tight junctions, require the drug be very potent; (b) primary skin irritation, consisting of the local inflammatory trio of erythema, edema, and pain, that is initiated primarily by the cells surrounding the dermal vasculature just below the dermal–epidermal junction; and (c) after repeated insult, sensitization, an immunological reaction in which recognition is initiated in the epidermis and is a systemic reaction.

Drugs must pass through the stratum corneum and epidermis to the blood vessels below the dermal–epidermal junction. The stratum corneum provides 90–95% of the diffusional resistance in the skin. Transdermal drug delivery avoids first-pass metabolism, provides continuous delivery for short half-life drugs, may circumvent GI side effects, and may avoid poor GI absorption.

Permeation through skin of lipophilic drugs is a classical problem in ideal solution theory [59] and may be related to the solubility in oil [60] or the melting point of the permeant [59]. There is an exponential dependence of the flux on the molecular volume [32,61] through its diffusion constant. While skin permeation has been limited to lipophilic compounds, a number of recent studies indicate that polar and ionic compounds may also permeate skin [62–64] and water solubility may also be important.

Enhancers to improve skin permeation have been a focal point of research [65]. Absorption of polar compounds may be enhanced by surfactants with hydrophilic head groups, or nonpolar and polar compounds when surfactants are combined with other solvents, such as diols or ethanol [65,66]. There is generally a correlation between the ability of a surfactant to improve skin permeation and skin irritation. Consequently, careful optimization of the formulation with respect to irritation and permeation may be required in the preclinical and early Phase I programs. Ethanol can increase the permeation of nonpolar species by increasing their solubility in the stratum corneum without altering their diffusion constants [67–69]. Ethanol is the only solvent used in a commercial transdermal system where the relationship between drugs, estradiol and fentanyl, and the solvent has been characterized [69–71].

Skin tolerability is often a limiting factor in the feasibility of transdermal delivery. Primary irritation, either acutely after a single application or cumulatively after repeated application to the same site, must be characterized in preclinical and human studies.

For drugs that transport across skin at the same rate, irritation may correlate with the pKa of the drug [72,73]. The choice of site of application may affect the sensitivity to the irritant. For example, the incidence of irritation on the buttocks from alcohol-containing transdermal estradiol placebos is substantially reduced compared to the abdomen [74]. Site-to-site bioequivalence must be established. Sensitization is a systemic immune response with typically severe erythema, edema, generalized rash, etc. The classical example is poison ivy. Transdermal clonidine is the most studied transdermal sensitizer to date [75], but transdermal nicotine is also a sensitizer in a small percent of the population. Fortunately, individuals sensitized to the transdermal route for these two drugs almost always have not reacted to oral delivery of clonidine or smoking cigarettes containing nicotine. While guinea pig or mouse-ear-swelling models are generally predictive of sensitization, they did not predict the clonidine or nicotine response in man. Moreover, the classical 2-week maximization paradigm for testing sensitization in man was too short to indicate the magnitude of the response. A 4-week induction period or 2 repeated 2-week induction periods separated by a 2-week rest period may be more appropriate. In preclinical testing GLP primary irritation in rabbits and sensitization in guinea pigs are the usual studies to screen the local tolerability. Studies of irritation, sensitization, phototoxicity, photocontact allergenicity, and bacterial proliferation are standard Phase II studies for transdermal systems. These are short-term exaggerated studies to identify potential problems and do not impact on the time line for development. However, if a problem is identified, larger studies to identify the incidence and severity of the tolerability problem in use should be included in the Phase III program.

The design of transdermal systems falls into two basic types: membrane controlled and monolithic. Since the skin is rate controlling for all commercial systems except the alcohol-containing transdermal estradiol and transdermal clonidine systems, both membrane-controlled and monolithic systems exhibit zero-order release *in vivo*. The common elements of the current transdermal systems are a drug reservoir, a backing that is impermeable to the drug over the system's lifetime, an adhesive and release liner to attach the system to skin with minimal tolerability concerns, and appropriate pouching to achieve the desired shelf-life. Technical problems that commonly affect stability or process validation and production are the uniformity of laminated components from batch-to-batch, migration or loss of components throughout the system during storage, and crystallization of a drug contained in polymers in a metastable state.

Iontophoresis, or the use of electrical current to drive drugs across the skin has recently received much attention as a means of increasing skin permeation and for temporal variation in drug delivery [76,77]. Iontophoretic permeation appears to occur through rare negatively charged pores of 20–25 Å radius with a surface charge of -0.05 C/m^2 [78]. The existence of such pores creates the possibility of peptide delivery, and several *in vitro* and *in vivo* studies in man have been reported [79,80]. Current ranges need to be restricted to limit skin irritation, and at higher levels, pain [81,82]. The therapeutic applications are only in early clinical trials including an iontophoretic patient-controlled analgesic system for fentanyl and an antiemetic [83]. Until Phase III, clinical trials are research on the device as well as the therapy. Early trials must concentrate on obtaining information about the device, *in vivo* delivery, and pharmacokinetics and, therefore, must be capable of multiple measurements. As the trials progress, the device must become smaller, narrower in scope, more rugged, patient friendly, and comfortable. While cost may appear to be a factor, markets requiring tens to hundreds of millions of disposable systems/year allow for fabrication of a single chip, and the cost may then be comparable to passive transdermal delivery. An interesting alternative to iontophoresis is electroporation in which large reversible decreases in the impedance of skin are produced by brief, high-voltage pulses [84].

All commercial transdermal systems to date use a generic drug, which allows for a new or more convenient therapy from its transdermal application. For these generics, pharmacokinetics and target plasma levels have been known at the inception of product development. The use of a generic allows a short feasibility phase of research, toxicology confined to the evaluation of local skin tolerability, a Phase I that typically includes 2–3 pharmacokinetic trials to optimize the performance of the dosage form *in vivo*, a pilot efficacy trial and the specified skin tolerability studies in Phase II, and 2 placebo-controlled, double-blind efficacy studies in Phase III. The final dosage form should be available for the start of Phase III. Large-scale adhesion and irritation trials may be part of Phase IV or in the actual Phase II trials. Such trials may be required as part of the European dossier. While improved patient compliance is typically a major advantage of transdermal dosage forms, surprisingly only one study with transdermal clonidine has been conducted [85].

The incorporation of a new molecular entity into a patch or other novel drug delivery system must have an excellent therapeutic justification, because the overall probability of success of the project is the product of the probabilities of success for both the delivery system and the new chemical entity. There may be cases where this is justified. For example, PHNO, a dopamine autoreceptor agonist that was examined for Parkinson's disease was being developed first orally and then as a transdermal [86]. The side effects from oral delivery served to terminate both projects, yet there was greater than 90% first-pass metabolism orally. An alternative analysis prior to any clinical study would be to either develop only the transdermal patch or terminate the project at the research stage.

C. Buccal Delivery

Buccal delivery offers many of the advantages of transdermal delivery, but may allow faster onset and is useful for a shorter duration, i.e., transdermal delivery is useful from 1 to 7 days while buccal delivery is typically from a few minutes to perhaps 12 hours. In contrast to the skin, the oral cavity is designed for some absorption and secretion, and consequently, the barrier properties and immunological activity are reduced as compared to the skin. Potential restrictions for the buccal route are its limited surface area, concerns of taste and comfort in a highly innervated area, the difficulties of adhesion to a mucosal surface for extended periods without the danger of swallowing or choking on a device, and potential bacterial growth or blockage of salivary glands associated with prolonged occlusion. Sublingual dosage forms have been developed for nitroglycerin [87], ergotamine [88], nicotine [89], buprenorphine [90], methyl testosterone [87], and nifedipine [91]. Oxytocin, a small peptide, has been shown to cross the buccal mucosa [92]. Controlled release devices are also being developed for local applications, in particular, the release of antibiotics from fibers that are placed in periodontal pockets [93].

Human oral mucosa is a stratified epithelium with specialized anatomical development. While the hard palate tends to have a cornified epithelial layer, the soft buccal mucosa is a nonkeratinized tissue (containing keratohyalin granules) with an average thickness of 580 microns [94]. Although certain rodents have a true stratum corneum in their buccal mucosa, no such layer exists in man. Compared to skin, there are a reduced number of Langerhans cells in the buccal mucosa, and these appear to process antigens in the same fashion as in the viable epidermis [95]. In contrast to dermal models, there is no validated model of local oral inflammation and sensitization, and a combination of buccal application and standard dermal animal models should be used to evaluate these issues.

The experimental paradigm of Beckett and Triggs [96] is the classical method for evaluating buccal absorption of drugs. With this method, a known concentration and volume of drug are kept in the subject's mouth for a fixed amount of time, spit out, and the drug absorption is calculated as the difference in the total amount of drug. *In situ* perfusion methods are also popular [97], but both methods have the same limitations: (a) absorption is not distinguished from metabolism and adsorption and (b) the solubility of the drug in water dominates the measurement. A result of this approach is the conclusion that unionized species dominate transport and that the flux follows the partition coefficient [98].

The polar shunt pathway for buccal transport has been largely neglected until recently. Sodium diclofenac in its ionized form has been demonstrated to permeate buccal mucosa rapidly in humans and in dogs [98–100]. Dipolar ions, i.e., angiotensin-converting enzyme inhibitors [101,102] and TRH [96, 103] also permeate extensively. In these latter studies, permeation was calculated by comparison of the AUC from buccal devices containing saturated solutions *in vivo* to intravenous infusion or from *in vitro* methods, such as Ussing chambers. Permeation through buccal mucosa is orders of magnitude faster than through skin, but perhaps a factor of ten slower than through intestinal or nasal mucosa [98,104].

Peptide and protein permeation through buccal mucosa has been reported based on pharmacodynamic measurements. The bioavailability of oxytocin administered transbucally was a few percent. Buccal tissue contains the typical aminopeptidases and degradation must be addressed [105,106]. Moreover, the extent of peptide permeation is unclear, and some histological studies indicate specific barrier layers to macromolecules, e.g., horseradish peroxidase [107]. Buccal tissue culture models are in development from hamster cheek pouch, a keratinized mucosa [108], and from canine mucosa [109], but the results are too early to evaluate. These models should permit careful evaluation of transport and biochemistry concurrently. Development of controlled-release buccal devices requires early and extensive *in vitro* and *in vivo* assessment of adhesion.

D. Nasal Delivery

Nasal anatomy is designed to provide sizable resistance to air flow and to control the temperature and humidity of inhaled air. In an adult, the surface with an area of about 180 cm^2 is lined with pseudostratified columnar epithelium. The blood perfuses the nasal cavity with a flow of 40 μL/cm for each 100 g tissue [110]. Nasal delivery is particularly convenient for local delivery of drugs, for treatment of allergic rhinitis and cold symptoms, and avoids hepatic metabolism. Trapped particles are removed by the mucociliary clearance with a mean turnover rate of 15 minutes [111]. Large particles have difficulty passing the nasal valve, a constriction. From *in vitro* studies of nasal mucosa in Ussing chambers, nasal mucosa is a leaky epithelium [112], and transport appears to be by parallel lipoidal and shunt pathways with oil and water solubilities and molecular weight providing an estimate of permeation [113]. While large proteins are not absorbed, small peptides such as the somatostatin analogs and oxytocin can show excellent bioavailabilities [114].

Drugs may be administered intranasally as aerosols, powders, or small particulates. Sterility, stability, toxicology, and effects on delivery of adjuvants should be evaluated [115]. Design of an inhaler device is also a key to reproducible dosing. Plasticizers and other excipients in gaskets and seals may interact with the formulation, and their effects must be evaluated [116].

Stability, bioavailability, and patient compliance may be substantially influenced by the actual device, and the device should be finalized by the latter stage of Phase II. For local delivery and potent drugs, accurate measurement of bioavailability is a concern, particularly for narrow therapeutic windows. Studies of the reproducibility of delivery within and among subjects are critical.

Screening of formulations may be performed *in vitro*. While the *in situ* rat perfusion model, in which inlet and outlet concentrations are measured, is the most popular model [117], sheep and primate models are to be preferred [118], although less convenient.

E. Pulmonary Delivery

While the trachea and bronchi are lined with pseudostratified columnar epithelium, the bronchioles are lined with columnar ciliated epithelium, and in the alveoli, the barrier is a thin capillary membrane. While drug delivery to the lung is classically for local therapy, pulmonary delivery is a major opportunity for systemic delivery of macromolecules including proteins and approaches to gene therapy [119].

Delivery of a drug to the lung is highly dependent on particle size and 1–2 μ is appropriate [119,120]. Dry powders are particularly useful to stabilize proteins. Loss of drug in the device and in the respiratory tract complicates the determination of bioavailabilities. Intratracheal infusions in rats are a useful test of the feasibility of pulmonary absorption [121]. The long-term inflammatory and immunological response to such delivery has yet to be characterized. As with novel delivery, patient compliance, bioavailability, stability, and particularly reproducibility, depend on the device, and the device should be finalized prior to the latter stages of Phase II.

F. Parenteral Delivery

For life-threatening diseases or those in which the quality of life is impaired, parenteral controlled-release administration either by injection or infusion pumps may be appropriate. For diseases where patient compliance, convenience, or repetitive administration by injection is an issue, the use of an implant may be appropriate. There are numerous depot formulations where drug delivery is controlled by solubility such as insoluble salts or emulsions. Direct infusion into physiological compartments, for example, intrathecal baclofen [122], may permit therapy for debilitating diseases. Miniaturization of mechanical devices and improved biocompatibility of materials are making these devices more acceptable, but the limitation is still the size of the reservoir for the drug. Clinical development is ongoing for products for spasticity with baclofen [122,123], patient-controlled analgesia [124], and diabetes [125]. The infusion pump must be registered as a device with an IDE and 510K, and then an IND and NDA must be filed for the delivery device for that drug and indication. Stability studies in the container and for beyond the period of use in the pump are required. As with iontophoresis, Phase I and IIa studies may be conducted with devices with broader capabilities, but specialized devices with safety and ruggedness built-in are required for Phase IIb and Phase III trials. Sterility and pyrogenicity must be adequately handled and evaluated in processing. Additional microbiological stability requirements must be included.

Implants have potential for treating diseases where patient compliance is an issue and where the drug is potent. Examples are naltrexone for drug abuse [126] and a number of other CNS and hormonal indications. For most pharmaceutical applications, subcutaneous implants must be easily removed intact for safety reasons to terminate drug therapy and pose long-term toxicological issues. Alternatively, microsphere implants may be used where the drug has a wide therapeutic window and few drug interactions. There are two basic approaches: diffusion controlled and chemically controlled where a reaction liberates the drug. In the diffusion-controlled case, the drug is typically dissolved or dispersed in a polymer and released by diffusion. There is currently a silicone-based implant marketed for contraception [47]. Osmotic and swelling-controlled variants of implants are also being developed. For most of these systems, the implant remains intact and removal is relatively simple. There are two main types of chemically-controlled systems: biodegradable and pendant chain. Examples of bioerodible polymers where the polymers degrade by hydrolysis or enzymatic cleavage are: D,L-lactic acid-glycolic acid copolymer (PLGA) [127], polyanhydrides [128], and polyorthoesters [129]. Since the biodegradable system is absorbed over its lifetime, there can be a significant advantage to the patient, but degradation must be reproducible for safety reasons. There are two commercial biodegradable PLGA-based systems for treatment of advanced prostate cancer: 3.6 mg goserelin acetate, an analog of luteinizing hormone releasing hormone, to be released over 28 days [47] and 7.5 mg leuprolide acetate, an analog of gonadotropin releasing hormone, to be released over 28 days [47].

Extensive studies of the degradation of the polymer and its byproducts are required to demonstrate that it is nontoxic, nonimmunogenic, and noncarcinogenic. Long-term safety studies are required. The pharmacokinetics should be extensively characterized in animal models. Obtaining the desired *in vivo* delivery profile for drugs with narrow therapeutic windows is quite problematic due to burst effects. Delivery *in vivo* may be governed largely by the surrounding tissue rather than the system. Reproducibility in scale-up and production must be carefully evaluated and has hindered developmental efforts. Removal of solvent can be problematic for PLGA based systems.

In pendant chain systems, the drug is chemically bound to the polymer and released by hydrolytic or enzymatic reactions. A spacer group varies the rate of release by controlling the hydrophilicity. The main advantage of these systems is its large capacity for drug (over 80 wt% loading). While bioerodible systems require full toxicological characterization of the polymer once, pendant-chain systems require these studies for every drug and spacer.

Acute and chronic inflammation and foreign-body reactions to implants are of great importance [130]. Much fundamental work centers on minimizing protein adsorption [131]. Investigations of the blood compatibility of materials have been adapted to accommodate subcutaneous implants, and similar tests of pathology and durability may be developed.

III. RECENT SUCCESSES AND FUTURE OUTLOOK

A. Recent Significant Product Introductions

During the last few years, several products based on novel drug delivery technologies have been introduced to the marketplace. Among them are Cardiazem

CD, a once per day oral formulation of diltiazem based on Elan's spheroidal oral drug absorption system and marketed by Marion Merrel Dow; Duragesic, a transdermal fentanyl patch developed by Alza and marketed by Janssen Pharmaceutica in 1991; Efidac/24, a once a day antihistamine based on Alza's Oros technology and marketed by Ciba Geigy in 1993; Minipress XL, a once per day antihypertensive formulation of prazosin based on Alza's Oros technology and marketed by Pfiser; and Testoderm, a transdermal patch of the male hormone testosterone, developed and marketed by Alza in 1993. Four transdermal patches delivering nicotine (Nicoderm, Alza-Marion Merrel Dow; Habitrol, Lohmann-Ciba; Prostep, Elan-Lederle; and Nicotrol, Cygnus-McNeil) were introduced in 1992. Procardia XL is a once-per-day oral formulation of the calcium channel blocker Nifedipine based on Alza's Oros osmotic technology, and Dilacor XR is a one-per-day oral formulation of diltiazem, based on Jago's Geometrix technology. Three of these products are discussed below in more detail.

1. Nicotine Transdermal Patch

In 1992 four Nicotine Transdermal Systems were introduced as aids to smoking cessation. The need for a system to alleviate the physical nicotine withdrawal symptoms was so great that the USA product sales for 1992 were over $600 million.

The transdermal nicotine patches were developed to continuously deliver low levels of nicotine to the systemic circulation, under the hypothesis that they would reduce the withdrawal symptoms and allow the smoker to concentrate on the behavioral aspects of the addiction. Habitrol, the leading nicotine system is a round, flat, 0.6 mm thick multilayer unit. Proceeding from the visible surface toward the surface attached to the skin are (a) a tan-colored aluminized backing film; (b) a pressure sensitive acrylate adhesive; (c) a layer containing a methacrylic acid copolymer solution of nicotine dispersed in a pad of nonwoven viscose and cotton; (d) an adhesive layer similar in composition to (b) above; and (e) a protective aluminized release liner that overlays the adhesive layer and must be removed prior to use [132].

Pharmacokinetic studies for all patches [133–137], comparison of the kinetics of skin patches versus the Nicorette Gum [138], effect of application site [139], and comparison of the kinetics of the four commercial patches [140] have been performed. Clinical, multicenter, and double blinded studies have been performed [141–143] showing that the Quit Rates were higher for those smokers using nicotine patches versus those using controls. In clinical trials where concomitant support was given, the Quit Rates in general were substantially higher with the groups using nicotine patches giving the best results. The patches were well tolerated, with mild itchiness and redness being the most common complaint [144].

2. Duragesic

Duragesic is a transdermal patch containing the opioid pain killer fentanyl and it was developed by Alza. The patch has a form-fill-and-seal drug reservoir and an ethylene–vinyl acetate membrane for the controlled delivery of the opioid [145]. The reservoir contains the drug in an aqueous ethanolic solution that has the dual purpose of enhancing the permeation of ethanol through skin and reducing the amount of fentanyl in the reservoir by limiting its solubility [146]. The later fact is significant because fentanyl is an abusable substance.

Duragesic was introduced in the marketplace by Janssen Pharmaceutica, Inc. in April 1991 for the control of chronic pain. It has a duration of activity of 72 hours and is removed from the skin 24 hours after application. The patch remains effective for 72 hours because fentanyl has a skin depot effect [147]. During its first year, Duragesic had sales of $25 million, more than doubling total fentanyl sales. In 1992 and 1993 the sales were $45 and $67 million respectively. As mentioned above, Duragesic has been approved for use in chronic pain but it has been investigated and found to be effective in the treatment of post-operative pain [148,149] as well. With over 40 million surgical procedures per year, the market for Duragesic is conservatively estimated at $500 million.

3. Procardia XL

Procardia XL extended release capsules were designed for once-a-day oral delivery of Nifedipine. Nifedipine belongs to a class of calcium channel blockers that interfere with the normal transmembrane flux of extracellular calcium on which vascular tissue depends for contraction and impulse generation [150] and it is used for the long term management of angina and hypertension [151].

Procardia XL was introduced in September 1989 by Pfizer to replace Procardia, an immediate release formulation designed to release 30, 60, or 90 mg Nifedipine T.I.D. By the time the patent expired in 1991 Pfizer had switched all its patients to Procardia XL. Procardia XL was designed by Alza and it is based on an osmotic push–pull pump system especially useful in delivering insoluble drugs, such as Nifedipine, in suspension [152].

Procardia XL is a bilayer tablet with the top layer containing the drug and the bottom layer containing a hydrophilic polymer, polyethylene oxide [153]. The bilayer is coated with a cellulosic semipermeable membrane and a hole is drilled by a laser beam on the drug side to allow for the release of the drug. In operation, water is osmotically imbibed in both layers, dispersing the drug and swelling the polyethylene oxide polymer, which pushes the dispersed drug through the laser-drilled orifice. This provides a predictable 24-hour zero-order release of Nifedipine with one-to-one correspondence between *in vivo* and *in vitro* results [152].

The success of the new formulation was such that even with strong generic competition Pfizer sales of Nifedipine increased from $700 million in 1989 to

$1.3 billion in 1993. Its success is based on the many advantages offered by the new formulation. Hilleman [154] performed clinical trials on 41 patients to compare efficacy, safety, compliance, and relative cost of treatment between Procardia XL and immediate release formulations. Procardia XL had fewer side effects (32% versus 58%), higher compliance rates (93% versus 76%), and lower cost of therapy ($45.71 versus $60.60). The lower cost of therapy is extremely important since managed care providers and many hospitals have implemented restrictive formularies in which cost is a major determinant of drug selection [155,156]. Clinical studies comparing Procardia XL to beta blockers Atenolol and Propranolol, with and without diuretics, were also performed [157,158]. It was concluded that Procardia XL was an effective, well-tolerated, once-a-day drug that provided a more favorable quality of life profile than did the beta blockers.

B. Future Outlook

Worldwide drug delivery system sales were $2.5 billion in 1991 and are growing at a rate of 35% per year [159]. In addition to the major pharmaceutical companies there are at least 29 companies in the United States spending over $200 million annually in research developing new products using transdermal, iontophoretic, nasal, blood-brain, liposome, polymeric, and monoclonal antibody technologies [160]. The growth mentioned above will be achieved through technological breakthroughs in several drug delivery areas.

1. Abrogation of Inflammatory Responses in Transdermal Delivery

The world market for drugs administered transdermally is predicted to grow from $1.6 billion in 1993 to $9.1 billion in 2003 [161]. The growth rate of 20% is faster than for most other routes of administration.

As mentioned above, several transdermal products have been outstanding technological and marketing successes. However, most drugs cannot be delivered transdermally because they do not permeate through the skin in amounts sufficient to administer a therapeutic dose or because they irritate or sensitize the skin. Furthermore, when chemical or physical enhancers are used to increase permeation, in most cases they also increase skin irritation and sensitization. It has been postulated that more than 80% of drugs will cause skin irritation or sensitization when administered transdermally [162].

Obermeyer et al. circumvented the irritation caused by chlorpheniramine delivered from cellulose triacetate membranes to humans [163]. The irritation, as well as the percutaneous absorption, were substantially reduced by reacting chlorpheniramine with undecylenic acid to form a fatty acid salt. The absorption of the salt was enhanced by dissolving it in a nonpolar nonvolatile solvent such as isopropyl oleate.

Patel and Ebert found that glycerine reduces the primary irritation of moderately irritating drugs and enhancer compositions consisting of solvents and envelope-disordering compounds [164]. Govil and Kohlman patented a nicotine patch containing an antipruritic to counteract pruritus observed with the transdermal administration of nicotine [165]. Antipruritics disclosed include bisabolol, oil of chamomile, chamazulene, allantoin, D-panthenol, glycyrrhetenic acid, corticosteroids, and antihistamines.

Corticosteroids have also been shown to suppress cutaneous delayed hypersensitivity [166,167]. Hydrocortisone and triamcinolone acetonide 21-oic acid methyl ester have been shown to counteract the sensitization potential of a variety of sensitizers, such as clonidine, scopolamine, tetracaine, chlorpheniramine maleate, naloxone, naltrexone, nalbuphine, levorphanol, hydromorphone, buprenorphine, and 1-chloro-2,4-dinitrobenzene.

Cormier was granted a patent for the elimination of irritation or sensitization caused by a drug that is metabolized by an enzyme in the skin to form an irritating or sensitizing metabolite [168]. The method involves the co-administration of a metabolic modulator capable of inhibiting the enzyme from metabolizing the drug, such metabolic modulators being selected from a group consisting of tranylcypromine and phenyl alcohols. Propranolol and tetracaine are shown to be drugs that should be co-administered with metabolic modulators.

Franz [169] was granted US Patent 5028431 for the suppression of irritant as well as allergic contact dermatitis by using agents that compete with the arachidonic acid biotransformation such as steroids, radical scavengers, vitamin E, and leukotriene receptor antagonists. Recently a series of patents [170–172] were issued for the prevention of both irritant and allergic contact dermatitis of drugs by coadministering an antigen processing inhibiting agent to inhibit the antigen processing of the drug in the lysosome. Ionophore and amphiphilic amines are disclosed as antigen-processing inhibiting agents including ammonium chloride, diethanolamine, and monensin. Treatment of sensitization has been significantly reduced by the topical administration of calcium flux inhibitors such as lanthanides and magnesium [173,174].

As indicated above, a lot of progress has been achieved during the last few years in this most important area of transdermal drug delivery, with much remaining to be accomplished. These accomplishments will come through systematic research and study of the inflammatory processes and agents responsible for the initiation of the arachidonic cascade as well as through the understanding of the cellular network and signaling cascade as it pertains to the development of irritation and sensitization.

2. *The Promise of Targeted Therapy*

The element of targeting or site-specific delivery is in the research stage. Carriers such as liposomes, colloidal particles, albumin, nanoparticles, or water-soluble polymer conjugates may be employed [21,175]. Particle filtration may be used to localize delivery to the lungs [176], but it is not always true that this localization targets the drug to the appropriate cells [177]. Many particles in the systemic circulation are rapidly cleared by the reticuloendothelial system (RES), specifically, the Kupffer cells of the liver [178]. The uptake or kinetics of uptake of these particles may be altered through surface coatings such as poly(oxyethylene) or poloxamers [179]. Water soluble macromolecular conjugates may include antibodies to target the conjugate, and then the drug may be released by lysosomal enzymes after being internalized into the cell [21,179]. Antibodies, lectins, rheoviruses, and immunotoxins are among the many strategies for targeting [180]. Gene therapy and antisense are clearly new therapeutic approaches requiring targeting. The difficulties in the analytical methodology have made quantitation difficult and kinetic/dynamic studies in this field are slow in coming. In the absence of analytical methodology, characterization by pharmacodynamic response can be so variable that drug development is risky until the results from large trials are obtained. The use of liposomes to deliver immunomodulators for cancer and antiviral therapy has been tested in several clinical trials [180].

We now focus on targeting with antibodies. Targeting with antibodies became possible with the publication in 1975 by Kohler and Milstein [181] of information on how large amounts of monoclonal antibodies (MoAbs) could be produced against specific antigen after *in vivo* immunization with the same antigen. Thus unlimited quantities of monoclonal antibodies directed against specific cell surface receptors could be affirmed. This new weapon, the "magic bullet," can then be directed on cell surface determinants present in tumor cells or other cells to be killed. The major advantage of targeting is that it delivers larger amounts of the toxic materials to the diseased site and smaller amounts to the healthy tissue.

Although MoAbs are cytotoxic themselves and can be used to kill cells, MoAbs linked to drugs and toxins are more effective. Many immunoconjugates of MoAbs with drugs, proteins, enzymes, and toxins have been produced [182–184].

Antigen specificity and the number of antigenic molecules per tumor cell are important for the adequate delivery of drug to kill the cell. Active drug will have to be released after the MoAb binding to kill the cell. Preferably, the immunoconjugate is endocytosed [185,186] where it can release its drug load by hydrolysis of the drug–MoAb linkage by low pH or by one of the lysosomal enzymes.

Conjugation through an intermediate carrier such as, dextran, poly L-glutamic acid, liposomes, and HPMA retains a higher degree of MoAb activity and much higher drug capacity [187–190]. In addition to the preservation of drug and antibody activity, the MoAb/Carrier system can (a) be used to incorporate different drugs with minimal alterations, (b) protect the drug because of encapsulation with the polymeric matrix, (c) deliver substantially higher amounts of drug than single conjugates, and (d) enhance efficacy of targeting, e.g., up to 100 MoAbs can be attached to a single liposome [191].

Although targeted therapy has exciting potential there are several technical problems that have to be overcome before commercial products can be developed.

- Antibodies may undergo conformational changes after conjugation, reducing their ability to bind to cell surface receptors.
- *In vivo* stability of the chemical linkages of immunoconjugates may not be adequate to preserve drug and antibody activity.
- Binding of the antibody to cell receptors may cause antigenic modulation and shedding or internalization of the receptors making subsequent treatment useless.
- Receptor molecules shed into plasma may bind to MoAbs before the conjugate has a chance to reach its target.
- Conjugates should have the ability to cross through several membranes, including the vascular barrier, and be able to permeate through the tumor.
- Repeat treatments may cause immunogenic reactions especially since human MoAbs are difficult to obtain.

Targeted therapy has been extensively studied for cancer therapy because the usage of chemotherapeutic drugs in the treatment of cancer patients is usually terminated by the toxic effects on normal cells. Thus MoAbs [192–196], drug/MoAb conjugates [197–201], and drug/inert carrier/MoAb conjugates [202–204] have been investigated in cancer therapy. Cancer drugs such as doxorubicin, daunorubicin, and vindesine as well as ricin and diphtheria toxin have been used with varied success [205–207]. Despite the high expectation, *in vivo* results have been rather disappointing probably due to the limitations mentioned above and the fact that (a) cancer cells are heterogeneous; if not all cells are recognized, some will survive and proliferate; (b) conjugates that are effective against a particular cancer in one patient may not be effective against the same type of cancer in another patient; (c) solid tumors are known to shed their receptors upon antigenic modulation rendering subsequent treatments useless; and (d) diffusion of the drug within the tumor can be problematic.

Recently some very encouraging studies have been presented from BR96-Doxorubicin conjugates [208]. BR96-DOX was evaluated against human lung adenocarcinoma, colon carcinoma, and breast carcinoma growing as subcutaneous transplants in athymic mice. Treatment with BR96-DOX consistently cured most mice bearing lung adenocarcinoma and colon carcinoma and complete and partial tumor regressions were produced in breast carcinomas. In contrast, DOX alone or DOX conjugated with nonbinding MoAbs did not show antitumor activity. Probably the care taken in the design of the conjugate is the reason for its success. For example, BR96 binds to a tumor-associated antigen that is abundantly (greater than 200000 molecules per cell) expressed on human tumors [209]. Second, the ability of the conjugate to bind antigen, i.e. its immunoreactivity, was tested and found to be as effective as that of unconjugated BR96 [210]. Third, it was shown that conjugate immunoreactivity was predictive of the antigen-specific cytotoxic potency [211]. Fourth, the BR96-DOX conjugate is rapidly endocytosed after binding to the cell receptors [209,212]. Fifth, a heterobifunctional linker, 6-maleimidocaproylhydrazone of Doxorubicin, was synthesized that imparts an acceptable stability at neutral pH but rapidly releases Doxorubicin under acidic conditions that mimic those of the lysosomal environment [213]. Human trials now in progress with this novel immunoconjugate, which if successful, would open up a new drug delivery approach of vast potential.

3. *Regulated Delivery to Satisfy Chronobiology*

Chronobiology deals with physiological functions that exhibit prominent rhythmic change. The daily rhythm, known as circadian, has been studied most extensively although high-frequency (ultradian, menstrual, and seasonal) rhythms have been well documented. Circadian rhythms have been demonstrated for over 100 variables in the blood, urine, and saliva [214]. Circadian rhythms also exist for body temperature, blood pressure [215], heart rate [216], and the plasma concentration of hormones [217]. The pulsed secretion of hormones has been described for insulin [218], somatostatin [219], luteinizing hormone [220], and several other peptides [221–223]. Many studies in a variety of pharmacological fields have shown a strong dependency of the onset of disease on circadian temporal rhythm. In asthmatics, episodes of dyspnea take place mainly between 2 and 7 a.m. and are 50-fold higher between 4 and 5 a.m. than between 4 and 5 p.m. [224]. Digestive tract rhythmicity has been described for many functions of the gastrointestinal tract, e.g. high gastric acid secretion rates in the evening hours and low in the morning hours [225,226]. Myocardial infarction [227], sudden cardiac death [228], thrombotic stroke [229], and arterial embolism [230] show a strong circadian rhythm with a morning peak and an evening trough. A circadian rhythm in all blood cell types has been well documented [231] including cells of the immune system such as B and T lymphocytes and natural killer cells [232–234]. Circadian rhythms have also been demonstrated for lymphocyte proliferation [235], as well as CD3 and CD4 epitope molecules at their surface [235], which may relate to cell reactivity to antigen exposure and may be critical to the fight against malignancies and other immune diseases [237–238]. Therefore, better management of patients could be obtained by including in the clinical protocol the application of the chronobiological aspects of the pathophysiology of the disease [239].

Pulsatile delivery can be employed for the delivery of the drug in accordance with the required temporal pattern. Pulsatile delivery can be achieved through sophisticated devices with the release profile achieved by some form of external trigger, as will be discussed below. It is important to recognize, however, that pulsatile release per se does not necessarily mean pulsatile concentration time profiles at the site of action. Drugs with the proper pharmacokinetics, e.g. short half-life and chronopharmacology [240,241] have to be considered in order to obtain the desired concentration–time profiles at the diseased site.

Several pulsatile delivery systems have been designed, all of which are in the experimental stage of development. External triggers used to accomplish pulsatile release include temperature, electric current, magnetism, ultrasound, and light.

At least three temperature activated systems have been described in the literature. Thermosensitive hydrogels have been prepared that exhibit reversible swelling–shrinking changes induced by temperature variations. Drug loaded into the hydrogel is released on shrinking in response to a programmed temperature change [242,243]. Acrylic pressure sensitive adhesives have also been prepared with side-chain crystallizable segments. Drug loaded in the pressure sensitive adhesive cannot be released until the temperature is increased above the melting point of the side chains [244].

A third concept uses the glass transition temperature of amorphous polymers as the trigger temperature. Since below the glass transition temperature no segmental rotation can take place, drug loaded in the polymer will not be released until the external temperature is brought above the glass transition temperature. By switching the external temperature above and then below the glass transition temperature of the amorphous polymer, a pulsatile on–off drug delivery can be obtained [245].

Another pulsatile system incorporates the drug, as well as small magnetic beads, into the polymeric matrix. When desired, the release rate is enhanced by an external oscillating magnetic field [246,247]. Magnetic field frequency and strength, as well as polymer composition and strength, and orientation of the embedded beads influence the release [248,249].

Externally applied ultrasonic irradiation has been shown to enhance the release of drugs from diffusion control membranes as well as bioerodible polymers [250,251]. The mechanism of drug release enhancement is the cavitation caused by the ultrasonic waves. The method has been tested *in vivo* in diabetic rats [252].

Pulsatile delivery has also been accomplished by making conjugates of targetable soluble polymers, e.g. HPMA copolymers with photoactivatable drugs such as porphyrins, phthalocyanines, and chlorins. The conjugates enter the cells by pinocytosis and accumulate in the lysosomes. At the desired time, the system can be switched on by external light of characteristic wavelength, which results in the formation of singlet oxygen that destroys the cell [253–255].

Iontophoresis uses an electric vield to increase the permeation of drugs delivered transdermallfy [256,257]. Permeation is proportional to the electric current. Therefore, pulsatile delivery can be obtained by an on–off switch in the circuitry, allowing electric current across the device [258]. Iontophoresis is further advanced than any of the other technologies mentioned above and several human clinical trials have been performed with, for example, nanopeptide leuprolide [259] and fentanyl and morphine for patient-controlled post-operative analgesia [259,260].

REFERENCES

1. Health Security, The President's Report to the American People. U.S. Government Printing Office, 1993.
2. T. Lusher and W. Vetter. *J. of Human Hypertension 4*: 43, 1990.
3. S. Ruggeri, et al. *J. Intern. Med. Res. 15*: 170, 1987.
4. E. Bantz, et al. *Annals of Allergy 59*: 341, 1987.
5. T. Pullan, et al. *Clin. Pharmacol. Therap. 44*: 540, 1988.
6. E. Gritz, et al. *Preventive Med. 18*: 711, 1989.
7. J. Bader. *J. Clin. Gastroenter. 11*: 525, 1989.
8. R. Stewart, et al. *Med. Clin. of N. America 73*: 1551, 1989.
9. J. Vandereychen. *Psychother. Phychosom. 50*: 182, 1988.
10. P. Denniston. Physicians GenRx. Data Pharmaceutica, New York, 1993, p. II–1221.
11. V. John, et al. *Br. J. Clin. Pharmac. 19*: 203S, 1985.
12. E. Barnhart. Physician's Desk Reference 45th ed. Medical Economics Co. Inc., Oradell, NJ, p. 454.
13. E. Barnhart. Physician's Desk Reference 45th ed. Medical Economics Co. Inc., Oradell, NJ, p. 669.
14. J. Shaw, et al. Rate Controlled Polymeric Therapy Utilizing Polymeric Membranes in Transdermal Delivery of Drugs. A. Kydonieus and B. Berner, Eds. CRS Press, Boca Raton, FL, 1988, p. 112.
15. S. Popli, et al. Transdermal Clonidine for Hypertensive Patients. *Clin. Therap. 5*: 624, 1983.
16. F. McMahon, et al. Clinical Experience with Clonidine TTS, in Mild Hypertension. M. Weber and C. Mathias, Eds. Steinkopff Verlag, Darmstadt, Germany, 1984, p. 148.
17. S. Campbell and M. Whitehead. The Controversial Climacteric. MTP Press, Lancaster, England, 1981, p. 103.
18. E. Barnhart. Physician's Desk Reference 45th ed. Medical Economics Co. Inc., Oradell, NJ, p. 853.
19. L. Laufer, et al. Estrogen Resplacement Therapy by Transdermal Estradiol Administration. *Am. J. Obstet. Gynecol. 146*: 533, 1983.

20. K. Steingold, et al. Treatment of Hot Flashes with Transdermal Estradiol Administration. *J. Clin. Endocrin. Metab. 61*: 627, 1985. Steady State Pharmacokinetics and Dose Relationship of Nicotine Delivered from Nicoderm. *J. Clin. Pharmacol. 33*: 161, 1993.
21. R. W. Duncan and L. W. Seymour. Controlled-Release Technology. Elsevier Advanced Technology, Oxford, 1989.
22. A. Kydonieus. Treatise on Controlled-Release Drug Delivery. Marcel Dekker, NY, 1992.
23. V. John, et al. *Br. J. Clinical Pharmacol. 19*: 203S, 1985.
24. S. S. Davis, J. G. Hardy, and J. W. Fara. *Gut 27*: 886, 1986.
25. M. Feldman, H. J. Smith, and R. R. Simon. *Gastroenterology 87*: 895, 1984.
26. J. H. Meyer, et al. *Gastroenterology 88*: 1502, 1985.
27. N. W. Read, et al. *Gut 27*: 300, 1986.
28. P. Mojaverian, K. Chan, A. Desai, and V. John. *Pharmaceut. Res. 6*: 719, 1989.
29. M. Lucas. *Gut 24*: 734, 1983.
30. M. L. Lucas and J. A. Blair. *Proc. R. Soc. London Ser. B 200*: 27, 1978.
31. J. G. Hardy, et al. *Int. J. Pharm. 48*: 79, 1988.
32. E. R. Cooper and G. Kasting. *J. Control. Rel. 6*: 23, 1987.
33. S. H. Yalkowsky. Techniques of Solubilization of Drugs. S. H. Yalkowsky, Ed. Marcel Dekker, New York, 1981, p. 1.
34. J. B. Dressman, G. L. Amidon, and D. Fleisher. *J. Pharm. Sci. 74*: 588, 1988.
35. G. L. Amidon, J. Kou, R. L. Elliot, and E. W. Lightfoot. *J. Pharm. Sci. 69*: 1369, 1980.
36. D. A. Johnson and G. L. Amidon. *J. Theor. Biol. 131*: 93, 1988.
37. R. L. Elliot, G. L. Amidon, and E. W. Lightfoot. *J. Theor. Biol. 87*: 757, 1980.
38. M. Rousset. *Biochim. 68*: 1035, 1986.
39. L. E. Riad and R. J. Sawchuk. *Pharmaceut. Res. 8*: 491, 1991.
40. R. M. Gilley, J. H. Eldridge, J. L. Opitz, K. Hanna, J. K. Staas, and T. R. Tice. *Proc. Int. Symp. Contr. Rel. Bioact. Mater. 15*: 123, 1988.
41. L. S. Lilienfeld and E. J. Zapolski. *Curr. Therap. Res. 33*: 692, 1983.
42. W. R. Good. Polymeric Delivery Systems. R. J. Kostelanik, Ed. Gordon and Breach Science Publishers, New York, 1978, p. 139.
43. K. Heilmann. Therapeutic Systems: Rate-Controlled Drug Delivery, Concept and Development, 2nd ed. Thieme-Stratton., NY, 1984.
44. R. Lasse. *Chemical Engineering Commun 6*: 1, 1980.
45. S. K. Singh and L. T. Fan. *Biotech. Prog. 2*: 145, 1986.
46. N. A. Peppas. *J. Biomed. Mater. Res. 17*: 1079, 1983.
47. Edward K. Barnhart. Physician's Desk Reference, 45th Edition: Medical Economics, Oradell, NJ.
48. K. Park, H. S. Ch'ng, and J. R. Robinson. Recent Advances in Drug Delivery. J. M. Anderson and S. W. Kim, Eds. New York, 1984, p. 163.
49. M. A. Longer, H. S. Ch'ng, and J. R. Robinson. *J. Pharm. Sci. 74*: 406, 1985.
50. H. Park and J. R. Robinson. *Pharmaceut. Res. 4*: 457, 1987.
51. J. D. Smart, I. W. Kellaway, and H. E. L. Worthington. *J. Pharm. Pharmacol. 36*: 295, 1984.

52. A. Silberberg and F. A. Meyer. *Adv. Exp. Med. Biol. 144*: 53, 1982.
53. N. Moranishi. *Int. J. Pharm. 4*: 279, 1980.
54. X. Ma, N. Santiago, Y. S. Chen, K. Chaudhary, S. J. Milstein, and R. A. Baughman. *J. Drug Target. 2*: 9, 1994.
55. J. A. Fix, K. Engle, P. A. Porter, P. S. Leppert, S. J. Selle, C. R. Gardner, and J. Alexander. *Am. J. Physiol. 251*: 6332, 1986.
56. K. Higaki, N. Takechi, M. Hashida, and H. Sezaki. *Chem. Pharm. Bull. 36*: 1214, 1988.
57. M. Murakami, K. Takada, T. Fujii, and S. Muranishi. *Biochim. Biophys. Acta 939*: 238, 1988.
58. E. J. Van Hoogdalem, H. J. M. Van Kan, A. G. deBoer, and D. D. Breimer. *J. Control Rel. 7*: 53, 1988.
59. E. R. Cooper. *J. Control Rel. 1*: 153, 1984.
60. A. S. Michaels, S. K. Chandrasekharan, and J. E. Shaw. *AICHE J. 21*: 985, 1975.
61. B. Berner and E. R. Cooper. Transdermal Delivery of Drugs, Vol. II. A. F. Kydonieus and B. Berner, Eds. CRC Press, Boca Raton, FL, 1987, p. 41.
62. G. C. Mazzenga and B. Berner. *J. Control Rel. 16*: 77, 1991.
63. D. C. Patel. Eur. Patent, EP0321870 (1989).
64. M. Sznitowska, B. Berner, and H. I. Maibach. *Int. J. Pharm. 99*: 43, 1993.
65. E. R. Cooper and B. Berner. Transdermal Delivery of Drugs, Vol. II. A. F. Kydonieus and B. Berner, Eds. CRC Press, Boca Raton, FL, 1987, p. 57.
66. D. C. Patel and Y. Chan. U.S. Patent 4,863,970 (1989).
67. B. Berner, G. C. Mazzenga, J. Otte, R. J. Steffens, R. H. Juang, and C. D. Ebert. *J. Pharm. Sci. 78*: 314, 1989.
68. B. Berner, R. H. Juang, and G. C. Mazzenga. *J. Pharm. Sci. 78*: 472, 1989.
69. B. Berner and P. Liu. Percutaneous Penetration Enhancers. E. W. Smith and H. I. Maibach, Eds. CRC Press, Boca Raton, FL.
70. S. Yum, E. Lee, L. Taskovich, and F. Theeuwes. Drug Permeation Enhancement. D. S. Hsieh, Ed. Marcel Dekker, NY, 1994.
71. P. S. Campbell and S. K. Chandrasekharan. U.S. Patent 4,379,454 (1983).
72. B. Berner, D. R. Wilson, R. H. Guy, G. C. Mazzenga, F. H. Clarke, and H. I. Maibach. *Pharmaceut. Res. 5*: 660, 1988.
73. B. Berner, D. R. Wilson, R. H. Guy, G. C. Mazzenga, F. H. Clarke, and H. I. Maibach. *J. Toxicol.—Cut. Ocular Toxicol. 8*: 1, 1989.
74. B. Berner and V. A. John. *Clinical Pharmacokinetics 26*: 121, 1994.
75. M. R. Holdiness. *Contact Dermatitis 20*: 3, 1989.
76. A. K. Banga and Y. W. Chien. *J. Control Rel. 7*: 1, 1988.
77. R. R. Burnette and B. Ungipipattanakul. *J. Pharm. Sci. 71*: 765, 1987.
78. S. M. Dinh, C. W. Luo, and B. Berner. *AICHE J. 39*: 2011, 1993.
79. M. B. Delgado-Charro and R. H. Guy. *Pharmaceut. Research 11*: 929, 1994.
80. M. C. Heit, N. A. Monteiro-Riviere, F. L. Jayes, and J. E. Riviere. *Pharmaceut. Res. 11*: 1000, 1994.
81. H. Molitor. *The Merck Report 52*: 22, 1943.
82. J. G. Webster. Medical Instrumentation. Houghton Miflin, p. 210, 1978.
83. J. B. Phipps, R. Haak, S. Chso, S. K. Gupta, and J. R. Gyory. *Proc. Int. Symp. Control Rel. Bioact. Mater. 21*: 170, 1994.

84. J. C. Weaver. *Proc. Int. Symp. Control Rel. Bioact. Mater. 21*: 15, 1994.
85. G. C. Brenche, Jr., J. M. Betts, V. M. Dowdy, L. S. Field, and C. K. Freis. *Am. J. Med. 91 (Suppl. 1A)*: 37S, 1991.
86. F. J. Grendas-Perez, P. G. Jenner, M. Nomoto, S. Stahl, N. P. Quinn, J. P. Parker, P. Critchley, and C. D. Marsden. *Lancet* 906, 1986.
87. Physician's Desk Reference, 43rd ed. Medical Economics Co., Oradell, NJ, 1989, p. 757, 1573.
88. V. L. Perrin. *Clin. Pharmacol. 10*: 334, 1985.
89. M. A. H. Russell, C. H. Feyerabend, and P. V. Cole. *Br. Med. J. 1*: 1043, 1976.
90. R. E. S. Bullingham, H. J. McQuay, E. J. B. Porter, M. C. Allen, and R. A. Moore. *Br. J. Clin. Pharmacol. 13*: 665, 1982.
91. K. Muller and M. Osler. *Acta Obstet. Gynecol. Scand. 46*: 59, 1967.
92. R. Duncan and L. Seymour. Controlled-Release Technologies. Elsevier Advanced Technology, Oxford, 1989, p. 72.
93. S. Y. Chen and C. A. Squier. The Structure and Function of Oral Mucosa. J. Meyer, C. A. Squier, and S. J. Gerson, Eds. Pergamon Press, Oxford, 1984, p. 7.
94. J. P. Waterhouse. The Structure and Function of Oral Mucosa. J. Meyer, C. A. Squier, and S. J. Gerson, Eds. Pergamon Press, Oxford, 1984, p. 109.
95. A. H. Beckett and E. F. Triggs. *J. Pharm. Pharmacol. Suppl. 19*: 31, 1967.
96. M. M. Veillard, M. A. Longer, T. W. Martens, and J. R. Robinson. *J. Control. Rel. 6*: 123, 1987.
97. N. F. Ho and C. L. Barsuhn. Buccal Delivery of Drugs. *Proc. Int. Symp. Control. Rel. Bioact. Mater. 16*: 24, 1989.
98. C. D. Ebert, V. A. John, P. T. Beall, and K. A. Rosenzweig. Controlled-Release Technology. P. I. Lee and W. R. Good, Eds. ACS Symp. Ser. 348: 310, 1987.
99. J. Cassidy, B. Berner, K. Chan, V. John, S. Toon, B. Holt, and M. Rowland. *Pharmaceut. Res. 10*: 126, 1993.
100. J. Cassidy, B. Berner, K. Chan, V. John, S. Toon, and M. Rowland. *Proc. Int. Symp. Contr. Rel. Bioact. Mater. 16*: 91, 1989.
101. E. Quadros, J. Cassidy, K. Gniecko, and S. LeRoy. *J. Control. Rel. 19*: 77, 1992.
102. E. Quadros, J. Cassidy, K. Rosenzweig, and B. Berner. *Proc. Int. Symp. Bioact. Mater. 15*: 325, 1988.
103. M. A. Longer, M. E. Dowty, and J. R. Robinson. *Proc. Int. Symp. Control. Rel. Bioact. Mater. 15*: 68, 1988.
104. S. J. Sjostedt. *Acta Obstet. Gynecol. Scand. 48* (suppl. 7): 1, 1969.
105. R. E. Stratford, Jr. and V. H. Lee. *Int. J. Pharmaceut. 30*: 73, 1986.
106. J. Cassidy and E. Quadros. *Pharmaceut. Res. 5*(Suppl.): S100, 1988.
107. C. A. Squier. *J. Ultrastruct. Res. 43*: 160, 1973.
108. M. R. Tavakoli-Saberi and K. L. Audus. *Pharmaceut. Res. 6*: 160, 1989.
109. E. Quadros, J. P. Cassidy, and H. Leipold, in press.
110. M. Bende, et al. *Acta Otolaryngol. 96*: 277, 1983.
111. G. S. M. J. E. Duchateau, et al. *Laryngoscope 95*: 854, 1985.
112. S. J. Hersey and R. T. Jackson. *J. Pharm. Sci. 76*: 871, 1987.
113. C. McMartin and G. Peters. Delivery Systems for Peptide Drugs. S. S. Davis, L. Illum, and E. Tomlinson, Eds. Elsevier, Amsterdam, 1985, p. 161.

114. B. G. Vickery, S. Anik, M. Chaplin, and M. Henzl. Transnasal Systemic Medication. Y. W. Chien, Ed. Elsevier, Amsterdam, 1985, p. 201.
115. S. Hirai, T. Yashiki, and H. Mima. *Int. J. Pharm. 9*: 173, 1985.
116. W. Petri, R. Schmiedel, and J. Sandow. Transnasal Systemic Medications. Y. W. Chien, Ed. Elsevier, Amsterdam, 1985, p. 161.
117. J. Seki, H. Mukai, and M. Sugiyama. *J. Pharmacobio-Drug 8*: 337, 1985.
118. J. P. Longnecker, A. C. Moses, J. S. Flier, F. D. Silver, M. C. Carey, and E. J. Dubovi. *J. Pharm. Sci. 76*: 351, 1987.
119. D. T. O'Hagan and L. I. Ilum. *Crit. Rev. Ther. Drug Carrier Systems 7*: 35, 1990.
120. I. Gonda. *Crit. Rev. Ther. Drug Carrier Systems 6*: 273, 1990.
121. J. S. Patton and R. M. Platz. *Adv. Drug Deliv. Rev. 8*: 179, 1992.
122. S. Kroin, R. D. Penn, R. C. Beissinger, and R. C. Arzbaecher. *Exp. Brain Res. 54*: 191, 1984.
123. R. D. Penn. Neurological Applications of Implanted Drug Pumps. *Ann. N.Y. Acad. Sci. 531*: 157, 1988.
124. G. Koning and F. Feith. Neurological Application of Implanted Pumps. *Ann. N.Y. Acad. Sci. 531*: 48, 1988.
125. W. Webster. Temporal Control of Drug Delivery. *Ann. N.Y. Acad. Sci. 618*: 544, 1991.
126. S. E. Harrigan and D. A. Downs. *NIDA Res. Monog. Ser. 28*: 77, 1980.
127. R. A. Miller, J. M. Brady, and D. E. Cutright. *J. Biomed. Mater. Res. 11*: 711, 1977.
128. K. W. Leong, B. C. Brott, and R. Langer. *J. Biomater. Res. 19*: 941, 1985.
129. N. S. Choi and J. Heller. U.S. Patent 4,093,709 (1978).
130. J. M. Anderson. *Trans. Soc. Artif. Intern. Organs 34*: 101, 1988.
131. J. D. Andrade, S. Nagaoka, S. Cooper, T. Okano, and S. W. Kim. *Trans. Soc. Artif. Intern. Organ 33*: 75, 1987.
132. P. Denniston. Physicians GenRx. Data Pharmaceutica, NY, 1993, p. II–1500.
133. S. Gupta, et al. Single and Multiple Dose Pharmacokinetics of Nicoderm. *J. Clin. Pharmacol. 33*: 169, 1993.
134. H. Ross, et al. Pharmacokinetics of Multiple Daily Transdermal Doses of Nicotine in Smokers. *Pharm. Res. 8*: 385, 1991.
135. J. Gorsline, et al. S
136. S. Keller, et al. Pharmacokinetics of a New Developed Nicotine TTS. *Arch. Pharmacol. 345* (Suppl. 1): R10, 1992.
137. S. Caspary, et al. Pharmacokinetics of Nicotine After Topical Application. *Arch. Pharmacol. 343*: R120, 1991.
138. J. Lane, et al. Pharmacokinetics of a Transdermal Nicotine Skin Patch Compared to Nicorette Gum. *Pharm. Res. 8* (No. 10 Suppl.): S208, 1991.
139. J. Gorsline, et al. Comparison of Plasma Nicotine Concentrations After Application of Nicoderm to Different Skin Sites. *J. Clin. Pharmac. 32*: 576, 1992.
140. Y. Chien, et al. Kinetic Evaluation of Transdermal Nicotine Delivery Systems. *Drug. Dev. Ind. Pharm. 19*: 295, 1993.
141. A. Christev, et al. Transdermal Nicotine for Smoking Cessation: Six Month Results from Two Multicenter Controlled Trials. *J. Am. Med. Assoc. 266*: 3133, 1991.
142. J. Foulds, et al. Effect of Transdermal Nicotine Patches on Cigarette Smoking: A Double Blind Crossover Study. *Psychopharmacology* (*Berlin*) *106*: 421, 1992.

143. J. Norregard, et al. Long Term Nicotine Substitution After Application of a 16 Hour Nicotine Patch in Smoking Cessation. *Eur. J. Clin. Pharmacol. 43*: 57, 1992.
144. J. Rose, et al. Four Week Tolerability of a Transdermal Nicotine Patch for Smoking Cessation. *Pharm. Res. 8* (No. 10, Suppl.): S209, 1991.
145. P. Denniston. Physicians' GenRx. Data Pharmaceutica, Smithtown, NY, 1993, p. II–865.
146. R. Gale, et al. Belg. Patent 0905568 (1987).
147. P. Plezia, et al. *Pharmacotherapy 9*: 2, 1989.
148. F. Holley and C. Van Stennis. *Br. J. Anaesth. 60*: 608, 1988.
149. R. Caplan, et al. *J. Am. Med. Assoc. 261*: 1036, 1990.
150. A. Fleckenstein, et al. A New Group of Compatible Calcium Antagonists. *Fluegers Arch. 307*: 25, 1969.
151. W. Frishman, et al. Calcium Channel Blockers in Systemic Hypertension. *Curr. Probl. Cardiol. 12*: 287, 1987.
152. D. Swanson, et al. Nifedipine Gastrointestinal Therapeutic System. *The American J. of Med. 83* (Suppl. 6B): 3, 1987.
153. A. Kydonieus, unpublished data.
154. D. Hillerman, et al. Conversion from Sustained-Release to Immediate-Release Calcium Entry Blockers: Outcome in Patients with Mild-to-Moderate Hypertension. *Clinical Therapeutics 15*: 1002, 1993.
155. J. Hinnan and Z. Grapes. Formulary Management Activities in Georgia. *Pand T. 17*: 475, 1992.
156. R. Plumridge, et al. The Effect of Hospital Formularies. *Drug Intell. Clin. Pharm. 18*: 652, 1984.
157. M. Testa. Parallel Perspectives on Quality of Life During Antihypertensive Therapy. *J. Cardiovascular Pharmac. 21* (Suppl. 2): 518, 1993.
158. W. Frishman, et al. The Nifedipine Gastrointestinal Therapeutic System in the Treatment of Hypertension. *Am. J. of Cardiology 64*: 65F, 1989.
159. Strategic Research Institute, On the Cutting Edge of Drug Delivery Systems Conference, October 1994.
160. Special Report on Drug Delivery. *Med. Ad. News* August 1993: 10.
161. Scrip No. 1888. P. J. Publications Ltd., January 14, 1994, p. 13.
162. T. Franz, et al. Transdermal Delivery, in Treatise on Controlled Drug Delivery. A. Kydonieus, Ed. Marcel Dekker, New York, 1992, p. 341.
163. A. Obermayer, et al. Transdermal Pharmaceuticals Containing Amines and Nonpolar, Non-volatile Solvents. Europ. Patent Appl. EP267051 (1989).
164. D. Patel and C. Ebert. Method for Reducing Skin Irritation Associated with Drug/Penetration Enhancer Compositions. U.S. Patent 4855294 (1989).
165. S. Govil and P. Kohlman. Transdermal Delivery of Nicotine. U.S. Patent 4908213 (1990).
166. A. Amkraut and J. Shaw. Prevention of Contact Allergy by Coadministration of a Corticosteroid with a Sensitizing Drug. U.S. Patent 5000956 (1991).
167. Rockefeller University. Glucocorticoid Carboxylic Acid Ester for Suppressors of Cutaneous Delayed Hypersensitivity. PCT Inst. Appl. W08809175.

168. M. Cormier. Method for Reducing Sensitization or Irritation in Transdermal Drug Delivery and Means Thereof. U.S. Patent 4,885,154 (1989).
169. T. Franz, et al. Article for the Delivery to Animal Tissue of a Pharmacologically Active Agent. U.S. Patent 5028431 (1991).
170. P. Ledger, et al. Reduction or Prevention of Sensitization to drugs. U.S. Patent 5120545 (1992).
171. M. Cormier, et al. Reduction or Prevention of Skin Sensitization by Drugs. U.S. Patent 5130139 (1992).
172. M. Cormier, et al. Reduction or Prevention of Skin Irritation by Drugs. U.S. Patent 5160741 (1993).
173. D. Wolfgang. Magnesium Salts as Topical Inflammation Inhibitors for the Skin. Ger. (East), Patent DD297062.
174. A. Grant. Suppression of Eczematous Dermatitis by Calcium Transport Inhibitors. U.S. Patent 5202130 (1993).
175. Site-Specific Delivery. E. Tomlinson and S. S. Davis, Eds. John Wiley, NY, 1986.
176. I. J. Fidler, A. Raz, W. E. Fogler, K. Kroh, P. Bugelsi, and G. Poste. *Cancer Res. 40*: 4460, 1980.
177. J. N. Weinstein, C. D. V. Black, J. Barbet, R. R. Eger, R. J. Parker, O. D. Hutton, J. L. Mulshinc, A. M. Keehan, S. M. Larson, J. A. Carrasquillo, S. M. Sieber, and D. G. Covell. Site-Specific Drug Delivery. E. Tomlinson and S. S. Davis, Eds. John Wiley, New York, 1988, p. 81.
178. L. Illum, N. W. Thomas, and S. S. Davis. *J. Pharm. Sci. 75*: 16, 1986.
179. J. Kopecek and R. Duncan. *J. Contr. Rel. 6*: 315, 1987.
180. I. J. Fidler. Site-Specific Drug Delivery. E. Tomlinson and S. S. Davis, Eds. John Wiley, New York, 1986, p. 111.
181. G. Kohler and C. Milstein. Continuous Cultures of Fused Cells Secreting Antibody of Predefined Specificity. *Nature 256*: 495, 1975.
182. B. F. Erlander. *Pharmacol. Rev. 25*: 271, 1973.
183. E. Ishikawa. *J. Immunoassay 4*: 209, 1983.
184. P. N. Kulkami, P. H. Blair, and T. Ghose. *Fed. Proc. 40*: 642, 1981.
185. R. Arnon and E. Kurwitz. In Durable Resistance in Crops. F. Lamberti, et al., Eds. Plenum Press, NY, 1983, p. 23.
186. R. K. Oldsman. *J. Clin. Oncol. 1*: 582, 1993.
187. G. F. Rowland. In Targeted Drugs. E. P. Goldberg, Ed. Wiley-Interscience, New York, 1983.
188. M. V. Primm, et al. *Cancer Immunol. Immunother. 12*: 125, 1982.
189. M. Muirhead, et al. *Blood 62*: 327, 1983.
190. R. Duncan, et al. *J. Cancer 55*: 165, 1987.
191. K. S. Houck and L. Huang. *Biochem. Biophys. Res. Commun. 145*: 1205, 1987.
192. G. F. Rowland, et al. *Protides Biol. Fluids 30*: 375, 1983.
193. J. Corvalan, et al. *Protides Biol. Fluids 31*: 921, 1984.
194. M. J. Embleton, et al. *Br. J. Cancer 43*: 582, 1981.
195. J. P. Brown, et al. *J. Immunol. 127*: 539, 1981.
196. J. T. Kemshed. *Hybridoma 1*: 109, 1982.
197. M. J. Embleton, et al. *Br. J. Cancer 47*: 49, 1983.

198. E. Hurwitz. *Cancer Reds. 35*: 1175, 1975.
199. H. E. Blythman, et al. *Nature 290*: 145, 1981.
200. I. S. Trowbridge and D. L. Domingo. *Nature 294*: 171, 1981.
201. T. Ghose and S. P. Nigam. *Cancer 29*: 1398, 1972.
202. L. D. Leserman, et al. *Nature 288*: 602, 1980.
203. G. M. Barratt, et al. *Biochem. Soc. Trans. 12*: 348, 1984.
204. G. F. Rowland, et al. *Nature 255*: 487, 1975.
205. M. V. Primm, et al. *Cancer Immunol. Immunother. 12*: 125, 1982.
206. D. G. Gilliland, et al. *Nat. Acad. Sci. USA 77*: 4539, 1980.
207. G. F. Rowland, et al. *Cancer Immunol. Immunother. 19*: 1, 1985.
208. P. A. Trail, et al. Cure of Xenografted Human Carcinomas by BR96-Doxorubicin Immunoconjugates. *Science 261*: 212, 1993.
209. I. Hellstrom, et al. *Cancer Res. 50*: 2183, 1990.
210. H. Zhao, et al. Determination of Immunoreactivity of Doxorubicin Antibody Immunoconjugates by a Le^y Competitive RIA. *Bioconjugate Chem. 3*: 549, 1992.
211. H. Zhao, et al. Immunoreactivity and Antigen-Specific Cytotoxicity of BR96 Immunoconjugates Synthesized from a New Heterobifunctional Linker, 6-Male-Imidocaproylhydrazone of Doxorubicin. *Proc. Am. Assoc. Cancer Res. 35*: 502, 1994.
212. D. Willner, et al. 6-Maleimidocaproylhydrazone of Doxorubicin—A New Derivative for the Preparation of Immunoconjugates of Doxorubicin. *Bioconjugate Chem. 4*: 521, 1993.
213. J. Garrigues, et al. *Am. J. Pathol. 142*: 607, 1993.
214. E. Kanabrocki, et al. Circadian variation in presumably healthy young soldiers, U.S. Department of Commerce, Doc. No. PB228427. National Technical Information Service, P.O. Box 51553, Springfield, VA (1974).
215. F. Halberg, et al. Blood pressure assessment in a broad chronobiologic perspective. In Heart and Brain. H. Refsum, Ed. Springer-Verlag, Berlin, 1988.
216. E. Halberg, et al. Plexo-serial linear-nonlinear rhythmometry of blood pressure, pulse, and motor activity by a couple in their 60's. *Chronobiologia 8*: 351, 1981.
217. D. Krieger. Rhythms in CRF, ACTH and Corticosteroids in Endocrine Rhythms. D. Krieger, Ed. Raven Press, New York, 1979.
218. D. Lang, et al. Brief, irregular oscillations of basal plasma insulin and glucose concentrations in diabetic man. *Diabetes 30*: 435, 1981.
219. J. Stagner, et al. Sustained oscillations of insulin, glucagon and somatostatin from the isolated canine pancreas during exposure to a constant glucose concentration. *J. Clin. Invest. 65*: 939, 1980.
220. A. Murdoch, et al. Determination of the frequency of pulsatile luteinizing hormone secretion by time series analysis. *Clin. Endocrinol. 22*: 341, 1985.
221. D. Koerker, et al. Synchronous sustained oscillation of C-peptide and insulin in the plasma of fasting monkeys. *Endocrinology 102*: 1649, 1978.
222. Y. Honda, et al. Growth hormone secretion during sleep in normal subjects. *J. Clin. Endocrinol. Metab. 29*: 20, 1969.
223. A. Frantz. Rhythms in prolactin secretion. In Endocrine Rhythms. D. Krieger, Ed. Raven Press, New York, 1979.

224. M. Warwock. Epidemiology of nocturnal asthma. *Am. J. Med. 85* (*Supl. 1B*): 6, 1988.
225. K. Vener, et al. Chronobiologic properties of the alimentary canal affecting xenobiotic absorption. *Ann. Rev. Chronopharmacol. 4*: 257, 1988.
226. J. Moore, et al. Circadian rhythm of gastric acid secretion in man. *Nature 226*: 5252 and 1261, 1969.
227. M. Smolensky. Human chronopathology in biological rhythms and medicine. A. Reinberg, Ed. Springer-Verlag, New York, 1983, p. 113.
228. D. Colantonio, et al. *Amer. J. Cardiol. 64*: 403, 1989.
229. J. Marler, et al. *Stroke 20*: 473, 1989.
230. H. Dewar, et al. *Br. Heart J. 49*: 133, 1983.
231. H. Brown, et al. The diurnal variations of blood leucocytes in normal and adrenalectomized mice. *Endocrinology 58*: 365, 1956.
232. T. Abo, et al. Studies of surface immunoglobulins on human B lymphocytes. *Clin. Exp. Immunol. 33*: 441, 1978.
233. T. Abo, et al. Studies on the bioperiodicity of the immune response. *J. Immunol. 126*: 1360, 1981.
234. E. Haus, et al. Chronobiology in hematology and immunology. *Am. J. Anat. 168*: 467, 1983.
235. F. Levi, et al. Circadian and seasonal rhythms in murine bone marrow colony forming cells affect tolerance for the anticancer agent 4-0 tetrahydropyranyladriamycin. *Exp. Hematol. 16*: 696, 1988.
236. F. Levi, et al. Seasonal modulation of the circadian time structure of circulating T and NK lymphocyte subsets from healthy subjects. *J. Clin. Invest. 81*: 407, 1988.
237. G. Magnus, et al. Circadian toxicology of cyclosporin. *Toxicol. Appl. Pharmacol. 77*: 181, 1985.
238. F. Levi, et al. Chronoimmunomodulation circadian circaseptan and circannual aspects of immunopotentiation or suppression with lentinan. In Toward Chronopharmacology. R. Takahashi, Ed. Pergamon Press, Oxford, UK, 1982, p. 289.
239. Reinberg, et al. Timing corticotherapy to biological rhythms to optimize treatment goals. *J. Asthma 25*: 219, 1988.
240. W. Ritschel. Chronopharmacokinetics. *Pharm. Int.* (*May*): 116, 1984.
241. L. Lesko, et al. Temporal variation in trough serum theophyline concentrations at steady state. *J. Pharm. Sci. 69*: 358, 1980.
242. Y. Bae, et al. A new thermosensitive hydrogel. *Makromol Chem. Rapid Commun. 9*: 1988.
243. Y. Bae, et al. Thermosensitive polymers as on-off switches for drug release. *Makromol Chem. Rapid Commun. 8*: 481, 1987.
244. E. Schmitt, et al. Side chain crystallizable polymer based drug delivery phenomenon. *Proc. Intern. Symp. Control. Rev. Bioact. Mater. 18*: 134, 1991.
245. A. Kydonieus, et al. Temperature activated controlled release. *Proc. Intern. Symp. Control. Rel. Bioact. Mater. 18*: 417, 1991.
246. D. Hsieh, et al. Magnetic modulation of release of macromolecules from polymers. *Proc. Natl. Acad. Sci. 78*: 1863, 1981.
247. E. Edelman, et al. In vitro and in vivo kinetics of regulated drug release from polymer matrices by oscillating magnetic field. *J. Biomed. Mater. Res. 21*: 339, 1989.

248. J. Kost, et al. Magnetically controlled release systems. *J. Biomed. Mater. Res. 19*: 935, 1985.
249. E. Edelman, et al. Regulation of drug release from polymer matrices by oscillating magnetic field. *J. Biomed. Mater. Res. 19*: 67, 1985.
250. J. Kost, et al. Ultrasonically controlled polymeric drug delivery. *Makromol. Chem. Macrom. Symp. 19*: 275, 1988.
251. S. Miyazaki, et al. Controlled drug release by ultrasound irradiation. *Chem. Pharm. Bull. 33*: 428, 1985.
252. S. Miyazaki, et al. External control of drug release. *J. Pharm. Pharmac. 40*: 716, 1988.
253. D. Ash, et al. Photodynamic therapy. *Br. J. Cancer 60*: 151, 1989.
254. J. Spikes, et al. Photodynamic therapy of tumours and other diseases using porphyrins. *Laser Med. Sci. 2*: 3, 1987.
255. K. Kopecek, et al. Targetable N-Z-hydroxypropylmethacrylamide copolymerchlorin conjugates. *Proc. SPIE 1203*: 144, 1990.
256. T. Bagniefski, et al. A comparison of pulsed and continuous current iontophoresis. *J. Controlled Rel. 11*: 113, 1990.
257. J. DeNuzzio, et al. Electrochemical and iontophoretic studies of human skin. *J. Controlled Rel. 11*: 105, 1990.
258. G. Lattin, et al. Electronic control of iontophoretic drug delivery. *Ann. N.Y. Acad. Sci. 618*: 450, 1991.
259. B. Meyer, et al. Electrically facilitated transdermal administration of a polypeptide: serum leuprolide concentrations in normal human volunteers. *Skin Pharmac. 2*: 120, 1989.
260. M. Ashburn, et al. Iontophoresis delivery of morphine for postoperative analgesia. *J. Pain Sympton. Manag. 7*: 27, 1992.
261. M. Ashburn, et al. The iontophoresis of fentanyl citrate in man. *Anesth. Analg. 78* (Suppl.): S12, 1994.

7

Computer-Aided Drug Design

Terry R. Stouch

Bristol-Myers Squibb Pharmaceutical Research Institute
Princeton, New Jersey

I. INTRODUCTION

This chapter defines computer-aided drug design (CADD), its role in drug discovery, and the personnel and computer resources that it requires. Some mention is made of its role in development as well as in biotechnology. The techniques and science that constitute this field will be only briefly discussed; a more thorough description is left to the references. The references cited here have been chosen to reflect the generality of this volume. Specific references to more detailed, technical literature can be found within these references.

Of course, computers are used in all data and instrument related areas of science and chemistry. In this chapter, however, we will not attempt to discuss and critique such wide-spread methods as statistics, curve fitting, and data management, but rather will discuss those areas of computational chemistry and biophysics that are specialties unto themselves and that are now routinely applied by research scientists primarily to the drug discovery phase of pharmaceutical R & D. These methods help medicinal chemists, biochemists, and molecular biologists to understand the atomic-level events involved in drug action and provide guidance in the design of new drugs. The methods are often broadly labeled as structure-activity relationships, molecular modeling, or rational drug design.

II. WHAT IS CADD?

Computer-aided drug design is difficult to define because, in actuality it encompasses many different fields with the commonality that the experiments and science are done on the computer, not in the laboratory, and the tools are not spectrometers and test tubes but chemical, physical, and biological theory as implemented by computer software. These fields include computer graphics, 3-dimensional models of molecules (molecular modeling), protein structure prediction and analysis, molecular motion (molecular dynamics simulation), molecular shape (conformational analysis), molecular property prediction, quantitative structure/property relationships (QSPR), structure-activity relationships (SAR; applied statistics, pattern recognition, and neural networks), database search, quantum chemistry (for predicting structure, properties, and reactivity), computer-assisted synthesis, protein/drug "docking," as well as others. Although many of these fields are related and overlap substantially, their size, scope, and intensity dictate that they embody several distinct specialties. For example, typically an expert in protein structure prediction is not also an expert in quantum chemistry. Also, the field of *force field* development (for molecular modeling) is so intense that typically an expert in this field will not be expert also in SAR studies.

Computer-aided drug design becomes a field unto itself partly through the application of these varied computational chemistry techniques to pharmaceutical discovery problems. However, since each method has the potential to provide a piece of the puzzle that provides the route to a new pharmaceutical, equally important to the definition of this field is the coordination of these diverse areas of expertise to maximize the synergy among them as well as between them and experimental methods. The CADD specialist must know what methods to apply, the reliability of the answers, and how those answers fit into the overall drug discovery process. Overall, the expectation is one of decreased time and effort spent in drug discovery.

An appreciation of the depth and breadth of the field and its cross-disciplinary nature can be obtained from several recent overviews and reviews [1–8].

III. WHAT INFORMATION DOES CADD PROVIDE?

Some of these techniques are used to predict the atomic-level structure and conformation (3-dimensional arrangement of atoms) of molecules both small (less than several hundred atoms) or large (thousands to hundreds-of-thousands of atoms as in biological molecules, such as proteins). Others are used to calculate a wide range of properties of these molecules, including reactivity, size, and solubility. Once obtained, structure-activity or structure-property relationship approaches find relationships between these structures and properties and either biological activities of the molecules or yet other properties. Rational drug-design is based on knowledge of the structure and mechanism of key regulatory proteins. The methods of protein secondary and tertiary structure prediction as well as molecular modeling and simulation assist in obtaining this information. Once protein structure is known, molecular "docking" and potential-energy function analysis help to evaluate the interaction and action of drug candidates and aid in planning further compound synthesis. *De novo* design helps to discover drug candidates from a consideration of only the protein structure. The overall goal in this work is to provide information to the discovery program that will accelerate the determination of the atomic structure of a new therapeutic agent.

IV. CADD TECHNIQUES

In a real sense, much of CADD can be considered to be an outgrowth and extension of the thought processes used by medicinal chemists, who in fact developed many of the approaches. The earliest applications of CADD assisted medicinal chemists in understanding those physical and structural features of molecules that contributed to their biological activity. By understanding these structure-activity relationships [SAR or Q(uantitative) SAR], the chemist can more directly target the most fruitful directions for synthesis. This information generally comes from examining a series of molecules whose biological activities are known and whose structures and properties are known or can be calculated. Such evaluation is always done by medicinal chemists during decisions about the progress of their synthesis. Computational methods assist this process by providing quantification and enhanced accuracy of the molecular properties and structures and by utilizing methods to derive quantitative relationships between the features and the biological activities. Originally, this latter stage was done through least squares or regression analysis. Later, other statistical methods, pattern recognition, neural networks, and genetic algorithms, or other methods of multivariate analysis (MVA) were applied. The result is an equation relating the properties of a series of molecules to their biological activities. The biological activity of a new compound can be predicted by inserting its properties into the equation. A number of introductory references are available [4–6].

In addition to the structural properties mentioned below, properties that can be calculated include geometrical quantities such as molecular volume, shape, and surface area. Electronic properties include electrostatic field, electron density, polarizability, and molar refraction. Bulk properties include boiling point, solubility in a range of solvents, and similarly, partition constants. Programs and algorithms are available for their calculation from a wide range of academic, government, and commercial sources [7].

The 3-dimensional shape of a hormone or drug is essential to its interaction with the binding site of the proteins that regulate physiology. Molecular mechanics techniques can, in many cases, rapidly provide very accurate representations of the three dimensional structures and shapes of molecules [9,10]. Molecular mechanics model building, driven by highly engineered "force fields" (potential energy functions), can often provide structures as accurate as experiment, but within fractions of a second [11,12]. The development of these force fields often require considerable time and expertise. When they are not available for the molecules in question, quantum mechanics can often provide structures within experimental error with substantially increased computation times (perhaps tens to hundreds of thousands of times more time) [13].

Most molecules are flexible and can obtain many (often many millions, even for small molecules) different conformations (3-dimensional arrangement of atoms in space). The determination of the *bioactive* conformation, that one which actually causes the biological effect, is often a principal pursuit of a drug discovery program [14,15]. Conformational analysis can be extremely demanding computationally. Once obtained, the structure of a bioactive conformer is often linked to the QSAR methods mentioned above.

Once the structures and conformations of molecules are known, they can be overlapped, compared, and visualized in ways only possible using computers and computer graphics (often called molecular graphics). A number of programs are widely available that perform these tasks. Differences in shape can often be related to differences in how molecules bind to regulatory proteins such as enzymes and receptors. Often such analysis is augmented by consideration of molecules' electric fields or other properties. In this way, a 3-dimensional hypothesis of the binding requirements of a particular protein can be developed. When joined with multivariate analysis, a 3-dimensional QSAR equation can be derived from the molecular models of a series of molecules and their known biological activities, similar to the relationships, mentioned above, derived for molecular properties [5].

The methods discussed above deal solely with the drug molecules, themselves. Recent advances in the methods of protein structure determination have allowed another course of action, structure-based (often called "rational") drug design (SBDD) [16–20]. In this approach, drug discovery is guided by knowledge of the biochemical pathways that one hopes to alter using drugs. Usually, this means understanding, at the atomic level, the *structure* and function of a particular protein, such as an enzyme or else a hormone receptor. The goal is to alter the protein's function, either by making it work better, or usually by inhibiting its function. Enzymes catalyze a transformation of substrate molecules; hormones attach themselves to receptors that signal their presence. Both types of proteins have binding sites for the hormones or substrates. Through SBDD techniques, drugs are designed through direct investigation of the protein and binding site in an effort to determine the optimal structural, electrostatic, and hydrogen-bonding interactions that will make for a good fit. For example, in order to replicate, the AIDS virus requires the proper functioning of the enzyme, HIV-protease, which cleaves a particular viral protein, its substrate. Much effort in anti-AIDS drug development has targeted this protein with the goal to develop molecules that fit into the binding site and prevent the enzyme from binding and cleaving its substrate [21].

Structure-based drug development relies heavily on the experimental fields of protein x-ray crystallography and protein nuclear magnetic resonance (NMR) to provide the atomic-level structures of the proteins. However, computational methods play important roles in the derivation of the structure from the raw data. Some are unique to the processing of the crystallographic or NMR data. However, molecular graphics, molecular mechanics, and molecular dynamics methods are heavily used to refine the solution to provide the final experimental model.

Unfortunately, often an experimentally determined structure of the desired protein is not available. The experimental approaches can be involved and often time consuming, sometimes requiring months or even years to determine a structure. Further, even with great effort, some proteins are intractable. The computational methods of protein homology model building, secondary structure prediction, and *de novo* 3-dimensional protein structure prediction are often used to provide approximate models [22–24].

Once the involved task of structure determination is completed, a protein can be studied using molecular graphics. The computational methods of force-field energy analysis and molecular dynamics simulations can then be used to learn about how the protein works and interacts with its substrate. Molecular "docking" can be used to computationally introduce new compounds into the protein in an effort to understand if they would function as drugs. *De novo* design methods are used to build, from scratch, "tailor-made" molecular models directly into the binding site [25].

Knowledge of protein structure is only the first step in understanding biochemistry, a multifaceted and dynamical series of events. Through molecular dynamics simulation molecular movement can be studied visually in a way unavailable by experiment [26–28].

The design of a molecule that binds well to a protein, although a substantial milestone, is only the first step in designing a drug. Bioavailability, how well a drug travels through the body, is critical for drug efficacy. The solubility of compounds in the body's various compartments and its transport between these compartments are key components of bioavailability. A number of methods that attempt to predict solubility in water, partitioning between aqueous and membrane phases, and movement within phases have been proposed [29]. Toxicity and other negative side effects have also halted the development of many promising candidates. The challenge of toxicity prediction has been the focus of many laboratories. Often, these approaches are identical to the QSAR methods mentioned above, used for the prediction of biological activities. In many cases, side effects are, in fact, just other biological activities. Sometimes, however, a single toxic response is actually due to a number of biochemical or physical mechanisms, all of which must be considered in predicting a response. Because of this, toxicity prediction can be very challenging [30].

Sometimes drug discovery is assisted by studying compounds with similar molecular structures or biological activity. Often, when looking for a place to start—a lead compound—a program might want to examine and evaluate many possibilities to find an optimum combination of activity, side effects, and of course novelty, for patenting purposes. Millions of small drug-sized molecules (less than a few hundreds of atoms) are known. Most pharmaceutical companies have hundreds-of-thousands of proprietary molecules. Additionally, the rapidly emerging field of combinatorial chemistry is already yielding thousands of new compounds in previously unthinkably short times [31–33]. Within these structures is a wealth of information and a company's proprietary molecules provide potentially unique and hence valuable information with which to compete in a very competitive world. Yet gleaning this data from the millions of known compounds is a daunting task. Storage, search, and retrieval of molecular information presents unique challenges to the development of computerized databases, which is a field unto itself [34,35].

Recent advances in molecular biology and protein and nucleic acid sequencing provide other database and "data-mining" challenges. These techniques now provide vast amounts of data on genomic structure and protein sequences and, it is hoped, will eventually provide the entire human genome. Included in this data will be the sequences of new, currently unknown, protein targets, such as key regulatory enzymes and receptors. A number of new companies have been formed for the purpose of extracting such sequences and a number of large companies have either purchased this information, have entered alliances with the smaller companies, or are developing their own effort. Coordinating this mass of information and providing rapid and convenient access to it requires the development of new software tools and easier use and access of old ones. Even more challenging is the task of shifting through the data to find the most promising pharmaceutical targets since identification and especially biochemical characterization of all of the protein targets in the near future will be impossible. This emerging field of *Bioinformatics* is making use of established approaches as well as extending these approaches to assist in the tasks of nucleic acid and protein sequence database development and search, protein identification, and protein structure prediction [36,37].

Although CADD is most often thought of as playing a role in drug discovery, the techniques of computational chemistry have also made inroads into other stages of pharmaceutical development. These include the use of structure-activity relationship methods for the prediction of toxicity of intermediates in chemical plants and the use of computer-aided synthesis in development efforts [38]. Although the fields lie beyond this review, computational methods are now routinely used in designing and optimizing chemical plants. Even apart from discovery efforts, molecular databases play an important role in information systems for archiving the large amount of data regarding the structures and biological activities of molecules that accumulates in a pharmaceutical company.

V. WHERE DOES CADD FIT WITHIN A DRUG DISCOVERY PROGRAM?

Computational methods do not replace experiment and will not do so. Rather, they can form a valuable partnership with experiment by providing estimates when experiments are difficult, expensive, or impossible and by coordinating the data that experiment provides. The intensity of the specialties that comprise CADD means that the computational specialist will not always be intimately versed in the chemistry and biology of the program at hand. The reverse is also true; it is unlikely that someone in the laboratory will have the same command of the computational approaches as the specialist. A close coupling between the computational specialists and experimentalists allows information to flow immediately and directly between the two. This helps the CADD specialist better understand the details of the problem and so refine his/her approach. It also provides valuable information to the experimentalist that helps to guide further experimental planning and potentially make this process more efficient. The synergy provided by this relationship means that it is difficult to imagine out-sourcing being as productive as in-house effort.

VI. IS CADD NECESSARY AND WORTH THE INVESTMENT?

Hopefully, by now it is clear that the questions that CADD hopes to answer are integral to a drug discovery program. As such, their answers are important to the thought processes of the experimentalists involved in the project. Especially when dealing with protein structures, computational approaches such as molecular graphics, molecular modeling, and protein/ligand docking are absolutely required. It is difficult to place a dollar figure on the time and effort that properly implemented CADD will save a company. It is not a direct route to new drugs, but rather provides a somewhat more detailed map to the goal. The hope is that by providing bits and pieces of information and by helping to coordinate that information, CADD will help to shave days and dollars off drug discovery projects. Conservative estimates are that overall, these techniques can save ten percent of a project's overall effort, more in some cases, less in others. Computer-aided drug design is often likened to analytical instrumentation. By themselves they do not discover new drugs, however the information that they provide is invaluable to the process. Boyd lists examples of the direct application of computational approaches to drug design [7]. Successes, especially in structure-based approaches, appear regularly in the literature and only a few are referenced here [21,39–45]. As mentioned below, CADD approaches can become only more powerful in the future with a consequential greater return on the investment.

VII. REQUIREMENTS

A. Personnel

How many people are required for a CADD effort and what should be their background? This depends largely on the company, its size, its efforts, and the problems that must be solved. Most large drug companies have groups of 8 to

20 computational specialists, chemists or biochemists that spend their time with computational methods and little to no time in the laboratory. Few reasonably sized companies have less than 3–5 specialists per site. Often this breaks down to 1 computational specialist per 15–20 medicinal chemists (not including the also requisite number of biologists and biochemists). Most of these are heavily utilized. Some advocate use of computational chemistry by nonspecialists. Computational chemistry software is readily available and much of it is easy for a beginner to at least start to use. However, the techniques are involved enough that should a novice want much depth or accuracy, he/she will have to spend a substantial amount of time learning the science and the methods. Many experimentalists have become excellent CADD practitioners. However, this is at the expense of their laboratory work and the time and effort spent in learning new fields.

Ideally, two factors determine the size of a group: the number of projects (related to number of chemists and biochemists) and the expertise required by the projects. It is not unreasonable to suggest that as a rough estimate a company could use one computational specialist per major focus; although because the expertise required by a project will change with time, a single individual might not necessarily be committed to solely to one project.

A critical mass of specialists is also important. Different skills are required at different times and the core disciplines of SAR, protein structure, molecular modeling, and quantum chemistry should be present. Many different computer programs are used in CADD and it is not unreasonable that one individual will be an expert in only a few of these. Further, the volume of software makes systems and software administration and maintenance time consuming and involved for a small group. Many departments have dedicated systems support groups. Further, as mentioned above, a unique problem often requires unique software and programming specialists can streamline an effort. The computational specialist in a one- or two-person group faces a substantial challenge. However, a small, highly focused company might not require all areas of expertise or a large amount of software. For example, a biotech company concerned with only a few related protein or peptide products will require someone skilled in protein structure/chemistry and perhaps molecular simulations but not necessarily an expert in chemical databases or quantum chemistry. The software required will scale similarly.

B. Software

Chemical software can be a considerable expense not only in its initial purchase but in yearly maintenance and upgrade fees. As mentioned, the many different fields that constitute CADD require different software. A number of protein analysis, quantum chemical, SAR, and modeling packages might be necessary.

With some exceptions, the easiest to use, most integrated (having multiple functions), and most polished software comes from commercial firms that can charge many tens of thousands of US dollars (USD) for individual programs and hundreds of thousands for a package of several related programs. Yearly maintenance and upgrade fees can range over 12–15 percent of that amount. Between the largest chemical software houses, there is much duplication and competition in the basics. However, each has some unique features, and this has prompted many companies to acquire conceptually identical software from several different firms.

Also, since CADD is an evolving field, software is not available for all eventualities. This means that most companies (and perhaps most computational chemists) will expend some effort in software development. Some software firms have attempted to overcome this issue by providing high-level programming command languages usable within their programs that provide access to chemical data and so save development time over writing all software in standard computer programming language, such as C or FORTRAN. Although this does save time, solving problems even with these command languages can require some effort and expertise.

It would be remiss not to mention that much of the chemical software available today, even the commercial software, was developed at academic institutions and very active development efforts continue there. Many market their software and almost always academic software costs are less than the commercial costs. A consequence is that this software is usually not as polished or "user-friendly" as commercial packages and support is not always guaranteed.

In summary, there is no single program or program suite for computational chemistry, although most of the vendors have the development of such a suite as their goal. Software must be chosen to fulfill a company's particular needs. Usually this software comes at considerable initial and yearly cost.

C. Hardware

It is a justifiable statement that CADL has become a routinely viable tool only with the advent of the current generation of scientific graphics workstations and recent generations of software. This being said, workstations have become a requirement and in a great many cases individual computational specialists have their own workstations. Recently introduced entry-level workstations can now be obtained for well under 50,000 USD. These are usually supported by larger multiprocessor or supercomputer compute-servers. Many of the principal approximations (and much research and effort) in computational chemistry and computational biophysics are due to lack of computer power. Recognizing this, many of the major pharmaceutical research centers have invested in fast supercomputers as compute engines in addition to a network of workstations for graphical visualization. At the time of this writing, Merck, Bristol–Myers Squibb, Pfizer, Dupont, Eli Lilly, and Hoechst, all have Cray supercomputers. Many others have substantial multiprocessor work stations.

The cost of hardware varies with need. A biotech firm that requires only protein homology building of a limited number of proteins and employs a single protein structure specialist could probably make due with one of the workstations mentioned above and so incur initial hardware costs of 100,000 USD (not including yearly maintenance fees). However a company with many diverse projects and 10 or more computational specialists will require considerably more and can incur computer hardware purchases of 5–10 million USD and many hundreds of thousands in yearly maintenance agreements.

VIII. PRESENT AND FUTURE

CADD has already made an impact and is integrated into successful research programs in many companies. However, although the successes of CADD have been significant, they at times seem modest. This is understandable since CADD (and most of its constituent fields) is a young pursuit. Much of it is still in development and retains an aura of basic research. Powerful computers, the engines of these methods, have only recently been routinely available. Also, in some respects the development of CADD has paralleled the development of the techniques of macromolecular structure determination (protein NMR and crystallography), which have also only recently become routinely and widely used. Chemical software, the other principal tool of CADD can do no more than track the progress of its underlying science. Also, mostly because of limited computer power, computational solutions always carry with them a certain level of approximation.

Luckily, however, diminution of these shortcomings is occurring rapidly and CADD techniques can become only more powerful and accessible. Computer hardware is becoming faster and cheaper. This will alleviate the need for many of the risky approximations that are currently employed. Also, the last few years have seen some impressive strides in the power and ease of use of CADD software. Software developers are continually working to develop better integrated and more user-friendly programs. Perhaps most important, the sciences that underlies CADD are intense areas of research that are constantly advancing and becoming better understood and more refined. Improved force fields will provide more accurate estimates of the interactions between proteins and drug molecules. The often ignored role of solvation and ionic strength in molecular conformation and biological interactions are being incorporated into calculations. New quantum chemical methods are under development that will provide more rapid determination of structure and properties. Understanding of protein structure and function is an intense field with daily advances.

IX. SUMMARY

CADD approaches aim to increase the speed and efficiency of the atomic-level design of new biologically active molecules by providing quantitative information about the structure and properties of molecules, intermolecular interactions, and relationships between properties and biological activity. It is a mixture of specialties that requires an substantial investment in personnel and specialized computer software and hardware. In many ways it is still an experimental and developing field, however, it already has had successes and enjoys routine use. In the future, due to improvements in CADD technology and software, as well as computer hardware, it stands to become an even more powerful tool and to play an even greater role in drug discovery.

X. ADDITIONAL SOURCES OF INFORMATION

Computational studies are routinely published in a wide number of journals and no one serves as a central repository. The *Journal of Medicinal Chemistry*, the *Journal of the American Chemical Society*, the *Journal of Computational Chemistry*, the *Journal of Computer-Aided Molecular Design*, the *Journal of Molecular Biology*, the *Journal of Chemical Information and Computer Science*, and *Computers and Chemistry* all have been repositories of drug-design studies and methodology. *Current Opinion in Structural Biology* has provided several reviews in computational methods and structure-based drug design [17–19]. Recently the computational chemistry literature has been reviewed [46]. Several books or series are available that deal with computational chemistry as a whole, drug design, or some aspect of computational chemistry [47–49].

There are about 7–10 software houses that deal largely or wholely in chemistry software (including Biosym/MSI, Inc., San Diego; Chemical Design, Oxon, UK; Daylight, Irvine, CA; Molecular Applications Group, Palo Alto, CA; Oxford Molecular, Oxford, UK; Tripos, Inc., St. Louis). This number has become dramatically smaller following numerous consolidations within the past few years. Many academic groups also market their software, usually at a lower price. The Quantum Chemistry Program Exchange has been a valuable repository of software that has been freely contributed by individuals and distributed for a nominal price [50]. Several publications provide listings of software and their availability [8,18,49,50,51].

A. Chemical Databases

There are a number of databases related to chemistry and computational chemistry available, both commercial and academic. The two most important and most widely used are the Cambridge Crystallographic Database (CSD), a compendium of the x-ray crystal structures of small molecules and the Brookhaven Protein Database (PDB) of protein structures from x-ray crystallography (primarily), NMR, and modeling.

REFERENCES

1. Medicinal Chemistry for the 21st Century. C. G. Wermuth, Ed. International Union of Pure and Applied Chemistry, Blackwell Scientific Publications, 1992.
2. Computer-aided Drug Design: Methods and Applications. T. J. Perun and C. L. Propst, Eds. Marcel Dekker, New York, 1989.
3. Perspectives in Drug Discovery and Design: Computational Methods in Drug Discovery, Vol. 1, Number 2. F. E. Cohen, W. Moos, Eds. ESCOM Science Publishers, Leiden, The Netherlands, 1993.
4. Y. C. Martin. Computer-Assisted Rational Drug Design. *Methods in Enzymology 203*: 587–613, 1991.
5. 3D QSAR in Drug Design: Theory, Methods, and Applications. H. Kubinyi, Ed. ESCOM Science Publishers, Leiden, The Netherlands, 1993.
6. Advanced Computer-Assisted Techniques in Drug Discovery. Volume 3 of Methods and Principles in Medicinal Chemistry. H. Van de Waterbeemd, Ed. VCH, Weinheim, Germany, 1994.
7. D. B. Boyd. Successes of Computer-Assisted Molecular Design. In Reviews in Computational Chemistry, Vol. 1. K. B. Lipkowitz and D. B. Boyd, Eds. BCH Publishers, New York, 1990, p. 355–372.
8. N. C. Cohen, J. M. Blaney, C. Humblet, P. Gund, and D. C. Berry. Molecular Modeling Software and Methods for Medicinal Chemistry. *Journal of Medicinal Chemistry 33*: 883–894, 1990.
9. D. B. Boyd. Aspects of Molecular Modeling. In Reviews in Computational Chemistry, Vol. 1. K. B. Lipkowitz and D. B. Boyd, Eds. VCH Publishers, New York, 1990, p. 321–354.
10. D. B. Boyd and K. B. Lipkowitz. Molecular Mechanics—The Method and Its Underlying Philosophy. *J. Chem. Ed. 59*: 269–274, 1982.
11. J. P. Bowen and N. L. Allinger. Molecular Mechanics: The Art and Science of Parameterization. In Reviews in Computational Chemistry, Vol. 2. K. B. Lipkowitz and D. B. Boyd, Eds. VCH Publishers, New York, 1990, p. 81–98.
12. U. Dinur and A. T. Hagler. New Approaches to Empirical Force Fields. In Reviews in Computational Chemistry, Vol. 2. K. B. Lipkowski and D. B. Boyd, Eds. VCH Publishers, New York, 1990, p. 99–164.
13. M. C. Zerner. Semiempirical Molecular Orbital Methods. In Reviews in Computational Chemistry, Vol. 2. K. B. Lipkowitz and D. B. Boyd, Eds. VCH Publishers, New York, 1990, p. 313–366.
14. M. Saunders, K. N. Houk, Y. Wu, W. C. Still, M. Lipton, G. Chang, and W. C. Guida. Conformations of Cycloheptadecane. A Comparison of Methods for Conformational Searching. *J. Am. Chem. Soc. 112*: 1419–1427, 1990.
15. A. R. Leach. A Survey of Methods for Searching the Conformational Space of Small and Medium-Sized Molecules. In Reviews in Computational Chemistry,

Vol. 2. K. B. Lipkowitz and D. B. Boyd, Eds. VCH Publishers, New York, 1990, p. 1–56.

16. C. E. Bugg, W. M. Carson, and J. A. Montgomery. Drugs by Design. *Scientific American 269*: 92, December 1993.
17. S. E. Ealick and S. R. Armstrong. Pharmacologically relevant proteins. *Current Opinion in Structural Biology 3*: 861–867, 1993.
18. W. C. Guida. Software for structure-based drug design. *Current Opinion in Structural Biology 4*: 777–781, 1994.
19. P. M. Colman. Structure-based drug design. *Current Opinion in Structural Biology 4*: 868–874, 1994.
20. C. L. M. J. Verlinde and Wim G. J. Hol. Structure-based drug design: progress, results and challenges. *Structure 2*: 577–587, 1994.
21. Dorsey, et al. L-735,524: The Design of a Potent and Orally Bioavailable HIV Protease Inhibitor. *J. Medicinal Chemistry 37*: Number 21, pp. 3443–3451, 1994.
22. J. Bajorath, R. Stenkamp, and A. Aruffo. Knowledge-based model building of proteins: Concepts and examples. *Protein Science 2*: 1798–1810, 1993.
23. M. Johnson, N. Srinivasan, R. Sowdhamini, and T. Blundell. Knowledge-Based Protein Modeling. *Critical Reviews in Biochemistry and Molecular Biology 29*: 1–68, 1994.
24. S. R. Krystek, Jr., W. J. Metzler, and J. Novotny. In Current Protocols in Protein Science. J. E. Coligan, B. M. Dunn, H. L. Ploegh, D. W. Speicher, and P. T. Wingfield, Eds. Protein Secondary Structure Prediction. John Wiley & Sons, New York, 1995, p. 2.2.1–2.2.11.
25. D. C. Roe and I. D. Kuntz. BUILDER Vol. 2: Improving the chemistry of a de novo design strategy. *J. Computer-Aided Molecular Design 9*: 269–282, 1995. Contains a brief review and comparison of methods.
26. J. R. Collins, S. K. Burt, and J. W. Erickson. Flap opening in HIV-1 protease simulated by "activated" molecular dynamics. *Structural Biology 2*: 334–338, 1995.
27. J. A. McCammon and S. C. Harvey. Dynamics of Proteins and Nucleic Acids. Cambridge University Press, New York, 1989.
28. D. Bassolino, H. E. Alper, and T. R. Stouch. Mechanism of Solute Diffusion through Lipid Bilayer Membranes by Molecular Dynamics Simulation. *J. Am. Chem. Soc. 117*: 4118–4129, 1995.
29. W. J. Dunn III, M. G. Koehler, and S. Grigoras. The Role of Solvent-Accessible Surface Area in Determining Partition Coefficients. *J. Med. Chem. 30*: 1121–1126, 1987.
30. T. R. Stouch and P. C. Jurs. Computer-Assisted Studies of Molecular Structure and Genotoxic Activity Using Pattern Recognition Techniques. *Environmental Health Perspectives 61*: 329–343, 1985.
31. E. J. Martin, J. M. Blaney, M. A. Siani, D. C. Spellmeyer, A. K. Wong, and W. H. Moos. Measuring Diversity: Experimental Design of Combinatorial Libraries for Drug Discovery. *J. Medicinal Chemistry 38*: 1431–1436, 1995.
32. Molecular Similarity in Drug Design. P. M. Dean, Ed. Chapman and Hall, London, 1994.
33. J. Singh, et al. Validation of Screening Immobilized Peptide Libraries for Discovery of Protease Substrates. *J. Medicinal Chemistry 38*: 217–219, 1995.

34. Y. C. Martin. 3D Database Searching in Drug Design. *J. Medicinal Chem. 35*: 2145–2154, 1992.
35. Y. C. Martin, M. G. Bures, and P. Willet. Searching Databases of Three-Dimensional Structures. In Reviews in Computational Chemistry, Vol. 1. K. B. Lipkowski and D. B. Boyd, Eds. VCH Publishers, New York, 1990, p. 214–264.
36. G. Casari, et al. Challenging times for bioinformatics. *Nature 376*: 647–648, 1995.
37. Firm to push computer-drug design links. *Chemical and Engineering News*, May 16, 1994.
38. W. L. Jorgensen, E. R. Laird, A. J. Gushurst, J. M. Fleischer, S. A. Gothe, H. E. Helson, G. D. Paderes, and S. Sinclair. *Pure Appl. Chem. 62*: 1921–1932, 1990.
39. Kim, K.-H., et al. *J. Am. Chem. Soc. 117*: 1181, 1995.
40. Shoichet, et al. Structure-Based Discovery of Inhibitors of Thymidylate Synthase. *Science 259*: 1445–1450, 1993.
41. M. von Itzstein, et al. Rational design of potent sialidase-based inhibitors of influenza virus replication. *Nature 363*: 418–423, 1993.
42. F. Cohen, et al. *Proc. Natl. Acad. Sci. USA 90*: 3583, 1993.
43. D. G. Alberg and Stuart L. Schreiber. Structure-Based Design of a Cyclophilin-Calcineurin Bridging Ligand. *Science 262*: 248–250, 1993.
44. P. R. Ortiz and J. J. De Voss. *J. Am. Chem. Soc. 117*: 4185, 1995.
45. S. Wang, et al. The Discovery of Novel, Structurally Diverse Protein Kinase C Agonists through Computer 3D-Database Pharmacophore Search. Molecular Modeling Studies. *J. Medicinal Chemistry 37*: 4479–4489, 1994.
46. D. B. Boyd. The Computational Chemistry Literature. In Reviews in Computational Chemistry, Vol. 2. K. B. Lipkowitz and D. B. Boyd, Eds. VCH Publishers, New York, 1990, p. 461–477.
47. K. B. Lipkowitz and D. B. Boyd, Eds. Reviews in Computational Chemistry, Vol. 1–6, VCH Publishers, New York, 1990. Future volumes are also planned.
48. D. M. Hirst. A Computational Approach to Chemistry. Boston, Blackwell Scientific Publications, 1990.
49. M. M. Ambos, B. R. Gelin, and A. B. Richon. The Computational Chemistry Yellow Pages. St. Louis, Custom Research and Consulting and Molecular Solutions, Inc., 1992. (Molecular Solutions, Inc., P.O. Box 32101, St. Louis, MO 63132).
50. Quantum Chemistry Program Exchange, Creative Arts Building 181 Indiana University Bloomington, IN 47405 USA Telephone: (812)855-4784 FAX: (812)855- 5539.
51. D. B. Boyd. Appendix: Compendium of Software for Molecular Modeling. In Reviews in Computational Chemistry, Vol. 1. K. B. Lipkowitz and D. B. Boyd, Eds. VCH Publishers, New York, 1990, p. 383–392.
52. D. B. Boyd. Appendix: Compendium of Software for Molecular Modeling. In Reviews in Computational Chemistry, Vol. 2. K. B. Lipkowitz and D. B. Boyd, Eds. VCH Publishers, New York, 1990, p. 481–498.
53. I. D. Kuntz. Structure-Based Strategies for Drug Design and Discovery. *Science 257*: 1078–1082, 1992.
54. T. R. Stouch. Structure-Activity Relationships Using Multivariate Analysis Techniques: Application to Topical Corticosteroids. In Topical Corticosteroids. H. I. Maibach and C. Surber, Eds. Karger, Basel, 1992, p. 93–127.

8

New Approaches to Nonclinical Biodisposition Studies

D. Bruce Campbell

Servier Research and Development Ltd.
Fulmer, Slough, England

I. INTRODUCTION

The pharmaceutical companies throughout the world are undergoing the biggest upheaval in their history. With mergers and buy outs, thousands of jobs have been lost and analysts feel that many small companies without a certain critical mass will either be swallowed up by the bigger fish or just sink to the bottom of the pool and disappear. In contrast, the larger companies have realized that they cannot afford to invest increasingly large amounts on research and not only are they critically appraising staffing levels, but also the questionable need of certain currently undertaken development studies. Costs are continuing to increase—a new drug costs between $200–300 million—but the returns in terms of new drugs are falling as governments everywhere are cutting their health care expenditures. Only a small fraction of drugs synthesized enter development and it has been estimated by analysts at Lehmann Brothers that less than 3% of all drugs that do finally reach the market achieve sales figures of $500 million within 5 years, the figures necessary to make the total investment worthwhile.

It has been previously considered that many drugs fail before they reach the clinical stage, and indeed, an earlier analysis of UK companies [1] suggested that more than 33% failed due to problems of kinetics, particularly absorption. More recent analysis [2] of North American companies has indicated that overall 68% of drugs fail during clinical trials, particularly those for CNS diseases, whilst drugs with clear efficacy endpoints, such as anti-infectives, are more likely to succeed.

There is therefore an increasing realization that preclinical studies must be reevaluated in terms of absolute needs and, with this in mind, recent draft guidelines were prepared for discussion at the Third International Conference on Harmonization (ICH3) in Japan in November 1995. These have reexamined the timings and minimal animal studies necessary to go rapidly into man for the first time without loss of safety. Unfortunately these guidelines do not address the need for preclinical biodisposition studies. There is thus no harmonized advice on this topic [3] despite the fact that such information is a cornerstone of drug development. New toxicokinetic guidelines [4] have provided a basis for taking a fresh look at which preclinical studies are absolutely necessary and seeing if we can incorporate new approaches to this discipline.

Table 1 New Approaches to Preclinical Biodisposition

Study	Methods	Information
QSAR and physicochemistry	Regression analysis Neural networks Expert systems Database libraries Data mining	Prediction of kinetics and metabolism Candidate choice
In vitro metabolism	Microsomes, cells, slices Expressed enzymes	Rates, routes, and profiles Specific cytochrome involvement Polymorphism, drug interaction, induction, inhibition
Scaling	*In vitro* *In vivo* (allometry)	Whole body clearance Clearance, volume, half-life
Pharmacology	PK/PD	Validation of animal model Effect extrapolation to human
	Tissue levels, microdialysis, PET, NMR	Validation of plasma/dynamic models
Toxicokinetics	PK/PD	Calculation of safety margins, first dose in man
	Population kinetics	Minimal sampling with fewer animals
Preclinical kinetics	Limited kinetics and metabolism Limited ADME and distribution	Basic IV and PO kinetics in few animals Balance and simple metabolic profiling Radioactive exposure calculation for man

This chapter investigates the changing face of preclinical biodisposition studies; the use of predictive artificial intelligence and expert systems; *in vitro* techniques; imaging to "see" inside the tissues; and how new statistical procedures, such as population kinetics, can make these investigations more cost effective (Table 1).

II. DISCOVERY

Although rational drug design for the discovery of new chemicals is still much used, it is being superseded by high throughput screening using combinatorial chemistry, where the emphasis is on producing increasing numbers of molecules closely related to the initial lead compound, but being altered progressively by addition reaction chemistry along well-defined structure activity relationships. This has allowed companies to not only synthesize whole libraries of new compounds (> 10,000) in a few weeks, but also to test them for up to 20 different activities at the same time. This enormous number of potential new molecules must be reduced to a handful of candidate drugs that can be taken into the costly development scheme. In the past, some basic pharmacology in a few animals together with limited acute toxicity was normally sufficient, but today there is an increasing reliance on kinetics and metabolic data to predict both efficacy and safety in man, providing additional information to make such a choice. But how can useful ADME information on the likely kinetics and metabolism in man be obtained at such an early stage and for potentially so many compounds?

A. Expert Systems

The amount of information that is now being generated in medical and pharmaceutical research is enormous. Keeping abreast of these data and trying to put them into some meaningful framework is becoming increasingly difficult. The complexities and interrelation of the physiological systems are too great for our minds to comprehend and we continue to myopically concentrate on one small area of interest without necessarily seeing how everything fits together. With the rapid advances in drug metabolism and kinetics the same problems are arising and we must turn to the new developing science of artificial intelligence and expert systems to progress more efficiently [5].

1. Quantitative Structure Pharmacokinetic Relationships (QSPR)

For many years, it has been possible to relate the measurements of the physicochemical properties of a compound within a particular series with its potential activity using Hansch-type relationships [6]. Since passive diffusion and nonspecific binding to macromolecules throughout the body are related to the same physicochemical measures, it follows that a comparable form of analysis could be equally applied to biodisposition [7,8]. Certainly for simple kinetic parameters, such as the volume of distribution, which is directly related to lipid solubility, QSPR can be successfully used as a predictor, even for those compounds that are not congeners within the same series [9]. However, these methods have rarely been used for other parameters such as clearance. These processes are dependent on active enzymatic reactions that are more related to the 3-dimensional structure of the molecule. However, in any one homologous series that is being screened, differences in metabolism may be dependent on relatively simple structural differences. Thus, for the glucuronidation of phenols, alcohols and benzoic acids, optimal rates of metabolism by UDP-glucuronyltransferase occur with compounds with a log P of 2.0 [10]—an optimal value found for many distribution and binding processes in the body [11]. Similarly, using principal-component analysis, Holmes et al. [12] were able to predict the extent of sulphate and glucuronide conjugation of a series of substituted phenols.

Recently certain computer software has become available to investigate these types of relationships using new algorithms. One such programme is TSAR (Tools for Structure Activity Relationships) from Oxford Molecular [13]. Using a structural-related molecular spreadsheet, it can not only calculate specific properties where necessary (charge properties; dipole moments, lipophilicity, Verloop indices; topological descriptors; Kier analysis, flexibility indices, and shape recognition, etc.), but also relate them to any measure, be it pharmacology, toxicology, or, for this discussion, kinetic and metabolic rates and pathways. Using a training set of data from a certain molecular series, univariate and multivariate analysis, such as principal-component analysis, discriminate analysis, hierarchical classification clusters, and neural networks [14] (see later), it is possible to predict the major endpoints of biodisposition for new compounds based on information from a few key structures. Others have used similar approaches in conjunction with fuzzy logic to obtain kinetic parameters from QSAR with some success [15].

A similar approach has been suggested [16] for the prediction of toxicity caused by the reactions catalyzed by the P450 cytochromes using a Computer-Optimized Molecular Parametric Analysis of Chemical Toxicity (COMPACT). Similarly, it is envisaged that with the increasing research on the structural interactions of drugs with cloned and amino acid sequenced cytochromes and other metabolic enzymes [17], QSAR will in the future be used to rapidly screen the thousands of drugs produced by combinatorial chemistry and predict which enzyme will metabolize which drug.

2. *Data-Based Expert Systems*

The approaches outlined above should be able to provide a guesstimate of certain kinetic parameters, providing that, in any one series, some data are already available for a few compounds. However, the prediction of which metabolic pathway is involved and what products will be formed will continue to be a problem. To overcome this, several expert systems and interrelational databases have been developed. Early systems, such as Xeno [18], have been reported but failed to be of general usefulness. Similar difficulties have been encountered for Metabol Expert [19] and Meta 2 [20], which give many possible metabolic pathways but provide little assurance as to whether the metabolites suggested actually can be expected when compared to real data [21]. These systems fail since they are dependent on the actual information in the

Xenobiotic Metabolism form version 1.0

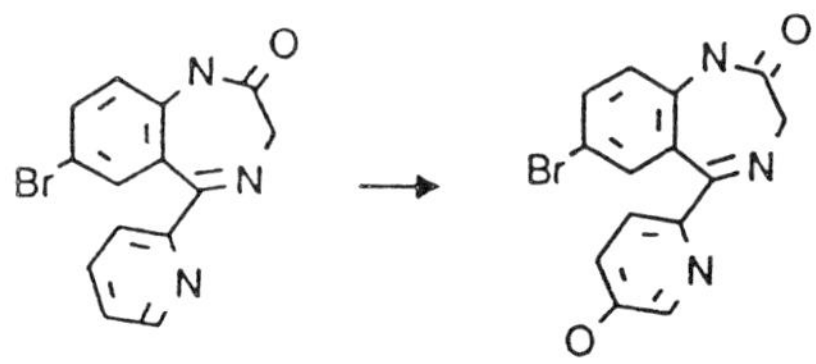

Regno: 152	Extreg: 20	Path: 20-F	Step: 1 Step	MDLNumber: RXME00000137

Ref	Species	Route	Excretion	Conjugates	Yield
1	Dog		Urine	Unspecified conjugate	
	Guinea Pig		Urine		
	Rat	oral	Urine	Unspecified conjugate	
	Rabbit	oral,	Urine	Unspecified conjugate	

Ref	Metabolic Step Literature References	Analytical Data
1	H Sawada, A Hara, J Pharm Soc Jpn, 9, p. 430, 1975	TLC, Ion Ex Chrom, IR, MS, NMR, Col Chrom, UV, Vis Spec

Fig. 1 Example of information obtained using "Metabolite," a data based search system from MDL. (From Ref. 22.)

database and have no learning possibility, which can be found in systems with baysian feedback or neural networks. Another approach recently adopted by Molecular Design Laboratories, MDL [22], called "Metabolite," is to search for metabolic routes found in the literature, capitalizing on their structure recognition system, used extensively in the chemical design of drugs. This relational database enables the scientist to search for metabolites by name, structure or functional group of interest, and provides information on all related papers, analytical methods, metabolic routes and structures, species differences and routes of elimination (Figure 1). With annual updates, this should be a tool with enormous benefit for the metabolic chemist, not only in the early stages of drug design, but later to search for potential minor metabolic pathways.

III. *IN VITRO* METABOLISM

There is increasing awareness of the potential usefulness of *in vitro* metabolism. In a recent survey [23], it was shown that more than 80% of UK companies are now undertaking such investigations at some time during drug development (Figure 2). Although most are undertaking *in vitro* metabolic studies prior to clinical trials, relatively few (17%) are using this approach to aid candidate drug selection. This situation will probably change since the information that can be acquired is valuable for choosing candidate drugs before taking them into full development, providing information on 1) the extent, rate and routes of metabolism; 2) the comparative metabolic profiles to choose the large species (dog or primate) to be used in long-term toxicity; 3) the isolation, production and identification of major metabolites for analysis and synthesis; 4) the clearance predictions to estimate the degree of first-pass metabolism and whole-body clearance (see scaling); and 5) identification of which enzyme is involved to predict potential clinical problems of polymorphism, drug interaction, inhibition, etc.

Several methods are currently being used: (a) microsomes, which have the advantage of ease of production, storage, and availability but do not have the ability to metabolize drugs by Phase II conjugation reactions or various oxidation reactions catalyzed by monoamine oxidase (MAO), flavin monooxygenase (FMO), etc.; (b) hepatocytes, which possess all metabolic capabilities but are difficult to produce and cannot be stored for more than 24–48 hours; (c) hepatic slices, which are good as metabolite "factories" but have similar draw-

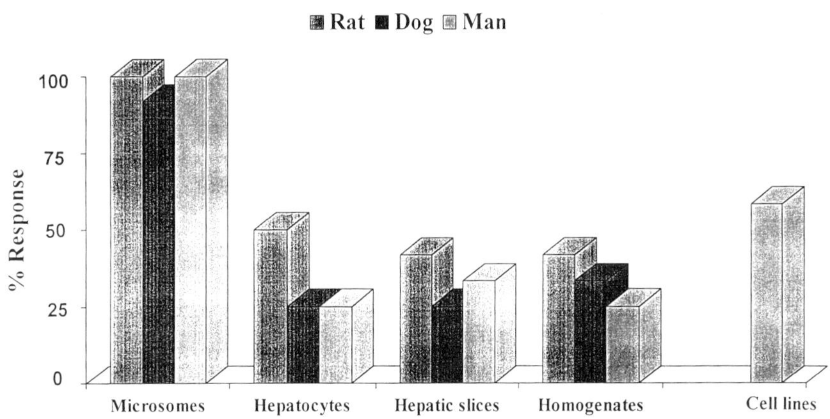

Fig. 2 The comparative use of *in vitro* metabolic methods used by UK pharmaceutical companies (n = 18) in different species. (From Ref. 23.)

backs to hepatocytes and are poor for rate measurements; (d) whole isolated organs, which are good for metab-olite production and physiological scaling but human tissues cannot be used; and (e) heterologous expressed enzyme systems using yeast, bacteria, or mammalian cell lines, which provide an idea of the specific enzyme involvement but not the total interrelationship of a whole tissue activity. One of the more important aspects of *in vitro* metabolism is the potential for the early prediction of human "kinetic difficulties."

IV. METABOLIC ISOFORMS AND KINETIC VARIABILITY

There are myriad factors that control the drug levels in individual patients [24], including environment, patient compliance, and genetic differences. Although we do not know the specific contribution of each, increasingly we are finding that genetic variation is a major contributor to the clinical variability in steady-state drug levels. Thus, in addition to providing early information on the rates, routes, and metabolic profiles and kinetic scaling, *in vitro* metabolic studies may give an insight into future kinetic problems that may occur by providing information on which specific enzymes the drug is metabolized and whether this enzyme is under polymorphic control. Genetic polymorphism occurs when the gene of an individual contains different codons that express a particular isozyme compared to the normal wild form. This can occur for a number of isozymes, including the cytochromes 2D6, 2C9, but also the nonmicrosomal enzymes, N-acetyl transferase, Glutathione-S-transferase, choline esterase, and others [25]. This detection of multiple "hidden" alleles in a number of enzymes provides an understanding of why there can be a large variability of metabolic rates, not just at the extremes, but within the normal distribution curve. It also shows that simple classifications into fast or slow metabolizers is a gross over-simplification of the real situation.

Thus for CYP 2D6, at least 19 different allele forms exist, producing extremes from ultrafast to very slow metabolizers and many variants in between [26]. A survey of UK companies [23] indicates that most have started to routinely screen their drugs for polymorphism using a variety of techniques (Fig. 3). These include *in vitro* methods such as (a) inhibition by a specific enzyme inhibitor; (b) metabolism by an isolated heterologous expressed enzyme; and (c) cross correlation of a genotyped bank of human microsomes and *in vivo* methods (a) kinetic measurements in geno- or phenotyped individuals using single or cocktails of compounds after single or repeated dose population screening, (b) polymodality of metabolic ratios, or (c) multiple interaction studies.

Up until recently, it was thought that animal *in vitro* metabolic studies could provide useful information, not only on the types of metabolic pathways, but also on the specific isozymes responsible for the metabolism in humans. Al-

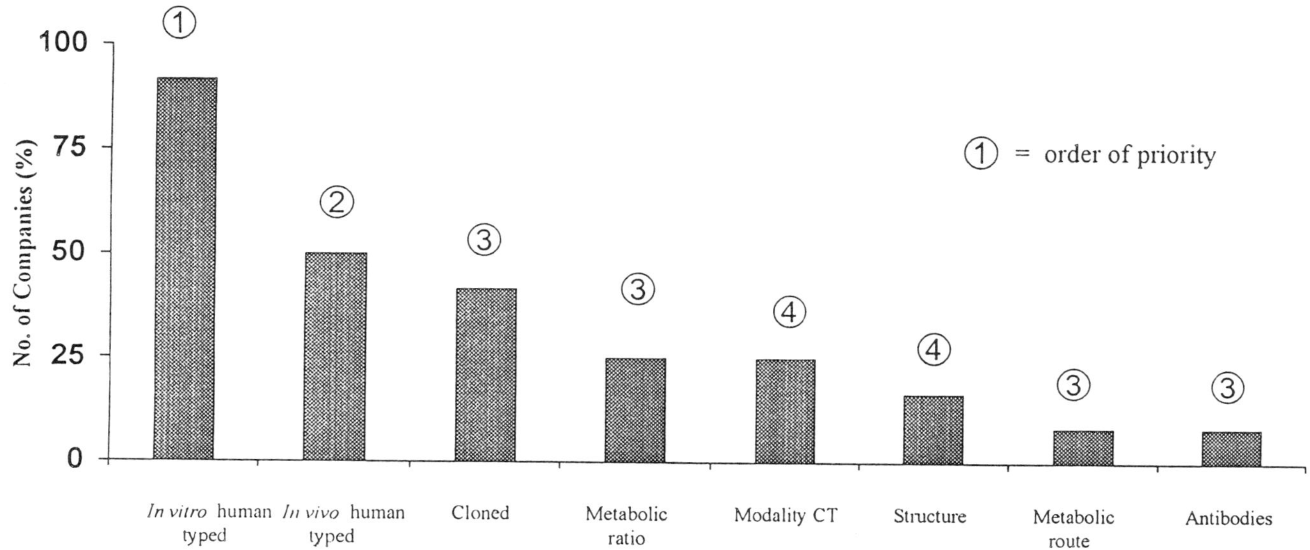

Fig. 3 Comparison of methods used by UK companies to measure polymorphism and the chronological order (①) in which they would be undertaken (from Ref. 23).

though this is partly true for the highly conserved enzymes such as CYP 1A or CYP 2E1, it is not the case for many others.

The major CYP enzyme in the rat is CYP 2C, whilst in the human it is CYP 3A4. In the rat, CYP 3A2 and CYP 2C show sexual dimorphism, but not in man. The enzyme CYP 2C11 exists as 50% of all hepatic P450 in the male rat, whilst CYP 2C12 is the major enzyme in the female [27]. Similarly, CYP 2D6 is not present in the mouse or rat, and in general, rodents are poor models for polymorphism [28]. Thus, researchers are becoming increasingly aware that human tissues or cell lines must be used for identification of metabolic enzyme involvement during early drug development. Human microsomes are readily available and can be stored for several months, but hepatic slices and hepatocytes have limited viability and must be used within 48 hours. Until recently, this has severely restricted their use, but now with the availability of cadaver livers direct from hospitals or from nonprofit commercial organizations [29], this problem has been largely overcome. Whether this situation will continue, as transplant services become more efficient, is questionable.

In addition to predicting the possibility of intersubject differences in kinetics due to the variability in the expression of enzyme, these early *in vitro* methods will identify the possibility of drug–drug interactions since certain isoforms have been shown to be inhibited (CYP 2D6) or induced by drugs (CYP 2E1 and alcohol) or environmental factors (CYP 1A1 and smoking).

Although more than 65% of UK pharmaceutical companies are starting to undertake these studies [23], there is some concern as to the importance that certain academics and regulatory authorities are placing on these results. All those replying to this survey said that if a drug was shown to be metabolized by an enzyme under polymorphic control, they would still continue with its development because there are many other factors that must be taken into account before rejecting such a drug. Reasons given for continuing the development include a wide therapeutic margin, alternate, more important, pathways, novel activity and clinical need, relationship between therapeutic plasma levels, and enzyme affinity constant. Fluoxetine and other specific serotonin reuptake inhibitors (SSRI), which are all metabolized by CYP 2D6, are but one example of a class of drugs that could have been discarded if *in vitro* metabolism had been used for screening. Also, hepatic metabolism is only one of many elimination routes and it is known that the GI tract has large amounts of CYP 3A4 [30]. For example, cyclosporin is extensively metabolized in the gastrointestinal mucosa before reaching the liver [31]. The brain also has appreciable levels of CYP 2D6 and may contribute to the activity of CNS drugs such as the antidepressants, dextromethorphan and codeine [32].

Alternative routes of elimination can become important in poor metabolizers, as has been shown for flecainide, which is extensively eliminated in the kidney thereby reducing potential side effects [33]. Similarly, alternative metabolic pathways can occur if there is a low metabolism by a particular genetically controlled pathway. An example of this is the metabolism of paroxetine by CYP 2D6, and although there are some differences in the steady-state levels between ultrafast and poor metabolizers, an alternative parallel metabolic route protects the poor metaboliser (PM) against dramatic increases in drug levels and adverse reactions [34]. Metabolic pathways (e.g., N-dealkylation) may be catalyzed by multiple enzymes, the extent depending on the relative amounts of enzymes present, making identification of specific mechanisms difficult. Thus, the gross differences in clearance, which could be expected in poor metabolizers for certain drugs, are often not found. In reality, the largest variability in enzyme levels in the liver occurs for CYP 3A4, which is not under genetic polymorphic control and, with the highest levels in the liver, can produce large variations in steady-state levels in clinical trials [35]. Thus, there is concern in the pharmaceutical industry that the regulatory authorities, sometimes with their own laboratories undertaking limited investigations, will view polymorphism as a box-checking exercise and beneficial drugs will be delayed or denied authorization because they are metabolized by a polymorphic enzyme [23].

There is another problem. What will the prescribing clinician do with this information? The knowledge that certain co-administered drugs are metabolized by the same enzyme and may produce adverse reactions is important information for the doctor, and *in vitro* metabolic studies will focus attention towards these potential problems. However, the possibility of altering the dosage in poor or ultrafast metabolizers or certain ethnic groups, e.g., is practically difficult: How would this information be generally available? There have been suggestions that all patients should be genotyped if they are to be prescribed certain drugs [36]. Although this may be possible within the hospital, in general practice it would not be feasible. There are also the implications of civil liberty. If this information is available to doctors or pharmacists, for example on "smart" identity cards, it would also become available to life insurance companies. They may decide to decline insurance coverage for a subject who is an ultra-fast metaboliser (UFM) to CYP 2D6 since this also increases the risk of liver cancer [37] or a PM to N-acetyltransferase, which increases the risk of bladder cancer [38] or a PM to CYP 2D6 and has a family history of Parkinson's disease [39]. The ramifications of these actions must be thought about carefully and it seems illogical to embark on detailed additional studies with already over stretched resources if the results are difficult to interpret or put into effect, and the methods of effecting change have not been properly considered.

V. SCALING

There is increasing awareness that a knowledge of animal kinetics and metabolism is of little value unless it can be extrapolated to humans. This is important for choosing the right candidate drug with the ideal kinetic profile for the medical application to be treated prior to full development and for choosing the first and subsequent doses in man. Two methods are being investigated with increasing success using both *in vitro* and *in vivo* approaches.

A. *In Vitro* Scaling

For almost 20 years, the possibility of predicting *in vivo* clearance from *in vitro* incubations has been discussed [40]. The more recent advances in *in vitro* metabolic methodology, together with the ability to identify and measure metabolites using HPLC linked with quadrapole MS–MS without the need to synthesize radioactive compounds, has dramatically improved the measurement of the rates of metabolism at an early stage in drug development. Recently, Houston [41] reviewed the available methods and, using published data, attempted to evaluate the accuracy of these predictions. There are 3 stages in the extrapolation from in vitro metabolism to whole body clearance (Figure 4).

The first stage is to calculate the total *in vitro* metabolic rate, either by measurement of drug disappearance—taking into account other potential losses: volatilization, binding to apparatus, instability, etc.—and/or by measurement of metabolic formation. This latter method, although preferable, is also more difficult since it must quantify all pathways. From rate curves, the maximum rate (V_m) and the Michaelis–Menten constant (K_m) for drug-metabolizing enzyme binding are calculated according to Equation 1:

$$\text{Rate of Metabolism} = CL_{int} \bullet C_e = \frac{V_m \bullet C_e}{K_m} \tag{1}$$

at low drug levels (<10% of C_e), and where CL_{int} is the intrinsic clearance (a measure of the metabolizing capacity of the organ, independent of other factors such as absorption or protein binding), and C_e is the concentration of drug at the enzyme site. In practice, the intrinsic clearance is measured in terms of the total amount of enzyme protein present and this will depend on whether the incubations are using microsomes, hepatocytes, hepatic slices, etc. Thus the second stage is scaling up from these to the whole liver by using certain factors that are dependent on the initial protein. These values are subsequently incorporated in Equation 2, which relates intrinsic and hepatic clearance (CL_H).

$$CL_H = \frac{Q_H \bullet f_u \bullet CL_{int}}{Q_H + f_u \bullet CL_{int}} \tag{2}$$

which uses the unbound free fraction in plasma (f_u) and hepatic blood flow (Q_H) of the animal being investigated. Lastly, other routes of clearance, such as renal elimination, must be included wherever possible, although this may

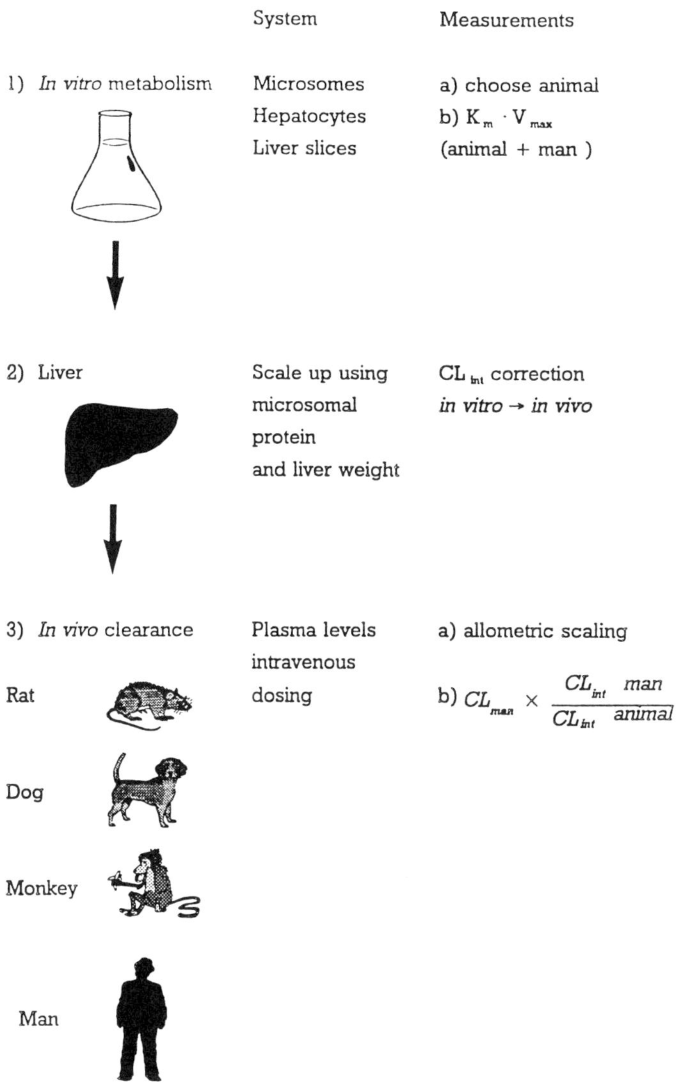

Fig. 4 Stages in the scaling up from *in vitro* to *in vivo* clearances.

be difficult to quantify if extra hepatic metabolism occurs in, for example, the gut wall or kidney.

$$CL = CL_H + CL_{GI} + CL_K + CL_{other} \tag{3}$$

Despite the difficulties of the methodology using this procedure and the many assumptions made with the calculation of both the *in vitro* and *in vivo* clearances, Houston [41] found in the published data on rats that the predictions were reasonably good. Using the incubations with microsomes, there was an overall mean overestimation of approximately 90% (median 40%), but ranged from –75 to 634% (Figure 5). Where comparative incubation methods were used in the same study, it would appear that hepatocytes gave similar predictive values to those of the microsomes, but hepatic slices gave consistently lower clearances. This is thought to be due to the inability of the drug to penetrate into the comparatively thick slices and be metabolized by all the metabolic protein present. The review by Houston [41] used data from rats, but extrapolations can similarly be made using human tissue [42,43]. However we in our lab have confirmed the findings of Houston that, for reasons not fully understood, the *in vivo* clearance of certain drugs may be poorly predicted, particularly those with a low clearance.

B. *In Vivo* Scaling

It is now generally well known that small animals will clear a drug or chemical faster than humans and, for this reason, the comparison of dosages to extrapolate pharmacological or toxicological studies [44] is often of little value. This is not surprising since small animals have relatively faster blood flow and larger organs than man when expressed as a percentage of body weight, and consequently clearance is more rapid and circulating levels of the administered compound are lower than could be expected in pharmacological and toxicological studies [45].

However since most mammals share similar physiological and biochemical actions, these differences in physiological rates and sizes for most processes in the mammalian body have been shown to be proportional to the body weight of the animal [46] and can be related by *allometry*, a word from the Greek meaning the measurement (*metry*) of changing size (*allo*). It has been shown that blood flow, organ size, metabolic and respiratory rate, and many other physiological and anatomical variables are related by the general allometric equation [47]:

$$Y = aW^b \tag{6}$$

where Y is the function to be measured, W the body weight of the animal, a the coefficient, and b the exponent. For mammals, whilst a is different for each

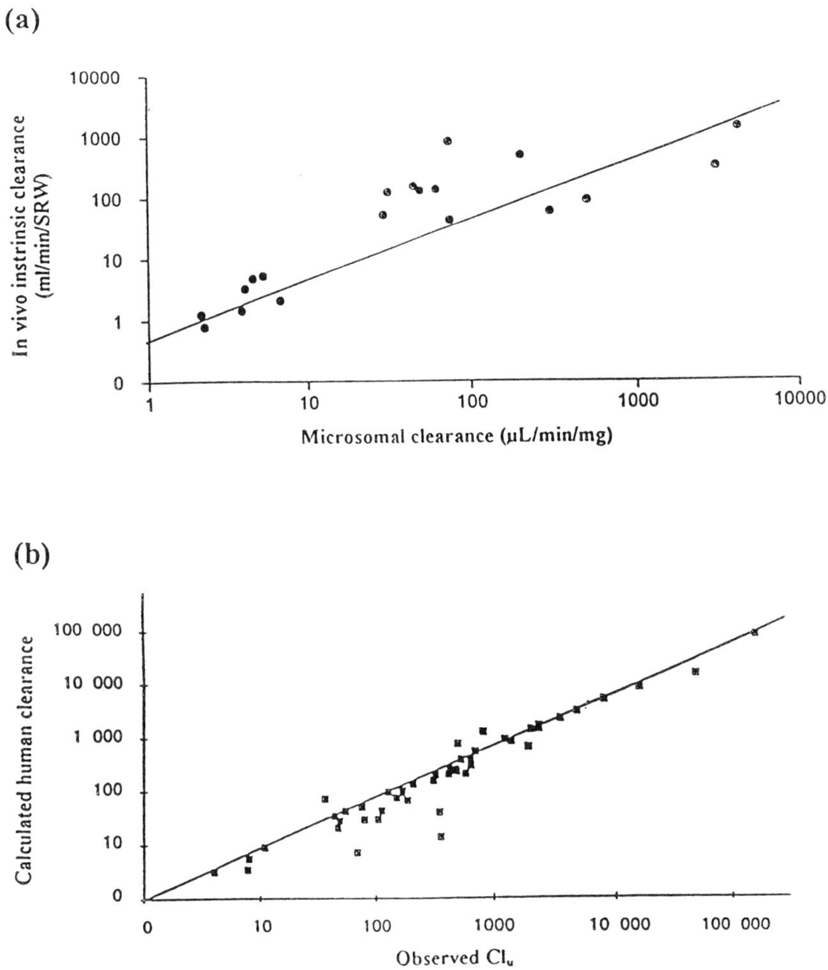

Fig. 5 Relationship between *in vivo* clearance in (a) rats compared with *in vitro* hepatic microsomal clearance with a line representing a 500 mg microsomal protein standard rat-scaling factor (from Ref. 41), (b) humans compared with that predicted from rat *in vivo* clearance using a maximum life potential (MLP) allometric scaling with the line of identity (from Ref. 48).

function and units used, b is approximately 0.6–0.8 for rates, flows, and clearances, 1.0 for volumes and organ sizes, and 0.25 for cycles and times. Thus metabolic rate can be calculated from $7.0 \cdot W^{0.75}$, liver blood flow from $37 \cdot W^{0.85}$, blood weight from $0.055 \cdot W^{0.99}$, and respiratory rate from $0.019 \cdot W^{0.26}$. Since the blood flows and the weights of the liver and kidney, the two major organs of elimination, can be similarly allometrically scaled, it follows that the same formula could, in principle, be used for extrapolation of the clearance of chemicals between species. This method works well for drugs that are poorly metabolized and those that are extensively renally cleared since renal clearance is primarily dependent on renal blood flow, which is allometrically scaled.

Indeed, it has been shown from a survey of the published literature on more than 20 drugs that the exponent b was 0.69 for clearance, 0.89 for volume, and 0.24 for half-life [48]. However, there was a large range of values ranging from 0.92–0.28 for clearance and, because of this unpredictability for certain compounds, allometric scaling has not gained wide acceptance. For some drugs, particularly those that are extensively metabolized but have a low hepatic clearance, such as phenytoin, antipyrine, or caffeine [49], where simple scaling provides poor prediction for man, an allometric correction using maximum life potential (MLP) has been used to improve the accuracy. Although the allometric approach using body weight alone is valid for many physiological functions, it is poorly predictive of longevity or maximum life potential in man. Using a derived equation based on body weight alone, humans should only live for 26.6 years, clearly an underestimate. In fact, Sacher [50] has shown that a better measure of life span can be calculated using not only body weight but also brain weight (Equation 7), and with this correction the MLP for man becomes 113 years [51].

$$\mathrm{MLP} = 185.4 \cdot BW^{0.636} \cdot W^{-0.225} \tag{7}$$

Simplistically, it has been suggested that these differences in longevity can be explained by the assumption that in any one species there is a predetermined or fixed amount of total "body metabolic potential" and once this is used up, the animal dies [52]. Boxenbaum [53] has extrapolated this concept to include intrinsic hepatic metabolism, suggesting that there is a certain quantity of "hepatic pharmacokinetic stuff" per unit of body weight available in a lifetime that can be related to the MLP by the following formula:

$$CL \cdot \mathrm{MLP} = c \cdot W^{b} \tag{8}$$

where CL is the unbound clearance, and c is a constant for each compound. Thus, the longer the animal lives, the slower this "stuff" is used up. Examination of the data available from 13 disparate compounds, where at least 4 species have been investigated, the MLP correction has produced good results with an exponent b equal to unity [48]. Thus, this would suggest that the relative clearance between species is directly proportional to their body weight (W) and MLP, and that animal ($CL_{(A)}$) and human clearance ($CL_{(H)}$) can be simply related according to Equation 9:

$$CL_{(H)} = CL_{(A)} \cdot [W_{(H)} \cdot \mathrm{MLP}_{(A)}]/[W_{(A)} \cdot \mathrm{MLP}_{(H)}] \tag{9}$$

Adopting this approach, it has been shown [48], using clearance values from published information on 60 different compounds, that generally good predictions, within ± 40%, can be made from rat (Figure 5), rabbit, or monkey clearance values, whereas the mouse data gave overall poor predictions, and dog data gave very poor predictions for a few compounds. In practice, using the information obtained from the intravenous administration to four rats or monkeys for a compound with a human clearance of 300 mL/min, the predicted range of values within 95% confidence limits would tend to fall between 240–360 mL/min. As the volume of distribution is normally directly proportionally to body weight, together with the predicted clearance value, the half-life can be simply calculated and all kinetic parameters necessary to simulate blood levels in man after repeated dosing can be made. Of course, there are exceptions and these are often due to differences in metabolic routes. Thus, this *in vivo* scaling should be undertaken in conjunction with the *in vitro* studies to improve the prediction accuracy by not only choosing the most appropriate species to use in the intravenous kinetics studies but also to compare the two calculated clearance values from each method and so provide better confidence in the data.

It can be envisaged that in the future using some or all of these approaches of QSAR, data bases, *in vitro* and *in vivo* scaling and metabolic routes, it may be possible to incorporate the data into cluster analysis or a neural network system [54] to achieve even better predictions.

VI. ARE ALL PRECLINICAL ADME STUDIES NECESSARY?

Although there is a perceived need to get a drug into man as soon as possible, harmonization of the timings and extent of preclinical studies has been difficult to achieve with no agreement reached on this subject at the recent ICH3 meeting [55], which could have been a useful opportunity to discuss in more detail the needs with regard to preclinical biodisposition. Unfortunately, this opportunity was missed and no more than a simple generalization was made. This omission should be put into the context that, unlike almost all other areas of drug development, no concise guidance is given for preclinical kinetics [2]. Admittedly, toxicokinetic guidelines have been agreed upon and this does provide a framework for the reevaluation of what studies are really necessary. These observations summarize a more detailed critique published elsewhere [56], which examines what preclinical studies are necessary.

The introduction of the measurement of drug levels during pivotal safety studies undertaken to GLP standards means that much of the important and useful animal biodisposition data is now available to design the studies and interpret and extrapolate the data to humans. Indeed, when we examine the other preclinical studies that have been undertaken in the past, we must question their relevance (Table 2). Recently, Warrender [57,58] undertook a survey of more than 80 companies in Japan, Europe and North America asking when and what preclinical ADME were undertaken. The results make for interesting reading. Certain studies such as enterohepatic recirculation (particularly in Europe), milk uptake, biliary cannulation (in Europe and the USA), induction and inhibition studies, pregnancy kinetics in nonrodent teratology species, and kinetics in special animal populations, and multiple dose balance studies (mostly in Japan), are all undertaken after the drug has been given to man for the first time but prior to marketing approval (Figure 6). Clearly these studies can provide little information to help the decision to go into man for the first time. Unless there is a particular need, as suggested by some specific toxicity, the fact that they are often undertaken at the end of drug development suggests that they are only completed as part of the checklist of regulatory requirements and not necessarily for any justifiable scientific necessity. For example, biliary circulation in rodents occurs with drugs with relatively low molecular weights (~ 250 MW) but, in man, rarely occurs for compounds with an MW lower than 500 and direct gastric secretion is probably a more important elimination route. Rarely is this an important issue in clinical pharmacokinetics. Milk transfer studies undertaken in animals cannot be meaningfully extrapolated to human infants because of differences in the frequency in weaning and the fat and protein composition. Approximations of likely infant exposure can be obtained from simple *in vitro* equilibrium dialysis of milk and plasma and a knowledge of the Pka of the compound [2]. Similar considerations hold for the implicit requirement for information on the kinetics in pregnant animals. Unless there

Table 2 What Information Does Toxicokinetics Provide?

1.	Design of safety studies
2.	Interspecies differences in kinetics
3.	Absorption
4.	Linearity (dose, induction, inhibition)
5.	Accumulation
6.	Exposure and safety margins for humans
7.	PK-PD relationships

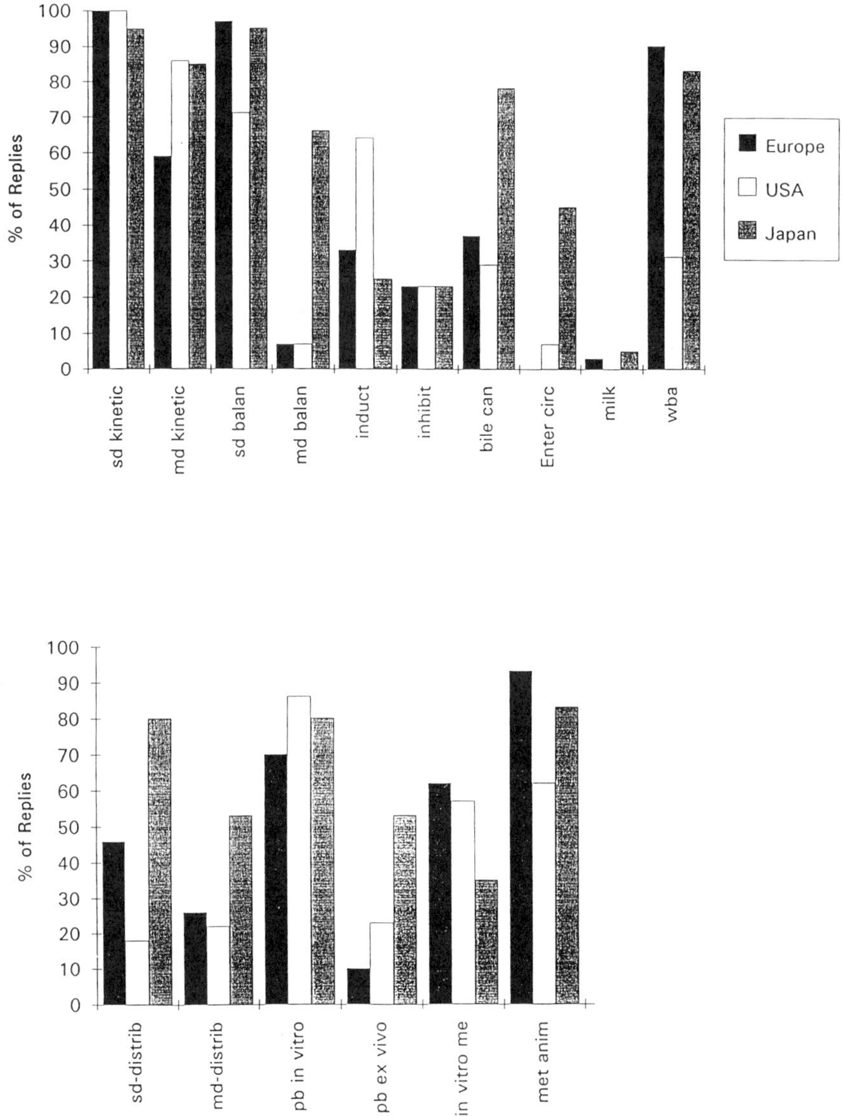

Fig. 6 Survey of the extent of nonclinical kinetics undertaken by companies in Europe, USA, and Japan before Phase I: sd = single dose, md = multiple dose, met = metabolism, balan = radioactive balance studies, induct = induction, inhibit = inhibition, enter circ = enterohepatic recirculation, distrib = distribution, spec anim = special animals, pb = species binding, can = cannulation, wba = whole body autoradiography. (From Ref. 58.)

is a specific problem, toxicokinetic information should be sufficient to allow comparative exposure to be calculated and little additional information in animals is necessary. If the drug were to be used in pregnant females, then considerably more investigations would be necessary, but not in rats. The need for detailed distribution studies has been partially addressed in the ICH2 guidelines [59]. In brief, tissue single-dose distribution in rats measured by whole body autoradiography (WBA) and image analysis and, increasingly, by photoluminescence [60], is mainly used to measure radioactive tissue exposure prior to the administration of a labeled drug to man. Repeat dose distribution, for a long time used in Japan, where radioactive studies in man are not undertaken, have now been restricted to those compounds where there are specific or likely problems of toxicity. However the new guidelines are unclear since they ask for distribution studies if unexpected accumulation in repeat-dose studies is found. Since the only repeat-dose studies necessary are those that will be done during toxicity studies, "unexpected" accumulation is likely to occur frequently when metabolic saturation occurs at the higher doses. Unless this is associated with some unexpected nonpharmacological toxicity, distribution studies would have little relevance since high levels can not simply be

Table 3 Essential Preclinical Biodisposition Studies[a]

Study[b]	Species	Information
In vitro metabolism	Toxicology species, human Expressed enzymes	Rates and routes Metabolite identification Candidate choice Whole-body clearance Cytochrome P450
IV kinetics	Rat, dog[c]	Basic kinetic parameters Allometric scaling
PO kinetics	Rat, (dog)	Absorption characteristics
Protein binding	Toxicological species human	Free-drug levels
Radioactive balance	Rat, (dog)	Elimination routes *In vivo* metabolism
Radioactive tissue distribution (WBA)	Rat	Exposure calculation for use of RA in human Unexplained toxicity

[a]Assuming Toxicokinetics studies undertaken according to ICH Guidelines (1993).
[b]Single doses studies.
[c]May be mice and monkey depending on species used in toxicology and if allometric scaling is used—see text for details.
( ) = May not be necessary if no unexplained problems.

related to toxicity. We should therefore rethink which preclinical studies are required before administering a drug to humans for the first time. These are actually relatively few (Table 3). After a suitable but not all encompassing analytical method is developed, the basic kinetics parameters (clearance, volume, half-life, and extent and speed of absorption) can be measured in a few (~ 4) animals, in rats and dogs (primates for allometric scaling). These measures will provide all that is necessary for the design of initial dose ranging studies and safety studies and to compare allometric scaling predictions with those from *in vitro* metabolism. *In vitro* metabolism studies should be undertaken in animal tissues to choose toxicological species and interpret results, and in humans tissues or cell lines to measure rates and routes of *in vivo* metabolism, identify and produce important metabolites, and predict possible clinical problems and interactions. Protein binding in the different species, in comparison with humans, is also required to express the exposure calculations in terms of free-drug levels, although few reports have systematically shown that this approach is actually necessary. Whether this should be done *ex vivo* with samples actually taken from the safety studies or *in vitro* has similarly not been extensively studied but will, no doubt, be dependent on the sensitivity of the analytical procedure. Animal radioactivity studies *in vivo* should be minimal and used to confirm *in vitro* metabolism by the species closest to man and to undertake single-dose distribution studies for the measurement of radioactive exposure prior to human isotope investigations. In general, it can be argued that little else is required unless some specific problem needs to be answered.

VII. BLOOD LEVELS AND EFFECT

Plasma or tissue levels and the derived pharmacokinetic parameters have little meaning unless they are related in some way to an effect, be it pharmacological or toxicological. For a long time, it has been generally assumed that there existed some direct linear relationship between drug concentrations and activity, such that doubling the one will lead to a corresponding increase in the other. This is rarely the case and even when it is the case, it is for only a small range of concentrations [61]. Indeed, it would appear that blood levels are another surrogate endpoint and too many assumptions are made about their relevance without justification. From Figure 7 and Table 4, it can be seen that measurement of circulating levels is far removed from the interaction at the receptor site.

The drug must dissociate from the binding to blood protein, pass through tissue membranes, and interact with nonspecific binding proteins before acting at its receptor. Despite the obvious importance of preclinical studies, particularly in pharmacology and toxicology, rarely is any attempt made to relate the

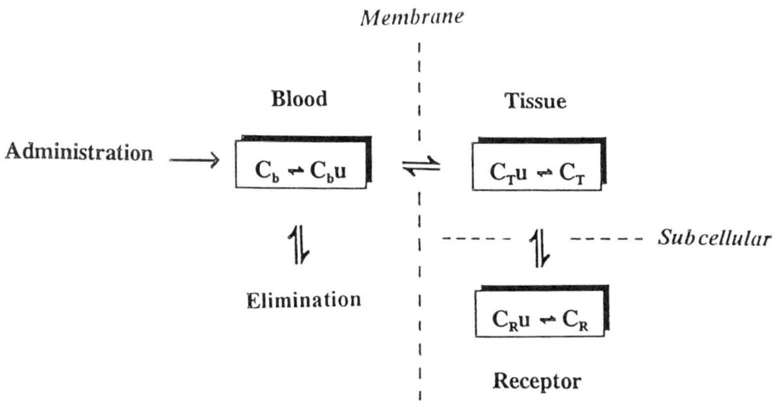

Fig. 7 Tissue uptake distribution and receptor binding of drug, where C is drug concentration, u is unbound, b is blood, T is tissue, and R is receptor.

drug exposure to activity and then, using this measure, extrapolate the results to humans [62]. Certainly in toxicology there are many routine biochemical, histopathological, and behavioural tests that are undertaken that could be related in some meaningful way to the exposure and this would serve as a reference for human studies. This is undertaken more routinely for anticancer agents that have important effects on white blood cell counts, and receptor based

Table 4 Some Assumptions for Plasma Kinetic Dynamic Relationships

Plasma kinetics	Dynamics
Plasma levels proportional to that at receptor	Effect is simply related to plasma concentrations
Receptor binding is reversible and is linear with dose and time	Measured effect or surrogate end point reflects clinical disease
Distribution is uniform and passive	No complex multiple receptor system or feedback control
Uptake is not affected by drug's activity	Little variability in subjects
No metabolism in tissue	Single dose reflects long term repeat administration
No interspecies differences in distribution	No interspecies differences in sensitivity

models [63] are used to calculate more accurately the first dose to man and thus to minimize the number of dose escalations [64].

One must question that if this is not done more frequently for all drugs then how relevant are animal safety studies? Certainly it is now well accepted that dosages cannot be compared from one species to another due to allometric differences in the rates of clearance, but similarly, we must not now simply accept plasma levels.

For example, it is assumed that the uptake into tissues is relatively the same for all species but this has never been systematically studied, presumably because of the difficulty of measuring the levels in humans. Recently, we have investigated the uptake of dexfenfluramine and its active metabolite into the brain of several species, including humans, and found that this is also dependent on the weight of the animal, such that the uptake by small rodents is four to six times higher than that in man (see details later) [48]. This has also been reported for other compounds, such as fluoxetine, and cannot simply be explained by differences in plasma protein binding. But how is it possible to measure the tissue kinetics in humans and can these difficulties by overcome?

A. Receptor-Based Models

Interrelating kinetic–dynamic data using nonlinear sigmoidal E_{max} models are now relatively easy to deal with because of the availability of computer programs. Thus data from animal studies can be rapidly assessed and used to compare from one species, strain, condition, etc. to another. This straightforward approach can be used for the majority of cases, even when multiple receptors are used [61,65], but it does assume that the drug is immediately in equilibrium with the receptor site and that there are few feedback controlling influences. To overcome the problem of hysteresis, when activity is not directly associated temporally with circulating drug levels, Sheiner and co-workers [66] have proposed the use of parametric models and nonparametric models [67] that link an "effect compartment" with a dynamic response. These methods are available using various computer programmes such as SIPHAR [68], PCNONLIN [69], ADAPT [70], TOPFIT [71], etc. With these models, it is possible to combine the changing kinetic profile with the dynamic activity, even if they are not directly in parallel. However, their very simplicity reduces their usefulness in describing the more complex drug effect that can occur.

B. Physiological Systems Modeling

The body is not a series of unrelated receptors and, although the empirical E_{max} models may be a useful starting point in describing drug action, they are gross oversimplifications of the real systems involved. Guyton, many years ago, described the time course of the feedback control following a sudden change in blood pressure. The resulting modifications of the cardiovascular system took seconds and minutes in the case of baroreceptors, hours in the case of vascular changes, and days in the case of renal function. Thus, to more fully understand the complexities of the effect of a medicine, it is also necessary to model these changes in conjunction with the changes in drug levels. The action of warfarin on blood clotting takes at least 24 hours due to the cascade effect on clotting factors. This can be modeled physiologically by building into a receptor-based model additional algorithms for the rate of synthesis and clearance of prothrombin [72]. The effect of cocaine on heart rate needs the additional physiological input of the circadian sinus rhythm of this frequency to adequately describe the resulting action of the drug [73]. Feedback control of a drug's action or tachyphylaxis is a well-known consequence of drug action

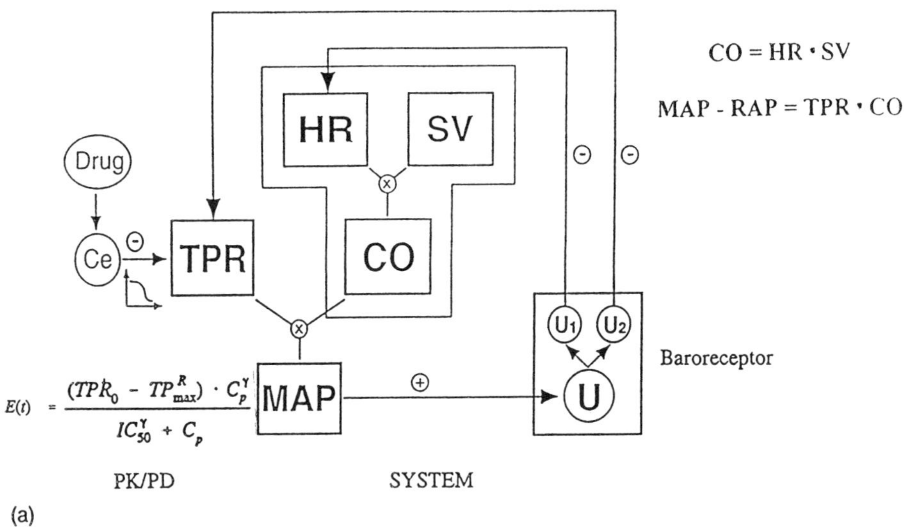

Fig. 8 (a) Physiological systems mathematical model for kinetic–dynamic relationships of the cardiovascular activity of Nicardipine, where TPR = total peripheral resistance, MAP = mean arterial pressure, HR = heart rate, SV = stroke volume, and CO = cardiac output. (b) Predicted (–) and actual (○, ◇, △) values for blood levels (C_p), total peripheral resistance (TPR), cardiac output (CO), and mean blood pressure (map) in human volunteers (n=6) following different infusion rates of Nicardipine using systems physiological model. (From Ref. 74.)

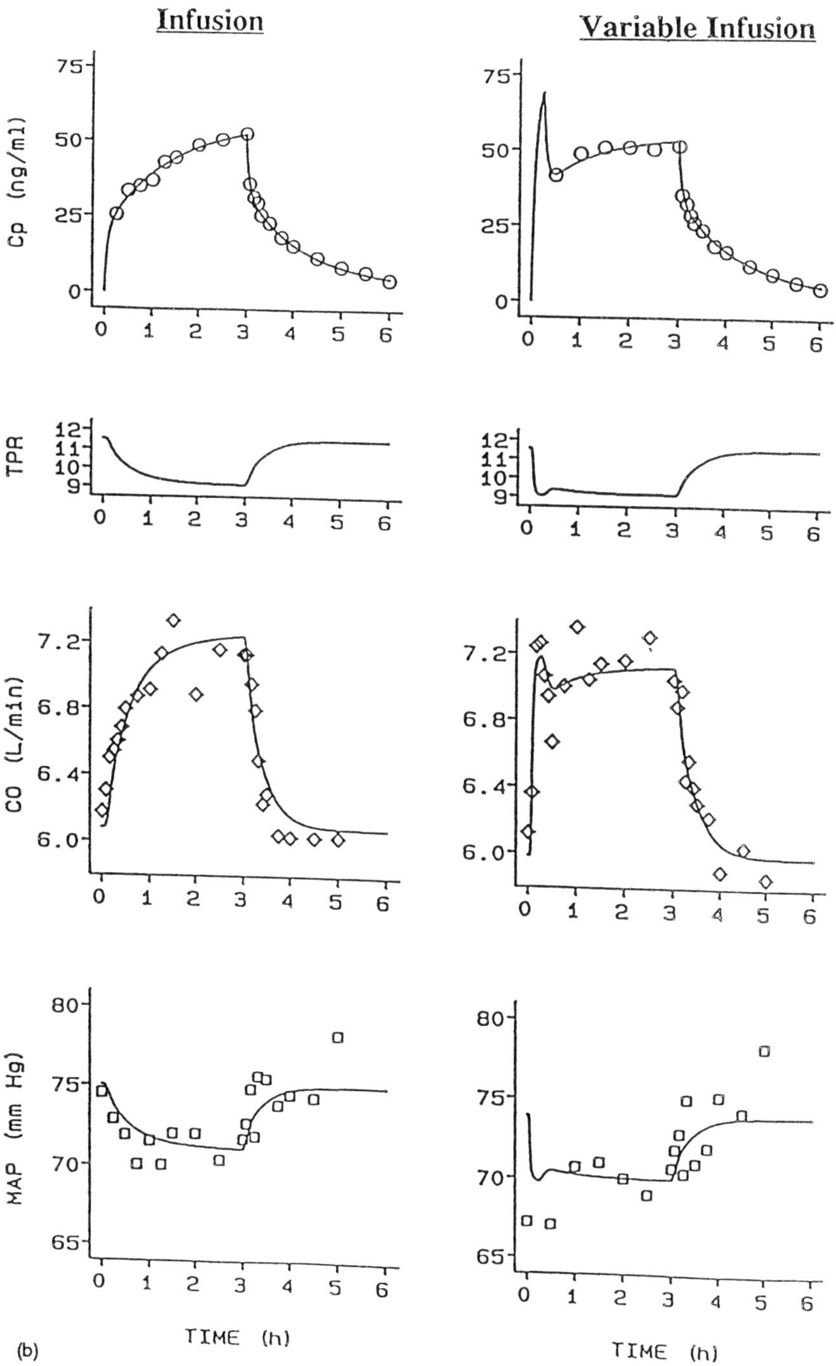

Infusion
Variable Infusion
Cp (ng/ml)
TPR
CO (L/min)
MAP (mm Hg)
TIME (h)
TIME (h)

(b)

but is poorly understood. For many drugs, this down regulation of the system can lead to important reductions in activity and can show marked subject variation depending on the severity of the disease. This effect can be modeled using a more complete systems approach. One such recent example has been the analysis of the effect of nicardipine on blood pressure incorporating total peripheral resistance, baroreceptors, cardiac output, and heart rate [74] (Figures 8a and 8b). Using this approach it was possible to show how individual compensatory mechanisms come into play to regulate blood pressure and to model the drugs action when administered rapidly after an intravenous injection or more slowly after an infusion.

Increasingly, it is becoming apparent that the rate of delivery of a drug can affect the ultimate action and that for both the calcium antagonists [75] and sulphonylureas [76] (Figure 9), rapid injection paradoxically produces shifts to the right of the E_{max} drug-level response curves suggesting rapid down regulation of the system to compensate for the immediate and excessive challenge. Only when these kinetic dynamic models are studied using the systems-based models of total control will we hope to understand the processes involved and the action of drugs.

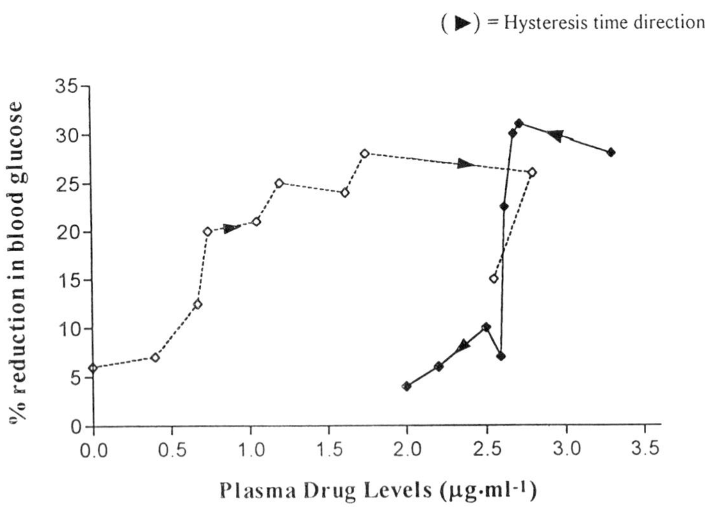

Fig. 9 Mean effect of gliclazide on the reduction of blood glucose levels over a 4-hour period after (◆) intravenous and (◇) infusion (3 hr) administration (65 mg) in humans (n = 3).

C. Neural Networks

The body is complex and scientists become increasingly focused on one small part without being able to comprehend how it actually functions together. In isolation, a drug may have a particular effect on a single locus of action but when multiple sites are implicated, especially when they intercommunicate, it becomes very difficult to disentangle the separate activities. Physiological and systems analysis may address some of these problems but for these to be useful it is necessary to define a specific model and then to test the assumptions proposed. For more complex systems, which cannot easily be understood, or more importantly to measure the component parts of the system, it is possible to use emerging methods of information analysis called neural networks. These attempt to emulate the brain's neuronal processing capability using artificial intelligence. A neuronal network consists of a network of artificial neurones that receive a certain number of independent input variables. If we use the control of blood pressure as an example, the inputs could be time, plasma drug levels, heart rate, peripheral resistance, diuresis, and cardiac output at rest and after different degrees of exercise. These are processed according to certain characteristics of the net such as the weighting or signal strength of each neurone or transfer function, which acts as a switch to allow the neurone to be activated. It does this according to predescribed input conditions that can be linear or a more useful sigmoidal exponential. After the input layer of neurones, there is a so-called hidden layer, which processes the results and minimizes the variance on incoming data from different nodes before allowing the data to be sent to the dependent-variable output layers. For our particular example, it could be blood pressure together with certain kinetic parameters.

As the network is trained, the characteristics of the net change according to the success of the output predictions. This is achieved by changing individual neuronal weights. As these adjustments become reinforced, prior old values are "forgotten" and the new memory is updated. This teaching process is undertaken by a supervised backward and forward propagation system improving on the estimates of the predictive output each time. Thus, the system is left to learn the dynamics of the net until certain preset conditions are met; e.g., all predictions will be within 15% of the observed value. Such an analysis is less than precise with a certain amount of error being inherent in the method, but with the introduction of fuzzy logic, which uses the imprecision of the neural net output, it can provide an optimized answer based on the ranges of predictions given [77]. Not surprisingly, these methods have found great use in predictive mathematical modeling for forecasting the weather, stock market, and horse racing, or for voice pattern recognition, writing, and images. The few studies that have so far been published do show that neural nets could have a useful application to kinetics [78,79] and dynamics [80,81] (Fig. 10), but they

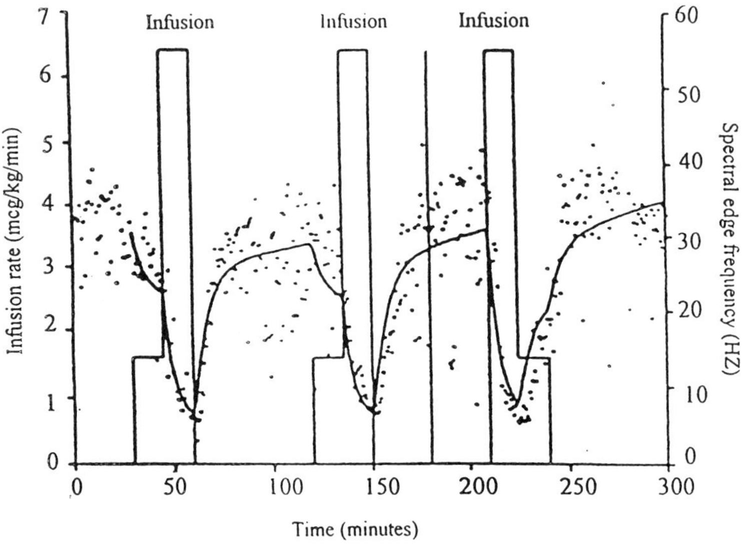

Fig. 10 Prediction of changes in spectral edge frequency for the hypnotic Alfentanil using neural networks (–) compared with measured data points (•) after different infusion rates (⌐⊓) in a human subject. (From Ref. 80.)

do have certain disadvantages. They may solve short-term problems of gaining information from complex unfathomable systems but they are still a black box providing little insight into the reasons for such interrelationships [82]. However at this stage, just to know that a relationship between drug levels and a complex activity can exist is enough to spur the scientist into further research to find out more details. Unquestionably, these new approaches will be used in the future for not only kinetics and metabolism, but for all areas of drug development.

VIII. TISSUE UPTAKE

As can be seen from Figure 7 and Table 4, one of the main assumptions when measuring plasma levels is that this directly reflects concentrations at the receptor site and that the same plasma tissue ratio exists in animals and man. Up until recently, it has not been possible to measure tissue levels without biopsy or sacrificing the animals, which makes human investigations impossible. Now, newer techniques of measuring both drug and activity *in situ* are being developed that could revolutionize kinetic–dynamic modeling. These include microdialysis and imaging techniques.

A. Microdialysis

Microdialysis techniques have been used to measure changes in drug levels and endogenous chemicals *in situ*. Small hollow plastic tubes are placed stereotaxically into specific parts of a tissue, particularly the brain, and low volumes of buffer are pumped through the system and "wash" out the chemicals to be analyzed using a flow-through HPLC, linked, if necessary, to a mass spectrometer. Once the animals have been acclimatized to the surgical procedure, this method has the advantage of measuring real-time changes of both drug and hormone or transmitter in close proximity to the site of action. However, although the probes are small, there is still local damage that may affect the results. Also, this technique can only examine a specific part of the brain and other areas that may be involved in controlling the system will be ignored [83]. However, the results are encouraging and have clarified the neuropharmacological action of drugs in terms of the turnover of neurotransmitters reflecting dynamic changes rather than the measurement of gross tissue levels.

B. Imaging

The newest techniques of nuclear medical imaging are for the first time bringing together all aspects of kinetic–dynamic modeling. These include (a) nuclear magnetic resonance (NMR), (b) positron emission tomography (PET), and (c) single photon emission tomography (SPECT). This chapter is not intended to discuss these methods in detail but instead to provide a brief overview and to show how they can be used in kinetics.

The NMR technique has been available for more than 20 years and exploits the magnetic properties of certain atomic nuclei, which, because they have an odd number of protons and or neutrons, will produce a small electromagnetic field [84]. The resonance frequency of a given atom in a magnetic field is fixed and can be measured by stimulating the atoms with radio waves and measuring the transmitted radio frequencies. The instrument determines amount of atom and its position within the body. Major atoms most commonly used are hydrogen to measure water and fluorine-19, but also include nitrogen-14, sodium-13, and potassium-19 [85,86]. This method has high resolution (1 mm) and can provide fine detail of the internal structure of the body, particularly in the brain. It can also measure energy and, therefore, metabolic changes using the phosphorus-31 associated with phosphocreatine and ATP and levels of creatinine, neutral amino acids, lactate, etc. These are very useful to assess loss of organ function, such as in a brain with Alzheimer's or Parkinson's disease. However, its use to measure drug levels is limited since there needs to be some specificity and, although hydrogen and nitrogen are present in many drugs, the levels of endogenous chemical would swamp the signal. But with fluorinated compounds, the naturally occurring ^{19}F isotope can be used with some success, and brain levels for the antidepressants fluoxetine [87] and trifluoroperazine [88] have been measured after chronic administration. Although NMR is mostly used with humans, recently brain levels of dexfenfluramine were measured using this technique both in the rhesus monkey and humans [89] and found to give similar values to those found by gas-liquid chromatography (GLC) analysis in post-mortem samples from both species.

The PET technique takes this concept one step further. By external body monitoring, it measures the decay of administered radio nucleotides that have an excess of positrons such as ^{11}C, ^{13}N, ^{15}O, and ^{18}F. The emitted positively charged positrons collide with the negative electrons in the tissue and send out simultaneously, at right angles, a pair of photons. Although for normal detection approximately 50–100 μC is administered, since radioactivity is annihilated with the collision and the emitted photons have such high energy (511 keV), they pass through the body safely with little tissue interaction. Externally, they can be detected by a circle of thousands of detectors. Because of the coincidence of the pair of photons, not only is this an absolute measurement of activity, similar to scintillation spectrophotometry, but also it has spatial recognition and 3 dimensional images of concentrations can be obtained. The images have less resolution (5–10 mm) than NMR, but when combined with the overlaid anatomical detail of NMR, these problems are minimized. The major disadvantage is the half-life of the radioisotopes, which range from 2 minutes for ^{15}O to 20 minutes for ^{11}C to 110 minutes for ^{18}F, and this means that starting with the enrichment of the isotope in a cyclotron, the synthesis and purification must all take place within a short time (1–2 hours from start to finish). However, with rapid and efficient reactions, robotized and automatic synthetic and separation techniques, this is possible for an increasing number of compounds. Again, as with NMR, the clinical usage of this method predominates, but large machines can be used for the larger primates and increasingly, PET scanners for small animals with sufficient spatial resolution are becoming available [90,91,92] and becoming realistically cost effective [93].

The SPECT technique has less spatial resolution than PET but has the advantage of, instead of imaging isotopes with ultrashort activities, using technetium-99 or iodine-123 with half-lives of 6 and 13 hours. But what is gained in this regard is lost in practice since molecules are much harder to make with these atoms compared to carbon or fluorine. However, often if a ligand is found to be useful for PET, a similar ligand with iodine attached for use with SPECT may have much wider usage. The cost of detectors may also be 5 to 10 times less than for PET, particularly for animal use [94].

But what can PET or SPECT do? Table 5 provides some general uses in drug development as a whole but specifically, for kinetics, it has far-reaching possibilities by integrating not only the kinetics at the site of action, but meas-

Table 5 Some Potential Uses of PET in Kinetics and Drug Development

Phase	Uses
Drug discovery and candidate choice	Species differences in receptor/enzymatic interaction and tissue energy changes Validation of disease animal model in comparison to humans
Pharmacokinetics and metabolism	Tissue, whole body, and excreta measurement when specifically required and other techniques are not possible Comparative kinetics and physiological modeling of toxic compounds in humans
Pharmacology	Relationship between plasma/tissue, active site levels and dynamic activity (receptor binding, endogenous chemical turnover, energy changes, etc.)
Toxicology	Measurement *in situ* tissue damage in humans in comparison to animal toxicology

uring specific binding and activity [95]. In addition, it can measure the energy and functional activity using ^{18}flurodeoxyglucose, which is useful in assessing disease states in tissues such as the brain or the heart. In pure kinetics terms, levels of a drug can be measured anywhere in the body in real time—for example, in the rat for phentermine [96], in the rabbit for fluconazole [97], in the monkey for dapoxetine [98], and in humans for cocaine [99]—but is particularly useful when other methods are not available. One example is for a new CFC replacement for an inhalation propellant, tetrafluoroethane. As a gas, conventional distribution studies in animals are difficult and, in humans, impossible, but by using 18F and PET scanning, the regional distribution and retention in humans could be investigated on a breath-by-breath basis (Figure 11) [100].

Perhaps the most important aspect of PET technology for the kinetics of the future is the measurement of the actual levels of the drug at the receptor site. Specific binding to the receptor can be obtained by obtaining an image before and after the administration of either an antagonist, which blocks the specific binding, or an inactive enantiomer, which has the same nonspecific distribution, but does not bind to the receptor. A subsequent experiment can relate plasma levels to activity at the receptor or some other measure of activity. This is particularly important when comparing animal models such as transgenic or receptor knock-out animals with human disease.

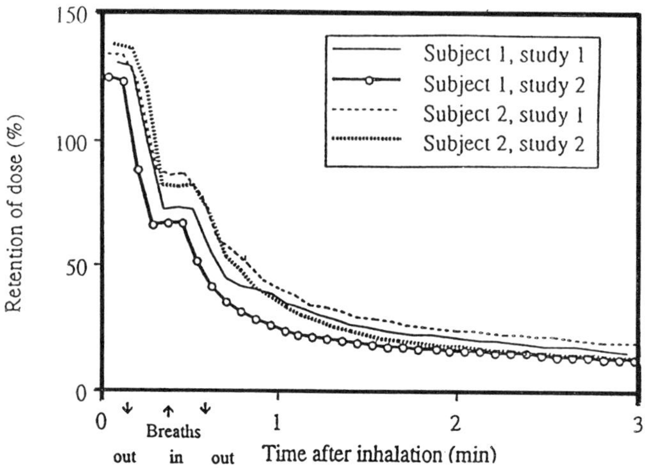

Fig. 11 Total body elimination of ^{18}F-Tetrafluoroethane after a single inhalation. (From Ref. 100.)

Although, for example, in the brain many subcortical regions show gross structurally and histologically similar features to those found in humans, there is a growing awareness that there may be important differences in neurotransmitter binding and types of receptors between animals. For example, both citalopram and imipramine show marked species differences in their binding in the amygdala and hypothalamus [101]. Similar species differences in receptor binding and distribution have been shown for ß receptor binding in the brain [102] and cholecystokinin (CCK) binding in rats and primates [103]. The 5-HT_{1B} receptor, although present in the rat, is absent in humans who have a 5-HT_{1D} receptor that is only different by two amino acids, but this confers differences in specificity. Brown fat that acts as a thermoregulator in rodents is present in infants but virtually absent in adult humans. These are but a few of the species differences now known to occur in receptor and physiological mechanisms.

Although there are still practical difficulties with the imaging methods, it is likely they will be used increasingly in drug development [104] to understand disease, validate animal models, and, importantly, improve kinetic–dynamic modeling by measuring both drug levels and activity directly at the receptor.

IX. POPULATION TOXICOKINETICS

The use of pharmacokinetic screens and population approaches to measure kinetic parameters using minimal sampling techniques has many advantages in drug development [105,106] and has been advocated by the FDA to improve information from large scale clinical trials [107]. There has been some reluctance to wholeheartedly embrace this idea, since many companies are not sure if the benefits outweigh the investment in time, money, and personnel. Many medical directors see this as an additional burden increasing the clinical kinetic workload. Not only will it be necessary to undertake pair-wise kinetics comparisons in disease group—elderly, hepatic, renal disease, etc.—but in addition, any new interactions that may be become apparent by the population analysis. However, this method can be used with all the advantages and few of the problems in preclinical toxicokinetics. In these safety studies, there is a need to measure exposure by estimating peak levels and the area under the curve. In dogs or primates, serial samples can be taken from the animals in the study, but this is not often possible from rodents. To overcome this difficulty, parallel or satellite groups are kept under the same conditions as the main study group but are only used for blood sampling and subsequent drug analysis. This considerably increases the number of animals and the number of kinetic analyses. Under these circumstances population kinetics can be used effectively [108] by taking only one sample from each of many animals but at different times (composite sampling), covering the whole of the dosing interval. These data can be analyzed together to define the average plasma level and the toxicokinetic profile for each dose with precision estimates by using population analytical methods [109,110]. These allow calculation of all measures of exposure without the inherent need to previously know exactly the profile or kinetics for each dosage in each species. The advantages are clear: in rats, there is no requirement for a satellite group, and in mice, the number of animals is greatly reduced. Similarly, the number of samples analyzed can be reduced 2–4-fold. In terms of management decisions, this approach is clearly cost effective, and should gain wider acceptance in the future. Indeed, minimal sampling techniques can be taken further to reduce the analytical load. We have found in our laboratories that, during carcinogenicity studies, when the drug is administered in the diet, only three samples are necessary to adequately describe the AUC with less than 10% error [111]. When the amount of food ingested by the animals over the previous 24 hours is taken as a correction factor, only one sample in the morning is necessary to obtain good estimates of exposure throughout the previous day. This method seems to have a wide applicability for a range of drugs with different half-lives [112]. Preliminary discussions with the Medicines Control Agency (MCA) in the UK would suggest that both population kinetics and minimal sampling techniques with suitable validation would be acceptable to the regulatory authorities.

X. SUMMARY

Regulatory requirements continue to increase despite harmonization, and kinetics may speed up drug development by "bridging" the gaps of knowledge between disciplines. But we have witnessed over the past few years some dramatic changes in biodisposition methodology and an understanding of what is important: improved analytical techniques, *in vitro* metabolism, enzyme expression, scaling, computational methods, and, for the first time, a core harmonized guideline for the acquisition of kinetic data from animal safety studies. These changes have allowed scientists to reassess what and when information is required. Some basic kinetics in a few animals can be obtained early in drug development but detailed ADME studies in multiple animal studies should be avoided unless undertaken to explain a particular problem. Emphasis on biodisposition studies must now be put into drug discovery, candidate choice, and getting into man as soon as possible. New predictive methods outlined here should be employed wherever possible to increase our knowledge of what is possible, and together with population approaches, all generated data on a new medicine should be interrelated to build up a complete and integrated profile. Perhaps the most exciting aspect of the future is the chance to make plasma concentrations more meaningful. They should not continue to be some undefined surrogate endpoint, but should be related to the activity at the site of action as early as possible in all preclinical studies, building on physiological systems control so that we can use pharmacological and toxicological pharmacokinetic–pharmacodynamic modeling and define more accurately the type of medicine and the dose for the individual patient. Kinetics, one of the youngest of the disciplines, is finally growing up and is being understood and accepted within the family of drug development.

Acknowledgment

I would like to thank Danielle Bowra for her artistic acumen and for patiently putting this paper together.

REFERENCES

1. S. Walker. On file Center for Medical Research Surrey UK, 1993.
2. J. A. DiMasi. Success rates for new drugs entering clinical testing in the United States. *Clinical Pharmacology Therap. 58*: 1–14, 1995.
3. D. B. Campbell and R. Jochemsen. Nonclinical pharmacokinetics and toxicokinetics. In International Pharmaceutical Product Registration: Aspects of Quality,

Safety and Efficacy—Chemistry, Pharmacy and Manufacturing. A. C. Cartwright and B. R. Matthews, Eds. Publ. by Ellis Horwood, Chichester, West Sussex, 1994.
4. ICH2. International Conference on Harmonisation Safety Topic S3A: Note for guidance on Toxicokinetics. The assessment of systematic exposure in toxicity studies. Draft 10 Step 4 document. EFPIA, Brussels, 1994.
5. D. A. Waterman. A guide to expert systems Reading MA. Addison-Wesley, New York, 1986.
6. C. Hansch. Quantitative structure-activity relationships in drug design. In Drug Design. Vol. 1. 1971. E. J. Ariens, Ed. Academic Press, New York, p. 271–342.
7. M. Gumbleton and W. Sneader. Pharmacokinetic considerations in rational drug design. *Clin. Pharmacokin. 26*: 161–168, 1994.
8. B. Testa and P. Jenner. A structural approach to selectivity in drug metabolism and disposition. In Concepts in Drug Metabolism, Part A. P. Jenner and B. Testa, Eds. Marcel Dekker, New York, 1980, p. 53–176.
9. R. A. Herman and P. Veng-Pedersen. Quantitative structure-pharmacokinetic relationships for systemic drug distribution kinetics not confined to a congeneric series. *J. Pharm. Sci. 83*: 423–428, 1994.
10. K. H. Kim. Quantitative structure-activity relationships of the metabolism of drugs by uridine diphosphate glucuronosyltransferase. *J. Pharm. Sci. 80*: 966–970, 1991.
11. C. Hansch, J. P. Bjorkroth, and A. Leo. hydrophobicity and central nervous system agents: on the principle of minimal hydrophobicity in drug design. *J. Pharm. Sci. 76*: 663–687, 1987.
12. E. Holmes, B. C. Sweatman, M. E. Bollard, C. A. Blackledge, C. R. Beddell, I. D. Wilson, J. C. Lindon, and J. K. Nicholson. Prediction of urinary sulphate and glucuronide conjugate excretion for the substituted phenols in the rat using quantitative structure-metabolism relationships. *Xenobiotica 25*: 1269–1282, 1995.
13. R. Lahana. Tools for structure activity relationships: a comprehensive software. *Human Exp. Toxicol. 14*: 522, 1995.
14. B. Ajay. A unified framework for using neural networks to build QSARs. *J. Med. Chem. 36*: 3565–3571, 1993.
15. S. Hirano, I. Nakagome, H. Hirano, F. Yoshi, and I. Moriguchi. Noncongeneric structure pharmacokinetic property correlation studies using fuzzy adaptive least squares: volume of distribution. *Bilo. Pharm. Bull. 17*: 686–690, 1994.
16. D. F. V. Lewis, H. Moereels, B. G. Lake, C. Ioannides, and D. V. Parke. Molecular modeling of enzymes and receptors involved in carcinogenesis QSARs and COMPACT-3D. *Drug Metabolism Revs. 26*: 261–285, 1994.
17. D. F. V. Lewis, B. G. Lake, and D. V. Parke. Molecular orbital-generated QSARs in a homologous series of alkoxyresorufins and studies of their interactive docking with P450s. *Xenobiotica 25*: 1355–1370, 1995.
18. XENO. A modular FORTRAN program runing on a Digital PDP-10 computer at the SUMEX-AIM (Stanford University Medical Experiment-Artificial Intelligence in Medicine) facility, 1980.
19. CompuDrug. Metabol Expert. Expert Advisory systems for the prediction of the metabolism of exogenous compounds in many different living organisms. CompuDrug Chemistry Ltd., Budapest, Hungary, 1990.

20. J. Talafous, L. M. Sayre, J. J. Mieyal, and G. Klopman. META 2. A dictionary model of mammalian xenobiotic metabolism. *J. Chem. Inf. Comput. Sci. 34*: 1326–1333, 1994.
21. M. Johnson. Assessing the reliability of methods for predicting drug metabolites. *J. Biopharm. Stat. 1*: 27–56, 1991.
22. C. Buchalter. Formula Searching in ISIS/Base. *Scientist's Desktop. A Newsletter for ISIS and CPSS Scientific Software Users. 3*:1, 1994.
23. D. B. Campbell and N. Marchant. Specificity and variability in drug metabolism: An industrial point of view. Paper to be published in proceedings of Cost B1 European Conference on specificity and variability in drug metabolism. Besançon, 10–12 May 1995.
24. E. S. Vesell. On the significance of host factors that affect drug disposition. *Clin. Pharmacol. Ther. 31*: 1–7, 1982.
25. A. K. Daly, S. Choleryon, W. Gregory, and J. R. Idel. Metabolic polymorphisms. *Pharmacol. Ther. 57*: 129–160, 1993.
26. U. M. Zanger, E.-U. Griese, B. Evert, and M. Eichelbaum. Function of the products of variant alleles for drug metabolising enzymes. Abstract L8. Paper to be published in proceedings of Cost B1 European Conference on specificity and variability in drug metabolism. Besançon, 10–12 May 1995.
27. R. Janeczko, D. J. Waxman, G. A. Le Blanc, A. Morville, and M. Adesnik. Hormonal regulation of levels of the messenger RNA encoding hepatic P450 2C (11C11), a constitutive male specific form of cytochrome P450. *Molec. Endocrinol. 4*: 295–303, 1990.
28. A. R. Boobis. Enzymatic studies in genetic polymorphisms of drug metabolism. In European cooperation in the field of scientific and technical research. G. Alvan, L. P. Balant, P. R. Bechter, A. R. Boobis, L. F. Gram, and K. Pithan, Eds. European Consensus Conference on Pharmacogenetics, Besançon, France, 24–15 October 1990. Commission of the European Communities, Luxembourg, p. 15–26.
29. J. A. Bardsley. Establishment of human tissue banks. *Human Exper. Toxicol. 13*: 435–437, 1994.
30. D. R. Krishna and U. Klotz. Extrahepatic metabolism of drugs in humans. *Clin. Pharmacokinetic. 26*: 144–160, 1994.
31. M. F. Herbert, J. P. Roberts, T. Pracksaritanont, and L. Z. Benet. Bioavailability of cyclosporine with concomitant riampisin administration is markedly less than predicted by hepatic enzyme inhibition. *Clin. Pharm. Ther. 52*: 453–457, 1992.
32. W. Kalow. Pharmacogenetic variability in brain and muscle. *J. Pharmac. Pharmacol. 46 (suppl 1)*: 425–432, 1994.
33. L. A. Siddoway, K. A. Thompson, C. B. McAllister, T. Wang, G. R. Wilkinson, et al. Polymorphism of propafenone metabolism and disposition in man: clinical and pharmacokinetic consequences. *Circulation 75*: 785–791, 1987.
34. S. Sindrup, K. Brosen, and L. Gram. Pharmacokinetics of the selective serotonin reuptake inhibitor paroxetine: nonlinearity and relation to the sparteine oxidation polymorphism. *Clin. Pharm. Ther. 51*: 288–295, 1992.
35. F. Macintyre, D. A. Smith, and P. E. Coates. Variability in human pharmacokinetics in volunteer studies and in the clinical situation. Abstract 25, 1996. Paper to be

published in proceedings of Cost B1 European Conference on specificity and variability in drug metabolism. Besançon, 10–12 May 1995.

36. G. Alván. Clinical consequences of polymorphic drug metabolism. *Fundam. Clin. Pharmacol. 5*: 209–228, 1991.
37. J. A. G. Agúndez, M. C. Lesesma, J. Benítez, J. M. Ladero, A. Rodríguez-Lescure, E. Díaz-Rubio, M. Díaz-Rubio. CYP 2D6 genes and risk of liver cancer. *Lancet 345*: 830–831, 1995.
38. R. A. Cartwright, R. W. Glashan, H. J. Rogers, R. A. Ahmad, D. Barham-Hall, E. Higgins, and M. A. Kahn. Role of N-acetyltransferase phenotypes in bladder carcinogenesis: a pharmacogenetic epidemiological approach to bladder cancer. *Lancet ii*: 842–845, 1982.
39. C. A. D. Smith, A. C. Gough, N. P. Leigh, B. A. Summers, A. E. Harding, D. M. Maranganore, S. G. Sturman, A. H. V. Schapira, A. C. Williams, N. K. Spurr, and C. R. Wolf. Debrisoquine hydroxylase gene polymorphism and susceptibility to Parkinson's Disease. *Lancet 339*: 1375–1377, 1992.
40. A. Rane, G. R. Wilkinson, and D. G. Shand. Prediction of hepatic extraction ratio from *in vitro* measurement of intrinsic clearance. *J. Pharmacol. Exp. Ther. 200*: 420–424, 1977.
41. A. J. Houston. Utility of *in vitro* drug metabolism data in predicting *in vivo* metabolic clearance. *Biochem. Pharmacol. 47*: 1469–1479, 1994.
42. B. A. Hoener. Predicting the hepatic clearance of xenobiotics in humans from *in vitro* data. *Biopharm. Drug Dispos. 15*: 295–304, 1994.
43. G. Ubeaud, C. Schmitt, D. Jaeck, T. Lave, and P. H. Coassolo. Bosentan: a new endothelin receptor antagonist: prediction of a systemic plasma clearance in man from combined *in vivo* and *in vitro* data. *Xenobiotica 25*: 1381–1390, 1995.
44. P. G. Welling and F. A. De La Iglesia. Drug Toxicokinetics: Drug and Chemical Toxicology Series No. 9. Marcel Dekker, New York, 1993.
45. D. B. Campbell and R. M. J. Ings. New approaches to the use of pharmacokinetics in toxicology and drug development. *Human Toxicol. 7*: 469–479, 1988.
46. E. F. Adolphe. Quantitative relations in the physiological constituents of mammals. *Science 109*: 579–585, 1949.
47. H. Boxenbaum. Interspecies scaling, allometry, physiological time, and the ground plan of pharmacokinetics. *J. Pharmacokin. Biopharma. 10*: 201–227, 1982.
48. D. B. Campbell. Sizing up the problem of exposure extrapolation: New directions in allometric scaling in toxicology of industrial compounds. H. Thomas, R. Hess, and F. Waechter, Eds. Taylor and Francis, London, 1995, p. 45–58.
49. M. Bonati, R. Latini, G. Tognoni, J. F. Young, and S. Garattini. Interspecies comparison of in vivo caffeine pharmacokinetics in man, monkey, rabbit, rat and mouse. *Drug Metabolism Rev. 15*: 1355–1383, 1984–85.
50. G. A. Sacher. Relation of lifespan to brain weight and body weight in mammals. In The Life Span of Animals. G. E. W. Wolstenholme and M. O'Connor, Eds. Little Brown, Boston, 1959, p. 115–141.
51. H. Boxenbaum and R. De Souza. Physiological models, allometry, neoteny, space time and pharmacokinetics. In Pharmacokinetics: Mathematical and Statistical Approaches. A. Peale and A. Resagno, Eds. Plenum, New York, 1988.

52. M. J. Boddington. An absolute metabolic scope for activity. *J. Theor. Biol. 75*: 443–449, 1978.
53. H. Boxenbaum. Time concepts in physics, biology and pharmacokinetics. *J. Pharm. Sci. 75*: 1053–1062, 1986.
54. A. S. Hussain, R. D. Johnson, N. N. Vachharajani, and W. A. Ritshel. Feasibility of developing a neural network for the prediction of human pharmacokinetic parameters from animal data. *Pharmaceutical Research 10*: 466–469, 1993.
55. ICH3 Harmonisation Meeting, Yokahama, Japan, November 1995.
56. D. B. Campbell. Are we doing too many animal biodisposition investigations before Phase I studies in man? A re-evaluation of the timing and extent of ADME studies. *European Journ. of Drug Metabolism and Pharmacokinetics 19*: 283–293, 1994.
57. A. Warrander. Harmonisation of preclinical metabolism and pharmacokinetic: Interim results of questionnaire. *ISSX Newsletter 12(1)*: 12–13, 1993.
58. A. Warrander. Around the world with 80+ companies—A review of toxicokinetic practices. *Drug. Inf. J. 28*: 281–283, 1994.
59. ICH2. Draft Consensus Text. Toxicokinetics: Guidance for Repeated Dose Tissue Distribution Studies. Released for consultation 27 October 1993 at Step 2 of the ICH Process, 1993a.
60. N. Motoji, E. Hatama, and A. Shigematsu. Radioluminography for quantitative autoradiography of 14C. E. *J. Drug. Metab. Pharmacokin. 20*: 89–105, 1995.
61. D. B. Campbell. The use of kinetic–dynamic interactions in the evaluation of drugs. *Phychopharmacology 100*: 433–450, 1990.
62. D. B. Campbell. The use of toxicokinetics for the safety assessment of drugs acting in the brain. *Molec. Neurobiol. 11*: 193–216, 1995b.
63. K. Kobayashi, D. I. Jodrell, and M. J. Ratain. Pharmacodynamic–Pharmacokinetic Relationships and Therapeutic Drug Monitoring Cancer Surveys 17: Pharmacokinetics and Cancer Chemotherapy Imperial Cancer Research Fund, p. 51–78, 1993.
64. J. M. Collins, C. K. Grieshaber, and B. A. Chabner. Pharmacologically guided Phase 1 clinical trials based upon preclinical drug development. *J. Nat. Cancer Instit. 82*: 1321–1326, 1990.
65. N. H. Holford and L. B. Shiener. Pharmacokinetic and pharmacodynamic modelling *in vivo. CRC Critical Reviews in Bioengineering* 5: 273–322, 1981.
66. L. B. Sheiner, D. R. Stanski, S. Vozeh, R. D. Miller, and J. Ham. Simultaneous modelling of pharmaco-kinetics and pharmacodynamics: application to d-tubocurarine. *Clin. Pharm. Ther. 25*: 358–371, 1979.
67. L. B. Sheiner. Modeling pharmacodynamics: parametric and nonparametric approaches. In Variability in Drug Therapy: Description, Estimation and Control. M. Rowland, L. B. Scheiner, and J. L. Steiner, Eds. Raven Press, New York, 1985, p. 139–152.
68. SIPHAR. Simed, 9211 rue G. Enesio, 94008 Creteil, France.
69. B. M. Barnhill. Micro NONLIN for MS DOS computers: Non-linear regression analysis. Pittsburgh PA, Elite Software, 1984.
70. D. Z. D'Arenio and A. Schumitzky. A program package for simulation and parameter estimation in pharmacokinetics system. *Computer Programs in Biomedicine 9*: 115–134, 1979.

71. G. Heinzel, R. Wolszczak, and P. Rhomann. Topfit version 2.0—Pharmacokinetic and Pharmacodynamic Data Analysis System for the PC. Gustav Fischer Verlag, 1993.
72. N. H. G. Holford. Parametric models of the time course of drug action in the *in vivo* study of drug action. C. J. Van Boxtel, N. H. G. Holford, and M. Danhof, Eds. Elsevier, New York, 1992, p. 61–69.
73. D. A. Noe and K. M. Kumor. A pharmacokinetic-pharmacodynamic model of heart rate during cocaine administration in humans. Clin. Pharm. Therap. 49: 426–432, 1991.
74. P. Francheteaud, S. L. Steiner, H. Merdjan, M. Guerret, C. Dubray, and P. Sassano. A mathematical model for dynamics of cardiovascular drug action with application to intravenous nicardipine in volunteers and hypertensive patients. Poster presentation, IOPHAR Symposium Measurement and Kinetics of *in vivo* Drug Effects, Noordwjik, Holland, 1990.
75. C. H. Kleinbloesem, P. Van Brummelen, M. Danhof, J. Faber, J. Urquhart, and D. D. Breimer. Rates of increase in plasma concentration of nifedipine as a major determinant of its haemodynamic effects in humans. *Clin. Pharmacol. Ther. 41*: 26–30, 1987.
76. D. B. Campbell. Unpublished, 1995c.
77. M. M. Gupta and D. H. Rao, Fuzzy Sets Systems 61 1, 1994.
78. M. E. Brier, J. M. Zurada, and G. R. Aronoff. Neural network predicted peak and trough gentamicin concentrations. *Pharm. Res. 12*: 406–412, 1995.
79. M. Costa, C. Della Pepa, P. Zara, and M. Eandi. Artificial neural networks for pharmacokinetic modeling (personal communication), 1995.
80. P. Veng-Pederson and N. B. Modi. Neural networks in pharmacodynamic modeling: Is current modeling practice of complex kinetic systems at a dead end? *J. Pharmacokin. Biopharm. 20*: 397–412, 1992.
81. J. Faro and S. Velasco. Studies on a recent class of network models of the immune system. *J. Theor. Biol. 164*: 271–290, 1993.
82. R. A. Siegal. Commentary on "Neural networks in pharmacodynamic modeling: Is current modeling practice of complex kinetic systems at a dead end?" *J. Pharmacokin. Biopharm. 20*: 413–418, 1992.
83. D. F. Morrison, P. M. Bungay, J. K. Hsiao, I. N. Mefford, K. H. Dykstra, and R. L. Dedrick. Quantitative microdialysis. In Microdialysis in the Neurosciences. T. E. Robinson and J. B. Justice, Eds. Elsevier, New York, 1991, p. 47–80.
84. S. Saini, R. B. Frankel, D. D. Stark, and J. T. Ferrucci. Magnetism: A primer and review. *American J. of Roentgenology 150*: 735–744, 1988.
85. C. B. Higgins, H. Hricak, and C. A. Helms, Eds. Magnetic Resonance. Imaging in the Body. Raven Press, New York, 1992.
86. I. L. Pykett. NMR imaging in Medicine. *Sci. Am. 246*: 78–89, 1982.
87. P. F. Renshaw, A. R. Guimaraes, M. Fava, J. F. Rosenbaum, J. D. Pearlman, J. G. Flood, P. R. Puopolo, K. Clancy, and R. G. Gonzalez. Accumalation of fluoxitine and norfluoxitine in human brain during therapeutic administration. *Am. Psychiatry 149*: 1592, 1992.
88. C. N. Karson, J. E. O. Newton, P. Mohanakrishnan, J. Sprigg, and A. Komoroski. Fluoxitine and trifluroperazine in the human brain: a 19F-nuclear magnetic resonance spectroscopy study. *Psychiatry Res. Neuroimaging 45*: 95–104, 1992.

89. P. F. Renshaw. Personal communication, 1995.
90. R. S. Miyaoka, T. K. Lewellen, and A. N. Bice. Dynamic high resolution imaging of rats: design considerations IEEE. *Trans. Nucl. Sci. 38*: 670–677, 1991.
91. P. D. Cutler, S. R. Cherry, E. J. Hoffman, W. M. Digby, and M. E. Phelps. Design features and performance of a PET system for animal research. *J. Nucl. Med. 33*: 595–604, 1993.
92. C. J. Marriott, J. E. Cadorette, R. Lecompte, V. Scasnar, J. Rousseau, and J. E. van Lier. High Resolution PET imaging and quantitation of pharmaceutical biodistribution in a small animal using avalanche photodiode detectors. *J. Nucl. Med. 35*: 1390–1396, 1994.
93. R. Hichwa. Are animal scanners really necessary for PET? *J. Nucl. Med. 35*: 1396–1397, 1994.
94. M. V. Green, A. Markowitz, T. E. Tedder, M. P. Andrich, E. S. Owens, and R. D. Neuman. SPECT imaging in small animals. *J. Nucl. Med. 33*: 852, 1992.
95. D. B. Campbell. Drug development and Positron Emission Tomography in Developments in Nuclear Medicine Vol 26: PET for drug development and evaluation. D. Comar, Ed. Kluwer Academic Publishers, Dordrecht, Holland, 1995, p. 1–24.
96. D. R. Elmaleh, H. Kizuka, R. N. Janson, G. S. Jones, L. W. Herman, and H. W. Strauss. Structure-localization relationships of 11C-labeled phentermine derivatives: Effect of aromatic substitution. *Appl. Radiat. Isot. 44*: 821–829, 1993.
97. E. Livini, A. J. Fischman, S. Ray, D. R. Elmaleh, N. M. Alpert, S. Weiss, J. A. Correia, D. Webb, E. R. Dahl, W. Robeson, D. Margouleff, R. Liss, H. W. Strauss, and R. H. Rubin. Synthesis of 18F-labelled fluconazole and positron emission tomography studies in rabbits. *Nucl. Med. Biol. 19*: 191–199, 1992.
98. E. Livini, W. Satterlee, R. L. Robey, C. A. Alt, E. E. Van Meter, J. W. Babich, W. J. Wheeler, D. D. O'Bannon, J. H. Thrall, and A. J. Fischman. Synthesis of [11C] dapoxetine. HCl, a serotonin re-uptake inhibitor: Biodisposition in rat and preliminary PET imaging in the monkey. *Nucl. Med. Biol. 21*: 669–675, 1994.
99. J. S. Fowler, N. D. Volkow, J. Logan, R. R. MacGregor, G. J. Wang, and A. P. Wolfe. Alcohol intoxication does not change [14C] cocaine pharmacokinetics in human brain and heart. *Synapse 12*: 220–227, 1992.
100. V. W. Pike, R. G. N. Tanner, F. I. Aigbirhio, C. A. J. Freemantle, S. L. Waters, B. C. Page, C. G. Rhodes, P. Olsson, B. G. Ventresca, and T. Jones. Study of disposition of a novel drug propellant 1,1,1, tetrafluoroethane in humans by labelling with fluorine-18 and whole body counting. In: PET for Drug Development and Evaluation. D. Comar, Ed. Kluwer Academic Publishers, The Netherlands, 1995, p. 341–353.
101. G. E. Duncan, K. Y. Little, J. A. Kirkman, R. S. Koplas, W. E. Stump, and G. R. Breese. Atoradiographic characterisation of [3H] imipramine and [3H] citalopram binding in rat and human brain: Species differences and relationships to serotonin innervation patterns. *Brain Res. 591*: 181–197, 1992.
102. G. E. Duncan, K. Y. Little, R. S. Koplas, J. A. Kirkman, G. R. Breese, and W. E. Stump. ß-adrenergic receptor distribution in the human and rat hippocampal formation: marked species differences. *Brain Res. 561*: 84–92, 1991.

103. C. Kohler and V. Chan-Palay. Cholecystokinin-octapeptide (CCK-8) receptors in the hippocampal region: a comparative in vitro autoradiographic study in the rat, monkey and the post mortem brain. *Neurosci. Lett. 90*: 51–56, 1988.
104. D. Comar (1995). PET for Drug Development and Evaluation. D. Comar, Ed. Developments in Nuclear Medicine, Vol. 26. Kluwer Academic Publishers Group, The Netherlands.
105. L. P. Balant, M. Rowland, L. Aarons, F. Mentré, P. L. Morselli, J. L. Steimer, and A. Vozeh. New strategies in drug development and clinical evaluation: the population approach. *Eur. J. Clin. Pharmacol. 45*: 93–94, 1993.
106. J. Grevel, B. Whiting, A. W. Kelman, and K. Kutz. Compilation of a clinical pharmacokinetic database for population analysis during drug development. *Pharma. Med. 2*: 127–136, 1987.
107. C. C. Peck, W. H. Barr, L. Z. Benet, J. Collins, R. E. Desjardins, D. E. Furst, J. G. Harter, G. Levy, T. Ludden, J. H. Rodman, L. Sanathanan, J. J. Schentag, V. P. Shah, L. B. Sheiner, J. P. Skelly, D. R. Stanski, R. J. Temple, C. T. Viswanathan, J. Weissinger, and A. Yacobi. Opportunities for integration of pharmacokinetics, pharmacodynamics, and toxicokinetics in rational drug development. *Pharm. Res. 9*: 826–833, 1992.
108. J. Van Bree, J. Nedelman, J.-L. Steimer, F. Tse, W. Robinson, and W. Niederberger. Application of sparse sampling approaches in rodent toxicokinetics: A prospective view. *Drug Inf. J. 28*: 263–279, 1994.
109. S. L. Beal and L. B. Sheiner. The NONMEM system. *Amer. Stat. 34*: 118, 1982.
110. R. P. Gomeni. Pharm: A population pharmacokinetic pharmacodynamic data modelling software. SIMED, Creteil, France, 1994.
111. R. Jochemsen, D. Bazot, M. H. Brillance, and M. Lupart. Assessment of drug exposure in rat dietary studies. *Xenobiotica 23*: 1145–1154, 1993.
112. L. Chasseaud. Personal communication, 1995.

9

Changes in Pharmacokinetics and Drug Metabolism Responsibility in Drug Discovery and Development

Peter G. Welling

Parke-Davis Pharmaceutical Research
Warner-Lambert Company
Ann Arbor, Michigan

I. INTRODUCTION

Pharmacokinetics is one of the many disciplines that contribute to the discovery and development of drugs. This was not always the case. Although the basic mathematics of pharmacokinetics were described in some detail almost 60 years ago [1,2], about 30 years went by before pharmacokinetics and the closely related discipline of drug metabolism started to make an appreciatable contribution to the understanding and management of drug action and also to the contents of applications to regulatory authorities for drug marketing. The rapid advances in the disciplines of pharmacokinetics and drug metabolism during the 1960s were a result of the combined influences of improved analytical methodology and the increased awareness by health care providers of the fundamental importance of pharmacokinetics in drug development and therapy. The major leap forward in pharmacokinetics during that period was due also to the ingenuity, foresight, and entrepreneurial skills of a number of scientists, predominantly in the United States, including Benet [3], Garrett [4], Gibaldi [5], Levy [6], Riegelman [7], and Wagner [8]. The combined influence of these individuals, and some others, provided a considerable driving force for the rapid evolution of pharmacokinetics.

Prior to 1960, pharmacokinetic data made only a minor contribution to regulatory marketing submissions. There was little appreciation of the importance of this type of information, little means to provide pharmacokinetic information in sufficient depth and detail, and the data could not be produced with sufficient speed to make a meaningful contribution, even when it was appreciated. The situation has changed remarkably since then. Pharmacokinetics and metabolism material is not only covered exclusively in several sections of regulatory marketing submissions, worldwide, but is also distributed throughout other sections of the documents to provide support for pharmacology, toxicology, and clinical material. In fact, toxicokinetics has emerged as a major new discipline, bridging toxicology and pharmacokinetics, and continues to play an ever-increasing role in the interpretation of toxicology data and prediction of toxicity profiles in animal species to humans.

The phenomenal growth of pharmacokinetics, toxicokinetics, and metabolism in pharmaceutical discovery and development research, from virtually nothing to providing major contributions, can be compared to the almost parallel growth of biotechnology. All of these disciplines have evolved rapidly and now make major contributions to pharmaceutical research and development (R & D). However, biotechnology has evolved in a well-defined discovery environment and has been marked by both successes and failures in the development of biologically based therapeutic agents. Pharmacokinetics, on the other hand, has no discrete boundaries. It contributes across the entire spectrum of activities ranging from early discovery to marketing authorization submission, and beyond to postmarketing support. This broad spectrum of responsibility places heavy demands on pharmacokinetics and metabolism expertise during the entire discovery and development process.

The intent of this chapter is to summarize the contributions that pharmacokinetics and metabolism make to drug discovery and development and to describe changes that are considered by this writer to be essential for these disciplines to continue to play a significant role in the total reengineering that must occur in pharmaceutical R & D in order for it to survive in an increasingly demanding and challenging environment.

II. INTERDISCIPLINARY INTERACTIONS

Pharmacokinetics and drug metabolism are among the most highly interactive disciplines in pharmaceutical R & D. This has both benefits and liabilities associated with it. Benefits include the ability of pharmacokinetics and metabolism scientists to contribute to a broad spectrum of research activities, ranging from initial discovery to final Phase 3 clinical studies, and beyond to marketing support. The major liability is that pharmacokinetics and metabolism activities are invariably dictated by events and decisions occurring in other disciplines. This is inevitable, can often be extremely frustrating, but provides a background for the many examples of procedures that need to be changed in the discovery and development process.

The essence of change, as applied to pharmacokinetics and metabolism interactions, must be associated with greater involvement of pharmacokinetics and metabolism scientists in preclinical and clinical strategic plans, together with judicious prospective planning and study design. This argument, while most relevant in this writer's mind to the areas of pharmacokinetics and metabolism, applies across all disciplines involved in the R & D process and necessitates discarding old concepts . . . "this is the way we do things. . . ." and replacing them with a faster, leaner, and more efficient and economically viable approach. This has to be achieved in the paradoxical environment of rapidly increasing demands and costs on the one hand and rigorous cost containment and overall reductions in health care costs on the other.

III. THE DYNAMICS OF CHANGE

The main problem when addressing change is that in most cases, by the time the elements of change in a particular environment have been identified and characterized, the change has most likely already occurred. Thus, in most cases, time is spent catching up with change rather than anticipating it. In order to be able to truly anticipate changes, such as the type of changes that are currently ravaging the pharmaceutical industry, one needs to step back and examine the larger picture of how change can influence a particular discipline and how that discipline in turn must change to productively contribute, and with greater efficiency, to reengineering the R & D process. The title of this section "The Dynamics of Change" is really a misnomer. Change, particularly that affecting industrial management, is rarely a gradual process but is rather quantum in nature and tends to occur "in einen Augenblick!" However the actual realization that certain changes have taken place is often gradual such that response to change, although often being considered as prospective, is almost always retrospective in nature; we invariably play catch up. If one cannot truly anticipate change, then in order to survive in the new "now existing" environment, an organization has to adjust and take compensating actions as rapidly as possible. Otherwise it will not survive in competition with others who may have either anticipated or rapidly adjusted to the new environment.

Such is the case with pharmaceutical R & D and, in particular, with the philosophical approach controlling the nature and extent of pharmacokinetics and metabolism contributions to the R & D process. The present situation, in which considerable pharmacokinetics and metabolism resources are wasted in endless assay development and validation, unnecessary kinetic modeling, wasteful and unnecessary preclinical and clinical pharmacokinetics studies, and sometimes mindless support of innumerable clinical studies, many of which are nonpivotal, duplicative, or unnecessary, is wasteful, ineffective, and economically suicidal. While the disciplines of pharmacokinetics and drug metabolism have expanded to a point where they can make meaningful contributions to a wide spectrum drug discovery and development of activities, the question has to be asked as to what extent the contributions provide necessary and useful information to the study of a particular compound and whether they are essential to support safety and efficacy claims in a drug-marketing submission.

IV. THE CURRENT SITUATION

The process of discovery and development of new chemical entities is summarized in Fig. 1 [9].

As a result of the combined effects of improved analytical methods, greater sophistication of pharmacokinetics and metabolism technology, and increased awareness of the usefulness of kinetic and metabolism data in the discovery process, these disciplines have become intimately involved in the design of new chemical entities. Drug metabolism now plays a critical role in the earliest stages of discovery, particularly *in vitro* metabolic screening using both animal and human enzyme sources. New chemical entities are also rarely elevated to "lead" status unless complete pharmacokinetic profiles, in particular absolute bioavailability, elimination half-life, clearance, and distribution volume, are

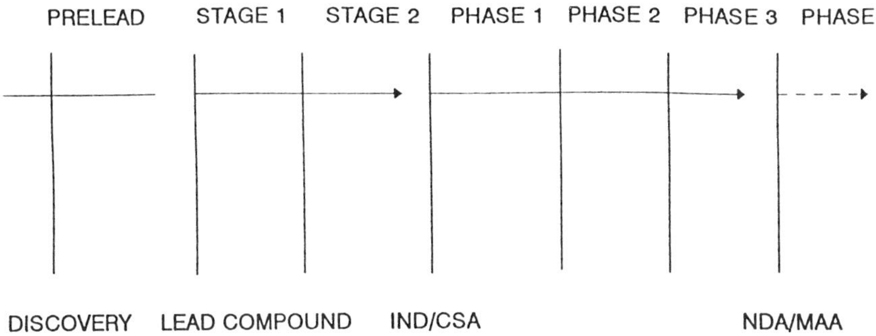

Fig. 1 Drug discovery and development process.

available. Kinetic and metabolic profiling continues throughout clinical development and an investigational new drug (IND) application routinely contains a considerable quantity of pharmacokinetic and metabolism data. While very little pharmacokinetic and metabolism data are officially required by most regulatory agencies, companies are generally too cautious to submit less than a fairly complete package. The spectrum of preclinical studies that may be conducted for IND submission, and beyond, is given in Table 1.

Table 1 Nonclinical Studies Involving Pharmacokinetics

Analytical development
Bioavailability, two species
Biopharmaceutical profile
Mass balance, two species
Autoradiography
Single-dose pharmacokinetics
Multiple-dose pharmacokinetics
Protein binding
Dose proportionality
Pharmacokinetic/pharmacodynamic relationships
Dose ranging, toxicology, two species
Short-term toxicology, two species
Long-term toxicology, two species
Metabolism work-up in toxicity species
Special toxicology studies

Apart from a wide range of pharmacokinetic and metabolism information, generally obtained in two or more animal species, an IND application contains an increasing proportion of toxicokinetic data. In fact the relatively new discipline of toxicokinetics, which has been the topic of several recent reviews [10, 11], has emerged as a major component of pharmacokinetics and metabolism support to the IND and also the new drug application (NDA) for marketing. It is now generally accepted that toxicology studies need to be conducted on a concentration-effect rather than a dose-effect basis and toxicokinetics and/or drug monitoring, depending on the circumstance, is now an integral (and expensive) component of essentially all toxicology studies [12]. Despite some obvious, and some perhaps less obvious, shortcomings to the assumption of a simple relationship between circulating drug levels and observed toxic effects [13,14], a considerable amount of useful information can nonetheless be derived from observed toxicokinetic–toxicodynamic relationships.

Toxicokinetic studies conducted early in a toxicology program are useful in order to provide complete kinetic profiles at toxicological doses in appropriate animal species, to guide subsequent dose regiments in longer term toxicology studies, to establish concentration-effect relationships at an early stage, to establish systemic drug bioavailability at toxicological dose levels, and to characterize saturation processes. Needless to say the toxicokinetic characteristics of a drug might differ from the pharmacokinetic characteristics due to differences in administered dose size and the resulting circulating drug and/or metabolite levels. Thus, the handling of toxicokinetic studies, and also the kinetic and metabolism results obtained, may be expected to differ in terms of compound solubility and stability, rate and extent of absorption, the degree of presystemic metabolism, rate and pathways of metabolism, and protein binding. In fact, any saturable process is likely to be influenced to some extent, contributing to differences between toxicokinetic and pharmacokinetic behavior.

Pharmacokinetic studies, and associated studies of pharmacokinetic–pharmacodynamic relationships, differ from toxicokinetic studies and associated toxicokinetic–toxicodynamic relationships in one other important aspect. Pharmacokinetic–pharmacodynamic relationships are frequently based on well characterized pharmacodynamic endpoints such as blood pressure, heart rate, etc., while toxicokinetic–toxicodynamic relationships are just as frequently based on unpredictable, poorly defined, and poorly understood toxicological endpoints. While preclinical pharmacokinetic–pharmacodynamic relationships are thus relatively easy to obtain, the nature of the relationship is unlikely to have a major impact on decisions to take the drug into humans. On the other hand, while toxicokinetic–toxicodynamic relationships are invariably difficult to obtain, and often even more difficult to understand mechanistically, these data are often critical for decisions as to whether or not the compound is safe to go into clinical trials. This paradox underscores the deemphasis that must occur in nonclinical pharmacokinetic studies, with far greater emphasis on toxicokinetic studies. Toxicokinetic–toxicodynamic data are critical for the preclinical to clinical transition; pharmacokinetic–pharmacodynamic data generally are not.

A. Clinical Pharmacology

The main objective during initial Phase I clinical pharmacology studies is to determine the safety of a new drug candidate in a small number of healthy individuals or, in the case of most anticancer agents and some other therapeutic classes, in selected patients. Compounds are routinely given as single rising doses and as multiple doses, and subjects are closely monitored for clinical signs and blood chemistry and also circulating levels of unchanged drug and/or metabolites. Other studies, for example, pilot bioavailability and food–drug interactions are also frequently conducted during clinical Phase 1.

These studies are routinely carried out by means of close collaboration between pharmacokinetics and clinical pharmacology scientists. The studies are data rich from both pharmacokinetic, pharmacodynamic, and safety perspectives and analysis is often conducted "on the fly," particularly in the single rising dose studies, so that compound blood or plasma levels and safety or activity data can be assessed before proceeding to the next highest dose. Depending on divisional organization, these responsibilities may be shared between two or more departments, for example, Pharmacokinetics, Clinical Pharmacology, and Biometrics, each depending on the other for data generation and integration, and probably represents the most intensive period of interdepartmental interaction and collaboration during the entire clinical development program. Overall, clinical Phase 1 may last between 6 months and 2 years, or longer.

B. Clinical Development

If a drug candidate is shown to be safe during Phase 1, it then proceeds into initial phase 2 and then into later Phase 2 and Phase 3 full-scale development. During Phase 2, the drug candidate is tested in small patient populations to further monitor safety and also to examine efficacy. Most Phase 2 clinical studies contain an extensive pharmacokinetic component. Such studies are summarized in Table 2.

The pharmacokinetics of a drug candidate are characterized after single and repeated doses in patients and additional information is obtained on dose proportionality, food effects, and possibly other interactions. Absolute systemic availability may be determined at this stage. Metabolism studies are initiated, together with mass balance. Thus extensive pharmacokinetic and metabolism characterization of the compound is obtained as it moves through

Table 2 Phase 2 Clinical Studies Involving Pharmacokinetics

Single-dose pharmacokinetics
Repeated-dose pharmacokinetics
Absolute systemic bioavailability
Food effects
Dose proportionality
Mass balance
Metabolism
Therapeutic monitoring during efficacy and safety studies

Phase 2 and into Phase 3 full-scale development. Simultaneously with Phase 2 and 3 clinical studies, additional nonclinical studies are conducted, including special studies such as placental transfer and excretion in milk and bile. However of far greater import is the continuation of metabolism characterization in toxicity species and also long-term general, carcinogenicity, and reproduction toxicology studies, together with associated drug monitoring. During this period there is considerable overlap and interdependence between nonclinical and clinical studies, particularly in the comparison of metabolism pathways in toxicity species and in humans, with consequent validation, or invalidation, of toxicity species relative to human safety.

A major activity during Phase 2, and continuing throughout the entire clinical development program, is that of therapeutic drug monitoring during efficacy trials. Consistent with the philosophy of mixed effect modeling [15], appropriate plasma and/or urine sampling during these studies can yield significant information regarding pharmacokinetics and concentration-effect relationships, both regarding efficacy and also tolerance to the drug, across a broad spectrum of patients.

The type of expertise generally required to carry out mixed effect modeling analyses has been available for many years, but their application has been plagued by the complexity of the statistics involved, difficulty of obtaining "good" data that are frequently generated in a noncontrolled clinical environment, difficulty in validating such data and also the pharmacokinetic and statistical computer software involved, problems in interpreting results of such data analysis, and, perhaps more critically, the ambivalent attitude of investigators and regulators regarding the value added by such analysis in a clinical program. Two opposing arguments have frequently been made. The first is that if pharmacokinetic and/or pharmacodynamic data are needed in a specific patient population then appropriate well-controlled studies should be conducted in that population. The counter argument is that such well-controlled studies are largely unnecessary and that sufficient pharmacokinetic and/or pharmacodynamic information can be obtained by combining data from various sources during clinical trials in order to identify and predict drug disposition and pharmacokinetic/pharmacodynamic relationships in specific populations. This author does not take issue with these arguments. However, the principal question that needs to be addressed, particularly in the current environment, is whether the mixed effect modeling approach actually adds value in terms of overall efficacy of the clinical drug development program. Regulatory agencies have not helped to resolve this question as their approach varies and often depends on the individuals currently making regulatory decisions. This area is fraught with advocates and skeptics. The degree of enthusiasm for mixed effect modeling almost invariably correlates highly with the mathematical expertise of individuals involved. Again, without taking issue, this writer's opinion is that, in the new cost-conscious drug development environment, mixed effect modeling will continue to be handled on a case-by-case basis and may evolve further as the associated computer software becomes more user friendly and less "exclusive" in nature. What is more doubtful is the extent to which such analyses become recognized as a necessary component leading to faster marketing approval of a new chemical entity. This hitherto has not been the case, and greater acceptance of the mixed effect approach will depend, to a great extent, on the actual value added relative to conventional approaches. Mixed effect modeling is currently regarded as a supplemental approach to the main thrust of clinical development programs, and specific studies in special populations continue to be the norm, whether associated with pharmacokinetic analysis or with establishing pharmacokinetic-pharmacodynamic relationships. Typical Phase 3 studies involving pharmacokinetics are summarized in Table 3.

Most Phase 3 clinical programs include between 4 and 8 drug interaction studies. Such studies, if justified, should always be carried out on the market image dosage form. The outcome of an initial food-drug interaction study may lead to additional studies. For example, if the systemic availability of a drug is

Table 3 Phase 3 Clinical Studies Involving Pharmacokinetics

Therapeutic drug-level monitoring of safety and efficacy trials
Special patient populations
Renal failure
Hepatic failure
Elderly versus young
Drug interactions
Bioavailability/bioequivalence of market-image versus clinical trial formulations

significantly increased or decreased by concomitant food intake, further studies may be required in which the time interval between drug administration and food ingestion may be varied to determine at what time interval the interaction loses significance.

Other drug interaction studies include coadministration with medications that may influence absorption or elimination, i.e., antacids, cimetidine, theophylline, probenecid, drugs that influence protein binding, and also drugs that are likely to be extensively coadministered in the patient population, particularly drugs in the same therapeutic class. Most regulatory agencies are sensitive to this topic and the number of these types of studies has increased during recent years. In many instances the number of drug interaction studies is dictated by a check list approach on a "what if . . ." basis. As will be described later in this chapter, this approach is cost ineffective. While some interaction studies are unpredictable, for example the type and extent of a drug–food interaction [16,17], many others may be predicted or discounted on a mechanistic basis dictated, for example, by the degree of protein binding, the extent of metabolism, the specific metabolism enzymes involved, and also on the presence or absence of active membrane transport. If these types of mechanistic guidelines are not applied, then the number of drug interaction studies conducted during a clinical development program will continue to expand to unrealistic and uneconomic proportions.

Relative bioavailability/bioequivalence between the dosage forms used in clinical trials and market-image dosage forms are often treated as check box items. However lack of equivalence between clinical and market-image formulations can have a disastrous impact on a development program possibly requiring the shifting of additional resources to reformulate and to conduct additional clinical bioequivalence trials. This sort of information should be generated as early as possible in a clinical development program. Achieving this may put considerable pressure on Product Development resources to develop the market-image formulation early, but is nonetheless a more attractive alternative than having to reformulate during the final stages of a development program and perhaps having to conduct additional clinical trials if equivalence between clinical and marketed formulations cannot be achieved.

V. THE NEED FOR CHANGE, RATIONALIZATION, EFFICACY, AND ECONOMY

As described in the introduction to this chapter, the disciplines of pharmacokinetics and drug metabolism have evolved to achieve their current high level of involvement in pharmaceutical R & D, and regulatory agencies worldwide demand an ever-increasing amount of pharmacokinetic and metabolism data.

While this has been professionally satisfying for practicing pharmacokinetics and drug metabolism scientists, one must ask the following questions: are too many of these types of data being generated for regulatory submissions and can whatever data are truly necessary be generated and handled more efficiently? The answers, in the writer's opinion, are yes on both counts. While kinetic and metabolism information is essential at all stages of a drug discovery and development program, too many data are being collected, often on a "nice to know" basis, and are too often handled inefficiently. Some pharmacokineticists fall into the trap of using pharmacokinetic data for convenience, as a surrogate, when other data such as clinical pharmacology or therapeutic endpoints cannot be readily obtained. Pharmacokinetic data are also not necessarily always easy to obtain. In many cases considerable analytical challenges have to be met before kinetic data can be generated, and correct interpretation of such pharmacokinetic data is often technically difficult. Nonetheless, the end result of pharmacokinetic data analysis is a body of highly quantitative information that can be interpreted, together with other information, to characterize the disposition and also kinetic–dynamic relationships of a compound. Unfortunately, such data are subject to misinterpretation or over interpretation, leading to incorrect or inappropriate conclusions and predictions. For example, poor systemic availability may be used as a basis to discontinue development of a drug candidate. However systemic availability may actually be unimportant depending on the site and mechanism of action, degree of tissue penetration, or a number of other factors that may impact the overall clinical efficacy of a compound.

Thus, while pharmacokinetics and drug metabolism are essential components of the discovery and development process, the extent of their utilization needs to be reassessed in terms of their relevance and efficiency of use. The following proposals might help to achieve this goal.

A. Prospective Planning

Given the pervasive nature of pharmacokinetic and metabolism science involvement in drug discovery and development, it is both logical and necessary for these disciplines to be involved during early planning stages. Too often a pharmacokineticist is required to act quickly to sudden and unexpected requests emanating from events and observations in other disciplines. Such requests are frequently unnecessary and always disruptive in that they require sudden shifts of resources from one program to another. These types of circumstance arise frequently, but could often be avoided if pharmacokinetic perspectives were included in advanced project planning. Resources can then be planned and assigned with reasonable consistency in order to provide optimum support consistent with overall priorities among competing or complimentary projects. Prospective planning helps to ensure optimum support to individual programs consistent with R & D priorities and to avoid wasteful "knee-jerk" activities. Prospective planning applies to all stages in R & D, from discovery through final compilation of regulatory documents, and represents one way, albeit a critical one, to streamline the process.

B. Discovery

Discovery teams are turning more and more to drug metabolism and pharmacokinetics input to assist in the design of new molecules. Such input may be extremely useful and could considerably shorten the discovery process. On the other hand, commitment of extensive pharmacokinetic and metabolism resources during discovery is potentially wasteful as only a very small percentage of new chemical entities is likely to reach clinical trials. Metabolism support at this stage must be based on utilization of computerized data banks to predict metabolism properties of molecules together with aggressive use of *in vitro* metabolism systems using animal and human source material to predict *in vivo* metabolic patterns. This type of work is currently labor intensive, but may not necessarily continue to be so. As metabolism technology advances to become more automated and miniaturized it should be entirely feasible to obtain metabolite characterization of new molecules within hours, with very limited resources.

While metabolism input into discovery is essential and is certain to increase, pharmacokinetics input, particularly bioavailability studies, are less useful, extremely labor intensive, and could be phased out or at least decreased without significant loss. In particular, the use of *in vivo* systemic availability as an initial screen to select a candidate for development represents a costly misuse of resources. It is far more economical, and frequently faster, to use a pharmacologic screen based on activity rather than a pharmacokinetic screen that involves the use of additional animals, multiple blood samplings, and development of analytical procedures for individual compounds. Pharmacokinetic analysis at the discovery stage is wasteful because it is only one of many factors that could affect the prospects of an early drug candidate.

In summary, during drug discovery there must be greater emphasis on rapid metabolism screens, possibly but not always requiring radiolabeled compounds, and far less emphasis on pharmacokinetics, which in many instances is both wasteful and inappropriate.

C. Nonclinical Development

As shown in Table 1, and as discussed earlier, a large number of nonclinical pharmacokinetics studies are conducted both before and after submission of an IND application. Some of these are essential; many are not. Emphasis in nonclinical research has changed from pharmacokinetics to toxicokinetics. Whether the pharmacokineticist accepts the notion or not, the most important activity of that discipline during preclinical development is to support toxicology studies. This type of support, although not yet clearly understood and often poorly characterized, is critical to support safety prediction from animals to man. Nonclinical studies predict human safety better than they predict efficacy.

Thus, many of the activities described in Table 1 should be deemphasized or dropped. Single- and multiple-dose pharmacokinetics and dose proportionality studies in animals may be of limited predictive value to humans and should be minimized. Autoradiography is not essential for every compound and should be restricted to those for whom information regarding tissue distribution of drug-related radioactivity is critical. Studies examining drug absorption in animals are an inefficient use of resources because of the generally poor predictability of these data to humans [18]. Similarly, extensive *in vivo* metabolite profiling in animals should become redundant as in vitro metabolism technology matures. Pharmacokinetic–pharmacodynamic interaction studies in animals may play a useful role for some compounds. However this is not universally the case. Even when good nonclinical pharmacodynamic data can be obtained, their relevance to the human clinical situation is uncertain.

While pharmacokinetic studies need to be deemphasized, greater emphasis will continue to be placed on toxicokinetic studies. As discussed earlier, toxicokinetic studies and establishing toxicokinetic–toxicodynamic relationships will continue to play an increasingly important role in nonclinical drug development. More use will continue to be made of these relationships to assess drug exposure in experimental animals and to link this with projected clinical safety margin. The major limiting factor in the evolution of these disciplines is the poor characterization and human predictability of toxicological endpoints. However, advances being made in the understanding of cellular pathophysiology and target organ susceptibility, together with increased knowledge of concentration-effect relationships, and also increased demand from regulatory agencies for such data to support drug safety claims, will continue to provide impetus for expansion of these activities [19]. It is unfortunate that any pharmacokinetics resources gained from downsizing nonclinical pharmacokinetic activity are likely to be lost, at least in part, due to increasing demands for toxicokinetic and toxicodynamic data. Some areas of pharmacokinetics and toxicokinetics involvement that should receive greater or less emphasis during preclinical discovery and development are summarized in Table 4.

D. Clinical Pharmacology and Clinical Pharmacokinetic Studies

The period during which a drug candidate is first administered to humans represents the first phase of a long and expensive clinical program, a great

Table 4 Areas of Toxicokinetic and Drug Metabolism Support That Warrant Greater or Less Emphasis in Nonclinical Discovery and Development

Greater emphasis	Less emphasis
Discovery	
Metabolism	Pharmacokinetics
Transport	Bioavailability screens
Pharmacologic activity screens	
Development	
Metabolism	Single- and oral-dose pharmacokinetics
In vitro interaction studies	Dose proportionality
Toxicokinetics	Bioavailability
Toxicokinetics/toxicodynamics	Food effects
	Autoradiography

proportion of which has considerable pharmacokinetic and metabolism involvement. As described previously, this is a difficult period involving intensive collaboration between clinical, pharmacokinetics, and statistical scientists. The focus of these initial studies is almost exclusively on safety, but they also have an extensive pharmacokinetic component.

Phase 1 studies provide preliminary safety and pharmacokinetic data essential for further development of a compound into Phase 2 and Phase 3. This segment of the clinical development program is unlikely to change, as is the pharmacokinetic component, due to the critical nature of the studies conducted. The only major change that has already occurred is that dose escalation, whether during single-dose or multiple-dose studies, is becoming increasingly drug concentration dependent. This places considerable demands on pharmacokinetics departments in that it requires rapid analytical turnaround to support concentration guided dose escalation. These early studies provide the first opportunity to initiate a clinical pharmacokinetic–pharmacodynamic database, which can be expanded as additional Phase 2 and 3 studies are conducted.

Metabolism work-up in humans is generally not done during Phase 1, but is usually started during Phase 2, continuing into Phase 3. With rapidly evolving metabolism technology, this delay in conducting human metabolic studies is no longer justified. While it may be appropriate to delay human mass-balance studies until clinical Phase 2, there is no reason why an initial metabolism profile should not be obtained, both in urine and plasma during Phase 1 studies. This will provide a critical comparison between metabolism profiles in toxicology animal species and man and will thus give an early indication of the relevance of the toxicity data to humans that could lead to possible changes in toxicology or clinical programs. It will "streamline" the system.

E. Clinical Development

Clinical Phases 2 and 3 are periods of close interaction between pharmacokinetics and clinical sciences. It is a period of considerable resource commitment and also the time during which the biggest changes in pharmacokinetic involvement are necessary.

Changes in pharmacokinetics resource commitment are a function of the number and types of clinical studies conducted and also the degree of pharmacokinetic involvement in individual studies. Prospective planning among clinical and pharmacokinetic disciplines is essential in order to achieve a more efficient and cost-effective clinical development program.

In most programs far too many clinical studies are conducted, sometimes to satisfy one or other opinion leaders in a specific and perhaps isolated market, but often also as a result of poor prospective planning. Regulatory approval of a drug for marketing is generally based on two or three pivotal safety and efficacy studies together with specific pharmacokinetic and/or pharmacodynamic studies such as food effect, interactions, and special populations. Most NDAs (New Drug Applications) contain far in excess of this. Some of the additional studies may be required for particular circumstances but many are wasteful, duplicative, or simply unnecessary. There is generally little reason why the same clinical study should be conducted in more than one country. A single study should be conducted under conditions that meet worldwide regulatory requirements. An extensive series of drug–food interactions studies is wasteful and can be avoided if initial studies are conducted correctly and if market-image formulations are available early in a clinical program. Drug–drug interactions should be limited to the absolute minimum and should be restricted, for the most part, to those interactions that are predicted from preliminary *in vitro* metabolism or binding screens. The concept of restricting the number of interaction studies would perhaps not be supported by marketing colleagues but is nonetheless mandatory for responsible cost containment. True pharmacologic or therapeutic interactions cannot readily be examined in a study conducted in a small number of subjects or patients and are best determined during large clinical trials, or subsequently during drug therapy.

Depending on the type of drug and therapeutic class, complete pharmacokinetic profiles should not be required for any study that is not specifically pharmacokinetically driven. Such data are nice to have but are not necessary for regulatory marketing approval. Drug level monitoring, which may also include metabolite monitoring, during clinical trials should be restrictive and sampling should be limited to that which is absolutely essential.

This depends, of course, on the philosophical approach to study design and analysis for a particular compound or compound class. When a conventional approach is used in which specific studies are conducted to characterize drug pharmacokinetics and pharmacodynamics in special patient populations, then plasma or urine sampling for drug analysis during general large-scale clinical safety and efficacy trials should be minimal and should be restricted to a small proportion of study sites. If, on the other hand, a mixed effect modeling approach is used to describe pharmacokinetics and pharmacodynamics in special patient populations, then studies in special populations are deemphasized and plasma and urine sampling in safety and efficacy trials needs to be more rigorous. As noted earlier, the place of mixed effect modeling in the analysis of clinical data continues to evolve. Its current contribution to NDA submissions tends to be nonpivotal but this could change depending on user friendliness of the kinetic and statistical computer software and the philosophical position taken by regulatory agencies.

One type of clinical study that has caused much controversy has been that of determining absolute systemic availability of orally administered compounds in humans. This writer has been involved in many debates weighing the benefits of obtaining these data against the risks. The benefits are clearly associated with complete pharmacokinetic characterization, with particular implications regarding interactions affecting absorption, first-pass presystemic clearance, and providing data that may be critical for novel dosage form development. The risks are principally associated with having to do additional intravenous toxicology and toxicokinetic studies and also a clinical absolute availability study, with all the associated costs, notwithstanding the potential for unexpected toxicity resulting from intravenous doses.

While the principal emphasis in this chapter has been to do fewer studies, particularly in clinical development, the case for obtaining absolute bioavailability data for an orally administered drug provides an exception. Despite the obvious risks involved, the absence of absolute bioavailability information for a new drug candidate is not only scientifically negligent in failing to describe a vital pharmacokinetic characteristic, but is also certain to give rise to repeated questions and challenges from regulatory agencies. Such questions are always contentious and, almost without exception, cause or contribute to delayed marketing approval of a new chemical entity. Carrying out clinical absolute bioavailability studies is both sensible and responsible from both scientific and safety perspectives and is favored or demanded by most regulatory agencies.

Some areas of pharmacokinetic involvement that should receive greater or less emphasis during clinical development are summarized in Table 5.

VI. SUMMARY AND CONCLUSIONS

Pharmacokinetics and drug metabolism have evolved to play critical roles in drug discovery and development. The increasing maturity of these disciplines, the relative ease of obtaining pharmacokinetic and metabolism data, and also

Table 5 Areas of Pharmacokinetic and Drug Metabolism Support That Warrant Greater or Less Emphasis in Clinical Development

Greater emphasis	Less emphasis
Early metabolism studies	Duplicative clinical studies
Absolute bioavailability	Multiple food-effect studies
Early systemic availability of market-image formulations	Unnecessary pharmacokinetic profiling in safety and efficacy studies
Pharmacokinetic–pharmacodynamic relationships and mixed effect modeling approaches*	Unnecessary and inappropriate interaction studies

*Compound specific. Depends on drug, therapeutic class, and regulatory position.

the tendency for companies to include as much data as conceivably possible in regulatory submissions, has led to often unreasonable demands on these disciplines.

If this trend were allowed to continue in pharmacokinetics and drug metabolism, as in every other discipline involved in the discovery and development process, then pharmaceutical research and development will rapidly become prohibitively cost ineffective. The recommendations for changes in pharmacokinetic and metabolism involvement described in this chapter are based on observations made during over a decade of experience in the pharmaceutical industry. While many attempts have been made to focus directly on pharmacokinetic and metabolism activities, the argument has frequently expanded, without apology, to other areas, in particular to clinical research where considerable changes and economies in developmental philosophy are needed. Attention has focused primarily on activities that, in the writer's opinion, need to be changed, either expanded or reduced. Other areas, not addressed here, work well and do not represent a "burning platform" for change [20].

It is worth noting that the objective of pharmacokinetic support for a drug development program should be to provide information that supports safety and efficacy claims. It is not, as appears often to have been assumed, to provide an exhaustively complete and in-depth pharmacokinetic and metabolism profile of a drug candidate under every conceivable situation. In this time of rationalization and need for responsible cost containment, it is imperative that emphasis in utilization of pharmacokinetic and drug metabolism resources be placed not on total pharmacokinetic and pharmacodynamic characterization, but rather on responsible and efficient application of limited resources to provide adequate support to ensure that a safe and efficacious drug is being introduced to the market.

REFERENCES

1. T. Teorell. Kinetics of distribution of substances administered to the body I. The extravascular modes of administration. *Arch. Int. Pharmacodyn. 57*: 205–225, 1937.
2. T. Teorell. Kinetics of distribution of substances administered to the body II. The intravascular modes of administration. *Arch. Int. Pharmacodyn. 57*: 226–240, 1937.
3. L. Z. Benet. General treatment of linear mammillary models with elimination from any compartment as used in pharmacokinetics. *J. Pharm. Sci. 61*: 536–541, 1972.
4. E. R. Garrett. The physicochemical and pharmacokinetic basis for the biopharmaceutical evaluation of drug biological activity in pharmaceutical formulations. *Acta Pharmacol., Toxicol., 29*: 1–29, 1971.
5. M. Gibaldi. Pharmacokinetics and clinical pharmacokinetics, 3rd edn. Lea and Febiger, Philadelphia, 1984, p. 330.
6. G. Levy and M. Gibaldi. Pharmacokinetics of drug action. *Ann. Rev. Pharmacol. 12*: 85–98, 1972.
7. J. C. K. Loo and S. Riegelman. New method for calculating the absorption rate of drugs. *J. Pharm. Sci. 57*: 918–928, 1968.
8. J. G. Wagner. Fundamentals of clinical pharmacokinetics. Drug Intelligence Publications, Hamilton, IL, 1975, p. 461.
9. P. G. Welling. Role of pharmacokinetics in drug discovery and development. In Pharmacokinetics of Drugs. P. G. Welling and L. P. Balant, Eds. Springer-Verlag, Heidelberg, 1994, p. 5.
10. A. Yacobi, J. P. Skelly, and V. K. Batra, Eds. Toxicokinetics and New Drug Development. Pergamon Press, New York, 1989, p. 246.
11. P. G. Welling and F. A. de la Iglesia, Eds. Drug Toxicokinetics. Marcel Dekker, New York, 1993, p. 408.
12. L. F. Chasseaud. Role of toxicokinetics in toxicity testing. In Drug Toxicokinetics. P. G. Welling and F. A. de la Iglesia, Eds. Marcel Dekker, New York, 1993, pp. 105–142.
13. A. M. Monro. Interspecies comparisons in toxicology: the utility and futility of plasma concentrations of the test substance. *Regul. Toxicol. Pharmacol. 12*: 137–160, 1990.
14. D. A. Smith. Integration of animal pharmacokinetic and pharmacodynamic data in drug safety assessment. *Eur. J. Drug Metab. Pharmacokin. 18*: 31–39, 1993.
15. J.-L. Steimer, S. Vozeh, A. Racine-Poon, N. Holford, and R. O'Neill. The population approach: rationale, methods, and applications, in clinical pharmacology and drug development. In Pharmacokinetics of Drugs. P. G. Welling and L. P. Balant, Eds. Springer-Verlag, Heidelberg, 1994, p. 405–451.
16. K. T. Kivistö, P. Ojala-Karlsson, and P. J. Neuvonen. Inhibition of norfloxacin absorption by dairy products. *Antimicrob. Ag. Chemother. 36*: 489–491, 1992.
17. J. X. Sun, A. Cipriano, K. Chan, M. Klibaner, and V. A. John. Effect of food on the relative bioavailability of a hypolipidemic agent (CGP 43371) in healthy subjects. *J. Pharm. Sci. 83*: 264–266, 1994.
18. J. B. Dressman and K. Yamada. Animal models for oral drug absorption. In Pharmaceutical Bioequivalence. P. G. Welling, F. L. S. Tse, and S. V. Dighe, Eds. Marcel Dekker, New York, 1991, p. 235–266.

19. F. A. de la Iglesia. Perspective and future directions of toxicokinetics in drug development. In Drug Toxicokinetics. P. G. Welling and F. A. de la Iglesia, Eds. Marcel Dekker, New York, 1993, p. 381–402.
20. D. R. Conner. Managing at the Speed of Change. Villard Books, New York, 1993, p. 92–97.

10

Anticancer Drug Development

Jim Cassidy

University of Aberdeen
Aberdeen, Scotland

I. INTRODUCTION

Unfortunately, the treatment of most common solid tumors in adults has not reproduced the encouraging improvements in response and survival demonstrated with chemotherapeutic intervention in the hematological cancers over the last 20–30 years. Many reasons can be cited for this disappointing state of affairs, but it is clear that for the common solid cancers (lung, colorectal, breast), in their advanced stages, chemotherapy is (at best) only palliative.

In view of the prevalence, mortality, social, and economic impact of cancer in the developed countries of the world, the importance of drug development in this area of medicine is self-evident. This is reflected in the level of activity and resource that is dedicated to anticancer drug development, both within the pharmaceutical industry and by governmental agencies. In spite of this expenditure of effort and money only a handful of new anticancer drugs have been marketed in the last 10 years. This is particularly true if one excludes derivative compounds, such as carboplatin, or those said to reduce particular toxicities of the parent, e.g., epirubicin. It is even more disappointing to note that, in terms of producing real impact on survival for a common solid tumor, cisplatin is unique (though Taxol may change this) over the last 20 years.

This has to be viewed as a failure of the drug development process. In this chapter I will attempt to highlight some of the unique problems of anticancer drug development (as opposed to other drugs). I will also address areas in which my personal view is that changes will be required to remedy this situation.

It is also worth stressing that our current armamentarium of drugs could be utilised more efficiently [1], with worthwhile improvements in our ability to palliate or even cure malignancies and I will highlight those areas where early development processes could be modified to optimise the eventual clinical utility of an anticancer drug.

A further level of complexity is given to anticancer drug development because of the widespread clinical use of combinations of cytotoxics. This is often not (never ?) addressed in the early development of cytotoxic agents. The complexities of this issue are beyond the scope of this contribution, but considerations of the therapeutic place of a compound have clear and important implications in strategic planning decisions within the pharmaceutical industry.

II. DRUG ACQUISITION

A. Analogue Development

A cytotoxic drug of proven clinical utility may be chemically modified to produce a series of derivatised molecules that are then tested for anticancer activity or toxicity profile relative to the parent compound. This approach may be considered to be a low-risk, low-tech way of drug development, but it has produced agents with improved spectra of activity or toxicity that have some clinical advantages (notably carboplatin). However, it does seem unlikely that such a strategy will lead to a significant increase in the potential for cancer cure by the new drug.

B. Screening

Initial large scale screening of compounds for anticancer activity was based on the long established mouse P388 leukaemia system. Around 10 years ago it became clear that too few clinically useful agents were emerging from the screen [2]. A new screen has been developed based on a large panel of *human* tumor cell lines. In tandem, new methods of analysis of data were developed, including COMPARE, which allows drugs to be selected based on differential cytotoxicity for particular groups of tumor cell types, possibly indicating novel mechanisms of action based on tumor specific biochemistry [3]. Many tens of thousands of compounds have now been screened by this system, and many thousands considered worthy of further investigation have been selected. It is usual to subject such compounds to second-level screening using human tumor xenografts in nude mice. A similar, but not identical system, has been adopted in Europe [4]. As yet it is too soon to know if such large-scale screening programs will be cost effective in terms of detecting new, active compounds with novel mechanisms of action.

C. Serendipity

In 1965 Rosenberg reported the chance observation that platinum complexes had potent biological activity. When *Escherichia coli* organisms were grown in culture containing a platinum electrode, bacterial growth continued but cell division was inhibited, giving rise to long filamentous bacteria. This eventually led to the demonstration of cisplatin antitumor effects in 1968, and hence to clinical development of that compound.

This story illustrates the importance of serendipity, but it is clearly not a strategic path that can be followed! Undoubtedly, we will continue to make these types of breakthroughs, and perhaps the message should be that all involved in drug development should be as open minded as possible. In addition, we should recognise that observations made outside our own fields of endeavour may have major importance. Since the very nature of cancer is a derangement of cell growth and behaviour such observations may conceivably arise from almost any branch of the biological sciences, and more particularly from the burgeoning field of molecular biology [5].

D. Rational Development

This is the most scientifically pleasing method of discovering a new anticancer agent. The process is dependent on the ability of biologists to define the nature of the molecular and biochemical changes that initiate and maintain the malignant cell phenotype. Using this knowledge, medicinal chemists and pharmacologists synthesise and screen molecules that may inhibit the phenotype.

This so-called "designer chemotherapy" is in its infancy, but many such compounds are in early clinical stages of development. The developments in this area have been greatly facilitated by the adoption of semiautomated robotic technology to allow rapid activity screening of lead compounds, and hence the development of structure-function models. Examples are inhibition of protein kinase C, tyrosine kinase inhibitors, and various inhibitors of the phospholipase signaling cascade. It remains to be seen whether this will yield more or better drugs than any of the other methods of drug acquisition.

III. ANIMAL TOXICOLOGY AS APPLIED TO ANTICANCER DRUGS

In contrast to other areas in medicine, most cytotoxic agents are by their very nature highly toxic substances. The potential for genotoxicity of an agent specifically designed to damage DNA is self-evident. In most clinical situations this is of no consequence, since we are attempting to *palliate* an incurable and lethal illness. However, in those tumors that are amenable to cure by cytotoxic therapy there is a substantial problem of induction of second malignancies, particularly leukaemia.

In high doses most current cytotoxics will be lethal in animal models due to bone marrow suppression, mucositis, cardiac or pulmonary toxicity. At present animal toxicology is only a very rough guide to the *types* of toxicity one might see in humans. This information is then used to build (what is hoped to be) appropriate screening in patients enrolled within the Phase I trials (e.g., cardiotoxicity in animals will lead to ECG or more intensive cardiac monitoring).

The major use of animal toxicology in oncology is to guide a safe starting dose for human Phase I trials. This subject has been extensively reviewed [6]. In the experience of the NCI-USA for the majority of compounds one tenth of the mouse LD_{10} was a safe starting dose (when expressed on a mg/m^2 basis). In Europe it is now common practice to confirm this in rats or another species to avoid undue toxicity at the starting dose.

The only other elaboration on this simple theme is the introduction of compound-oriented toxicity testing. In principle, this involves animal testing using a route and schedule that is intended for clinical use rather than the more empiric use in classical toxicology (such as IP or repeated IV administration). This has resulted in both a reduction of the number of animals used and in some cases a substantial reduction in the number of patients needed for completion of the Phase I trials [8].

This system is not ideal since rodents (and other lower species) have quite different biological and biochemical profiles to humans. This problem may be circumvented when we know the mechanism of action of drugs, but potentially could be a major problem for drugs with unknown novel mechanisms. The best example of this phenomenon is in the clinical development of thymidylate synthetase inhibitors (TSI). Thymidylate synthetase is the major focus of activity for 5-fluorouracil, and many new agents have been synthesised to produce more efficient TS inhibition. The toxicity of TSI is dependent on extracellular fluid thymidine levels, and since this is 10-fold higher in mice compared to patients [9], the use of murine toxicology would be entirely inappropriate.

As we head towards drugs that are not DNA-targeted and that have more specific enzyme inhibitory function, it is to be hoped that we will adapt our strategies even further. Conceivably, Phase I trials could be performed with dose escalations and starting doses based on expected enzyme inhibitory activity.

It is clear that the days of extensive animal testing of cytotoxic drugs are now behind us. Our aim should be to limit this phase to the minimum needed for safety in human studies.

IV. METHODOLOGICAL ISSUES IN PHASE I TRIALS

Phase I trials in oncology are unique in that healthy volunteer studies are entirely inappropriate because of the cytotoxic and genotoxic nature of the drugs. This leads to a selection bias for patients that tends to reflect the investigator's practice or prejudices, although standard guidelines do exist that serve as a template for most Phase I protocols [7].

Although traditional Phase I trials are predominantly toxicology in humans, the temptation remains to bias patient accrual to those tumor types in which activity is expected (e.g., colon cancer for thymidylate synthase inhibition). The demonstration of a hint of activity in Phase I will often be the deciding factor in the progression to Phase II. Hence, there is an understandable desire to select those more likely to respond. This may be reasonable for a TSI, but what of a compound with an entirely unknown or novel mechanism? In my opinion it is more desirable to include as many tumor types as possible. This introduces an element of randomness that may not be inappropriate, since it is not inconceivable that a TSI may affect renal cancer or melanoma that may not traditionally be seen as 5-Fluorouracil sensitive.

A. Patient Selection

Certain criteria of patient selection are standard, including:

1. Histological confirmation of malignancy no longer amenable to established forms of therapy,
2. Age 18 or over,
3. Performance status (ECOG-Zubrod scale) <3,
4. Normal hematology (WBC $\geq 4000/mm^3$ and platelets $\geq 100{,}000/mm^3$),
5. Life expectancy of more than 12 weeks, and
6. Informed consent for entry to the trial.

In addition the following are normally excluded:

1. Antitumor therapy within the last 4 weeks (6 weeks for nitrosoureas or mitomycin C),
2. Pregnancy, or women of child bearing potential not taking adequate contraceptive precautions,
3. Patients with intercurrent illness or complications of malignancy (e.g., hypercalcaemia),
4. Patients with psychotic disorders or other psychiatric complaints that might inhibit informed consent or follow-up, and
5. Patients with major organ dysfunction at a site of likely drug toxicity (e.g., cardiotoxicity).

B. Selection of Starting Dose

In drugs that produce toxicity in animal species we rely heavily on this information to establish what is hoped will be a safe starting dose. As discussed previously this is conventionally taken as $^1/_{10}$ of the LD_{10} (in mg/m^2) in the mouse. Prior verification in another species that this dose is safe is usually performed before initiation of patient dosing. This approach has proven to be safe in most instances, but occasionally unusual or unpredictable toxicities such as headache are observed even at the entry dose [10]. Some investigators now feel this starting dose may be too low. In a review of 45 Phase I drugs Penta et al. [11], found that the median range of maximal tolerated dose (MTD) to starting dose for all drugs was 20, with a median number of eight dose-escalation steps to reach the MTD. Even more worrying was the finding that for drugs with nonhaematologic toxicity the median ratio of MTD to starting dose was 30; necessitating a median of 9 dose-escalation steps.

Whilst it is morally laudable to pick a safe starting dose, one must also remember that patients enter Phase I trials with some hope of anticancer response. Thus wasteful exploration of doses that are too low for toxicity may deny patients the possibility of response, which is almost always experienced at the highest dose levels [11]. In my own clinical practice, with a number of competing Phase I protocols, patients often elect to enter those studies that are at or are close to MTD and will be more reluctant to go for entry dose levels. We urgently require methods of dose selection that minimise patient numbers at low doses and accelerate escalation to the MTD.

C. Selection of Schedule

The choice of schedule of drug administration may be crucial for a number of reasons. A drug may have different levels of activity with different administration, one example being Etoposide (VP-16) [12]. It is theoretically possible that a drug may be incorrectly abandoned as inactive when a more appropriate schedule would reveal anticancer action. Toxicity may be quantitatively or qualitatively different with alteration of schedule; such as with taxotere, where nonhematological toxicity (mucositis) was clearly schedule dependent [13]. This may also lead to erroneous decisions on the future development of the drug. Even when a drug is active and toxicity acceptable with one schedule in early clinical trials, this may not be the *optimal* schedule, and it may take many years to investigate this point in clinical practice [14] with grave consequences for individuals not exposed to the optimal schedule in the meantime.

The relevance of animal data to patients with respect to schedule is questionable. Occasionally data do exist on mechanism of action, cycle specificity, or pharmacokinetics that will argue for particular administration parameters. Pragmatic and financial constraints limit our ability to explore very prolonged infusions, 3–4 times daily chronic IV, and other "inconvenient" schedules. All too often the empirical approach will prevail with IV bolus dosing once every 3 weeks as the initial selected schedule.

It is possible that a more detailed preclinical investigation of pharmacokinetics and pharmacodynamics, or development of assay systems that measure the biological effect of the drug on its target, could help to guide our choice of schedule. However, there is an understandable reluctance on the part of pharmaceutical companies to initiate even more preclinical studies for an agent with a high risk of not becoming a product. In addition, clinicians are so desperate to try any new agent in this patient population that they will accept much more limited preclinical data than is customary for noncytotoxics and will push for the most convenient schedule for patients, sometimes to the exclusion of clear scientific data that an alternative schedule is likely to be more active.

D. Dose Escalation Scheme

Again, in the absence of good predictive animal model systems, dose escalation is often based on empirical formulae, the most widely used being a modified

Fibonacci scheme. Three patients are treated at the starting dose and, in the absence of toxicity, a series of dose escalations is applied in successive cohorts until toxicity appears. Thus if level 1, the starting dose, is X_1, level 2 is X_1 + 100%, level 3 is X_2 + 67%, level 4 is X_3 + 50%, and levels 5 and above are X_n + 30%. Three patients are usually treated at each dose level but additional patients are entered at a given dose if significant toxicity is documented. More conservative dose escalation steps (i.e., 30% or less) proceed after the observation of WHO grade 2 toxicity [7]. This scheme can be time consuming and wasteful of precious resources, particularly when the MTD is significantly higher than predicted by animal studies and if sporadic events in early doses are wrongly attributed to drug effects, thus slowing down escalation.

Two recent innovations are finding increasing application in an attempt to improve our current methodology, these are known as PGDE (pharmacokinetically guided dose-escalations) and CRM (continuous reassessment method).

PGDE was originally proposed by Collins et al. [15]. The European Organisation for Research and Treatment of Cancer (EORTC) produced guidelines for its use in Phase I in 1987 [16] and since then it has been prospectively evaluated in a number of Phase I studies (reviewed by Graham and Workman [17]). The aim of PGDE is to reach a target AUC (area under the plasma concentration-time curve) in humans in 4–7 steps. This target AUC is derived from the AUC at the LD_{10} in mice, and the assumption is made that discrepancies between the LD_{10} in mice and the MTD in man are similar. Implementation of PGDE is highly dependent on suitable (rapid) analytical methodology and expertise, but these are almost always available on site or at the pharmaceutical research establishment. Although PGDE does have limitations it has the potential to reduce escalation steps. It is only through continued prospective evaluation that the true worth of PGDE will be revealed.

CRM is based on use of all available data to predict the MTD. In other words the preclinical data are modified and reassessed with each patient's experience to update the estimate of MTD. Prior to patient dosing a probability distribution for the MTD and dose toxic-response model are selected. These may be modified by pharmacokinetic or other data. The "new" MTD is calculated after each individual patient has been treated with the new agent using the methods of O'Quigley et al. [18] and Faries [19]. This allows for just one patient to be treated at each dose level, which may not save time but will reduce the number of patients exposed to low (inactive) doses. The method is also sufficiently flexible to re-accelerate escalation if sporadic events at lower dose levels are not repeated in individuals given higher doses as the trial progresses. This methodology is in its infancy but again could radically alter our current practice.

One further approach is to use pharmacokinetic and pharmacodynamic information to define the maximal tolerated systemic exposure of a drug [20].

This type of approach has the added advantage that such pharmacodynamic data would be invaluable in attempting therapeutic drug monitoring or adaptive feedback control of drug dose for individual patients at a later stage in the development process.

E. Patient Monitoring

Since the Phase I study is designed to have toxicological endpoints, it is of paramount importance that *all* forms of toxicity be fully evaluated. It would also be particularly onerous if patients had to undergo repeated investigations that are time consuming, potentially hazardous, or very expensive. So a compromise is usually reached that encourages vigilance against toxicities predicted for the drug. The physician must always be alert to unexpected sequelae, and it is essential to investigate any untoward events as fully as possible since the future development of the drug will be discontinued in the face of unusual or severe toxicity profiles, unless they can be adequately explained and circumvented. Patients should be cared for in an environment where all the necessary facilities for resuscitation are available, and an experienced physician should be in attendance. The investigator should bear in mind that omissions at this stage may have serious consequences for a larger patient population in Phase II studies.

F. Definition of Study Endpoints

The Phase I study is complete when the maximally tolerated dose is established for ambulatory patients. Doses should be recommended for Phase II in both good- and poor-risk patients (usually based on performance status and marrow reserve from prior therapy).

The definition of the maximally tolerated dose is usually that dose that produces tolerable and reversible toxicity in $^3/_6$ patients. Over the last few years our concept of "tolerable" toxicity has changed, and in particular with hematological toxicity our definition has become more aggressive. This reflects our ability to manage pancytopenia better than before due to broad spectrum antibiotics and use of hematological growth factor support (such as G-CSF).

Various problems exist with the use of the MTD as it is currently defined. Phase I is usually capable of picking up acute toxicity, but since few patients have more than 3–4 cycles of therapy Phase I will not be a good indicator of cumulative or late toxicity. The concept that "more is better" has become accepted dogma in oncology, but it is clear that many biological agents have bell-shaped dose-response curves; that is, with increase in dose beyond some optimal level there is a *reduction* in response.

As we move away from agents with DNA as the main locus of activity it is likely that we will encounter novel (nonhematological) toxicities, and those toxicities may or may not be related to the mechanism of anticancer activity. One potential solution is the adoption of so-called biological endpoints. Put simply, this involves an *in vivo* assessment of the drug target, such that if 100% inhibition (possibly of an enzymic process) has been obtained dose escalation would cease even in the *absence* of toxicity [21]. This strategy is not without problems but could help in a number of ways with some of the more empirical factors in Phase I evaluation.

V. PHASE II TRIALS

The main emphasis of Phase II trials is to identify any antitumor activity of the new compound. This is tested by exposing cohorts of patients with particular tumor types to the dose and schedule defined in the preceding Phase I trials. In addition, the toxicological data in humans are improved by experience in Phase II. This is particularly true of the longer term effects and multiple cycle actions that are usually not well characterised in Phase I. This helps to define the therapeutic index of the new agent [22].

Many of the methodological issues pertinent in Phase I have to be revisited in designing Phase II trials. This particularly applies to patient selection; should we select patients with early metastatic disease that have had minimal prior exposure to cytotoxics (thereby improving the chances of observing activity)? Or should we only allow those patients who have been shown to be intractable to standard therapies to be entered into investigational drug studies? Since, for the majority of common solid cancers at the advanced stage, chemotherapy is given with palliative intention I feel that it is perfectly justifiable to enter minimally or non-pretreated patients, with the proviso that such patients are closely monitored and at the first signs of tumor progression can be switched to standard therapy. This approach has been applied to both lung cancer and breast cancer in recent years with no apparent detriment in terms of overall survival time of such patients.

It would be nice to evaluate activity in a wide spectrum of tumor types, in order to avoid missing anticancer action in rarer tumors. However, each Phase II will be expensive, and there must be some limitation to the availability of patient numbers in rare conditions. In practice this dichotomy is resolved by financial considerations; usually only those tumor types that are common enough to provide a prospect of financial return, should the drug be marketed, may be tested in Phase II. This explains the relative lack of Phase II activity testing in cervical cancer in North America (which is now being emulated in Europe), despite the global impact of this disease. Occasionally a particular tumor type may be selected from preclinical activity profiles or by similarity with existing agents, for example colorectal cancer with TS inhibitors.

How many patients should be entered in Phase II? In the Early Clinical Trials Group (ECTG) of the EORTC, such trials usually have a two-stage design. In the first stage, 14 evaluable patients are entered for a particular tumor type. If no response is observed the trial is closed. This approach ensures that if the aim is to identify a drug with at least 20% response rate, the chance of rejecting it wrongly is 0.044 [23]. In the second stage (if one or more responses are seen in the first stage) up to 11 additional patients are entered to estimate the response rate with a standard error of 10%. Whilst this approach is commendably rapid, and allows ECTG to run multiple Phase II trials, it may miss activity less than the 20% level, which may still be better than existing drugs (e.g., in colorectal cancer). Also low-level activity may prompt a re-examination of the preclinical and Phase I data to seek better dosing/schedules and may encourage programs of analogue development to attempt to improve on anticancer activity. It is therefore not uncommon to observe Phase II trials involving fifty or more subjects, and the limits are again arbitrary or dictated by economic constraints.

Since the demonstration of anticancer activity is so essential at this stage, great care should be taken to ensure that only those patients with measurable disease be entered and that methods of assessment be applied meticulously, preferably with external independent review of radiological images, etc.

Most Phase II trials have been open label, nonrandomised studies. In those drugs that have ready made comparators (i.e., prodrugs or analogues of existing drugs) it may be appropriate to consider a randomised design of the new drug versus the standard agent, thus allowing an early comparison of therapeutic index [24], which is usually a registration prerequisite for such drugs.

Increasing amounts of resource and effort have been put into the use of pharmacokinetics and pharmacodynamic modeling in early clinical trials of anticancer drugs. Such detailed study has definite benefits if the compound progresses to product license application [25], but is expensive, and particularly so if the compound is abandoned. Much recent effort has gone into developing limited sampling strategies as early as possible to reduce the burden on clinical and analytical resource. This has been particularly true of one of the taxanes, Taxotere, which is currently in global Phase II–III programmes [13,26]. I think it is fair to say that this scale of pharmacokinetic/dynamic input is unique and is watched with great interest by others to determine the cost benefit of this exercise, before it could be accepted as the norm.

VI. PHASE III TRIALS

Few drugs reach this stage in comparison to the huge numbers of compounds screened for potential anticancer effects!

The concept of comparison of the new drug with the accepted best available treatment is common to all medical research. The problem in oncology is that there is in general no consensus as to the best available therapy. In fact, in some cases the "best" may be supportive care with no exposure to cytotoxics at all. Even in tumor types where some consensus does exist (e.g., platinum plus an alkylator in ovarian cancer), there is considerable regional, national, or international variation, which makes design of large-scale international collaborative Phase III studies particularly difficult.

In view of the numbers of patients required for statistical validity in Phase III trials, it is unusual for them to be performed in single institutions (or even single countries). This compounds the problems of assessment of anticancer response as discussed previously, and necessitates the adoption of the most incontrovertible endpoints such as survival time as the primary objectives in oncology Phase III trials.

The rapid pace of change in oncology may lead to the "best" treatment at the start of Phase III being considered wholly inadequate by the time the results of the trial are mature. It is also particularly difficult from both a moral and practical standpoint to perform a placebo-controlled trial in cancer patients, as few such patients will accept the possibility of placebo therapy for a lethal condition.

VII. NEW CHALLENGES FOR DRUG DEVELOPMENT IN ONCOLOGY

The explosion of knowledge about the control of cell division, motility and death that is evident in modern cell and molecular biology must be integrated into the practice of cancer medicine.

It is almost inconceivable that useful new drugs will not result from this expansion of knowledge [27]. However, it is unlikely that the traditional drug development path described in this chapter will serve us efficiently in identifying drugs with novel (non-DNA) mechanisms of activity. The history of cytokine development (such as Interferon) should serve as a warning in this respect. I believe that the current system is too heavily dependent on toxicological endpoints, based on the hypothesis that you have to do some harm to do some good in treating cancer. If this were entirely true patients experiencing the worst toxicities should have the best outcomes, and this is patently not true to any practising oncologist.

New cytokines, signal transduction inhibitors, protein biosynthesis inhibitors, cell adhesion promoters, and antimetastatic and antiangiogenic molecules are all in early clinical trials. I think it unlikely that we will be able to unify such diverse mechanisms under one clinical trial strategy, and this will become even more complex as we reach further back into control of DNA translation and posttranslational mechanisms of protein synthesis regulation.

One unifying principle may be attainable. We should strive whenever possible to design trials that look at the relevant actions of drugs and attempt to measure such actions (or some surrogate of action) as accurately as possible in those individuals who volunteer for early clinical trials of potential novel antitumor agents. Thus if we are testing a Topoisomerase inhibitor, would it not be possible to measure inhibition of the enzyme in the tumor or some surrogate tissue, and to define activity in terms of enzyme inhibition rather than the incidence of life-threatening toxicities?

The future of cancer treatment is inextricably linked with the drug development process. We must find ways of getting the best out of the massive efforts in this area.

REFERENCES

1. J. Cassidy. Chemotherapy administration: Doses, infusions and choice of schedule. *Annals of Oncology 5*: 525–530, 1994.
2. J. M. Venditta. The National Cancer Institute drug discovery program, current and future perspectives: A commentary. *Cancer Treatment Reports 67*: 767–772, 1983.
3. K. D. Paull, R. H. Shoemaker, L. Hodes, et al. Display and analysis of patterns of differential activity of drugs against human tumour cell lines: Development of mean graph and COMPARE algorithm. *J. Natl. Cancer Inst. 81*: 1088–1092, 1989.
4. S. P. Langdon, H. R. Hendricks, B. J. M. Braakhuis, et al. Preclinical phase II studies in human tumour xenografts: A European multicenter follow-up study. *Annals of Oncology 5*: 415–422, 1994.
5. R. Sykes. Innovations on the Pharmaceutical Industry. *BMJ 309*: 422–423, 1994.
6. C. K. Grieshaber and S. Marsoni. Relation of preclinical toxicology to findings in early clinical trials. *Cancer Treatment Reports 70*: 65, 1986.
7. EORTC New Drug Development Committee: EORTC guidelines for phase I trials with single agents in adults. *European Journal of Cancer and Clinical Oncology 21*: 1005–1007, 1985.
8. J. M. Collins, C. K. Grieshaber, and B. A. Chabner. Pharmacologically guided phase I clinical trials based upon preclinical drug development. *J. Natl. Cancer Inst. 82*: 1321, 1990.
9. A. L. Jackman, G. A. Taylor, A. H. Calvert, et al. Modulation of antimetabolite effects. Effects of thymidine on the efficacy of the quinazoline-based thymidylate synthetase inhibitor CB3717. *Biochem. Pharmacol. 33*: 3269, 1984.
10. J. Cassidy, C. Lewis, A. Setanoians, L. Adams, D. J. Kerr, A. H. Calvert, G. W. Brown, A. J. Pateman, E. M. Rankin, and S. B. Kaye. Phase I trial of GR 63718A. *Br. J. Cancer 60*: 457, 1989.
11. J. S. Penta, G. L. Rosner, and D. L. Trump. Choice of starting dose and escalation for phase I studies of antitumour agents. *Cancer Chemother. Pharmacol. 31*: 247–250, 1992.

12. R. Comis. Oral etoposide: a developing role. *Eur. J. Cancer 27(Suppl. 2)*: 5348, 1991.
13. D. Bissett, A. Steanoians, J. Cassidy, M. A. Graham, G. A. Chadwick, P. Wilson, V. Auzannet, N. Le Bail, S. B. Kaye, and D. J. Kerr. Phase I and pharmacokinetic study of taxotere (RP 56976) administered as a 24 hour infusion. *Cancer Research 53*: 523–527, 1993.
14. J. Cassidy. Chemotherapy administration: doses, infusions and choice of schedule. *Annals of Oncology 5(Suppl. 4)*: 25–30, 1994.
15. J. M. Collins, D. S. Zaharko, R. Dedrick, et al. Potential roles for preclinical pharmacology in phase I clinical trials. *Cancer Treat Rep 70*: 73–80, 1986.
16. EORTC pharmacokinetics and metabolism group. Pharmacokinetically guided dose escalation in phase I clinical trials. *Eur. J. Can. Clin. Oncol. 23*: 1083–1087, 1987.
17. M. A. Graham and P. Workman. The impact of pharmacokinetically guided dose escalation strategies in phase I clinical trials: Critical evaluation and recommendations for future studies. *Annals of Oncology 3*: 338–349, 1992.
18. J. O'Quigley, M. Pepe, and L. Fisher. Continual reassessment method: a practical design for phase I clinical trials in cancer. *Biometrics 46*: 33–48, 1990.
19. D. Faries. The modified continual reassessment method for Phase I cancer clinical trials. *Proc. of Amer. Stat. Assoc.* 1991.
20. W. E. Evans, J. H. Rodman, M. V. Relling, W. R. Crom, G. K. Rivera, C. B. Pratt, and W. M. Crist. Concept of maximal tolerated systemic exposure and its application to phase I-II studies of anticancer drugs. *Medical and Paediatric Oncology 19*: 153–159, 1991.
21. J. Cassidy. Biological end points in early clinical trials of antineoplastic drugs. *CRC Beatson Laboratories Scientific Report* 21–23, 1993.
22. S. K. Carter. Study design principles of the clinical evaluation of new drugs as developed by the chemotherapy program of the National Cancer Institute. In The Design of Clinical Trials in Cancer Therapy. M. Staquet, Ed. Brussels, Editions Scientifique Europeennes, 1973, p. 242–247.
23. G. Schwartsmann, J. Wanders, I. J. Koier, et al. EORTC New Drug Development Office co-ordinating and monitoring programme for phase I and II trials with new anticancer agents. *Eur. J. Cancer 27*: 1162–1168, 1991.
24. F. M. Muggia, M. Rozencweig, M. J. Stawuet, and W. P. McGuire. In Methodology of Phase II Trials in Cancer. S. K. Carter and Y. Sakurai, Eds. New anticancer agents. Springer, New York, 1980.
25. S. B. Kaye, P. Workman, M. A. Graham, J. Cassidy, and D. Jodrell. Pharmacokinetics and early clinical studies of selected new drugs. *Cancer Surveys 17*: 371–395, 1993.
26. J. Cassidy and S. B. Kaye. New drugs in clinical development in Europe. Haematology/Oncology Clinics of North America 8: 289–303, 1994.
27. J. Carmichael. Cancer chemotherapy: identifying novel anticancer drugs. *Br. Med. J. 308*: 1288–1290, 1994.

11

Clinical Pharmacology in Drug Development: A View to Future Effectiveness

J. Robert Powell, Alan Bye, and Paul D. Rubin

Glaxo-Wellcome Inc.
Research Triangle Park, North Carolina

I. INTRODUCTION

The success, efficiency, and wisdom exhibited in bringing new drug therapy to treat unmet therapeutic needs of patients is the direct result of the vision, leadership, and skill of many types of people . . . Among them is the clinical pharmacologist. Clinical pharmacologists contribute to the development of life-saving or pain-alleviating therapies in multiple ways:

- assisting discovery scientists in focusing on therapeutic targets and selecting screens or surrogates that are likely to predict the desired activity in humans.
- designing the early clinical development program to determine both pharmacodynamic (safety and efficacy surrogates) and pharmacokinetic milestones.
- collaborating with preclinical development scientists to both screen and test new chemical entities (NCEs) in preparation for human testing.
- designing, conducting, and analyzing studies leading to dosage regimen recommendations throughout development.

The actual work and leadership in each of these areas is collaborative with a wide variety of other disciplines. Indeed, no activity is the universal domain of the clinical pharmacologist. The core skills needed are usually not embodied in one person.

The quality of this work has a direct impact on achieving the desired effect for the patient, the clinician's confidence in the reliability of the drug and its supporting information, and the investor's confidence in the future value of the company.

Clinical pharmacology is currently practiced across the industry in a heterogeneous manner that makes it difficult to find the clinical pharmacologist who has expertise in all the above areas. Large companies tend to have larger clinical pharmacology departments that focus on both science and process. Smaller, one-drug companies may have no clinical pharmacologist and may never consider the value of interspecies scaling for estimating the first human dose, physiologic models to predict human absorption, preclinical-to-clinical links in surrogate dynamic markers, or high-intensity clinical pharmacokinetic/dynamic (PK/PD) studies to estimate dosage regimens. Indeed, little time may be spent in Phases I and II before moving to the pivotal clinical trials.

The perspective taken in this discourse is that of the large company challenged with simultaneously investigating a hundred discovery targets and developing a similar number of drugs, new indications, and dosage forms while maintaining a large marketed product portfolio. In this environment both science and process become critical to finding, developing, and supporting drug therapies. An assumption made is that while drugs can be developed without clinical pharmacology expertise, there is value in employing and enhancing this resource.

The purpose for this discourse is to describe both a scientific paradigm and an organizational model for applying clinical pharmacology skills in drug development and to make recommendations for moving into the future.

II. CURRENT ENVIRONMENT

The marketplace has changed the way drugs will be developed. The high cost of development and the prospect of greater profits for true advances in unmet therapeutic needs is driving the industry to

- consolidate into larger, multinational entities,
- focus on novel ideas for new drugs,
- rapidly increase R & D productivity several fold, and
- question the core competencies (i.e., skills, intelligence) needed to retain versus contract out.

These changes have a direct impact on how clinical pharmacology is conducted in drug development. The high cost of getting a drug to market has risen from $80 M in 1970, to $350 M in 1988 [1], to about $500 M in 1995. Increasing costs to discover new drugs combined with decreasing profitability are forcing companies to increase productivity. In effect, do more with about the same or less resources by working smarter.

Investigating past practices gives clues about the areas that could become more productive. Common reasons for drugs failing during clinical development are unfavorable pharmacodynamics (poor efficacy, unacceptable toxicity), pharmacokinetics (poor absorption, short elimination half-life), and a poor market forecast. Before 1990, the information needed to know if a NCE was likely to be successful as a drug was not known until the results of the clinical Phase III studies were completed (Figure 1). By then all the money had been spent. Now companies are attempting to predict an NCE's success back in the discovery-to-early-clinical development phases both through new technologies for synthesizing and screening NCEs and linking information more effectively to make better decisions. Large contract research organizations are allowing the discovery companies to shift their internal resources to the early core phases.

The work environment is becoming increasingly chaotic. Companies are continuing to acquire, merge, and reorganize at an increasing rate. Even now the largest pharmaceutical company only controls about 5% of the global market. The challenge is increasingly difficult for individual scientists to maintain their research and development focus, to develop their skills and careers, and

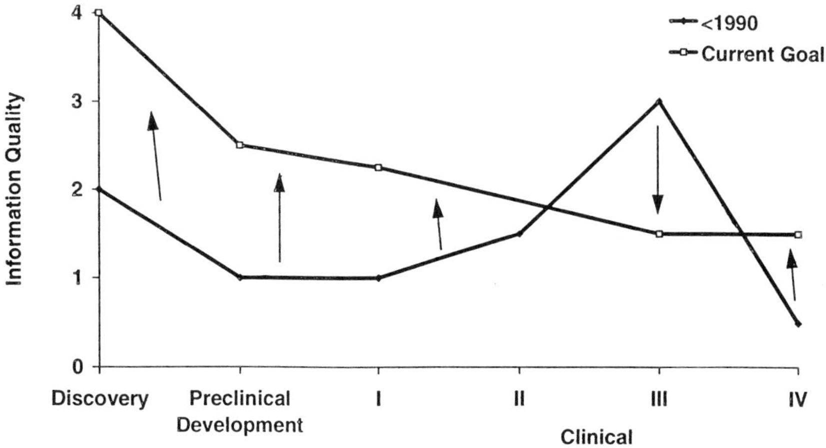

Fig. 1 Conceptual view of information quality over the research and development phases. Values above 1 in information quality are increasingly smarter, 1 is break-even, and below 1 is unsmart.

to achieve balance between the work and other aspects of their lives. The contract between the company and the employee is in flux.

III. THE CHALLENGE

From a clinical pharmacologist's perspective the challenges are that there are likely to be an ever-increasing number of drugs coming through the pipeline that are targeted to treat previously poorly treated or untreated diseases using new pharmacologic concepts. The resource to get the job done will not expand proportionately. This must be accomplished in an environment where change is more common than stability. However, a clear advantage to work in a changing environment is that experimentation with new concepts or technologies is easier to introduce. It is less common to defeat new ways of working in favor of tradition.

To succeed in this environment, it will require understanding the R & D strategy, defining the clinical pharmacology core competencies, acquiring and developing new scientific skills, and creating a strategy for deploying, recycling, and supporting people in the drug development process.

IV. CORE COMPETENCIES

Core competencies are defined as the collective learning in the company, the coordination, the diverse R & D skills, and the integration of numerous technology streams [2]. It is about organizing the companies' work and delivering value. Part of core competence is a commitment to working across organizational boundaries.

A small pharmaceutical company might have only one core competence: the technology or biology that brought forth their product. For a contract research organization the core competence might be data-flow automation or excellence in the conduct of in-house Phase I studies. Other services might be added to the companies as they grow, but if integral core competencies are not grown in parallel, the quality of these additional services may not be as great as the original.

Large pharmaceutical companies may not have defined well their core competencies in the past. However with the less favorable economic climate, companies are being forced to determine what core competencies should be retained. This decision must be based upon which of these competencies is central to future success. It is then easier to devise a strategy for managing and assignment of internal versus external resources.

Clinical pharmacology is considered a core competency in many pharmaceutical companies. In order to assist in selecting the drug candidate with discovery scientists, to set the Phase I plan, to agree to the preclinical plan prior to taking the chemical into humans, and to collaborate with clinicians downstream on dose recommendations, there are three scientific areas of mastery:

- clinical pharmacokinetic/dynamic theory and application,
- disease biology-pharmacology-clinical medical axis, and
- clinical trial design, conduct, and information access.

To meet the challenge, people with these skills who are working to the same mission need to be organized so that they can form focused early-development teams. Traditional pharmaceutical industry structure has people with these skills working in different departments and, at times, competing on the same project rather than developing a close partnership. There may be a competitive advantage for companies that bring together and grow these skills for the focused mission of drug discovery and development. The challenge is in how to do it.

V. APPLICATIONS OF SCIENCE TO DRUG DEVELOPMENT

A series of clinical case studies follow to demonstrate the value of applying biopharmaceutic and integrated pharmacokinetic/dynamic principles to solve drug development problems. The cases are meant to demonstrate the value of applying science as opposed to empiricism in approaching common issues. It is also intended to demonstrate the close collaboration needed between clinical pharmacologists and scientists in discovery research, drug metabolism, bioanalysis, pharmaceutics, clinical research, and academia.

Problem 1: An oral drug solution from an investigational effervescent tablet was found to be only 50% as well absorbed as the marketed tablet. Why did this occur? Could an alternative solution be made that is bioequivalent to the tablet? This problem was thought to be odd in that drugs from oral solutions are generally thought to be absorbed as well or better than from tablets since there is no restriction from dissolution.

When this problem occurred it was known that ranitidine is about 50–60% absorbed and that the absorption profile is frequently characterized by double peaks over a 4-hour period. A study had just been completed where ranitidine was administered by a tube into the stomach, jejunum, and cecum [3]. The results demonstrated ranitidine was virtually not absorbed after leaving the small bowel (Figure 2).

Of the many possibilities investigated, it was noted that the ranitidine absorption pattern from the oral solution was different from the tablet in that the absorption portion of the curve terminated earlier for the solution. One of the ingredients in the solution, sodium acid pyrophosphate (SAPP), was thought to be present in a large enough quantity to be speeding small bowel transit time and possibly sweeping the drug past the site of absorption. Clinical studies then found that a ranitidine solution without SAPP was as well absorbed as the tablet. The addition of SAPP to the ranitidine solution decreased absorption by 50% and produced a profile similar to the first bioavailability study. Gamma scintigraphy confirmed that SAPP was decreasing small-bowel

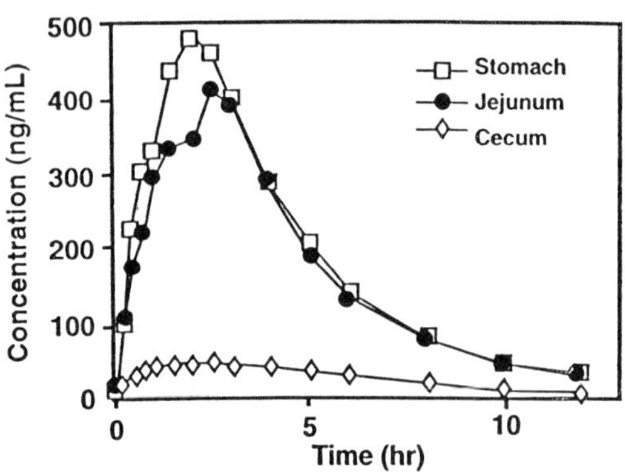

Fig. 2 Ranitidine mean (n=8) plasma concentration versus time after giving 150 mg by nasogastric tube into the stomach, jejunum, and cecum.

transit time from 4 hours to 2 hours [4]. Collaborative studies between drug metabolism and clinical pharmacology groups on the mechanism of ranitidine absorption using cultured human Caco-2 cells showed absorption to be paracellular and not transcellular [5]. The collaboration of pharmaceutics and clinical pharmacology led to a new effervescent tablet that is bioequivalent to the marketed tablet and is now on the market.

This experience helped create several systematic changes in the way we develop drugs. Determining the characteristics of gastrointestinal absorption site using intubation techniques now is performed commonly when either the drug is not well absorbed or is likely to be considered for alternative formulations (e.g., controlled release, suppository). This simple study helps predict the feasibility of developing other formulations and shows physiologic restrictions in absorption processes. By routinely knowing the drug's solubility, permeability (e.g., Caco-2 [6]), and human hepatic intrinsic clearance (e.g., human hepatocyte [7]), it is possible to select drugs from research that are likely to be well absorbed. Low oral bioavailability accounts for a large proportion of drugs that fail in Phase I. By integrating this information into a physiologic absorption model, both time and money can be saved.

Problem 2: Can the maximally tolerated dose by predicted from lower doses for a cancer drug in the first Phase I dose-escalation clinical trial?

During the first single-dose escalation studies in humans it is useful to predict the dose associated with the maximal effect or the maximally tolerated effect from lower doses. When a surrogate or direct measure of pharmacodynamic effect is available, this prediction can be done by fitting the dose or drug concentration-response data to a model (e.g., sigmoid Emax, linear regression). Benefits include sparing patients excessive toxicity and increasing study efficiency by decreasing dosage increments.

The synthetic topoisomerase I inhibitor GG211 is being developed for various solid-tumor cancers. The initial single-dose escalation study to determine the maximally tolerated dose was conducted at two sites in the United States and Europe using the same protocol. Following intravenous administration the active lactone form is converted to an inactive acid by a pH-dependent process. During dose escalation, key safety information (e.g., platelets, neutrophils) was accumulated from both sites by clinical research scientists and blood samples were analyzed at the company within days of collection from patients. The pharmacokineticist graphed and computer fit the data that was then interpreted by the development team led by a company oncologist. Information collected and analyzed by the company was routinely shared with the clinical sites. An objective was to predict the dose that would produce a drop in the blood platelet count not exceeding 75,000/mm^3 and neutrophil count not exceeding 750/mm^3.

Figure 3 shows the fit of the relationships between the day-4 GG211 lactone area under the blood curve and the nadir in both the absolute neutrophil and platelet counts using a sigmoidal Emax model [8]. From this type of information the development team was able to anticipate the maximally tolerated dose before it was achieved and adjust doses along with the clinical investigators. Other analyses of the data found that there was not a relationship between the pharmacodynamic effect and either prior treatment with other bone-marrow suppressing drugs or the clinical site. During the trial there was reason to believe that both factors were influencing response.

To achieve this benefit the company oncologist, pharmacokineticist, study monitor, and bioanalyst functioned as a coordinated team to plan the data flow and analysis. The partnership with the clinical sites included an open sharing of the information collected and analyzed centrally. Benefits gained from this style of Phase I study include sparing patients from unwanted toxicity, more efficiently selecting doses based upon information gained from prior doses, and possibly decreasing the time needed to conduct the study. The experience gained pointed to the need for electronic remote data-entry systems for clinical pharmacology studies. Collecting the information from the clinical sites was performed manually by the clinical research scientist. If the patient information in the case record form is accumulated and graphed electronically as it is collected from the patient, efficiency, productivity, and quality would increase.

Problem 3: When a target subpopulation (e.g., children, elderly, hepatic failure) is likely to need a different dose from the primary population due to either altered drug pharmacokinetics or dynamics, how should the dosing recommendation be developed?

Traditionally, dosage recommendations for special populations result from either a pharmacokinetic study when dynamic differences are considered unlikely or perhaps a clinical trial when the population is large, the drug's therapeutic index is low, and/or dynamic differences are suspected. When pharmacodynamic differences are considered more likely, dosage recommendations for these special populations may be delayed at the time a drug comes to the market due to the expense and time needed to conduct clinical trials. Performing a high intensity PK/PD study may allow dose recommendations to emerge earlier by indexing PK/PD findings to the dosing recommendation in the primary population.

Remifentanil is an esterase metabolized opioid drug with a very high clearance and short elimination half-life of about 5–10 minutes that is being developed for clinical anesthesia. The drug was designed to allow the anesthesiologist to dial in the desired anesthetic effect by changing the intravenous infusion rate. The objective was to minimize delays in achieving the desired pharmacodynamic effect by changing the infusion rate during surgery and to shorten the postoperative recovery period awaiting the anesthetic effect to dissipate.

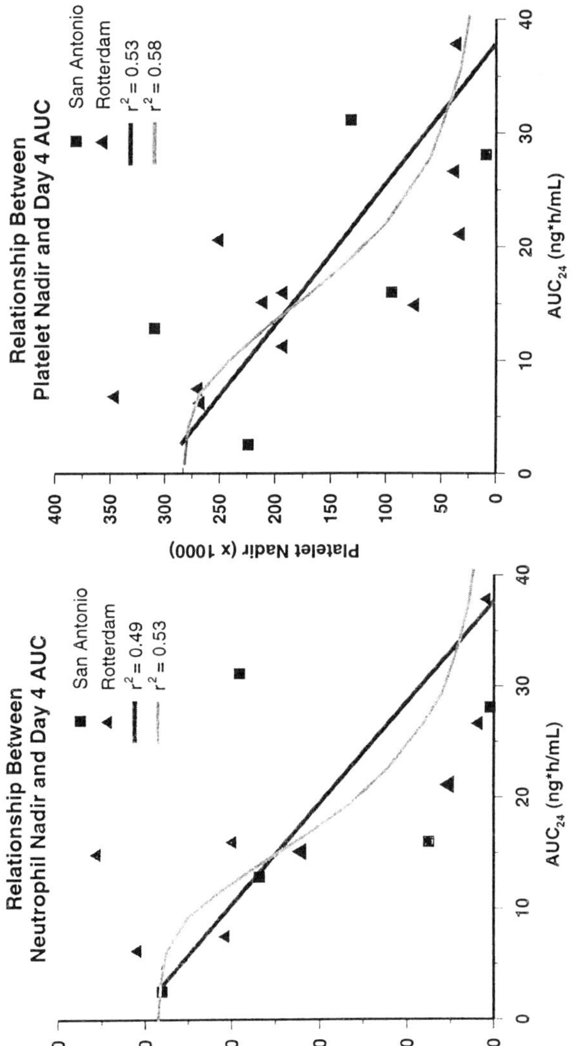

Fig. 3 GG211 (topoisomerase I inhibitor) area under the blood lactone concentration on day 4 of dosing versus absolute neutrophil nadir and platelet nadir in cancer patients from San Antonio and Rotterdam. The data were fit to both a sigmoidal Emax and a linear regression model.

The remifentanil dose-finding strategy was driven by predicting doses in healthy volunteers from animal PK/PD studies and predicting doses in clinical efficacy studies for patients undergoing anesthesia from healthy-volunteer PK/PD studies. Dynamic measurements in animals and human included rod-induced pain, minute ventilation, EEG spectral edge, visual analog, and psychomotor tests. Dynamic measures used in patient-efficacy studies included loss of consciousness time, incision response, major surgical response, and post-surgical spontaneous ventilation time and analgesia. Links between these responses and with other drugs of the same pharmacologic class (i.e., fentanyl, sufentanil, alfentanil) showed that remifentanil acted in a predictable fashion and met the initial design criteria.

The relationship between remifentanil blood concentration and EEG spectral edge in a healthy volunteer is shown in Figure 4 [9]. Dosing recommendations in patients are generally based on the results of the clinical efficacy studies. By confirming predictability in studies linking animals to humans and volunteers to patients, the development team was able to improve the dose recommendations by conducting several high-intensity PK/PD studies in various special populations using EEG spectral edge and minute ventilation as dynamic measures. Dosage considerations based upon patient age, gender, and the presence of hepatic disease are partially derived from a comparison of PK/PD outcome measures in these populations to those in healthy volunteers and recognizing the established link to the clinical outcome measures. This development program required close collaboration amongst the bioanalyst, preclinical pharmacologist, clinical pharmacologist, monitors, Phase II/III clinical staff, and academic anesthesiologists.

Problem 4: Pharmacokinetic drug interactions are often reported once a drug is marketed. This often stimulates a clinical and regulatory interest to consider dose label changes. When the interaction is thought to be potentially clinically insignificant, how should this be studied to determine the need for additional dosing recommendations?

The lead article in a major medical journal reported ranitidine increased blood ethanol levels by from 30.5 mg/dL to 40.9 mg/dL after an oral ethanol dose of 0.3 g/kg (about 1.5 12-oz beers). The authors concluded patients treated with the combination should be warned of possible functional impairment [10]. The legal limit for driving while intoxicated is either 80 or 100 mg/dL depending on the state. However, measurable physiologic or psychological changes can be detected at alcohol levels below these limits. Media and regulatory interest was heightened both in that the article was published on New Year's Day and that ranitidine is frequently taken to counteract the gastrointestinal upset associated with a hangover.

To address concern over this interaction, two studies were conducted. Having noted that the published study used only 7 subjects given one dose and that

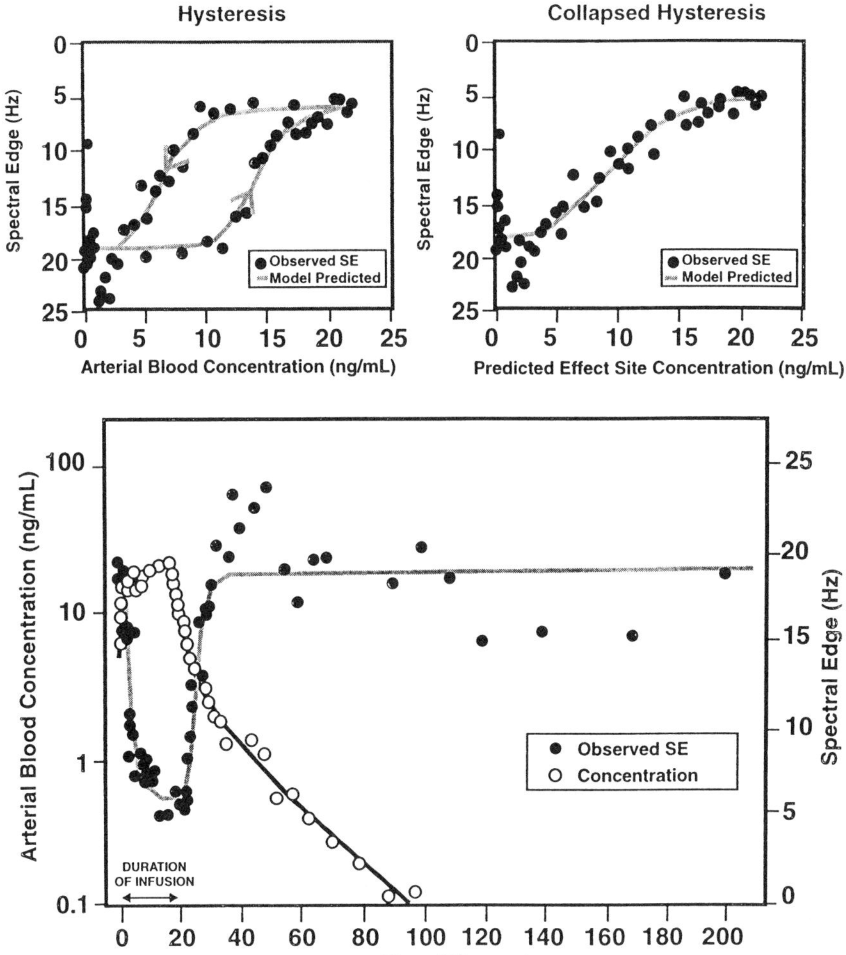

Fig. 4 Bottom fit curves remifentanil arterial blood concentration versus EEG spectral edge in a healthy volunteer given a 20-minute infusion. The upper left curve shows the hysteresis and the right curve shows the collapsed curve after fitting.

the analytical measures were varied, a new study was conducted in 18 adults given 3 alcohol doses (0.15, 0.3, and 0.6 g/kg). The same experimental conditions were employed with and without ranitidine, but with a sensitive, specific ethanol assay covering the concentration range [11]. This study found that while no interaction could be determined at the two higher doses (contradicting the publishing findings), ranitidine did increase the peak blood-alcohol concentration following the 0.15 g/kg dose from 13 mg/dL at baseline to 16 mg/dL. The largest single individual change at this dose was from 16 mg/dL at baseline to 26 mg/dL with ranitidine.

There is little literature on the pharmacological or clinical relevance for incremental changes in blood alcohol at such low concentrations. A PK/PD ethanol study on cognitive performance was conducted by giving a 20-minute intravenous ethanol infusion. This simulated oral absorption to volunteers targeting peak ethanol-blood concentrations of 0, 13, 26, and 80 mg/dL, respectively [12]. The study was randomized, double-blind, placebo-controlled, and crossover in design. While a decrease in cognitive performance could be detected at the highest ethanol-blood concentration, a pharmacodynamic difference could not be detected between the 13- and 26-mg/dL blood levels (i.e., most sensitive subject from the previous study) (Figure 5).

While it is common to find pharmacokinetic drug interactions with marketed products, deciding on the need to warn patients or change the label can be difficult when the clinical relevance of the change in drug exposure is not known. These publications often conclude with wording such as "While the clinical relevance for the interaction is not known, patients should be warned

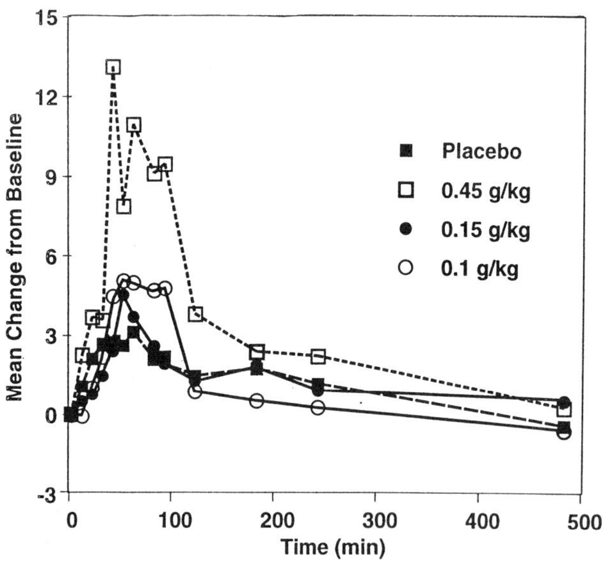

Fig. 5 Mean divided-attention tracking scores (n=8) at moderate difficulty level following ethanol doses as listed in the panel.

of the potential toxicity (or subtherapeutic effect) when the drugs are coprescribed." Warning patients of all potential drug interactions may lead to information paralysis on the part of both the patient and clinician. The addition of dynamic testing goes a large step further in assessing the clinical relevance of drug interactions.

Problem 5: How can preclinical information be used to target drug interactions studied during clinical drug development?

There has been a historical tendency to perform drug interaction studies of new drugs with many drugs having a potential to be concurrently administered. This can lead to a number of drug interactions being presented within the NDA that do not confer a safety concern. Providing drug interaction information early in the development program allows patients taking potentially interacting drugs to be entered into clinical trials earlier. An alternative strategy to studying all potential interactions is to perform clinical drug interaction studies only with drugs where it is reasonable to assume a dynamic interaction of clinical significance or a kinetic interaction that is predicted from preclinical models.

By mapping out the elimination mechanism in animals and human tissues or cells, it is increasingly possible to predict which elimination clearance interactions are likely to occur clinically. Mapping out the metabolic pathway including the predominant cytochrome P450 isozymes allows the scientist to plan a drug interaction program more logically and to conserve resources. When the drug is primarily eliminated by renal clearance mechanisms, the isolated perfused rat kidney preparation provides a system for predicting human drug interactions.

Lamivudine (3TC) is a new nucleoside analogue being used to treat patients with HIV infection. Early in the preclinical program is was known that the primary clearance mechanism for lamivudine is renal secretion and that the drug would be routinely coadministered with a variety of other antivirals and antibiotics that are also primarily eliminated by the kidney. It was decided to select drugs for clinical interaction studies by using an isolated perfused rat kidney screen and to support the clinical efficacy program with population pharmacokinetics to detect other large interactions not specifically studied. This preclinical model found that trimethoprim produced a large decrease in lamivudine renal clearance, whereas AZT, ddI, and ddC did not [13]. A clinical study then found coadministration of trimethoprim/sulfamethoxazole to HIV infected patients taking lamivudine produced a 45% increase in the lamivudine serum concentration and a 35% decrease in renal clearance (Figure 6) [14]. Lamivudine did not significantly alter the pharmacokinetics of either trimethoprim or sulfamethoxazole. Since lamivudine has a wide safety margin, no change in the dosing strategy was recommended as a result of this drug interaction.

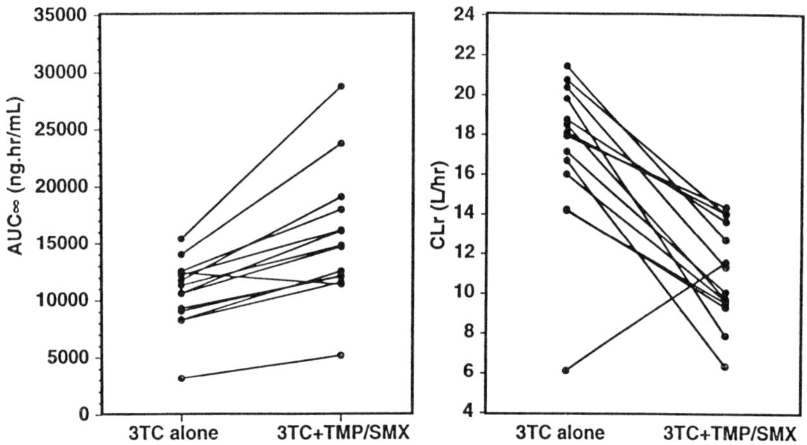

Fig. 6 Individual plots of the lamivudine (3TC) area under the serum concentration time curve (AUC) and renal clearance (CLr) with and without coadministration of trimethoprim (TMP)/sulfamethoxazole (SMX).

VI. CURRENT AND FUTURE NEEDS

To improve clinical pharmacology effectiveness in helping select new drugs for unmet therapeutic needs and better advising on how to use them, improvements need to occur in better use of the skills and technologies available now (management/organization), developing new scientific techniques, and developing people for a career in clinical pharmacology.

VII. MANAGEMENT/ORGANIZATION

The value in a well-managed and organized company should be that it facilitates and unlocks the ability of people to work toward the company's mission. Developing better drugs more efficiently and making more money for investors probably meets the mission statement for many pharmaceutical companies. Yet the statistics on performance indicate in aggregate the pharmaceutical industry has room to improve. One index that should be relevant for clinical pharmacology is that by 1993 only 17.2% of new chemical entities with an IND filed from 1964 to 1989 had been approved for marketing in the United States [15]. The reasons given for stopping further clinical testing that emerged following the IND filing were lack of safety (27%) within 2 years, lack of efficacy (46%) in 2 years, and commercial or poor market forecast (23%) in 4 years. While the study did not specify reasons for failing efficacy, poor pharmacokinetics (e.g., absorption, half-life, variability) may account for a large proportion. Improving on success while minimizing these reasons for failure can be the management value added.

Historically, many companies have organized in silos around functional skills (e.g., clinical pharmacology, drug metabolism, toxicology, etc.) focusing inward and missing the broader systems view (the big picture). In this case both process and functional skills are combined in the silo. More recently there has been movement to empower project teams to move projects across functional groups. In the team-based environment the team takes ownership of the project, while the functional areas are responsible for staffing and supporting teams. When there are many project teams, it is important for the functional groups to share best practices reaching agreements on the type of information that will be routinely collected, the order in which it will be collected, and how it will be used to help the project team make decisions. Information networks form in a more horizontal direction.

Expanding on the learn/confirm model advocated by Sheiner [16], Figure 7 might be the mission for the drug development project team. The simplest project team mission might be to create a development plan for the NCE. Teams should also be committed early to create models, to set hypotheses, and to create the target product label. Learning occurs as information is collected. If the information is not consistent with the original models or hypotheses, the plan may be adjusted. Eventually, either the information is declared in the form of a NDA or the project is stopped.

Rewards for project teams are more common for achieving the development plan milestones on or before the planned date than for learning and adjusting to the information gained. Shifting from a time-based to a learning-based reward system is central to meeting the future R & D challenge [17]. Creating models is inherently appealing because they focus people on the critical

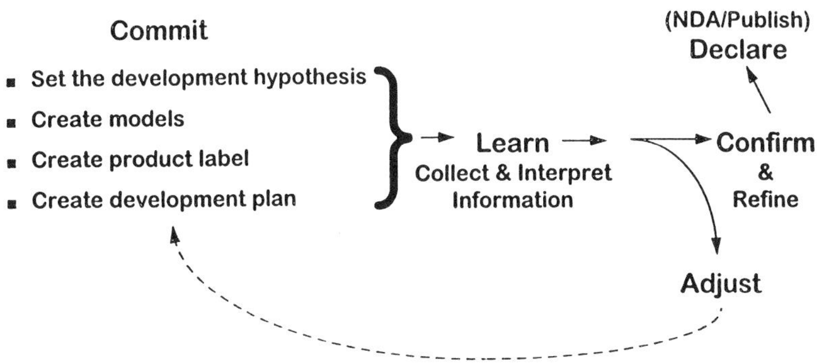

Fig. 7 Drug development team mission and learning process.

decision types (e.g., pharmacodynamic, pharmacokinetic, pharmacoeconomic), organize the information collected, commit people to think about how the information will be used before it is collected, predict reality before it is measured, and create a framework for learning when the information does not fit the model. Working models tend to minimize the information and resource expenditure that is needed to make a decision thereby leading to efficiency.

An example of the potential value for models is in the drug absorption process. Creating a human drug absorption model could allow only those drugs that are capable of being absorbed to be selected from discovery research for development (Figure 8). A physiologic model that incorporates solubility, caco-2 permeability, and human hepatocyte intrinsic clearance might be used at the discovery/development interface for NCE selection in addition to the relative potency and selectivity of the chemical candidates. By incorporating such a model, chemicals might be selected based upon the overall balance of these critical characteristics. The model might also create the basis for engaging academic researchers to improve the model by developing other cultured cell lines from other regions of the gastrointestinal tract, adding gut-wall metabolism, and predicting the influence of food on absorption by incorporating the presence of bile and changes in portal blood flow. Development and "ownership" for this model would cut across basic research, drug metabolism, formulation development, and clinical pharmacology. This wisdom developed across scientific disciplines should be transparent to the NCE project development team in that absorption problems would be less likely.

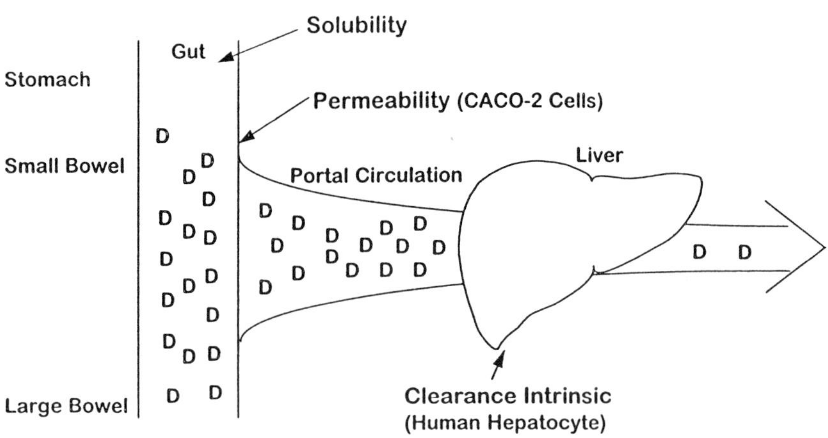

Fig. 8 Human absorption model.

Managing the type of information collected and knowing how it will be used should be a critical advantage in drug development. Figure 9 diagrams a macroperspective for collecting PK/PD information from discovery research to NDA filing. This integrated drug development concept was recommended by Peck et al. [18]. Creating this type of framework allows the scientist to understand the relationship of their contribution to the whole process. This orderly supply of information will feed the project team and prompt them to make decisions. The "models" provide an effective means for the skill areas to infuse wisdom into the project team.

Managing and organizing the information flow is critical to making rapid development decisions in early clinical development. In a sense, the most important value for clinical pharmacology information is in making rapid, effective drug development decisions within the company either in the form of a go/no go decision or in designing subsequent studies. While the studies tend to be small in patient numbers, there are many protocols that usually do not take more than weeks to complete the clinical portion. Using remote data entry for all clinical data and collecting analytical information closer to sample collection from the patient should allow development decisions to be made more rapidly and study reports to be issued within weeks of the last patient studied as opposed to months or years. A close partnership between the clinical pharmacology clinical monitor, data management, and information technology staffs is required to accomplish this goal.

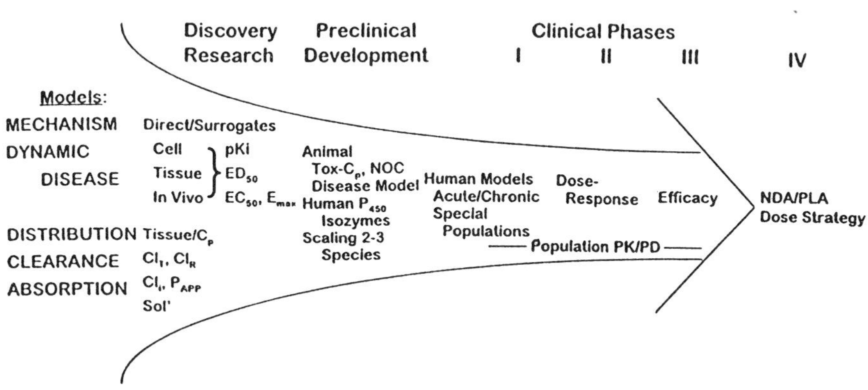

Fig. 9 PK/PD information flow paradigm from discovery research to the NDA/PLA dosing strategy.

VIII. SCIENCE

Changes in pharmacokinetic and dynamic science will likely be driven by changes in technology. Measuring drugs in ever lower concentrations, imaging labeled drugs in body regions in real time, and the ability to continuously collect blood or tissue concentrations from probes will change the way pharmacokinetic information is analyzed and reported.

Biochemical, cellular, and clinical measures of drug effect need to be planned during the discovery phase for new therapeutic target areas. Clinical pharmacology needs to have access to preclinical scientists to establish these measurement techniques. Research is just now beginning to understand the disease surrogate versus time surface in the presence of no treatment or the existing therapy. The CD4 and viral burden versus time data collected in HIV infected patients with and without antiviral drugs serve as a model for understanding drug effect over the time cycle for the disease (Figure 10) [19]. Approval to market drugs in the future is likely to be more influenced by this type of information for both acute and chronic diseases. As with chemical drug assay validation criteria, there is a need to develop a better understanding of the criteria used to validate pharmacodynamic surrogates.

IX. PEOPLE

Developing oneself is a commitment each person must make. The environment created must foster career development, scientific and otherwise. Departments

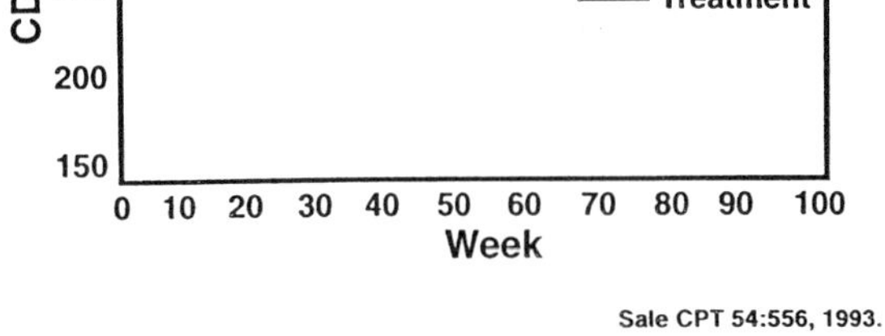

Fig. 10 Estimated time course for CD4 cell count for the average HIV patient in weeks from study entry. Upper curve is for active treatment with AZT and the lower curve is for placebo treatment. (Source: Ref. 19.)

that are known to be "stable," where no one ventures to other disciplines and new people are rarely hired, might rest somewhere between sedentary and moribund. While people need to develop in the core competencies and in team-based behaviors, there will always be the need to develop new skills.

Two of many areas to consider for cross-training or hybridizing are pharmacokinetics and biostatistics and also clinical monitors (CRSs) and data managers. For example, in the past pharmacokineticists and biostatisticians have collaborated on issues such as decisions in bioequivalence testing. Both groups are currently engaged in analyzing pharmacodynamic information, but in remarkably different ways. Pharmacokineticists tend to look at single-dose PK/PD or Phase II/III population models. Biostatisticians tend to focus more on hypothesis testing for large efficacy trials. If a hybrid "clinical statisticokineticist" was developed, companies might become more creative in developing more efficient and relevant designs and analyses for Phase II and III trials. The idea of creating disease models and searching for drug effect over time should be natural area of mutual scientific interest.

In collecting the information from clinical pharmacology studies, the clinical monitor tends to throw the case report forms over the wall to the data manager. From that point forward the ownership of the data, the cleanup, and database entry process gets murky, often resulting in long delays in reporting the final data and submitting the final report. Data quality, access, and speed for decisions and reports could be catalyzed both by cross-training in disciplines and expanding the career path. This new hybrid clinical study and data flow person might speed data-collection format from paper to computer and maintain continuous responsibility for data integrity and access.

X. CONCLUSION

The science disciplines that are the foundation of clinical pharmacology in the drug development environment are pharmacodynamics, pharmacokinetics, and biopharmaceutics. These skills are blended with medical specialties and aspects of biostatistics. The clinical experience gained in experimenting on healthy people and patients is a unique aspect within the pharmaceutical company, particularly when a drug-study unit is part of the function. The decision process to administer a new chemical to a human for the first time is pharmaceutical medicine. Long-term practitioners develop an unwritten wisdom that their colleagues depend upon. They assess the safety of new chemicals that might as easily be a poison as a life-saving drug. While most drugs have been discovered and developed by drug companies, the new science that underpins clinical pharmacology has been developed by academic centers. Industrial clinical pharmacologists apply the science to sorting out useful drugs from poisons and placebos and then recommending how they should be dosed. Investing in academic programs to train new scientists and develop new scientific methods and models will be key to our future success.

REFERENCES

1. J. A. DiMasi, R. W. Hansen, and L. Lasagna. Cost of innovation in the pharmaceutical industry, *J. Health Economics 10*: 107–142, 1992.
2. C. K. Prahalad and G. Hamel. The core competence of the corporation, *Harvard Business Rev.* 79–91, 1990.
3. M. F. Williams, G. E. Dukes, W. Heizer, Y. Han, D. J. Hermann, T. Lampkin, and L. J. Hak. Influence of gastrointestinal site of drug delivery on the absorption characteristics of ranitidine. *Pharm. Res. 9*: 1190–1194, 1992.
4. K. M. Koch, A. F. Parr, J. J. Tomlinson, E. P. Sandefer, G. A. Digenis, K. H. Donn, and J. R. Powell. Effect of sodium acid pyrophosphate on ranitidine bioavailability and gastrointestinal transit time. *Pharm. Res. 10*: 1027–1030, 1993.
5. L. Gan, P. Hsyu, J. F. Pritchard, and D. Thakker. Mechanism of intestinal absorption of ranitidine and ondansetron transport across Caco-2 cell monolayers. *Pharm. Res. 10*: 1722–1725, 1993.
6. P. Artursson and J. Karlsson. Correlation between oral drug absorption in humans and apparent drug permeability coefficients in human intestinal epithelial (CACO-2) cells. *Biochem. Biophys. Res. Comm. 175*: 880–885, 1991.
7. B. Hoener. Predicting the hepatic clearance of xenobiotics in humans from in vitro data. *Biopharm. Drug Disposit. 15*: 295–304, 1994.
8. R. L. Kunka, J. R. Ekcardt, J. Verweij, S. P. DePee, D. Littlefield, K. A. Selinger, P. Beranek, P. Collis, and P. S. Wissel. Use of pharmacokinetics as a tool in predicting toxicity of GG211, a new topoisomerase I inhibitor. *Clin. Pharmacol. Ther. 57*: 175a, 1995.
9. T. D. Egan, C. F. Minto, H. J. M. Lemmens, D. J. Hermann, K. T. Muir, and S. L. Shafer. Remifentanil versus alfentanil: comparative pharmacokinetics and pharmacodynamics in healthy adult male volunteers. *Anesthesiology*, in press.
10. C. DiPadova, R. Roine, M. Frezza, R. T. Gentry, E. Baraona, and C. S. Lieber. Effects of ranitidine on blood alcohol levels after ethanol ingestion. *JAMA 267*: 83–86, 1992.
11. A. Bye, L. F. Lacey, S. Gupta, and J. R. Powell. Effect of ranitidine hydrochloride (150 mg bd) on the pharmacokinetics of increasing doses of ethanol (0.15, 0.3, 0.6 g/kg-L). *Brit. J. Clin. Pharmacol.*, in press.
12. S. K. Gupta, E. H. Ellinwood, K. T. Muir, S. Hege, C. Kleoudis, and J. R. Powell. Ethanol pharmacodynamics at low blood concentrations. *Am. J. Therapeut. 3*: 1–8, 1995.
13. K. R. Sweeney, P. Hsyu, P. Statkevich, and D. R. Taft. Renal disposition and drug interaction screening of (–)-2'-deoxy-3'-thiacytidine (3TC) in the isolated perfused rat kidney. *Pharm. Res. 12*: 1958–1963, 1995.
14. K. H. P. Moore, G. J. Yuen, R. H. Raasch, J. J. Eron, D. Martin, P. K. Mydlow, and E. K. Hussey. Pharmacokinetics of lamivudine administered alone and with trimethoprim/sulfamethoxazole. *Clin. Pharmacol. Ther.*, in press.

15. J. A. DiMasi. Success rates for new drugs entering clinical testing in the United States. *Clin. Pharmacol. Ther. 58*: 1–14, 1995.
16. L. B. Sheiner. The intellectual health of clinical drug evaluation. *Clin. Pharmacol. Ther. 50*: 4–9, 1991.
17. L. B. Sheiner. A new paradigm for clinical drug development. Submitted.
18. C. C. Peck, W. H. Barr, L. Z. Benet, et al. Opportunities for integration of pharmacokinetics, pharmacodynamics, and toxicokinetics in rational drug development. *Clin. Pharmacol. Ther. 51*: 465–473, 1992.
19. M. Sale, L. B. Sheiner, P. Volberding, and T. F. Blaschke. Zidovudine response relationships in early human immunodeficiency virus infection. *Clin. Pharmacol. Ther. 54*: 556–566, 1993.

12

Contracting CROs into Your Organization: New Strategies for New Challenges

Gary D. Lightfoot
Pharmaco International Inc.
Austin, Texas

John R. Vogel
John R. Vogel Associates, Inc.
Oldwick, New Jersey

I. INTRODUCTION

> This is as strange a maze as men e'er trod;
> and there is in this business more than nature
> Was ever conduct of; some oracle
> Must rectify our knowledge
>
> William Shakespeare
> *The Tempest*

Those who are now negotiating the unfamiliar, often rocky terrain of today's drug development environment may do well to remember that they are not the first to face new—and sometimes frightening—challenges. After all, every age of radical change in business and industry plucks us from our familiar surroundings and plunks us down in a strange new landscape. If we are human, our first responses may be fear, panic, and resistance to change; if we are wise, these soon give way to hope, excitement, and a sense of new possibilities. The key is to explore the new world with open and observant minds, looking to those who have gone before us and gleaning from their experiences the strategies we must master to negotiate the terrain successfully.

Just as the Industrial Revolution completely redefined the environment in which goods are manufactured and produced, and just as the PC Revolution wholly transformed the face of the landscape of communications, so now has the Global Revolution begun to alter the shape of our vast arenas of business and industry, ushering us into the twenty-first century.

The effects of the Global Revolution reach into virtually every area of business and industry today, including health care and medicine. The process of drug development is no exception; in fact, it profoundly exemplifies the radical shift from the highly structured, largely self-contained corporate entities of recent history to the increasingly global, essentially boundaryless "virtual corporations" engendered by the Global Revolution.

This tempest of change presents immense challenges to those who are involved in developing new drugs today. The following material is intended to help by providing a better understanding of the forces at work, a clearer view of their effects, and, most importantly, some practical advice for successfully maneuvering through this "strange maze" in which we find ourselves, particularly with regard to the rise of CROs as a significant force in the new drug development environment.

A Note on Terminology For purposes of this discussion, we define a CRO—or contract research organization—as an entity that provides drug development companies with services that those companies traditionally have done in-house.

II. DEFINING THE LANDSCAPE: GENERAL AND INDUSTRY-SPECIFIC TRENDS AFFECTING THE DRUG DEVELOPMENT ENVIRONMENT

A. The Effects from Without

The ever-increasing sophistication of technology in communications, transportation, and other areas that enable us to connect with each other across geographical and other boundaries has served to make those boundaries less meaningful in business and industry today. After all, if you can fax or fly to France on a moment's notice, what does it matter if your factory is in San Francisco?

In a world in which physical boundaries mean less, the traditional structures of business and industry make it more difficult to compete. The corporate model of a self-contained, closed entity, its unique culture, standards, and procedures guarded zealously against intrusion, no longer suffices. In a world in which people, information, and resources move more quickly than ever, the traditional structure is inherently slow to react. In a world of global opportunity, this structure is isolated and unconnected. In a world of rapid change, this structure is inflexible and rigid. The strength and permanence that were its attributes in another age are now its weaknesses.

Finally, in drug development, as in every area of business today, the phenomenon of a world growing smaller and moving faster has placed demands for change on business structures that cannot be—and have not been—ignored. The effects can be seen in the widespread reengineering and downsizing which, while not always easy or painless, are making today's companies much smaller and less unwieldy.

The development of increasingly sophisticated technology, the demand for faster and more flexible responses to global opportunities, the trend toward reengineering and downsizing—all these factors have given rise to a new kind of business structure described by business writers William H. Davidow and Michael S. Malone, among many others, as the "virtual corporation" [1]. It is what Jan Hopland (whom *Business Week* credits with probably having coined the phrase) describes as an enterprise that uses collaborations with others to marshal more resources than it would ordinarily have on its own [2].

In a "virtual" enterprise, the smaller, more flexible, and more efficient downsized entities join forces with each other to respond more quickly and effectively to new opportunities. Such an enterprise can (and some would say, must) exist because a world with fewer meaningful boundaries demands a business organization with fewer boundaries—one in which the lines between internal and external interests are less defined and in which the ability to be fast and flexible is more valued than the ability to protect and defend the integrity of a rigid, impenetrable structure.

In the business of drug development, we see the idea of the virtual corporation reflected in the trend toward increasing contracting in of CROs, and forming unprecedentedly close relationships with them, to recognize and respond to drug development opportunities more effectively than would ordinarily be possible.

According to many business observers, learning to work within "virtual" relationships is going to be vital to remaining competitive in the future, not just for drug development companies, but for all kinds of businesses. Journalist Julie Cohen Mason, for one, contends that "in today's global marketplace many companies are discovering that their long-term survival may depend on the partnerships they build with other companies" [3]. Rosabeth Moss Kanter of the *Harvard Business Review* concurs. "Alliances between companies, whether they are from different parts of the world or different ends of the supply chain, are a fact of life in business today," she says. ". . . being a good partner has become a key corporate asset. I call it a company's *collaborative advantage*" [4].

B. The Effects from Within

So far, we have examined the influence of trends in the business world in general on drug development. But there are also industry-specific circumstances driving change in drug development. Industry observers Michael Schlander [5] and Jenny Hone [6] have pointed to various factors such as loss of capitalization, cost containment, increasing therapeutic substitutions, and shorter patent lives as being among some of the key influences on pharmaceutical companies' decisions to downsize in order to operate more efficiently and flexibly.

Downsizing inevitably means having to do more with less—less staff, less space, less money. For drug development companies, it can mean lower R & D budgets, the loss of in-house expertise in key therapeutic areas, and fewer resources with which to mount large-scale, fast-track projects. This can make it difficult, if not seemingly impossible, for clinical groups to put together the right mix of resources—MDs, statisticians, CRAs, medical writers—to develop new products successfully.

Adding to the pressure of doing more with less is the increased globalization of drug development. Since most compounds are now being developed on a global basis, a company needs not only the right mix of skills and experience, but also the right people in the right countries. The ability to get to market on time may depend on the ability to carry out studies in different parts of the world simultaneously—and few companies today have the resources to do that efficiently, if at all.

These circumstances may be specific to drug development, but their effect is the same as that of the general trends toward downsizing and globalization: a greater willingness to make up for lost resources by contracting to CROs to carry out drug development projects.

III. CONTRACTING OUT VERSUS CONTRACTING IN: FROM VENDOR TO VIRTUAL CORPORATION

A. The Potential for a New Relationship Between Sponsor and CRO

The use of a CRO is hardly revolutionary; pharmaceutical companies and other drug developers have been farming out work to contract organizations for years. What is different is the potential nature of the relationship between the sponsoring entity and the CRO, specifically the potential for the CRO to become an integral and vital part of—an extension of, really—a company's drug development team.

Of course, there will always be times when it is perfectly appropriate simply to contract out certain aspects of a drug development project, without regard to the potential for extended involvement on the part of the CRO. But in a downsized, globalized environment, sponsors also have the opportunity to consider the possibility of contracting in—or compensating for reduced staff, resources and expertise—by finding a CRO with complementary experience and making that CRO an integral part of the drug development project team.

This suggests a radical shift in thinking about the role of CROs in the drug development process, but one that is a natural outgrowth of the aforementioned general and industry-specific changes in the drug development environment today.

B. The Advantages and the Pitfalls of Contracting In

1. *The Advantages*

Under the right circumstances (as detailed in the next section of this chapter), a CRO may have a great deal to offer the drug development company, including

- a broad range of clinical experience
- multiple areas of therapeutic expertise
- global resources and experience
- an established research team
- access to qualified investigators
- the resources to start up studies faster
- specialized technology
- flexible systems
- access to patients
- efficient processes
- expanded development capacity

Drawing on these capabilities can give the drug development company not only more resources, but also more flexibility. The company can augment its own internal expertise to get the most effective mix of resources for a particular project—and it can change the mix as necessary to meet the demands of different projects—without the tremendous costs of maintaining a huge, all-purpose organization in-house. The company could even contract in more than one CRO, virtual-corporation-style, if a particular project warranted bringing together complementary strengths from several different organizations.

2. *The Pitfalls*

Sure, the advantages sound hard to beat. But there are also potential risks to contracting in a CRO, including

- loss of control over studies
- budget overruns
- inadequate CRO resources and expertise
- late, inaccurate, or otherwise unusable results
- conflicts between SOPs
- incompatible corporate cultures
- failures in communication
- lack of rapport with key people

- people who oppose partnerships
- lack of control over personnel decisions
- reduced contact with investigators

If contracting in is beginning to sound more risky than advantageous, do not stop reading now. Yes, there are risks. But as Christopher Ball, CEO of a biotech company in the Pacific Northwest, points out, ". . . despite the many risks, contract research poses as many (if not more) benefits and opportunities" [7]. The key lies in understanding the risks and managing them intelligently and effectively; we will discuss some effective strategies for doing so in subsequent sections of this chapter.

IV. WHETHER AND HOW TO CONTRACT IN: THE DECISION-MAKING PROCESS

A. Evaluating the Need for a CRO

The process of choosing a CRO begins with defining specific needs within an organization. The most common circumstances under which a CRO might be considered include

Fig. 1 Illustration of how a small pharmaceutical or biotechnology company might allocate resources for drug development, combining its own internal resources with outside resources to create an efficient "virtual company" structure. The internal resources listed on the left comprise the company's core areas of expertise. Next, the mix of internal and external resources shown here reflects how the company could augment its internal resources with outside resources in particular areas to manage the actual development process efficiently. Finally, purely external resources could be used to manufacture and market the drug—perhaps even as a consequence of selling rights to the new product to a third party—once development is complete.

- insufficient capacity or personnel to handle a major increase in workload or a backlog of work
- lack of special facilities to conduct key aspects of a new project
- movement into a new therapeutic area in which internal staff has little expertise

B. Traditional Strategies for Contracting Out to a CRO

Once it is determined that a CRO can help in circumstances such as those described in the preceding paragraph, the sponsor must determine what strategy to pursue for using the CRO. Traditional strategies include

- temporarily augmenting staff by hiring a CRO to help with a backlog or an increase in workload (for example, hiring additional monitors from a CRO to help internal monitor staff carry out an unusually large project)
- farming out certain aspects of a study to a CRO that has the special facilities to handle them (for example, using a CRO with a purpose-specific lab to handle HIV-positive or other special-need samples for which the sponsor has no comparable facility)
- using a CRO in areas in which the sponsor has little experience (for example, using a CRO with expertise in CNS studies to handle certain aspects of a schizophrenia study)

These are all traditional strategies that represent methods of contracting out, rather than contracting in. They may be characterized as follows:

- *Limited use of CRO resources.* The sponsor hires the CRO to supply specific resources to meet a particular need, without regard to larger areas of experience or expertise offered by the CRO.
- *Central control at sponsor level.* The CRO simply carries out the sponsor's directives, often with little or no access to information about the larger context in which the work is taking place.
- *Urgency often a primary basis for selection of CRO.* The decision to use a CRO is based not on proactive planning for future needs, but on a reaction to an immediate crisis; the CRO may be selected largely, if not wholly, on the basis of who can start work sooner.

C. The Alternative of Contracting In

While traditional strategies continue to be perfectly adequate in certain circumstances, their value is becoming increasingly compromised by the general and industry-specific trends shaping the drug development environment.

As sponsor organizations continue to reorganize into leaner, less unwieldly, more flexible entities, their internal resources continue to shrink, making it more and more difficult to handle all major project demands internally. The solution may be to look to a CRO not just to help out on the periphery of a project, but to join in with the sponsor as a partner in it, acting as a virtual extension of the sponsor's resources and capabilities.

In contrast to contracting out, the strategy of contracting in a CRO as a project partner may be characterized as follows:

- *Potentially extensive use of CRO resources.* The sponsor may choose a CRO with a broad range of experience and expertise in planning, carrying out, and completing drug development projects, and exploit that experience and expertise throughout the project.
- *Decentralized control.* In planning and managing resource, budgetary, and time requirements, the sponsor shares control with the CRO, providing ample information and access to enable the CRO to contribute to the decision-making process.
- *Performance as a primary basis for selection of CRO.* Rather than choosing a CRO based on who can get the job started fastest at the best cost, the sponsor makes CRO selection decisions based on the CRO's track record of quality, speed, and dependable performance.

D. The Key Differences Between the Traditional View and the Alternative

Perhaps the best way to sum up the preceding material is to say that the difference between traditional "contracting out" and the alternative of "contracting in" is the difference between seeing a CRO as a back-up resource and seeing a CRO as a partner. Reactions to crises tend to drive the former; by contrast, proactive planning characterizes the latter.

Tradition: The CRO as Back-up	Alternative: The CRO as Partner
In-house staffing based on expected workload	In-house staffing based on core needs
CRO used when in-house resources become inadequate	CROs included in resource planning
Crisis management atmosphere	Proactive planning for CRO involvement
CRO viewed as back-up to in-house staff	CRO viewed as complement to in-house staff
Scope of CRO services used is limited	Full resources of CRO considered for use
Major concern: time	Major concern: total performance
Results often unfavorable	Results often favorable

E. Some Examples of CRO Studies

How do you know which opportunities are good ones for contracting in a CRO? Here are some examples of instances in which contracting in offers important advantages at different points in the drug development process.

New Therapeutic Class: Phase I and/or Early Phase II. Contracting in a CRO with experience in a new therapeutic class speeds up development and brings the sponsor up on the learning curve quickly with a minimum investment.

Phase IIIB. By having a CRO do the study while the sponsor completes Phases III and regulatory submission, two key activities happen simultaneously, saving valuable time. In some companies, it would be extremely hard to resource both at once.

Large Global Phase III. The CRO works with a small team from the sponsor to plan and implement studies while the rest of the sponsor's resources accelerate completion of Phase II and development of output tables and final report outlines for global submissions.

Global Product Development via Virtual Corporation. A small team from the sponsor works with two major CROs to pursue an aggressive development timeline even when few in-house resources are available for the project.

V. CHOOSING TO CONTRACT IN: STRATEGIES FOR SUCCESSFUL CRO SELECTION

Although the characteristics of a close CRO–sponsor relationship would indicate that choosing to contract in may offer a relationship of potentially far more value, it is still a relatively new approach and, as such, may be considered with understandable trepidation about the risks of such close involvement with an outside source.

While contracting in may extend the capabilities of the sponsor far beyond what would ordinarily be possible, it remains of considerable importance to question how the sponsor can minimize the risks involved in the process.

This section is given over to specific steps the sponsor must take to ensure that the company enjoys the full advantages of contracting in and, at the same time, avoids the potential pitfalls.

The key concepts throughout the process of risk management are preparation, information, communication, clarity, and trust. The strategy associated with these concepts is threefold: define specifications clearly, choose the right CRO to meet them, and manage the relationship appropriately.

A. The Importance of Study Specifications

Study specifications identify the activities required to initiate, conduct, analyze, and report the results of a clinical study [8]. An accurate list of study specifications is an important tool for selecting the right CRO for a project and for successfully managing the relationship with that CRO during the project. (See sample outline.)

The process of preparing study specifications is a multi-disciplinary one involving a team of specialists from within the company who can address the various aspects of the study, such as protocol development, case report design, database design, study locations and so forth. In certain cases (such as when a decision about which CRO to use has already been made, based on past experience with the CRO), the CRO itself may even be a part of the team that prepares the specifications. By making the CRO a part of the process when appropriate, the sponsor can be sure that the CRO fully understands the scope and demands of the project, since it will have been involved in the process of establishing them.

Sample Outline of Specifications for a Clinical Study

A. Description of the product

1. Generic name
2. Dose form
3. Projected therapeutic indication

B. Details of the study

1. Study objective
2. Experimental design
3. Patient population
4. Projected dropout rate
5. Total number of patients
6. Statistical power
7. Clinical setting
8. Number of clinical sites

C. Regulatory status

1. Purpose of the study
2. Regulatory phase
3. Type of regulatory submission

D. Materials and service

1. Prepare study materials (list specific activities)
2. Initiate study (list specific activities)
3. Conduct study (list specific activities)

4. Data Management and Analysis (list specific activities)
5. Other (specify)

E. Milestones and timelines

1. Approve protocol
2. Obtain institutional review board approvals
3. Hold multi-investigator meeting
4. File regulatory submission
5. Ship clinical supplies
6. Complete 25% of the projected patients
7. Complete 50% of the projected patients
8. Clean up all data
9. Approve integrated study report

Clear and carefully thought out study specifications are of inestimable value to both the sponsor and the CRO. They can help the sponsor assess internal needs, identify cost and time issues, and establish criteria for CRO selection. They can help the CRO become familiar with project goals, break down tasks for line-item bidding and timelines, and choose the appropriate format for responding to an RFP. Most importantly, they can provide a standard by which to evaluate a CRO and a benchmark by which to measure the CRO's performance during the project. For all these reasons, it is imperative to develop study specifications early and to supply them to all the key players—both within the company and at the CRO—as quickly as possible.

B. Qualifying CROs

Once study specifications are complete, the sponsor can begin to prepare a list of potential CROs, using whatever resources are available for preparation of such a list, from existing databases to recommendations of colleagues.

With basic information about CROs in hand—size, facilities available, areas of therapeutic experience—it should be fairly simple to use the study specifications to eliminate those which do not meet the most basic criteria, such as those which are not large enough to handle a project, or do not have the facilities to carry out key aspects of the project, or have no experience in the therapeutic area on which the project focuses.

Once those CROs that are clearly unsuited for the project are eliminated, the sponsor can move on to applying the following criteria to determine which CROs warrant an RFP for the project, employing telephone and personal interviews with key CRO personnel, studying CRO literature, and seeking input from colleagues. The goal at this point is to obtain general answers in all of the following areas.

- *Alliance potential.* Are the CRO's business objectives compatible with those of the sponsoring organization? Is there a basis for mutual benefit in a relationship between the sponsor and the CRO?
- *Comprehensiveness of resources.* Does the CRO have the facilities and staff to handle all the different aspects of the project outlined in the study specifications? Do the personnel have the expertise and experience to work as a true extension of the sponsor, rather than just as a vendor?
- *Record of quality service.* Has the CRO historically performed to the standards of accuracy, efficiency, and timeliness that the study specifications demand? Is documentation available to support this history?
- *Extent of experience.* Roughly how many studies in the therapeutic area being considered has the CRO performed? How many of these studies were of the same type and size as the one the sponsor proposes?

The sponsor can then move on to evaluating CROs which meet these basic qualifications.

C. Evaluating CRO Proposals and Choosing the Right CRO

Choosing a CRO to contract in may be one of the toughest decisions a sponsor will ever make; it does, after all, involve buying something that does not yet exist and that will not exist until the commitment to buy has been made. As such, it is ultimately based on faith and trust, and it unavoidably involves some degree of risk. This material is intended to help show how a sponsor can minimize that risk by taking care to gather as much solid, pertinent information as possible on which to base a decision.

In addition to reviewing any proposals or other written materials a CRO submits for consideration, the sponsor should request a visit to the CRO, to get a firsthand look at facilities and conduct on-site interviews with key personnel. Like the development of study specifications, this should be a team effort; sponsor personnel representing different disciplines should visit the CRO as a team, and then split off from each other to conduct one-on-one interviews with their CRO counterparts [9].

The accompanying chart lists general areas of information about the CRO that the sponsor should address in the decision-making process. These categories should, of course, be tailored to the specific situation, and the sponsor should set specific standards for each one.

CRO Evaluation Criteria
Capabilities
Needed range of services, facilities, and equipment
Global capabilities
Reliable record-keeping systems
Adequate security measures
Personnel
Needed range and mix of expertise and experience
Appropriate extent of expertise in therapeutic class
Ability to participate in collaborative strategic planning
Good training program in place
Quality of Work
History of experience in appropriate therapeutic area
Record of on-time and accurate results and reports
Regulatory History
Results of FDA inspections
Experience with regulatory submissions
Financial Considerations
Proven financial stability and resources
Financial independence from other sponsor organizations
Able to provide sponsor maximum value for cost proposed
Standards and Ethics
SOPs meet appropriate standards
QA program in place
Good business practices in place
Confidentiality assurances
Compatibility
Corporate culture compatible with sponsor's
Flexibility in business practices to meet sponsor needs
Previous positive experience with sponsor

At this stage, the information-gathering process should go beyond contact with the CRO to include discussions with CRO bankers or venture capitalists, scrutinization of financial statements, and the pursuit of other avenues of information. Only by gathering as much relevant data as possible can a company make the most informed choice.

VI. MAKING IT WORK: HOW TO LAY THE GROUNDWORK FOR A SUCCESSFUL PROJECT RELATIONSHIP

What makes a relationship between a sponsor and a contracted-in CRO work to its fullest potential? It depends entirely on the willingness of both parties to let the following attributes define the relationship.

- long-term contracts based on quality as well as speed
- a mutual vested interest in each other's future
- a long-term strategic orientation
- top-rank support for the relationship in both groups
- reciprocal relationships based on sharing strengths
- coordinative management styles based on collaboration

All of these attributes reflect a significant shift in the nature of the relationship between a sponsor and a CRO. Accordingly, some structural and procedural changes on the sponsor's part should be considered, to create the ideal environment in which these characteristics can grow and flourish.

A. Company Organization: Redefining the Structure

Any company that is considering working closely with CROs on a significant portion of its drug development activities should consider looking at an organizational structure that reflects the nature of its relationships with CROs.

Charles Handy, in *The Age of Paradox* [10], suggests a "doughnut" organization (Fig. 2) with a solid core that contains the company's internal resources and core competencies and a space surrounding the core that contains others who are needed to perform key functions that arise on a periodic basis.

This "most curious doughnut" [11], with its solid center and surrounding space, is a fitting model for the development phase of the pharmaceutical or biotech company's efforts. At the core are the essential internal components of the company, such as key full-time employees, core competencies (drug discovery, for example, along with financial and regulatory affairs), and organizational and management resources. In the surrounding space, outside parties can move in and out to meet changing company needs that exist beyond the

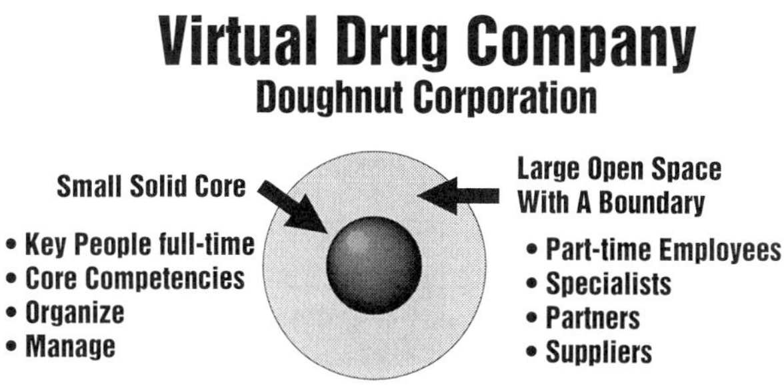

Fig. 2 The "doughnut" organizational structure into which pharmaceutical or biotech product development fits in well. Adapted from Charles Handy. *The Age of Paradox*.

solid core. These outside parties can include just-in-time resources, consultants, suppliers, and partners, like CROs.

Handy positions the doughnut, with its flexible open space around the core, as a useful alternative to the traditional, rigid organizational chart that has historically defined corporate structure.

B. Personnel: Developing New Skills

When a company is working closely with a CRO, the personnel it assigns to the project frequently need to develop skills that they may not have been called upon to utilize in their current positions.

For instance, in the sponsor–CRO relationship, a CRA at the sponsor company moves from actively doing the tasks to managing people at the CRO who implement tasks under the CRA's direction. Similarly, research physicians may be communicating concepts to their CRO counterparts, who then develop the protocols and manage day-to-day patient safety issues.

Often, the person at the sponsor company is expected to manage the study at one or two levels higher than those to which they were previously assigned. They may be paired with personnel at the CRO who need advice and direction that they are not normally asked to provide. The CRO personnel may in fact even have more experience in the project than the sponsor personnel who are providing them with direction.

To avoid potential problems in this area, sponsors would do well to choose for close work with CROs those people who have previously shown skills or aptitudes in the "C"s: conceptualizing, coordinating, consolidating, and communicating. Furthermore, they should make sure that these people understand what is expected of them and that they have the resources they need—training, mentoring, or other programs—to develop these skills fully.

C. Procedures: The Best of Both Worlds

It is important to keep in mind that there exists a fundamental difference in the way a sponsor's development team functions operationally and the way a CRO development team does, since one works in a single-client environment and the other works in a multi-client environment.

In the sponsor team's single-client situation, it is possible to develop unified SOPs and to standardize many aspects of the drug development process across various therapeutic groups and projects. In the CRO's multi-client environment, on the other hand, SOPs and systems must be much more flexible, since they must deal with a wide variety of unique client environments.

How can the sponsor and the CRO bridge the gap created by this situation? It may seem like a simple either/or proposition: either the CRO duplicates the sponsor's SOPs or the sponsor acquiesces to whatever seems to be the most efficient of the various methods the CRO has developed. But a better solution may be to work closely together to come up with a mix of standardized and customized processes that will best meet the sponsor's needs. This approach, while challenging, can bring together the best of both worlds, to the benefit of both parties. It requires a big commitment to open communication, a strong ability to engage in joint problem-solving, and the willingness to work out, within the new procedural standards, processes for dealing with project changes that occur.

VII. MEASURING RESULTS: END-OF-STUDY EVALUATION OF THE CRO

You have done everything right: the study specifications, the CRO selection, the adaptation to new ways of doing business. So how did it go? To answer that, you must have two things: (a) reasonable expectations for results and (b) performance milestones, set up at the beginning of the process, against which to measure results.

The following are some touchstones you might consider using in developing criteria for CRO performance evaluation:

- performance in meeting stated goals
- performance on specific services
- CRO strengths and weaknesses affecting the project
- actual versus projected costs
- effective CRO–sponsor personnel communications
- flexibility in meeting sponsor needs

A CRO that does well in all those categories at the end of a study is certainly worth cultivating a continuing close relationship with for work on future studies. If a CRO does not do well, examine why and whether it would be possible and worthwhile to seek improvements in those areas for the sake of possible future projects.

Building and maintaining an ongoing relationship with a good CRO can ultimately pay off in improvements in many areas that will benefit the sponsor company. For example, it has been demonstrated that database development cycle times will tend to grow shorter and shorter with every subsequent project on which a sponsor collaborates with the same CRO, as illustrated in Fig. 3.

VIII. BEYOND THE PROJECT AT HAND: LONG-TERM RELATIONSHIPS WITH KEY CROs

Contracting in dictates a radical shift in the way sponsors use CROs: the sponsor moves from farming out work based on crisis management to forming a

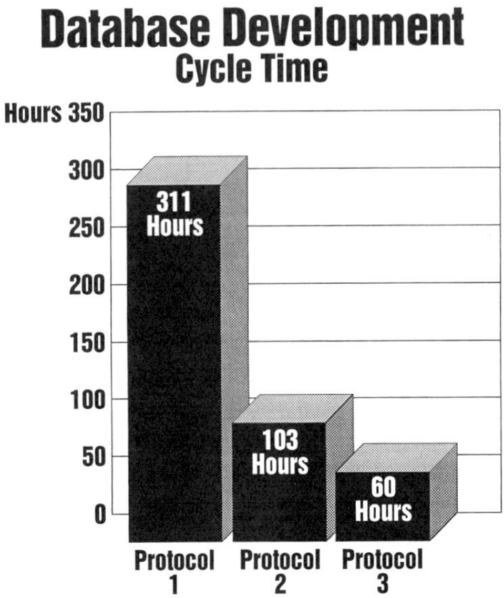

Fig. 3 Database development graph showing how shorter, more efficient cycle times may be achieved in the process of working with a CRO. Courtesy of Pharmaco LSR, Austin, Texas.

few select relationships based on long-term mutual benefit. Making a change of this magnitude may not be easy, but it can be extremely rewarding over the long term.

Through significant relationships with a few key CROs, the sponsor gains the flexibility and the resources to respond quickly and compete effectively wherever and whenever opportunity presents itself in the new drug development environment.

In a time of unprecedented industry redefinition, contracting in may mean the difference between being battered by the storms of change and enjoying smooth sailing into the future.

I'll deliver all;
And promise you calm seas, auspicious gales
And sail so expeditious that shall catch
Your royal fleet far off.

William Shakespeare
The Tempest

REFERENCES

1. W. H. Davidow and M. S. Malone. The Virtual Corporation. HarperCollins, New York, 1992.
2. J. A. Bryne. The Virtual Corporation. *Business Week.* February 8, 1993, p. 103.
3. J. C. Mason. Strategic Alliances: Partnering for Success. *Management Review.* May 1993, p. 10.
4. R. M. Kanter. Collaborative Advantage: The Art of Alliances. *Harvard Business Review.* July–August 1994, p. 96.
5. M. Schlander. A Strategic Role for CROs. *Pharmaceutical Executive.* February 1994, pp. 74–84.
6. J. Hone. The rise and pull of CRO partnerships. *Scrip Magazine.* March 1994, pp. 32–34.
7. C. Ball. Thinking Outside the Lines: Selecting a Contract Research Agency. *Bio-Pharm.* November–December 1993, p. 42.
8. J. R. Vogel and S. R. Nelson. Achieving results with contract research organizations: determining the study specifications. *Applied Clinical Trials 2*: 70–76, 1993.
9. J. R. Vogel and M. I. Linzmayer. Achieving results with contract research organizations: evaluating and selecting CROs. *Applied Clinical Trials 2*: 36–41, 1993.
10. C. Handy. Summary of the Age of Paradox, Soundview Executive Book Summaries, 16 (8, part 1), 1994, p. 5.
11. C. Handy. Summary of The Age of Paradox, Soundview Executive Book Summaries, 16 (8, part 1), 1994, p. 4.

13

The Role of Clinical Research Organizations in Drug Development

Albert J. Siemens

ClinTrials Research Inc.
Research Triangle Park, North Carolina

James E. Higgins

Health Decisions, Inc.
Chapel Hill, North Carolina

I. CHALLENGES FACED BY THE PHARMACEUTICAL INDUSTRY

Global economic pressures and access to advanced technologies in the 90s have spawned a revolution in how business is being conducted throughout the world. Changes in the pharmaceutical industry are the epitome of this fact.

Public concern about the rapidly escalating costs of health care, particularly in the USA and Europe, reached a fever pitch in the early years of this decade. Prescription drugs, a highly visible component of health care expenditures, came under especially heavy attack. Consequently, the five largest pharmaceutical markets in the world grew by only 3–8% in 1992 [1] compared to a +10% growth historically (see Table 1). Similar sluggish performance was registered in 1993 and 1994, with Germany and Italy actually experiencing a market size reduction [2,3].

Legislation in Europe in 1993 required pharmaceutical price cuts of 2.5% for three of the next five years in the UK, reductions of 5% in France, and an equivalent amount in Germany on products that are exempt from reference pricing, while Spain and Portugal demanded a 3% reduction, and Denmark and Norway introduced reference pricing. Meanwhile in Italy, 700 products were removed from the reimbursement list [4]. In the United States, the proposed legislation for Health Care Reform in 1993, though not passed, projected sales losses of 11%, industry tax rates greater than 55% of pretax income, with the total cost of the legislation equating to 25% of the industry's R & D investment [5].

Not only has the industry encountered pressures on sales revenue, it has also recognized major increases in R & D expenses [6] as shown in Table 2. The growing complexity of product development and the demands of regulatory agencies have contributed substantially to these increases. According to the Boston Consulting Group, the average number of patients in clinical trials per New Drug Application has almost tripled from 1321 in 1981–1984 compared

Table 1 Five Leading National Pharmaceutical Markets, 1992

Market	Est.Market Value ($B)	% World Market	% Growth
United States	48.2	29	6
Japan	29.4	18	3
Germany	14.0	9	5
France	12.1	7	8
Italy	10.0	6	5

Source: Ref. [1].

Table 2 Total Estimated R & D Expenditures by Major Pharmaceutical Companies

Year	Total estimated expenditure ($B)
1970	0.6
1975	1.1
1980	2.0
1985	4.1
1990	8.4
1993	12.6

Source: Ref. [5].

with 3567 in 1989–1992 while, over the same period, the average number of clinical studies per NDA increased from about 30 to 60 and the number of pages per NDA increased from approximately 45,000 to 90,000 [7].

A further challenge to pharmaceutical companies is the shrinking of the period of marketing exclusivity [8] as indicated in Table 3. The examples shown and the well-known marketing approvals in rapid succession of multiple products in each of the antidepressant, anticholesterol, and antiinfective classifications in recent years emphasize that the competition in drug development is intense.

II. RESPONSES TO THE CHALLENGES

These numerous major challenges have stimulated dramatic responses from the industry. Most noticeably perhaps, pharmaceutical companies have taken steps to become as consumer oriented as possible as exemplified by the acquisition

Table 3 Period of Exclusivity Shrinking

First launch (drug/year)	Second launch (drug/year)	Exclusivity (years)
Inderal/1968	Lopressor/1978	10
Tagamet/1975	Zantac/1983	8
Seldane/1984	Hismanal/1988	4
Zofran/1991	Kytril/1992	1

Source: Ref. [8].

of Medco, a mail-order pharmacy business, by Merck at a cost of US $6B. Similarly, SmithKline Beecham acquired Diversified Pharmaceutical Services Inc. for US $2.3B and Pfizer aligned with Caremark International Inc. and Value Health Inc. Moreover, traditional research companies, such as, SmithKline Beecham, Hoechst, Marion Merrell Dow, Rhone Poulenc–Rorer, Upjohn, and Ciba–Geigy among others, have moved into the generic drug business. In addition, the over-the-counter market is now being pursued aggressively by the major companies. For example, Merck and Johnson & Johnson formed Centra Healthcare in the UK to market Pepcid whereas Warner–Lambert and Glaxo formed a joint venture to market Glaxo prescription medicines [5,9,10].

On the research side, the industry is adopting more efficient means of identifying and optimizing new product leads such as robotic screening methods, structure-based *de novo* drug design, combinatorial chemistry, and the use of diversity libraries that include small organic molecules through oligomers and natural products [8]. However, as the most sophisticated and efficient approaches available to any one pharmaceutical company have not been adequate to ensure a healthy product pipeline, virtually all companies have turned to joint ventures, mergers, and acquisitions for survival. Importantly, one of the key participants in these initiatives has been the biotechnology industry; innumerable agreements have been signed between pharmaceutical and biotechnology firms in the first half of this decade [11].

Irrespective of source, the most promising product leads are now typically incorporated into global development programs. The goal is to reduce the number of redundant clinical trials, reduce the time to market, and reduce the overall cost of drug development in the interest of enhancing profitability. Today the global approach to product development is often essential for maximum return on R & D investment. International regulatory harmonization efforts, the development of worldwide reporting requirements for adverse drug reactions, and a gradually increasing uniformity in clinical practice are all facilitating the global development process.

III. ENTER THE CLINICAL RESEARCH ORGANIZATION (CRO)

In spite of the strategies that have been embraced on both the R & D and sales ends of the pharmaceutical business domain, the profitability and ultimate survival of the industry could not be achieved without radical restructuring and downsizing of the work force. Over 30,000 layoffs were announced in 1993 in the pharmaceutical industry. This trend has continued into 1995. In parallel, pharmaceutical, biotechnology, and medical device companies exhibited an ever-growing commitment to conduct their clinical research programs through contract research organizations (CROs) on a worldwide basis. It has been estimated [12] that CROs have captured up to a third of the available clinical research market.

A. CRO Definition

In the broadest sense, a CRO is any organization that provides a service for pharmaceutical, biotechnology, or medical device sponsors in support of a clinical research project or program. The CROs range from a single self-employed consultant through companies of over 1,000 staff members. Not surprisingly, the services provided by an individual will generally be highly focused, such as statistical analysis, protocol, and report preparation, or medical, scientific, or regulatory consultation. In contrast, the larger companies are likely to provide comprehensive product development services ranging from R & D planning and design through complete clinical program implementation, analysis, report preparation, and, ultimately, regulatory submission. Depending upon a client's need, all components of these services or a select subset may be provided. As the barriers for entry into the CRO business were originally not substantial, the majority of companies, both large and small, were initiated by medical, scientific, or business professionals with prior experience as employees of the major pharmaceutical, biotechnology, or medical device companies.

B. CRO Origins

The concept of retaining expert consultation at various stages in the development of a pharmaceutical product is not novel; it was already common in the 1960s. Substantial organizations that were dedicated to Phase I studies began appearing in the 70s, including Quincy Research Center, Harris Labs, and Medical and Technical Research Associates in the United States, and Guy's Drug Research Unit and LAB in the UK and Germany, respectively. Pharmaco LSR, although being a relative latecomer to provide Phase I services, with operations beginning in the mid 80s, rapidly incorporated Phase II–IV services into its portfolio. Other Phase I units have gradually developed services in Phases II–IV as well, whereas other organizations such as Besselaar, Quintiles, and ClinTrials Research were initially formed to focus on Phase II–IV programs.

Based on the specialties of company founders and their early associates, many companies initially developed specific niche services, such as data management and biostatistics at Quintiles, a central nervous system emphasis at Cato Research and International Clinical Research Corp., and oncology at Theradex. In contrast, ClinTrials Research and Besselaar were formed from the outset to support the full clinical development process encompassing regulatory, medical, project management, clinical monitoring, data management, biostatistics, and report preparation functions.

C. Multinational Expansion

In response to the global demands for clinical research services from the established multinational pharmaceutical industry and the rapidly evolving international orientation of biotechnology companies, the major U.S.-based CROs began offering international services in the mid-to-late 80s, some based on internal growth and the establishment of European offices such as Besselaar, Quintiles, and ClinTrials Research. Others, such as Parexel and Pharmaco entered Europe through acquisition or joint venture. The strategy of mergers and acquisitions, though uniquely challenging to manage, has become the most common approach to expansion in the 90s as it provides rapid access to additional expert resources in new markets and facilitates the integration of new services such as preclinical and clinical laboratories as well as drug packaging and supply. The acquisition route is not limited to U.S.-based CROs as European companies such as Biodesign Institute for Clinical Research and Innovex have made acquisitions in the United States in recent years.

Although the early focus of CROs was on the U.S. and European markets, recent years have seen expansion into Australia, South East Asia, Japan, South Africa, Israel, Eastern Europe, Russia, and Latin America, in concert with client demands. Japan represents a potentially major growth market for CROs, not only because of the increasing demands of Japanese pharmaceutical companies to develop products in the United States and Europe, but also as a result of increasing medical, business, and an expected regulatory acceptance of CRO participation within the country.

Great strides have already been taken in Japan including, among others, the acquisition of U.S.-based Institute for Biological Research and Development (IBRD) by Koraya, a Japanese pharmaceutical distributor; the announced initiation of activities by other leading U.S. and European CROs; the establishment of CMIC Co., Ltd. and MediScience Planning, K.K. as two leading Japanese CROs; and a long history of Japanese Phase I units such as Sekino Research Institute and Osaka Pharmacology Research Clinic (OPHAC). However, major challenges still exist in Japan. For example, two CRO associations have been established, one that represents Phase I companies and another, the Japanese CRO Association, that is limited to organizations providing clinical research services from Phase II–IV. Moreover, Koseisho, the Japanese drug regulatory agency, has not formally endorsed the use of CROs. Nonetheless, the third international conference on harmonization (ICH-3) in Yokohama in late 95 is expected to facilitate a greater harmony in how pharmaceutical product development is carried out in the United States, Europe, and Japan, including the use of CROs.

D. Rationale for Using CROs

In the early years of the evolution of CROs, pharmaceutical companies often contracted out work that represented a narrow scope or was of a small scale; if the contracted job was of greater magnitude, it was likely considered to be of secondary importance, such as studies to support product launch or marketing, product line extension, or the development of a secondary indication. This practice was potentially a reflection of the lack of confidence sponsors had in the service providers at the outset. On the far end of the spectrum some product development managers contracted out the most difficult projects either in the hope of capitalizing on the specific capabilities and expertise of the selected CRO or, in the worse case, to avoid criticism in the event of failure had the project been handled by the company's internal resources.

During the late 80s and early 90s, pharmaceutical sponsors often enlisted the support of CROs upon encountering a crisis that may have resulted from unanticipated delays in study conduct due to a variety of internal or external factors, inadequate resource planning, or poor program management. Over the past few years, however, the crisis mode has largely been replaced with much more reasonable proactive planning to involve a CRO, whether the project is of top or secondary priority. Pharmaceutical companies have determined that CROs are a valuable, flexible source of qualified resources and specialized expertise and often can increase the speed of project performance. Most importantly, the use of CROs helps manufacturers to control R & D expenditures, particularly as outsourcing represents a variable rather than a fixed cost.

Pharmaceutical companies have now wholeheartedly incorporated the CRO into product development programs from R & D planning through product licensing, Phase IV trials, postmarketing surveillance, and outcomes research. This maturation has occurred most rapidly in the United States, but the same phenomenon is now also seen in Europe, Australia, and other countries that require country-specific trials as a prerequisite for product registration. As noted above, progress is being made in Japan as well.

The evolution of biotechnology companies has occurred almost coincidentally with the development of CROs. As those companies have generally been research-based, having little or no clinical development expertise or plans to develop the capacity, they have benefited greatly from, and contributed substantially to, the sophistication of CROs. Indeed, those biotechnology companies that have elected not to develop products through a licensing arrangement with pharmaceutical firms, have virtually depended on CROs exclusively, particularly when taking products in development from the United States to Europe and other countries.

With the ever-increasing regulatory demand for the approval of medical devices, particularly in the United States, many medical device companies who had not built a substantial clinical research infrastructure are now also turning to CROs for study support.

E. Preferred Supplier Relationships

Another clear indicator of maturation in the CRO industry is the development of preferred supplier relationships or strategic alliances between pharmaceutical companies and one or a few CROs who have generally been selected on the basis of their specific expertise plus scope, capacity, and quality of service. Many companies who had adopted the use of CROs over the past 10 to 15 years suddenly have found themselves working with as many as 40 or 50 individual service providers often with no central or standardized mechanism for the selection, contracting, or management of the CROs, resulting in inefficiencies and lack of control.

Today, many major U.S.-based CROs have entered into preferred supplier agreements with one or more sponsors. The preferred supplier relationships have many specific advantages for the sponsor, such as

- Increased efficiency of the initial proposal and bidding process as a result of a reduced number of bids to review and a clear understanding of the scope of work that can best be achieved through a close and long-term working relationship between the parties.
- Elimination of study-specific contract negotiation as the long-term relationship is typically governed by a master agreement that spells out terms and conditions and simply requires the addition of a specific task order with an approved budget to initiate a new project or activity.
- More rapid study start-up as a result of the advantages listed above plus reduction in the time required for identifying and training human resources, transferring standard operating procedures, technologies, and systems (e.g., in project management, communications, data transfer).
- An established confidence in the operating philosophies, processes, and capabilities of the CRO and key staff members.
- Benefits from advanced technologies, enhanced operating systems, and growing staff expertise while progressing from one project to another.
- Cost savings as a result of the efficiencies noted above plus a clear understanding of service rates, the program budget, and a reduction in the risk of cost over run.

The CRO in such a relationship also accrues important benefits including

- A substantial reduction in the time and cost of the bidding and contracting process.
- Improved predictability in the source and potential volume of revenue.
- A reduced risk in recruiting and building an experienced work force.
- Improved ability to understand the requirements and expectations of the client.
- Ability to respond rapidly and confidently to requested changes in scope during the course of the project.
- Customized management information and reporting systems for the client.
- Access to technologies that are developed among the two parties.

The full value of preferred supplier relationships or strategic alliances can only be achieved through an open and continuing planning and review process involving both sponsor and the CRO. This process can be achieved via close collaboration at two primary levels, namely (a) through project-specific team(s) that handle the planning and implementation of the project scope of work, and (b) a bipartisan executive review committee that monitors and ensures the continued development of the overall intercorporate relationship.

F. Keys to Success

Whether governed by an ad hoc project-specific contract or a preferred supplier agreement, there are a few key factors that facilitate the success of a project that is conducted through the support of a CRO.

- Explicit definition and agreement on the scope and duration of work.
- A written contract between the CRO and sponsor that is based on a win-win philosophy; each partner must be accountable while neither is placed at inappropriate risk.
- A sophisticated, well-experienced approach to project planning and budgeting by both the CRO and the sponsor.
- Clearly identified project leaders and responsibilities.
- Demonstrated ability by CRO in project leadership and management.
- Clearly identified lines of communication.
- An established process for performance measurement and reporting.
- Recognition that the CRO is a service provider and, accordingly, must be professionally responsive and flexible while assuring compliance with regulatory and ethical business requirements.
- Understanding of any subcontracting that the CRO may be required to do during the project.
- CRO reference checks prior to contract award.
- Financial stability of the CRO.

IV. PROJECT IMPLEMENTATION

The technical functions that CROs carry out, such as project management, clinical monitoring, drug safety reporting, biostatistics, medical writing, etc., are typical of the pharmaceutical development process and are well known by professionals in the field. These activities will not be addressed here, but it is of utmost importance to recognize that all required functions and activities must be appropriately integrated into the sponsor–CRO project team.

Keeping in mind the keys to success that are summarized above, it is essential that the CRO and sponsor work together as a team that has common goals. This requires that the team clearly understands all of the project's specifications and expectations, and in some extreme instances, it might be necessary to help the pharmaceutical sponsor identify specific expectations. Virtually all clients differ to some extent, some requiring only process support while others look to the CRO for leadership and guidance.

Each member of the team must not only be competent to carry out specific tasks, but must also buy into the concept of teamwork. Importantly, the project leaders, one generally at the CRO and a counterpart in the client company, must coordinate the activities of the entire team and must facilitate communication among team members. Fortunately, the advent of a myriad of electronic communication tools for video, voice, text, and data have dramatically facilitated this vital exchange of information. The technology per se, however, will not ensure communication success; rather a commitment to utilize these tools is key.

As study data are often key deliverables in a CRO–sponsor relationship, and since data management technology is often being enhanced through the cooperation of these two parties, a review of key issues in data management follows.

A. Data Retrieval and Review

The interface between clinical monitoring and data management is blurred and overlapping rather than a distinct line. Most studies use paper to capture original or source data. The appropriate data are then transferred manually to paper case-report forms. Study monitors visit clinical sites to verify, among other things, that source data were accurately transcribed from one document to another. Currently, the primary transfer point between clinical monitoring and data management is the delivery by or through monitoring of paper-based case-report forms. However, advances in data capture and transfer technology are changing the ways clinical monitoring and data management are being performed, and CROs are playing a major role in the change. In some instances CROs are taking the lead in developing new approaches while in others, particularly through preferred supplier and strategic alliance relationships, sponsors and CROs are capitalizing on shared capabilities to enhance these technologies [13].

Over a decade ago, desktop computers were installed at clinical sites to be used as study management and data collection devices. That study sites were in the best position to monitor and transfer to an electronic format the data from their patients seemed clearly logical. The clinical site computers were linked to a central study computer for harvesting, reviewing, and integrating data. Clinical monitors were to review electronic data harvested from the study sites and to use site visits to verify source documents, query questionable data entries, and ensure compliance with regulatory requirements. This general approach to data collection and monitoring was named remote data entry (RDE).

The concept of RDE is sound but how and when to use it was initially not well understood. For each success there were failures. Some of the failures were so major that RDE is no longer used by many sponsors. Yet, the appeal of the idea that data can best be reviewed and validated at the source of collection and near the time of collection has, along with the availability of new technology, spawned new systems to manage data that are being collected from many distributed sites.

Powerful notebook computers, some with touch screens, are used as combination data collection instruments and data entry/validation processors. As data are entered at the site, the software checks the logic and consistency of the entry and reports the results of the electronic review almost immediately. The site can review the electronically checked data and make edits as appropriate. An electronic audit trail of all edits is maintained. Entered data and audit logs can be harvested remotely by the monitoring site for review and for integration with other study data. If there is a requirement to maintain a paper case-report form, a copy of the electronic form can be printed and filed.

An increasing number of CROs and sponsors are managing clinical trials by relying on images of case-report forms that have been transmitted from remote study sites to a central location. The images can be reviewed on a computer monitor and queries/comments can be added to the image. The annotated image can be transmitted back to the study site for review and clarification. This cycle can continue until the information sent by the site satisfies the requirements of a visual review. The initial, intermediate, and final transmitted images can be stored and are available for cataloging, linking to the clinical database, and further review. In addition, the "clean and complete" case report forms are available to be entered into an electronic database by a combination of traditional key data entry and electronic character recognition. As the data are entered into the clinical database and once entry is complete, they are subjected to electronic verification (logic and consistency checks). The electronic validation will generate queries that require resolution before the data can be assumed clean.

Fax/image-based approaches allow the preliminary visual review of the quality of the data to be shared between the study site and the monitoring site in an ongoing manner without the monitor visiting the site. Nonetheless, monitoring visits for source data verification, some resolutions of queries generated by electronic validation, and review of adherence to good clinical practice are still required.

Finally, a growing number of clinical sites are implementing electronic patient record systems for all patients seen. For those patients who are also participating in a clinical trial, there is the opportunity to transfer electronically the source data to an electronic case report form (Figure 1). Data transferred this way will be precise and the need to compare the source to the case report form is eliminated.

B. Capture and Transfer of Data Generated Outside the Clinic

Safety lab data are required for almost all studies and data from speciality labs as well as daily diary data are required in many trials. Traditionally, safety lab data generated by a local lab and patient daily diary data were transcribed onto the case report form at the study site. Data generated from an automated analyzer by central laboratories and most speciality laboratories are routinely transferred electronically.

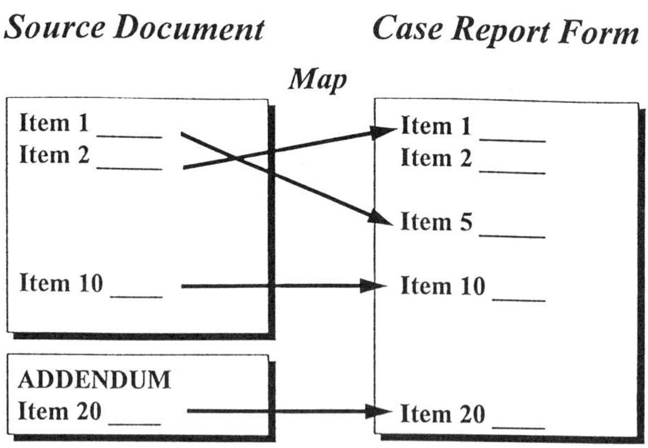

Fig. 1 Electronic mapping of data from a clinic record (source data) to a case report form (clinical trial data).

Electronic patient diaries are available in two primary formats. Patients can record information daily on a variety of small electronic devices. Data recorded on these devices can be read remotely from the clinic site and/or downloaded from the device when the patient visits the clinic. Alternatively, patients can use a telephone keypad to answer diary questions asked by an automated telephone system. Patients can call in to the system or be called. Daily harvesting and review of diary data provides a timely means of monitoring the progress of the study.

Databases containing information about quality of life and cost of care are sometimes assembled from data obtained outside the study clinic. Quality of life data are often collected daily and can be part of a daily diary that could be transmitted via an electronic device. Cost of care data may need to be collected from many different sources. Hospitals, clinics, and pharmacies usually have an electronic record of their charges and, in some studies managed by CROs, cost data have been transferred to the study database electronically.

C. Access to Data

Several CROs and sponsors have developed information systems that will allow study databases to be warehoused in a read-only environment for access by both internal and external users. Query tools can be made available through a menu when the data are viewed or data can be downloaded to local environments where existing, sometimes unique, tools are available for special purpose reviews. The data can be refreshed as often as new data are processed. Since data are warehoused, processing of new data and review of current data can proceed independently and unencumbered by read-only users (Figure 2).

D. International Databases: Integration of Data

Many CROs with an international presence are positioned to support sponsors with multipurpose international databases. An international database for a product could be used to support regulatory filings in different formats in different countries. The key to providing this flexibility is the coordination of the types of data that will be collected in the international studies. If the primary outcome and safety endpoints are all collected using the same or essentially similar definitions, then the success of the data integration is made much more likely. The same variable collected in multiple studies will be assigned a unique name in the integrated database. Laboratory values reported in different units will be converted or normalized according to their magnitude relative to their study-site-specific normal ranges. Safety, therapy, and other data that need to be dictionary coded, will be coded using the same dictionaries.

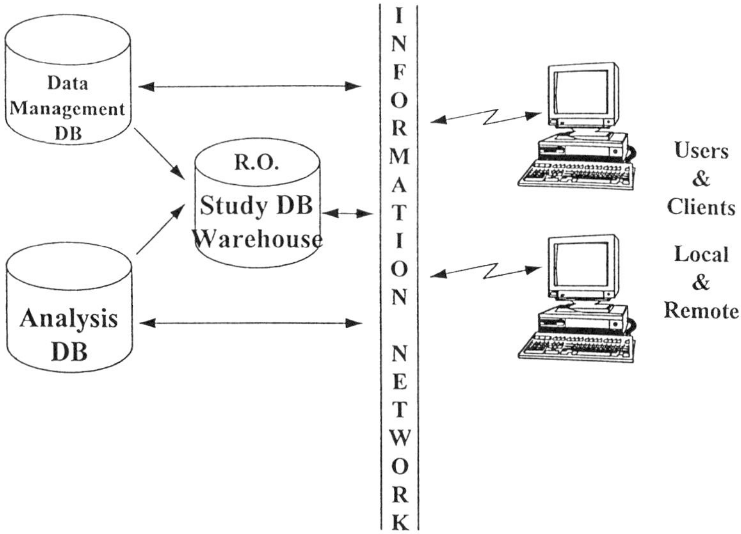

Fig. 2 Information system design that allows data management and analysis databases (DB) to be shared with local and remote users and clients as a read only (R.O.)

Common variable names and definitions simplify the task of programming the data displays and analyses. Statistical planning and programming should be centralized but have input and review from the dispersed team. Specifications for the analysis should be detailed and drafted in parallel with the final stages of protocol planning or, at the latest, when the database structure is being developed. Unless there are compelling reasons not to, data should be displayed in the same manner across all the studies included in a particular regulatory filing. A core set of computer programs can be developed to cover all the common study definitions. If definitions need to vary according to the destination of a regulatory filing, then the set of core programs can be made specific to the requirements.

If the database is designed as an integrated database, then mixing and matching study data for a regulatory filing should be limited only by the specific requirements of the filing. The international database can be warehoused and accessed in the manner described earlier in the discussion on access to data.

E. Support for Regulatory Filings and Marketing Efforts

In general, the support offered by CROs does not end with a regulatory filing. The version of the warehoused integrated-study database used with each regulatory filing is archived, but the study database continues to evolve. Data from ongoing studies continues to flow into the database to be prepared for safety updates. Queries by regulatory authorities of the data that were filed [assuming that a Computer-Aided New Drug Application (CANDA) was not filed or was inadequate or improperly used] can be directed by the CRO/sponsor to the archived database or the authorities can be given access to the appropriate data warehouse.

The integrated database will also be the primary source of information for marketing. A plan for general information dissemination can be a component of the overall plan for the development of the drug. That plan might include preparation of abstracts, presentations at symposia, and submissions to peer-reviewed journals. Specifications of analysis and data display requirements can be prepared in a manner similar to that used for preparing specifications for regulatory submissions. The use of statistical and programming time will be both more efficient and of better quality if the efforts specific to general information dissemination occur in parallel with those for regulatory submissions.

V. CONCLUDING OBSERVATION

CROs have truly become an integral component of the drug development process. While it can be expected that pharmaceutical and biotechnology companies will continue to depend on their highly qualified scientists, physicians, regulatory experts, planners, marketing experts, and managers for their unique skills and direction setting, they will rely on CROs to execute the process of drug development in the most efficient manner while achieving standards of excellence.

REFERENCES

1. Glaxo Annual Report, 1992.
2. Glaxo Annual Report, 1993.
3. Glaxo Annual Report, 1994.
4. I. Schofield. Corruption And Cost Containment In Europe. *Scrip Magazine Jan*: 7, 1994.
5. M. Dower, 1993—A Year To Retrench, Restructure, Rethink. *Scrip Magazine Jan*: 2, 1994.
6. Trends In U.S. Pharmaceutical Sales and R&D. *1990–1993 PMA Annual Survey Report.* Pharmaceutical Manufacturers Association, 1993, p. 6.
7. S. Engel and J. F. Jalkiewicz. Mixing Up A New Formula. *Med. Ad. News 12(15)*: 3, 1993.
8. R. B. Giles. Blending Business Boundaries. *Pharmaceutical Executive 13(11)*: 46, 1993.

9. D. C. Ruriani and S. Engel. Introduction. *Med. Ad. News 13(7)*: 3, 1994.
10. Med. Ad. News Staff. In OTC Market, Joint Ventures Work Best. *Med. Ad. News 13(9)*: 1, 1994.
11. R. Davison. Research Alliances in 1993. *Scrip Magazine Jan*: 36, 1994.
12. The CRO Industry. Wertheim Schroder. *May*: 3, 1995.
13. M. J. Rosenberg and J. R. Haldi. Accelerating Drug Development with Electronic Data Collection and Processing. *Sci. Comp. & Auto. 11(12)*: 13–17, 1995.

14

Understanding Drug Development and Registration in Japan

W. J. C. Currie

Merck & Co., Inc.
Rahway, New Jersey

I. INTRODUCTION

The sales of pharmaceuticals in Japan, in United States dollar terms, are second only to those in the United States [1]. The significant price reductions occurring in the developing managed-care environment of the United States and the strength of the yen are likely to reduce the U.S. lead. Thus it is not surprising that U.S. pharmaceutical companies are eager to register and sell their drugs in Japan. Differences in the regulatory requirements that have been noted between these two countries have been viewed as barriers to free and fair trading in pharmaceuticals. These issues are not new, and to resolve them the Market-Oriented, Sector-Selective (MOSS) talks [2] were set up between government officials of both countries. Although progress has been made and the talks continue, many differences remain. Among these is the fact that Japan insists that drugs developed elsewhere undergo, on the one hand, repeat dose-range finding and pharmacokinetic studies in Japan and, on the other, a comparative drug study. These requirements are purportedly based on the possibility of genetic variation in drug handling between Japanese and non-Japanese patients.

There is, concededly, a trend in the United States and the European Union (EU) towards the evaluation of pharmaceuticals in an increasing number of subgroups [3]. Differences noted in the dose response or ADME (absorption, distribution, metabolism, excretion) data may well suggest that additional clinical investigations are necessary. However, where no differences are noted it is difficult to justify a repetition of the Phase III program within the confines of technical registration.

The MOSS initiative was spearheaded by representatives from the U.S. Department of Commerce, since the Japanese requirements were perceived as a barrier to free and fair trading. These representatives were not, however, equipped to debate the scientific aspects of these requirements. With the advent of the International Conference of Harmonization (ICH) [4,5] movement, it is hoped that this technical group could address such matters.

Within the ICH process there are five steps defined in the path to harmonization. Once selected for harmonization, the topic is worked on by the appropriate Expert Working Group (Step 1) and their deliberations are sent to the ICH Steering Committee (Step 2) who consult the participating regulatory bodies (Step 3) before submitting final recommendations to the three regulatory groups (Step 4) for incorporation into the regulations (Step 5) [6].

As in most countries, the Japanese regulatory decision-making process is less transparent than that in the United States. However, this impediment to registration like those posed by the drug development process and regulatory requirements, will lessen as the United States, EU, and Japan increasingly harmonize drug approval. Although the major impetus to harmonization may be improved commercial access for global marketing, other benefits include earlier availability of new medicines and reduced sacrifice of animals for duplicate studies to satisfy national variations in regulatory protocols. Thus the Japanese requirements for drug approval, like those of other nations, appear to be passing a threshold of significant transition.

II. THE REGULATORY PROCESS

The Japanese Pharmaceutical Affairs Law (PAL) covers pharmaceutical development for registration and matters pertaining to manufacturing, licensing, adverse-reaction reporting and reexamination among others. Rewritten in 1960, the law subsequently has been revised on several occasions. An official English version of the most recently updated Japanese regulatory process and requirements is available [7]. Revisions, subsequent to the publication of this edition, have as their principal objectives the support of the research and development of orphan drugs and ensurance of earlier approval of highly needed drugs by fast-track examination. These planned activities were calculated to increase the workload of the Koseisho, while it is known that the Japanese government has ruled, some years ago, that there would be no increase in the number of government employees. As a consequence, to ensure that the necessary time would be available to achieve these objectives, a clear reduction of certain aspects of the regulatory work within the Ministry of Health and Welfare (MHW) had to be planned. To this end the MHW has enlisted the assistance of the Lyakuhin Kikou, a nongovernment, nonprofit, public organisation originally established as the instrument through which those who suffer severe drug-related injury could have their cases evaluated and appropriate compensation offered from funding provided by the pharmaceutical industry. The Lyakuhin Kikou is the Japanese for Pharmaceutical Organization and its full title is The Organization for Drug ADR Relief, R & D Promotion and Product Review (Lyakuhin Fukusayo Higai Kynsai•Kenkyu Shinkou Chosa Kikou). As part of these drug law revisions of April 1994 the Lyakuhin Kikou, reinforced by the transfer of some Koseisho officers, will review all applications for the registration of generic drugs. Having done so, the Lyakuhin Kikou recommends action to the MHW. Additionally, the Lyakuhin Kikou has been charged with monitoring compliance with Good Laboratory Practice (GLP) and aiding orphan drug development. To this end, it utilises the money it generates from its generic drug evaluation fees. An orphan drug has been defined in Japan as a product that will make a significant contribution to the health and well being of a population of potential patients whose number does not exceed 50,000. The developer can receive significant subsidies and tax benefits. The MHW was assisted by a relaxation of regulations; as of April 1, 1994, all newly approved medications designated for subsequent reexamination and orphan drugs have had the interval from licensing to reexamination extended to 10 years from the previous 6 years. The MHW will further permit the extension of the validity period of the license for the manufacture or importation of drugs from 3 to 5 years and the expansion of items for which approval is not required (e.g., some raw materials). A number of recently approved NCEs have had their reexamination extended to 10 years.

The manufacturer of a product deemed essentially identical to an existing one, that is, a me-too product, may submit a New Drug Application (NDA) during the 10 years prior to the reexamination of the original product, but data may be required from the postmarketing surveillance program that is being conducted by the first applicant to evaluate further the risk-to-benefit ratio. Without obtaining these data from the original applicant, filing of an NDA would seem to be not possible. Currently this would appear to effectively increase the market exclusivity period for an innovative product to 10 years. However, the definition of what constitutes a me-too product has still to be tested. In line with this change from 6 to 10 years, records of and materials used in all tests included in the registration application must be retained at least till reexamination. Although this can accentuate storage problems, it is a small price for an innovative company to pay for such potential benefits.

In Japan, NDAs are submitted to the MHW by way of the pharmaceutical section of the Prefectural Government Office within the business district of the applicant, and if no objections are raised, the NDA is forwarded to the MHW. Responsibility for the regulation of pharmaceutical products is situated within the Pharmaceutical Affairs Bureau (PAB), which is one of nine within the MHW (Figure 1). The PAB provides the necessary framework and administration to facilitate the drug regulatory process by auditing the drug dossiers to ensure that the data are complete and satisfy the Japanese guidelines [8]. On completion of review by the PAB, a meeting takes place to advise the pharmaceutical company of any deficiencies in content or format within the NDA that must be put right before the review can progress. This frequently requires several meetings with submission of supplemental data by the sponsor. Once the PAB declares the NDA acceptable, it is passed to the appropriate subcommittee of the Central Pharmaceutical Affairs Council (CPAC) for detailed scientific and medical review. Some drugs may be examined by more than one subcommittee; a combination product containing a new chemical entity (NCE) will be referred to the subcommittee on combination drugs and to the appropriate subcommittee for new drugs. These subcommittee reviews are conducted by highly experienced members of the Japanese scientific and medical communities, drawn from the universities, research institutes, and hospitals. All communication between these reviewers and the pharmaceutical company is conducted via the Koseisho officer and familiarisation with the file usually takes the Koseisho officer 2 to 3 months. Since the company is not permitted to present data or defend a new drug application (NDA) before the reviewing committees and subcommittees of the CPAC, it is critical that the Koseisho officer be as well versed as possible on the file content. Although the final decision on a drug approval rests with the Minister of Health and Welfare, it would be unusual for the Minister or a Koseisho officer to disagree with the recommendations of the CPAC. The Koseisho officers are not a major part of this decision-making process but fulfill the important role of informed conduits between the company and the committees; therefore these officials cannot enter into any agreements or commitments, pertaining to the scientific evaluations of the application, with a pharmaceutical company during the approval process.

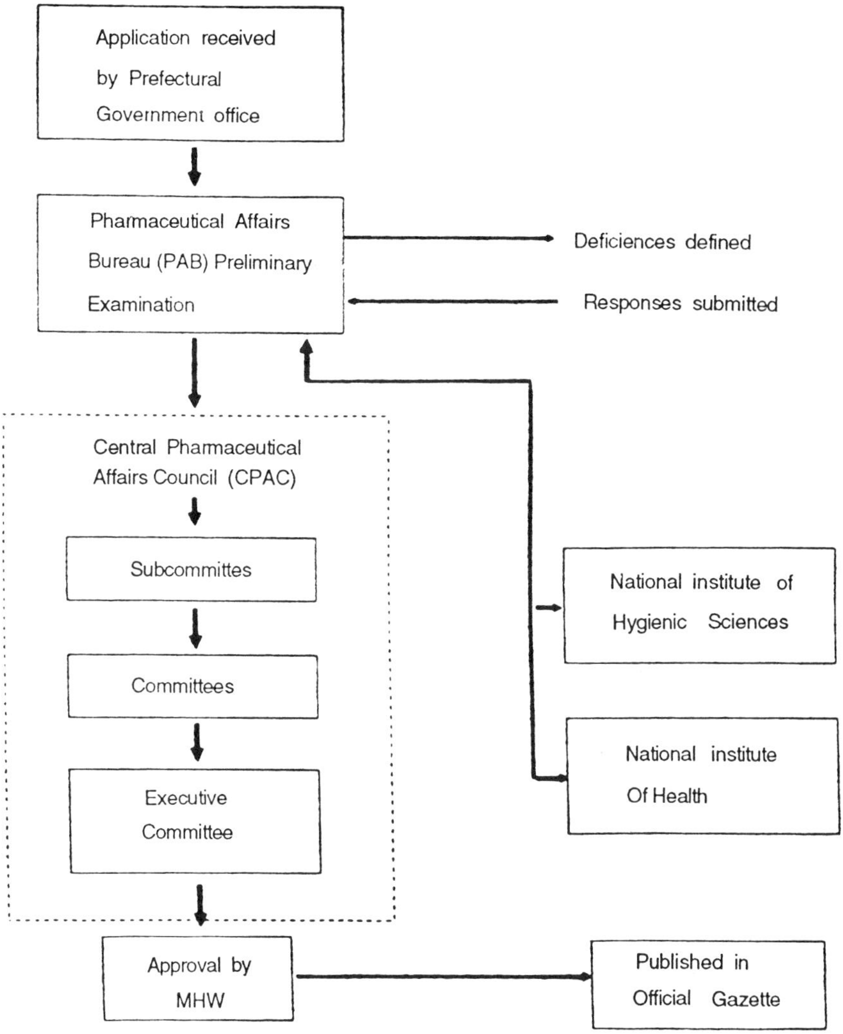

Fig. 1 Procedural flow chart for a new chemical entity submitted to Ministry of Health and Welfare (MHW).

In parallel with the review, drugs containing a new ingredient are also referred to the National Institute of Hygienic Sciences (NIHS) or the National Institute of Health (NIH). Among the functions of the NIHS is the testing and analysis of drugs, whereas the Japanese NIH conducts tests on specifications for antibiotics and biological products and have strong representation on the committee on antibiotic products.

A drug is defined as "new" if at the time of application for a manufacturing or import approval it is designated as different (by chemical structure of the active ingredient, desired indication, or planned dosage, etc.) from those already approved in Japan. The significance of the definition is that new drugs are subject to postapproval clinical investigation. Applications to manufacture or import a drug must be made through the pharmaceutical sections of the prefectural government office of the district where the business is situated. For all drugs, except nonprescription medications with government defined approval standards and some raw materials the prefectural governor transmits the application to the MHW for evaluation.

Each of the four subcommittees of CPAC for new drugs meet twice monthly whereas the other subcommittees generally meet monthly. A subcommittee will deliberate on one to three drugs during any one session, and a product is likely to be reviewed on several separate occasions. Only when the subcommittee is satisfied with a product's quality, safety, and efficacy will it proceed to the next stage in the review. An NCE passes to a special committee on new drugs that meets once every 3 months and reviews 10 to 15 products per session. Products that pass the scrutiny of these special committees advance to the executive committee, which usually meets 1 month after the special committee session. The most senior committee in the decision tree, the executive-committee membership is draw from senior or former members of Japan's leading pharmaceutical, medical, scientific, and health department institutions. It is responsible for making recommendations to the Minister of Health and Welfare. The number and type of subcommittees and committees are shown in Figure 2. The therapeutic areas of responsibility of each of the four subcommittees for new drugs is shown in Table 1.

When the MHW has approved a drug the sponsor is notified by its Prefectural Government Office. This involvement of the Prefectural Office is to ensure its awareness of the application since it shares responsibility with the Inspection and Guidance Division of the PAB, under whose oversight it is charged with ensuring the manufacturer's adherence to Japanese Good Manufacturing Practice (GMP). The GMP was incorporated into the regulations and has been enforced since September 1980. The Drugs Division of the PAB is responsible for monitoring compliance with Good Clinical Practice (GCP). As noted, the Lyakuhin Kikou now has responsibility for monitoring compliance with GLP; however, when conducting inspections to ensure adherence

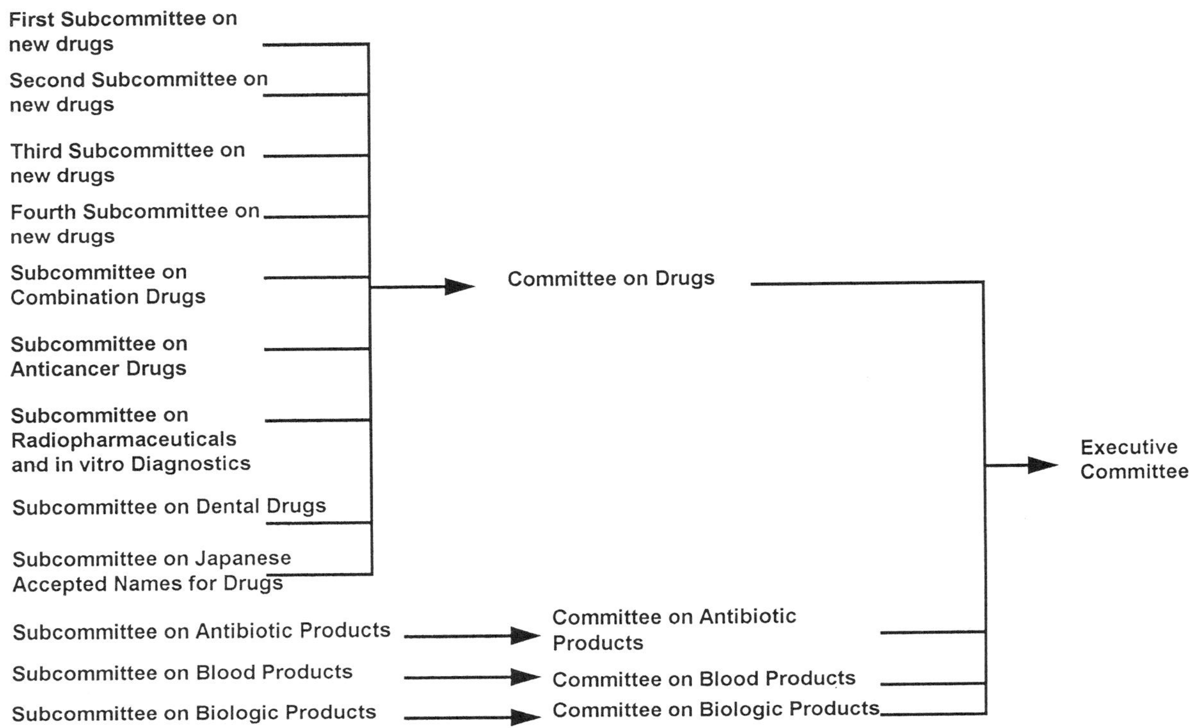

Fig. 2 The subcommittees and committees of the Central Affairs Council.

Table 1 The Subcommittees on New Drugs: Division of Therapeutic Responsibility

First subcommittee	Gastrointestinal
	Genitourinary
	Hormonal
	Topical
Second subcommittee	Cardiovascular
Third subcommittee	Central nervous system
	Sensory organs
	Respiratory
	Allergy
Fourth subcommittee	Antibiotics
	Chemotherapeutic agents

to GLP, the Lyakuhin Kikou does seek the cooperation of the appropriate Prefectural Office.

If one excludes the time taken for the pharmaceutical company to respond to questions, the regulatory process from application to approval for a new drug averages 13.9 months, with the longest time, during the 1980–92 period, being 21.8 months [9]. Overall, branded generics take less time than new entities, usually less than 12 months. If one compares the United States and the European performance, these times are by no means unfavorable.

As in the United States, generally new medicines in Europe are evaluated for marketing approval on the basis of quality, safety, and efficacy. Although the fourth hurdle, cost, often an issue in European approvals, is absent, the Japanese government has, over the past several years, contained pharmaceutical costs by frequently mandating cost reductions of established products. Such practice accords with its policy of holding down the health fund payments to hospitals and health care workers even though both the government and union health funds have enormous reserves.

For those contemplating drug registration in Japan, a number of general points are worth contemplating. A significant point of deviation from the requirements of other agencies is that the majority of data contained in a Japanese NDA must be published [10]. This is part of a philosophy of minimizing government responsibility for drug evaluation. They have elected to have neutral third parties do the work. To this end clinical studies must be conducted by independent investigators with a neutral supervisory investigator, as will be seen, and NDAs are evaluated by an assembly of independent advisors, as previously stated. The evaluation of study results by independent journal referees was designed as part of the same process. However, with the resultant pressure for publication and subsequent registration, non-peer-review journals created a niche in the market place by speedily publishing all that was submitted. Another point of note is that in the NDA, all the data must be presented in Japanese. Translation, if necessary, must be done with care to ensure scientific accuracy of the data and its interpretation. All translations must be accompanied by a copy in the original language. Translation of large dossiers is both time consuming and very expensive. All copies of every data report supporting an application for approval to manufacture or import a drug must bear an original signature of the person who conducted the tests, and, to verify his or her qualifications, a copy of that person's curriculum vitae must be included. The suitability of all institutions supplying test results must also be verified by submission of detailed statements, including a full floor plan, indicating all equipment and its layout [11]. Considerably more detail than required for other regulatory agencies is necessary and includes the origin, details of discovery, and the process of development of the drug. To evaluate possible novelty in comparison to other drugs in the same therapeutic class, the sponsor must submit a tabulation of such features as dosage and administration, warnings, precautions, and adverse reactions. These data are to be gleaned from the company's worldwide development program, which is somewhat surprising given the weight placed on local Japanese comparative studies. A vital part of a Japanese NDA is the highly condensed summary of approximately 200 pages.

III. QUALITY NEEDS

Data requirements for assessing the physicochemical properties, standards, and test methods must include the demonstration of the molecular structure of the active substance and quality-control specifications for the active substance. To demonstrate uniformity of the production process, results from the testing of at least five lots of new drug substance and of the finished product must be submitted, and each quantitative test has to be conducted in triplicate. This multiplicity of testing to set product specifications creates a heavy workload and may ignore an extensive database developed outside of Japan. Although the Koseisho is now slowly accepting data generated to its protocols outside of Japan [12], this does not resolve the issue of potential, substantial duplication of data generated elsewhere for a protocol not requiring the same degree of repetition.

The guidelines for stability testing were amended in 1991 [13] and further amended for medicines containing an NCE in 1994 [14]; their differences from those of the United States have been reviewed [15]. The expiration dating of a product is based on real-time storage testing. However, the Koseisho will accept an NDA during the course of the long-term (3-year) storage testing if the interim results reveal a shelf-life of not less than 1 year, the accelerated testing estimates stability for at least 3 years, and the final long-term storage results will be submitted before approval [16]. Additionally, the bulk drug substance and the finished product should be studied under varying light, temperature, and humidity exposures. Any resultant degradation products must be identified as precisely as possible and their toxicity and general pharmacology tested.

Japan is a party to harmonization of stability requirements that has now reached Step 5 in the ICH process. The Koseisho has accepted protocols both for long-term stability testing (temperature and relative humidity 25°C and 60%, respectively) and for accelerated testing (40°C and 75%, respectively). However, there are no standards for light testing. Japan has taken a number of initiatives on this topic of standardization of light testing and an early draft guideline was issued in December 1993. This is an official ICH draft still designated as at Step 1.

A requirement unique to Japan was the need for an assay for the arsenic content of all medications. For medications that do not contain arsenic, the development and validation of such a test is difficult to justify. Through the ICH, Japan has agreed to forgo the requirement for an arsenic assay of bulk drug substance.

In Japan, pharmaceutical inspectors are prefectural government officials, and they have three major duties: to inspect in accordance with GMP, to watch for unlicensed and adulterated drugs, and to control false, exaggerated advertising. To meet these obligations, they conduct regular on-site inspections of manufacturers, importers, pharmacies, and all other premises where drugs are sold. If a problem is detected, the officials will conduct intensive inspections of the offender. Officials based at Japan's ports used to conduct detailed inspections of all imported drugs. As a result of international concern, this potential trade barrier has been significantly modified. Currently drugs with import approval and investigational drugs for clinical trials where the study protocol has been submitted to the MHW are cleared inwards through customs; however, the government insists that as part of quality assurance importers shall perform quality testing for each lot and retain the results in the import office. Since April 1994 it is no longer necessary to report the results to the pharmaceutical officials of the importer's prefecture. Such testing is likewise required of Japanese pharmaceutical companies who manufacture off-shore and subsequently import. Such off-shore manufacturing is common practice for several economic reasons.

IV. PRECLINICAL NEEDS

A recent publication prepared under the supervision of the NDD of the PAB clearly discusses, with useful explanatory notes, the Japanese animal toxicology requirements [17]. These include the need for single- and repeated-dose studies, reproductive and developmental toxicology, mutagenicity, carcinogenicity, and antigenicity studies. These testing requirements are defined as guidelines and data will not be rejected simply because the methodology employed is not in accordance with Japanese guidelines. However, given the sponsor's inability to discuss the program beforehand with the real decision makers (who sit on the subcommittees and committees), as is readily available with the Food and Drug Administration (FDA), and Japan's failure to recognize formally other protocols, rejection of data not collected in strict adherence to Japanese protocols must be viewed as a distinct risk. Thus, it is difficult to see how one can interpret the "guidelines" as other than mandates at this time.

Guidelines covering general pharmacology studies necessary for a Japanese NDA were published in 1991 [18]. These guidelines present basic concepts and fundamental tests to be applied in general pharmacology studies that should be conducted in the research and development of new drugs with diverse pharmacologic effects. Such tests are conducted to study the desired treatment effect and any unwanted effects that may predict adverse reactions during subsequent human exposure. However, the Japanese guidelines do not simply ask for identification of effects in addition to the desired effect, but specify several specific areas of investigation (Table 2). Also in 1991, the Koseisho issued guidelines on animal pharmacokinetics [19]. In addition to general international requirements, the Japanese guidelines have two routine requirements: determination of the pharmacokinetics of metabolites of the test medication and of the distribution of the medication in the body, assessed by whole-body autoradiography.

These additional preclinical needs are not only a challenge for harmonization but are also a potential source for delay in the development program of a new medicinal compound.

Agreement was reached at the First ICH on regulatory requirements [4] to abandon the LD_{50}, a test requiring identification of the dose that will be lethal to half the animals tested. This test, of questionable value, will no longer be a

Table 2 General Animal Pharmacology

Effects on general activity and behavior
Effects on the central nervous system
Effects on the autonomic nervous system and smooth muscle
Effects on the respiratory and cardiovascular systems
Effects on the digestive system
Effects on water and electrolyte metabolism
Other important pharmacological effects

regulatory requirement for new medicines in the United States, EU, or Japan. The Japanese guidelines were the first to be amended, in accordance with this agreement, in August 1993. It was recommended that the LD_{50} be replaced by increasing dose tolerance studies in two rodent species by both the recommended (usually oral) and intravenous routes. If the compound has very poor solubility, the peritoneal route may be substituted for the intravenous. These studies will result in the use and sacrifice of significantly fewer animals.

Although comment has not, as yet, appeared in the official regulatory guidelines, it is understood that Japan no longer requires single-dose studies in nonrodents. This is an important step, since this requirement was unique to Japan.

While the value of repeated-dose testing beyond 6 months has been questioned [20], such testing is a regulatory requirement for a number of agencies, including the FDA and the Koseisho. In Japan, repeated-dose testing for 12 months is required only for new medicines expected to be administered to humans for periods in excess of 6 months [17]. At the First ICH there was consensus that 12-month toxicity studies in rodents could be reduced to 6 months where carcinogenicity studies are required. Encapsulated in the Japanese guidelines, 6-month repeated-dose toxicity studies have been accepted by the agencies of all three regions. Although the FDA continues to demand 12-month repeated-dose toxicity studies in the nonrodent, Japan like the EU accepts a 6-month duration.

A regulatory requirement that is more rigorously adhered to in Japan than elsewhere is the need to establish a nontoxic dose within the framework of the toxicity studies.

With regard to reproductive toxicology, as a consequence of the First ICH, it was agreed among the United States, EU, and Japan to recommend mutual recognition of their respective current guidelines. However, there were high hopes of a tripartite proposal of harmonisation [21,22]. Prior to the Second ICH a tripartite, harmonized guidelines on reproductive toxicology achieved Step 4 status and has been incorporated into the local regulations of all three regions soon. This is a very significant achievement.

Currently the three regions lack uniformity for selection of dosage, the requirements for carcinogenicity studies, exceptions to these requirements, and requirements when the route of administration or chemical form is altered. The rationale and criteria for carcinogenicity testing made progress between the First and Second ICH and guidelines (ICH Step 5) on dose selection for such studies are now available. Additionally, guidelines for when carcinogenicity studies are needed are currently at Step 2 in the process. Although these measures will not propose answers to all the problems, they do go a long way towards this end and are encouraging.

Two further documents presented at the Second ICH have now reached Step 5 and are likely to alter the preclinical requirements for registration in

Japan; they cover toxicokinetics and when to conduct repeated-dose tissue distribution studies.

The former may improve the ability of animal toxicology studies to predict possible adverse events in man; currently their relevance is questioned [23]. Whereas there is general agreement on the registration requirement for single-dose tissue distribution studies there is no consistency regarding the requirement for repeated-dose tissue distribution data.

Currently, the Japanese do not require a mammalian cell gene mutation assay. The three tests required for genotoxicity evaluation are a bacterial gene mutation test, *in vitro* cytogenetics, and *in vivo* tests for genetic damage. The Japanese regulations clearly state these to be the minimum requirement and encourage additional tests. Thus harmonization will likely be achieved by the Koseisho recommending all four tests as occurs in the United States and EU.

In the clinical development of drugs in Japan, before a single-dose human study can be undertaken, a 1-month preclinical toxicology study must be conducted. This is twice as long as the U.S. requirement. The duration of toxicity studies required to support the use of a test drug for varying lengths of human usage in Japan is shown in Table 3. Additionally, before conducting a single-dose male volunteer study in Japan, it is usually necessary to have completed a preclinical male fertility study (Segment 1) that has an in-life phase of 10 or more weeks. Although the guidelines do not require completion of this study before Phase I, the responsible Institutional Review Board (IRB) or the investigator, usually does. The unique Japanese requirement for Segment I male fertility studies before the conduct of single-dose studies on male volunteers in Japan has, as yet, not been resolved by the ICH initiatives. Japanese regulatory circles are aware that the Segment I male fertility study is of poor predictive value. This requirement is unique to Japan, and its value is debatable. The rat, which is used in this study, produces a marked excess of sperm and thus the test is believed by many to be less sensitive than the evaluation of

Table 3 Preclinical Requirements

Duration of dosing in toxicity study	Duration of human exposure
1 month	Single dose or repeat dosage not exceeding 1 week
3 months	Repeated dosing exceeding 1 week and to a max. of 4 weeks
6 months	Repeated dosing exceeding 4 weeks and to a maximum of 6 months
12 months	Repeated dosing exceeding 6 months or where this is deemed to be appropriate

testicular weight and histology that constitute part of the routine toxicology assessment. At such an early stage in the development cycle, the drug is made by a pilot process and is usually in limited supply. The need for twice the amount to conduct a 4-week rather than a 2-week study and for the 10-week male rat fertility study can cause a significant program delay. Removal of this barrier to harmonization is a likely outcome of future discussions on fertility testing.

Before entering a female into a clinical study, it is necessary to have completed the entire reproductive program, which consists of studies of fertility (Segment I), teratology (Segment II), and late gestation and lactation (Segment III). This represents approximately a 2-year time frame. Although the U.S. regulations state the need for Segments I and II and the demonstration of efficacy in male patients, where appropriate, before entering females into the program, the present U.S. trend is toward relaxation of the requirements to encourage investigation of the drug in a larger number of females during product development. This trend has probably more to do with the powerful Women's Lobby in the U.S. than any other single factor: there is no equivalent Japanese lobby.

Three additional requirements unique to Japan are necropsies in acute toxicity studies, with additional histology where macroscopic abnormalities are detected; an acute toxicity study for identified degradates of the test medication; and antigenicity tests. The last include skin-sensitization and photo-sensitization studies for topical preparations, in addition to the minimum requirement for all medications of active sensitization of guinea pigs, passive cutaneous anaphylaxis in rabbits or guinea pigs, and passive hemagglutination with use of sensitized rabbit serum.

Nonclinical data accumulated from studies conducted outside Japan are accepted by the Koseisho provided that they comply with the appropriate regulations [24,25], and that adequate information is supplied regarding the facility and scientists where the studies were conducted. A statement from the program director that the data have been collected and prepared in accordance with Japanese GLP guidelines, or their equivalent, is essential. Japan has mutual recognition of GLP inspections with most other major regulatory agencies. Japan has adhered to GLP [26] since 1983, its data are acceptable internationally, and it accepts all GLP data generated in other major pharmaceutical research countries.

A significant point of deviation from the requirements of other agencies is that the majority of the toxicology data contained in a Japanese NDA must be published. Since toxicology data are frequently published in non-peer-review journals, it adds nothing to the quality assurance of these data. The requirement also raises concerns regarding both confidentiality and the possible exploitation of these data to register a copy product by a third party. Also as mentioned, in the NDA, all the data must be presented in Japanese, accompanied by a copy in the original language.

V. CLINICAL NEEDS

The Japanese regulations covering the clinical program correctly stress its importance in evaluating the test medication, the need to ensure the use of appropriately experienced physicians at adequately equipped hospitals, and the need to ensure adherence to procedures, such as the Declaration of Helsinki, to ensure patient protection. Although these are consistent with most other parts of the world, there are differences in the conduct of clinical trials in Japan, both in organizational and philosophical terms. The industry sponsor enters into a contractual agreement with a medical institution in which the study is to be conducted and the investigator in charge of the study is directly responsible for the clinical trial. When several investigators in several institutions are involved, a supervisory investigator is appointed with responsibility for the oversight of the entire trial. The supervisory investigator need not be affiliated with any of the participating institutions. Unlike the Western hemisphere, this supervisory investigator is legally responsible for the part of the development program that he supervises. He is responsible for ensuring the ethical and scientific validity of the study and is authorised to finalize and amend the protocol and to request additional information, such as additional preclinical data. All scientific and study-related communications with the sponsor are channeled through the supervisory investigator, who also is responsible for inspection of completed clinical report forms and the preparation of the study report.

For each clinical study of an NCE, a clinical trial notification (CTN) must be submitted to the Koseisho. This document contains information about the

- rationale for the study;
- preclinical data;
- previous clinical study results;
- control and manufacturing data; and
- draft protocol.

The CTN must be submitted to the Koseisho no later than 4 weeks before the commencement of the study. Although it is their right, it is unusual for the Koseisho to comment. As in other countries, the duration of clinical trials with NCEs depends on the preclinical toxicity data. These durations are listed in Table 3, and additional requirements have been discussed under preclinical needs.

Japanese clinical development programs may involve smaller patient numbers than Western programs, although this is becoming less common. Japan presently is flexible in its requirements. For a chronic-use adult therapy, the

Koseisho would expect the drug to have been studied in approximately 500 patients, with at least 50 having been on therapy for 12 months and with at least 100 over 65 years of age. Special postmarketing surveillance arrangements exist to identify rarer adverse reactions. In an attempt to address the lack of consensus on duration of exposure and patient numbers required to evaluate safety of an NCE, the ICH has produced guidelines that have now reached Step 5. Japan has agreed with the United States and EU that, for chronic-use therapy, 300–600 patients should be treated for a minimum of 6 months and that no fewer than 100 patients should have been treated for at least 1 year. While the United States and EU feel, based on retrospective data, that a total of 1500 cases is acceptable, the Japanese have pressed for a prospective evaluation before reaching final decision, since their retrospective data are not compatible with that collected in the United States and EU. Such data should be available by 1996. The reviewing committees of the PAB presently consider that data on 1000 patients (with a range of 500 to 1500 or more for vaccines and oral contraceptives) would be appropriate to evaluate the safety within the NDA for an NCE.

The clinical development program is divided into three phases. The guidelines state that, in an ethical and scientific clinical program, the data generated in each phase should be carefully evaluated before permitting progression to the next phase. Phase I consists of a single rising-dose study, a short multiple-dose study, and a food-interaction study. Although the Japanese PAL does not mandate a food-interaction study for all oral medications, it is clearly recommended that such a study be carried out before the commencement of Phase II.

Phase II consists of a prepilot study, a pilot study, and a dose-ranging study. The prepilot study is not mentioned in any of the guidelines but is carried out at the instigation of the supervisory investigator with the objective of familiarizing the investigators with the NCE before commencing the full pilot study. For products already investigated outside of Japan and for which data are available, this step is generally omitted. The pilot study is considered to be a probe for efficacy, safety, and initial dosage evaluation and is conducted as an open, dose-escalation trial of 6- to 8-weeks' duration in about 30 to 40 patients. This is followed by the dose-range-finding study, which is often double blind, but may be conducted as an open study, in a maximum of 100 outpatients for 8 to 12 weeks. The value of both the prepilot and pilot studies before the dose-ranging study has been questioned. Although the Japanese clinical trial guidelines refer to early double-blind studies, they are advised only "when possible."

On the other hand, during Phase III, strong emphasis is placed on double-blind comparative studies with registered compounds having similar indications. A double-dummy approach to blinding is not uncommon as it obviates the need to conduct bio-equivalence studies that are necessary if the formulation used is other than marketed. Although the Koseisho may change the guidelines to strengthen the use of placebo comparison, senior investigators who control the protocol content would probably strongly resist such efforts. Where a registered therapy exists, Japanese physicians are not well disposed to placebo studies. Similarly Japanese patients, whose medication is paid for by their health fund, may be prepared to try an investigational product with potential benefits over that currently available, but they are less willing to enter a study where there is a fair chance that they will receive a placebo. However the general attitude is changing with the Koseisho favoring the conduct of Phase III studies to incorporate a placebo. While the demand to demonstrate statistical superiority or equivalence (to be discussed later) would require smaller studies when the new drug is compared to a placebo rather than a comparator drug with a good efficacy rate, such a change would not be without drawbacks for the pharmaceutical company. Studying a new drug against a placebo may align the price against the most expensive drug in that therapeutic category. To increase the ability to obtain a 3% premium, however, it is better to test against that drug and show superior efficacy. Under the current reimbursement system, this 3% advantage may be crucial to the success and survival of the company.

The current Japanese guidelines encourage investigators to conduct more scientifically correct studies, including the determination of decision criteria before the commencement of a trial, demonstration of statistical equivalency in the comparative studies (in preference to showing no statistical difference between groups), and the recruitment of more patients from fewer centers [27,28]. The use of more patients from fewer centers is not occurring and will require either the New Drug Subcommittee or the Special Committee to reject all studies failing to enroll at least 10 patients per site. Until this happens the present practice will continue because the investigators do not want to change and the studies are controlled by them according to Japanese GCP. In contrast the Special Committee has begun rejecting files not showing at least equivalency (on a statistical basis) against the comparative drug. However, in private discussions the Koseisho has made it clear that drugs that fail to show statistical equivalency may nevertheless be approved if evaluated usefulness (a Japanese assessment incorporating both efficacy and safety data) is demonstrated. This may be achieved by having a drug with a new mechanism of action or a demonstrated superiority in safety. It is likely that this may be an interim measure to rescue some NDAs during the early days of implementation of the need to demonstrate, at least, statistically based equivalency.

Where a test medication is being developed in more than one dosage strength or in more than one presentation, such as tablets and capsules or liquid, patients must be entered on all dosage strengths and formulations. The

PAL suggests that for each additional formulation, data on not fewer than 40 cases in not fewer than two institutions should be submitted. Guidelines for the clinical evaluation of 11 categories of drugs are available (Table 4); however, only the first 7 have easily available English translations. Efforts to deviate from the outlined course of clinical trials or their design regularly causes difficulties, in part because of the dominant role of the supervisory investigator.

The ability to use foreign data is limited at present and those inclined to use it in a Japanese NDA should consult beforehand with members of the NDD of the PAB. The PAB Notification 660 sets out the conditions necessary for acceptance of foreign data [29]. Foreign clinical trials must meet the Japanese clinical practice standards or be applicable to medical care as carried out in Japan. They should have been conducted by experienced researchers from reliable medical institutions and the results, as with the preclinical data, should be published. In addition, individual patient case records and statistical analysis records of the study must be available for inspection. Given all this, foreign clinical data are only accepted in relation to safety information. Currently one must conduct the ADME and dose-range-finding studies and a full Phase III program within Japan. Yet it would not be unreasonable to expect that if the ADME and dose-range-finding studies conducted in Japan agreed with the results from such studies conducted outside Japan, that the Koseisho would accept Phase III data conducted elsewhere to GCP standards. There is support for such a move within the Koseisho; however, there is little corresponding enthusiasm within the powerful Senior Physician Lobby.

In Japan there is a distinct reluctance to use a surrogate marker in trials defining dosage, unless the hypothesis supporting its use as a predictor of the desired effect has been proven. Thus in a global development program, if one

Table 4 Guidelines for Clinical Evaluations Are Available for Eleven Categories of Drugs

Antihypertensive drugs (established in 1979 and amended 1989)
Antiarrhythmic drugs (established in 1984)
Antiangina pectoris drugs (established in 1985)
Analgesic, anti-inflammatory drugs (established in 1982 and amended 1985)
Oral contraceptives (established in 1987)
Cerebral vasodilators (established in 1987)
Antihyperlipemies (established in 1988)
Antidepressant drugs (established in 1988)
Hypnotic drugs (established in 1988)
Drugs for heart failure (established in 1988)
Anticancer drugs (established in 1991)

wished to include Japan, the inability to use a biochemical marker in place of a late onset endpoint for dose-range-finding studies could add considerable time to the clinical development program or require, as at present, that the dosage be reevaluated in Japan.

However, irrespective of conditions met, the requirements to conduct clinical trials defining ADME and administration and dosage within Japan will almost certainly not change in the foreseeable future. This opinion is based on the Japanese declared belief that differences in race, environment, and medical care practice may affect such studies and thus the acceptance of foreign data. The Koseisho and physician establishment quote such differences as the frequency of slow acetylators of isoniazid between Japanese and Caucasians, which, in the case of isoniazid, does result in a different adverse-reaction profile. Although there are few documented examples of such differences, the Japanese position is that such differences cannot be excluded for an NCE and that foreign data may not accurately reflect the true adverse-reaction frequency and severity and thus the benefit-to-risk profile in Japanese. Furthermore, they quite the frequently documented lower daily dosages of prescription medication in Japan than in other countries, such as the United States. In part, this is based on a philosophical difference in the approach to drug development. In the United States, emphasis is placed on the need to develop a sufficiently large dose to ensure substantial efficacy for the patient. The tendency in Japan is to develop a lower dose that will demonstrate a degree of efficacy while minimizing associated side effects.

In December 1993 the Koseisho published a Guideline for Clinical Trials of Drugs Used in the Elderly [30]. In general these are consistent with the United States, EU, and ICH guidelines. The one substantial difference is in Paragraph 4.1, which states that before conducting clinical trials in the elderly, it is desirable to examine the pharmacokinetics, the efficacy, and the safety of the drug in nongeriatric patients, that is, those under 65 years of age. It is hoped that the guideline will permit some flexibility since there are circumstances where the studies may reasonably be done in parallel or where the drug is targeted primarily to the elderly and thus these parameters might be investigated in the elderly before, or instead of, a younger age group. The guideline clearly supports the option that pharmacokinetic information can be obtained either through formal studies or the so-called pharmacokinetic screen. The latter has been under discussion since the U.S. FDA discussion paper of 1983 [31]. Although pharmacokinetic screening has some merit, difficulties reside in identifying possible problems after completion of Phase III, plus the logistics of the larger number of assays involved. Generally, it will be more efficient to identify potential age-related differences in Phase II and incorporate dosage alterations, if necessary, into the Phase III program. The ICH guideline on drug evaluation in the elderly has reached Step 5 (Second ICH) and should be adopted into the national guidelines of Japan as well as of the United States and EU.

In general concept, no major differences in GCP guidelines exist between Japan, the United States, and EU; in 1995, at the Third ICH, comprehensive, harmonized GCP guidelines are expected to be released for discussion.

VI. OTHER ISSUES

In October 1993 the Koseisho issued a discussion document promoting the development of a Summary Basis of Approval (SBA) Document for new drugs and thus showed a willingness to improve transparency of the approval basis for new drugs by CPAC in Japan. From March 30, 1994, SBAs will be developed for innovative Japanese products and orphan drugs. It is likely that the practice will spread to cover all newly registered products, including those of foreign origin. Additionally, it brings Japan into harmony with such transparency activities in the EU and the United States.

The Koseisho has become much more receptive to the inclusion within the Japanese physician's package circular of safety information derived from foreign data. Overall there is now little difference in this Japanese document from that in the other countries, with the exception of format and the quoting of local clinical study results. Entry Guidelines for Precautions for Use of Ethical Drugs [32] were updated in 1994 [33] in response to serious hemopoietic adverse reactions that resulted from an interaction between the antiviral agent sorivudine and fluorouracil type agents. The object of the guidelines was to increase the awareness among health professionals of drug interactions and adverse reactions. To this end, the section on drug interactions must be placed directly before the adverse-reactions section. Additionally, where the interaction has caused a serious and irreversible event or resulted in a fatality, its importance must be stressed by additionally entering it in the warning, general precautions, or contraindications section, as appropriate. Such entries must also be clearly placed on the covers of ethical drug physician's circulars of all new drug approvals. A two-year period was given for updating other circulars. As a result, the amount of safety information, including the listed adverse drug reactions (ADRs), has considerably increased in Japanese circulars. During development of a new compound that Koseisho has become more interested in being kept appraised of the status of foreign programs with particular reference to safety.

Significant changes have occurred in adverse-reaction reporting in Japan as it moves to position itself with those who have the most developed surveillance. Investigational adverse drug reactions are reported to the NDD of the PAB, while those occurring with marketed drugs are processed by the Safety Division.

The GCP [34] requires an investigator-in-charge to ensure the speedy reporting of all serious drug reactions that occur during clinical investigation to the head of the medical institution, the supervisory investigator, and the sponsor. It is the sponsor's responsibility to ensure the immediate reporting of all serious ADRs and deaths suspected of being drug related to the NDD. This applies to such foreign events as well as domestic incidents. All other ADRs should be reported in the NDA. Equally, for marketed drugs, the time for reporting serious ADRs, including foreign events, that cannot be predicted from the package circular, is 15 days from awareness. Also reportable in 15 days are events where the severity or frequency is greater than the package circular indicates. In the event of a death thought to be due to an unexpected ADR, the company must immediately advise the Safety Division by fax and follow up within the 15-day time frame. A 30-day time period is permitted for other serious ADRs and for nonserious, unexpected events. It is important to note, however, that while the above are the current requirements, physicians are tending to change their practice and report all serious adverse events and deaths to the Koseisho. Whether or not an adverse event is related to a drug treatment is a judgment call, and the tendency to pass the responsibility for making such judgments to the Koseisho is increasing. This is especially so in pre-NDA clinical trials.

The guidelines on the Standard for Good Post-Marketing Surveillance Practice (GPMSP) was revised in June 1993 and took effect on April 1, 1994. It is likely that this will place Japanese postmarketing surveillance (PMS) among the best available by laying down procedures and requirements that should ensure the reliability of the data. It requires the product's manufacturer to set up a department independent of sales and marketing that can effectively function without hindrance from any quarter within the company. Staff must meet certain education and training requirements and are responsible for the collection of safety, efficacy, and quality data for all marketed drugs, from physicians and allied medical groups. They must assess and analyze the information, decide on any action, and ensure dissemination to health care practitioners, as necessary, by such means as changes to the package circular and "Dear Doctor" letters. The name of the manager of this department must be provided to the Koseisho as their communication link. All studies necessary to help in the evaluation of safety are designed by this group and, if conducted by others within the company, this group must maintain supervisory control and ensure that all PMS trials are carried out in compliance with GCP. The MHW will carry out inspections to confirm validity of data and ensure that the company is complying with GPMSP.

To compensate for the limited clinical data for evaluation of drug safety at the time of marketing approval, in 1979 the MHW instituted a system for the reexamination of safety at either 4 or 6 years after approval as part of the revisions to the Pharmaceutical Affairs Law [35]. The company must submit all efficacy and safety data gathered since approval in a prescribed manner [36]. Drugs with an active ingredient or a combination prescription medicine not already approved underwent reexamination after 6 years from approval; however, since April 1, 1994, this has been extended to 10 years for many new medicines. Reexamination is necessary after 4 years for a product having the same active ingredient and route of administration as an already approved drug but with an additional indication or in a different dosage. As noted, it is difficult to register a drug that is a copy of a product in the original's reexamination period; thus, the extension of the period to 10 years is of distinct commercial value.

As occurs in many other markets, Japan requires all pharmaceutical products to undergo a periodic reevaluation of efficacy and safety every 5 years. For products requiring reexamination, reevaluation begins after that process has been completed. A reevaluation subcommittee advises the company when reevaluation is required, and the company has 4 months to submit the data for assessment. It is unusual for a drug to be removed from the market as a result of periodic reevaluation. Ad hoc reevaluation is conducted when a potential problem arises requiring urgent resolution.

A review of the Japanese approach to drug development and regulatory approval demonstrates significant differences from that in the United States and EU. Given the sensitivity surrounding the subject of public safety and medicines and the cultural variance between nations, it should be no surprise that Japan, the EU, and the United States have developed different approaches to the achievement of the same goal. A desire for harmonization of drug development and regulatory requirements and thus for the facilitation of regulatory acceptance of foreign data is not a new topic between the United States and Japan. The cooperative study for health and welfare that began in 1974 involved the exchange of information on pharmaceutical affairs, GMP, and GLP. This was followed by the MOSS discussions about acceptance of foreign data and aspects of harmonization that have been taken up by the tripartite endeavor of the ICH. Harmonization is not a one-way street and requires giving as well as receiving; with regard to Japan the will is there, at least in the Koseisho, but the rate of progress will be influenced by the senior Japanese physicians who sit on the decision-making committees of the CPAC. Although laws and guidelines may read alike, harmonization will require all parties to interpret the words similarly. History teaches us that the achievement of the latter is likely to require much longer than the agreement about the written word.

REFERENCES

1. Pharmaceutical Industry in Japan 1992. Japan Pharmaceutical Manufacturers Association, July 1992.

2. Department of the Treasury: Report on Medical Equipment and Pharmaceuticals Market-Oriented, Sector-Selective (MOSS) Discussions, January 1986.
3. W. J. C. Currie and R. W. J. Currie. Registration of Drugs, Encyclopedia of Pharmaceutical Technology. Marcel Dekker, Inc., in press.
4. P. F. D'Arcy and D. W. G. Haron, Eds. Proceedings of the First International Conference on Harmonization. A Queen's University of Belfast Publication, 1992.
5. P. F. D'Arcy and D. W. G. Haron, Eds. Proceedings of the Second International Conference on Harmonization. A Queen's University of Belfast Publication, 1994.
6. Plenary Session: Background to the Conference. Second International Conference on Harmonization, 1993, p. 4.
7. Drug Registration in Japan, 5th ed. Yakuji Nippo LTD, Tokyo, Japan, 1993.
8. PAB Notification, No. 698. May 1980.
9. PMA Survey of NDA Processing in Japan, 1993. Pharmaceutical Research and Manufacturers of America, Internal Report.
10. PAB Notification, No. 698. May 1980.
11. PAB Notification, No. 970. October 1976.
12. PAB Notification, No. 774. October 1983.
13. PCD Notification, No. 43. February 1991.
14. PCD Notification, No. 30. April 1994.
15. G. Melien. Stability studies in the E.C., the U.S. and Japan. *Reg. Affairs J. 2*: 878–883, 1991.
16. PCD Notification, No. 43. February 1991.
17. Guidelines for Toxicity Study of Drugs Manual. Yakuji Nippo LTD, Tokyo, Japan, 1994.
18. NDD Notification, No. 4. January 1991.
19. PAB Notification, No. 6. January 1991.
20. C. E. Lumley et al. An international appraisal of the minimum duration of chronic animal toxicity studies. *Hum. Exp. Toxicol. 11*: 155–162, 1992.
21. R. Bass et al. Draft guidelines on detection of toxicity to reproduction for medicinal products. *Adverse Drug React. Toxicol. Rev. 3*: 127–141, 1991.
22. C. E. Lumley. Proposal for international guidelines for reproductive and developmental toxicity testing for pharmaceuticals. *Adverse Drug React. Toxicol. Rev. 2*: 143–153, 1991.
23. Report of working group on relevance of animal toxicology for predicting human adverse events, 1992. Pharmaceutical Manufacturers Association of Japan, Internal Report.
24. PAB Notification, No. 970. October 1976.
25. PAB Notification, No. 315. March 1982.
26. PAB Notification, No. 313. March 1982.
27. NDD Notification, No. 43. June 1992.
28. NDD Notification, No. 20. March 1992.
29. PAB Notification, No. 660. June 1985.
30. NDD Notification, No. 104. December 1993.
31. R. Temple. Food and Drug Administration's Guidelines for Clinical Testing of Drugs in the Elderly. *Drug Information Journal 19*: 483–486, 1985.

32. PAB Notification, No. 153. February 1976.
33. PAB Notification, No. 999. January 1994.
34. PAB Notification, No. 874. October 1989.
35. Pharmaceutical Affairs Law, Article 14-2. October 1979.
36. PAB Notification, No. 189. December 1983.

15

Increasing the Effectiveness of Clinical Pathology Testing and Its Value to Drug Development in Europe

Dai Davies and Karolyn Jackson

Zeneca Pharmaceuticals
Cheshire, England

I. THE ROLE OF CLINICAL PATHOLOGY IN THE DRUG DEVELOPMENT PROCESS

Clinical pathology encompasses the two major disciplines of hematology (with coagulation) and clinical chemistry; the latter often being subdivided into blood chemistry, urine chemistry, and hormone determination. Traditionally, these two disciplines have often been supported in separate laboratories with their own complement of staff and responding to separate line management. Integration of the disciplines is rare, often leading to a lack of overall appreciation of the total clinical pathology picture. A similar situation exists in the Health Service where separate departments receive and analyse samples and invariably report separately the patient's clinical chemistry or hematology results to their investigating physician. In clinical practice this approach is usually satisfactory since it is more common for a physician to be investigating or monitoring a single illness, e.g., anaemia, and rarely requires results for both hematology and clinical chemistry simultaneously.

The safety assessment of drugs, both preclinically and during the initial phases of clinical development, requires a totally different approach. In toxicology the studies are designed to screen for adverse changes in clinical pathology in healthy animals following the administration of a novel drug entity. Animals are rarely clinically ill and detection of subclinical target organ toxicity is required. Both clinical chemistry and hematology are routinely monitored and blood samples are often taken from the animals for both disciplines at the same time. Similarly, Phase I clinical trials are usually performed in healthy volunteers and, although they are not intended as "human toxicology studies," both clinical chemistry and hematology are monitored at frequent intervals. An integrated clinical pathology report, encompassing the results from both disciplines, is clearly the most appropriate approach for these safety assessment studies.

A. Clinical Pathology and Preclinical Studies

Invariably, the role of a clinical pathology laboratory in the pharmaceutical environment is seen as principally to support toxicology studies. With a few notable exceptions, most regulatory authorities simply state the need for appropriate clinical pathology testing in toxicology studies without specifying exact requirements. It is not our intention in this chapter to discuss the merits of various tests and procedures for use in preclinical safety assessment and the reader is directed to Evans [1] where animal clinical pathology testing is discussed at length. Suffice to say that, before most new drugs are marketed, extensive animal toxicology studies will have to be completed.

A standard general toxicology package will include one or more short-term studies of 7 to 28 day's duration in both a rodent and nonrodent species; a 3- or

6-month study in two species; a 12-month dog study, and 2-year oncogenicity studies in both rats and mice. All of these studies, with the exception of the oncogenicity studies, will include blood chemistry, hematology, and urine chemistry at study termination and, ideally, at intervals during the dosing period. For a typical 6-month rodent study, 80 animals (10 per sex per group) will be bled and urine collected during week 1 (optional), and at months 1, 3, and 6. For rodent studies, the volume of an interim blood sample rarely exceeds 1.2 mL for rats and, for mice, a terminal sample of <1 mL is not uncommon. With such small volumes it is essential that samples are assayed as soon as possible for blood chemistry in order to avoid concentration artifacts due to evaporation. The small volume of rat blood usually available for hematology evaluation and the instability of coagulation samples dictate the immediate analyses of these samples in order to produce valid results. Consequently, near-animal testing is essential and every facility performing toxicology studies should have immediate access to their own clinical pathology laboratory.

B. Clinical Pathology and Clinical Trials

The clinical development program of a new pharmaceutical agent traditionally includes three distinctive phases with an increasing number of individuals being progressively exposed to the drug with increasing dose levels and for an increasing duration. The preceding toxicology studies must be adequate to characterise any potential toxic effects and *in vitro* mutagenicity studies should have been completed prior to initial exposure of the drug to man and the conduct of any clinical trial.

Each clinical phase has clear purposes with Phase I trials, usually being performed in a small number of healthy volunteers, targeted at safety assessment and initial tolerance studies. Phase II trials, which include up to 500 patients, are a combination of efficacy and tolerance studies while the final Phase III programs aim to expose 3000–5000 patients by means of several large multicenter multinational trials. Ethical, medical, and regulatory considerations demand that clinical studies are supported by a recommended program of toxicity studies although the requirements do vary between countries and continents. The European Commission (EC), with up to 15 participating member states, is aiming to produce new legislation controlling certain aspects of clinical trials and pulling together a number of the new guidelines to supplement the GCP guidelines issued in 1991. Changes are necessary since each European Union (EU) country has rules on clinical trial authorisation but they are all different. Satisfying these divergent rules cause developers major problems and starting multicenter, multinational trials can take 6 to 9 months longer in Europe than in the United States.

In line with these proposals, the International Conference on Harmonization (ICH) has generated guidelines on the “Technical Requirements for the

Registration of Pharmaceuticals for Human Use" that have come into effect in Europe, the United States, and Japan. In principle the duration of the animal toxicology studies conducted in 2 species should equal or exceed the duration of treatment intended in the clinical trial. Phase I studies of up to 2 weeks require the support of a repeated-dose toxicity study in 2 species for a duration of at least 2 weeks. For subsequent phases and the marketing approval stage, two 1-month toxicity studies would support clinical trials of up to 2 weeks duration. Three-month toxicity studies would support clinical trials of up to 1-month duration and 6-month studies would support the extended clinical trial and fulfill marketing approval requirement if chronic toxicity or carcinogenicity studies are on-going. Completed oncogenicity studies are required only for marketing approval where prolonged use of the drug is anticipated or where there is reasonable cause for concern. In the case of drugs intended to treat life-threatening or severely debilitating disease the oncogenicity studies can be completed postapproval. The evaluation of clinical pathology parameters is an integral and essential part of every clinical trial. The monitoring of volunteers and patients is particularly intense during Phase I and Phase II trials with due note being taken of any clinical pathology changes observed in the toxicology studies. As confidence in the safety of the drug increases the frequency and scope of the clinical pathology testing will reduce such that, for Phase III/IIIb trials, there may be a need only to monitor a few key safety parameters (see Figure 1).

The conduct of clinical trials is a complex process requiring the integration of various key components to produce data suitable for regulatory submission. One of these key components is the clinical pathology safety or efficacy data that often represents between 40 and 60 % of the final submission document. The quality of the clinical pathology data must be of the highest standard, principally in order to provide a reliable and valued service to the patient and physician. However, clinical trial objectives require us to look beyond local quality standards to those standards that can be achieved on a much broader scale in order to provide consistency across multicenter clinical trials. There are a number of variables that can influence the production of laboratory data: methodology, instrumentation, reagents standardization, and assay temperature, to name a few. Standardizing the way in which the laboratory data is produced will have a significant impact on the overall quality of the clinical pathology contribution to clinical drug evaluation.

C. Integration of Preclinical and Clinical Support

The vast majority of Pharmaceutical Companies see the clinical pathology support of preclinical and clinical studies, with the possible exception of some Phase I trials, as being entirely separate. If toxicology studies are performed "in house" then it is impractical, for reasons of sample volume, to out-source

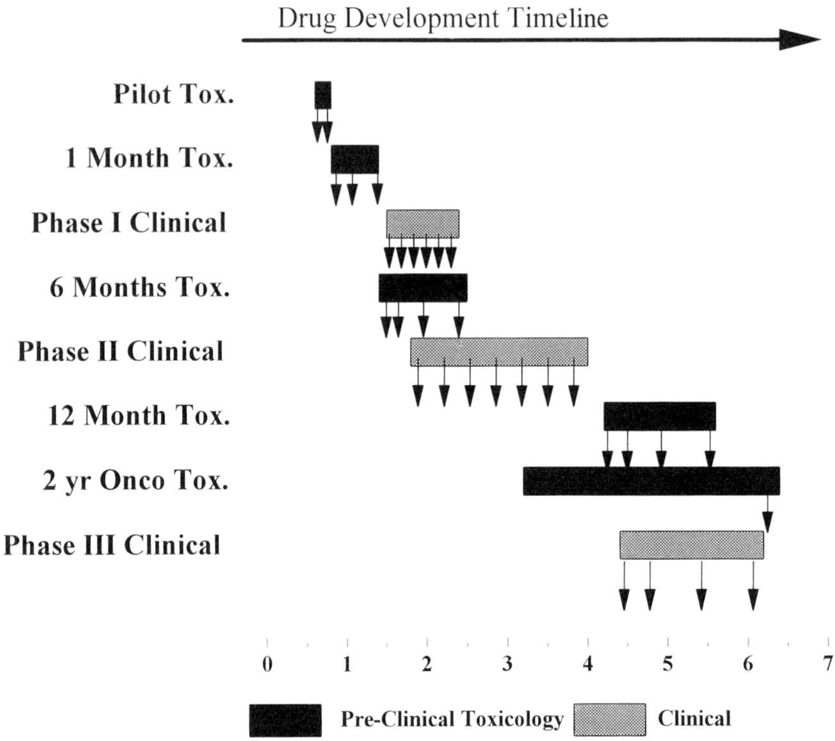

Fig. 1 Diagrammatic representation of the preclinical and clinical phases of drug development. Note the overlap in the development phases and the need for clinical pathology monitoring (indicated by arrows) throughout the process.

the clinical pathology. For clinical trials, on the other hand, traditionally all the clinical pathology is performed at local laboratories or contracted to regional or central laboratories. The advantages and disadvantages of the use of various types of laboratories for the support of clinical trials will be discussed in this chapter. We will also identify the need for establishing good relationships with external laboratories and describe the pitfalls that need to be avoided to successfully and efficiently complete the clinical pathology contribution to a clinical drug development program.

At Zeneca, the clinical pathology laboratory has supported Phase I clinical pharmacology trials for more than 2 decades. The test profiles can be extensive

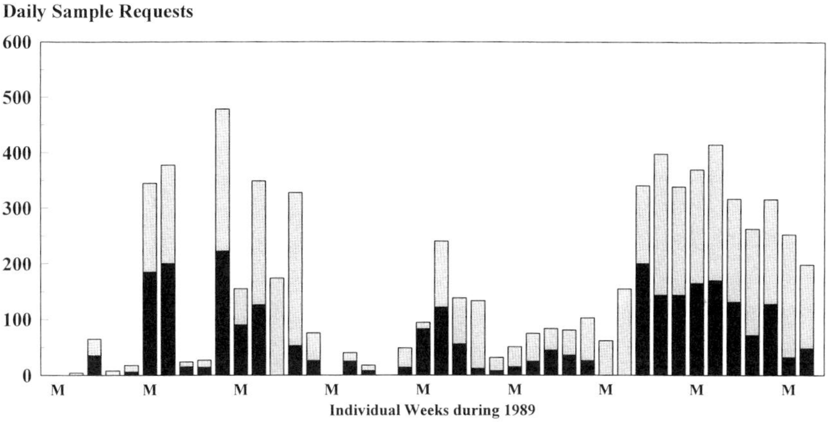

Fig. 2 Typical daily workload pattern for clinical chemistry (hatched bars) and hematology (solid bars) for a two month period in 1989.

and specifically tailored to the pharmacology of the drug but the core safety profile is similar to that for preclinical toxicology studies; however, the laboratory is required to report the results from these trials within 5 hours of sample receipt. As illustrated in Figure 2, during the period 1980–1990 the daily workload for the laboratory was quite variable. It was not uncommon for the laboratory to be faced with periods of inactivity punctuated by periods of frantic exertion when several studies came to fruition simultaneously. During these periods of inactivity, staff occupied themselves with method development and evaluations; however, unless the laboratory has an active clinical pathology research program, such activities may not be cost effective. Clearly, most laboratory managers will wish to even out the workload. By the very nature of the timed sampling procedures for toxicology studies, the limitation of the number of compounds in predevelopment and availability of animals rooms, it is unlikely that a laboratory can significantly improve its efficiency by simply relying on the efficient management and appropriate staggering of toxicology studies.

At Zeneca, the option of supplementing the toxicology workload with blood samples from the company's own clinical trials was considered. During the period 1980–1990 the majority of all Phase I trials were performed in-house using Zeneca volunteers; Phase II and III trials were performed in both Europe and North America. For the European trials, the clinical pathology was performed by local laboratories at the trial centers and the results were returned to headquarters for manual punching into the clinical database and subsequent statistical analysis. It was our belief that the efficiency and cost-effectiveness of the Zeneca laboratory would be improved by the laboratory supporting Zeneca's European clinical programs and that the company would also directly benefit by having consistent quality data, validated on an on-going basis and electronically transferred to the clinical database. There was also a clear target of saving 3 months on the historic norm for the reporting of clinical trials. This chapter describes how the laboratory coped with the demands of Phase II and Phase III clinical trials, provides some performance data, and discusses the cost benefits of integrating the clinical pathology support of toxicology and clinical trials in the one laboratory.

II. THE CHOICE OF CLINICAL PATHOLOGY LABORATORIES

Within Europe 4 types of laboratories exist that are regularly used to support clinical trials:

(a) A *local laboratory* is used by investigators for routine sample testing; it is usually located close to the investigator site and is often a hospital laboratory. For more specialized tests, these laboratories may send their samples to a larger specialized laboratory.

(b) A *regional or national laboratory* is used by all investigators in a multicenter trial conducted in a certain region or country. These are, invariably, contract laboratories that organize an efficient national sample transport system and result-reporting procedure.

(c) A *network of laboratories* consisting of several regional laboratories may be used in multinational trials. There would usually be one laboratory per country that would perform the majority of requested routine tests. These laboratories may choose to perform the more specialized or esoteric tests at a single central laboratory. In order to gain maximum benefit from such a network of laboratories it is essential that each laboratory operates to the same standard and procedures and makes every effort to coordinate their quality control procedures, instrumentation, methodologies, reagents, reporting procedures, and database formats.

(d) A *central laboratory* is used by all investigators in a trial covering a very large region, a whole continent, or the whole world. These laboratories are faced with the challenge of providing single correlated testing methodologies and standardized technical databases but, unlike the networked laboratories, these have to be managed on a global basis. Large Contract Research Organizations (CROs)—such as SciCor and SmithKline Beecham Clinical Laboratories—have established, in the past few years, laboratories in North America and Europe, and there appears to be an intention to provide similar facilities in South Africa, Australia, and Japan. These laboratories can offer real-time, online access to national, pannational and global trial data providing a worldwide combinable trial database, national and remote safety reporting, and worldwide protocol management. When using such laboratories the sponsor should ensure that the same instrumentation and reagents are being used throughout the study and that the same methods, and even the reagent lots, are used at all the CRO's facilities.

In a survey conducted by Odel et al. [2], based on 27 clinical research decision makers, there was a difference in the usage of the three main types of laboratory (local, regional, or central) depending whether the relationship was with a pharmaceutical sponsor or a CRO. The pharmaceutical sponsor favored the use of local laboratories at the expense of using a central laboratory while the reverse was the case for CROs.

	Percent Laboratory Utilization		
	Local Labs	Regional Labs	Central Lab
By Pharmaceutical Sponsor	40%	32%	28%
By CRO	26%	28%	46%

From both the investigator's and sponsor's point of view, the patient's welfare and management needs are paramount. It may, therefore, be preferable to use a local laboratory when the study involves treatment of some acute disorders in which rapid turnaround time for tests may be necessary for directing patient care (e.g., for chemotherapy patients where the dose depends on the hematology results). Another situation where the use of local laboratories for routine analysis is preferable is in the treatment of critical care patients (e.g., clinical trials with antibiotics or anesthetics). Similarly, if a patient becomes acutely ill on a trial then a local laboratory should be used ideally with back-up samples being sent to the central laboratory to maintain the database without compromising patient care. Routine analyses should be done at the local laboratory but more specialized tests should be performed by the laboratory contracted to support the trial. It must be stated in the protocol how this data is to be handled and whether it will be included in the clinical trial database.

Within Europe, custom and practice may also influence the decision as to the type of laboratory to be used. In France, for example, there are more than 3000 private laboratories, and many general practitioners involved with Phase IV studies provide patients with a test request and entrust them to visit the local laboratory of their choice. The laboratory sends the results back to the investigator, who also receives a percentage of the fee charged for the analysis. Furthermore, many French GPs have no facilities for taking blood samples and these investigators often make it a precondition that the central laboratory must provide its own team of nurses who are properly equipped to perform the extra functions required.

Other considerations in selecting the type of clinical laboratory appropriate for a particular trial include (a) The geographical scope and the scale of the study: the more centers that are involved, the more will the selection of a central laboratory be favored; (b) The phase of the clinical development: generally it is considered that local laboratories are more suitable for the short turnaround time required for Phase I trials or some specialised Phase IV studies. For Phase II and III trials however, there is probably a strong preference for the use of central laboratories; (c) Previous experience with a laboratory; (d) Short-term costs and long-term cost effectiveness; and (e) The quality of the laboratory service.

III. QUALITY, ACCREDITATION, AND DATA ARCHIVING

In the mid-seventies the Food and Drug Administration (FDA) issued regulations defining Good Laboratory Practice (GLP) in order to ensure the quality, standard, and integrity of drug development studies in animals. Although few regulatory authorities outside the United States actually require compliance with GLP for samples assayed from clinical trials, the pharmaceutical industry in general expects compliance with the principles of GLP when carrying out trials in hospital or contract laboratories. There is no compulsion on local laboratories, whose prime concern is to diagnose ill health, to comply with GLP, and all too often difficulties are encountered by the sponsor in obtaining appropriate documentation and certification from such laboratories.

For contract laboratories it is expected that they will comply with the requirements of GLP and, in the United States, also participate in programs conducted by the College of American Pathologists (CAP) certification or Clinical Laboratory Improvement Amendments of 1988 (CLIA) certification. In Europe, the EU produced a document governing the conduct of clinical trials and requested that these be conducted in accordance with Good Clinical Practice (GCP). Within this regulation it is inferred that all laboratory activities in support of clinical trials should be performed according to the principles of GLP. It is also desirable, for both investigator and sponsor, that clinical trial samples are assayed in an accredited laboratory. In Europe, a laboratory may be accredited by complying with the standards of ISO 9000, EN 45000, or standards set up by organisations within a specific country. In the United Kingdom laboratories can be accredited by the Clinical Pathology Accreditation (CPA) whose inspectors ensure that the laboratory is in compliance with CPA standards.

When work is performed at a contract laboratory it is important that the sponsor's quality assurance staff perform regular audits to verify consistency and compliance. They should ensure that standard operating procedures (SOPs) are in place and that equipment, staff training records, service records, and maintenance contracts are adequate to ensure the integrity of the trial. They should also ensure that all samples are identified throughout the process, that all documents are dated and signed, and that all raw data is archived. For the analytical procedures, the QA personnel should ensure frequent calibration of all methods, daily testing of precision and accuracy prior to sample analysis, and a demonstration of quality control checks throughout the day to detect any drift in methodology. Validated methods and procedures should be used at all times and particular attention should be paid to investigators or laboratories that are running specialised or novel tests to ensure that the method is fully documented, validated, and acceptable to regulatory authorities.

It is also appropriate that the sponsor receive quarterly quality-control reports on key laboratory parameters throughout the course of the trial. These reports allow the sponsor to monitor that the laboratory remains "in control" and that the patient data will remain consistent from one month to the next. This consistency is especially important if the analysis being performed is used as a measure of drug efficacy. In such cases, examining trend analysis reports may be appropriate to guard against any drift or bias in the results. Similarly, laboratories should be actively discouraged from using cheaper generic reagents for "in house" assays since this is not in the best interest of the sponsor. Proprietary reagents should always be used so that any variation in a patient's laboratory results are due to a treatment effect and not to an artifact associated with a methodological imbalance over time.

Diligent monitoring of key laboratory results can also avoid surprises, such as a laboratory changing its methodology without the consent of the sponsor. Changes to testing methods mid-trial can leave the sponsor guessing which tests were run with which methodology and whether the data can be combined. The laboratory should always inform both the sponsor and the investigator of any intended change in methodology or reference range and, prior to any such decision, the laboratory should have validated the new method and have clearly demonstrated that there was no significant bias in the results derived from the old and new method. In an extreme illustration, Hill [3] described how a central laboratory involved in monitoring an antiretroviral drug trial changed its methodology for evaluating viruses between visit 1 and the end of the trial. The new method only detected 20% of the viruses present compared to a 100% detection with the original method.

Probably the most difficult task related to Good Clinical Practice is protecting source documentation against destruction. As mentioned above, the European Union directive (91/507/EEC) not only indicates that clinical trials must be conducted in compliance with GCP but also that patient files and other source data should be kept for the maximum period of time permitted by the hospital, institution, or private practice where the records are stored. The European GCP guideline specifies that pharmaceutical companies, investigators, and clinical centers involved in trials must keep patient files and other source data for at least 15 years and longer if possible. The sponsor also has responsibility for retaining other documentation pertaining to the trial but clearly the area of greatest potential for noncompliance resides with the local clinical pathology laboratories.

IV. PROGRESSIVE RESTRUCTURING OF CLINICAL PATHOLOGY AT ZENECA TO SUPPORT CLINICAL TRIALS

In 1989, Zeneca's clinical pathology laboratory had a complement of 21 staff, 19 of whom were analysts working in either the blood chemistry, urinalysis, or hematology units. In that year 35,000 analytical samples were analyzed with 80% being generated from animal toxicology studies with the remaining from Phase I clinical trials. As illustrated in Figure 2, the daily workload at this time was quite variable and efficiency was compromised during periods when there were few or no samples for analysis.

In order to provide a steady flow of work and to improve clinical standards it was decided that the laboratory would start to support U.K. Phase II trials, and later to expand to Phase II and III support throughout Europe. The initial trials went well, with the laboratory following a steep learning curve, and by the end of 1991 the laboratory had supported 12 single-center and 5 multicenter trials in 5 European countries. As displayed in Table 1 and Figure 3, clinical trial support rapidly increased such that, by 1995, of the 71,000 samples analysed 53% were human samples submitted by 967 clinical trial centers located in

Table 1 Growth in Clinical Pathology Workload in Support of Clinical Trials (1990–1995)

	1990	1991	1992	1993	1994	1995
Clinical workload as a percentage of laboratory total	20.8%	39.5%	50.2%	70.3%	73.6%	52.8%
Laboratory total workload (samples/yr)	39,250	46,113	58,405	75,961	84,599	71,170
Total number of centers supported during the year	9	47	325	450	753	967
Total number of countries	1	5	15	17	18	20

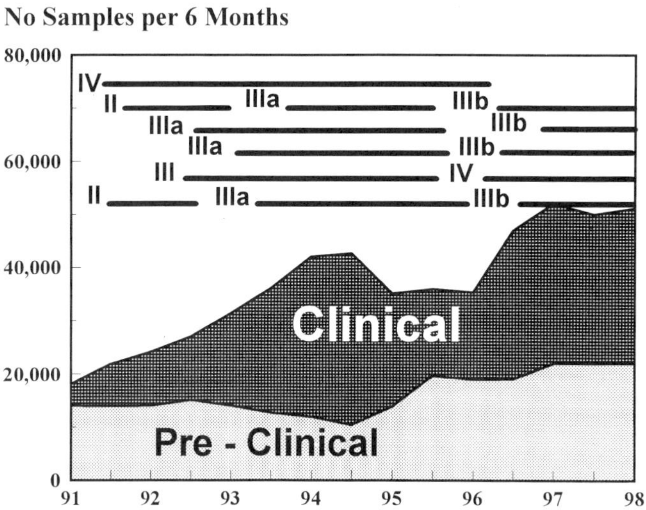

Fig. 3 The graph shows the increases in the annual workload for the laboratory, apportioned to the preclinical and clinical support. The bars indicate the duration of various clinical trials with the roman numerals indicating the phase of development. Late-stage development compounds, supported by the laboratory, are each represented by one of the horizontal tracks.

20 European countries. For the 120 single-center clinical trials completed during 1992–95, 64 were supported by the laboratory. A further 32 pan-European multicenter trials were also supported during the same period.

During 1994/95 samples were received from 6,770 patients from 809 separate centers. Because of the way centers and patients are recruited into a clinical trial and the way investigators organise their patient visits, the clinical pathology laboratory has only the broadest idea of how many samples can be expected on a given day. As illustrated in Figure 4, which shows the daily workload between July 1994 and June 1995, the participation of a large number of investigators produces a reasonably even workload of about 150 ± 30 samples each day. The laboratory still has to cope with the cyclical nature of toxicology samples but, at least, the laboratory has samples to analyse every day.

A. Laboratory Changes Required to Accommodate the Additional Workload

One major proviso for undertaking the support of clinical trials was that no significant increase in manpower would be allowed. For sample analysis, this

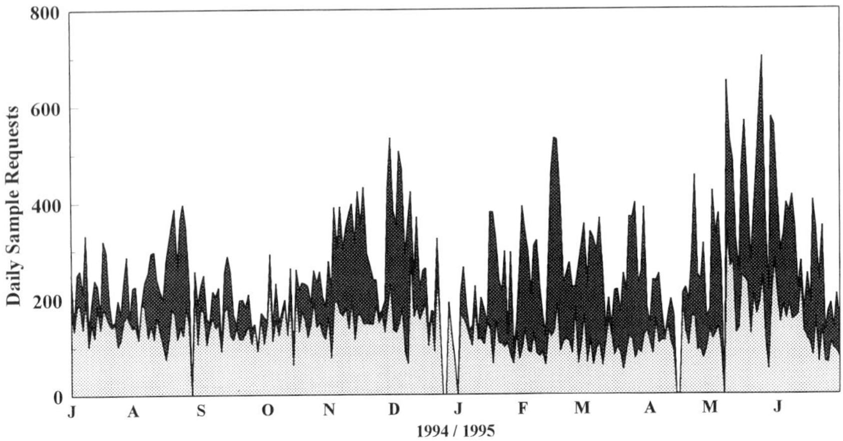

Fig. 4 Daily workload for the period July 1994 to June 1995 is displayed. The clinical workload is represented by the light stippled area while the darker area represents the pre-clinical toxicology workload for the laboratory.

was achieved by integrating the three disciplines under one management and adopting a policy of training all the staff to work in all areas under the guidance of specialized leaders. This approach provided maximum flexibility for resourcing the laboratory and each member of staff works 3 months before rotating into another discipline or to another activity within the same discipline. The majority of staff enjoyed the variety that the rotation offered and, in any one year, an individual may be a trainee in one area and acting as a trainer in another.

In order to fully meet the needs of our clinical program it was necessary for us to develop an expertise in endocrinology and the assay of surrogate markers. A nonisotopic, automated immunoassay analyzer was the only capital purchase made to support clinical trials. As instruments were replaced, however, analyzers of higher capacity and faster throughput were purchased at minimal extra cost. The purchase of "state-of-the-art" high-specification equipment also benefitted toxicology since analytical turnaround times were reduced by 75% and new assays, developed for clinical trials, could be modified for use with animals.

It soon became clear, in order to effectively support clinical trials, that the laboratory had to provide much more than just an analytical service. The administration of blood sample packs and transport, patient result management and the administration of patient demography details were all key activities that had to be supported. The first was achieved by developing an effective partnership with a contract packer, who provided and distributed trial specific phlebotomy packs while, for sample transport, a world renowned courier company was contracted to achieve the effective pan-European transportation of samples to the laboratory.

Improving patient data management was achieved by the installation of a new computerised Laboratory Information System whose extensive and easily accessible electronic database allowed efficient demographic management. Extensive use of barcodes on documents and samples aided sample tracking while the automated report printing and electronic faxing of results supported the same day reporting of results. Customized reports provide monthly updates on the number of patients screened and enrolled into a study and history prints provide details of recorded patient demography information. All clinical trial data is automatically transmitted over night to the Medical Function and recent enhancements have allowed trial data to be electronically transferred to CROs involved in Trial Center Management or Trial Data Statistical Analysis.

Laboratory personnel actively participate in pretrial protocol review meetings; training sessions for the CRAs involved in center monitoring and pretrial investigator meetings where the investigator can directly resolve any clinical pathology issue. Although the laboratory is fully GLP certified, in order to further reassure our investigators, clinical pathology accreditation was sought and awarded, without reservation, in 1992.

The support of these administrative activities has necessitated an expansion in staff numbers and a realignment of administrative activities with two staff

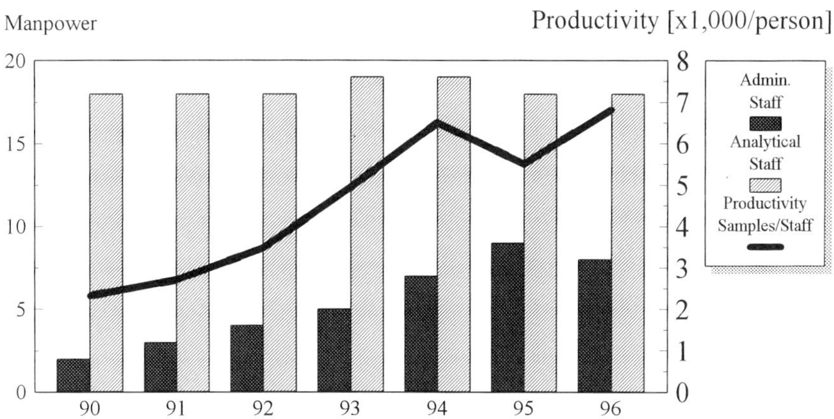

Fig. 5 The number of laboratory staff employed for either administration (dark bars) or sample analyses (gray bars) are shown for the period 1990 to 1996. The increase in productivity (i.e., number of samples analyzed per individual) is also displayed.

a.

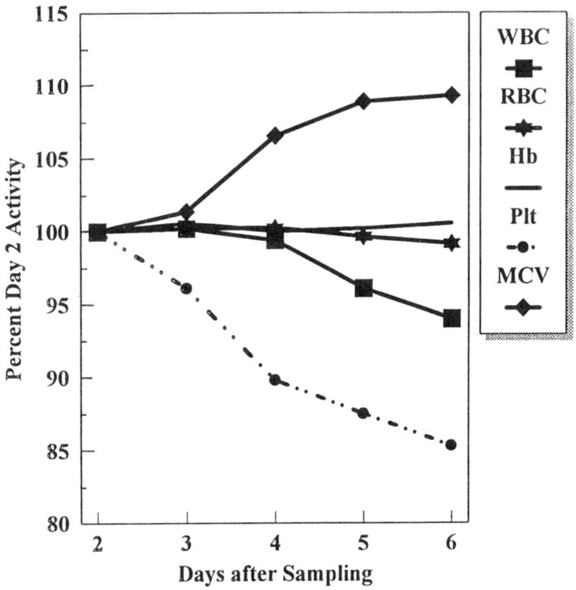

Fig. 6 Forty-seven human samples were analysed on day 2 (i.e., the day after being taken) and re-analysed daily for a further 4 days. (a, above) The percentage change from the day-2 values for 5 key hematology parameters. (b, opposite) The mean absolute white blood cell count and the counts for neutrophils (Neuts), lymphocytes (Lymphs), monocytes (Monos), eosinophils (Eos), and basophils (Baso) are displayed for the 5 days the samples were analysed. The number of valid results on each day are given in the inset box.

being responsible for all IT activities and a further two providing appropriate Quality Control and Quality Assurance support. Although the laboratory's manpower has been increased by 35%, the number of samples received by the laboratory has doubled over the same period and the laboratory's analytical productivity has increased from 2.32 (in 1990) to 6.5 × 1,000 samples analyzed/person in 1994 (see Figure 5).

B. Sample Stability for Clinical Chemistry and Hematology Analyses

With the exception of our Phase I samples, all other clinical trial samples are transported overnight to the laboratory. The vast majority of our samples are transported at ambient temperature and transport with dry ice is only considered necessary where poor sample or test stability dictates, e.g., evaluation of coagulation times. Provided the plasma or serum samples are separated from

b.

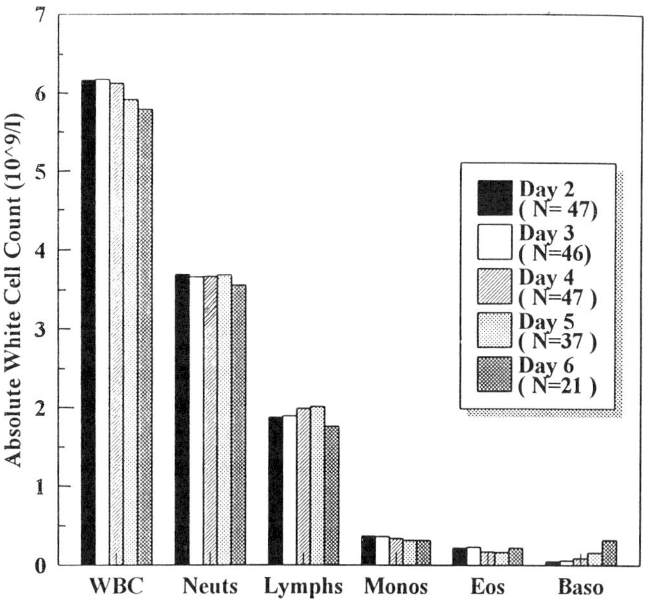

the blood cell at the trial center, all routine clinical chemistry tests are stable for at least 5 days and the serum shows no clinically significant reduction in enzyme activities or analyte concentration up to this time.

Traditionally there has always been concern about the stability of hematology samples and the reliability of assessing samples following their transport to a central laboratory. The assessment of white cell differentials is the least reliable in older samples and many trial protocols require the investigator to prepare blood films that are sent with the blood sample to the laboratory for manual assessment using a microscope. At Zeneca, the purchase of the Technicon H*1, and later the H*3, have dispensed with the need to prepare blood films. The Technicon H* series of analyzers use flow cytometry in combination with a biochemical marker to identify white blood cells. As part of the laboratory's evaluation and commissioning of the H*3, 47 trial samples that had been collected the previous day from clinical trial patients were evaluated and a full blood count and differential count determined. These samples were left on a labora- tory bench under a polystyrene igloo and were reanalyzed daily over a further 4 days. The hematology results of greatest clinical interest are presented in Figures 6a and 6b. With the Technicon H*3 the hemoglobin, red cell and white cell counts change by less than 5% over 4 days. A 10% increase in the MCV was observed while the platelet count fell by 15%. A white cell differential count was reported for every sample up to day 4 but the instrument failed to give a valid result for 10 five-day-old samples and 26 samples 6 days old. When the H*3 provided a valid result, the values for WBC and the white cell differential—for all but basophils—were similar to the day-2 results, even when the samples were 5 or 6 days old.

V. CLINICAL PATHOLOGY SUPPORT OF PHASE I: SAFETY AND TOLERANCE TRIALS

Phase I trials tend to be of a limited nature and usually each trial is performed at a single center. A few pharmaceutical companies run their own Phase I trials "in house" while the majority contract these to CROs that specialize in these types of trials. At this stage the volunteers are intensively monitored and it is essential that the investigator receives the laboratory results as soon as possible after dosing and certainly before the volunteer is administered a further dose of the new drug.

Consistency of tests results between laboratories is less critical for these trials and only becomes an issue if a trial is performed at multiple centers, each using their own local laboratory. The critical issue is the turnaround time between the sample being taken and the investigator receiving the laboratory results for review.

Phase I clinical trials often deal with novel therapeutic agents and novel therapeutic targets, therefore non-routine laboratory support is often required. Surrogate marker data, as an indicator of drug efficacy, is becoming more widely accepted by regulatory authorities. Some of these surrogate markers are commercially available (e.g., prostate specific antigen [PSA] for monitoring prostate cancer patients) while others, such as urinary 3-methyl-histidine for monitoring muscle breakdown, require a more specialized approach. For a novel surrogate marker, the credibility of the laboratory to perform the analysis is very important and the sponsor should seek reassurance, possibly by means of published papers, that the individual assigned to the assay is competent. Local laboratories, while comfortable in providing routine safety testing data, may not be the right choice to analyze these markers.

At Zeneca, the majority of Phase I trials are performed in the Clinical Pharmacology Unit on site using a volunteer population of Zeneca employees. Sample transport to the laboratory is not a problem and all analyses are reported on the day samples are received. Recently more Phase I trials are being contracted to specialized CRO Clinical Units, sometimes at more than one location. All these samples are also analysed by the Zeneca laboratory but special transport arrangements are necessary to ensure that the samples are received and analyzed on the day of sampling, preferably by early afternoon. The laboratory then endeavors to ensure that the results are transmitted overnight to the investigator for his consideration the next morning.

VI. CLINICAL PATHOLOGY SUPPORT OF PHASE II AND PHASE III TRIALS

A. Views of Investigators on the Use of Local Versus Central Laboratories

Irrespective of the nature of the trial most investigators would prefer to use the center's local laboratory. The investigator would, therefore, have no concerns about sample preparation, transport delays, test values, units and ranges, or the turnaround time for the results. He might, however, have concerns about the local unavailability of "special tests" stipulated in the trial protocol, of having to conduct an audit of the local laboratory, or of having to ensure local archiving of laboratory data for a minimum of 15 years. These concerns do not exist when using a central laboratory but they may be replaced by doubts about the validity of the test results. Although investigators like the consistency of the data from a central laboratory there is usually an initial concern because of the difference in the results received from the central laboratory compared to those received from his/her local laboratory. In most cases this is due to methodology differences between the two laboratories but differences in the test results units (e.g., uKat/L or IU/L for serum enzyme activity) and the laboratory reference range may add to the investigator's doubt. Sample degradation during transport is often a concern of an investigator but in reality degradation is so small that it rarely presents a clinical problem (see Table 2).

B. Views of Sponsors on the Use of Multiple Local Laboratories

Provided that critical care of the patient is not an issue, the disadvantages for the sponsor of using several local laboratories for a multicenter trial far outweigh the advantages. The disadvantages of using multiple local laboratories can be categorized as being related to either methodology or logistics. Two examples illustrating the type of methodological problems that can arise have been presented by Bloom [4]. In a particular clinical trial the protocol required serologic testing to identify acute infection with certain micro-organisms known to be insensitive to the antibiotics being tested. Unfortunately it was not established before the start of the trial which method should be used by the laboratories to evaluate antibody production. Therefore, some laboratories used total immunoglobin, IgG or IgM, some used nephelometry, while others

Table 2 Advantages and Disadvantages of Using Local and Central Laboratories

Local Laboratory	Central Laboratory
Perceived advantages to the investigator: Fully conversant with laboratory operation, fully conversant with reporting style No sample transportation delay No sample preparation Fast reporting time	**Perceived advantages to the investigator:** "Special test" data available quickly Local laboratory audit not required Local archiving not required Laboratory operating to principles of GLP
Perceived advantages to the sponsor: The investigator has confidence in his laboratory No transportation cost Fast local reporting time for safety data	**Perceived advantages to the sponsor:** No "special test" data constraints Consistent methodology across multiple sites Consistent reporting Laboratory operating to principles of GLP Complete audit trail Single analytical charge Data validation at source Electronic data may be available Improved data integration and statistical analysis Single laboratory site audit Complete study overview Close monitoring of adverse events
Perceived disadvantages to the investigator: "Special test" data availability constraints Local laboratory audit may be required Local archiving will be required for minimum of 15 years	**Perceived disadvantages to the investigator:** Not confident with the system Not conversant with laboratory operation Unfamiliar with reporting style Unfamiliar with reporting units Sample preparation required before transportation Sample transportation procedures to be followed Delay in data reporting
Perceived disadvantages to the sponsor: "Special test" data availability constraints Inconsistent methodology across multiple sites Inconsistent reporting style Integration of data very time consuming	**Perceived disadvantages to the sponsor:** Investigator uncomfortable with the system Investigator training required Sample transportation cost Clinical Research Associate training required

Table 2 Continued

Local Laboratory	Central Laboratory
Laboratory may not be operating to principles of GLP	Courier reliability must be established and maintained
Laboratory data audit trail may be incomplete	Higher direct cost of analysis
Poor notification of methodology changes	Higher up-front costs
Data validation required at sponsor site	
Manual data input at sponsor site	
Multiple laboratory site audits may be required	

used electrophoresis or radial immunodiffusion. The data was, therefore, of little value because it could not be pooled. Another common problem in Europe is that the local laboratories run their serum enzyme assays (i.e., liver transaminases and alkaline phosphatase) at different temperatures and with different reagents. These differences in testing conditions can greatly influence how much enzyme activity is measured and thus pooling the data would be impossible, short of normalizing the values (see Table 3).

Local laboratories, whose primary concern is rarely the support of clinical trials, have been known to change reporting units and reference ranges mid-trial, thus making it difficult to pool data, even at a single center. The inherent variability in test values, associated with the use of multiple laboratories, can

Table 3 Differences in Laboratory Reference Ranges for Alkaline Phosphatase for a Single Age Range

Laboratory	Country	Laboratory values
SciCor	U.S.A.	31–110 IU/L
Ulleval	Norway	60–275 IU/L
ABL	Holland	35–140 IU/L
Cortes	Spain	150–500 IU/L
Holste	Germany	0–190 IU/L
Zilver	Holland	30–95 IU/L

also potentially mask adverse clinical pathology changes related to the administration of the new drug entity.

Logistical difficulties for the sponsor relate to the need to audit several laboratories to ensure compliance with GCP, including the local archiving of raw data. Electronic transfer of laboratory results from local laboratories to the sponsor is uncommon, resulting in labor intensive manual data entry, data checking, and validation; all of which add time and additional resource to the completion of the clinical trial and the reporting process.

C. Views of Sponsors on the Use of Central Laboratories

Current trends in pharmaceutical clinical trial management have forced many companies to use central laboratories because multicenter Phase II and III trials are becoming increasingly global in scope and larger in scale. These trials often entail novel therapeutic agents for which special or experimental assays are needed to demonstrate safety and efficacy. While there may be some reluctance on the part of investigators to move away from the use of local laboratories, the benefits of using a central laboratory to the sponsor and thus to the overall cost effectiveness of the trial are persuasive.

There is little doubt that the data consistency obtained by analysing 100,000 samples at one central laboratory is significantly superior to that for 1,000 samples analysed at 100 laboratories. It is also believed that regulatory approval is much easier if a higher proportion of results are obtained from the same laboratory. In order to achieve this advantage the central laboratory must guarantee standardization of its methodology and analytical procedures and compliance with the European Union's GCP guidelines and the principles of GLP. For logistical reasons there may be more than one central laboratory located in different countries but the standards and principles they work to have to be identical. Several large clinical Research Organizations are structured in this manner and they guarantee global consistency with single methodology, instrument type, reporting format, etc. for all their central laboratories, throughout the course of a trial. Combining or merging of laboratory data from multiple central laboratories and across multiple trials, in order to establish a longitudinal safety and efficacy database, becomes feasible and highly desirable.

The quantity of clinical pathology data produced during a multicenter multinational trial is significant and the speed and efficiency with which it can be assembled, interpreted, and reported are becoming more critical as the pressures increase on pharmaceutical companies to contain development costs and progress drugs rapidly to the market. Rapid access to data is no longer a luxury but an absolute necessity allowing the interim assessment of safety and efficacy. Therefore, the efficient electronic transfer of laboratory data to the sponsor is essential to reduce cost and time by eliminating hours spent transcribing and reviewing transcribed data. Validating at source, patient demography, test selection and visit structure will reduce the time spent on checking at later stages of report compilation, thus reducing the time needed to prepare data for statistical analysis. As indicated by Odel [2] 30–50% of all data resolution queries (DRQs) concern laboratory data. Since some DRQs may take up to 80 days to resolve, remote data entry and electronic data transfer can have a significant impact on reporting time.

D. Establishing Central Laboratories in Europe

Central clinical pathology laboratory testing was once dismissed as unworkable in Europe. Strict border controls, combined with enormous cost and grave logistical difficulties of transporting specimens across a continent, were regarded as insurmountable problems. A concept that was embraced by U.S. trial organizers in the mid-1980s was considered inappropriate for a continent as linguistically, politically, and culturally diverse as Europe. It is only in the past 3 to 4 years that we have seen companies like SciCor, SmithKline Beecham, and Medinet establishing central laboratories in Europe. Although cultural differences and language difficulties are not easy to overcome, the essential abolition of strict customs control within the European Union in January 1994 has significantly relieved transport difficulties.

While open borders have helped, both sponsor and central laboratories need to devote a significant amount of effort to ensure the efficient collection and delivery of samples to the laboratory. Although the courier system in Europe is not as well developed as in the United States most difficulties arise because of language differences and the lack of understanding of each other's business. Some general physicians, who are already overworked and stretched to the limit, find it difficult to cope with the additional administrative burden of arranging collection, filling out forms, and handing specimens over to the courier. Some courier staff, on the other hand, fail to appreciate the urgency with which blood samples should be collected and delivered. For the successful utilization of central laboratories in Europe the sponsor must address these issues by easing the administrative burden on the investigator and communicating effectively with the courier. The practical difficulties can be classified as taking samples, sample packing/documentation, and sample transportation/delivery. In order to avoid jeopardizing the delivery of clean samples for analysis and rendering any testing service null and void, the following must be agreed with the investigator before the start of the trial and the procedures established.

1. *Taking Samples:*

(a) Clinical trial center may not have a centrifuge to separate serum/plasma, so one must be provided.

(b) Training must be given in the sample-preparation procedures.
(c) The central laboratory must provide all syringes, tubes, and needles to take blood samples in a trial specific phlebotomy kit.
(d) Accurate recording of patient and visit identity on both tubes labels and accompanying sample documents is essential.

2. *Sample Packaging:*

(a) Training of on-site personnel in using the kit and packaging must be given.
(b) It must be ensured that kits and packing supplies arrive on time at each center and are resupplied throughout the trial.
(c) It must be ensured that the investigator uses the supplied kits and does not revert to hospital supplies.
(d) It must be ensured that all appropriate documentation is provided (e.g., air way bills, customs declaration, any biohazard documentation, and International Air Transport Association regulations are completed and signed by the correct authority).
(e) Any dry-ice packaging must be more than adequate for the expected transit time.
(f) Where possible, preprinted documentation must be provided and simplified courier contact arrangements made in order to minimize investigator inconvenience.

3. *Sample Transport:*

(a) Transport time from different locations must be agreed upon with the courier and guarantees of alternative routing in the event of problems must be established and agreed upon.
(b) Latest collection times for each center must be agreed upon and it must be ensured that the investigator is aware of the time.
(c) Time delays are common in airport security and for samples being stored in dry ice, there is the additional requirement of topping them up. Delays in airport security are usually due to incomplete documentation. All questions must be answered in full and no abbreviations should be used in the responses.
(d) Investigators must be provided with clear instructions on how the samples should be stored in the event of the courier not collecting or the collection time being missed.
(e) Tracking of samples in transit must be implemented to avoid any sample loss.
(f) An effective working relationship with one or more couriers must be established with an understanding that additional costs may be incurred in an emergency to guarantee sample delivery.

VII. PERFORMANCE MEASURES FOR ZENECA'S CLINICAL PATHOLOGY LABORATORY

One of the key advantages of centralized testing is to eliminate the discrepancies that can arise when assays are performed in different laboratories. At Zeneca every aspect of clinical pathology testing is standardized such that

(1) The same sample collection tubes are used by every center for all clinical trials.
(2) Every new instrument is checked for correlation against the old instrument. If a significant difference exists between the instruments, the old instrument will be retained to support the existing trials but samples from any new trials will be analyzed on the new instrument.
(3) Change of methodology and reporting units are only acceptable in extreme situations, or when a new instrument is commissioned, and with the consent of the senior trial physician and biometrician.
(4) "Normal" patient clinical pathology values are viewed annually but changes to the laboratory reference ranges are only considered on a 5-year cycle in consultation with senior clinical personnel.
(5) The laboratory boasts of a stable workforce of highly qualified staff most of whom have worked in the laboratory for over 15 years and all have a minimum of 5 years experience.
(6) Strict internal, quality control surveillance is maintained under the direction of a dedicated quality control officer. Multiple control samples from external quality control schemes, which also provide peer-group comparisons, ensure that accuracy and precision are maintained throughout long-term clinical trial programs. During 1995 the laboratory was ranked in the top 2% of 986 laboratories participating in a U.K. QC scheme for clinical chemistry.

These quality assurance procedures ensure the consistency of the laboratory data thus allowing longitudinal comparison between different clinical phases of the same drug or transverse comparisons for similar phases of different drugs. It is believed that the quality, data consistency, and sound data management offers a significant benefit to Zeneca's drug development process.

Other key performance measures, directed more towards satisfying the needs of our investigators, are (a) sample transport time, (b) promptness of reporting, (c) completeness of the reporting, and (d) competitive charges.

A. Sample Transport Time

There are few courier companies that can offer a truly pan-European service. The majority of couriers are nationally based with reciprocal agreements for transport between countries. Where a courier covers many countries they may have pricing structures dictated by the country where the pack originates thus making accounting a nightmare and price negotiation virtually impossible.

Over the years the laboratory has worked hard towards establishing a good working relationship with one commercial courier company. This company, in turn, has allocated a U.K. based accounts manager specifically to meeting the needs of the laboratory and both parties see the relationship as a working partnership. All transport arrangements and queries are handled through the accounts manager who resolves issues with the regional manager in each European country. The laboratory holds a list of names of key courier staff in each country and in each major European region a member of the local Zeneca staff is nominated to coordinate and resolve local transport arrangements (e.g., collection addresses, courier contact telephone numbers, latest pick-up times, etc.).

For the period July 1994 through June 1995 over 8,000 individual samples were transported to the laboratory from 17 European countries; a further 1,953 were delivered from U.K. centers by the mail service. Since the pattern of sample collection reflects the working practices of the investigators, it may be of passing interest that, throughout Europe, investigators see significantly less clinical trial patients on Friday compared to other days. More importantly, the transport times from each European country (collection date to delivery date) are displayed as actuals and percentages in Figures 7a and b. Individual differences exist, which appear to be independent of the distance from the U.K. Overall 6,553 samples arrived the day after collection while a further 2,548 arrived the following day (i.e., 36 hours after the blood was taken). Less than 3% of the samples were more than 60 hours in transit.

B. Result Reporting Times

The laboratory provides a single patient report that includes the results for all the tests protocolled for that patient visit. A report is automatically generated when all the analyses are complete and authorized but, for specific trials, an interim report will always be printed on the day the samples are received. Each report is faxed to the investigator with faxed copies going to the CRA at headquarters for trial awareness and to the monitoring CRA responsible for the clinical trial center. While the promptness of the reporting will depend on the number of analyses requested, more significant is the requirement to perform endocrine or surrogate marker assays. For 1,053 samples analyzed for a trial requiring only clinical chemistry and hematology, 78% of all completed reports were faxed on the day of sample receipt, a further 11% were faxed the next day. For another trial where 4 peptide hormone assays were requested for each sample, of the 5,777 analyzed, 64% were reported in full and faxed the same day and further 18% were faxed the next day.

a.

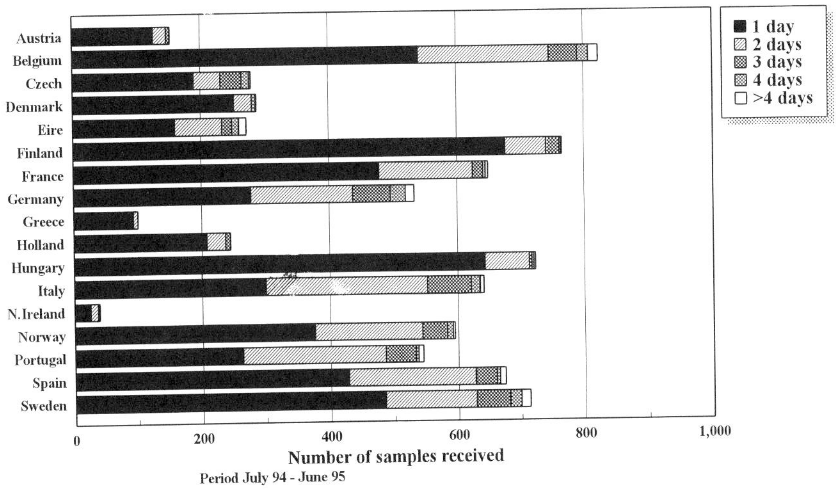

b.

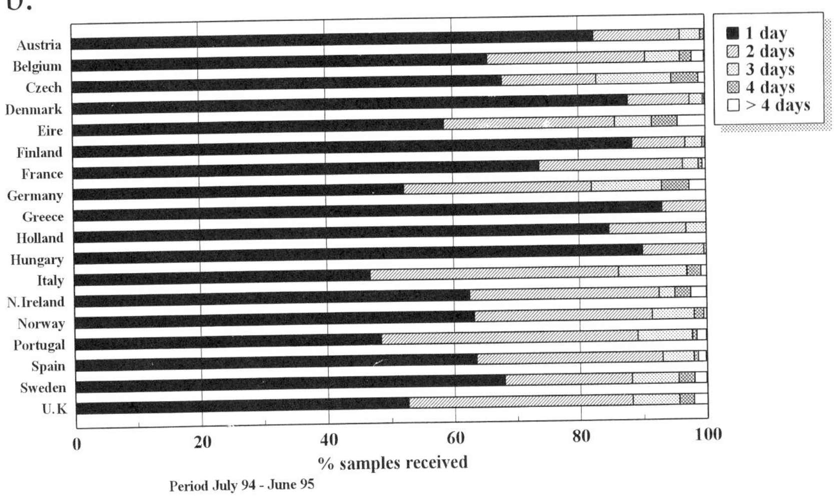

Fig. 7 The transit time for the transport of clinical trial samples from the countries of mainland Europe are displayed as either the actual number of samples received (a) or as a percentage of the samples from each country (b). Samples arriving on day 1 had been taken the previous day at the trial center, day-2 samples had taken between 36 and 48 hours to be transported. The actual number of samples from the U.K. (1953 in total with 1,028 arriving on day 1 and 695 on day 2) are not displayed in (a) as the data would distort the graph.

C. Completeness of Results Database

To be able to provide a result for every protocolled test for every sample received would be ideal for both the investigator, concerned about patient welfare, and the trial biometrician. This ideal situation, while possible for Phase I trials performed "in house," is rarely achievable for transported samples because of such factors as poor quality samples, samples too old for analysis, broken tubes or leaked samples. In assessing the frequency of "no test result," 148,355 test requests for clinical chemistry, hematology or endocrine analyses, received over a 12 month period, were examined. A valid numeric result was reported for 98.3% of the tests requested. For the remaining 1.7% (i.e., 2,513 tests), where no result was possible, 70% related to hematology, mostly due to old or clotted samples, while lack of clinical chemistry results was usually due to broken or leaked tubes.

D. Competitive Charges

Irrespective of whether the laboratory charges the Medical Function (i.e., sponsor) for clinical trial support, the actual cost of performing the test and providing the total service has to be calculated and compared to external contract prices. In 1994 the laboratory commissioned Technomark Consulting Services Ltd to perform a survey of the clinical pathology pricing in the U.K. and the rest of Europe. Responses were received from 23 contract laboratories (14 from the U.K.) and each was requested to prepare costings for a Phase II trial with 50 investigators, 5,000 sample packs; to report the results and any analytical trends for 5,000 sample analyses for clinical chemistry; hematology, 4 hormones, and PSA as a tumor marker; and the electronic transfer of the data back to Zeneca. They were not requested to supply a cost for sample transport; for providing CRA monitoring of the centers, or perform any management of the trial data (i.e., demography checks and error corrections).

The survey shows there to be a wide variation in price between laboratories (Figure 8). The U.K. prices are on average lower than those in the rest of Europe, but the two ranges do overlap. The lowest price received was £117K, the highest £639K, a factor of 5.5 between lowest and highest. Within each individual category of analysis there was equally wide variation (clinical chemistry: £27.5K–£169K; hematology: £14K–£59K; endocrinology: £37.5K–£360K, and PSA: £15K–£121K); more remarkable were the charges for producing the reports ranging from £500 to £50,000 while the cost of supplying the sample packs ranged from as little as £0.08 to £20 each.

The Zeneca laboratory's costing for this trial was £213K (i.e., 6th lowest cost).

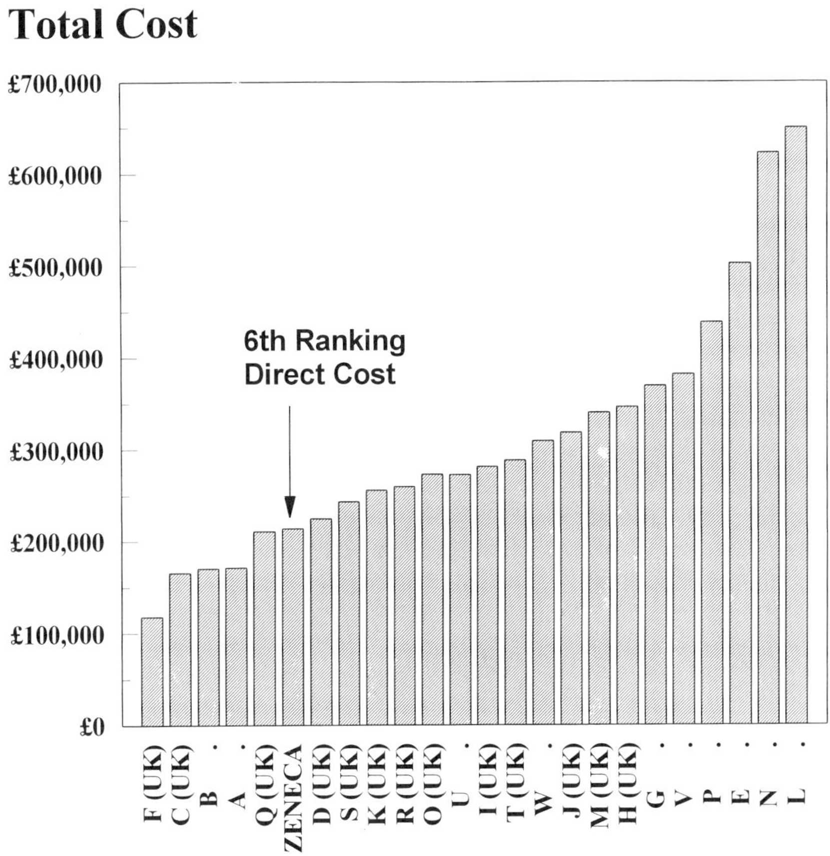

Fig. 8 The cost of clinical pathology service provided by the Zeneca laboratory compared to 23 contract laboratories costing an identical Phase II trial. The contract laboratories are identified by letter and (UK) indicates the laboratory was based in the United Kingdom rather than mainland Europe.

VIII. DIRECT COST AND INDIRECT COST BENEFITS

Although it may be inconvenient for the sponsor's Accounts Department to have to deal with multiple local laboratories, the direct cost is usually significantly less than had the analysis been performed at a central laboratory. The "up front" costs are also significantly greater with a central laboratory but it must be recognized that only between 25–30% is allocated against the analytical cost. The residual direct cost goes to cover additional services, some of which are listed in the following:

Education and instruction of personnel at the study sites;
Providing consistency checks between sites;
Organizing and managing sample transportation;
Specimen management: analyzed in house, by another facility, saved in a repository; and
Study management by providing monthly updates on
- numbers of patients screened and enrolled into a study,
- patient progress—number of patients that have reached a particular visit number,
- trend analyses that follow the results from screening and periodic laboratory tests,
- a broad glimpse of the data 2–3 months in advance of final database output,
- the resolution of demographic inconsistencies between visits and preventing such data problems from accumulating,
- manually entering trial data generated from local laboratories to allow sponsor to have timely access to the data, and
- data archiving.

A. Added Value Associated with Efficient Data Processing

It is important that an efficient electronic communication link is established early between the sponsor and the central laboratory. The key events in the stages of data processing are listed below and it is in both parties' interest to ensure that the principles are adhered to.

1. Data Entry Timings

Laboratory data should be transferred electronically once patients are randomized and other details from the CRF have been validated and entered onto the medical database.

2. Query Turnround Timings

In a multicenter study, it is not unusual for laboratory data queries to comprise the majority of the total queries on the data collected. Take the case of a multicenter study consisting of 60 sites, each of which has a designated laboratory. Each laboratory has patients unique to it and the units and reference ranges often differ from laboratory to laboratory, according to their own methodology of measurement and sample patient population. Each laboratory has at least 2 sets of lab ranges (one for each sex), and some laboratories may change one or two of their ranges during a trial of several month's duration or change reporting units due to new equipment. The laboratory data, therefore, has to be checked against more than 130 corresponding sets of laboratory ranges; in eradicating the bulk of these ranges by the use of a central laboratory, the total number of queries sent to a center can be drastically reduced.

As experienced by Fenning [5] laboratory queries amounted to as much as 46.5% of total queries in one multicenter trial using over 12 individual laboratories, and the total duration of the query process was 89 working days.

3. Retrieval of Data Timings

If a central laboratory is used, then retrieval and analysis becomes a single process, with no need to convert units or examine against separate reference ranges. The safety and efficacy profiles become simpler to understand because all parameters have been measured by the same method with the same units and compared against the same reference range. There are more options and more statistical power in this greater pool of results.

4. Analysis Timings

With the central laboratory there is no need to program each center's results with their related units into their individual tables. Consistency of the data set will require less data manipulation, important with the move towards electronic CANDAs.

B. Hidden Cost Benefit Associated with Reduced Development Time

When comparing the cost of different laboratories sufficient account should be taken of the real value of using a central laboratory as compared with local laboratories. In the worst case scenario, if it is not possible to merge the data obtained from the different laboratories, resolving the problem can add months to the development process at a very high price? The hidden cost benefit of using a central laboratory is evident in the time saved to get to the marketplace: each day potentially representing a million dollars in sales. A full cost benefit analysis should, therefore, include the time that is saved by achieving an earlier market launch of a new product associated with improved efficiency and a more reliable regulatory package.

Placing a figure on this saving is not easy since many factors influence the speed at which a trial can be completed and reported (e.g., the priority assigned to the trial). For a drug with a yearly return of $100 million, a saving of a few weeks for a pivotal trial on the critical path in a drug development program can amount to several million dollars. The time saving due to improved data management associated with the use of a central laboratory is considered to be in the order of 10–15%.

IX. ZENECA LABORATORY'S HIDDEN COST BENEFIT

A. More Efficient Use of Laboratory Resources

The principal responsibility of the laboratory is to support Zeneca's preclinical safety evaluation program. Because of the small volume of blood available from most of our animals for analysis it is important that all samples are analysed on the day of sampling. Unfortunately, although every effort is made to provide a steady flow of samples, by the very nature of preclinical development, this is not always possible. As seen in Figure 4, large daily fluctuations in animal toxicology samples are observed. The support of clinical trials was, therefore, seen as an opportunity to fill the workload troughs by utilising the spare capacity of the laboratory. Table 4 displays a summary of the data presented in Figure 4 (with public holidays excluded). While the average number of samples for toxicology and clinical samples were similar the daily variation (expressed as a percent of standard deviation/average) for the toxicology samples is more than double that for the clinical samples. When the data are combined, the daily average is doubled but the daily variation remains very acceptable. At least 82 samples are received daily and, although the maximum number of samples at 701 is high, for the 251 days when samples were received, only on 26 occasions did the number of requests exceed 400 samples. These results support the position that the additional clinical samples have been absorbed without compromising the ability of the laboratory to support the toxicology work. In fact, by ensuring that samples are received daily, the analytical performance of the laboratory has improved since individuals remain motivated and the instruments are run more efficiently.

B. Economy of Scale and Common Resources

The doubling in the number of samples analysed over the past 5 years has significantly reduced the laboratory's cost per test. This has been partly achieved by increasing productivity (i.e., same staff salary for more work) and partly because a greater discount can be negotiated with both instrument and reagent

Table 4 Daily Samples Received by Zeneca Laboratory Between July 1994 and June 1995

	Clinical samples	Toxicology samples	Total samples
Minimum number	52	0	82
Maximum number	342	456	701
Daily average	139	129	268
(Standard deviation, SD)	47	96	110
Daily variation (SD/average)%	33.7	74.0	40.9

manufacturers. As seen from Figure 9, the actual cost per test has been reduced by 35% over the past 5 years (more if inflation is taken into account), and this cost reduction, achieved because of the additional clinical samples, is of direct cost saving on the toxicology studies.

As we have seen, the doubling in the workload did not result in an increase in analytical staff. In fact, with the exception of purchasing an immunoassay instrument, a fax machine and additional filing system, no other purchases were made specifically to support the clinical work. All other instruments, although of a slightly higher capacity than needed solely for toxicology, are used for all samples. The physical size of the laboratory has not increased, equipment service and maintenance contracts remain the same, electricity and services remain unaltered, but the telephone costs have more than trebled.

One significant hidden benefit of being part of a large organization like Zeneca is that the laboratory gains the advantage of corporate rates agreed between Zeneca PLC and the courier company. Based on the total value of business generated by the company the cost of transporting samples to the laboratory is significantly less than if the laboratory was negotiating courier prices in isolation. The saving in a given year can be in excess of £100K.

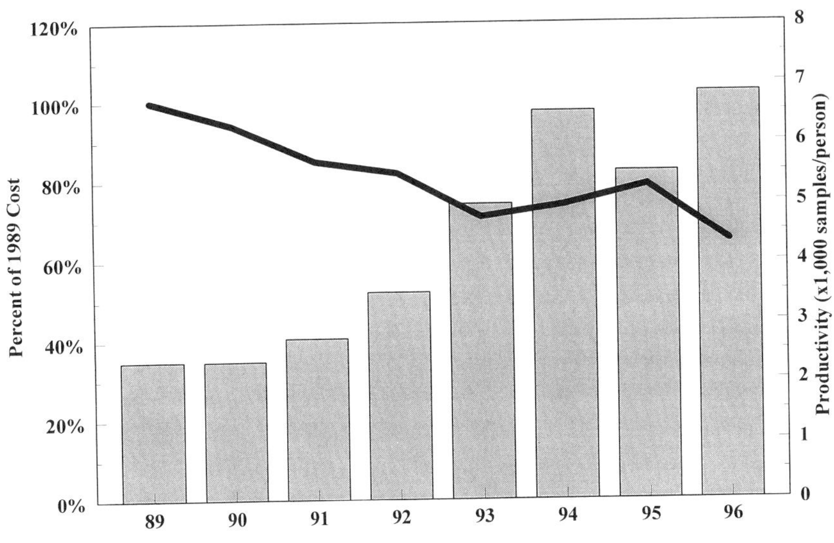

Fig. 9 Reduction in the actual cost of analysis (consumables and laboratory salaries) over 8 years as a percentage of the 1989 cost. The vertical bars display the increased laboratory productivity over the same period.

C. Reduced Reporting Time

Barnett and James [6] have examined the overall performance of the clinical trial cycle time by examining the time taken to complete the 6 stages of the trial cycle: protocol writing, trial start-up, subject enrollment, data cleaning, analysis, and report writing. The average total cycle time for the 1,000 clinical trials surveyed—from protocol start to approval of the final study report—was more than 200 weeks (3 years, 10 months). Although it is commonly believed that the cycle time is affected by the phase of the clinical trial, the authors found very little difference in cycle times between Phase I, Phase II, and Phase III trials. Aside from the differences in patient enrollment times, the other processes took roughly the same amount of time in each phase. What was more surprising was the observation that the completion of the three final stages (i.e., data cleaning, analysis, and reporting) took an average of 47, 16, and 44 weeks, respectively, almost as long as the subject enrollment stage.

Since the reporting of clinical trials is, in most cases, on the critical path for the successful and speedy submission of an MAA regulatory package, the duration of the final three stages in Barnett and James' survey appear excessively long. A similar performance measure has been defined for Zeneca clinical trials. The interval between the "Last Patient Completing the Protocol" and the "Completion of the Statistical Evaluation of the Trial" (i.e., the data cleaning and the analysis stages combined) have been determined and are presented in Table 5 and Figure 10. For multicenter trials completed since 1991, the median interval between "patient complete" and "statistics complete" was 22 weeks for trials where the clinical pathology was performed at local laboratories and 12.5 weeks where the trials were supported by Zeneca's laboratory.

Table 5 Overall Duration Between Last Patient Complete and Statistics Complete

	Zeneca Central Laboratory				Outside Laboratories			
Indication	N	**Median**	Mean	SE	N	**Median**	Mean	SE
All indications	**20**	**12.5**	**14.22**	**3.62**	**49**	**22**	**22.96**	**2.58**
Antiasthmatic	7	**12**	16.00	3.49				
Anticancer	4	**11**	10.25	1.78				
Anticancer	2	**10**	10.00	0.00	6	**20.5**	34.67	13.62
Anesthetic					7	**23**	25.86	7.35
Antibiotic					21	**22**	26.43	2.98
Anticancer					9	**22**	20.44	2.65
Cardiovascular	3	**18**	17.33	0.98				
Cardiovascular	2	**16.5**	16.50	3.18				
Anticancer	2	**13**	13.00	0.71	6	**18**	22.00	4.68

Data for multicenter trials with Regulatory Phase compounds for trials completed after 1991.

This saving of 9.5 weeks for 20 key trials had a significant impact on the time taken to prepare and issue the final trial report and reflects on the ease and speed with which data was transferred to the Medical Database, the consistency of the results, and the accuracy of the patient demography data.

X. ESTABLISHING RELATIONSHIPS AND AVOIDING PROBLEMS

A. Relationships

There are many strategies which a Pharmaceutical Company can adopt to support clinical trials. In its simplest form the sponsor can establish a direct link with a central laboratory while, alternatively, the sponsor may contract the

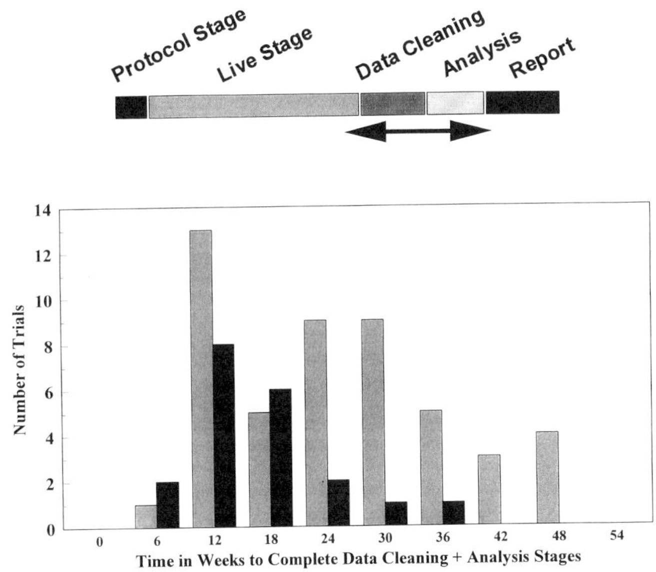

Fig. 10 Typical stages of a clinical trial. The period between the "last patient completing the protocol" and the "statistical analysis complete" (indicated by the double headed arrow) identify the start of the data cleaning stage and the end of the analysis stage. The total time, in weeks, to complete both stages, are displayed as an incidence bar chart where the number of trials in each 6-week interval are displayed. The gray bars display the results for trials where the clinical pathology was performed by outside laboratories while the solid bars display the results for trials supported by the Zeneca laboratory. All were multi-center trials completed since 1991.

whole trial to a CRO who will establish working relationships with one or more clinical pathology laboratories. Over the past few years we have seen in Europe more complex relationships being established between sponsor, one or more CROs responsible for managing the trials, a separate CRO responsible for data management and a central laboratory with links to a specialist laboratory. Traditionally CROs were mainly used for study monitoring and local recruitment for the Phase III/IIIb and Phase IV trials. In a recent survey of CRO usage, Getz and Vogel [7], it was noted that use of CROs for Phase II work had not increased between 1992 and 1994 and remained at about 16%. The use of CROs for study monitoring had increased from 59% to 94% but significantly more CROs were used for data management (from 5% to 94%) and statistical analyses (from 10% to 77%). In this survey, 64% of companies said they gave major project responsibilities to more than eight CROs at any one time. The other 6 said they preferred to use a limited number of CROs.

A sponsor who has developed a good working relationship with a particular central laboratory should think very carefully before contracting additional partners. Such relationships are based on mutual understanding and trust, underpinned by good communication. Central laboratory personnel should be involved with the pretrial meeting with the sponsor to review and resolve any outstanding issues before the trial begins. Attendance at the pretrial investigator meeting is mutually beneficial for the laboratory personnel to gain a better understanding of the aims and design of the trial and for the investigator to meet and communicate with the individual who will be providing their test results.

When using a laboratory for the first time the sponsor should identify individuals who will interface directly with designated personnel at the central laboratory. These individuals should allow plenty of time to get to know their counterparts and should arrange a laboratory tour to get to know and understand the laboratory's procedures (e.g., sample tracking, report formats, barcoding, etc.). Ideally, the sponsor's representatives, possibly a CRA, should personally get to know the study director at the laboratory; the data management staff both at the laboratory and in-house; the QA/QC people both at the laboratory and in-house; and the laboratory management in order to ensure appropriate resources are available for the laboratory to support the trial and to resolve any problems. At this stage it is also appropriate for members of the sponsor's Quality Assurance group to check laboratory procedures.

B. Operational Pretrial Checks at Central Laboratories

It must be remembered that, although "time is money," adequate time not spent setting up a trial properly can cost even more time and money later.

A simple check-list may help to avoid the major problems and it is important that all systems are running smoothly before the trial starts.

1. Getting Samples to the Central Laboratory

(a) What are the courier arrangements?
(b) Does the investigator need a centrifuge and are there any potential problems with blood sampling (e.g., in France)?
(c) Are there standardized request forms; are they easy to use; are they barcoded?
(d) What are the laboratory's policy about sample packs and expiry dates; are they replaced automatically or by request?
(e) If samples are to be transported frozen will the laboratory provide dry ice and appropriate shipping materials and guidelines to ensure that the samples are still frozen when they arrive at the laboratory?
(f) Will the laboratory arrange training for the study nurse to explain the importance of sample collection, packaging, shipment, and documentation?

2. Sample Analysis at Central Laboratory

(a) Quality work should be assumed but inspect the laboratory, request quality control records for assays to be utilized in the trial, particularly specialized tests. During the trial request regular updates.
(b) Does the laboratory have efficient specimen handling procedures; timely data access and acceptable turnaround time?
(c) Check the test capability of the laboratory. If some work is to be subcontracted will the additional sample transport have an impact on the quality and speed of response, i.e., additional sample degradation?
(d) Does the laboratory have a global presence; if so, is there consistency in testing methods among sites and over time?
(e) For each parameter included in the trial protocol the sample stability period should be discussed with the central laboratory. For those parameters (e.g., bicarbonate; blood gases or ESR) which show biological stability for only a few hours, what arrangements have been made to analyse the samples near the investigator site?

3. Reports

(a) Agree on the format to be used.
(b) Agree on units and reference ranges and ascertain how these are determined.
(c) What are the procedures for abnormal results, are there abnormal flagging conventions; how do they track and highlight patients whose results go outside stipulated ranges, e.g., 3× ULN (upper limit of normal)?

(d) Are abnormal results tracked and does the laboratory monitor for key events?
(e) Can different flagging criteria be applied to specific patient visits or to different therapeutic areas?

4. Data Management

(a) Check the electronic transfer of data, agree on the coding to be used, and ensure procedures are in place regarding cleaning header demography and the electronic transfer of results.
(b) Expect flexibility so that the laboratory conforms (at a price) to the wishes of the sponsor.
(c) Obtain guarantees that the format is not changed without the sponsor being informed and agreeing to the change.

C. Avoiding Problems

It is important to involve the central laboratory early at pretrial investigator meetings so that any problems can be resolved. The meeting also provides an opportunity to build confidence between the Investigators and laboratory. The real bottom line is to avoid any surprises, either way. A laboratory protocol, which specifies the logistics of the trial, should be agreed on and should include contract costs, terms and conditions, responsibilities, the procedures to be followed by the laboratory (e.g., sample handling), and instructions to investigator on what to do and what to expect. It is important that the laboratory protocol should clearly define: the expectations from different parties, the timelines for the different activities, and the responsibilities of the different parties. Ensure that any specialised test is fully validated and documented and that the laboratory has the proven expertise to perform the tests.

Investigator buy-in is another major factor that should not be dismissed lightly. Historically, investigators have shown a reluctance to work with a central laboratory but attitudes are changing. On occasions it may be necessary to take investigators to the central laboratory to show them how highly proficient and sophisticated these facilities are in order to address their queries and allay their concerns.

Two areas of potential conflict are (a) divergence from agreed timeline (i.e., the time from the collection of samples to the delivery of final report) and (b) total cost and budget over-runs. There should be no surprises and all costs should be agreed up-front and stipulated in the contract. It is, however, prudent to agree up-front how much extra the laboratory can spend in an emergency to ensure sample integrity if the sponsor cannot be contacted.

Finally, it is important that the investigator/study nurse's life is made as easy as possible by:

(a) Avoiding poor phlebotomy kits; ideally these should be bar coded so that no labeling of tubes is required and the kits should come pre-prepared. In addition to including labels, the instructions of what should be done with the samples should be in the form of an investigator study handbook.
(b) Pre-printed transport forms should be provided and easy phoning arrangements made.
(c) Storage of supplies can be a problem if the investigator is involved in several trials: consider the phased delivery of supplies.
(d) Provide legible results with reference ranges and clear out-of-range flagging on forms that can go directly into a CRF without the need to transcribe the data.
(e) A 24-hour, toll-free telephone number into the laboratory should be provided so that the investigator can phone if there are any problems.
(f) Good pretrial planning is essential and, ideally, the center coordinator or trial nurse should be involved in addition to the trial investigator.

XI. LABORATORY RELATIONSHIPS AND DATA MANAGEMENT

A. Effective Relationships Within Zeneca

The successful management of Zeneca clinical trials depends on good working relationships between the laboratory and other Zeneca personnel involved with clinical trial management.

Good working relations have been established with two key operational groups, CRAs and Data Associates. Regular meetings, laboratory tours, and training sessions all help to build and maintain mutual confidence and understanding. The close proximity of the laboratory to the Medical Function allows the rapid resolution of queries and personal contact avoids most misunderstandings. Good communication and direct access to clinicians, therapeutic team leaders, and biometricians help the processes of agreeing on the trial protocol, maintaining awareness of key events during a clinical trial, trial progress, and laboratory result or reference range queries.

As diagrammatically displayed in Figure 11, the laboratory is centrally placed and is a focus for effective communication at key stages of clinical trials. A considerable amount of time and effort is devoted to maintaining good working relationships.

B. Effective Relationships Within Europe

Zeneca Pharmaceuticals has 8 major Pharma offices and a further 10 smaller Pharmas located throughout Europe. Each of these Pharma offices have Medical

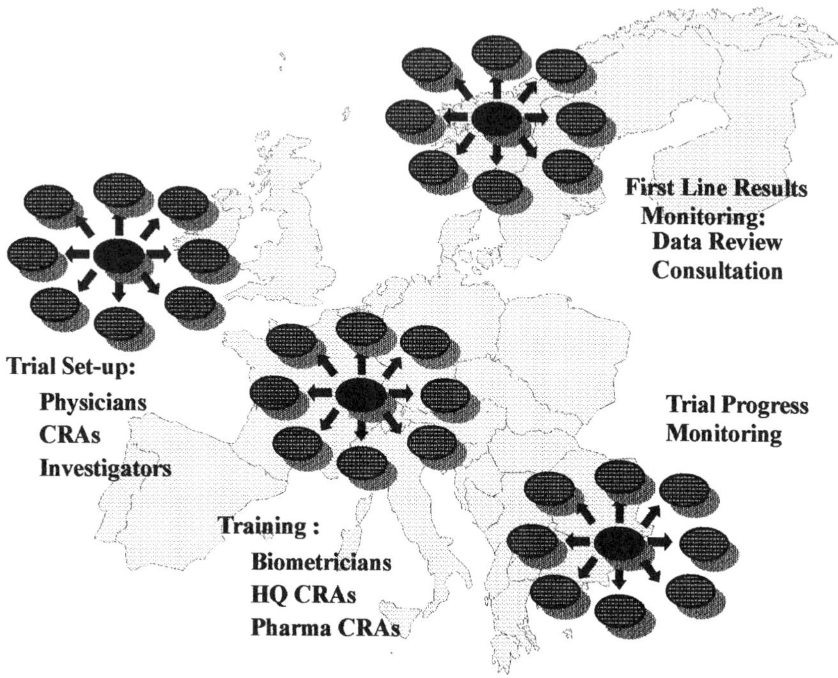

Fig. 11 Key relationships: the solid ellipse shows the laboratory in a central position interfacing with several teams, both at headquarters and with Pharma personnel.

Advisors and CRAs, the difference being reflected in the number of individuals being employed. Most of the major Pharmas also have a Quality Assurance Unit. Good working relationships with these individuals are essential in order for the laboratory to effectively support pan-European clinical trials. As illustrated in Figure 12, all regions of Europe are covered by these Pharma offices with the major Pharmas being located in France, Germany, Spain, Holland, Belgium, Scandinavia, Italy, and the U.K.

The Pharma Medical Advisors directly resolve most issues raised by the investigator or they function as a local intermediary for the laboratory to provide the appropriate information. There are no language difficulties to hinder communication and the Medical Advisors are familiar with the local customs and working practices. It is the local Pharma CRAs who are responsible for the conduct and monitoring of clinical trials in Europe. At the start of a trial the laboratory provides the CRA with an investigator brochure, customized

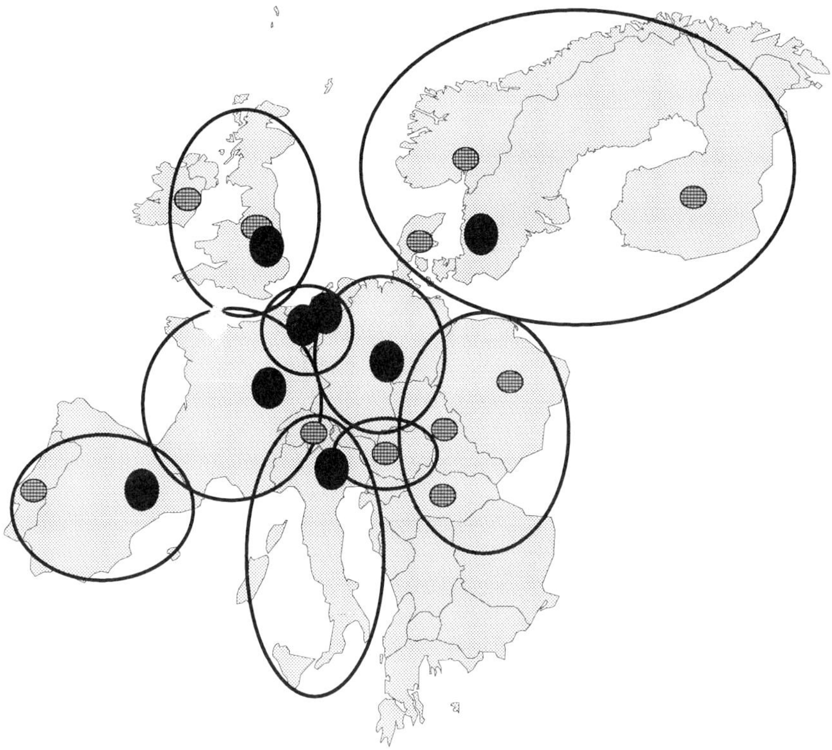

Fig. 12 Zeneca has 8 major Pharma offices (dark dot) and 10 minor Pharma Offices (hatched dot) located in the European countries displayed. These broadly have responsibilities displayed within the ellipses. These Pharma offices have a complement of Medical Officers, CRAs, and Quality Assurance personnel.

trial handbook, courier and transport documentation, and the phlebotomy packs. The CRA will distribute these to their investigators as well as perform all the required training of the center personnel in the identified procedures. These CRAs also resolve most logistical problems, including any sample transportation issues, directly with the local Courier representatives. Again cultural and language difficulties are avoided by allowing fellow Nationals to interpret and resolve queries.

The Pharma CRAs are in regular contact with the laboratory and attend training and refresher sessions when they visit Headquarters. Regular User Group Meetings with European representatives are held where common issues, policies and service reviews can be discussed and difficulties resolved.

C. Patient Review and Database Management

The laboratory acts as an initial sieve to identify any major clinical pathology changes. In addition to reviewing every report, electronic flags can be set against key parameters, specific to each therapeutic area, allowing immediate action to be taken to inform the appropriate individuals. A quick response is always important on such occasions and the information is phoned or faxed immediately. Follow up review can be easily arranged and the flexibility of the laboratory computer allows additional related information to be extracted quickly. As confidence in the laboratory has grown over the years, more and more responsibility for identifying important changes in the data is placed with the laboratory personnel reviewing the results.

Early identification of errors and inconsistencies in patient demography details and the pro-active approach adopted to resolve these issues, ensures that errors are quickly corrected. The ease of communication within the company, both at headquarters and with the European Pharmas, ensure that issues are addressed and resolved within days. Joint Working Practice Procedures have been agreed on between the laboratory and Medical Function personnel, including the Pharma CRAs. These standard procedures avoid confusion and the documents related to data amendments are fully covered by the procedures and comply with GCP. All clinical pathology requests are completed in triplicate, a copy of each form being retained by the investigator. Each CRA will check the accuracy of these requests during their center monitoring visit and also retain a copy. Any patient demographic amendments must carry the investigator signature before they can be actioned by the laboratory. Any other type of amendment must be substantiated by the CRA using validated documentation. Although, apparently labor intensive, the procedure ensures accuracy and thus avoids any unnecessary and unwelcome delays at the end of the trial.

XII. WHAT OF THE FUTURE?

Although somewhat behind our American colleagues, the way clinical trials are supported in Europe has changed significantly over the past few years. The trend is clearly away from the use of local laboratories towards multicenter multinational trials supported by large central laboratories providing worldwide uniformity in data management and analytical procedures. Expansion of these central laboratories into regions beyond the continents of Europe and America is set to continue, allowing clinical trials to be run on a truly global basis. Global databases, holding all laboratory data for a clinical trial, will soon be the norm and it is likely that those CROs with a global presence will be the guardians of the data and will manage it on behalf of their sponsors. Sophisticated data management tools will aid global data review and trend analysis, providing the sponsor with the means to detect adverse events and monitor drug efficacy. Direct access for investigators to assess their own data will become mandatory, thus resolving many issues related to turnaround times and errors associated with patient or visit mis-identity and CRF transcription.

As the influence of central laboratories on the drug development process increases it will become more and more critical that these CROs respond to the needs of the sponsor. Greater flexibility for data management, customized reporting, and data transfer will become the norm and the central laboratory may need to take responsibility for management of locally derived laboratory data. Surrogate markers and novel assays, not commonly associated with clinical pathology, will need to be embraced with enthusiasm, thus relieving the sponsor of the responsibility of finding a reliable alternative that has the required expertise and credibility to perform the assay. Partnerships will probably become more common as CROs seek "preferred supplier" status.

The Zeneca laboratory is not seeking to expand its support of Zeneca clinical trials outside Europe and is not seeking to offer its services to other pharmaceutical companies. The cost benefit of the laboratory depends on a delicate balance between animal toxicology and clinical trial support. Any increase in the latter, demanding additional resources, or compromising the ability of the laboratory to effectively analyse toxicology samples would disturb such a balance. As clinical trials become more global it would be of benefit to both Zeneca and the laboratory to achieve an integration of its European database with that produced by a CRO prepared to support Zeneca trials in the rest of the world. Such an approach would allow our investigators to have direct access to their own data and allow them interrogation of the database. More importantly, it would allow Zeneca to reap the benefit of conducting unified global clinical drug development programs.

In Memoriam:

This chapter is dedicated to the memory of my uncle, Ellis Jones of Blaenau Ffestiniog, a gentle and caring person who fell ill during the preparation of this chapter and died on the day it was completed. [D.D.]

Mwyach ni chawn dramwy'r llwybrau,
Drwy y grug i'r llynnoedd pell,
Camu wnaethost, gyfaill annwyl,
Tros y ffin i fyd sydd well.

—J. D. R.

REFERENCES

1. G. Evans, Ed. *Animal Clinical Chemistry*: A primer for Toxicologists. Taylor & Francis Press, London, 1996.
2. G. Odel, K. Schloemer, M. Harvey, and R. Malcolm. Cost-effectiveness of laboratories. *Applied Clinical Trials 4*: 32, 1995.
3. A. Hill. The pros and cons of using a central laboratory versus a local laboratory. Personal Communication presented at central laboratories, "Blood brothers or spin doctors?" organised by ACRPI on December 1995 at the Royal College of Pathologists, London.
4. J. C. Bloom. Issues in the selection and use of centralised laboratories. *Applied Clinical Trials*. April Supplement 1, 1995.
5. C. J. Fenning. Optimizing the use of a central laboratory in Europe. *Applied Clinical Trials 3*: 28, 1994.
6. S. T. Barnett and J. A. James. Measuring the clinical development process. *Applied Clinical Trials 4*: 44, 1995.
7. K. A. Getz and J. R. Vogel. Achieving results with CROs: Their evolving role in clinical development. *Applied Clinical Trials 4*: 32, 1995.

16

New Marketing Authorization Procedures in the European Union and the Impact on Regulatory Strategy

Vaila M. Marshall

Pfizer Central Research
Kent, England

I. INTRODUCTION

The Single European Act was adopted in 1987 to create a European Market without internal frontiers to promote the free movement of goods, services, capital, and people. The new legislation for Marketing Authorizations in the European Union was created to further these goals of the single market. The legislation has created a European Agency for the Evaluation of Medicinal Products (EMEA) and there will be three procedures for registration of products: the centralized, decentralized, and national procedures. These new procedures will change the process of obtaining marketing authorizations in Europe in a dramatic way and will have a significant impact on the Regulatory Affairs strategy and functions within the pharmaceutical industry and national Regulatory Agencies.

The two previous European approval systems, the concertation procedure [1] and the multistate procedure [2,3], have provided experience on which to build the new procedures. A critical difference between these and the new procedures, however, is that decisions from these two procedures were not binding on national Member States resulting in differing decisions, whereas in the new systems the decisions are binding. Thus, as we move through the transition and national procedures have a more limited role, we will have evolved into a truly European approval process. This chapter will explain the role of some of the main bodies involved in the new system, the procedures themselves, and the impact this will have on regulatory strategies in development of new products.

II. THE LEGISLATION AND IMPLEMENTATION DATES

The legislation underpinning the future marketing authorization systems in the European Community takes the shape of a Regulation and three Directives for human and veterinary medicinal products. Regulation 2309/93 of 22.7.93 [4] sets out arrangements for a European Agency for the Evaluation of Medicinal Products (EMEA) and for the new centralized procedure that will lead to a community authorization valid in all 12 Member States. Directive 93/39/EEC of 14.6.93 [5] amends earlier Directives 65/65 [6], 75/318 [7], and 75/319 [8] and sets out the decentralized procedure for human medicinal products that, based on the principle of mutual recognition, will allow extension of approval in one Member States to others. This procedure is also called the mutual recognition procedure. The second Directive 93/41/EEC of 14.6.93 [9] repeals the original Directive 87/22/EEC [1], which set up the concertation procedure. A third Directive 93/40/EEC [10] sets out the decentralized procedure for veterinary medicinal products. These products are also covered in the Regulation 2309/93. There will be no further discussion of veterinary products in this chapter although broadly the same procedures apply. National authorization procedures will continue although their use will become more limited as will be explained below.

The decision to place the Agency in London was taken in November 1993. Both the new centralized and decentralized procedures were effective from January 1, 1995. During the period 1995–1998, a transition period will operate. The most significant aspect of the transition period is the possibility for Member State Regulatory Authorities to suspend assessment of a dossier if they note another Member State has the dossier under active examination. The strategic significance of this procedure will be discussed later.

From January 1, 1998, the decentralized procedure will be fully in operation. This means that if the product is authorized in one Member State, other Member States must either take the assessment report of the original country into account and mutually recognize the decision or they can raise serious objectives for referral to the EMEA. From 1998 applications under national legislation will be focused on assessment of products for one-country marketing only and maintenance of products approved nationally before the new procedures. Pharmacovigilance and inspections (Good Manufacturing Practice [GMP], Good Laboratory Practice [GLP], Good Clinical Practice [GCP]) will also continue to be the responsibility of Member States although coordination may take place through the EMEA.

The national Regulatory Authorities will of course also be fully involved in the new procedures as first-country approvals for the decentralized procedure will have been the result of a national examination. In addition, the national Regulatory Authorities will be supporting the new procedures and the EMEA by providing experts to assess the products.

III. EUROPEAN MEDICINES EVALUATION AGENCY STRUCTURE AND TASKS

The overall structure of the European Medicines Evaluation Agency (EMEA) is laid out in Figure 1. The main tasks of the EMEA are:

1. Coordination of the scientific evaluation of the quality, safety, and efficacy of medicinal products;
2. Transmission of assessment reports, Summaries of Product Characteristics (SmPC), labels, and package leaflets or inserts for these medicinal products;

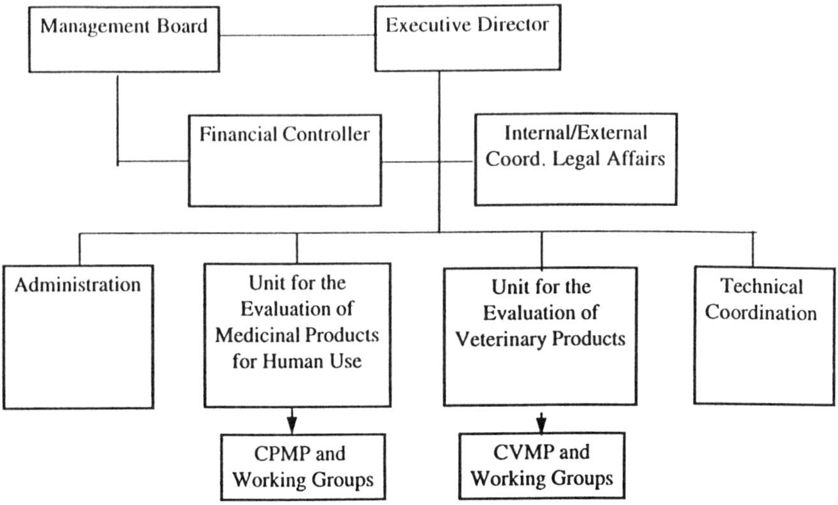

Fig. 1 EMEA structure.

3. Formation of a central point where coordination of the supervision of pharmacovigilance can take place; reporting will continue through Member States;
4. Coordination of verification of compliance with Good Manufacturing Practice (GMP), Good Laboratory Practice (GLP), and Good Clinical Practice (GCP); inspections will still take place through the Member States;
5. Provision of technical and scientific support to cooperation between the Community, Member States, international organizations (such as IFPMA, WHO, etc.), and third countries;
6. Recording of the status of marketing authorizations;
7. Provision of technical assistance for maintenance of a public database on medicinal products;
8. Provision of information to health care professionals and the public about medicinal products that have been evaluated by the Agency; and
9. Advising of companies on the nature and extent of the various tests and trials necessary to develop new products.

The Executive Director is responsible to the Management Board. This Board consists of two representatives from each Member State, two representatives from the European Commission, and two representatives appointed by the

European Parliament. One of the main functions of the Board is to oversee the activities of the Agency particularly concerning the budget. The Secretariat will provide the technical and administrative support for the Committee for Proprietary Medicinal Products (CPMP). Initially, this staff will be about 100 in 1995. The Secretariat will report to the Executive Director, Fernand Sauer, who was appointed in June 1994 and whose responsibilities encompass day-to-day administration of the Agency, management of the budget, and support of the CPMP.

The CPMP is the scientific committee and consists of two members nominated by each Member State—these members should have experience in the evaluation of medicinal products. This Committee previously existed under the old procedures but was reformed in January 1995. The members may be accompanied by a maximum of three experts at each meeting. The main task of the CPMP is to provide the scientific opinion on the authorization and renewal of medicinal products including pharmacovigilance opinions when emergency measures such as urgent labeling changes or removal of the product from the market are required. The CPMP may also establish working parties and have access to expert groups to support them in execution of the tasks. Various working parties have been formed, i.e., pharmacovigilance, biotechnology, safety, quality, efficacy, and ad hoc groups have been formed on anti-infectives, AIDS, oncology, and blood products. The experts available to the CPMP are proposed by the Member States and must have proven experience in the assessment of medicinal products. Some of the areas where they could support the CPMP are

- scientific evaluation of medicinal products;
- transmission of assessment reports, Summaries of Product Characteristics, labels, package leaflets or inserts for those products;
- coordination between Member States of the supervision of authorized products (particularly pharmacovigilance);
- coordination between Member States of verification of Good Manufacturing Practice, Good Laboratory Practice, and Good Clinical Practice; and
- advice to companies on nature and extent of tests and trials during development.

IV. PROCEDURES

A. Centralized Procedure

The Centralized procedure should offer direct and quick access to the European market for innovative new products. Its use is mandatory for biotechnology

Table 1 Part A

Medicinal products developed by means of one of the following biotechnological processes
—recombinant DNA technology;
—controlled expression of genes coding for biologically active proteins in prokaryotes and eukaryotes including transformed mammalian cells; and
—hybridoma and monoclonal antibody methods.
Veterinary medicinal products, including those not derived from biotechnology, intended primarily for use as performance enhancers in order to promote the growth of treated animals or to increase yields from treated animals.

Annex, Part A of Council Regulation (EEC) 2309/93 of 22 July 1993.

products. Such biotechnology products are delineated in Part A of the Annex to the Regulation 2309/93, see Table 1. The procedure is also open by choice to products classed as "high technology" (Part B of the Annex to Regulation 2309/93) and new active substances, see Table 2.

A single European Marketing Authorization will be granted through this procedure and it will apply throughout the European Community. The authorization is renewable every 5 years on provision of a dossier containing up-to-date information including pharmacovigilance. The authorization also carries 10 year's exclusivity against cross referral to the data by another applicant. Once a product is authorized under the centralized procedure, further applications related to that product (e.g., new indications, new dosage forms, and variations to the authorization) must be filed under the same procedure.

The full procedure is explained in the Notice to Applicants currently under revision and expected to be reissued by mid-1996 [11]. The procedure itself, as detailed in the draft, is explained diagramatically in Figure 2. The main points are discussed below.

1. Verification of Part B Status

In the case of products possibly falling under the Part B classification, the applicant must apply for a ruling that the product concerned will be accepted for Part B by the Agency. This may be done at the time when the company is consulting the Agency on the development plans (e.g., for a very innovative product). Otherwise it will be necessary, even before the dossier is finalized, to provide a 2–3-page document describing the properties of the product in which the innovative character is described. The Agency will then advise on acceptability for Part B.

Table 2 Part B

Medicinal products developed by other biotechnological processes which, in the opinion of the Agency, constitute a significant innovation.
Medicinal products administered by means of new delivery systems which, in the opinion of the Agency, constitute a significant innovation.
Medicinal products presented for an entirely new indication which, in the opinion of the Agency, is of significant therapeutic interest.
Medicinal products based on radioisotopes which, in the opinion of the Agency, are of significant therapeutic interest.
New medicinal products derived from human blood or human plasma.
Medicinal products the manufacture of which employs processes which, in the opinion of the Agency, demonstrate a significant technical advance such as two-dimensional electrophoresis under microgravity.
Medicinal products intended for administration to human beings containing a new active substance which, on the date of entry into force of this regulation, was not authorized by any Member State for use in a medicinal product intended for human use.
Veterinary medicinal products intended for use in food-processing animals containing a new active substance which, on the date of entry into force of this regulation, was not authorized by any Member State for use in food-producing animals.

Annex, Part B of Council Regulation (EEC) 2309/93 of 22 July 1993.

2. Prefiling

Prior to filing an application the EMEA should be notified 4 months before of the pending submission. The firms proposal for rapporteur can be given at this stage. It is likely the rapporteur and corapporteur will then be appointed by the CPMP 3 months before filing.

3. 210-Day Assessment of the Application

Upon submission of the dossier to the EMEA, a validation or "check-in" procedure will take place within 10 days* and before the beginning of the 210-day period. If deficiencies cannot be rectified within 1 month the dossier will be returned to the applicant.

Assessment of the dossier by the rapporteur and corapporteur (who is a member of the CPMP) and their teams of experts should take place within 210 days. The experts who will support the rapporteur/corapporteur will be selected from the expert list and will be agreed by the CPMP, but support is

*All days are calendar days unless specifically stated.

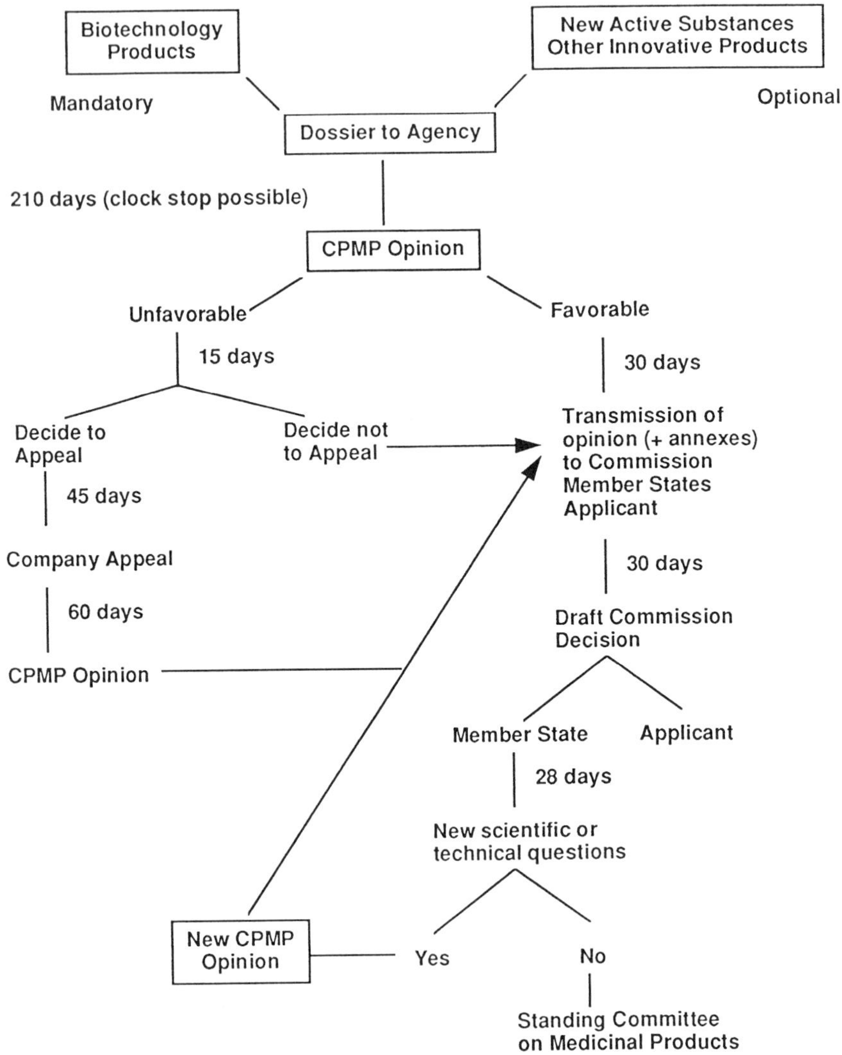

Fig. 2 Centralized procedure.

also given from the Member State Regulatory bodies. The decision on the rapporteur/corapporteur is taken by the CPMP; however, proposals by the applicant will be taken into consideration.

Within 70 days the rapporteur and corapporteur will circulate their draft assessment report to the CPMP and company; the CPMP will establish by 120

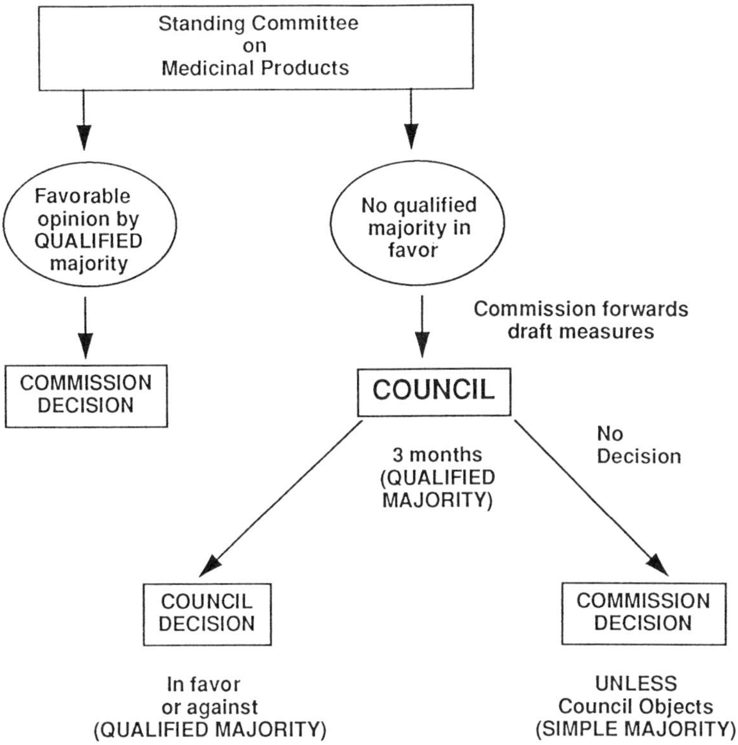

days issues for the applicant to clarify. The clock can stop at this stage for the applicant to submit comments in writing. The Notice to Applicants draft suggests 6 months is the maximum to reply, and if longer is needed, liaison with the Agency is essential to decide how to progress. After the rapporteur prepares the conclusions from the written comments, the CPMP will conclude the evaluation and adopt the opinion within 210 days. At this meeting of the CPMP the applicant can give an oral explanation. Useful guidance on oral explanations are given in the Notice to Applicants. At the time of issuing the opinion, it is necessary to have the SmPC and patient insert available in all 12 community languages.

4. Appeal

In the event of an unfavorable opinion, the applicant has 15 days to decide if they will appeal and a further 45 days to send in the written grounds for appeal. An unfavorable opinion includes the cases where the SmPC should be amended as well as more fundamental issues concerning quality, safety, and efficacy—so it is likely that appeals will be very frequent. The CPMP has 60 days to consider the appeal and reissue an opinion. It is possible that additional experts may be involved at this stage.

5. Decision

The CPMP provides a scientific opinion and the conversion of this opinion to a decision takes place through the Commission using the Standing Committee on Medicinal Products. The Commission has the right to change the decision but must give detailed explanations of their reasons. This decision is sent to the Member States and the applicant. Member States are allowed 28 days to raise, in writing, important new questions of a scientific or technical nature that have not been addressed in the opinion delivered by the Agency. If this happens the procedure may be suspended and the matter referred back to the Agency for further consideration.

It is to be hoped that in most cases the Member States will not be objecting at this stage and the Standing Committee (which is composed of Member State representatives) will be able to deliver their opinion in writing. The opinion is delivered by a qualified majority, which means that each country has a weighted vote according to the population size of the country.

If the vote is unfavorable or if no opinion is delivered, the Commission has to submit a proposal to the Council of Ministers relating the measures to be taken. The Council also votes by a qualified majority and after 3 months the Council could vote in favor or against or take no decision in which case the Commission adopts their original opinion unless the Council has decided against the measures by a simple majority. Details of the decision procedure are published by the Commission. The final decision will be published in the Official Journal of the European Communities.

6. European Public Assessment Report (EPAR)

The EMEA makes available on the Internet the European Public Assessment Report for the product and the reasons for its opinion. This report will have any information of a commercially confidential nature deleted from it by the applicant.

7. Variations

The CPMP must also be consulted in cases of proposed variations (i.e., changes to the details in the marketing authorization application dossier) to products approved through the centralized procedure. A Regulation has been issued covering the variation procedure for products approved through the centralized procedure [12].

There will be two types of variation:

1. A "minor" variation (Type I)—these are defined in Annex 1 to the Regulation and are generally small changes to chemistry and pharmacy and some administrative changes. A guideline details the supporting data needed for the variation. These Type I variations should be submitted to the Agency and if the company receives no queries within 30 days the variation can be implemented, i.e., this is a "notification" system. If there are queries the applicant has 30 days to amend the application; if this cannot be done, the application is rejected.
2. "Major" changes are termed Type II variations; they are not defined as such being all changes which are not a Type I or requiring a new application (for which there is a definition in Annex II of the Regulation). A Type II variation will be assessed in the Agency within 60 days. Within that time the applicant may be requested to provide more information; an extra 60 days are allowed for this. This can be extended both by the applicant or by the Agency. If the opinion is favorable the decision to approve is taken through the procedure described previously for a full application (IV A.4.). An unfavorable opinion can result in an appeal followed by the decision as described for the full procedure.

B. Decentralized or Mutual Recognition Procedure

The objective of this procedure is to facilitate access to a single market through the principle of mutual recognition of an authorization issued by one Member State (Reference Member State) by the other Member States. Only in the case of serious objections on the quality, safety, or efficacy of the product would the matter be referred to the EMEA for a single binding decision on the area of disagreement. The procedure results in a series of national harmonized authorizations as opposed to one authorization in the centralized. The procedure is not available for products of biotechnology (Table 1) but is open by choice to new active substances, products classed as high technology (Table 2), and all other products.

The procedure can be initiated either by the company or by a Member State. The full procedure is explained in the Notice to Applicants currently under revision and expected to be reissued by mid-1996 [11]. A diagrammatic representation of the procedure is given in Figure 3 with the main points of note discussed below.

1. Originating Application and Mutual Recognition

The application to the Reference Member State (RMS) should be evaluated within 210 days by national procedures and an assessment report produced plus the Summary of Product Characteristics (SmPC). These documents are

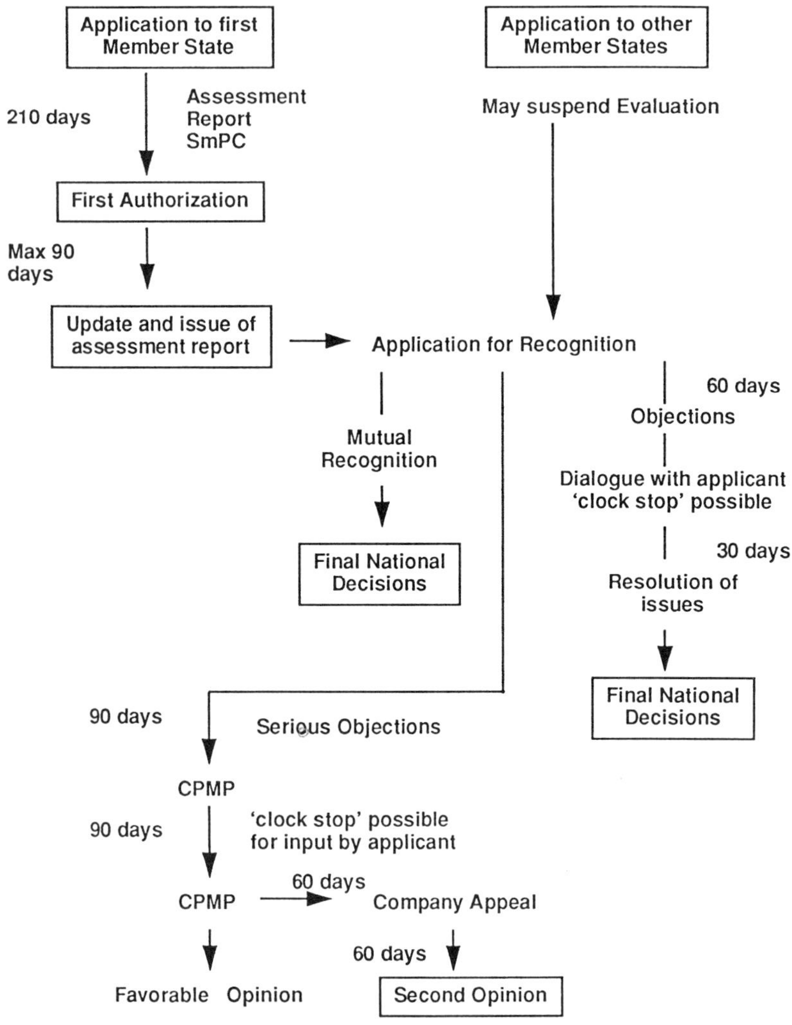

Fig. 3 Decentralized procedure.

essential for the procedure to progress to the mutual recognition phase with the second wave of countries so it will be important that they are available as soon as possible. The Member States are allowed 90 days to produce the up-to-date assessment report. Only a few national regulatory authorities are able at present to evaluate a product within a 210-day period so this will be one of a series of important points in selection of this first country by the company (see Section VII). Once the assessment report and SmPC are obtained by the

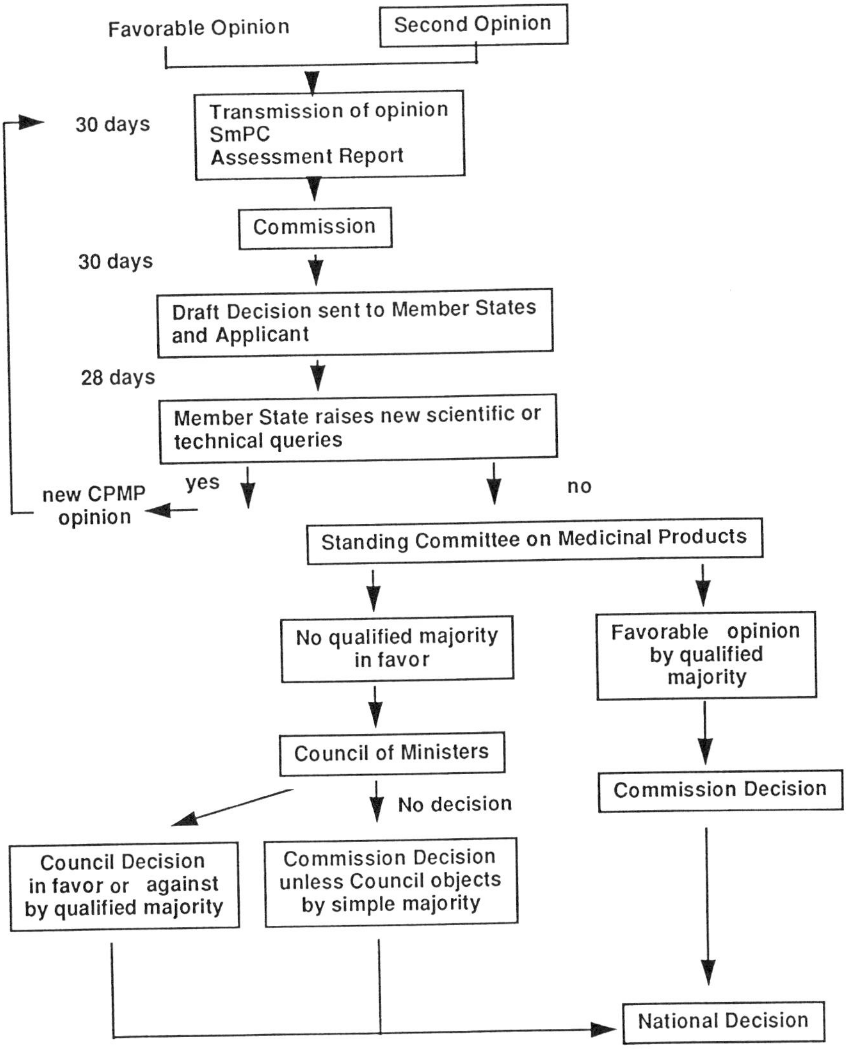

second countries and this is acknowledged to the RMS, the clock starts on the next phase (90 days) of the procedure.

If the principle of mutual recognition works, it should be possible to obtain recognition of the initial authorization within this 90 days and the national authorities should then issue the national decisions. At the present time, it is not clear how long the national bodies will take to issue the authorizations.

Mutual recognition had rarely happened during the old multistate procedure and although there appears to be a will to make it work now, it can be expected that in some cases significant objections will still be raised by some Member States. In order to allow time to resolve these between Member States and the applicant, the new procedures state that the Member States have agreed to notify these objections within 60 days so that there is a chance to still have all queries resolved with the applicant within the remaining 30 days—this is an ambitious time frame and will depend on the applicant being able to respond quickly.

Allowing for some time between the first approval and starting up the second part of the procedure (90 days) the total time could be 390 days (210 + 90 + 90 days). This could be shorter if less than 90 days are required by the first Member State to update the assessment report. The amount of time the company takes to update the dossier and distribute it to the second wave of countries will of course also determine the total time taken.

2. Arbitration

In the event that there is still disagreement, the matter must be referred to the CPMP to undertake a scientific evaluation. This should take place within 90 days. The CPMP will appoint a rapporteur from one of its members to lead the evaluation of the disagreement. This rapporteur may be from the originating country or may be another member (perhaps from an objecting Member State?). Other experts may also be appointed to assist. At the beginning of this 90-day period, the clock can be stopped to allow the applicant to prepare comments in writing. Subsequent to submitting these it will be possible to have interaction with the rapporteur to know if any issues remain. An oral explanation by the applicant will be possible at the CPMP meeting. Useful guidance on the conduct of oral explanations is given in the Notice to Applicants.

3. Appeal

After the issue of the opinion there is the possibility of appeal if the opinion was unfavorable. An unfavorable opinion not only covers the possibility of rejection but also it may request a Summary of Product Characteristics change or special conditions attached to the authorization. Appeals are therefore quite likely, given the frequency of SmPC changes made during the assessment processes now. During the appeal, a different rapporteur will generally be appointed to make the assessment and an oral explanation is available again to the applicant.

4. Decision

A legally binding decision on all Member States then has to take place. This is the same procedure as described under the centralized procedure, but with the issue of national authorizations.

5. Initiation by a Member State

Although the procedure described above, initiated by the applicant, will be the most used for full or abridged applications, there are other cases where referrals may be made to the CPMP using the same procedure. These are briefly described below.

As mentioned earlier, from January 1, 1995, when a Member State notes that an application for authorization is under active examination in another Member State, it may decide to suspend examination of the dossier and to wait for the assessment report of the first Member State. If the Member State decides not to recognize the decision of the other Member State, the matter of disagreement will be referred to the CPMP as described above. This facility will continue even after January 1, 1998. From January 1, 1998, Member States must take into account the assessment report from another Member State on that medicinal product and either recognize the decision or refer the objections to the CPMP—i.e., the decentralized procedure is fully in operation.

6. Article 11 Referrals

Article 11 of Directive 75/319/EEC as amended states that where divergent decisions have been made on a product that has been the subject of several applications for marketing authorization in the Member States, the matter may be referred to the CPMP. The referral may be made by either one or more Member States, the Commission, or the company. The objective of Article 11 is to provide a mechanism for resolution of divergent national decisions that will hinder free movement of medicinal products in the Community. Although these divergent decisions will gradually disappear through the new procedures, there could still be divergence during the transition until 1998. The scope and procedure for Article 11 referrals are covered in detail in the Notice to Applicants.

7. Article 12 Referrals

Article 12 of Directive 93/39/EEC covers the cases where the interests of the Community are involved and the Member States, the Commission, or the company may refer the matter to the CPMP for an opinion before decisions are taken on granting an authorization or suspending, withdrawing, or varying one. This Article has already been used for several pharmacovigilance matters. Referrals are made on a case-by-case basis and must be in the interests of the Community; apart from pharmacovigilance cases the Article is likely to be used for products that are of high importance to protection of public health but that are *not* eligible for the centralized procedure. Again the objective, scope, and procedure are covered in detail in the Notice to Applicants.

8. Variations

The CPMP must also be consulted in cases of proposed variations (i.e., changes to the details in the marketing authorization application dossier). A Regulation is issued covering the variation procedure for products approved through the decentralized procedure [13].

There will be two types of variation:

1. A "minor" variation (Type I)—these are defined in Annex 1 to the Regulation and are generally small changes to chemistry and pharmacy and some administrative changes. A guideline details the supporting data needed for the variation. These Type I variations should be submitted simultaneously to all countries where the product has been authorized. The Type I procedure is a notification system—if the applicant has not received queries within 30 days then the variation is accepted and can be implemented. The Member State who examines the variation and could receive objections from the other Member States is termed the reference Member State and can be specified by the applicant. If the other Member States have objective grounds for nonacceptance of the variation they must inform the reference Member State within 20 days so the applicant can receive the objections within 30 days. The applicant then has 30 days to amend the application. If the applicant does not amend the application it is rejected. If the rejection resulted from divergent positions of the Member States, the applicant has the right to refer the matter to the EMEA.
2. A "major" variation (Type II) is not defined as such; it is all changes which are not a Type I or a new application (for which there is a definition in Annex II of the Regulation). Type II applications must go through a formal approval procedure within 90 days with the reference Member State leading the assessment. The possibility exists for the applicant or Member State to extend the time by up to 60 days for provision of more information. In the event of objections from one or more of the other Member States, a full arbitration procedure with the CPMP takes place as described earlier for a full application.

C. National Procedure

Although registering products for marketing in more than one country nationally will disappear after January 1998, the national regulatory bodies still have many functions. Correspondingly, national regulatory groups within companies will still have several functions. Listed below are some of the functions of the Member State regulatory bodies in the new systems:

- to assess new medicinal products as Reference Member State for decentralized procedure;
- to provide members of CPMP and other Committees (Standing Committee, Pharmaceutical Committee) in the European system;
- to provide experts for the EMEA working groups and experts lists;
- to authorize national applications;

- to maintain products registered before January 1, 1995 (variations, renewals, etc.);
- to handle adverse drug reactions;
- to authorize clinical trials (where legislation demands it); and
- to inspect (GMP, GLP, and GCP).

This is by no means a complete list but illustrates that the Member States have an important and continuing role to play in the new procedures as well as still having many activities locally. This new emphasis has resulted in the recent reorganization of many regulatory bodies in the European Union to enable them to carry out their new functions.

V. FEES

A Council Regulation on Fees [14] was issued in February 1995. The Agency has discussed the intention to be self-financing, with fees as the main source of revenue, within 3–5 years. Figure 4 details the present fees.

VI. COMPUTER ASSISTED PRODUCT LICENCE APPLICATIONS (CAPLAs)

Although various national Regulatory Agencies have been accepting and experimenting with Computer Assisted Product Licence Applications (CAPLAs),

	ECU
Centralized Procedure	**140,000**
Additional strengths/forms	**20,000**
to a total of	***200,000***
Generics	**70,000**
Additional strengths/forms	**10,000**
to a total of	***100,000***
Extensions	**40,000**
Type I Variation	**5,000**
Type II	**40,000**
Renewal	**10,000**
Inspection	**10,000**
Transfer of MA holder	**5,000**
Arbitration	**30,000**

Fig. 4 Council Regulation Fees.

primarily consisting of the clinical data at this stage, there is no policy from the EMEA on full electronic submissions, although this can be expected with time. It should still be possible, of course, to file CAPLAs to Reference Member States in the decentralized procedure if they wish to accept it. At present, it is also possible to submit Part 1A, 1B, and 1C of the dossier only in an electronic form to many Member States. At present, the priority of the EMEA is towards building a network for exchange of pharmacovigilance and administrative information between Member States and the Agency.

VII. IMPACT OF NEW PROCEDURES ON REGULATORY STRATEGIES

Although there has been the possibility of filing applications through a "European System" for many years few companies have taken up this opportunity and most applications, including those for new active substances, have been filed nationally. Indeed, even for those applications that have used the new procedures, because of the structure of the existing legislation and the fact that the decisions are national, a harmonized outcome (especially SmPC) has often not been achieved. In terms of regulatory strategy for a company, this has tended to perpetuate individual country applications and strategies.

Some of the major changes that will influence strategies brought about by the new legislation are

1. Binding decisions on the Member States—resulting in no national deviations to the SmPC. This occurs through the issue of one European Marketing Authorization from the centralized procedure for all of the European Union; mutual recognition in the decentralized procedure implies acceptance of the SmPC as authorized in the originating Member State. If arbitration takes place changing that SmPC then the newly agreed one will be binding on all Member States including the originating country.
2. It will be necessary to file exactly the same dossier in all countries. In the decentralized procedure the applicant is required to "certify" that the dossier is the same.
3. After 1998, separate national assessments and decisions are, in effect, no longer possible for products where applications are being made in more than one country.
4. Approval will be obtained for all of Europe at once (except for the first country in the decentralized procedure) with implications for launch strategies. Pricing and reimbursement decisions will still be conducted on an individual national basis.
5. If the time frames for the procedures are respected, approvals could be obtained relatively quickly for all of Europe in contrast to the previous

staggered situation. This has implications for conduct of studies to support pricing and reimbursement in individual countries and many of these will now have to be started at least during Phase III development.

The strategic impact of one dossier for Europe, one final assessment (at least in the centralized procedure), and one decision is therefore very high and obtaining a fast approval for applications with optimal labeling has to be a key goal for a pharmaceutical company. Consideration to strategic implications will need to be given through the drug development process, during the approval process, and postmarketing. This chapter is only dealing with the former two.

During drug development the following are some issues to be considered.

- Contact must be developed with a potential Reference Member State country for the decentralized procedure. As the choice of country rests with the applicant it will be important to discuss the application with the selected country before filing to obtain their support. It may also be advisable to consult with one or a few countries during the drug's development (e.g., end Phase II) if there are issues that the company feels need clarification or advice; any differences in medical practice between countries should be identified and a strategy developed for ensuring this does not influence approval. Although clinical data are acceptable from all over Europe and from third countries, it may be advisable to consider having data available from the company's key European countries.
- The choice of rapporteur for the centralized procedure is made by the CPMP but proposals by the applicant are taken into account, so again it will be important to have established the support of members of the CPMP during development.

Within the company decisions will have to be made at the appropriate time on the procedure to be used and, in the case of the decentralized procedure, the Reference Member State—many factors may influence both decisions and will to an extent be both product and company specific. Some influencing factors are listed in Tables 3 and 4. In making these decisions, it will be important to build an "in company" procedure to ensure all "interested parties," e.g., subsidiaries, are involved as the decision could have considerable business implications. In formulating a regulatory strategy an important factor will be the scope of the dossier, e.g., are all indications well supported? Given the nature of the procedures and the need for 15 countries to reach a consensus on the data presented, the regulatory strategy should seek to identify areas of possible weakness likely to cause discussion, queries, or dissension in the assessment and consequent delay in the process. In the initial years it will be vital to obtain information on the performance of the procedures for all applications in order to assist decision making on choice of procedure. This information may well

Table 3 Factors Influencing Choice of Procedure

Type of Product	
Biotechnology	Centralized
NAS[a]/High Tech	Decentralized or centralized
Others	Decentralized
Does it classify as "High Technology"?	
Previous submissions on same product if it is a line extension	
Previous submissions by other companies in same therapeutic area	
Performance of Procedures	
Marketing needs (e.g., marketing foreseen in all of Europe or only selected countries)	
Involvement with other companies (codevelopment, comarketing)	
Medical practice differences?	
Acceptance of indications in all countries?	
Internal work load / allocation of dossiers between procedures	
Implication of protection from second applicant	

[a]New Active Substance.

be published by the Agency but probably with some delay so it will be essential for each company to have its own network of information from colleagues.

Once the dossier is filed it will go through a "check in" process to ensure completeness. This is not as detailed as the "Refusal to File" process in the FDA but nevertheless incomplete applications will not be accepted into the process for evaluation. During the evaluation process questions should arrive at the company in a more coordinated, concentrated fashion than now and there will be defined time frames for answering these. It will be important therefore that possible queries have been identified beforehand and some pre-

Table 4 Factors Influencing Choice of Originating Member State

Experienced Health Authority as first country
Health Authority experienced with indication
Opinion leaders present in the country
Clinical trials conducted in the country
Time to approval
Good appeal system
Possibility of presubmission dialogue and good liaison during the procedure
Experience of Drug Regulatory Affairs Department in the subsidiary
Pricing and other marketing considerations
Obtaining good quality postmarketing information quickly.

paration done to be able to answer them. In addition, the project team needs to be kept together in order to have dedicated resource for answering the queries. This will be particularly important in the decentralized procedure to avoid the arbitration step if at all possible; the more prepared the applicant is to deal with Member State objections in the first 90-day period (see IV B.1) the better the chance of mutual recognition being achieved.

Oral explanations before the CPMP will be a feature of the new procedures and it will be important to have staff with the necessary skills of negotiation besides their scientific skills. As more than one language may be spoken in a CPMP meeting, it could also be useful to have staff with fluency in more than one European language.

VIII. CONCLUSION

The new marketing authorization system is having a considerable influence on the regulatory strategy for companies. Contrary to old practices there is a need to submit the same dossier to all countries, one assessment by the CPMP is carried out (at least in the centralized procedure), and both procedures result in a binding decision on all Member States. With the entry of Austria, Sweden, and Finland into the European Union in 1995, the size of the market covered by this regulatory system is considerable. Strategic decision making in the Regulatory Affairs Department and its full involvement in the development process will become a key factor in the success of the company's business.

ACKNOWLEDGMENTS

I wish to acknowledge the considerable support of my secretaries, Aisling Blagg and Tracy Warman, and the internal Pfizer reviewers of this chapter.

REFERENCES

1. Council Directive 87/22/EEC of 22 December 1986 on the approximation of national measures relating to the placing on the market of high technology medicinal products particularly those derived from biotechnology.
2. Second Council Directive 75/319/EEC of 20 May 1975 on the approximation of provisions laid down by law regulation or administrative action relating to proprietary medicinal products.
3. Council Directive 83/570/EEC of 26 October 1983 amending Directives 65/65/EEC, 75/318/EEC, and 75/319/EEC on the approximation of provisions laid down by law, regulation, or administrative action relating to proprietary medicinal products.
4. Council Directive EEC No. 2309/93 of 22 July 1993 laying down Community Procedures for the authorization and supervision of medicinal products for human

and veterinary use and establishing a European Agency for the Evaluation of Medicinal Products.
5. Council Directive 93/39/EEC of 14 June 1993 amending Directives 65/65/EEC, 75/318/EEC, and 75/319/EEC in respect of medicinal products.
6. Council Directive 65/65/EEC of 26 January 1965 on the approximation of provisions laid down by law, regulation, or administrative action relating to proprietary medicinal products.
7. Council Directive 75/318/EEC of 20 May 1975 on the approximation of the laws of Member States relating to analytical, pharmacotoxicological, and clinical standards and protocols in respect of the testing of proprietary medicinal products.
8. Second Council Directive 75/319/EEC of 20 May 1975 on the approximation of provisions laid down by law, regulation, or administrative action relating to proprietary medicinal products.
9. Council Directive 93/41/EEC of 14 June 1993 repealing Directive 87/22/EEC on the approximation of national measures relating to the placing on the market of high technology medicinal products, particularly those derived from biotechnology.
10. Council Directive 93/40/EEC of 14 June 1993 amending Directives 81/851/EEC and 81/852/EEC on the approximation of laws of the Member States relating to veterinary medicinal products.
11. Notice to Applicants for Marketing Authorization for Medicinal Products for Human Use in the Member States of the European Community Volume IIA (in revision—draft only available). Previous version July 1993—III/3567/92.
12. Commission Regulation No. 542/95 of 10 March 1995 concerning the examination of variations to the terms of a marketing authorization falling within the scope of Council Regulation (EEC) No. 2309/93.
13. Commission Regulation No. 541/95 of 10 March 1995 concerning the examination of variations to the terms of a marketing authorization granted by a competent authority of a Member State.
14. Council Regulation (EC) No. 297/95 of 10 February 1995 on Fees Payable to the European Agency for the Evaluation of Medicinal Products.

Index